GALENA PUBLIC LIBRARY DISTRICT

P9-DDL-766

Galena Public Library
DISTRICT

In honor of

Janet Jonjack
"25 Year Employee"

Given by the Staff
of the Galena Public Library

2011

Also by Elizabeth Bishop

North & South (1946)

A Cold Spring (1955)

The Diary of "Helena Morley" (translation) (1957)

Brazil (with the editors of *Life*) (prose) (1962)

Questions of Travel (1965)

The Ballad of the Burglar of Babylon (1968)

The Complete Poems (1969)

An Anthology of Twentieth-Century Brazilian Poetry
(edited with Emanuel Brasil) (1972)

Geography III (1976)

The Complete Poems: 1927–1979 (1983)

The Collected Prose (edited by Robert Giroux) (1984)

One Art: Letters (edited by Robert Giroux) (1994)

Exchanging Hats: Paintings (edited by William Benton) (1996)

Edgar Allan Poe & The Juke-Box:
Uncollected Poems, Drafts, and Fragments
(edited by Alice Quinn) (2006)

Elizabeth Bishop: Poems, Prose, and Letters
(edited by Robert Giroux and Lloyd Schwartz) (2008)

Words in Air: The Complete Correspondence
Between Elizabeth Bishop and Robert Lowell
(edited by Thomas Travisano with Saskia Hamilton) (2008)

Poems (2011)

Prose (edited by Lloyd Schwartz) (2011)

Elizabeth Bishop and

The New Yorker

SEPT. 12, 1978 l.c. M Hendle M l.c. VERY SOON nc 2571

DEC 11 1978

white #

#6

NORTH HAVEN

(In memoriam: R.T.S.L.)

[Robert Lowell]

white space

white #

I can make out the rigging of a schooner
a mile off; I can count
the new cones on the spruce. It is so still
the pale bay wears a milky skin, the sky
no clouds, except for one long, carded, horse's-tail.

white #

The islands haven't shifted since last summer,
even if I like to pretend they have,
drifting, in a dreamy sort of way,
a little north, a little south or sidewise,
and that they're free within the blue frontiers of bay.

This month, our favorite one is full of flowers:
Buttercups, Red Clover, Purple Vetch,
Hawkweed still burning, Daisies pied, Eyebright,
the Fragrant Bedstraw's incandescent stars,
and more, returned, to paint the meadows with delight.

white #

The Goldfinches are back, or others like them,
and the white-throated Sparrow's five-note song,
pleading and pleading, brings tears to the eyes.
Nature repeats herself, or almost does:
repeat, repeat, repeat; revise, revise, revise.

roman commas

white #

Years ago, you told me it was here
(in 1932?) you first "discovered girls"
and learned to sail, and learned to kiss.
You had "such fun," you said, that classic summer.
("Fun"—it always seemed to leave you at a loss...)

You left North Haven, anchored in its rock,
afloat in mystic blue. And now—you've left
for good. You can't derange, or re-arrange,
your poems again. (But the Sparrows can their song.)
The words won't change again. Sad friend, you cannot change.

Elizabeth Bishop

#

11 pt.
27 picas;
set line
for line;
indent
turned
lines
one em

11 pt
caps &
sm. c.
set on
1 line

roman commas
and 6 pts

no lead
no rest

l.c. ||||
l.c. |||
l.c. ||

l.c.
l.c. ||

Stet

Stet

tn.

white #
l.c.

white #

11 pt caps
& sm caps
fl. right with
longest line
above.

Elizabeth Bishop and

The New Yorker

THE COMPLETE CORRESPONDENCE

Edited by Joelle Biele

FARRAR, STRAUS AND GIROUX

NEW YORK

Farrar, Straus and Giroux
18 West 18th Street, New York 10011

Copyright © 2011 by the Alice H. Methfessel Trust
Introduction and selection copyright © 2011 by Joelle Biele
All rights reserved
Distributed in Canada by D&M Publishers, Inc.
Printed in the United States of America
First edition, 2011

Correspondence originating at *The New Yorker* reprinted courtesy of
The New Yorker/ The Condé Nast Publications Inc.

Frontispiece and images on pages 1, 25, 243, and 293 courtesy of
the New York Public Library.

Library of Congress Cataloging-in-Publication Data
Bishop, Elizabeth, 1911–1979.
    Elizabeth Bishop and The New Yorker : the complete correspondence / edited by
Joelle Biele.— 1st ed.
        p.   cm.
    Includes index.
    ISBN: 978-0-374-28138-0 (hardcover : alk. paper)
    1. Bishop, Elizabeth, 1911–1979—Correspondence.   2. New Yorker (New York, N.Y. :
1925)   3. Poets, American—20th century—Correspondence.   I. Biele, Joelle, 1969–.
II. New Yorker (New York, N.Y. : 1925)   III. Title.

PS3503.I785Z484 2010
811'.54—dc22

                                                            2010005677

Designed by Jonathan D. Lippincott

www.fsgbooks.com

1   3   5   7   9   10   8   6   4   2

Contents

Introduction · *vii*

A Note on the Text · *lxi*

ONE: 1934–1946 · 1

TWO: 1947–1961 · 25

THREE: 1961–1967 · 243

FOUR: 1967–1979 · 293

Acknowledgments · *403*

Index · *405*

Introduction

"I sort of see you surrounded with fine-tooth combs, sandpaper, nail files, pots of varnish, etc.—with heaps of used commas and semicolons handy, and little useless phrases taken out of their contexts and dying all over the floor," Elizabeth Bishop mused upon learning that her friend Pearl Kazin had landed a copyediting job at *The New Yorker* in March 1953.[1] Bishop had published her first poem in the magazine in 1940 when it was already well on its way to becoming legendary, not just for the things it printed but also for its way of bringing them to print. In *The New Yorker*'s offices above Forty-third Street, Bishop found a series of admiring editors, including Charles Pearce, Katharine White, and Howard Moss. The kind of commentary they provided their writers is arguably unparalleled in American literary history. In public Bishop rarely articulated poetic theory, but in letters to *The New Yorker* she discussed the ideas behind her poems while sharing news about her travels and passing along anecdotes about her life in Brazil. On her editors' part, these letters show Pearce's polite encouragement of the young writer, White's serious approach and thoughtful diplomacy, and Moss's wonderful wit and deep appreciation of her work. With the back and forth of hundreds of letters, Bishop's deepening friendship with her editors became sustaining. Her relationship with the magazine strained, however, when she attempted pieces that were more experimental or involved sexuality, and as a result, after fifteen years of detailed correspondence and steady encouragement, she canceled her first-reading agreement from 1961 to 1968. Yet, no matter how much Bishop struggled with *The New Yorker* in private, she retained a great deal of affection for its famous mysteries and was grateful for her editors' insightful reading. Their questions pushed her in directions she might not otherwise have taken and at times changed her work in dramatic ways. When asked about publishing, Bishop once remarked, "I'm rather against professionalism—(I only wish I could type better—) and really often think I would have preferred the days when poems just got handed around among friends.—"[2] Submitting to the magazine was the closest she came to handing poems around as her address changed from New York to Key West to Saratoga Springs and Washington, D.C., from Rio de Janeiro, Petrópolis, and Ouro Prêto to Seattle, San Francisco, Cambridge, and, finally, Boston. Bishop has often been portrayed as an orphaned wanderer, but that is not entirely true. There was one constant in her writing life, and that was her place at *The New Yorker*.

In the fall of 1939, just a few months before Bishop sent "Spleen" (later titled "Cirque d'Hiver") to Charles Pearce, then poetry editor at *The New Yorker*, she confessed to her friend Ted Wilson, "I can't think of any place to send poetry anymore."[3] With "The Monument" on its way to James Laughlin and his *New Directions Yearbook in Poetry and Prose*, she thought *The Southern Review* was a possibility for some Key West stories and poems. Bishop had long absorbed the ethic that her mentor and friend Marianne Moore had imparted to her. Each time Bishop left Moore's Brooklyn apartment, nickel for her subway fare in hand, she left determined "to work harder, not to worry about what other people thought, never to try to publish anything until I'd done my best with it, no matter how many years it took—or never to publish at all."[4] When Bishop sent Pearce "Spleen," it wasn't her first submission to the magazine; she had sent poems while a senior at Vassar College in 1933. From her Poughkeepsie dorm room, she quipped to her old classmate Frani Blough, "Personally I find that *The New Yorker* sends things back quicker than any other publication, quicker than the twinkling of an eye, so quick it's quite painless."[5] Within a year of graduation she had an acceptance, an anonymous "Talk of the Town" story concerning a note from a domestic servant, a series of which the magazine had been featuring in its opening pages.

"Cirque d'Hiver" ran in the January 27, 1940, issue, and Bishop was pleased by its prominent position. In the front of the book, the section that had no advertisements, Bishop's poem sat inside Geoffrey T. Hellman's profile of *Scientific American* publisher Orson D. Munn and was surrounded by small drawings of a dancer, horse, and key, neatly if excessively illustrating the poem. With the publication of "Cirque d'Hiver," Pearce began to court the poet. A recent arrival at *The New Yorker*, "Cap" Pearce had come to Forty-third Street from Harcourt Brace. The first editor hired to deal exclusively with poetry, he apparently used the procedure that founding editor

Harold Ross and lead fiction editor Katharine White established for discovering new talent. Running through lists of promising writers and their publications, he approached poets and followed up in more or less regular intervals after their poems appeared. After learning that Bishop had opted out of Laughlin's anthology of young American poets—she hoped to publish a volume of her own and didn't want to serve as "Sex-Appeal," as the only woman in the book—he urged her to reconsider.[6] He even read her poetry manuscript for his own press, the recently founded Duell, Sloan and Pearce, and, though enthusiastic, gave her what she felt was a "by no means uncertain refusal."[7] What Bishop received from Pearce before he left *The New Yorker* in 1944 for the Army were basically form letters asking for poems and regular rejections of those poems. Looking for new work, Pearce sent Bishop the same note he had sent to Russian émigré Vladimir Nabokov the day before: "We'd be particularly grateful to see a manuscript of yours in the mails one of these fine mornings."[8] After he turned down poems such as "Letter to N.Y.," Bishop ended up submitting her story "The Housekeeper," which was accepted, under the pen name Sarah Foster, the name of her paternal grandmother.

What finally allowed Bishop to break into *The New Yorker* were Katharine Sergeant Angell White and the Houghton Mifflin Poetry Prize Fellowship. White, a senior fiction editor at the magazine, agreed, along with poet-critic Horace Gregory, to serve as judge for the fellowship in November 1944. With a purse of one thousand dollars, the fellowship was aimed at young writers hoping to publish their first books, and Houghton Mifflin wrote Bishop asking her to submit. Bishop mulled the competition over with Marianne Moore, and by January, Moore, John Dewey, and Edmund Wilson wrote letters on her behalf, as Houghton Mifflin required. Dewey was Bishop's neighbor in Key West, and his daughter Jane was one of Bishop's lifelong friends, her quiet house in Havre de Grace, Maryland, serving as one of Bishop's favorite retreats. Wilson, who often advised Bishop on publishing matters, was a writer at the magazine and at that time the husband of Bishop's former classmate Mary McCarthy. By the time White received her first batch of manuscripts the following March, she was already familiar with Bishop's work. That winter Wilson approached her about Bishop's poems, and she followed the poet in the literary reviews and asked for contributions. When White made her top picks, however, Bishop's manuscript was not among them. When editor Ferris Greenslet learned of White's choices, he let her know he disagreed. He planned to meet with the judges in his office off

Boston Common in May, and by the end of that month the trio decided on Bishop as the winner. White wrote Bishop a warm letter of congratulations, one that suggests she did not read Bishop's manuscript until after speaking with Greenslet in late spring. Since she had only recently returned to full-time work after working half-time from her home in North Brooklin, Maine, she suggested Bishop send the poems she had previously submitted. White wanted to bring Bishop and the other new poets she read into the magazine. In her memo about the fellowship's outcome, White reported "'North & South' was, to my mind and without question, the best of any of the manuscripts I read." Given White and Ross's long-standing debate over the use of serious poetry—she wanted it, he didn't—she carefully pitched the young poet, admitting that Bishop's poems were not necessarily best for *The New Yorker*. "She may not be a great poet but she has a very real poetic gift and we ought to have her in the magazine."[9] In fact, White felt *North & South* put Bishop among the best poets of the day, but she measured her words until Ross agreed to publish her work.

White, then Katharine Sergeant Angell, came to *The New Yorker* in the summer of 1925, six months after the February 21 issue found its way to the city's newsstands with the bemonocled dandy Eustace Tilley on its cover. At thirty-two, Angell was looking for work that dealt with writing, a love of hers since she was a child in Brookline, Massachusetts, and a Bryn Mawr undergraduate editing *Tipyn O'Bob* and *The Lantern*. In the last three years she had worked as a translator, a shopkeeper, and an errand girl, publishing articles and book reviews in *The New Republic*, *The Atlantic Monthly*, and *The Saturday Review of Literature*. With a lead from a weekend neighbor in Snedens Landing, New York, Angell applied for a job as a manuscript reader. Apparently, Ross hired her on the spot for a part-time position. Within a few weeks Angell was reading full-time; within a few months she was editing; and within a year she was the magazine's top literary editor, a position she held for the next twelve years. She was, along with Ross, Wolcott Gibbs, Ralph Ingersoll, James Thurber, and her future husband, E. B. "Andy" White, part of the magazine's original "nucleus."[10] There was almost no part of the magazine in which she was not involved. Developing art and story ideas, making layout suggestions and tracking submissions, reviewing previous issues for improvement and nurturing her writers, and occasionally writing pieces of her own, she is credited with expanding the magazine's range. Peter Arno's graceful drawing of White—her long hair whisked into a flowing bun, cigarette smoke rising above her head—evokes this period with the intensity of White's gaze, her entire body focused on the subject before her.

"All the signs of her work were around her wherever she went," Roger Angell, her son by her first marriage and a longtime editor at the magazine, recalled. "She carried one of those big brown portfolios—it was stuffed with galleys and manuscripts, and she always had brown pencils scattered around, and big erasers and eraser scrubbings and cigarette ashes."[11] White's devotion to the magazine was as unquestioned as her vision was large. Describing their life together, Andy White said, "The light burned late, our bed was lumpy with page proofs, and our home was alive with laughter and the pervasive spirit of her dedication and her industry."[12]

White loved the wry give-and-take between herself and the magazine's original editors, particularly with Ross. Much has been written about Ross, not just by his biographers Dale Kramer and Thomas Kunkel, but also by friends and staff members in memoirs, novels, and plays, the most famous account being James Thurber's *The Years with Ross*. A year after dropping out of high school to write for *The Salt Lake City Tribune*, Ross found himself a tramp reporter, hoboing his way from town to town, drinking and gambling with friends, and writing for such papers as *The Sacramento Union*, *The Panama City Star and Herald*, and *The New Orleans Item*. As managing editor of *Stars and Stripes*, Ross got to flex his editorial skills and develop his business acumen in Paris during the First World War. In a prelude to his evenings at The Algonquin Hotel in New York, he met with fellow reporters at Nini's in Montmartre, where they imagined their lives after the war and tossed around ideas for a witty tabloid based in New York.

Once the magazine was under way, Ross became a man about town, appearing in New York City gossip columns and cartoons and profiled in *Fortune* and *Harper*'s. Through the Algonquin's "vicious circle," he built a network that combined talented journalists and artists with the silk-stockinged East Side, helping him build the magazine during its early years. All the while he played cards, sometimes for incredibly high stakes, with the Thanatopsis Literary and Inside Straight Club. Jane Grant, Ross's first wife, believed he enjoyed "acting the goon," yet on paper he was utterly droll.[13] His friends loved to joke about his thick black hair that stood on end, his big hands, his big feet, and his suits that never seemed to hang straight. His general unease around women, his lack of formal education, his western roots, and his fondness for profanity all came in for a ribbing. White professed that, after working with Ross for twenty-five years, nothing he said could hurt her feelings and vice versa. "Actually I delight in these exchanges and we tell each other 'You're bats!' without the slightest ill will."[14] White could give as good as she got, and one can hear him waiting for her comeback to this memo: "As to your sharp-shooting of the issues, and your recent memo about this, I say do it your way. I deplore your way, but since you can't do it another way, I'll settle on it."[15]

Without question, White's most important contribution to the magazine was bringing serious poetry and fiction to its pages, helping turn the "fumbling and impoverished new weekly" into a magazine of sophisticated satire and high polish.[16] As William Shawn, Ross's successor, said in White's 1977 obituary, "When Ross knew what he wanted and didn't know how to get it, he began turning to Katharine. When he didn't know quite what he wanted, he turned to her to find out what it was. When he was unsure of himself, he was sure of her. Before long, she was his most valued collaborator. More than any other editor except Harold Ross himself, Katharine White gave *The New Yorker* its shape and set it on its course."[17] Lobbying Ross to broaden his taste, she regularly courted potential writers with letters and notes. White once said her perfect *New Yorker* writer was Jane Austen, and this emphasis on gentle irony and observation, what James Thurber called "playing it down" in portrayals of the white upper and upper-middle classes is key to understanding what she would take for the magazine.[18] White was influential in bringing into the fold not just Bishop and Nabokov but other young writers such as Nadine Gordimer, Elizabeth Hardwick, Mary McCarthy, Adrienne Rich, and Jean Stafford. That she had her blind spots becomes clear when we learn she told Howard Moss she believed *The New Yorker* had published every important poet except, perhaps, T. S. Eliot and Edna St. Vincent Millay. White's biographer, Linda Davis, stresses that White's writers were devoted to her. Bishop was part of this admiring group, always pointing to her personal and professional relationship with White when anyone inquired about submitting to the magazine. To her Yaddo friends Kit and Ilse Barker, she said:

> As you know, she is quite a good friend of mine and has been extremely nice to me, and I don't think you could have a better person interested in you—she fights for what she likes, and I think her taste is less "safe" and conservative than the rest of them's.—I think *she* got them to take my very long story all by herself and also fought, with the poetry editor [Moss], on his side, I mean—for a long poem . . . And I've always found her criticism intelligent and to the point—not insulting![19]

A gifted close reader, White could often be seen lunching with one of her writers at The Algonquin, ordering a martini before heading to her office to review the latest manuscript. White wrote gracefully about the placement of a comma, the choice of a word, the breaking of a line, and how these details changed a poem or story's meaning. White felt it was her first duty, and the first duty of every *New Yorker* editor, to become involved in the life and work of "*every* person one comes in contact with at the magazine."[20] As Angell said, "She'd worry about her writers' health, money, happiness, their success, their children. She was a terrific worrier—she was a major-league worrier—and for an editor to be a major-league worrier is a wonderful thing."[21] In Bishop's case, it was her health, particularly her asthma, that White asked after. Her urge to take on writers in such a thoughtful though always professional way was a natural part of her personality. Its outgrowth was the "personal-editorial letter," White's other major contribution to the magazine. Whether dictating letters in New York or into "a horrible machine called a Soundscriber" from her home in Maine, she developed close working relationships by sending these notes.[22] As "mother hen of the Fiction Dept.," writing this letter was something she wanted all of her editors do. "It's a New Yorker method I've always been proud of and it is rare among magazines."[23] William Maxwell agreed, and upon retiring he told White, "I did my best to emulate your deep concern for both the literary and personal problems of your writers [. . .] the belief that the magazine was best served by what best served the writers I was working with. Which idea I got from working with you."[24]

Because White often expressed her ideas with a certain force, she developed something of a reputation. It was a reputation she was not unaware of, and it is one that has persisted after her death. After Mary McCarthy signed her first-reading agreement, White asked if she would like to be addressed as "Mrs. Wilson" or "Miss McCarthy." "I don't suppose it matters much, legally," she sighed. "For my own part I wish you and your husband and Andy and I could get on less formal terms than Mr. and Mrs. _____ There must be something particularly formidable about me which makes people call me Mrs. White indefinitely."[25] White felt strongly that all members of the fiction department should express their "ideas in loud clear tones." She didn't believe in "being polite or sparing feelings" when it came time to gather opinions for a vote. She was aware this attitude created problems. To Maxwell, she conceded, "I realize that some of the newer members of the staff take my forcible remarks (especially the spoken ones) too seriously & that I err on the side of not being tactful enough—also after 25 years I know damn well I'm often wrong in an opinion & it doesn't bother me to be told so."[26] Bishop knew of White's reputation around the office. Yet whenever her friend Pearl Kazin (later Bell) relayed some bit of office gossip, Bishop defended her editor. "I know, others have said the same things about Katharine, and yet she really couldn't be kinder or more sympathetic editorially—considering the position they're all in—than she has been to me."[27] Angell elaborates:

> If she was formidable, if people were scared of her, it was because she was so good at what she did, and she knew so much, and she was in the middle of everything—not because she'd been given power but because she assumed that this was where she belonged, because she cared so much. She was intensely, *intensely* interested in the work. It was the main event of her life—*The New Yorker*, and *New Yorker* writers, and what was in the magazine. It wasn't a matter of power. It was about what was on the page or what could be on the page if something worked out.[28]

White was modest about her contribution to *The New Yorker*. When poetry reviewer Louise Bogan emphasized White's *"great share"* in the magazine's success, White demurred. "As for my share in *The New Yorker*'s excellence—it is, as you know, just a small share and there are *countless* people who are also responsible for what good stuff we do publish—more responsible than I in recent years."[29] She felt all editors should be writers but doubted her own abilities, despite her early articles, book reviews, and highly praised column, "Onward and Upward in the Garden." Bogan chided White after one of these episodes, "You underestimate your own powers and importance; certainly your career has been creative in the true sense; and remember how helpful you have been (Andy too) to poets and writers at large, when they seemed to faint and fail!"*[30]

White was Bishop's editor, ally, and occasionally, her self-described "whipping boy." She was instrumental in Bishop's receiving the Lucy Martin

---

*White's anxiety over her role continued into retirement, called up by Tom Wolfe's notorious *New York Herald Tribune* articles, "Tiny Mummies! The True Story of the Ruler of 43rd Street's Land of the Walking Dead!" and "Lost in the Whichy Thicket," and Brendan Gill's memoir *Here at The New Yorker*. Though Wolfe did not directly refer to White, his attacks on the quality and kinds of stories run in the magazine clearly upset her. Putting it even more bluntly than Bogan, Shawn warmly contended after Wolfe's articles appeared, "Numberless writers have written better because of what you were able to give them, and many editors, including me, have been able to be of more service to writers and artists because of what you have taught them. In your integrity and passion and dedication and generosity, in your energy and never-ending youth, you have inspired us all" (Shawn to White, June 7, 1965, Bryn Mawr College Library).

Donnelly Fellowship from Bryn Mawr, the fellowship that let Bishop set sail for South America in 1951. White could be gentle in her suggestions to Bishop and she could be firm; she could deftly deploy the passive voice and drop in tentative phrasing to cushion her concerns. In her first letters as Bishop's editor, White carefully went through "Large Bad Picture" and called the poet's attention to passages that confused her fellow editors. Looking at the last two stanzas of the poem, she began:

> The question has been raised as to whether you mean by the "it" of the first line (and that of the second also) the sun or the calm harbor. As it is worded it refers to the sun and I believe you mean it to. But this belief of mine shakes a trifle when I read and wonder whether you mean the sun or the harbor as the boats' possible destination. Possibly what is obscure here therefore is the word destination rather than the "it's"?

White's sense of decorum appealed to Bishop, and she readily agreed to White's reading and made the correction and used "destination" in the second line of the last stanza. White could also politely, and at times apologetically, relay comments from Ross and other fiction editors; but in passing them on, she also showed her agreement. In his reading of "Large Bad Picture," Ross queried the "large aquatic animal" in stanza six. White outlined his concern:

> The last two lines of this stanza have bothered some readers who do not understand what you mean here. I take it you are referring to the many seals on the Labrador coast but perhaps you could work out a way to say this which won't stop anyone. Mr. Ross hopes you can name the animal—says he didn't realize there were large aquatic animals on the northern coasts. All this may sound too literal by far, but I do hope you may want to reconsider this stanza as a whole. The poem is so good and so humorous too that it would be good to have it clear to all. However, if you cherish the stanza as now worded, just say so and we'll reconsider the queries.[31]

White made it clear that this suggestion, along with other concerns, factored into the acceptance of the poem. Bishop's response was typical of what she would do when the magazine asked her to be more literal. She set out her intentions and offered some stumbling alternatives.

I am trying to describe a picture and the sounds are imaginary, just for effect. There are no animals in it—although if there were they might perfectly well be something inappropriate. If you would prefer it this way, the 1st line of that stanza 1st read "One can imagine their . . ." etc. But when one exclaims at a picture one doesn't say, "Can't you just imagine you hear the birds," etc., one says "You can just hear," etc. . . . As alternatives, though, I'd be willing to have the stanza go "One can imagine . . .", or, for the last line, "as a large unseen aquatic animal breathes." However I do think that the way it is now is much better than either of those.[32]

Regardless of what Bishop says, it is surprising that there are no animals because the stanza suggests there are. The magazine went along with her argument, but head fiction editor Gustave Lobrano let her know they were not entirely pleased. "We're disposed to accept your original wording in the reference to the breathing of the large aquatic animal," he allowed—not exactly a capitulation.[33] For this poem to have gone through, White must have exerted her influence as she continued to do in the years to come. White not only argued on Bishop's behalf during the submission process, helping stories like "In the Village" and long poems like "Manuelzinho" find their place, she kept pieces like Bishop's unfinished travel essay on Sable Island reserved for years, despite Shawn's inquiries and other writers asking for the assignment.

As she did with all her authors, White regularly asked how Bishop's work was progressing while requesting new poems. It was her way of showing concern and making plans for future issues. She had to periodically gauge the "bank," the wall of typed note cards showing pieces awaiting publication, and write reports for Ross and Shawn. Seeking Bishop's essay on Sable Island and anything else she might have on hand, White declared, "I hate to act like a whipping boy, but honestly, it is wicked to see anybody so talented as you not producing and I can't help having the uneasy feeling that you have a lot of stuff up your sleeve that you have not sent us just because you feel that it is not perfect yet."[34] When White wrote this letter in November 1954, her concern was not unfounded. Bishop had not submitted any new poems since "The Shampoo," which had been rejected the previous summer; all she offered were promises. After receiving White's letter, Bishop promptly told friends, "Mrs. White of *The New Yorker* is furious with me because I am doing a translation and not finishing up 'Sable Island,' so I must get that off, too."[35] Bishop's letters continued to express her annoyance with White's "efforts to get me to 'produce,'" speaking more to her own insecurities than to anything else.[36] By the following spring, however, Bishop was on her way to completing an unprecedented amount of work. Having completed a third of her translation of *The Diary of Helena Morley* and finished with the proofs for *A Cold Spring*, Bishop started to submit poems as she had never done before, with "The Squatter's Children," "Manners," "Filling Station," "Questions of Travel," "Sestina," "Manuelzinho," and "The Wit" all coming to White and Moss within the next year. Anxious complaints aside, Bishop was grateful to White for her encouragement. Clearly moved by White's 1955 letter announcing that she was stepping back from the magazine, Bishop wrote, "I don't know much about the workings of *The New Yorker*, nothing at all, really, but I do know it was wonderful to feel that there was someone there I knew and liked and who couldn't have taken a kinder, or more personal, or more meticulous interest in everything I sent in."[37] When White filled in for Moss during his 1959–1960 leave of absence, Bishop submitted "The Riverman." In a compliment that White modestly declined, Bishop wanted to dedicate the poem to her. As Bishop remarked near the end of her life, White "was unfailingly kind and generous to me, and unfailingly perceptive about my work."[38]

As well as being Bishop's editor, White was Bishop's friend. The two saw each other socially in New York and made plans for a picnic when Bishop spent the summer in Stonington, Maine, in 1948. Bishop visited the Whites in North Brooklin on her way back from Sable Island in 1951 and went into their barn with Andy White to see the web that would be Charlotte's. After Bishop left for Brazil, she saw White whenever she returned to New York, and White, along with Moss, helped her look for places to stay. During her 1957 trip, Bishop and her partner Lota de Macedo Soares went to White's farmhouse for dinner with Robert Lowell and Elizabeth Hardwick when visiting the Lowells in Castine. Of their visit, White related:

Both Elizabeths looked beautiful and we had a fine and very sober evening. Elizabeth Bishop seems to me healthier and more good-looking than I've ever seen her: she's svelte and chic and free of asthma. Whether she's *happy*, I can't say. I thought she was beginning to worry because she had not written anything while on this trip, but it's natural enough that she hadn't been able to. She had given up on going to Nova Scotia, as they had originally planned, and I was sorry for that because I am so anxious to have her write some more Nova Scotia short stories.[39]

When White prepared to leave the fiction department she worried about losing touch with her writers. Bishop promised their friendship would continue. "And for heaven's sake don't feel you are 'giving up' any friends! That must be just an additional fantasy of the present moment, as you must know quite well and nip in the bud immediately!"[40] The two continued to correspond after White left the magazine in 1961. Although they made plans to see each other when Bishop began summering on North Haven, Maine, there is no record of their seeing each other after Bishop's 1957 trip. As White had worried after her, Bishop worried after White and her rapidly declining health. Upon White's death in 1977, she said in her sympathy note to Andy White, "It breaks my heart to think of how much she suffered physically—"[41]

In November 1946, White suggested to Ross a first reading contract for Bishop that would cover poetry, fiction, and travel essays. In place for the last several years, the agreements stated that writers would send all work listed on their contracts to *The New Yorker* before attempting to publish it elsewhere. The magazine guaranteed writers a minimum rate per line of poetry or per word of prose and usually paid 25 percent above that, in addition to quarterly cost-of-living adjustments and a signing bonus each time the agreement was renewed. White preferred the word "agreement," "especially in talking to writers, rather than *contract*, which has a foreboding sound, it seems to me."[42] White proposed the agreement to Bishop soon after their first lunch at The Algonquin. Years later Bishop admitted to Andy White that she had felt shy and frightened at this meeting. In presenting Bishop to Ross, White described Bishop as "a literate, literary person, intelligent, [who] really has something on the ball." Having recently bought "Large Bad Picture," "Little Exercise," and "Chemin de Fer," in addition to the earlier "Cirque d'Hiver," White told Ross Bishop's poems were "better than average—mostly serious but several with a light touch." There was the sad figure of the failed artist, cabin boy turned schoolteacher, whose vision was grander than his skill in "Large Bad Picture," the subtle variation of tone that provided the necessary humor in the otherwise devastating "Little Exercise." There was the inherent comedy of the lovelorn hermit shooting off his gun as his pet hen says "chook-chook" in "Chemin de Fer" and the dry self-recognition in the flitting mechanical horse "fit for a king of several centuries back" in "Cirque d'Hiver." "She sends things around to little magazines and may not want to promise us first sight, but I could try. She is broke she says. Also is shocked that our poetry payments are so much less for on the basis of time put in the writing than our prose rates."[43] Ross approved the agreement, and White showed her enthusiasm for Bishop's work by arguing for a higher rate than was proposed. "I myself think \$1.75 a line too low for her and believe that any thing at all of hers we'd buy would be worth \$2.00." White acknowledged that some of Bishop's poems would be inappropriate for the magazine, but anything she published should be at that rate. "Her last book puts her right up with the best poets—(serious)." But Bishop seemed "somewhat dubious of signing up for poetry" and wanted to talk it over with Ferris Greenslet at Houghton Mifflin.[44] Greenslet was enthusiastic about the agreement, mentioning poet Helen Bevington's success with the arrangement. "I think your proposal from *The New Yorker* means business for you," he said. "We, of course, have no objections, only cheers."[45]

In its 1924 business prospectus, *The New Yorker* announced it would "carry each week several pages of prose and verse, short and long, humorous, satirical and miscellaneous."[46] While poetry wasn't one of the first issue's major components—there were only two poems—on page 21 readers could find the first installment of Arthur Guiterman's "Lyrics from the Pekinese." Musing on everything from the "u" in women's dresses to U.S. senators composing "demagogerel" in Washington, the well-to-do dog could turn a mean rhyme from the comfort of his satiny pillow, pairing *"gedenken"* with "Omnipotent Mencken" and "tabasco" with "David Belasco." *The New Yorker*'s poets delighted in satire and found nothing too small to write about. Even the lowly amoeba got his ode. Mixing traditional forms with everyday language, they showed a playful love of contrast and titled their poems "Lines to a Modern Refrigerator," "Lines on Anyone's Lines Along Certain Lines," and "Poem of Gratuitous Invective Against New Jersey."[47] The magazine ran parodies of poets such as T. S. Eliot, James Whitcomb Riley, Edwin Arlington Robinson, and John Greenleaf Whittier. Parodies eventually made way for travesties and poems like Ogden Nash's "I Will Arise and Go Now," his take on W. B. Yeats's "The Lake Isle of Innisfree."[48] The magazine also ran addresses to poets, like the one to Ezra Pound from a creative writing teacher. After reading *A Draft of XXX Cantos*, the teacher tells Pound to try again:

> If a student of mine should hand in to me
> Such pretentious nonsense,
> I should give him (or her)
> A very low mark:
> In fact, a C–[49]

Poetry clubs and literary teas were also the subject of satire, as were poets and poetasters. Poets were to be pitied for their wringing of hands, their flowery, overwrought language, and, well, for their inability to find friends at train stations. Taken all together, poetry in *The New Yorker* demonstrated a profound reaction against the decorous and formal verse of the previous century and against the challenges of literary modernism. Its editors wanted poetry that was smart but not difficult, that was witty and light on its feet. They wanted the poet and the poem to maintain good form, in all its senses, and most important, they wanted poems to sound like talk. The work they published was a precursor of the plain style that came to dominate American poetry by the 1970s, and not surprisingly, that style found a home in the magazine.

In 1929, White persuaded Ross to publish what the magazine called "serious" poetry soon after he agreed to publish "serious" prose. It wasn't an easy sell. Ross had little interest in anything other than light verse for his young weekly's pages. White recalled, "It was a concession on his part to run any serious verse."[50] When White began contacting poets, she was met with surprise. "Really I didn't know that *The NYer* was interested in poetry as poetry," William Carlos Williams wrote.[51] Indeed, balancing "Sand" and "Lake," or serious and light verse, was a source of tension for the rest of White's and Ross's careers. With the onset of war in Europe, editors did not want to be accused of being aloof, as their critics charged during the Depression, and they cut back on humorous writing and increased the number of serious poems. In fact, the entire magazine changed and its tone became more somber. The magazine ran poems that reflected the growing angst before the bombing of Pearl Harbor with W. H. Auden's "Song," Stephen Vincent Benét's "Nightmare for Future Reference," and Louis MacNeice's "Barroom Matins."[52] It also published poems from soldiers like Karl Shapiro and Peter Viereck and printed others that gave the view from home. This turn in *The New Yorker* did not go unnoticed, and its poetry became to gain recognition, both in print and informally between colleagues. Stanley Edgar Hyman remarked in *The New Republic*, "*The New Yorker*'s serious verse, like the serious fiction, is surprising both for its quality and its degree of social content." Louise Bogan told Morton Zabel, former editor of *Poetry*, that *The New Yorker*'s poetry "is alive," after he dismissed it.[53]

Complicating the debate over poetry was Ross's early declaration that *The New Yorker* "will be the magazine which is not edited for the old lady in Dubuque." Ross, White, and Shawn—indeed, all the editors—maintained that what they chose to print was based solely on what they liked to read.

White recalled, "We did not work or write for anyone but ourselves, and Ross and all the rest of us never thought whether our readers would like this, that or the other. It was a rule, in fact, that we were never to consider our readers. We were only to consider the merits of the manuscript in question and publish what *we* liked."[54] Fiction and fact pieces aside, White simply did not have the kind of latitude in publishing poetry that she described. In rejecting Bogan's poem "Hypocrite Swift," White said, "Mr. Ross feels that it presents a literary knowledge and background that most of our readers would not have and that it would not be understandable to many people who read it."[55] Editors, particularly Pearce, would occasionally refer to the magazine's view of its readers. In responding to "What Are Years?" which Moore had submitted at his request, Pearce asked for clarification in what was most likely the first stanza.

You probably realize how literal minded we are, and how anxious we are to avoid printing anything which might confuse or puzzle our readers. I didn't have trouble understanding what you were getting at in the three lines alongside of which I have run my pencil, but this part of the poem would, we think, present something of a problem to most of our readers, and I wonder if you would care to change the poem and say what you have in mind in a more direct and simple fashion.[56]

When Bishop heard of Moore's rejection a few weeks after "Cirque d'Hiver" appeared, she fired off, "What I think about *The New Yorker* can only be expressed like this: *!@!!!@!*!!"[57] She later continued, "I simply can't understand *The New Yorker*—or yes, perhaps I can—they want all *New Yorker* poetry to sound like *New Yorker* poetry, on & on . . ."[58] Bishop would have "Varick Street" and "Faustina" rejected on similar grounds. None of the editors liked writing rejections, and Maxwell told White that after he retired he felt "more light-hearted because I am not writing letters that begin, 'I am extremely sorry but the vote was against . . .' "[59] White agreed. "I know what you mean about a distaste for writing 'The vote was against' to one of one's dearest friends, and sometimes time after time."[60] In addition to being too difficult and too elliptical, poems were also rejected for being too dramatic or too archaic, or for having to be read with a dictionary. Sometimes editors placed the blame right at Ross's cantankerous feet. Speaking of the third stanza of "The Deceptrices," Maxwell told Williams, "Ellipses and indirection and implication, even in poetry make him nervous. *What*, he wants to know, is too soon gone?"[61]

Ross died on December 6, 1951, and five weeks later, Shawn, then managing editor of the Fact Department, took his place. With a notice posted on the editorial floor, Shawn's new position became official on January 21, 1952. Having come to the magazine researching "Talk of the Town" stories in 1933, Shawn was revered for his skillful editing. He led *The New Yorker* until 1987, when he was fired by S. I. Newhouse in Condé Nast's huge shake-up of the magazine. As in control of the final product as Ross had been, Shawn was a quiet, less flamboyant presence but a presence that was no less mistakable. As Moss once said, "He has the ultimate authority."[62] Despite making no major changes in his first ten years, he agreed to White's request to expand the place of serious verse. As time went by, the magazine committed itself to using its high rates to get the best writing it could afford. *The New Yorker* never lavished money on poetry the way it did on prose, but it did pay significantly better than its competitors. It was at this time that the magazine began regularly publishing Bishop, Robert Graves, Howard Nemerov, Theodore Roethke, William Stafford, and Richard Wilbur. Under this strategy, the magazine's reputation continued to grow, leading Karl Shapiro, then editor of *Poetry*, to remark that he regarded *The New Yorker* as "one of the few places where a poet can be in the right company and get a proper reward and audience all at once."[63] White sent out feelers almost immediately, contacting Bogan and Bishop and inviting E. E. Cummings and Wallace Stevens to submit. Careful not to make promises, she let them know that Shawn "likes more *kinds* of poetry than Ross did."[64] White confessed to Bogan:

> I know that you've never thought highly of most of the poems we did publish and I imagine that you are aware of what our limitations have been in the past in that field. Such poetry—as distinct from light verse—as we did publish was always more or less on sufferance. Therefore I never dared ask certain poets to contribute as I felt almost too awkward to ask them to submit their work.[65]

White especially wanted to see Auden and Moore in the magazine. She had pursued them several years before, but having rejected poems such as "September 1939" and "Four Quartz Crystal Clocks," she worried about hard feelings. Bogan was delighted with the policy change and agreed that Auden and Moore would be a good match for the magazine. White wrote Auden directly and appealed to him for poems. "Now, I think, we can have more leeway, though being the kind of magazine we are, I suppose we shall never be able to use the more abstruse or experimental poetry of the literary reviews or special poetry magazines."[66] White approached Moore through Bishop, and eventually Moore, like Auden, came to be a regular contributor. Although change was slow at first, by the time White retired in January 1961, the number of poetry submissions had risen substantially. A rush of young poets saw their debut, and readers began finding poems from James Dickey, Ted Hughes, William Meredith, W. S. Merwin, Anne Sexton, John Updike, David Wagoner, and James Wright.

When Bishop came to *The New Yorker* in 1946, she came not just to its pages but also to its particular approach to editing. In addition to his love of humor with a bright sheen and stories packed with facts, Ross's newspaper-style editing was his great and enduring legacy. While the process could be painstaking and at times downright aggravating, *The New Yorker*'s writers ended up thankful for their editors' meticulous reading and respected their dedication to clear and conversational writing. Bishop found *The New Yorker* superbly edited and complained of mistakes she saw in other magazines. Ross spent a considerable amount of energy developing this approach, and there was nothing too small for him to consider. With *Webster's* and Fowler by his desk, Ross fired off memos, sometimes blunt, sometimes elaborate, and always humorous, with the latest rules for his editors to follow. Style sheets on where to place commas in dialogue, how to use (or not use) periods in acronyms, and when "Oh!" was more appropriate than "O!" found their way to editors' in-boxes, telling them to query words and phrases such as "vague," "a little," "oddly enough," "pretty," "innards," and any adjective ending in "-ish." "I think the word 'fabulous' should be regarded with great suspicion. It seems suddenly to have become a fad word and, worse, a *Vogue* word; it is said to appear on every page of *Vogue* in every issue."[67] At times Bishop could even sound like Ross. She made a list of forbidden words for her Harvard students and on reading over her friend May Swenson's poem "All That Time," she cried, "I can't BEAR the word 'like' used instead of 'as if.' But perhaps you have decided in favor of that use of it?—In which case there's nothing much I can say, because it is a possibility—But please look at Fowler, page 325, I just hate it—"[68]

The sheer volume of Ross's style memos and joking bombast contributed to Thurber's series "Our Own Modern English Usage" and Wolcott Gibbs's unpublished spoof "Theory and Practice of Editing *New Yorker* Articles." Gibbs's "scholarly document," as White called it, begins with a parody of Ross: "The average contributor to this magazine is semi-literate; that is, he is ornate to no purpose, full of senseless and elegant variations, and can be relied on to use three sentences where a word would do. It is impossible to lay down any exact and complete formula for bringing order out of this under-brush, but there are a few general rules."[69] Muffling her chuckles, when White passed "Theory and Practice" on to recent hire Gus Lobrano, she said, the rules are "absolutely sound."[70] One of the first rules was "pegging" a story's location, owing to Ross's theory that readers assumed *New Yorker* stories took place in New York. "If it doesn't, if it's about Columbus, Ohio, the lead should say so. 'When George Adams was sixteen, he began to worry about the girls' should read 'When George Adams was sixteen, he began to worry about the girls he saw every day on the streets of Columbus' or some-thing of the kind. More graceful preferably." Bishop came up against this rule during the editing of her stories "Gwendolyn" and "In the Village," so when she suggested her friend Ilse Barker send White some work, she added, "They would probably want their standardized kind of information-giving beginning—'In the Black Forest just before the first World War' or some-thing on that order . . . 'My mother'—not quite so explicit, of course, but *placing* the thing—and I bet if you can manage to do that [. . .] Katharine would like them."[71] Beyond pegging, poems and stories should not be about writers or the writing business, as Bishop learned with the rejection of "Rachel and the U.S.A. School of Writing." Foul language (and "functional references") had to go unless absolutely necessary. As far as humor went, the magazine did not do puns. Fowler's *English Usage* was the grammar guide, "but don't be precious about it," Gibbs warned. Editors did query these points on a regular basis, and many pieces were rejected because they did not measure up. Poems were subject to the same checking that prose was, and the legal department read poems, as they did everything else, for libel. Poets sometimes tried to beat *The New Yorker* to the punch, explaining where their information came from. Otherwise, they were left to track down their sources after the fact. The editors understood how their questions came across. To Auden's remark that the staff was somewhat daft, Maxwell said, "The description is accurate enough."[72]

Although White said these rules applied during Ross's years but not Shawn's, that's not quite true. Several of Gibbs's points became issues for Bishop while Shawn was editor. Violating rule eighteen brought the trou-bling rejections of "The Shampoo." In reviewing the difficulty that stories containing drunkenness and adultery posed for the magazine, Gibbs con-cluded, "Homosexuality [. . .] is definitely out as humor, and dubious in any case." "The Shampoo," an affectionate lyric of washing her beloved Lota de

Macedo Soares's hair, was the most openly gay poem Bishop had attempted to publish to date. White let Bishop know the votes were mixed. Things were set up so that if White did not want a poem, she rejected it immediately and did not show it to her fellow editors. Saying that the votes were mixed probably made White a "yes." If she wanted a poem, she showed it to another editor, most likely Moss, since he dealt exclusively with poetry; but if he was away, she would show it to someone else. It didn't matter whether the other editor agreed or not because the poem then went to Shawn, who had final say. Who the second reader of "The Shampoo" was is unclear—Moss was in the office—but Shawn had to have said no. After questioning some wording in the second stanza, White said sheepishly, "But I guess the deciding factor was that this sort of small personal poem perhaps doesn't quite fit into *The New Yorker*."[73]

From the very beginning, Bishop took her rejections in stride. Of a special issue of *Westminster Magazine* (1935) she remarked, "The fact that Ezra Pound has left out my poems along with the others does not distress me very much, except that it probably marks the beginning of a long period of such discriminations."[74] But the rejection of "The Shampoo" was something else. She wrote Pearl Kazin, her *New Yorker* friend who had spent time in Brazil, about White's letter. "Yesterday she returned a little poem which I think I'll enclose just to see what *you* think and maybe you'll understand it better than she did being acquainted with some of the details. It won't make literary history either, but I did think it was easy enough to understand."[75] She fiddled with the poem for a couple of days and then wrote Kazin again. "Here is the little poem Mrs. White couldn't understand—I have changed three words, though, since she returned it. I wonder if I am in honor bound to return it to them because of the three words before I send it someplace else?"[76] The version in Bishop's papers which runs closest to the comments in White's rejection letter has the second and third stanzas as:

> And all the heavens will attend
> as long on us.
> You are, dear friend,
> demanding and too voluble;
> and look what happens. For Time is
> nothing if not amenable.
>
> The shooting stars in your black hair
> in swift formation

are flocking where,
so straight, so soon?

The other parts of the poem are the same as it was eventually published. Bishop changed "demanding and too voluble" to the alliterative and playful "precipitate and pragmatical" and the "swift formation" of stars to a "bright" one, highlighting the streak of white in Lota's long, dark hair. Bishop also combined the first and second sentences and adjusted the verb tense, "You are" to "you've been," in the second stanza, giving the poem more speed while lessening the declarative quality of the stanza's first two lines. The same day she sent the revised poem to Kazin, she sent it to Karl Shapiro at *Poetry*. Shapiro's reply was short and quick. "I never thought I'd see the day when we would reject a poem of yours but we do so daringly today. I hope that our courage will be rewarded with a long poem of yours."[77] What added to the sting was the lack of response from friends, including Moore. To Swenson she worried, "No one but you and one other friend have ever even mentioned *The Shampoo*, I don't know why—I sent it to a few friends and never heard a word and began to think there was something indecent about it I'd overlooked."[78] As she had with rejected poems in the past, she thought about revising the poem, making it "more elaborate—a stanza or two more—because it does sound now as if something were left out."[79] The version she sent to Kazin was eventually published by *The New Republic*.

Bishop's play with sexual identity was also the likely reason for Moss's rejection of "Exchanging Hats" in 1955. After it appeared in John Ciardi's poetry selection for *New World Writing*, her friend James Merrill wrote a praising note, to which Bishop replied. "I am glad you liked Exchanging Hats because I was afraid it was a good idea completely spoiled in the writing."[80] Despite writing a number of love poems after submitting "The Shampoo" and giving at least one of them as a gift, it wasn't until she sent Moss "One Art" in 1975 that she attempted to publish one again. Likewise, she held off publishing anything that could be read as dealing with sexual identity until submitting "Sonnet" in 1977.

When White stepped aside as Bishop's editor in January 1956, poet Howard Moss came to take her place. A native New Yorker, Moss had worked briefly as a book reviewer at *Time* magazine and served as an English instructor at Vassar College before holding an editing position at the soon-to-be-defunct *Junior Bazaar*. After *Junior Bazaar* folded, the twenty-six-year-old Moss learned of an opening at *The New Yorker* from recent arrival Peter De Vries, whom Moss had known from *Poetry* when studying at the University of Wisconsin. As part of his application, Moss had to edit several anonymous stories. One, he could tell, was Vladimir Nabokov's. "I made some notes, things I would ordinarily have changed, like the word 'perish.' Somebody 'perished.' In any other story, I would have changed that to 'died,' but in view of the overall tone of Nabokov, I wouldn't touch it. You don't tamper with people who know what they're doing. I knew even that much back then and I suppose that's why I got the job."[81] Moss was hired in 1948, and two years later, he asked Ross about working exclusively with poetry. Moss and White shared responsibility for the poets as she quietly coached him for the position. By the time White retired in 1960, Moss had full command of the magazine's poetry, buying poems from a multitude of poets and priding himself on publishing unknown writers every year. Regular contributors who arrived early in their careers include Louise Glück, Seamus Heaney, Philip Levine, Sharon Olds, Robert Pinsky, Stanley Plumly, Dave Smith, Mark Strand, Derek Walcott, and Charles Wright. With poems from John Ashbery, Paul Blackburn (son of early contributor Frances Frost), and Diane Wakoski, Moss continued White's push to extend the magazine's range, but how far he could go ultimately rested with Shawn. Like White, Moss developed lasting friendships with many of the writers he published. Not one to write the "editorial-personal" letters she did—he usually kept his office letters to the point and saved his personal correspondence for home—he regularly lunched with writers at The Algonquin and the Teheran and met them for drinks at the Iroquois. By his death in 1987, he had become one of the most influential editors of his generation.

Although his selections had grown more eclectic, Moss was particularly welcoming of the plain style—broadly, a narrative poem that uses Wordsworth's "language of real men" in a concentrated and often elevated way to find beauty in everyday events. There was no room in *The New Yorker*'s pages for the linguistic experimentation of the Beats or Objectivists, nor was there room for the sheer length of John Berryman's "Homage to Mistress Bradstreet," the playful 4/4 blues of Langston Hughes's "Mean Old Yesterday," or the raw female anger of Sylvia Plath's "Daddy." That the magazine could be shortsighted comes out in Moss's rejection, month after month, of almost every poem found in Plath's posthumous collection *Ariel*. The "family magazine," as Bishop called it, maintained its manners and continued to turn down poems using what can only be called bodily subject matter.[82] Galway Kinnell flat-out retracted "The Porcupine" after Moss suggested he change "he shits on the run" to "he defecates." "There's nothing I can do but tell you about it," Moss said with some embarrassment about Shawn's policy.[83] Moss loved *The New Yorker*, but he was also conscious of its limitations, leading him to joke about starting a magazine called *Not The New Yorker* for all the impressive work he had to reject. Many poets understood Moss's situation. Anne Sexton dryly noted with her submission of "In Celebration of My Uterus" and "The Nude Swim" that it was highly unlikely he would take either poem.[84]

Despite its strictures, by the late fifties, publishing in *The New Yorker* was a mark of success. Aurelia Plath recalled a phone call from her daughter a few years before her death, "her voice vibrant with joy—'I've *arrived*, mother! A *New Yorker* acceptance, at last!'"[85] The number of submissions continued to rise, and by the late 1970s, *New Yorker* historian Ben Yagoda asserts, "there was no doubt that American poets would rather be published in *The New Yorker* than any other journal."[86]

Moss edited poetry the same way his colleagues edited prose, with a keen eye and a sharp pencil. "The words in poems are no more sacred than words in anything else," Moss said on more than one occasion. It was a credo that would have certainly met with Ross's approval. "I will often make suggestions on changes, cuts, different punctuation. I would never edit without the approval of the author, but I feel quite free to make suggestions for improvement if we are seriously interested in his work. Think of what Pound did for Eliot, after all."[87] Moss was known for his excellent ear, and drumming his fingers on his desk, he looked for places where a poem went on too long, where it sped up or slowed down, where it digressed or changed its tone.

> My most important function is to spot irrelevance, that point when an idea, or motif, or a tone wanders off course. An irrelevance is not a leap of the imagination, but an editor has to be very careful in discriminating between them, because sometimes, it is the very stuff we read poetry for—the surprising elevation, the rug pulled out from under our feet, the illumination by a second reference, another subject, of what the man there is after.[88]

As the department grew in stature, Moss's longtime assistant Vickie Karp found herself reading up to a thousand poems a week while Moss edited the ones the magazine bought, tracked proofs, monitored the bank, and handled innumerable small business details. His hectic schedule led to one of his long-standing jokes: the sight of his office desk. To his friend Richard Wilbur he jested:

My desk looks like nothing I've ever seen. Or I think even human eyes have seen. There are hundreds of poems, proofs, protests, angry revisions, carbons, postcards suggesting revisions in poems I didn't know we'd bought, attacks, personal revelations, checks, contracts, tickets to shows that have expired, notes, memos, and changes of address certain people I can't even remember have moved. Pray for me.[89]

The fatigue of his job got to him, even in dealing with Bishop. In a note to his lifelong friend John Malcolm Brinnin, Moss related a recent conversation during which he and Bishop made plans to meet during an upcoming trip to Boston. "But then we discussed a semicolon in a new poem of hers at some length—disheartening."[90] Moss had expressed this sentiment in one form or another from early on. Sometime during the mid-fifties Brinnin considered applying for a position at the magazine. Moss dissuaded him, saying he would have to face "the drudgery of picayune and maddening editing" every day. "It *is* drudgery and I think the close kind of meaningless detail work would make you unhappier, probably, than a real crap job."[91]

Moss saw himself as a writer first and an editor second. Well noted for his elegant handling of form, elegiac tone, and sparkling wit, Moss wrote poetry, criticism, and plays and edited a number of anthologies and collections. His poems appeared regularly in *The New Yorker*, and they went through the same editorial process of acceptance, rejection, and queries that his poets' work did. Moss garnered several major awards, including the National Book Award for his *Selected Poems* in 1972. Yet, from the start of his career, he struggled with his job as editor and its impact on his writing and reputation. In a letter of recommendation, Brinnin told Yaddo director Elizabeth Ames that Moss hoped to complete his second book at the Saratoga estate. "As you no doubt know, he is poetry editor for *The New Yorker* and while he likes the job and is able to do much good for poetry in that position, the high pressure under which he must work tends to sabotage his own efforts."[92] Eventually, Moss was able to arrange his schedule so he came into the office only two days a week with his summers off, providing him with time to write. Like other *New Yorker* editors, he also took leaves of absence to pursue his poetry and plays. "How I would love to be yanked out of the NYer for two years and do nothing but write!" he exclaimed to Brinnin.[93]

Working at the magazine did have its rewards. Moss deeply enjoyed working with poets and learning from their work. An exciting new poem could lift his spirits for weeks. He was troubled, however, by the "confusion between me as an editor and me as a poet. The distinction is very clear to me."[94] His position often put him on the spot with other writers. "I'm afraid I've forgotten what not being on one is like," he confessed. "Everywhere I go I am greeted by poems. I am waiting for the ultimate dinner party at which, when I lift up my napkin, there will be a double sestina lying on my plate."[95] Moss loved the swirl of the city's literary life—his letters to Brinnin are full of cocktails, dinners, and parties—but it also wore him down. Moss could show his work in progress to few people with much trust. Of compliments he received, he admitted, "I can't tell whether people really mean it or just want to get into the NYer."[96] White understood the feelings Moss had about his job and its effect on his writing. From time to time he would half consider leaving the magazine. After she received a copy of *Finding Them Lost*, she tried to cheer him on: "The one reason I think you are so good a poet is that you do not write poetry every minute and your other work— prose and editing—keeps you from writing too *much* poetry and sending it out for publication."[97]

Moss and Bishop had a warm friendship but not an intimate one. They met some time before September 1945 through the painter Loren MacIver. Moss wrote Brinnin soon after their meeting. "I had a lovely dinner with Elizabeth Bishop, Loren and others. Elizabeth and I get along wonderfully well, and I have a feeling it's going to be a very good relationship for me. I'm having dinner with her again this week."[98] The pair shared a love of good food and good music, a breezy, soft-shoe humor, and a circle of friends. They saw each other whenever Bishop was in New York and later made plans to meet in Europe. Bishop regularly invited Moss to her home in Brazil, and even though he never went, he gave her address to friends and writers traveling in South America, including the young Mark Strand. Once Bishop moved to Cambridge, they saw each other in New York and Boston and met from time to time at Brinnin's beach house in Duxbury, Massachusetts. Moss was affectionate and charming in his letters, even writing "Letter to an Imaginary Brazil" as a gift, and Bishop was witty and talkative in hers, responsive to his work and gracious about his praise. In their surviving letters neither Moss nor Bishop discuss their personal lives. Bishop never seems to have griped to him about *The New Yorker* the way she did to Pearl Kazin, talked about her financial worries, or shared her increasingly stressful situation with Lota. Moss never seems to have shared *his* complaints about work or the pressures and anxieties of publishing, let alone mentioning family or relationships.

Enthusiastic about Bishop's poetry since first reading it, Moss told Brinnin, "I just finished reading Elizabeth Bishop's book which is superb. I have the utmost love for it—it's so original, so clean, and so beautifully new. I think I could live happily with *Look Stranger, Deaths and Entrances*, and *North & South*."[99] His feeling never wavered and he took pleasure in reading poems like "Anaphora" and "Little Exercise" with friends. Bishop was "one of the few that never gets stale for me. And my admiration for her poems continues unabated. To me, she's the best, the one I read most for enjoyment. Let Merwin and Lowell and . . . Ginsberg . . . go on being major. I know what I like."[100] He threw the spotlight on her whenever he had the chance, despite his policy of not writing about the people he edited. "I was so crazy about her work that I couldn't avoid writing about it."[101] In thoughtful essay-reviews, he praised her indirect and sympathetic approach, her restraint, and her lack of self-absorption. In reviewing *Questions of Travel*, Moss singled out her clear-eyed vision in addition to her intuitive sense of form and selection of detail. In one of the most astute comments about her poetry, he described her work as "revolutionary, not 'experimental.'"[102] To his young contributors, Moss used Bishop as a kind of gold standard. After all, he kept her photo displayed in his wall of poets above his office desk. In explaining his rejection of "A Point of Distance," Moss told Strand, "We liked many things in it, of course, but our main objection was that instead of merely using the resources of prose, the way Elizabeth Bishop does, say, this often becomes prose itself—or so it seems to us."[103]

Within a few years of starting her first-reading agreement, Bishop hoped to publish poems elsewhere. She wanted to see work in *Botteghe Oscure, Evergreen Review, New World Writing*, and *Poetry*. Editors often asked Bishop to submit, but because of her contract she had to wait for *The New Yorker*'s rejection. When John Ciardi wrote from *The Saturday Review* and later *The Nation*, Bishop felt she couldn't promise anything because she wrote so few poems and because she had "some 'commitments.'"[104] When Bishop eventually sent him "Exchanging Hats" for *New World Writing*, she bantered, "Here is a small escaped poem."[105] Her contract was even the source of some gentle goading. Philip Rahv, who had published Bishop regularly in *Partisan Review*, never gave up on her work and always expressed his wish that she return to its pages. "Your writing is better than ever, and I do wish you'd 'liberate' some of them from *The New Yorker*'s grasp and send them to us."[106] Bishop was particularly keen on appearing in *Poetry*. Since 1950 she had wanted to send work to Karl Shapiro.

> I had a poem ["The Prodigal"] I was sure *The New Yorker* wouldn't want & I wanted to send it to you. They boggled for a week at its indelicacy but finally took it—they were very decent, said I could have it back if I wanted it for my next book, but, alas, since they pay on acceptance and since I needed the money for my fare to NS—I let them take it. I still hope to send you some things soon though—I'm trying to wind up all the poems for the book before I go and there should be 2 or 3 I shd think—unless I'm really a wage-slave.[107]

After Shapiro requested a submission for the fortieth anniversary issue, Bishop responded, "I shall do my *damnedest* to get you something by Aug 1st—I never *have* any 'unpublished works' though—no 'works' at all. I've been wanting to send you something for 2 years now, & I *am* writing you one & hope it reaches you, this time."[108] The next month she sent White "The Mountain," not so subtly hinting she wanted it to go to *Poetry*. At the same time she alerted Shapiro that something might be coming his way. "I feel as if I were staying home from a grand costume ball," she cried like a wry Cinderella.[109] At Bishop's behest, White promptly rejected the poem and forwarded it to Shapiro, who ran it in the anniversary number. Bishop included "The Mountain" in the first printing of *A Cold Spring* but eventually distanced herself from the poem and removed it from later printings.

Along with finding a change of venue, Bishop wanted to reorient her work. After reading a batch of Robert Lowell's poems that included "My Last Afternoon with Uncle Devereux Winslow" and "Sailing Home from Rapallo," she confessed, "It is hell to realize one has wasted half one's talent through timidity that probably could have been overcome if anyone in one's family had had a few grains of sense or education . . . Well, maybe it's not too late!"[110] She considered writing fewer descriptions and more directly about herself. She also began to voice concerns about *The New Yorker*'s effect on her writing. After reading her Yaddo acquaintance Calvin Kentfield's story, "A Good Example," Bishop wondered whether publishing in the magazine led to sentimental writing. "Oh dear—what is always supposed to happen to NY-er writers maybe does happen. Perhaps I can be saved because I write so seldom?"[111] In addition, Bishop started to feel *The New Yorker* was pigeonholing her as a South American writer, and she bridled at this perception. Her concern came from her editors' queries, which "have been just too silly lately."[112] This charge was aimed at White and Shawn for, among other things, continually asking her to identify the location of her poems. When White suggested including "Brazil" in the title of "Song for the Rainy Season," as was done for "Brazil, January 1, 1502," Bishop refused. "I don't want to become a local-color poet any more than I can help."[113]

Reviewers had identified Bishop with *The New Yorker* since *North & South*. While only four of its thirty poems appeared in the magazine, Selden Rodman believed Bishop's "sophisticated innocence now and again recalls standard *New Yorker* light verse."[114] Vocalizing her growing discomfort with the association, after receiving the *Partisan Review* Fellowship in 1956, Bishop told Rahv, "With any luck at all I hope to get a group of non–*New Yorker* poems done this winter to send you. They take some rather unlikely things sometimes, though—in spite of Mr. Gregory! (However, in general, I agree with him.)"[115] Bishop is referring to Horace Gregory's essay-review "The Poetry of Suburbia," which takes numerous jabs at *The New Yorker* through comments on recent books by Adrienne Rich and Richard Wilbur. Calling it "the handbook of the suburban matron," Gregory, who had published poems in the magazine in the forties and had been one of Bishop's early and pivotal supporters, says its "quasi-serious verse" is nothing but formulaic. The *New Yorker* school, Gregory contends, relies on "certain verse forms used with enough caution to be recognized at once, certain images within the verses that recall the 'happy-bitter' experience of childhood, the joy of collecting toys and the discovery that toys are perishable, the country places visited at home, and the holiday from suburban security in Europe."[116] Gregory was not alone in what he saw. These criticisms had been leveled before, and they would be leveled after: that *The New Yorker* featured bourgeois poets writing for bourgeois readers. Likewise, Lowell, a *Partisan* regular, believed the magazine showed "no particular continuity of excellence" because of its use of light verse. "There just seems no point in printing there."[117] These comments from Lowell and Gregory, on the heels of *Partisan*'s negative review of *A Cold Spring*, must have hit a nerve and kindled her recurring self-doubt.

From the beginning, Bishop was pleased by the rate she received from *The New Yorker*. She had always hoped to supplement her modest inheritance with publication fees, and *The New Yorker*'s line rates were encouraging in this regard. After "Cirque d'Hiver" appeared, she confided to her college friend Frani Blough (now Muser), "They've asked me for more and I hope I'll be able to supply them because they pay one dollar a line."[118] Yet Bishop prided herself on not sacrificing her art and would hold on to a poem until it was just right. "I had a poem and a letter for K White—took them to the PO—changed my mind about one line in the poem and brought it back—now it's stuck for another five years, I suppose—and I'm desperate for CASH!"[119] With the sale of "Gwendolyn" and "In the Village," Bishop realized the money she could make writing prose. The magazine's prose rates were an attraction, and they could leave writers incredulous once their checks arrived. "Well, a few more stories to *The New Yorker* and I can rocket to the moon if I care to, it seems to me," Bishop bandied to Lowell.[120] Despite her worries about soul selling, saying she was "going to stick to absolutely unsellable (to the NY-er) subject matter as the only way of playing safe—" Bishop began trying to write stories for extra income.[121] She even planned a "detective story to make money from 'Ellery Queen'" and declared her hopes "to jump at least three income tax brackets" with prose in 1955.[122] With Brazil's inflating cruzeiro and Lota's assets tied up in real estate and lawsuits, Bishop wanted to contribute to the household and take Lota on a much-needed trip. The pressure she put herself under came out in mumbling to Lowell that she was supposedly "at home to work and make us money . . ."[123] She eventually submitted "Rachel and the U.S.A. School of Writing" and an essay on her trip with Aldous Huxley and his wife Laura Archera to the new capital city Brasilia. She worked on the essay for several months and even had Lota's friends do some fact-checking, but *The New Yorker* rejected it, as they had her story. Bishop was not surprised: she knew one of its main faults was the lack of quotes from Huxley. Bishop told her doctor Anny Baumann, "I feel it was rather *dumb* of me to put in so much time on it. However, the chief loss is that we'd hoped to start the garage on the proceeds! Now I'll work on something more my natural bent . . ."[124]

As Bishop had written "The Mountain" for *Poetry*, she wrote "The Riverman" for *The New Yorker*, but not for the same reasons. There was no grand anniversary issue, no "Best of . . ." in which she wanted to appear. For the last few years, Bishop had been busy translating *The Diary of Helena Morley* and working on her Brasilia essay in addition to her usual voluminous correspondence with friends and family. When she sent Moss "The Riverman" in June 1959, she had not finished any poems for publication in almost three years. Although she was happy to be writing poetry, and even hoped to complete a book by the following year, she was not happy with the poem. The 158-line "Riverman" was part of a group, and she sent it to Moss first, thinking he "might take it if the other better ones didn't come at the same time!—and it seems to have worked."[125] The magazine's acceptance telegram lifted her spirits and Bishop offered to dedicate the poem to White, but she was quickly embarrassed by the poem (Lota hated it). She confided to Kazin, "I'm afraid I was feeling desperate about NY and money—"[126] Her anxiety seemed to have reached a new pitch, and she wondered if she was worrying poetry "right out of existence."[127] Bishop also seemed uncomfortable with the way she had composed the poem. "I actually just lifted whole phrases out of a couple of chapters [of Charles Wagley's book *Amazon Town*] and stuck them together—scarcely anything of my own."[128] Mixed with this unease was her feeling that "The Riverman" was inauthentic, as she had not taken a trip on the Amazon herself: that trip was to come, the following year. It's as if she could hear Marianne Moore urging her "not to worry about what other people thought, never to try to publish anything until I'd done my best with it, no matter how many years it took—or never to publish at all." Yet, at the same time Bishop was struggling with these issues, so was her mentor. Moore, now a regular contributor, confessed to Moss, "I don't quite bear out my advice to beginners, 'pay no attention to acceptances and rejections. Write what you, yourself, like and be loyal to it!'"[129]

With Moss away, William Maxwell sent Bishop her contract renewal in October 1960. But, unknown to him, she had more or less made up her mind to leave the magazine. Like any publication, *The New Yorker* came with a certain reputation. Over the years it had been the subject of numerous articles and commentaries, many of them published in *Partisan Review*, and the attitudes expressed therein were often some variant of Horace Gregory's. At times Bishop went so far as to try to separate herself from the magazine, calling it "that rigidly 'nice' sheet."[130] When she described "In the Village" to the Barkers, she said it was "completely autobiographical (although not in the usual NY-er manner)—I've just stuck a few years together."[131] Bishop never specifically defined what that "manner" was, but critics often described *New Yorker* fiction as understated and conversational, citing Anton Chekhov and Katherine Mansfield as its models. Stories tended to share a certain reminiscent mood, which came out in long descriptive passages and fade-to-black endings. After *The New Yorker* took "In the Village," Bishop was worried. "At first I thought it was my best, but after they took it naturally I had serious doubts. However, they keep assuring me it is extremely 'experimental' for them."[132] What Bishop objected to in *The New Yorker* was perhaps what she objected to in a lot of women's writing, the "She-has-such-a-*lovely*-home" boasting.

They are secretly pointing out, for you to admire, their beautifully polished old silver, their taste in clothes, their intellectual and, frequently, social standing, their husbands, etc.—and ultimately their sexual irresistibility . . . (Men writers do this last of course, but not in such a sly way). It's the "How nice to be nice!" atmosphere that gets to me, and I think women writers must get quite away from it before they ever amount to a hill of beans . . .[133]

As practitioners of the style, Bishop included, among others, *New Yorker* regulars Mary McCarthy, Jean Stafford, and Eudora Welty.

Growing more unhappy with the magazine, Bishop announced to Kazin, "It is getting to be like reading a quilt—eating a quilt, I mean—full of starchy fillers and 'enough water to properly prepare' etc."[134] *New Yorker* historian Yagoda agrees, characterizing this period, with the exception of John Cheever and the young John Updike, as bland. Bishop noticed a lack of variety in its offerings and was tired of finding the same writers week after week. She was especially disappointed in its recent fiction. Pointing to J. D. Salinger's "Seymour: An Introduction," she was bothered by the rumor that Salinger's stories ran untouched. (In this case, Shawn edited "Seymour," instead of the fiction department). To Kazin, also a story writer, she said, "WE MUST write some stories for the *NYer*—we could do better than what they've been printing lately blindfolded, I'm sure."[135] Bishop was further dissatisfied with its poetry, finding some poems guilty of "false refinement."[136] After reading Moore's "Carnegie Hall: Rescued" and "Tell Me, Tell Me," Bishop echoed her sentiments from 1940 when Pearce rejected "What Are Years?": "It has taken *The New Yorker* sadly long, I think, to discover that there is a *real* New-Yorker, *New Yorker* poet—just the kind of thing they must have dreamed of when they were younger and better—sophistication, wit, up-to-date,—and informed—all the New York qualities it seems to me they've been losing, themselves, lately."[137]

Bishop did not single out *The New Yorker* in her complaints. Her criticism extended to most contemporary poetry. An avid reader of little magazines and literary reviews, more and more of what she read was "just well-written and *voulu*."[138] "I get so depressed with every number of POETRY, *The New Yorker*, etc.," she explained to Lowell. "So much adequate poetry all sounding just alike and so *boring*—or am I growing frizzled small and stale or however you put it? There seems to be too much of everything—too much painting, too much poetry, too many novels—and much too much money, I suppose—(Although I certainly welcomed mine.) And no one really feeling anything much . . ."[139] Only once did Bishop obliquely reveal her discontent to the magazine in agreeing with Moss on the dullness of recent poetry. Bishop also felt the magazine did not take many risks in subject matter. Still stung over the rejection of her Brasilia essay, she believed, she was disappointed in her editors' unwillingness to let her take a stand on the upcoming presidential election in her poem "From Trollope's Journal." To Kazin, she half jokingly complained, "*Your* magazine rejected my poem about the city of Washington—as I thought they might—I think they thought I was attacking Eisenhower! (which I was, more or less)."[140] She told Swenson she supposed her editors rejected the poem because they feared "to annoy their Republican readers."[141] Bishop was discouraged by what she saw, but she could still be approving. She wrote Kazin, "And yet—and yet—for what it is it is still damned good, Pearl—and maybe New York itself has lost that smart Big City-ness it used to have."[142]

Bishop was objecting to a sense of gentility that other regulars also found problematic. Their complaints echoed those of Gregory a few years earlier. Unlike Bishop, they openly argued with their editors about the magazine's narrow range of subjects and its exclusion of individual words. When Roethke submitted "Dirge" to White in February 1959, he said, "Here's a bitter anti-war poem that would probably involve a major policy decision—or would it?—by the magazine."[143] Protesting the Korean War, Roethke compiles a list of things he "would praise" and draws parallels between those who lead empty lives in the States and the Korean people and the American soldiers overseas. The poem does not shrink from the stench of the dying, the suffering of the combatants and noncombatants, nor does it flinch from the anxiety provoked by war for each of these groups. "Dirge" received a polite rejection. Later that year, Richard Wilbur began disputing the parameters his editors were placing on language. When editor Rachel MacKenzie let Wilbur know the magazine wanted to buy "October Maples," she also let him know that White and Shawn did not want the word "irradiated" in the penultimate line. It had the "wrong connotation."[144] Wilbur balked: "I don't comprehend the objection, and I can't see the 'wrong connotation.' Has the word been taken over by the advertising-men? Is there an irradiated bread? Are there irradiated sheets? If so, poetry should reclaim the word and treat it properly, not shy away and let the ad-men have it."[145] When Shawn continued to stand by his objection, Wilbur continued at length in a letter to MacKenzie:

Not to be embarrassing, I do think that Mallarmé is right, & that one of the poet's functions is to purify the words of the tribe. Now, how can you purify the words of the tribe if you don't use them, and correct the bloody tribe by using them properly? To shudder away from any word is to start establishing a special diction or permissible lexicon; and one which is bound to dwindle, because one shudder leads to another. The next thing you know you're talking to someone's periphrastic aunt, or writing poems which begin, "A garden is a lovesome thing, God wot." I know you know all this, and I'm sure Mr. Shawn does, but that makes it *worse*. Ignorantia non excusat, but it's nicer than knowing error.

See here, I don't mean to be nasty; certainly not to you. But one has so few principles nowadays that one jumps at the chance to be outraged. Oughtn't *The New Yorker* to realize that gentility, which always has a keen sense of what words are "spoiled," is the essence of vulgarity? Let's have a little disdain, for heaven's sake. Can a magazine be funny or brilliant and at the same time so careful?[146]

Shawn read Wilbur's letter, reread "October Maples," and bought the poem. Shawn told MacKenzie "that if we were ever to establish a permissible lexicon we would destroy ourselves—and the poem stays, irradiated."[147]

Like anyone else, Bishop noted the dichotomy between what was on *The New Yorker*'s pages and what was in its margins. Although Ross and Shawn famously kept the editorial and business departments separate—they even worked on different floors—it was impossible for readers not to see the luxurious ads lounging alongside the black-and-white copy. Bishop worried about how those ads played into the reading of her work. After "Manuelzinho" ran in the May 26, 1953, issue, she told Lowell, "Somehow when he appeared just now, in *The New Yorker*, he seems more frivolous than I'd thought—but maybe that's just the slick, rich surroundings."[148] The poem was published in the front of the magazine, hence no advertising, but the issue had the usual ads for Mark Cross, Henri Bendel, and Brooks Brothers. What was actually around "Manuelzinho" was in fact quite helpful in reading it. Placed inside Robert Coates's story "Return," the poem was encircled by cartoons that poked fun at the upper and upper-middle classes and the strivers who longed to join their ranks. In a Peter Arno drawing a well-fed Texan slouches next to his frowning wife, his longhorn tie paired with her big bubble pearls while the other airline passengers sleep beside them. "Look, honey," he explains, "I can't complain to the stewardess about every itty-bitty thing. It's not like we were in our own little old plane." Turn the page and three Perry Barlow women stand in the rear of a meeting hall. After being introduced, one politely exclaims, "Oh, Mrs. Penecrest! Aren't you the new green split-level?" Turn the page again, and there's Bishop's poem; facing it, two well-heeled matrons leave a production of *Richard III* in a James Mulligan cartoon. "At least now I know where 'My kingdom for a horse' comes from," one says brightly to the other, clutch bags in hand. This was the paradox of *The New Yorker*: as its ads urged an expensive lifestyle on its readers, its cartoons tweaked the very buyers of those goods. In the context of the drawings, the speaker of "Manuelzinho" was very much one of the women in the drawings, more sympathetic because of Bishop's exhaustive detail but just as much a subject for humor as her incompetent gardener.

Eventually, Bishop began to see her association with *The New Yorker* as a hindrance to her continued growth and found the need to step back from its pages. When she sent Maxwell the news the following summer, she emphasized her interest in writing experimental poetry and prose. She would rather not send the magazine work it was bound to reject. In a separate letter to Moss, Bishop said she felt she "should branch out a bit more—as I undoubtedly should have done before, I suppose—"[149] For Bishop, leaving *The New Yorker* marked the beginning of a period that would eventually result in her autobiographical and formally innovative last collection: *Geography III*. Although Bishop promised *The New Yorker* more poems and stories, to others she indicated her intention of selling them only the occasional story. She downplayed the breaking of her agreement, mentioning it to few friends. In her letters to Maxwell and Moss, Bishop made no mention of her rates, but it was a deciding factor. The previous summer Bishop vented to Kazin, who left the magazine soon after Bishop, "I have just realized (I'm a bit slow) that my rates haven't changed since 1948—don't you think I might ask for a big raise IF I renew that contract this fall? I may not do it—it depends on finances, work on hand, etc.—but I wonder if there's any way you could look into rates for me without appearing to? Or is it too difficult?"[150] In fact Bishop's rate had been raised in 1954, from $2.00 to $2.30 per line for poetry, and unknown to her, she was one of the highest paid poets publishing in the magazine. It was her prose rate that was toward the very bottom. In 1946 she signed on at fourteen cents per word for the first 1500 words (later for the first 2000 words) and seven cents for every word after. In 1954 it was raised to sixteen cents over eight. Bishop did ask for a raise a few months after breaking her contract, and her minimum was raised to $2.50 per line. On editor Robert Henderson's recommendation, *The New Yorker* continued to send her cost-of-living adjustment checks. Bishop submitted poems, as she had promised, but not with the same regularity.

After breaking her contract, Bishop sent "First Death in Nova Scotia" and "Sandpiper" to Moss, but "Twelfth Morning; or What You Will" went to *The New York Review of Books* through Robert Lowell, and a group of prose poems, "Rainy Season: Sub-Tropics," went to Robie Macauley at *Kenyon Review*. Focusing her attention on the country where she had made her home, Bishop was busy collecting information for her Time-Life series book *Brazil*, drafting prose sketches for her unfinished travelogue, and translating Brazilian writers João Cabral de Melo Neto, Clarice Lispector, and Carlos Drummond de Andrade. Translating proved a way to earn extra money, and after she approached White about submitting her Lispector stories, Shawn lifted Ross's ban on publishing translations. As far as her own poetry went, Bishop found herself in a slump and muttered, "I am so tired of all this false praise of *poetry*, 'distinguished writing'—blah blah blah—from publishers, the Nyoer."[151] Meanwhile, Bishop and Moss stayed in touch, and she sent him a couple of poems, including "The Burglar of Babylon" and "Under the Window: Ouro Prêto." Moss loved "Under the Window" and sent word round. To Strand he beamed, saying, "She's written an absolutely marvellous poem about it, which, happily, she sent to us."[152] Bishop waited over a year to see the poem in print, but she shrugged, rationalizing, "it is one way of making some money."[153] Then, in the summer of 1967, Bishop quietly contacted Moss and asked to resume her contract. The papers were drawn up immediately. She reported to Lilli Correia de Araújo that she was busy writing poems, "all in the hopes of making lots & lots of money" for Casa Marianna, the colonial house she was restoring outside Ouro Prêto.[154]

After Bishop resumed with the magazine, she continued to see prose, particularly reviewing, as a way to add to her income. She had tried her hand at critical writing before, with short reviews of Gwendolyn Brooks's poetry and Emily Dickinson's letters. When Bishop asked Moss about Louise Bogan's position as the magazine's poetry critic in February 1970 after learning of Bogan's death, she had not published any critical writing since looking at Walter de la Mare's anthology *Come Hither* for *Poetry* in 1958. It wasn't the first time she had inquired about the job; she had sounded out White in 1956. White told her the magazine wasn't looking for anyone new, but she would keep Bishop in mind should Bogan decide to step down. On hearing Bishop's proposal, Shawn immediately said yes, and Bishop was thrilled. To Anny Baumann she whispered, "I have another piece of news to tell you—it isn't all settled yet, so please don't tell anyone at all. I think I'm taking on the job of poetry reviewing for *The New Yorker*—something I'd really like to do. It is just 4 or 6 times a year—and one can write about what one wants to, I gather, so I think I could do it all right, and it would be a small source of 'security' (much needed) . . ."[155] By summer's end, Bishop had received almost forty books, and she was beginning to feel overwhelmed. Journalistic prose and working under a deadline were antithetical to her method of composition. She had struggled with reviews before. After completing her piece on *Come Hither*, she confessed to *Poetry* editor Henry Rago, "I have a real block about writing reviews and I should really never undertake them, I'm afraid."[156]

Bishop felt it was essential to provide critical evaluation in her commentary, but she also found it difficult to do. In writing reviews and blurbs, she often worried about repeating what someone else had already said. She summed up her difficulty to Baumann: "Writing any kind of prose, except an occasional story, seems to be almost impossible to me—I get stuck, am afraid of making generalizations that aren't true, feel I don't know enough, etc., etc."[157] When drafting her first piece for *The New Yorker*, she asked James Merrill whether *The Firescreen* had already been reviewed; she wanted to include it in her article. Bishop never completed the piece, nor did she finish pieces on recent books by Denise Levertov and William Carlos Williams. Moss grew dismayed. "E. Bishop called to ask for advice—she won't be able to do a poetry review until January. (I wonder if ever.)"[158] After a couple of years, Moss's patience had reached its limit and he began suggesting alternatives to Shawn. "Unless we do something I think poetry reviews in The NYer will simply go down the drain."[159] By 1973, Moss said, the magazine "decided to act as if it were over" and they never referred to the matter again.[160] From then on, Bishop only mentioned selling poetry, giving readings, and teaching as a way "to get along."[161]

The lag between acceptance and publication was something that had always bothered Bishop about *The New Yorker*. Poems and stories were often printed seasonally, and although the policy officially changed during Shawn's tenure, internal reports on the poetry bank show that many poems were still categorized this way. White disagreed with this approach, Mary McCarthy recalled, and knew it was odd that a story with spring flowers, for instance, couldn't run in the fall.[162] Poems slugged "Anytime" were at particular disadvantage because the magazine was always making room for seasonal poems or for poems in upcoming books. "The Riverman," bought in July 1959, was originally scheduled for that September but was pulled for James Kirkup's "Sendai Sequence" and had to wait until space became available the following April. But even seasonal poems could be at a disadvantage if their imagery was too similar to other recent poems. White told Roethke "The Storm" would have to wait almost two years because she had just bought Bishop's "Electrical Storm," which had to wait until *it* was in season. With the poetry bank swelling year after year, the magazine had more work than it could hope to publish in any timely way. Editors knew waiting unsettled writers, but there was nothing they could do except buy fewer poems. "It's always been my dream to find the slate wiped clean, so I can make a completely fresh start," Moss said. "If only I could get all the poems I want to buy into print promptly, without being haunted by the thought of all the ones waiting to be published."[163] Bishop generally waited four to ten months for publication, but as the number of poems on the bank rose, her wait lengthened. After Moss held "In the Waiting Room" for a year, Bishop offered to return her check so she could try placing it elsewhere, saying she would not renew her contract unless it guaranteed a three-month wait. The poem ran the next month, and they came to a six-month agreement. But several poems were held over the six-month limit, leading her to mutter about "Poem," "It will be in *The New Yorker*, but God knows when, they're so slow—"[164] What irked her more was that Moss's poems appeared once every few months. Waiting for "Sonnet" to appear, she shared this poem with friends:

> All our poems
> rest on the shelf
> while Howard publishes
> himself.[165]

Despite her discomfort with reviewing and irritation over scheduling, Bishop's last twelve years at *The New Yorker* were happy ones. She was writing with renewed vigor, her poems went easily through the editing process, and her work enjoyed increasing recognition. *The New Yorker* showered her with flowers when she received the prestigious Neustadt International Prize for Literature. She was elected to the American Academy of Arts and Letters in 1976 and received the National Book Critics Circle Award for *Geography III* in 1977. Moss accompanied her to readings and lectures in New York, wrote appreciatively of her work, and regularly raised her rates until they passed $4.90 per line of poetry and fifty cents over twenty-five for prose. She had become one of the magazine's most cherished writers.

When Bishop submitted her poems to Moss, they were still very much in process, as they had been with White. There were changes to be made and suggestions to be heard from almost everyone involved before they were pasted onto the page, run off the press, and delivered to city stoops and far-away mailboxes. The arrival of Bishop's poems always brought an excited stir to the office, a feeling that came from working with a master. After Moss approved a poem and reviewed it with another editor, he sent it to Shawn with their opinions. Bishop then answered any editorial queries about individual words or lines, and once they were resolved, Moss notified Bishop of the acceptance, passed along any other questions, and had a check drawn up and in the mail. Before bringing her manuscript to the copy desk for typesetting instructions and a "slug" signaling when and where the poem was to appear, Moss made punctuation changes and corrections in line with Fowler and the poem was set in galley proof with copies going to the proof room, the checking and legal departments for queries, and to Shawn for additional review. After everyone read the galleys and sent them back to Moss, he reviewed their questions and decided which ones Bishop should consider. Moss then sent the annotated galleys to a collator, who combined the approved questions onto an author's proof. The proof was then sent to Bishop, who could take or leave whatever suggestions remained. White's overall process seems quite similar to Moss's. It does appear, however, that during White's time intermediate galley proofs were not made up, since Bishop refers to individual editor's remarks in letters to friends and White mentions crossing off queries, suggesting that Bishop could see suggested changes before they were incorporated into the text. On the few surviving author's proofs one can see the proof room's punctuation queries and the checking and legal departments' questions. What about adding a comma after "I love you"? they ask alongside "The Burglar of Babylon." "Not on maps," they say next to the Tantramar marshes in the margins of "The Moose." Is there a real Mr. Swan? they ask on "Santarem."[166] And there were commas, commas, commas. "Commas in *The New Yorker* fall with the precision of knives in a circus act, outlining the victim," Andy White once quipped.[167] As Bishop told Swenson with some lingering disbelief, "They once put 23 commas in a long poem of mine—settled finally for 8 or 9."[168]

While Bishop did not take all of the proofreaders' suggestions, she did take almost all of Moss's. Moss gave suggestions for punctuation early in their correspondence, but as the years passed, he provided less and less. This is not to say that he did not continue to edit her work—he did—but it was up to Bishop to notice changes already incorporated into the proof and to make a decision on his edits before sending it back. Most of Moss's changes make her punctuation conform to the house style, the same style that was applied to everything else in *The New Yorker*. Moss's changes were part of Shawn's philosophy that the entire magazine should be of a piece, and since White made similar changes at the same stage, it suggests that the procedure went all the way back to Ross. Even after the editors began to relax their stylistic strictures for poetry, Moss continued referring to Fowler in editing Bishop's work, owing to the concern that for a poet as exacting as Bishop, any deviation would look like a mistake on her part or a typographical error on the magazine's. Once asked about Moss, Bishop downplayed his editing, saying that Moss had "never been in any way a 'prime editor.'" She was sure he would agree. "He has just accepted almost everything I've ever sent him, but I believe other people [at the magazine] fuss occasionally about punctuation, spelling, and so on!" suggesting that she did not entirely understand his role.[169] Bishop could be very tough-minded about her poems, but she could also lack confidence in punctuation, calling it her "Waterloo."[170] Like other poets, she admired Moss's taste and was willing to be advised. Some changes may not have been worth the battle, and others she may have considered unimportant. Having just been over positioning dashes in "Questions of Travel" with *The New Yorker*, she said to Ciardi in regard to "Exchanging Hats," "I believe the punctuation is correct—but people have different ideas about punctuating dashes at the beginning of lines, and whatever the rule at *New World Writing* may be it won't matter to me if they change this a bit."[171] Bishop struggled from time to time with aspects of *The New Yorker*'s house style, but when it came time to collect her poems, she retained, with very few exceptions, all of Moss's changes for her books.

From the very beginning, almost all of the editing of Bishop's work involved punctuation. Bishop often used her punctuation to trace the movement of thought and announce changes in tone. Take "Cold dark deep and absolutely clear," which occurs twice in "At the Fishhouses." When going over the galley proofs, White removed most of the proofreader's queries, asking Bishop to look over a few suggested commas. "I only left in the ones I thought would really help the reader but you may not agree. In this case it should be as you want it."[172] Bishop agreed to all of the changes except adding serial commas to those two lines, politely pressing for her unconventional use. "For some reason or other it seems more liquid to me without them and I think in this case the sense is plain enough without them, don't you?"[173] It's worth noting, however, that Bishop apparently agreed to inserting commas in a parallel line in the poem's final sentence. In her last extant draft, the sentence runs:

> It is like what we imagine knowledge to be,
> dark salt clear moving, utterly free,
> drawn from the cold hard mouth
> of the world, derived from the rocky breasts
> forever, flowing and drawn, and since
> our knowledge is historical, flowing, and flown.

"Dark salt clear moving, utterly free," served to echo the earlier "Cold dark deep and absolutely clear" line. Since it looks like *The New Yorker* changed the comma after "be" at the end of the first line to a colon, perhaps Bishop felt the inserted commas complemented the definitive feeling the line now had, even though it lost some of its swelling quality.

In addition to leaving out serial commas, Bishop would balance ellipses and periods with dashes. In the same draft of "At the Fishhouses," Bishop punctuated lines fifteen to twenty-one in what became the third stanza as:

> Cold dark deep and absolutely clear,
> the clear gray icy water . . .—Back, behind us,
> the dignified tall firs begin.
> Blueish, associating with their shadows,
> a million Christmas trees stand
> waiting for Christmas.—The water seems suspended
> above the rounded gray and blue-gray stones.

When the poem was published in *The New Yorker* the dashes were missing. But here, at least, the dashes serve to interrupt the painterly reverie for a direct description of the landscape, and then return to the deepening pull of the sea. The dashes link the first two lines to the last two, bringing the reader back to the idea of "Cold dark deep"; removing them makes the poem more linear, so that it no longer turns back on itself. Bishop's punctuation shows a more deliberate play with the poem's traditional structure, the speaker working out the conflict before coming to a final resolution. This doubling of punctuation is something Bishop used frequently in her letters. With it, she seems to have had in mind specific ways of conveying tone and showing lapses of time, turning from or returning to something she wrote about before. In the later dream poem, "Sunday, 4 A.M.," Bishop describes the disorienting feeling between sleeping and waking on a damp night. Stars above her head, the speaker conflates one person with another and hears a voice from "somewhere" that may be coming from her past. Bishop submitted the first two lines of the seventh stanza as "Dream dream confronting,— / now the cupboard's bare." The comma with the dash makes for a lengthy pause, especially considering that it comes at a line break. It trails off with a questioning "Dream dream confronting" . . . what? The speaker attempts to come to a conclusion. While she can't, the dash leaves her dwelling on the idea. When Moss took out the dash, he shortened the questioning and the movement of thought.

Moss could add or remove something as seemingly small as a dash, comma, or colon to dramatic effect. As in the editing of "At the Fishhouses," the serial comma in the opening line of "First Death in Nova Scotia" was an issue. Bishop submitted the first line as "In the cold cold parlor", which Moss changed to "In the cold, cold parlor", a correction Bishop kept. The comma slows down the movement of the line, making the room grow colder by degrees, and makes the voice clearly in that of the adult remembering the death of her two-month-old cousin.

Bishop was a big fan of the colon with all its powerhouse effects; *The New Yorker* was not. The colon, like all punctuation, was to be used rationally and sparingly, not for its musical or dramatic effects. In taking the colons out of Bishop's poems, Moss made them less declarative and more conversational. By smoothing out some of her more abrupt phrasing, he changed the rhythm and, in the end, the voice of her poems. In "One Art," her powerful villanelle about loss, Bishop uses the form's repetitive structure to escalate the poem's emotional stakes, the loss of small items leading to the loss of one's past and, finally, to the loss of the beloved. The speaker insists, as the form requires she must, that "losing isn't hard to master" and that "loss is no disaster." The opening stanza becomes the basis for the poem's fundamental irony, and the speaker has to force herself to write the poem's final line. Bishop submitted the opening stanza as:

The art of losing isn't hard to master:
so many things seem filled with the intent
to be lost their loss is no disaster.

Bishop's colon at the end of the first line serves as a declaration, as it did in "Five Flights Up," giving a definitive point to lines two and three. The speaker clearly knows where she's going. As he had done in "Five Flights Up," Moss took out the colon at the end of the first line and inserted a semicolon. Again, he made a line sound more like talk, evened out its tone, and put the poem in action. Like a signpost, the colon says the speaker is headed in a particular direction; the semicolon gives her the possibility of wandering.

Bishop always made changes to her poems after submitting them, what she called her "second-thought habit."[174] She had been revising poems in midstream since the beginning of her career. After going over the proofs of her *Trial Balances* poems with Marianne Moore, she decided to change "ye" to "you" in "Valentine II" and "topography plays" to "topography displays" in "The Map."[175] She often sent her editors revised poems a few days after her initial mailing and occasionally asked them to insert changes on submitted manuscripts. To Ciardi, she sent a slightly revised version of "Exchanging Hats" for *New World Writing*. "I wasn't satisfied with those aunts—now I think they will do, and since I am being precious I feel I might as well be good and precious while I'm at it . . ."[176] Her "Pajama'd aunts" became "Ananadrous" ones; her "Aunt so extrovert and slim, / with such dancing eyes" became "Aunt exemplary and slim / with avernal eyes." She also changed the line "he thinks what might a mitre matter" to "he means . . ." before going back to "thinks" in proof.[177] Her revisions could lead her to an internal debate that could last for weeks. After changing "an indistinct philosophy" in "Crusoe in England" to "a faltering" and then "a stammering" one, she finally found the adjective she wanted: "miserable." Bishop was always apologetic when sending these changes and often used humor to deflect any annoyance she might be engendering. When sending Moss the author's proof of "The Moose," she allowed, "I am a fuss-budget—but you already knew that."[178]

Sometimes *The New Yorker*'s queries prompted Bishop to make additional changes to her poems. In writing "The End of March," Bishop labored over the third stanza. Her poem of longing for an impossible home, "The End of March" is set on a Duxbury, Massachusetts, beach near John Brinnin's home where the speaker takes a walk on a cold and windy day. As usual, when it came time for the author's proof, her discussion with *The New Yorker* centered on punctuation. "The End of March" had an usually large number of questions since it was not edited according to house style before it was set in proof. Bishop had submitted this section as:

> I wanted to get as far as my proto-dream-house,
> my crypto-dream-house, that crooked box set up on pilings,
>   shingled green
> —a sort of artichoke of a house, but greener
> (boiled with bicarbonate of soda?)
> protected from spring tides by palisades
> of—are they railroad ties.

Moss drew Bishop's attention to her hyphens, dashes, and commas. "In stanza 3 the proof readers say the dashes aren't coordinate, and suggest putting a comma after 'green,' taking out the dash before 'a sort of,' and leaving the dash before 'are they railroad ties?'"[179] Looking over the proof with Moss's letter, Bishop agreed to the proofreader's changes. The proof does not survive, but the proofreader must have also suggested taking out the comma between "icy" and "off-shore" in the first stanza and removing the hyphens from "sea-birds" and "off-shore," something Bishop and her editors had debated since she began publishing:

> I suppose Webster has it about the words "seabirds" and "offshore" &
> I really should get another dictionary besides the Oxford, which leads
> me to such variations, usually. The dash before "a sort of artichoke",
> etc., shd. also come out with a comma after "green"—I like the
> comma after "icy", however, and have put one in after "far" in the
> next to last line of the third stanza. It should have been "a palisade"—
> my mistake, I think. Everything else seems all right.[180]

Bishop agreed to the revisions in the third stanza but argued that other lines should stay the same. The ungrammatical comma after "icy" gave the poem the pacing she wanted and modified "rackety," lending a temperature to the sound instead of the wind. Adding the comma after "far" in the sentence "And that day the wind was much too cold / even to get that far, / and of course the house was boarded up" opened the pause at the end of the line and filled it with a mixture of unstated disappointment and acquiescence, thus re-creating the speaker's experience of time.

If Bishop was lucky, she could also make changes after proof. Sometimes her revisions were a simple matter of straightening out the facts. Four months after correcting proof for "At the Fishhouses," Bishop wrote from Nova Scotia to change the codfish scales that lined the tubs to herring. "They fished for both fish at the place I had in mind, and the scales of both were everywhere, but only herring scales would produce the effect that particularly struck me."[181] Bishop apologized and included the revised lines, which arrived in time for the August 9 issue. Other times, the changes had a much bigger impact. Bishop wanted to replace the fourth stanza of "The End of March" before it was published. When drafting, she did not significantly revise this stanza; she arrived at the main image of the stones on the beach and the sun in the first draft and never strayed too far from her original idea. Her decision may be due to the fact that she had already made use of the sun in the closing of another poem, the abandoned "Apartment in Leme, Copacabana." In "Apartment in Leme," written for Robert Lowell, the speaker walks along a littered beach early one New Year's morning. A running dog and two bathers leave their tracks in the sand. She ended the poem with the sun rising slowly, "metallic, two dimensional," suggesting a kind of reluctant hope for the figures standing at the open mouth of the cold sea. In "The End of March," Bishop let the blurring of the weather, the move from winter to spring, suggest renewal instead of using the New Year with all its symbolic weight. Bishop did not bring the prints on the beach into "The End of March" until the fifth draft, and she played with the phrasing after she had the first half of the stanza down. The lion sun had "grandiose footprints," "classical, big foot-prints," and, finally, "big, majestic paw-prints."

After *The New Yorker* bought the poem, Bishop sent Lowell a copy in September.

> Here's a bit of description, for what it's worth—it started out as a sort of joke thank-you-note—John B was so appalled when I said I wanted that ugly little green shack for my summer home! (He doesn't share my taste for the awful, I'm afraid.) This is the only copy I can find— & I may have more changes already—& shd. probably make a lot more. Suggestions welcome—even to tearing it up. (No—I can't— I've already spent the N Yorker check.)[182]

Bishop gave Lowell an opening here in a way she rarely did. At least in letters, she only asked him for help with "From Trollope's Journal" and "In the

Waiting Room." While praising the poem, Lowell offered some tentative criticism:

> The meter I see is steadily iambic . . . any number of terrific seemingly tho quiet details—you arrive at your castle safely. I am troubled by one thing, a sort of whimsical iambic Frost tone to the last five lines or so, tho I think they are needed. New lines might make a fine poem into one of your finest. Nothing else needed, I think.[183]

Bishop received Lowell's comments after returning the author's proof, and she agreed, "more or less." "I like the very last line all right—but three or four just before that have been bothering me and I wanted to change them around—it may be partly a matter of placing them differently—leading up to the last line in a different way."[184] Bishop located the problem in the first five lines of the stanza. It was an issue of positioning the poem for the closing image. She began rewriting the lines and within a couple of days sent them to Moss. "I'm afraid I'm being a nuisance—but I don't think I have done this kind of thing very often, have I? The last stanza of THE END OF MARCH never pleased me, so this morning I've made some changes that I think improve it a lot. I hope you'll agree."[185] Moss, accommodating and supportive of Bishop as always, responded, "I think the changes in THE END OF MARCH are all splendid, and they are being put into proof. The ending is much more beautiful this way and yet nothing essential is changed."[186] Bishop changed the lines from:

> The sun came out for just a minute
> and for a minute the embedded stones
> showed what colors they were
> and all those high enough threw out long shadows,
> individual shadows, then pulled them in again.

to:

> The sun came out for just a minute.
> For just a minute, set in their bezels of sand,
> the dim, occasional stones,
> were all of different colors,
> with all those high enough throwing out long shadows
> and, after a minute, pulling them in again.

l

Bishop slowed the stanza's movement by breaking one sentence into two, dwelling on the image of the stones by adding a line, and shifted from the simple past of "threw" and "pulled" to participial phrases, expanding the image even further. The changes emphasized the connection between the movement of the shadows and the lion sun batting the kite out of the sky. Nonetheless, Bishop was still not satisfied and wrote the stanza again:

> The sun came out for just a minute.
> For just a minute, set in their bezels of sand,
> the drab, damp, scattered stones
> were multi-colored,
> and all those high enough threw out long shadows,
> individual shadows, then pulled them in again.

First the "dim, occasional" stones became "drab, damp, scattered" and "all of different colors" became "multi-colored." She then went back to the lines she submitted to Moss in July to wrap up the sentence, removing the participles and taking out the third reference to "minute" that she added in the October version. In this final version, Bishop extends the moment with the steady beats of "drab, damp, scattered stones" while she lifts the weight of the "d's" with the bright quality of the adjective "multi-colored." If she had stayed with "different colors," perhaps the "d" sounds would have been too heavy and pulled the end of the poem down. With the long pause after "multi-colored," she creates a resonance for the full dash before the final tercet. This change keeps the poem in action, instead of letting it come to rest, the rhythmic pauses generating an open ending.

By sweating through the last stanza, Bishop kept the movement of the poem fluid, letting it slide from association to association. The next time she heard from Lowell, he apologized for making suggestions:

> My suggestions for the end of your poem must have been troublesome. I think I've spent more futile hours trying to perfect something satisfactory—always pressing and invisible, the unimagined perfect lines or ending, for there it usually falls. Often I've given up, and wondered why I ever found fault. There are the experiences we haven't had, working in a spool factory etc. and can't imagine, and there are others like the end of Lycidas where all the experience is easily ours, but we can't turn to it or find the right sound. I've just spent a week or more on three lines which finally ended in changing the

position of two words. (I did other things). I hope you won't bother anymore, you were probably right all along.[187]

Perhaps his suggestions were troublesome, but they were worth it. Bishop was pleased with the new stanza, and to an ailing White she commented, "Thank you for liking the Duxbury poem—I did have a much better last stanza that I forgot to send to Howard until it was too late."[188] After all of her effort on the stanza, fine-tuning it like a violin, Bishop turned to her experience by turning slightly away from it. She let a turn of phrase, a line break, and a pause create experience instead of confronting it head-on.

She made small changes to a number of poems after they ran in *The New Yorker*. Sometimes she went back to the version she had originally submitted. She removed a stanza break her editors added to "Cape Breton," changed "a" back to "the" in the title of "Song for the Rainy Season," and returned most of the punctuation, notably the dashes at the start of her lines, to "A Cold Spring." Other times she returned to her original spelling, preferring her *Shorter Oxford English Dictionary* to *Webster's*. She also made changes based on questions that came up during the editing process. During the querying of "View of the Capitol from the Library of Congress," one issue was the color of the musicians' uniforms, which Bishop described as "brilliant blue." Ross questioned their color: one staffer labeled it a dull, post-office blue and another called it a light powder color. White defended Bishop's choice, and the adjective stayed, but in *A Cold Spring*, Bishop changed the color to "Air Force blue," creating a nice echo of the previous line: "On the east steps the Air Force Band / in uniforms of Air Force blue." She also changed the hyphen between "*boom-boom*" to a dash in the final line, having reviewed her options with White. When a proofreader asked why "Red Sea" was in initial caps in "The Moose," Bishop explained, "I liked Red Sea with a capital, two capitals—otherwise it loses its good old Baptist significance entirely and is just descriptive—and it isn't the 'sea', anyway—it's the Bay of Fundy *looking like* the Red Sea (which it does, that is, if the Red Sea is RED.) 'Led them with unmoistened foot / through the Red Sea waters . . .' (I'm afraid you aren't apt to be familiar with one of my favorite hymns!)"[189] When she published "The Moose" in *Geography III*, she put "Red Sea" in lower case, as the proofreader suggested, perhaps thinking the capital letters were too heavy-handed and the idea was understood.

Bishop could also rethink a poem after it appeared in *The New Yorker* and do more extensive revision. In the drafts of a poem like "North Haven," her elegy for Lowell, one can see Bishop keeping one of Moss's changes, going back to some of her original phrasing, and making additional corrections of her own. The speaker describes what has changed and what has not for her dear friend. She submitted the second stanza as:

> The islands haven't shifted since last summer,
> even if I like to pretend they have,
> drifting, in a dreamy sort of way,
> a little north, a little south or side-wise,
> and that they're free within the blue frontiers of bay.

In a December 1978 issue of *The New Yorker* the stanza ran as:

> The islands haven't shifted since last summer,
> even if I like to pretend they have—
> drifting, in a dreamy sort of way,
> a little north, a little south, or sidewise—
> and that they're free within the blue frontiers of bay.

Moss had pulled out the commas from the ends of the second and fourth lines for dashes and added a comma between "south" and "or" to the fourth line. Taking the hyphen out of "side-wise" was something that probably came up with the proofreaders. When the poem was later printed as a broadside by Lord John Press, the stanza became:

> The islands haven't shifted since last summer,
> even if I like to pretend they have
> —drifting, in a dreamy sort of way,
> a little north, a little south or side-wise,
> and that they're free within the blue frontiers of bay.

Bishop brought the fourth line back to the way she originally had it and worked with Moss's addition of the dash to the second line, bringing it down to the start of the third, making a stronger break from the humorous tone of the first two lines to the lilting observation of the following three. The most noticeable change, however, is with the wildflowers and birds. Bishop had submitted the poem using initial caps—"Buttercups, Red Clover, Purple Vetch". Upon receiving her proof, Bishop called Moss to question why they were put into lowercase. Although he convinced her to leave the poem the way it was, once she saw "North Haven" in print, she felt the switch was a mistake and decided to have the broadside made in order to highlight her allusion to Spring's song at the end of Shakespeare's *Love's Labours Lost*. Bishop even wanted to make changes to poems after they came out in her books, saying to Sybill Estess, "I have re-written the 1st stanza of that old poem, LARGE BAD PICTURE, which seems to have given you [. . .] trouble. It now says clearly the picture was painted by a young boy when he came back from being a cabin-boy in those northern places. This version will appear, I hope, in any future printings!"[190] As she says in "North Haven," "Nature repeats herself, or almost does: / *repeat, repeat, repeat; revise, revise, revise.*" The creative process for Bishop was something that remained always in motion.

Elizabeth Bishop died of a cerebral aneurysm on October 6, 1979. Bishop's partner, Alice Methfessel, asked Bishop's mutual friend Lloyd Schwartz to read "Sonnet" at the memorial service on October twenty-first; they could not find a copy among her papers, however. Schwartz called Moss, who dictated the poem over the phone. When the poem appeared in *The New Yorker* the following week, Alice, Schwartz, and Frank Bidart were stunned. Moss read the opening to Schwartz as "Caught—the bubble / in the spirit-level, / a creature divided", but it ran as "contrarily guided". No one had seen that line. Alice contacted Moss about the difference, and he explained that what he had read to Schwartz was the galley, the intraoffice version, not the proof. He wrote a letter saying he was enclosing a photocopy of the proof with the change in Bishop's handwriting, but neither the copy nor the original appear to survive. Bishop had not shared the revised version of "Sonnet" with the group, as was her usual practice. Schwartz in particular felt that Moss was capable of talking Bishop into changes she did not want to make, as with removing the capital letters in "North Haven." When Alice, Schwartz, and Bidart met with Robert Giroux about *The Complete Poems,* they made a unanimous decision that "a creature divided" was better than "contrarily guided" and published the poem that way.

The New Yorker's commitment to Bishop's work has never waned. Moss rejected "Efforts of Affection," a remembrance of Moore assembled by Giroux from Bishop's notes and fragments, which he felt wasn't Bishop's best prose, most likely because her feelings toward Moore remained unresolved. It was the only piece of hers he ever rejected. But he published her stories "A Trip to Vigia" and "The U.S.A. School of Writing." He also wrote a glowing review of her collected prose, saying now, like her poems, "it is spontaneous and perfect." The magazine also featured poems dedicated to her by friends, a profile by her former student, poet Dana Gioia, and, later, an essay on Bishop's life in Brazil by Schwartz. When Moss died suddenly in 1987, her picture still hung above his desk.

With Shawn's blessing, Alice Quinn became poetry editor. A newcomer to the magazine, Quinn, who held the post until 2007, was as devoted to Bishop's work as the editors who came before her. When editing what would become *Edgar Allan Poe & The Juke-Box*, Bishop's uncollected drafts and fragments, Quinn published many new texts as they emerged from Vassar's archives and private collections. The posthumous poems cover everything from listening to a new stereo to star watching on a summer night, but the ones that predominated in Quinn's choices were the love poems Bishop never chose to make public. "Dear, my compass / still points north", "Close close all night / the lovers keep", and "Breakfast Song" all have the same affection that is found in the comfortable intimacy of "The Shampoo." "A lovely finish" and "Vague Poem" are marked by an aching frankness in their celebration of the female body. In these years, the magazine also ran excerpts of her letters and letters written to her and reproduced photographs of her and her watercolor paintings. At the closing event of the 2002 *New Yorker* Festival, the magazine organized a reading of Bishop's poems that would be included in Quinn's forthcoming book. Jorie Graham, Seamus Heaney, Robert Pinsky, and former student Katha Pollit, among others, read to a packed house at Town Hall. The theater stands only a block away from the offices where she first began sending her poems almost seventy years before.

Before she died, Bishop drew what may be her only surviving self-portrait, an outline of her left hand. The hand has two rings, one that looks like a puzzle ring on the pinky and a bright stone labeled "Imaginary" on her ring finger. In the center of the drawing she wrote, "With best wishes, rheumatically, Elizabeth Bishop." As a response to Keats's poem "This Living Hand," Bishop's drawing depicts her hand not as one of earnest grasping that will haunt the beloved's days and nights. Yet, in her witty and reserved way, she also grapples with lost opportunities and impending death. Her hand is knobby and arthritic, playful and open, the hand of the poet, choosing details, shaping images, and crafting lines, dwelling in the possibility of the sentence and where its rhythms might take her.

1. Elizabeth Bishop to Pearl Kazin, March 7, 1953, Vassar College Library.
2. Bishop to Anne Stevenson, February 18, 1965, Washington University Library.
3. Bishop to Ted Wilson, June 27, 1939, Beinecke Library, Yale University.
4. Bishop, *The Collected Prose*, edited by Roberrt Giroux (New York: Farrar, Straus and Giroux, 1984): 137.
5. Bishop to Frani Blough Muser, December 12, 1933, Vassar College Library.
6. Bishop to Marianne Moore, December 15, 1939, Rosenbach Museum and Library.
7. Bishop to James Laughlin, August 9, 1940, Vassar College Library.
8. Charles Pearce to Bishop, June 16, 1942, *The New Yorker* Records, New York Public Library.
9. Katharine White to Harold Ross and Gustave Lobrano, June 18, 1945, *The New Yorker* Records, New York Public Library.
10. White to Ross, August 27, 1931, *The New Yorker* Records, New York Public Library.
11. Nancy Franklin, "Lady with a Pencil," *The New Yorker*, February 26 and March 4, 1996: 183.
12. E. B. White, "The Art of the Essay I," *Paris Review*, Fall 1969: 83.
13. Jane Grant, *Ross, The New Yorker, and Me* (New York: Reynal, 1968): 219.
14. White to William Maxwell, n.d. [early 1950s], Bryn Mawr College Library.
15. Ross to White, n.d. [White dates memo at around 1939], Bryn Mawr College Library.
16. E. B. White, 83.
17. William Shawn, "Katharine White," *The New Yorker*, August 1, 1977: 72.
18. "James Thurber: The Art of Fiction," *The Paris Review Interviews*, vol. II, edited by Philip Gourevitch (New York: Picador, 2007): 22.
19. Bishop refers to "In the Village" and "Manuelzinho." Bishop to Kit and Ilse Barker, June 14, 1956, Princeton University Library.
20. White to Ruth Rogin, November 19, 1976, Bryn Mawr College Library.
21. Franklin, 184.
22. White to Jean Stafford, June 30, 1949, *The New Yorker* Records, New York Public Library.
23. White to Maxwell, July 27, 1970, Bryn Mawr College Library.
24. Maxwell to White, August 6, 1976, Bryn Mawr College Library.
25. White to Mary McCarthy, April 22, 1944, *The New Yorker* Records, New York Public Library.
26. White to Maxwell, n.d. [early 1950s], Bryn Mawr College Library.
27. Bishop to Kazin, February 10, 1953, Vassar College Library.
28. Franklin, 183.
29. Louise Bogan to White, January 23, 1949; White to Bogan, February 3, 1949, *The New Yorker* Records, New York Public Library.
30. Bogan to White, June 2, 1954, Bryn Mawr College Library.
31. White to Bishop, August 31, 1945, *The New Yorker* Records, New York Public Library.
32. Bishop to Lobrano, September 10, 1945, *The New Yorker* Records, New York Public Library.
33. Lobrano to Bishop, September 27, 1945, *The New Yorker* Records, New York Public Library.
34. White to Bishop, November 2, 1954, *The New Yorker* Records, New York Public Library.
35. Bishop to Barkers, November 12, 1954, Princeton University Library.
36. Bishop to Kazin, April 23, 1955, Vassar College Library.
37. Bishop to White, December 20, 1955, *The New Yorker* Records, New York Public Library.
38. Bishop to E. B. White, July 27, 1977, Cornell University Library.
39. White to McCarthy, August 19, 1957, *The New Yorker* Records, New York Public Library.
40. Bishop to White, December 20, 1955, *The New Yorker* Records, New York Public Library.
41. Bishop to E. B. White, July 27, 1977, Cornell University Library.
42. White to Ross, February 6, 1950, *The New Yorker* Records, New York Public Library.
43. White to Ross, November 4, 1946, *The New Yorker* Records, New York Public Library.

44. White to Hawley Truax, November 22, 1946, *The New Yorker* Records, New York Public Library.

45. Ferris Greenslet to Bishop, November 28, 1946, Vassar College Library.

46. Ben Yagoda, *The New Yorker and the World It Made* (New York: Scribner, 2000): 39.

47. Arthur Guiterman, "Ode to the Amoeba," November 5, 1932: 76; William Rose Benét, "Lines to a Modern Refrigerator," October 26, 1935: 71; David McCord, "Lines on Anyone's Lines Along Certain Lines," February 22, 1941: 56; Robert Lax, "Poem of Gratuitous Invective Against New Jersey," July 6, 1940: 18.

48. February 7, 1948: 28.

49. Lee Wilson Dodd, "A Draft of *XXX Cantos*," *The New Yorker*, May 20, 1933: 55.

50. White to Elizabeth Perlmutter, June 14, 1975, Bryn Mawr College Library.

51. William Carlos Williams to White, October 12, 1930, *The New Yorker* Records, New York Public Library.

52. W. H. Auden, "Song," April 15, 1939: 21; Stephen Vincent Benét, "Nightmare for Future Reference," April 2, 1939: 19–20; Louis MacNeice, "Barroom Matins," January 4, 1941: 24.

53. Stanley Edgar Hyman, "The Urban *New Yorker*," *The New Republic*, July 20, 1942: 92; Bogan to Morton Zabel, September 5, 1941, *What the Woman Lived: Selected Letters of Louise Bogan, 1920–1970*, edited by Ruth Limmer (New York: Harcourt, Brace, Jovanovich, 1973): 233.

54. White to Perlmutter, August 13, 1975, Bryn Mawr College Library.

55. White to Bogan, May 7, 1931, *The New Yorker* Records, New York Public Library.

56. Pearce to White, January 29, 1940, *The New Yorker* Records, New York Public Library.

57. Bishop to Moore, February 19, 1940, Rosenbach Museum and Library.

58. Bishop to Moore, February 24, 1940, Rosenbach Museum and Library.

59. Maxwell to White, January 18, 1976, Bryn Mawr College Library.

60. White to Maxwell, February 6, 1976, Bryn Mawr College Library.

61. Maxwell to Williams, June 16, 1939, *The New Yorker* Records, New York Public Library.

62. "Craft Interview with Howard Moss," *New York Quarterly*, Summer 1973: 48.

63. Karl Shapiro to White, March 17, 1952, *The New Yorker* Records, New York Public Library.

64. White to Bogan, February 18, 1952, *The New Yorker* Records, New York Public Library.

65. Ibid.

66. White to Auden, March 7, 1952, *The New Yorker* Records, New York Public Library.

67. Ross, March 25, 1947, *The New Yorker* Records, New York Public Library.

68. Bishop to May Swenson, March 9, 1964, Washington University Library.

69. Walcott Gibbs, "Theory and Practice of Editing *New Yorker* Articles," Bryn Mawr College Library.

70. White to Gustave Lobrano, n.d. [1936 or 1937], Bryn Mawr College Library.

71. Bishop to Ilse Barker, June 14, 1956, Princeton University Library.

72. Maxwell to Auden, April 17,1945, *The New Yorker* Records, New York Public Library.

73. White to Bishop, July 2, 1953, *The New Yorker* Records, New York Public Library.

74. Bishop to Wilson, February 10, 1935, Beinecke Library, Yale University.

75. Bishop to Kazin, July 10, [1953], Vassar College Library.

76. Bishop to Kazin, "Next Day" [July 11 and 19, 1953], Vassar College Library.

77. Shapiro to Bishop, August 4, 1953, University of Chicago.

78. Bishop to Swenson, September 6, 1955, Washington University Library.

79. Bishop to Swenson, September 19, 1953, Washington University Library.

80. Bishop to James Merrill, June 5, 1956, Vassar College Library.

81. "Howard Moss: An Interview," Robert Leiter, *American Poetry Review*, September/October 1984: 27.

82. Bishop to Moss, March 30, 1971, Berg Collection, New York Public Library.

83. Moss to Galway Kinnell, May 10, 1966, *The New Yorker* Records, New York Public Library.

84. Anne Sexton to Moss, September 26, 1966, *The New Yorker* Records, New York Public Library.
85. Aurelia Plath to Editor, March 23, 1963, *The New Yorker* Records, New York Public Library.
86. Yagoda, 383.
87. "Howard Moss," John Baker, *Publishers Weekly*, March 26, 1973: 27.
88. Leiter, 27–28.
89. Moss to Richard Wilbur, September 8, 1965, *The New Yorker* Records, New York Public Library.
90. They were probably discussing the proof of "North Haven." Moss to John Malcolm Brinnin, October 4, 1978, University of Delaware Library.
91. Moss to Brinnin, n.d. [probably mid-1950s], University of Delaware Library.
92. Brinnin to Elizabeth Ames, February 17, 1950, Yaddo Records, New York Public Library.
93. Moss to Brinnin, May 13, 1958, University of Delaware Library.
94. Leiter, 28.
95. Moss to Brinnin, November 6, 1963, University of Delaware Library.
96. Moss to Brinnin, April 7, 1961, University of Delaware Library.
97. White to Moss, June 9, 1965, Berg Collection, New York Public Library.
98. Moss to Brinnin, n.d., University of Delaware Library.
99. Moss to Brinnin, n.d., University of Delaware Library.
100. Moss to Brinnin, n.d. [late 1950s?], University of Delaware Library.
101. Leiter, 31.
102. *Minor Monuments: Selected Essays* (New York: Ecco Press, 1986): 136.
103. Moss to Mark Strand, January 27, 1961, *The New Yorker* Records, New York Public Library.
104. Bishop to John Ciardi, January 17, 1955, Vassar College Library.
105. Bishop to Ciardi, September 27, 1955, Vassar College Library.
106. Philip Rahv to Bishop, January 15, 1956, Vassar College Library.
107. Bishop to Shapiro, July 21, 1951, University of Chicago Library.
108. Bishop to Shapiro, July 9, 1952, University of Chicago Library.
109. Bishop to Shapiro, August 17, 1952, University of Chicago Library.
110. Bishop to Robert Lowell, December 14, 1957, *Words in Air: The Complete Correspondence between Elizabeth Bishop and Robert Lowell*, edited by Thomas Travisano and Saskia Hamilton (New York: Farrar, Straus and Giroux, 2009): 247–48.
111. Bishop to Barkers, Monday morning, 1958, Princeton University Library.
112. Bishop to Kazin, December 26, 1960, Vassar College Library.
113. Bishop to White, July 17, 1960, *The New Yorker* Records, New York Public Library.
114. Selden Rodman, "Carefully Revealed," *The New York Times Book Review*, October 27, 1948: 18.
115. Bishop to Rahv, November 26, 1956, Boston University Library.
116. Horace Gregory, "The Poetry of Suburbia," *Partisan Review*, Fall 1956: 547.
117. "Robert Lowell: The Art of Poetry," *The Paris Review Interviews*, vol. II: 86.
118. Bishop to Muser, November 1939, Vassar College Library.
119. Bishop to Kazin, May 18, 1960, Vassar College Library.
120. Bishop to Lowell, July 28, 1953, *Words in Air*: 143. Bishop was paid $1,712.50 for "In the Village," which is about $13,700 in today's money.
121. Bishop to Kazin, August 19, 1953, Vassar College Library.
122. Bishop to Kazin, October 7, 1954, Vassar College Library; Bishop to Lowell, November 23, 1955, *Words in Air*: 172.
123. Bishop to Lowell, December 11, 1957, *Words in Air*: 241.
124. Bishop to Anny Baumann, December 4, 1958, Vassar College Library. *The New Yorker* published "The U.S.A. School of Writing" after Bishop's death in the July 18, 1983, issue.
125. Bishop to Kazin, July 4, 1959, Vassar College Library.

126. Bishop to Kazin, November 12, 1959, Vassar College Library. At her line rate of $2.50 and her 25 percent bonus, Bishop was probably paid $493, or $3,630 in today's money.

127. Bishop to Kazin, September 9, 1959, Vassar College Library.

128. Bishop is referring to Charles Wagley's book *Amazon Town*. Bishop to Kazin, January 6, 1960, Vassar College Library.

129. Moore to Moss, February 8, 1959, *The New Yorker* Records, New York Public Library.

130. Bishop to Barkers, September 8, 1955, Princeton University Library.

131. Bishop to Barkers, February 25 or 26, 1954, Princeton University Library.

132. Bishop to Lowell, December 5, 1953, *Words in Air*: 149.

133. Bishop to Barkers, February 28, 1955, Princeton University Library.

134. Bishop to Kazin, July 13, 1960, Vassar College Library.

135. Bishop to Kazin, April 9, 1958, Vassar College Library.

136. Bishop to Swenson, June 4, 1958, Washington University Library.

137. "Carnegie Hall" was later called "Glory"; it appeared in the August 13, 1960, issue; "Tell Me, Tell Me" appeared in the April 30, 1960, issue. Bishop to Moore, January 5, 1961, Rosenbach Museum and Library.

138. Bishop to Swenson, October 17, 1960, Washington University Library.

139. Bishop to Lowell, October 1960, *Words in Air*: 344.

140. Bishop to Kazin, September 14, 1960, Vassar College Library.

141. Bishop to Swenson, March 8, 1961, Vassar College Library.

142. Bishop to Kazin, July 13, 1960, Vassar College Library.

143. Theodore Roethke to White, February 22, 1959, *The New Yorker* Records, New York Public Library.

144. Rachel MacKenzie to Wilbur, December 14, 1959, *The New Yorker* Records, New York Public Library.

145. Wilbur to MacKenzie, December 15, 1959, *The New Yorker* Records, New York Public Library.

146. Wilbur to MacKenzie, January 2, 1960, *The New Yorker* Records, New York Public Library.

147. MacKenzie to Wilbur, January 6, 1960, *The New Yorker* Records, New York Public Library.

148. Bishop to Lowell, June 7, 1956, *Words in Air*: 178.

149. Bishop to Moss, June 28, 1961, Berg Collection, New York Public Library.

150. Bishop to Kazin, July 13, 1960, Vassar College Library.

151. Bishop to Kazin, September 2, 1961, Vassar College Library.

153. Moss to Strand, October 22, 1965, *The New Yorker* Records, New York Public Library.

153. Bishop to Lowell, March 3, 1967, *Words in Air*: 614.

154. Bishop to Lilli Correia de Araújo, August 8, 1967, Vassar College Library.

155. Bishop to Baumann, March 7, 1970, Vassar College Library.

156. Bishop to Henry Rago, April 15, 1958, University of Chicago Library.

157. Bishop to Baumann, September 1, 1955, Vassar College Library.

158. Moss to Brinnin, December 7, [1971?], University of Delaware Library.

159. Moss to Shawn, n.d., Berg Collection, New York Public Library.

160. *Remembering Elizabeth Bishop*: 275–76.

161. Bishop to Lowell, January 14, 1973, *Words in Air*: 736.

162. Linda Davis, *Onward and Upward: A Biography of Katharine S. White* (New York: Harper and Row, 1987): 172.

163. Baker, 27.

164. Bishop to Grace Bulmer, n.d. [1972], Vassar College Library.

165. Lloyd Schwartz, "Elizabeth Bishop, 'Sonnet,'" Soundings, *The Atlantic Online*.

166. The proof of "The Moose" is held in *The New Yorker* Records.

167. E. B. White, 79.

168. Bishop to Swenson, March 20, 1953, Washington University Library.

169. Bishop to Sybill Estess, April 17, 1976, Vassar College Library.

170. Bishop to Moss, January 20, 1951, *The New Yorker* Records, New York Public Library.

171. Bishop to Ciardi, November 9, 1955, Vassar College Library.

172. White to Bishop, February 25, 1947, *The New Yorker* Records, New York Public Library.

173. Bishop to White, February 28, 1947, *The New Yorker* Records, New York Public Library.

174. Bishop to Moss, November 8, 1955, *The New Yorker* Records, New York Public Library.

175. Bishop to Ann Winslow, November 21, 1934, University of Wyoming Library.

176. Bishop to Ciardi, November 9, 1955, Vassar College Library.

177. *New World Writing* Archive, Beinecke Library, Yale University.

178. Bishop to Moss, July 7, 1972, Berg Collection, New York Public Library.

179. Moss to Bishop, September 24, 1974, *The New Yorker* Records, New York Public Library.

180. Bishop to Moss, September 30, 1974, *The New Yorker* Records, New York Public Library.

181. Bishop to Poetry Editor, July 8, 1947, *The New Yorker* Records, New York Public Library.

182. Bishop to Lowell, September 3, 1974, *Words in Air*: 767.

183. Lowell to Bishop, October 6, 1974, *Words in Air*: 769.

184. Bishop to Lowell, October 18, 1974, *Words in Air*: 771.

185. Bishop to Moss, October 22, 1974, Berg Collection, New York Public Library.

186. Moss to Bishop, October 24, 1974, *The New Yorker* Records, New York Public Library.

187. Lowell to Bishop, December 18, 1974, *Words in Air*: 776.

188. Bishop to White, April 14, 1975, Bryn Mawr College Library.

189. Bishop to Moss, July 7, 1972, Berg Collection, New York Public Library.

190. Bishop to Estess, May 10, 1976, Vassar College Library.

A Note on the Text

The vast majority of these letters come from *The New Yorker* Records housed at the New York Public Library. Others come from Elizabeth Bishop's, Howard Moss's, Katharine and E. B. White's personal papers housed at Vassar College, The Berg Collection at the New York Public Library, Bryn Mawr College, and Cornell University. *The New Yorker* seems to have saved almost every letter, postcard, and telegram from Bishop; however, very few of her editors' original letters survive. What is here are unsigned carbon copies that were held in Bishop's file at the magazine. Likewise, Katharine White and Moss appear to have saved most of Bishop's personal letters, but she seems to have lost many of theirs. The gap is most noticeable in letters from Moss, but there are also gaps in the letters from White. Likewise, neither Bishop's correspondence with Charles Pearce outside *The New Yorker* nor any of Pearl Kazin Bell's personal letters to Bishop appear to survive.

In preparing these letters for publication, I have used the ideas set forth by the textual scholar Jerome McGann in *A Critique of Modern Textual Criticism* (1983). With the exception of correcting spelling errors, I have made few changes. Bishop had a preference for the *Oxford English Dictionary* and hyphenated words. I have maintained her punctuation and italics, since she often used them to create the effects of speech. I have also maintained her inconsistent capitalizations and abbreviations for things such as "*The New Yorker.*" Bishop usually proofread her letters before sending them. I have incorporated her corrections. When her corrections or additions did not fit into the syntax of a particular sentence, I left her plus signs and asterisks in place. I have also regularized the presentation of dates and originating location. In letters mailed from *The New Yorker*, I have relied on Bishop's salutation to determine how to sign her editors' names.

The footnotes rely heavily on Bishop's manuscripts housed at the New York Public Library and Vassar. Bishop's submitted manuscripts with editorial corrections begin appearing in 1951 but not with any regularity until 1964, after which all of the manuscripts survive. When Bishop and her editors discuss her proof, I refer either to the submitted manuscript or to the last extant draft. In some cases no manuscripts survive. The only proofs to survive are those of "The Burglar of Babylon," "Crusoe in England," "The Moose," and "Santarem."

In citing the changes to Bishop's manuscripts before they were set in galley proof, I have not included spelling corrections, the transposition of commas inside quotes, or changes in possessive form. In citing Bishop's changes to her poems after they appeared in *The New Yorker*, I have included only those that were discussed during the editing of her poems at the magazine. The few additional changes are cited in Candace MacMahon's *Elizabeth Bishop: A Bibliography, 1927–1979*.

In quoting Bishop's and her editors' changes to individual sentences and lines, I have left all punctuation intact, with the exception of changing double quotes to single quotes. I put any necessary commas and periods that are not on the manuscripts themselves outside the closed quotes in order to be clear about exactly which elements Bishop and her editors are discussing. This decision has led to such combinations as .", and ,", and ;". When I discuss a word as a word or a phrase as a phrase and punctuation is necessary, I put the punctuation inside the closed quotes. I have noted any deletions I have made with ellipses inside brackets.

Bishop, White, and Moss frequently refer to their reading in their correspondence. For magazine and newspaper articles and for poems and stories in recent periodicals, I have given authors' names, titles, and dates of publication. For books, I have cited first editions.

All of the mistakes in this book are mine.

One

1934–1946

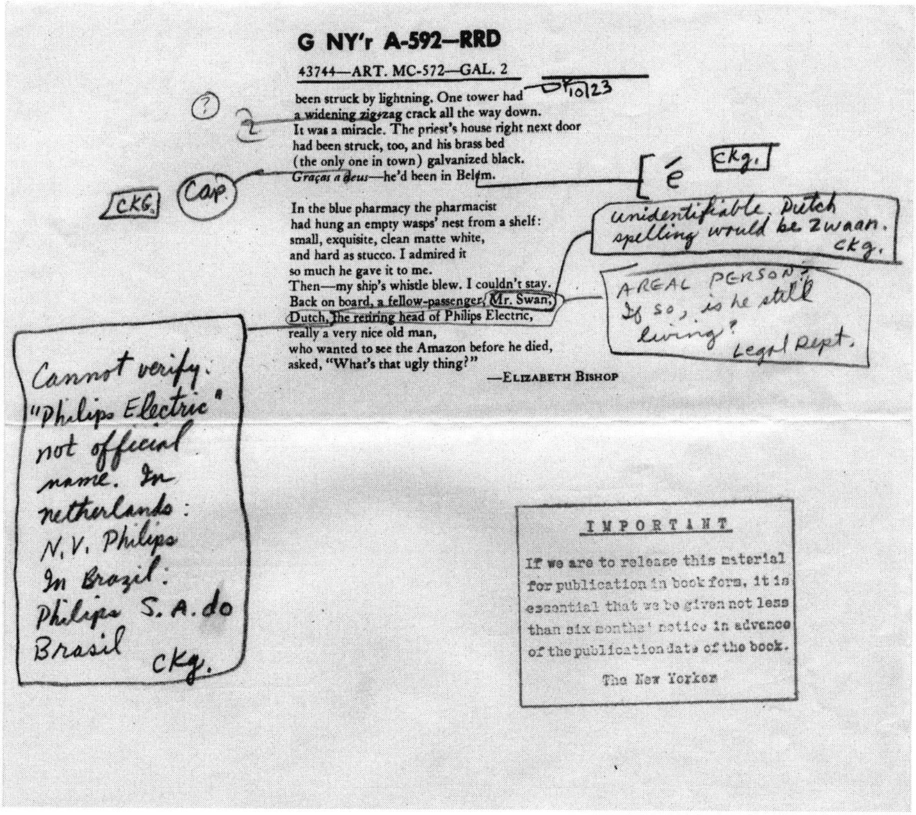

G NY'r A-592—RRD

43744—ART. MC-572—GAL. 2

been struck by lightning. One tower had
a widening zig-zag crack all the way down.
It was a miracle. The priest's house right next door
had been struck, too, and his brass bed
(the only one in town) galvanized black.
Graças a deus—he'd been in Belém.

In the blue pharmacy the pharmacist
had hung an empty wasps' nest from a shelf:
small, exquisite, clean matte white,
and hard as stucco. I admired it
so much he gave it to me.
Then—my ship's whistle blew. I couldn't stay.
Back on board, a fellow-passenger, Mr. Swan,
Dutch, the retiring head of Philips Electric,
really a very nice old man,
who wanted to see the Amazon before he died,
asked, "What's that ugly thing?"

—ELIZABETH BISHOP

Handwritten annotations:

? 2 · CKG. · Cap · 10/23 · é CKG.

unidentifiable. Dutch spelling would be Zwaan. ckg.

A REAL PERSON? If so, is he still living? Legal Dept.

Cannot verify. "Philips Electric" not official name. In netherlands: N.V. Philips In Brazil: Philips S.A. do Brasil CKg.

IMPORTANT

If we are to release this material
for publication in book form, it is
essential that we be given not less
than six months' notice in advance
of the publication date of the book.

The New Yorker

The New Yorker
25 West 45th Street
New York, New York
November 2, 1934

Dear Miss Bishop:

We are enclosing a check for five dollars for your anecdote about the message from the servant, which we are using soon in a short Talk of the Town story. Thanks for writing us.

Very truly yours,
THE NEW YORKER[1]

The New Yorker
25 West 43rd Street
October 27, 1939

Dear Miss Bishop,

I am pleased indeed that you submitted a poem to us recently for I had liked your work and had planned to write to you inviting you to submit poems here. SPLEEN has been gladly accepted and here is our check for it. Proof will be mailed to you soon. There's only one change we much insist upon. The title *Spleen* doesn't seem to us to suit the poem at all and I'm sure you will be able to find one that is more appropriate.

Won't you send us other poems whenever you can?

Cordially,
Charles A. Pearce

1 The most likely candidate for Bishop's story is "Reassurance" (November 10, 1934). "Talk of the Town" stories were always rewritten, in this case by editors Francis Steegmuller and Harold Ross. There is no way to know at this time what Bishop originally submitted. The letter was probably signed by Donald Wharton, an editor in the "Talk" department, since the initials "D.W." appear at the bottom of the page.

624 White Street
Key West, Florida
November 1, 1939

Dear Mr. Pearce:

Thank you very much for the check for my poem which came yesterday. I agree with you that the title SPLEEN is poor, and I suggest instead the title HISTORY. Will that do? I think it will help to clarify the meaning as well.

I shall be very glad to send you more poems when I have some that I think you might be able to use. Thank you for asking me.

Very truly yours,
Elizabeth Bishop

November 7, 1939

Dear Miss Bishop,

We're still not happy about the title for your poem. We think that HISTORY tends to reveal the pleasantly surprising ending and wish you'd find a title that wouldn't do that.

Those who know about such things tell me that some of your punctuation changes are most improper and I gather that the only one that seemed entirely correct was the deletion of the comma in the second line of the last section.

I hope you will have some other poems to send me one day soon.

Cordially,
Charles A. Pearce

November 14, 1939

Dear Mr. Pearce:

I am sorry to have been so much trouble to you with my poem. I think however, I have at last found a good title: *Cirque d'Hiver*. Will that do?[1]

I hope to send you a little group of short poems quite soon. Thank you for correcting my punctuation.

Very truly yours,
Elizabeth Bishop

---

1 In discussing the poem with critic Anne Stevenson, Bishop said the title came from the Cirque d'Hiver, which had "a team of little trained ponies wearing ostrich plumes, etc.—but I think the title referred to the mood more than anything else" (March 20, 1963, Washington University Library).

November 17, 1939

Dear Miss Bishop,

Thanks for the new title. We think CIRQUE D'HIVER is fine.

As usual at this time of year, there's a special need for long one-column poems. We'd all be especially grateful to you if you could help us out.

Cordially,

Charles A. Pearce

January 24, 1940

Dear Miss Bishop,

CIRQUE D'HIVER appears in this week's issue. I am pleased to say that it has been given a prominent place in the magazine.

Cordially,

Charles A. Pearce

March 4, 1940

Dear Miss Bishop,

Enclosed is a paragraph from a letter I received from Marianne Moore. I thought you'd appreciate her comment on CIRQUE D'HIVER.

I haven't yet received a decision on SUNDAY MORNING, but I hope I will have word for you by the end of the week.

It occurs to me that I am still holding on to that collection of your poems and short stories. You haven't by any chance changed your mind about the [James] Laughlin anthology? He'd be immensely pleased if there would be any way in the world for you to change your verdict.

Cordially,

Charles A. Pearce

March 14, 1940

Dear Miss Bishop,

I am sorry indeed to report that SUNDAY MORNING has been voted down. After a good deal of discussion it was decided that the poem was a little too remote for us—or rather that having printed at least two verses about Florida in the past two weeks, we couldn't go another.

Thanks a great deal for letting us see it and please try to understand why we've had to decide against it.

Cordially,
Charles A. Pearce

April 8, 1940

Dear Miss Bishop,
Sorry to say LETTER TO N.Y. doesn't seem right to us.[1] Thanks as ever for letting us see it.

Cordially,
Charles A. Pearce

November 19, 1940

Dear Miss Bishop:
It seems a long while since we've seen any new poems by you. I do hope you'll be sending us some one of these days.

Sincerely,
Charles A. Pearce

January 29, 1941

Dear Mr. Pearce:
It was very kind of you to write to ask me if I had any poems to send to the NEW YORKER some time ago, & I should have answered sooner, except that I thought if I waited I possibly *would* have some poems that you might like. I am enclosing the only thing I have just now that I think the NEW YORKER might like—but probably will not—but I hope to be able to send you several more sometime in February.

Sincerely yours,
Elizabeth Bishop

February 4, 1941

Dear Miss Bishop:
We all liked this one ["Poem on Dolls"], but felt it was far too special—

---

1 *Harper's Bazaar* published the poem in the September 15, 1940, issue.

or perhaps I should say personal—a statement for us to print. It was good to hear from you again, and I look forward to seeing the other poems you have promised us "sometime in February."

Sincerely,

Charles A. Pearce

March 7, 1941

Dear Miss Bishop:

Apparently THE STREET BY THE CEMETERY is one The New Yorker is unable to use.[1] I am sorry the decision has turned this way. It's a good poem, I think, and I hope I'll be able to see it in print soon.

Sincerely,

Charles A. Pearce

March 14, 1941

Dear Miss Bishop:

I'm afraid that we still feel the same way about this ["Sunday Morning"] as we did when we first read it some months ago. Thanks again for letting us have a chance to reconsider it.

Sincerely,

Charles A. Pearce

March 18, 1941

Dear Mr. Pearce:

I don't seem to be having very much luck with you lately, and I am very embarrassed & sorry to have sent you the same poem twice without realizing it! I am enclosing another short poem ["A Cancelled Dream"], & if you do not care for it, I shall wait until possibly I can send you a "group." Thank you for your patience.

Sincerely yours,

Elizabeth Bishop

1 A handwritten, crossed-out poem with this title appears in Bishop's papers at Vassar. It appears in *Edgar Allan Poe & The Juke-Box: Uncollected Poems, Drafts, and Fragments*, edited by Alice Quinn (New York: Farrar, Straus and Giroux, 2006: 43).

April 1, 1941

Dear Miss Bishop:

I am afraid we didn't feel that this one quite came off, though we liked parts of it very much. Thanks very much, as ever.

Sincerely,

Charles A. Pearce

February 4, 1942

Dear Miss Bishop:

It's a long time since we've seen any poems of yours and I hope you haven't forgotten our interest in you. Is there any chance that we can see some new ones one of these days?

Sincerely,

Charles A. Pearce

June 16, 1942

Dear Miss Bishop:

A very long time has gone by, it seems to us, since we've had the privilege and pleasure of seeing a new poem of yours. Our need for verse is greater than it has been for a long while, too, so that we'd be particularly grateful to see a manuscript of yours in the mails one of these fine mornings. Is there any hope of that?

Sincerely,

Charles A. Pearce

October 28, 1942

Dear Miss Bishop:

I am sorry indeed to say that we cannot use this poem about the slot machine ["The Slot Machine"]—at least, not in its present form.[1] It doesn't seem quite precise enough (I believe that is the right word), just to use as light verse and also, as it stands, it is a bit too long, we feel. If you feel

---

1 A handwritten, unfinished poem title "The Slot Machine" is in Bishop's papers. It begins: "It is hard to imagine / the world without women".

tempted to try a revision of this, and I hope you will, please let us have a chance to see the result, won't you?

Sincerely,

Charles A. Pearce

Murray Hill Hotel
Park Avenue, 40th to 41st Streets
New York
November 23, 1942

Dear Mr. Pearce,

I hate to trouble you about this, but just before I left Mexico City the 22nd of October I sent you a poem called "The Slot-Machine." I haven't heard anything from you about it. So much of my mail from there was lost, I have discovered, and the forwarding services were so poor, that I thought I'd ask you if you ever received it, or if I just didn't receive the rejection slip. I know how prompt *The New Yorker* usually is about such things so I think something must have gone astray. Could you let me know your decision, or shall I send you another copy of the poem? I hope to send you some more, also a little group of sketches, fairly soon.

Very truly yours,

Elizabeth Bishop

November 25, 1942

Dear Miss Bishop:

Thanks a lot for your note of November 23rd. Enclosed is a copy of the letter I sent you on October 28th. I do hope you will be willing to let us see a revised version of THE SLOT MACHINE. Sorry that the original letter couldn't have reached you in Mexico City on time.

Sincerely,

Charles A. Pearce

623 Margaret Street
Key West
December 12, 1942

Dear Mr. Pearce,

Here is a bit of "seasonal" light verse ["A Bitter Day—Key West"].[1] I shall try the "Slot-Machine" again. I am sorry about the manuscript, but it is next to impossible to get a typewriter repaired here at present.

Very truly yours,
Elizabeth Bishop

December 26, 1942

Dear Mr. Maxwell,

Thank you very much for your kind note. I have been working on a few short sketches which I had thought of submitting to you and now when they are finished—next month, I think—I shall be very glad to.

Sincerely yours,
Elizabeth Bishop

January 5, 1943

Dear Miss Bishop:

It's been decided that we cannot use A BITTER DAY—KEY WEST, I regret to say. Many thanks, though, for letting us see it.

Sincerely,
Charles A. Pearce

April 14, 1943

Dear Miss Bishop:

Isn't it a very long time since we've had the privilege of considering a new poem of yours? And is there any chance of seeing something soon? I do hope so.

Sincerely,
Charles A. Pearce

1 A handwritten poem with the titles "A BITTER DAY," "Key West," and "A 'NORTHER'" appears in Bishop's papers from the 1940s. Bishop submitted the same poem, titled "A Norther," calling it old, to Howard Moss in June 1961. The poem had one change. In stanza three, line two, she changed "chilling sea" to "tepid sea". It appears in Bishop's Collected Poems (New York: Farrar, Straus and Giroux, 1983: 202).

May 13, 1943

Dear Miss Bishop:

What about those prose pieces that you spoke about last December?
Hopefully yours,
William Maxwell

September 9, 1943

Dear Miss Bishop:

I am sorry indeed to tell you that we will not be able to use FULL
MOON: KEY WEST, but thank you a very great deal for letting us see it.[1]
Sincerely,
Charles A. Pearce

October 11, 1943

Dear Miss Foster:

Here's our check for your Housekeeper piece which we all liked so
much.[2] An author's proof, containing such editing as we felt was necessary,
will be forwarded to you before the piece is published. And meanwhile, we
hope you'll send us something else.
Sincerely,
Gustave S. Lobrano

November 17, 1943

Dear Mr. Pearce,

Perhaps you will be able to use these songs, or some of them ["Song for a
Colored Singer," "Song for Sina," "Lullaby for a Not Very Bright Child,"
and "Lullaby"]. They were all written originally for colored singers, so that
explanations as to what race is supposed to be singing were unnecessary.
However, in those in which it might make a difference, I think either the title
or the context makes it clear.
Very truly yours,
Elizabeth Bishop

---

1 A typed poem with this title and several handwritten corrections appears in Bishop's papers. Bishop wrote "about
1943" on the manuscript. A version of it appears in *Edgar Allan Poe & The Juke-Box* (59). Because of the return
address, the poem was typed sometime during or after 1944, and its relationship to the submitted poem is unclear.
2 Sarah Foster was Bishop's paternal grandmother's name.

November 30, 1943

Dear Miss Bishop:

I wish we could use one of these new ones, but the verdict is fairly unanimous that these fall outside our bailiwick.[1]

It was kind of you to let us see them and I hope you'll try us again soon.

Sincerely,

Charles A. Pearce

April 14, 1944

Dear Miss Bishop:

You must know by this time how anxious we are to have a poem of yours in The New Yorker again, but LARGE BAD PICTURE doesn't seem quite to work out for us. Please be forgiving and send us something else soon.

Sincerely yours,

William Maxwell

June 14, 1945

Dear Miss Bishop:

Congratulations on the Houghton Mifflin Fellowship Award! It was a deep satisfaction to me that your book won by a unanimous vote and I want to tell you how much pleasure and excitement the book gave me. It is a distinguished volume and I am lucky to have had the chance to vote for it. For awhile there as a judge, I was rather gloomy, but the horizon lightened when your manuscript turned up.

Switching from my role as judge, one I never felt quite at ease in or suited for, to the more familiar one of being an editor of The New Yorker, I want to ask whether you would not care to send to The New Yorker any hitherto unpublished poems from your Houghton Mifflin Book. I am not at all sure which ones have been published or whether, among those which have not, there are any which would seem suitable for The New Yorker, but I feel almost sure there must be a number. Won't you let us have a chance to read the lot—even poems which you might have previously sent the magazine? Since your book is not to come out until January (or so Ferris Greenslet writes me) we would have time to publish some of the poems before then,

---

1 *Partisan Review* published "Song for a Colored Singer," "Song for Sina," "Lullaby for a Not Very Bright Child," and "Lullaby" in its Fall 1944 issue.

if the other editors voted with me in liking them. As you know from my letter of last winter, The New Yorker has been hoping for contributions from you.

Not long ago I was talking about you with Mary McCarthy. I know she will be very happy to hear of your award. Edmund Wilson, too. We talked about your work this winter before he went abroad. I hope I can see you sometime when I get back to the office in the fall. During the summer, I do my New Yorker work at long distance.

Sincerely yours,

Katherine S. White

August 31, 1945

Dear Miss Bishop:

We were delighted to receive your two poems and like them both, though we have a few queries on "Large Bad Picture", which I am returning now for your consideration. The check for "Little Exercise" should reach you soon but it will come direct from the office as this is my last day before a month's leave of absence.

Here are our problems on "Large Bad Picture":

1) The question has been raised as to whether the "n's" of this line should be in caps or lower case. I think in New Yorker type that our capital N looks more like the n's most fine black birds make, but it should be left to you to decide whether you want your image to be visual as well as mental. This is a minor point and can be worked out when you receive your author's proof.

2) The last two lines of this stanza have bothered some readers who do not understand what you mean here. I take it you are referring to the many seals of the Labrador coast but perhaps you could work out a way to say this which won't stop anyone. Mr. Ross hopes you can name the animal—says he didn't realize there were large aquatic animals on the northern coasts. All this may sound too literal by far but I do hope you may want to reconsider the stanza as a whole. The poem is so good and so humorous too that it would be good to have it clear to all. However, if you cherish the stanza as now worded, just say so and we'll reconsider the queries.

3) The question has been raised as to whether you mean by the "it" of the first line (and that of the second also) the sun or the calm harbor. As it is worded it refers to the sun and I believe you mean it to. But this belief of mine shakes a trifle when I read on and wonder whether you mean the sun or

the harbor as the boats' destination. Possibly what is obscure here therefore is the word destination rather than the "it's"?

Since I shall be on vacation and since we hope you'll want to fuss with the poem a little and send it back soon, will you please write Mr. G. S. Lobrano about this. If you decide against any revision at all, will you send the poem back to him so that we may have another chance at it? I'd be rather grateful if you would.

I'm enclosing some clippings which you have no doubt seen already, but I send them along in case you have not.

I take it that the two new poems are to be used in "North and South". It would seem to me that they belong there. If you do plan to include them in the book, will you please write Mr. Lobrano the probable publication date so that we may know about scheduling the poems for the New Yorker to appear before the book deadline.

I hope that these are just the first of many more poems to come to us from you. And thank you for your earlier letter to me.

Sincerely yours,

Katharine S. White

P.S. I see that I haven't begun to say how much "Little Exercise" delights me.

September 10, 1945

Dear Mr. Lobrano:

Mrs. White has asked me to write to you about the enclosed poem, since I believe she is away on holiday.

I am sending the copy I sent first as well as the new one so that you can see the objections and the one change I have made.

As to (1):—after looking at all the *n*'s in New Yorker type I still think that the lower case n is best. (Mrs. White suggested a capital.) I was thinking of course of a written n, like this *n n n n* that is why I said "scribbled". No printed n looks *like* that, but I still think that the lower case one gives the idea best without any attempt at representation.

(2) I am trying to describe a picture and the sounds are imaginary, just for effect. There are no animals in it—although if there were they might perfectly well be something inappropriate. If you would prefer it this way, the 1st line of that stanza 1st read "One can imagine their . . ." etc. But when one exclaims at a picture one doesn't say, "Can't you just imagine you hear the

birds," etc., one says "You can just hear," etc. . . . . As alternatives, though, I'd be willing to have the stanza go "One can imagine . . .", or, for the last line, "as a large unseen aquatic animal breathes." However I do think that the way it is now is much better than either of those.

(3) I think Mrs. White was quite right about this stanza being confusing and I believe I have straightened it out.

I have written to Houghton Mifflin Company to find out the scheduled publication date of my book and I shall let you know as soon as I hear from them so that you may use the other poem before then, and this one, if you care to use it.

I hope this will be satisfactory to you.

Sincerely yours,

Elizabeth Bishop

P.S. I'll be at the above address for at least the next six weeks.

September 11, 1945
[postcard]

Dear Mrs. White: thank you very much for your letter & for sending the clippings—I had seen only one of them. I have improved the poem somewhat, I think, & sent it back to Mr. Lobrano. I have written Houghton Mifflin & will send on the publication date as soon as I know it. I don't want to trouble you any more now & hope you are having a pleasant holiday.

E. Bishop

September 27, 1945

Dear Miss Bishop:

I'm very pleased to be able to report that we've put through "Large Bad Picture" with the one change you made.[1]

You are quite right, of course, about the lower case "n's" being more appropriate, and we're disposed to accept your original wording in the reference to the breathing of the large aquatic animal.

I'm very sorry that illness prevented my letting you know before this about the poem. Many thanks for it, and we're looking forward to seeing

1 After suggesting to a friend that he turn some notes into "a series of New-Yorker-style sketches" because of the pay, Bishop added, "I sold them some rather light poems the other day—but of course nobody wants to send them anything really 'good'" (Bishop to Johnny [no last name], October 1, 1945, Vassar College Library).

more soon. Also, we'll be grateful for word about the book publication date when you know it.

Sincerely,

Gustave S. Lobrano

Dear Mr. Lobrano,

Houghton Mifflin has written me that they expect to bring out my book around March, 1946.

I am glad you can make use of "Large Bad Picture" and thank you for the check. I wonder if sometime you could let me know about the system by which The New Yorker pays for poetry? Is it page-space? I can't seem to figure it out from my own experiences and I'm afraid it is of some importance to me.

I hope you are quite recovered from your illness.

Sincerely yours,

Elizabeth Bishop

October 12, 1945

Dear Miss Bishop:

Here is your author's proof of "Large Bad Picture." The checking department says it should be "strait" not "straits" but if you prefer the sound of the latter, I don't think we need to be too literal.[1] The punctuation queries are for your consideration only—please do as you like.

Thank you for the change on the last stanza. I think all your decisions on our queries were right.

We hope for another poem soon.

Katharine S. White

P.S. I was so glad to have your postcard. I see that they sent the check for this poem to your New York address. I hope I'm right in thinking that this should go to Florida.

---

1 White is referring to the first line, which ran as: "Remembering the Strait of Belle Isle or".

16

October 20, 1945

Dear Mrs. White:

I am returning the proof today, and I have changed "Straits" to "Strait"—how mortifying. It seemed to me that the suggested changes in punctuation would both have been too noticeable as interruptions, but I am not very good at it and I am sure you probably have real authorities, so it will be quite all right if you prefer to restore the changes.

Yes, this is my address for the next few weeks. I hope to send you a few more poems before I leave. Thank you for all your kindness.

Sincerely yours,
Elizabeth Bishop

February 20, 1946

Dear Miss Bishop:

We like the last poem very much indeed—your impoverished scenery and your hermit—and I enclose our check for "Fine Examples." Our only doubt is about this title which, frankly, we don't quite understand. Possibly you would be willing to try another title when you return the proof, which I enclose now. Do you intend to include this poem in your book? We need to know this because of scheduling.

I'm wondering whether you won't have lunch with me some day. I'd love to have a chance to meet you and to hear about plans for your book and so on. Do you ever come up to this region at noontime? If you would like it, we could lunch at the Algonquin which is right across the street from this office. It would have to be before March 14, when I expect to go away for a couple of weeks.

Sincerely yours,
Katharine S. White

46 King Street
New York
February 25, 1946

Dear Mrs. White,

I am so glad you can use the little poem and I agree with you about the title's not being very clear. I shall send the proof back as soon as I can think of something better—at present all that occurs to me is "Old School

Ties" . . . I don't believe I shall use it in the forthcoming book so I guess there is no hurry about it, is there?

I'd be delighted to have lunch with you and any day after this week would be all right for me. When I returned to town I found I had a telephone at last—the number is WAlker 5-1706, if it would be more convenient for you to call than to write.

Sincerely yours,
Elizabeth Bishop

March 11, 1946
[Western Union Telegram]

=I SEEM TO HAVE THE FLU AND AM AFRAID I WILL BE UNABLE TO KEEP OUR LUNCHEON APPOINTMENT TODAY I HOPE VERY MUCH TO MEET YOU ON YOUR RETURN FROM FLORIDA=

E BISHOP.

March 11, 1946

Dear Miss Bishop:

I'm awfully sorry that you have flu. As a matter of fact, I'm walking around three-quarters sick myself so I would not have been good company for lunch. I look forward to seeing you after the 1st of April. In the meantime perhaps you'll have some poems to send us. I hope so.

Sincerely yours,
Katharine S. White

March 27, 1946
[addressed to "Poetry Editor"]

Dear Sir:

I am returning the proof to you today of my poem originally called "Fine Examples". I have changed the title to "Chemin de Fer" and I hope that will meet with your approval.

I should like to use both this poem and another one of mine that you now have called "Large Bad Picture" in my forthcoming book which Houghton Mifflin has just told me is being "rushed through the presses." I'm not sure how long that takes but shall try to find out and let you know—I imagine six weeks or so at the quickest.

I am sending the proof in the regular envelope but thought I had better write to you separately.

Very truly yours,
   Elizabeth Bishop

Dear Mr. Maxwell:

You may remember that some time ago you asked me to submit some stories to The New Yorker? This ["The Farmer's Children"] I am afraid is not at all in your line but since once in a while I notice that The New Yorker does publish something rather "out of character" I thought I might submit it to you anyway.

Sincerely yours,
   Elizabeth Bishop

April 4, 1946

Dear Miss Bishop:

I'm back from my vacation and I'm hoping that perhaps we can get together for luncheon before too long. Do you want to call me up sometime next week to make a date? I'd set a date now except that I have to have some x-rays and the appointments have not yet been made.

We have put down on our records the fact that both of your poems which we have on hand are to be included in your book and must be used soon. Would you please let us know the exact publication date of the volume as soon as you hear it?

Since I was writing you anyway and since I also handle fiction, I, rather than Mr. Maxwell, am writing you about your story, "The Farmer's Children." We have all of us read it with a great deal of interest and think it is extremely well written but our final decision, I'm sorry to say, is that it is rather remote for us. We can't help feeling it is more suitable for a literary magazine than for The New Yorker. As you said in your letter we do sometimes use stories that are "out of character." In fact we really do not feel that we have quite so definite a pattern or character as some of our critics imply. This statement may, I'm afraid, seem to be refuted by our rejection of your story. But we don't always reject literary stories or farm stories by any means, so it might be more honest to say that this particular story didn't appeal to us quite enough to compensate for its remoteness in spite of its merits and its considerable charm. I hope you won't be entirely discouraged with us and will have another story to send us soon. I have a strong feeling we will be able to use your fiction, if you let us see some more of it.

Sincerely yours,

Katharine S. White

May 21, 1946

Dear Miss Bishop:

I have been sick so I haven't called you up to try for lunch again. I'm afraid I'll have to let it go for this spring but this is just a line to say that although I shall be in Maine after the first of June, I shall still see any poems you send in. I hope you'll [have] many poems to send us.

Sincerely yours,

Katharine S. White

May 30, 1946

Dear Mrs. White,

Thank you for being so patient—I have been sick, too, and am going away for a while but I shall hope to see you in the fall. I also hope to send you a group of poems very shortly.

Sincerely yours,

Elizabeth Bishop

October 2, 1946

Dear Mrs. White,

I don't know whether you are back in town yet or not but I thought I would send you the enclosed poems ["Argument" and "Full Moon, Key West"] anyway and maybe you will be able to use them. I asked Houghton Mifflin to send you a copy of my book when it came out [in August] and they said they had already done so—I hope you received it safely.

I am in town now for the next two months at least and do hope I shall be able to meet you sometime this trip. Are you feeling better after your holidays?

Sincerely yours,

Elizabeth Bishop

Dear Miss Bishop:

I owe you an apology for not thanking you long ago for the copy of "North and South." My only excuse is that it arrived just as we were getting moving from Maine to New York and since getting here I've been lost in the effort of trying to furnish an unfurnished apartment. The volume, in print, seems to me even finer than it did when I read it in manuscript and already I have read and reread it. I was delighted by Louise Bogan's review for it expressed my own opinion so much better than I could. I have never spoken to her about your work and, because I value her opinion, I was happy to find that she approved the choice of the judges of the contest and that she liked your book so much. Edward Weeks' review seemed to me incredibly stupid. I missed Marianne Moore's but intend to look it up.[1]

Now after all this, it is particularly sorrowful for me to have to report that in a mixed vote here on your two latest poems, the "no's" have it. The sticking point for those who voted no on the Key West poem seemed to be the second stanza with its prolonged and slightly loose sentence structure. Everyone liked the first stanza. The other more personal poem some thought was not so good for our purposes as your poems usually are. I therefore return now "Argument" and "Full Moon, Key West" with many regrets and many thanks to you for having let us see them. Do be forgiving and send us something else soon.[2]

I'm glad to hear that you are in New York and hope that you will be able to lunch with me this time. I could do it almost any day in the week beginning October 28. Would you want to name a day and come to this office (20th floor) about 12:30?

Sincerely yours,

Katharine S. White

October 20, 1946

Dear Mrs. White,

Thank you for your kind remarks about the book. I was pleased with Miss Bogan's review, too—in fact I have been very lucky in that respect so far. It is quite all right about your returning the two poems—it probably was not a

1 Louise Bogan, "Verse" (October 5, 1946); Edward Weeks, "Prize Poet," *The Atlantic Monthly* (August 1946); and Marianne Moore, "A Modest Expert," *The Nation* (September 28, 1946). Weeks was the editor of *The Atlantic* from 1938 to 1966.
2 *Partisan Review* published "Full Moon, Key West" in its January/February 1947 issue.

very wise selection for me to have made, & I shall try to send some other things soon.

Would Thursday the 31st be all right for you for lunch? I shall write it down anyway & then you can let me know if it is not. I hope you have been able to find the furniture all right—the extraordinary thing is to have found the apartment!

Sincerely yours,
    Elizabeth Bishop

October 22, 1946

Dear Miss Bishop:

Lunch on Thursday, the 31st, will be fine for me. Why don't you stop here at the office a little before 12:30 (25 West 43rd Street, 20th Floor) and then we can go across the street to the Algonquin for lunch. Perhaps you hate the Algonquin but it is so near the office that we use it quite a lot. I look forward to seeing you.

Sincerely yours,
    Katharine S. White

November 25, 1946

Dear Miss Bishop:

Here are two copies of the first reading agreement that I told you about when we talked. I also enclose the check we shall give you (to bind the bargain) in case you decide to sign the agreement. If you do, please keep one copy of the letter for yourself and sign and return the other copy. I hope that Mr. Greenslet will think the plan a good one for you. We really want to have first look at your poetry but I understand perfectly that you feel that much poetry you have written would not be for us. We can promise you prompt reading and you could send the poems on to another magazine if we did not want them. I hope that the advantages of the plan will outweigh the disadvantages in your mind. If either you or Mr. Greenslet want further explanation about how the arrangement works out in detail I hope you will ask any questions you may have about it. Please give him greetings from me.

Sincerely yours,
    Katharine S. White

December 1, 1946

Dear Mrs. White,

Here is the contract. Mr. Greenslet seemed only too pleased.

I am enclosing three very old stories, all rather sad, I'm afraid. I believe you saw and rejected one called "The Farmer's Children." I'm now trying to re-write it for Harper's Bazaar—I think that will be perfectly all right, will it not, since it was rejected, and also before this contract? My best story, I think, is one called "In Prison".[1] I haven't a copy of it but it has just been reprinted in the "Partisan Reader." I also have one or two articles you might be interested in seeing—one unpublished one—both about Florida, and I shall send them to you when I can obtain copies. These things enclosed I'm afraid really will not give you a very good idea of my prose.

I wonder if you would be kind enough to send them back to me when you have read them? I am sorry to bother you but they seem to be the only copies I have and I must send them on to Houghton Mifflin.

Thank you for your letter and I hope that this will work out well for everyone.

Sincerely yours,
Elizabeth Bishop

December 9, 1946

Dear Miss Bishop:

Thank you for the clippings of the stories which I found very interesting. I am returning them now and realize how precious they must be to you if they are your only copies. We are particularly interested in the Florida articles of course, since they are factual and we hope you may be able to do some factual pieces for us on your trip. If you can get copies, do send them along and particularly the unpublished one.

There can be no objection to your rewriting "The Farmer's Children" for Harper's Bazaar. I still remember the story vividly and think it an interesting one and I wish we could have been persuaded that it was up our street.

It's splendid that you have signed the agreement and that Mr. Greenslet approved. I hope that the arrangement will work out happily for all of us and I'm sure it ought to.

Sincerely yours,
Katharine S. White

1 *The Partisan Reader: Ten Years of Partisan Review*, edited by William Phillips and Philip Rahv (1946).

Two

1947–1961

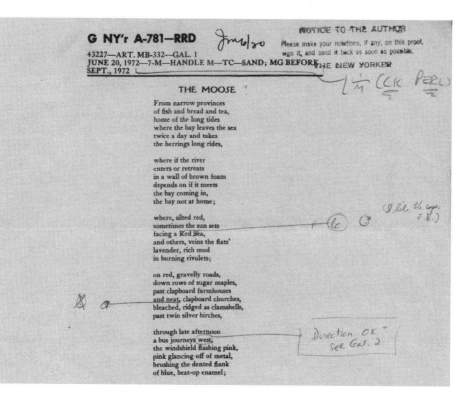

G NY'r A-781—RRD

43227—ART. MB-332—GAL. 1
JUNE 20, 1972—7-M—HANDLE M—TC—SAND; MG BEFORE
SEPT., 1972

NOTICE TO THE AUTHOR
Please make your notations, if any, on this proof,
sign it, and send it back as soon as possible.

THE NEW YORKER

THE MOOSE

From narrow provinces
of fish and bread and tea,
home of the long tides
where the bay leaves the sea
twice a day and takes
the herrings long rides,

where if the river
enters or retreats
in a wall of brown foam
depends on if it meets
the bay coming in,
the bay not at home;

where, silted red,
sometimes the sun sets
facing a Red Sea,
and others, veins the flats'
lavender, rich mud
in burning rivulets;

on red, gravelly roads,
down rows of sugar maples,
past clapboard farmhouses
and neat, clapboard churches,
bleached, ridged as clamshells,
past twin silver birches,

through late afternoon
a bus journeys west,
the windshield flashing pink,
pink glancing off of metal,
brushing the dented flank
of blue, beat-up enamel;

46 King Street
January 15, 1947

Dear Mrs. White,

Thank you for the clipping from the Tribune,—no I hadn't seen it and of course I agree with Selden Rodman, too. Oh dear, it would have been so pleasant to make Mr. Gannett "catch fire" as he puts it . . .[1]

The piece on Florida proved to need more work on it than I had thought. I am working on it but chiefly on a number of poems I want to get done before I go away. I am enclosing two ["Varick Street" and "Faustina, or, Rock Roses"]. I am afraid you will not be able to use either of them but I shall send you a group fairly soon some of which may be practical for you. However you might possibly like *Varick St.*

You said in your last letter that you would be willing to send things on to my next choice after The New Yorker. I am going to take advantage of this offer this time at least, but this is why. Randall Jarrell has asked me to send him some poems before he leaves The Nation, April 1st, I think, and I should like to get some to him right away. So if you cannot use either of these would you please be kind enough to let me know and to send one or both on to him at The Nation? And thank you very much.

I hope you are well—

Sincerely yours,

Elizabeth Bishop

---

1 Bishop is referring to Lewis Gannett, "Books and Things," *New York Herald Tribune* (December 13, 1946). Gannett reported that Selden Rodman had written him in response to his statement that 1946 "was the most arid year in American literature since our renaissance began thirty-odd years ago." Rodman believed Gannett would not have made that claim had he read Bishop's *North & South* and Robert Lowell's *Lord Weary's Castle*. Gannett replied: "I glanced through one, read the other, caught fire from neither, and wrote nothing about them."

January 20, 1947

Dear Miss Bishop:

I was much interested in "Varick Street" and "Faustina" but the consensus is that they don't belong in The New Yorker and might prove too difficult for our readers. I'm therefore sending them on to Randall Jarrell saying that you asked me to. To you I send our thanks for the poems and very real regrets. We look forward to seeing the others you say you are working on.[1]

Sincerely,

Katharine S. White

February 13, 1947

Dear Mrs. White,

Here is, I am afraid, another unusable poem ["At the Fishhouses"] that I should like to get out of your way and mine. I am doing quite a bit of work these days however and have quite a large group almost done, one or two of which I feel you may like. Thank you so much for sending the things on to Mr. Jarrell. As soon as I finish the group I mentioned I shall get to work on the prose.

Sincerely yours,

Elizabeth Bishop

February 17, 1947

Dear Miss Bishop:

We think that "At the Fish Houses" is a very beautiful poem and one that we are delighted to be able to buy and use when summer comes. Far from being unusable it has given us a great deal of pleasure. The check and proof will be along soon.

I look forward to the large group of poems you speak of and also the prose when you get to it.

Sincerely,

Katharine S. White

---

1 *The Nation* published the poems in its February 22 and March 15, 1947, issues.

February 25, 1947

Dear Miss Bishop:

Our proofroom, which has a highly conventional idea of punctuation, had scores of punctuation queries on the Fish Houses poem, but we have eliminated the major portion of them, since your lack of punctuation is purposeful and adds to your effect. Will you please study the few commas now suggested and see whether you approve. I only left in the ones I thought would really help the reader but you may not agree. In this case it should be as you want it.

Sincerely,

Katharine S. White

February 28, 1947

Dear Mrs. White,

I think the proof looks very nice and thank you for your help with the punctuation. I have left in all your changes except the commas between "Cold dark deep" that occurs twice. For some reason or other it seems more liquid to me without them and I think in this case the sense is plain enough without them, don't you? I notice that quite a few tails of p's, y's, etc. are missing but I imagine that is just because it's proof.

Also, thank you for Miss Bogan's number—she was very nice.

Sincerely yours,

Elizabeth Bishop

April 25, 1947

Dear Miss Bishop:

We are going to use your story "The Housekeeper", which we bought so long ago, this summer—or at least plan to now. I was amazed to find that it had been held all these years. When it went through I was working at long distance in Maine and I must disclaim having anything to do with the editing. Since it's not signed with your name it's possible that you don't care about the way the piece was edited and possibly you gave permission for editing changes at that time. I haven't had a chance to look up the correspondence. In any case I send it to you in fear and trembling lest it displease you terribly. I hope it won't. It suits the powers that be here and I myself reread it and thought it a charming story. I hope it will reach you before you leave and that you can let us have it back of course, or that if you wish to have changes made you will call me up and we can get together on it. The insert at (1) was put in for clarity because apparently most people misread the story and that Mrs. Sennett was simply working as housekeeper in Mr. Curley's summer cottage. I'm sure you meant that she owned the cottage herself. If you can think of a more adroit way of making this clear, I hope you won't hesitate to do it.

Faithfully yours,
Katharine S. White

D. B. MacLeod's
Briton Cove, Cape Breton
Nova Scotia
July 8, 1947

Dear Sir:

I have just this minute realized that there is a bad mistake in my poem AT THE FISH-HOUSES which you are going to publish sometime this summer. I've already corrected proof for the poem and only hope it is still possible to make these two very necessary corrections. I referred to layers of codfish scales stuck to the tubs, etc., when actually codfish have rather negligible scales and it was herring scales that I meant. They fished for both fish at the place I had in mind, and the scales of both were everywhere, but only herring scales would produce the effect that particularly struck me.

Lines 21 and 22 should read:

> The big fish tubs are completely lined
> with layers of beautiful herring scales
> and, etc. . . .

I hope it is not too late to make these changes and I am very sorry to have been so careless.[1]

Thinking that Mrs. White may be away I am addressing this to the "Poetry Editor" and hoping that it will reach the right person as soon as possible. My address will be the one above for the next three weeks at least.

Very truly yours,
Elizabeth Bishop

---

1 In the last extant draft, the lines read: "The big codfish tubs are completely lined / with layers of beautiful codfish scales" (Vassar College Library).

October 17, 1947

Dear Miss Bishop:

We're hoping for some poems from you and prose pieces too. Is there any chance? I don't know where you are or what you've been doing but hope that you had a good summer and were able to write. If you have anything on hand, I hope you'll let us read it for a manuscript from you would start the winter season well for us.

Sincerely yours,

Katharine S. White

907 Whitehead Street
Key West
November 4, 1947

Dear Mrs. White,

I went to Nova Scotia again this summer, to Cape Breton, & I have almost completed two poems about it, one somewhat on the order of the Fishhouses one that you published. As soon as they are done, I shall send them along to you.

I had just got back to New York when by great good fortune Pauline Hemingway offered me her guest house here until she gets back from California in January, so I got away from the city just as fast as I could.[1] I have two projects for prose pieces which might possibly be of interest to you. One is the trip around the "out islands" of the Bahamas, that I may have spoken to you about. The other is a trip I think I shall be able to take on the schooner that goes from here to Grand Cayman getting green turtles. It is a rather fascinating industry and I think should make quite a nice article. I am also working on two stories which I intend to send you. I shall probably be here working on poetry & stories till around the first of the year, then go on these two trips. I shall certainly be sending you some poems in a week or so, & I hope you'll be able to use one or two of them, anyway.

I hope you had a nice summer & are very well. I just missed meeting Karl Shapiro in Washington on my way down & I was sorry to.

Sincerely yours,

Elizabeth Bishop

---

1 Pauline Pfeiffer Hemingway was Ernest Hemingway's second wife. They were married from 1927 to 1940.

November 25, 1947

Dear Mrs. White,

I am returning the [first reading] contract to you and have signed it for another year. Thank you very much for the check and for the bonus, too. I hope maybe this year you will receive a little more work from me.[1]

I don't believe you could have received the letter I wrote you when I first got down here, about three weeks ago. In it I said that I hope to send you a couple of poems, at least, in a week or so, one somewhat on the order of the fishhouse one, but a little more serious. I also said, I think, that I had some idea of going on a turtle-schooner from here to Grand Cayman, and hoped to be able to write a piece about the green turtle industry that might perhaps be of interest to you. At present that plan isn't going very well; the captain of the schooner doesn't care about taking ladies along. He says he's a 'moral man'—he's a Mohammedan—but 'sailors sometimes go too far.' But I may get to Cayman yet one way or another and also I am going on a trip around the 'out islands' of the Bahamas. Some of these trips should produce something you might like, I should think. I also am at work on a couple of stories.

In case you didn't receive my first turtle picture I'll enclose another one. I hope you are well—

Sincerely yours,
Elizabeth Bishop

December 2, 1947

Dear Mrs. White,

It occurred to me that you might like this for your "Incidental Intelligence" dept.—or to illustrate the hard life of the poet. A current magazine

1 Earlier that year, memos had gone back and forth over Ross's decision to change the magazine's poetry rates. Ross wanted to pay for poems by their width. White balked at the idea and attempted to shame him by saying his scheme would make *The New Yorker* the laughingstock of the literary world. "Andy, when he heard of it, said he was going to write a poem with the longest lines ever known and with a title called something like 'On Learning That *The New Yorker* Pays More for Wide-Measure Verse than for Narrow-Measure Verse" (White to Ross, August 4, 1947, Bryn Mawr College Library and *The New Yorker* Records). Ross, however, would not back down. "It's the only way I, for one, can operate," he confessed. "We pay for everything else by space—or at any rate we measure everything, and space is one factor—and we should unquestionably pay for poetry that way, too" (Ross to White, September 9, 1947, *The New Yorker* Records). Ross combined the earlier system of giving writers letter grades to determine their fees with this one. A report on Bishop's contract revealed that her rate of: "$2 per line is half way between 'B-plus' and 'A-minus' for verse not over one column wide and is equivalent to 'C-plus' ($1.95) for verse not over one-and-one third columns wide" (Mason to Truax, November 12, 1947, *The New Yorker* Records). The magazine continued to struggle with how to pay for poetry for years.

('47, to be exact) wrote me this: *"Our rates for poetry are slightly variable but basically related to about $1 a line."*

Sincerely,

Elizabeth Bishop

December 3, 1947

Dear Miss Bishop:

Thank you for the signed agreement. We look forward to the promised poems, really earnestly. If you do take the trip on the turtle schooner, that certainly sounds like a piece that would be of interest to us, and also of course we'd like to see your story of the trip through the Bahamas, if it turns into a piece. In your earlier letter, which it was stupid of me not to answer—somehow it got filed before I answered it—you mentioned that you were working on two stories that you intended to send us. We very much hope to see these too.

Faithfully,

Katharine S. White

December 8, 1947

Dear Miss Bishop:

The oftener one rereads that sentence about '47's verse rate the more wonderful it is. However, before we even considered whether it would be cricket to use it, we'd have to know whether we could do so legally. If it came to you in a prospectus or on a mimeographed sheet, or if it is from a form letter to writers, perhaps we could. But if it came to you in a personal letter, signed by an editor (or by anyone for that matter), we could not quote it verbatim because, by law, letters belong to the sender, not the receiver. Won't you therefore let me know the circumstances? This letter business is odd but sometimes, remembering the foolish letters I must often write, I am grateful for the law. Thank you for the incidental intelligence anyway. There is no law to prevent your having passed that on—only the words themselves are sacred.

A letter like this of mine is another example of how to complicate a poet's life!

Sincerely,

Katharine S. White

630 Dey Street
Key West
January 5, 1948

Dear Mrs. White,

Yes, my letter from '47, '48, rather, *was* a personal one and I'm sorry to have bothered you with it. Another item in the 'poetic life', interesting to me, at any rate, is my publishers' giving me as a Christmas present a book called 'The Basic Cookbook.'[1] I have a feeling they probably give their novelists an 'Advanced' cookbook . . . I shall send you a group of poems shortly and in the meantime perhaps you will be able to use this one ["A Summer's Dream"] but maybe not since it is rather gloomy—With best wishes for your New Year,

Sincerely yours,
Elizabeth Bishop

January 21, 1948

Dear Miss Bishop:

Here's your check for "A Summer's Dream," a poem that we admire. You've succeeded wonderfully with your effect I think.

I passed on your little item about the cook book to the Notes and Comment department thinking it might make a little paragraph. Do you mind? Your name wouldn't be used, of course, if they wanted to use it, which they may not, because such material depends upon how it strikes the fancy of the person who rewrites it and upon how he writes it. We look forward to more poems soon—and what about the stories?

Sincerely,
Katharine S. White

March 29, 1948

Dear Miss Bishop:

This is just to remind you that we are longing for some more poems and for some prose pieces too. I am going to be out of the office because of an operation on my spine but William Maxwell will be at my desk and he is a great admirer of your work. Do send us something.

Sincerely,
Katharine S. White

1 Marjorie Heseltine and Ula M. Dow Keezer, *The Basic Cookbook: A Completely Revised and Enlarged Edition of Good Food Made Economical* (1947).

April 8, 1948

Dear Mr. Maxwell,

I recently had a letter from Mrs. White asking me for some work and saying that I should submit it to you while she is away. I am enclosing two poems, neither of which, I'm afraid, you'll be able to use . . . The one called 'The Bight' may be possible, I don't know. Mrs. White has been kind enough, in the past, to send work that she found inappropriate to the New Yorker on to other places for me. I wonder if you would find it too much trouble to send the 'Over 2000 Illustrations' one on to Partisan Review for me, and 'The Bight,' if not usable, back to me, since it will eventually be part of a Key West group? Or just send them both back to me.

Maybe I should have mentioned before to Mrs. White that although I have a contract with you I am having a short poem and essay in the Marianne Moore no. of the Quarterly Review, neither of which I sent to the New Yorker first.[1] They are both such specialized, done-for-the-occasion things that I thought it wouldn't matter, and also both were requested before I signed a contract.

If you are writing or seeing Mrs. White, please give her my regards and tell her I am sorry she is ill.

Sincerely yours,

Elizabeth Bishop

April 19, 1948

Dear Miss Bishop:

Here is a check for the periodical cost-of-living adjustment which I'm sure Mrs. White has explained to you and so I won't go into it. Mr. Ross likes "The Bight" as we all do, and a check for it will come along to you in a few days. The other poem I'm still waiting to hear from him about.

Sincerely,

William Maxwell

April 26, 1948

Dear Mr. Maxwell,

My friend, Mrs. Pauline Hemingway, and I have been amusing ourselves in our spare time here by collaborating on some little stories. They mostly

---

1 "For M.M." ["Invitation to Miss Marianne Moore"] and "As We Like It," *Quarterly Review of Literature* (Spring 1948).

grew out of anecdotes she has told me about her life in Arkansas twenty or thirty years ago. We have been doing it more or less for fun but I have decided to send one ["The River Rat"] on to you to see if you think there is any possibility of making New Yorker material out of it. We have a couple more and ideas for several more—one trouble is that some of the tales just don't seem credible, although they are perfectly true.

I should be very grateful if you could give me an opinion. I expect to send you a couple of stories under my own name shortly.[1]

After this, for a while, my address is 46 King Street, New York 14, New York.

Thank you very much.

Sincerely yours,

Elizabeth Bishop

May 3, 1948

Dear Miss Bishop:

I'm ever so sorry but the vote was finally against "Over 2000 Illustrations" which I liked particularly but the other editors found too difficult for a general magazine. I'm very sorry, because it seemed to me to have some really wonderful descriptive passages, and a profound idea. I'm sending it along to Philip Rahv, as you suggested.[2]

The story that you and Mrs. Hemingway worked on together didn't seem right for us, either in content or in form. Since you are contemplating other pieces with Mrs. Hemingway, perhaps you'd like to stop by the office and talk about this one. That you are about to send us two of your own stories is very good news. We'll be looking forward to them.

Sincerely yours,

William Maxwell

May 13, 1948

Dear Miss Bishop:

Our style expert says we can't grant two of your requests on the proof of The Bight. The italic subtitle is against the style of the magazine, and the lower case "g" in the fourth line from the end is, he says, against English and

---

1 Bishop submitted the story under the name "Katharine Burns."

2 *Partisan Review* published the poem in its June 1948 issue.

would look monstrous.[1] I don't know what "against English" can possibly mean, and personally, I like things that look monstrous. But these two details would, it seems rock the foundations of the magazine, and I hope you won't mind our leaving them the way they are.

Cordially yours,

William Maxwell

September 22, 1948

Dear Miss Bishop:

I'm awfully sorry to discover that we've been holding this story so long. Mr. Maxwell I think kept it, after notifying you that it wasn't right for us, in case you wanted to discuss it or others in the same group with him. He left the office some time ago, and I didn't know the story was here until just now.[2] I also see by the correspondence he had with you last spring that you were planning a couple of short stories of your own. I hope they're still on the way, and that we'll have the opportunity to see them soon.

Sincerely,

Robert Henderson

November 10, 1948

Dear Miss Bishop:

We seem to run into only bad luck about our meetings. I'm just back from the dentist—I have a frightful job of dentistry ahead after all this illness— and he did something to my teeth that requires my attendance there on Tuesday, the 16th, at 12:30. He's a very busy man and couldn't fit me in for a long time if I didn't come then. This means I shall have to ask you whether you'd have lunch with me late that day—say 1:30—and the nearest place to the dentist is Longchamps Restaurant at Madison and 59th Street. If Longchamps isn't too repellent to you, how about meeting me there, and if you can't do it that day, I'll hold Wednesday, the 17th, open until I hear from you. I tried to reach you by phone but got no answer. Perhaps you'd be good enough to call me up tomorrow.

Apologetically yours,

Katharine S. White

1 In the last extant draft, the line runs: "Click. Click. goes the dredge," (Vassar College Library). It ran as: "Click. Click. Goes the dredge,". Bishop maintained the change for *A Cold Spring* but put the subtitle, "On My Birthday", back into italics.

2 Maxwell left on July 1 for a trip to Europe. He returned in October.

November 16, 1948

Dear Miss Bishop:

Here is the agreement I forgot to bring you. It is just like last year's. Please send us one copy signed and keep the other. I also enclose the one hundred dollar check that goes with the contract. Last year this check was for $135 because it included the "cost of living adjustment" described in paragraph 3, but this year we have paid such adjustments quarterly and you've received two checks, one in May and one in August.

Don't forget to send the new poems! You are right that "The Bight" has not been run. We are saving it for winter.

Hastily,
Katharine S. White

46 King Street
November 18, 1948

Dear Mrs. White,

Here is the contract and thank you very much for the check.

Thank you also very much for a very enjoyable luncheon. I'm afraid I was suffering from New York-itis that day and feel that I probably talked my head off and said all sorts of things I shouldn't have. I hope not.

I may not be able to get the things typed and off to you until I get down to Florida—probably the 1st week in December—but I shall send them just as soon as I can.

Sincerely yours,
Elizabeth Bishop

611 Frances Street
Key West
January 12, 1949

Dear Mrs. White,

I don't know whether you could possibly be interested in another plain description from me or not, but I am sending it ["Cape Breton"] along. I shall send you some more poems in about a week, and those stories I mentioned at least before the winter is over—I've only wanted to work on poetry since I got back.

I think the two last Thurber stories have been wonderful—particularly the correspondence with the publisher—so *true*—and I also enjoyed the Nabokov.[1]

I do hope you are keeping well.

Sincerely yours,

　　Elizabeth Bishop

January 20, 1949

Dear Miss Bishop:

"Cape Breton" is a beautiful and magical poem and we are delighted to have it. We want to buy it of course and I am writing now only about one small section in it, the meaning of which bothers us a little. There have been various interpretations. If you feel that the four lines that I have marked of Stanza 2 on the enclosed copy of the poem are just as you want them to stand, we'll run them that way, but if you would want to clarify them a little, we'd be grateful.[2] Just what is your meaning here? Do you mean that the interior regions have little to say for themselves except in the songs of birds and except for the fact that on this Sunday you describe so exactly the fishermen who live in the little houses of the back country are mending their torn fish-nets? We realize that the lines are put in for texture, as in a painting, and for general atmosphere as well as exact description and that you may want to keep your ellipsis. Some have read the lines as if the "their" which has no antecedent applied to the birds whereas others have thought the songs were the songs of the men mending their fish-nets. I myself think it applies to the regions. All this, I'm afraid, will sound frightfully literal to you but though we would prefer to have it entirely clear we will, as I said, accept it your way.

I can't tell you what pleasure this poem has given me—given all of us here as a matter of fact. It is a perfect portrait of a countryside, a wonderfully exact description of that kind of seacoast and a most distinguished poem as well. I hope you'll let me know right away how you feel about this passage and whether you want it to stand as written. You know one of Mr. Ross's

---

1 Bishop is probably referring to James Thurber's "A Friend of the Earth" (June 4, 1949) and "Joyeux Noël, Mr. Durning" (July 2, 1949) and Vladimir Nabokov's "Portrait of My Mother" (April 9, 1949).

2 In the last extant draft, the four lines that correspond to White's question are:

　　Which regions now have little to say for themselves
　　except in thousands of light song-sparrow songs floating upwards
　　freely, dispassionately, through the mist, and meshing
　　their brown-wet, fine, torn fish-nets. (Vassar College Library)

fetishes is that he understand every poem we publish. Sometimes we've published ones he doesn't understand but we try to make clarity an aim even so which is why I'm bothering you.

I told Thurber what you said about his stories and he was much pleased and so will Nabokov be. It's good news that you have some more poems to send and also that the stories may be written this winter.

We have half planned a trip to Cape Breton this summer and your poem makes me all the more anxious to go.

Faithfully yours,

Katharine S. White

February 1, 1949

Dear Mrs. White,

I have nothing against clarity, you know, and I think you were quite right to question that passage. All I meant by it was that the effect of the (literally) thousands of song-sparrow songs floating up above the unseen mysterious landscape of the interior, and meeting each other, was *like* (with some vague connection between the color of the birds and the color of the fish-nets used there, I suppose) a torn fish-net floating in the air.

I think it could be fixed in this way:

> like the admirable scriptures made on stones by stones,
> —and these regions now have little to say for themselves
> except in thousands of light song-sparrow songs floating upwards
> freely, dispassionately, through the mist, and meshing
> in brown-wet, fine, torn fish-nets.

Would that do it? Or I suppose there could be another *like*, *like* brown-wet, fine, etc. . . . But I'm afraid that makes many too many likes and somewhat spoils the effect I had in mind. But if it has to be *like*, all right, because I think that would make it perfectly obvious, don't you? But I really think that *in* makes it clear—I've asked a couple of people, who read it without any explanation from me and 'got' it, just to see.

There is so much to say about Cape Breton it is hard to stop, but I felt a lot of the other things went better together in another kind of poem and this was my 1st general impression. If you do go there be sure to tell me; although it is two summers ago I was there I think I might be able to tell you about one or two nice places to stay & things to see. Thank you for your very kind letter, and I hope this makes the poem clear enough.

Sincerely yours,

Elizabeth Bishop

P.S. *"their"* referred to "songs".

February 4, 1949

Dear Miss Bishop:

It is wonderful to have a poet as amiable as you are about a literal query of the sort I made. We are most grateful to you for the rewording of those lines and I have put the poem through with the version you prefer. If it hits any queries for clarity from Mr. Ross, who is the final reader on all proof, I'll write you about it and will suggest your second version. I agree with you that your first version of the revision is better and that it ought to be kept that way and I shall so argue. I'll be sending you a check and a proof soon but I wanted to thank you at once. If all contributors were as amiable, life would be much easier for me.

Hastily yours,

Katharine S. White

February 16, 1949

Dear Miss Bishop:

Here is your author's proof of "Cape Breton." There are very few problems about it but there is one that you can help us with and that is when is the best season to use it. I can't be absolutely sure when daisies come in Cape Breton. If we use it in summer, say July or August, your next to last stanza poses a problem because if Cape Breton is at all like Maine there are no flags flying even on weekdays during the summer holiday. Wouldn't it be safe to use the poem about the middle of June? Or is this too early for the feel of the poem?

All the other matters are minor ones of punctuation and in this case they are mostly author's choice. I think our proof department tends to want us to over punctuate poetry and I've removed a lot of their questions.

I am beginning to feel the onset of summer and the rush for accommodations. Some time when you get a moment in the fairly near future, would you want to write me about good places to stay in Nova Scotia? It now looks as if Andy and I would go off there for the month of July and we'd like to travel around some but have a couple of good spots to stay in because neither of us are people who like motoring for motoring's sake. Perhaps the best thing to do would be to go to one spot and settle down and motor about from it. We don't care about fancy food but we do want it to be good to eat and in general we prefer a place where you don't have to be terribly clubby with other people. A simple boarding house is always all right except where it has become bastardized. I'd be awfully grateful for any tips you wanted to give us.

I hope you didn't miss seeing "The Bight" in last week's issue. I like all of your poems so much that I never can decide which are my favorites.

Sincerely,

Katharine S. White

April 18, 1949

Dear Miss Bishop:

Here is the check due you for the cost of living adjustment on the quarter ending March 31. I am not quite sure where you are, but hope that this note will be forwarded.

I am extremely grateful to you for your long and detailed letter about Nova Scotia. It has been of enormous help to Andy and myself and it now looks as if we were going to make the trip to Nova Scotia. We shall start in the car from North Brooklin and work our way up the coast slowly, because I can't drive too far in a day. We're using that book of where to stay as a kind of guide, but your hints are particularly useful, and we'll try to avoid the towns you say to skip. I think we'll probably end up at Margaree or Ingonish and stay a longer time at one or the other place than anywhere else. We may go to Shelbourne (?) to see whether we can get a small boat built there.

Did I ever thank you for the proof? I think all is in order on it and that it now reads as you want it to. It is that poem of yours that makes me feel I just *must* get to Cape Breton. We may take your suggestion of calling John MacDonald.

I *have* been to Haiti at the time of the American occupation. It was absolutely unspoiled (except by the American marines) and some time I hope I can persuade you to tell me all about it as it is today. When you come back to New York could we have lunch, or could I get you to the apartment for dinner some night? We shall be here until about May 15. When do you return?

Katharine S. White

c/o Frankenberg
61 Perry Street
New York
July 10, 1949

Dear Mrs. White,

I hope you're off in Cape Breton or some other place that's relatively cool. I have three poems all just about done that I'll send you and one at least I think maybe you'll be able to make use of. This one ["O Breath"] I'm pretty sure you won't. Will you send it back to me, or else kindly send it along to Partisan Review? My address is very uncertain so I'm just using the one above for the time being.

I hope you're well and I'm sorry I missed seeing you in New York.

Sincerely yours,
    Elizabeth Bishop

July 14, 1949

Dear Miss Bishop:

Mrs. White is on her vacation just now, but the rest of us have read "O Breath," and, I'm sorry to say, agree that it isn't right for The New Yorker, as you yourself suspect. I'm sending it to Mr. [William] Phillips at Partisan Review, since your address is uncertain, and I'll forward your note to Mrs. White when her holiday is over. Thank you for sending the poem in. We'll be eager, of course, to see the ones you say are on the way.[1]

Sincerely,
    Robert Henderson

August 10, 1949

Dear Miss Bishop:

I wish I'd been able to see the poem that was sent on to the Partisan Review during my vacation, and am exceedingly sorry that it proved to be one we could not use. Instead we must live in hopes of receiving soon the three poems you told me were "all but down."

I am perfectly delighted about the news given in the clipping that I enclose, and we all send you our warmest congratulations on this honor. I can't think of any poet who deserves the appointment [as Poetry Consultant

1 *Partisan Review* published the poem in its September 1949 issue.

to the Library of Congress] more. When do you begin your term? I know that Louise Bogan very much enjoyed her work when she was consultant on poetry, and Karl Shapiro, too, though I think he was less enthusiastic than Louise, perhaps partly because he was less temperamentally suited to such a position.[1]

I have been meaning to write you that we never did get to Nova Scotia. It was a terrible disappointment. Our plans were all made and we had accommodations secured along our route, all the way to Ingonish, when only two days before we were to leave, we had a disaster here on our farm which meant that we had to stay right at home. The man who has worked for us for seventeen years and who is our mainstay in keeping the farm running fell unconscious on his scythe. By a miracle he did not cut himself but we had a most frightening time. It proved to be a diabetic coma—and at 53 years old, he'd never had any indication before of diabetes. We got him to the hospital in time and he's slowly getting better, but we could not leave not knowing how he would get along and besides, had to stay here to carry on without him. He isn't well enough to work—perhaps he never will be but the doctor hopes he will.

I have not yet seen the new Martha Foley volume of short stories but gather from the reviews that your short story is one of the few good ones in it.[2] I gather, too, that it is the story about the farm children which we rejected once. I always was grieved about that rejection.

Is there any chance of your coming to Deer Isle this summer? Joe, my eighteen year old son, is a counselor at a camp in Canary Cove and if you do happen to be in Stonington, perhaps he could sail or drive you over here. He gets a half day off once in a while, and has a Model T there and also a small sloop, both of which get him home satisfactorily. Would you want to chance the trip in either conveyance?

Faithfully,

Katharine S. White

Yaddo
Saratoga Springs, New York
August 24, 1949

Dear Mrs. White,

How I wish I *were* in Maine. Instead I decided to try this famous place for

1 Bogan was the library consultant from 1945 to 1946 and Shapiro from 1946 to 1947.
2 "The Farmer's Children," *The Best American Short Stories* (1949).

the month of August. One month I think, is not enough to get used to the strangeness of it all and start writing poetry—at least not for me—I think some do better, and painters seem to do best of all. I may feel a little gloomy about it at the moment because I am in bed with what they think is a case of *mumps*, of all things, and feeling my desirability as a 'guest' ebbing every second. However I'm much better today so maybe it isn't mumps after all, or a very slight attack of them.

Thank you so much for sending me the clipping. I'm not sure how I'll be at such a job, but I do know some of the people who have held it, and surely next year couldn't prove to be as difficult as I imagine the one Léonie Adams is just concluding. I'm supposed to get there about the middle of September. I'm leaving here the first and shall be in New York for a week or ten days. For your sake I hope you'll still be in North Brooklin, but if you are in New York I hope maybe I'll be able to see you.

I'm sorry you didn't get to Nova Scotia, but rather glad you didn't get to Cape Breton in that heat—I did once & it's particularly maddening to be hot that far north and where there isn't much ice, etc. The sad story of the man who worked for you takes me right back to similar events in Nova Scotia when I was little.

I would have adored to have sailed from Stonington—in fact I wish I were doing it right this minute. I have got some work done here in spite of my ungraciousness about it all and shall really be sending something in a week or so.

Mrs. Ames, the woman who runs Yaddo, tells me that Jean Stafford is going to write a piece about Saratoga Springs for you. It would make a wonderful one, I think; it's a fascinating place and right now 'cheaper' than any place I've ever seen including Miami. But she should put in the races, I think—for the first time I've been reading Audax Minor and feeling in the know.[1]

I do hope you've been well.

Sincerely yours,

Elizabeth Bishop

October 27, 1949

Dear Miss Bishop:

Your first reading agreement expires next month and I am sending you a

---

1 George Ryall wrote his *New Yorker* column "The Race Track" under the pseudonym Audax Minor.

new one together with the $100 check, hoping that you will want to sign an agreement for next year. This is just like your old one, I believe, and we have even left in Paragraph 1 the words "including travel essays." I imagine that now you are in Washington you may not be contemplating travel but we have always hoped to have this sort of material from you and it occurred to me that you might travel in the summer. Will you sign one letter and keep the other— that is if you want to sign at all. It would be an awful blow if you didn't.

I am anxious to see you and I hope you will let me know ahead of time when you are coming to New York so that I may take you to luncheon. I feel that I have a lot to talk about with you even if it's only about the trip we didn't take. I am anxious to know how you like the job. Naturally we hope for some more poems, if you get time to write any, but don't think that signing an agreement puts you under obligation to produce any. We are quite willing to give you an agreement just on the chance you *might* write something for us during the year.

In reply to your last letter written on August 24th from Yaddo, I am not sure whether Jean Stafford is definitely going to do a piece on Saratoga Springs or not but I can find out the next time I see her if you should happen to want to do one. I would be much interested to know what the place is like now. It's wonderful to think that you read Audax Minor. Lots of people ask me why we continue to run that department. I myself never fail to read it though I haven't been to a horse race in years.

Faithfully,

Katharine S. White

Library of Congress
Washington, DC
January 14, 1950

Dear Mrs. White:

I don't know whether you'll be able to make use of this ["Verdigris"] or not—I have another, about Washington more directly, that I'll try to send you after next week.[1] I only hope people won't think I'm talking about TIME

1 An undated version of this poem appears in *Edgar Allan Poe & The Juke-Box* (186). A typed version dated February 9, 1950, appears in the *Poetry* magazine papers. Bishop made two handwritten corrections on the manuscript. In stanza one, line three, she changed "Time turns green" to "Time grows green" (the same as in *Edgar Allan Poe*), and in stanza four, line two, Bishop crossed out "Justice" and wrote "Freedom" (the version in *Edgar Allan Poe* has "Justice"). In the February 9 version, in stanza six, line one, Bishop also did not capitalize "seas" in "seas of Greece."

magazine. I have a feeling I should have written to you some time ago but I'm not sure whether it was just to thank you for the contract or what. One thing I know I have had on my mind is to thank you or your magazine for the campaign against radio broadcasting in the station—*here* we have it in the trolley cars and busses and it is really pure torture.[1] Every day I say to myself now you CAN read and forget it, if you try—but it's really impossible and I'm spending all my salary on taxicabs just to escape it. I had an awful little interview with some lady from the Boston Post a while ago—I don't know whether it's appeared yet or not. It didn't go too well, but when she asked me if I had any "pet peeves" I said, yes, I certainly had, & said that I thought radio on the trolleys, etc., was an infringement of human rights and dignity, and also mentioned the New Yorker's stand, etc.[2] It is particularly painful here, I think—thousands of government workers being carted off to work every morning and being *forcibly soothed* all the way—as bad as "1984". Sometimes I think they get their programs mixed—once at 8:30 A.M. I found I was listening to a crooner singing "When Day is Done." Well, I mustn't get worked up . . .

A friend of mine here just had the same back operation you had—she is doing extremely well, I think, but apparently was extremely surprised when she tried to stand up for the first time.

I am liking my job quite well—it's all a little unbelievable, though. I do hope you are well. If you ever get down here do please come to see me.

Sincerely yours,

Elizabeth Bishop

January 20, 1950

Dear Miss Bishop:

It seems incredible that I should be sending you back a poem when we have been so longing to have one from you. Your villanelle, "Verdigris," drew a mixed vote but the "no's" won out in the end. I simply hate to have to send it back to you but it does seem to the majority to be obscure and not to have quite the simplicity and neatness that a villanelle should have.

---

1 During the fall of 1949, *The New Yorker* ran several "Talk of the Town" stories on the background music and commercials playing in Grand Central Terminal. The articles and commuters' complaints led to a highly publicized hearing, after which the broadcasts stopped.

2 "This is the first time she has been in Washington and the only thing she doesn't like about it is the heavy traffic and the music they play on the street cars. Thinks it's an infringement on personal liberty and has been driven to taking taxis to work to keep her peace of mind." Sally Ellis, "U.S. Poetry Chair Holder Tells How She Courts the Muse," *Boston Post Magazine* (January 8, 1950).

I hope you will show that you forgive us by coming right back with another poem. That would comfort me enormously if you would. And of course I must wistfully ask again for those stories. Aren't you going to have some prose to send us too?

I sent your paragraph about the radio broadcasting on to Mr. Ross and to my husband, who wrote the editorials on that subject. We all think that Mr. Ross has won a wonderful victory and that it wasn't so light and insignificant a one as most newspapers and news magazines thought it to be. Once they start things of that sort, it's bound to carry on. Andy was much interested to hear what you said about broadcasting in Washington trolley cars and busses. He'd had reports from a friend there but he hadn't heard the thing in action.

If you get to New York any time, do save a lunch for me—or a dinner at our house.

Sincerely,
    Katharine S. White

January 23, 1950

Dear Mrs. White:

Thank you for your kind letter & please don't feel badly about having to return the poem! It was just one of those hunches that I guess didn't work—& on studying it some more I think probably in order to make the meaning clear it will have to be turned into a *double* villanelle! I should certainly try to send you some more things soon. I really have had almost no time for my own work, but I think I'm going to have more from now on.

I meant to say this in my other letter but I don't believe I did, or did I? Wallace Fowlie has written a little article about Max Jacob, for "Poetry" Magazine, & they asked me to provide a few translations of Jacob's poetry to go with it. They may not use them, & the poems, aside from the translation, aren't much good, anyway—but I don't believe this will be any infringement of my contract with you, will it?[1]

Please feel that I don't mind your turning down the poem a bit.

Sincerely yours,
    Elizabeth Bishop

1 *Poetry* published Bishop's translations of "Rainbow," "Patience of an Angel," "Banks," and "Hell is Graduated" in its May 1950 issue.

Dear Miss Bishop:

As you suppose, it is of course no infringement of your agreement with us to translate the Max Jacob poem for *Poetry*, but we thank you for telling us about it. I'm very grateful to you too for your gentle letter about the villanelle.

Yours,

Katharine S. White

Saratoga Springs

October 22, 1950

Dear Mrs. White:

I am enclosing two slight poems that you might be able to use ["View of the Capitol from the Library of Congress" and "Little Exercise"]. It is nice to be free from the Library and working again, and as soon as my new typewriter arrives (I don't like the type of this borrowed one) I'll send you a crazy story you also might possibly be able to use, although I'm afraid it will be too morbid. Also some more poems shortly.

The desk poem may be mis-titled, but I was afraid "Desk at Night" made it entirely *too* clear. I had one poem you printed called "Little Exercise" and I'd like to use it again—but I'd be grateful for any suggestions.

With best wishes, and I hope you are well—

Elizabeth Bishop

November 1, 1950

Dear Elizabeth Bishop:

It was a great pleasure and happiness to receive some poems from you and I enclose our check for "View of the Capitol"—a poem we admire. It is a delight. On the other hand I must reluctantly return "Little Exercise," which has caused a lot of discussion, but the final decision was against asking you for clarification. I for awhile thought that it might be made clear enough for us by a new title and by, perhaps, some change in the second stanza where we are sure about the unicyclist (or flatter ourselves we are) but not so sure about the rest. Anyway the final feeling is that the poem perhaps belongs in another publication and that it would not be fair to ask you to change it so that it would be easy to comprehend. You ask for my advice about the title and perhaps it's impertinent of me to give it now that our vote has gone against the poem but I'll plunge in anyway and say I do think you need some amplification, at least of "Little Exercise." For example, one reader, who read the poem but not your letter about the alternate title, at first read the poem as a description of a surrealist painting. I wish you could keep the present title and add something to it this way—"Little Exercise: Typewriter at Night," not those over explicit words or course but some such thing—something that did not diagram it. I'm not sure whether "Desk at Night" would work. It was slightly misleading to me anyway since, to me, the word *desk* never suggests a typewriter if only because I always have my typewriter on a separate table, not on my desk. I think most people do. I hate to send this poem back.

I also now enclose a new first reading agreement for you and the check that goes with it. Perhaps I should have asked you first whether you wanted the agreement renewed. I certainly hope so. This one, I'm told, is just like last year's.

Do send us the "crazy story" right away. I can't wait to read it, and all of us feel the same way about the story and also, of course, the new poems. It is so good to have you contributing again.

One more thing: would you have any interest in applying for the fellowship described in the enclosed pamphlet? I feel almost certain that you would detest the idea of living all year in the academic atmosphere, but the reason I send along the announcement and the application blank is that I have a letter from the President's office at Bryn Mawr asking me for nominations and telling me that under certain circumstances they would not require the holder of the fellowship to live at Bryn Mawr. Apart from this residence thing, there seem to be no strings attached. Let me know if it should happen to interest you and I'll write them at Bryn Mawr but you yourself would of course have to send in your application before January 15.

Do let me know if you come to New York. It seems years since I've seen you.

Faithfully,
Katharine S. White

November 3, 1950

Dear Mrs. White:

I'm so glad you liked the little poem about the Capitol—I must tell you, only please don't repeat it, that I think I wrote it because the Assistant there once told me that the Library had always been disappointed because none of the Consultants had ever been inspired to write about the Library! Of course, this is scarcely what they had in mind, but I have a more serious one under weigh—which will disappoint them even more, I'm afraid.

Perhaps "Steps" in line 6 should be capitalized—those steps seem to be national institutions.

I agree with you perfectly about the other number & am just sorry that you wasted so much time over it. After I mailed it I started going over some old things & realized I had three or four such little conundrums—which is what they are—and that in a group they'd be much more effective.—& probably easier to get. Anyway, when I piece them all together I'll send them again and then I can try them someplace else. (The unicyclist is a typewriter eraser, that's all.)

I am very pleased to sign the contract again, & surprised to be invited to, my output has been so negligible. However, things do seem to be taking a turn for the better.

My new typewriter came a few days ago, but then I had to go up to Trudeau to visit a sick friend & just got back last night. It is a wonderful toy—a gift—I just can't get over it and as you see I haven't mastered the magic margins yet, or else they need adjusting. I'll get busy on the story today, though, and try to get it to you next week.

I think it would be nice if you called me Elizabeth.

Sincerely yours,

Elizabeth Bishop

I'm pretty sure you won't be able to use this story—but I have 3 or 4 others going & eventually one might do—

Miss Bogan is very funny about the Ciardi anthology—that's exactly the way I felt about it—a "shake-down"—[1]

November 6, 1950

Dear Mrs. White:

I realized after I had written you that I'd forgotten completely to mention, or thank you for sending, the information about the Bryn Mawr Fellowship. The forms are very simple, for once—I think possibly I might try to fill them

---

1 Bogan reviewed *Mid-Century American Poets*, edited by John Ciardi (1950) in the November 4 issue. Bishop is referring to this passage: "In his introduction, he treats modern poetry to a firm, common-sense lecture before proceeding to subject his poets to one of those thoroughly positivist questionnaires that are guaranteed to chill every scrap of wit and fancy out of the persons questioned. He shakes each poet, as it were, to discover whether any ideas will fall free." Bishop's essay "It All Depends" appeared in the book along with poems from *North & South*.

out, etc., and it's awfully kind of you to have thought of me—I'll be needing the money pretty soon, I'm afraid. However, as you say, the one catch would be—if one by any chance got it—living there, which I don't think I'd like very much. I'd been hoping to get abroad for a few months somehow. I think, if all goes well, I'll be staying on here until sometime in March. This doesn't seem to give any specific dates—and of course I'm well taken care of till then. I guess it can't do any harm to try.

I have two small anecdotes that might possibly be of interest to you, although probably I should send them to different departments. 1. On my trip to Saranac I passed a large roadside restaurant—neon-sign at night—called "Long Expected Resturant." 2.—which is seasonal, & I should have written when it happened. I was on my way to the hairdresser's in Washington and passed by a building that was being sand-blasted. They seemed to have stopped for the moment, and there were those canvas affairs hung up, etc., so I didn't make a detour but walked directly below. Just as I got there the sand-blasting started up again. A few minutes later the hairdresser ran his fingers over my scalp and said "Ah! Madame has been to the beach!"

There are quite a few things I seem to have collected to send you, including the story, but the typing is way ahead of me. This week I hope to get off a batch, though. Here is an old old dream ["The Owl's Journey"] that doesn't seem to want to grow any longer.

Sincerely yours,
Elizabeth Bishop

—And the shoe-shine parlor I frequent in Saratoga displays a sign that says: "Shoes shined off feet 5¢ extra."[1]

November 10, 1950

Dear Mrs. White:

I can't seem to stop writing you!

I'd like to get this little group of poems out of the way. There should be four, actually,—you refused one, and it appeared by itself, by mistake, in Partisan Review. Then you refused 3—which Partisan already has set up— they sent me the proof a while back and I asked them to withhold publication until I'd fussed over the others some more. I'm pretty sure it isn't the kind of

---

1 All three items were eventually used in "The Talk of the Town": untitled (October 13, 1956); "False Scent" (January 27, 1951); untitled (August 21, 1954). They were edited by Geoffrey T. Hellman.

thing to interest you and if you reject #1 & 2 I suppose I'll send them on to PR—which may not like them, either, as far as that goes. I'm just sick of looking at them.[1]

In the poem about the owl I sent you I have made two changes to improve the meter. In the 8th line it should be just "collaboration"—without the "a" in front of it, and in the last line I've changed it to "—But the dream has never got any further."[2]

Sincerely yours,
Elizabeth Bishop

November 14, 1950

Dear Elizabeth:

I am going to send off this proof even though we seem to have so many of your poems still on the griddle here—I mean without final decisions. I had hoped to be able to give you an answer on "The Owl's Journey." I might ask you, about that poem, whether a vague stirring of memory that three of us here seem to have has any basis in fact. Is there a picture, say, from Audubon, or from a nursery picture book, or from an old chromo, or even from Blake, that was the basis of your dream? If there was, it might be interesting and clarifying to put it in the subtitle. However, it may be purely a dream but I wish you'd write me about it. Perhaps this is just something on the fringe of everybody's subconscious and not in an actual picture at all.

The Partisan Review group of poems is going the rounds now and I'll let you know about them later.

I did want to add one note about the Bryn Mawr Fellowship. Did I tell you that they wrote me from the President's Office that they would very likely make an exception on the matter of living on the campus if there was a good reason for the writer not to. They seemed to think that travel might be a reason for not being there and it seems to me your wish to travel has particular point in your case, or would to anyone who knows your poetry. Therefore, I would not hesitate to express that need in your application. If you were awarded the $2500, it would be a nice help toward travelling. So if it

1 It is not entirely clear to which poems Bishop is referring. The fourth poem of the group is most likely "O Breath," which *The New Yorker* rejected and at Bishop's request forwarded to *The Partisan Review*, which ran it in September 1949. There is no previously unaccounted-for poem that would be "3." For this submission, *The New Yorker* Records show three poems under the title "Rain Towards Morning."
2 In the last extant draft, lines seven and eight are: "—The adventure's miniature and ancient: / a collaboration thought up by a child." The last line is: "—But the dream never got any further." (Vassar College Library).

does interest you enough to apply, I would state quite plainly that you hope to go abroad. I take it that the term of the fellowship would be the college year October 1951 to June 1952, but the application must be in before this coming January, 1951.

I have sent your three items for Talk of The Town to that department and will let you hear.

Now to revert to this author's proof [of "View of the Capitol"]. I have left on the proof the punctuation queries for your consideration. Mark out the ones you do not want. In the second stanza, I am told by the grammarians and stylists that it should be either "east steps," with no capitals, or "East Steps," with both words capitalized and there seems to be some doubt whether these particular steps are well enough known to justify capitalization at all. Again this is your decision.[1] Then comes up the matter of the color of the Air Force band's uniforms. It turns out that they are a dull blue, a postman blue. I contend that they must, even so, have looked a brilliant blue to you and, if so, that you should be allowed your "brilliant" but I did think you ought to know they are actually a gray-blue in case you'd forgotten it.[2]

If you do get down from Yaddo, let me know. Another letter soon about the other poems.

Yours,

Katharine

November 16, 1950

Dear Mrs. White—or Katharine—

The story about the owl is really rather strange and I guess I'll go ahead & bore you with it—I've never been able to see any way of getting it into the poem, though. A long, long time ago, when I was a child, I had that dream or maybe just imagined it—I had certainly never seen any such picture, never saw Blake or Audubon—to my conscious recollection, although as you say it might have been in a nursery book. At college I had a friend (now with the Museum of Modern Art) who drew & painted very well; and I told her about the owl & the rabbit and asked her if she'd make a picture of it.[3] She tried and tried and did a lot of pen & ink drawings but somehow either of us were ever

---

1 Bishop had submitted the phrase as "East steps".

2 The question of the uniforms' color came from one of Ross's queries: "Fact matter: Is the uniform of the Air Force band brilliant? Mr. [Hobart] Weekes, old Air Force man, says they were dull blue in his day, as he recalls—sort of a postman's blue." White replied, "The 'brilliant' must be allowed to poet I think—It is how they looked to her in the sun—" (November 7, 1950, *The New Yorker* Records).

3 Margaret Miller.

satisfied with them. After graduation she had a scholarship in art at New York University, and one of her courses was illuminated manuscripts, with Meyer Schapiro. Well, I've forgotten exactly where & how she found it—I think in the British Museum, but I'm not sure, but she'd know—she came across, in the margin of a very early English manuscript—I think 12th century, but again I'm not sure—the exact picture I had had in mind all those years, and she was able to get me a tracing of it. Exactly the way I'd imagined it—the rabbit running diagonally to the left, the owl seated facing a little the other way, etc. It was just in simple outline drawing, although the MS had painted illuminations in it. I was so pleased and mystified I decided to use it as a kind of seal, and I even had one of those gadgets made, at great expense, that make an impression in the paper. It's in storage now, or I'd give you a sample. As I write this it all sounds as if I were making it up—but I guess it really isn't the kind of thing one makes up.

I can't seem to do any more with it than that brief poem. I suppose there might be a subtitle something to the effect that it was an "Early dream, later found in the margin of a –cent English, or Saxon or whatever it was—I could find out—MS." But maybe that's stupid.

About the Air Force band's uniforms—I know the regular air-force blue color—but once they came and played right *in* the Library & it struck me they looked a different blue and awfully bright. But I'm probably wrong, and it may have been just the general effect of all that marble and those potted palms. Everything else is fine—I'd like a little more space if I could have it between the "booms", but I've indicated that on the proof.[1]

Everything goes like a house afire here only I'm still behind with that typing.

My idea would be to try to go abroad this spring & summer, if I can earn, save, etc. enough money—then I'd be quite willing to take up residence in Bryn Mawr in the fall & winter for as long as they thought necessary. Anyway, it's awfully kind of you to have thought of it, and I undoubtedly have very slight chances. I think Marianne Moore should be the first, somehow, & suggested it to her, but she seems to have reasons against it—work—but I should think she could do it there, & she certainly must be one of their prize alumnae.

Sincerely yours,
Elizabeth

1 When the poem ran in the July 7, 1951, *New Yorker*, "east steps" remained in lowercase and the uniforms were still "brilliant blue." Bishop changed the uniforms to "Air Force blue" when she published the poem in *A Cold Spring*. She also removed the comma after "dim" in stanza three, line one, and returned to her original spelling of "gold-dust" in stanza four, line two.

Dear Elizabeth:

Your story of the owl and the rabbit is so strange that I keep brooding on it. As Howard Moss says, the whole thing gets into the realm of one of those Duke University experiments in the psychic. We have fussed and fussed as to how to bring your explanation into a subtitle but just do not believe it would work to try to do so. Probably the poem should be published just as it is, with no explanations, but the general opinion here, I'm sorry to say, seems to be against using that way in the New Yorker since some seem to feel that the poem is too personal for us. What I really wish is that you would write an essay for a literary publication that would include the poem and tell the whole story about the dream, the illuminated manuscript, etc., etc., much as you told it to me in your letter. I really do wish you'd do this for I'd love to read such a piece and I'm sure many others would. I really wonder whether there ever was an illustration in a nursery book that could have been derived from the 12th century picture and that might have been at the back of your dream and at our memories of such a picture. *Why* did three of us here think we had seen such a picture—Moss, Maxwell, and I? Perhaps we had better get the Duke experimenters to work on us all.

I therefore return "The Owl's Journey" sadly. And sadly, too, poem number 2 from the group of which you have already sold one to the *Partisan Review*. We think that the group should go together and that any single poem would not be right for us.

I have one more thing to bother you about, which is your request that we put more space around the dash of "boom-boom" in the last line of "View of the Capitol." It can't be done, the experts say, as it will look only like a printer's error, or, at best, like sloppy printing. Perhaps there are other ways of doing it if we knew what effect you wanted to get. For instance:

The gathered brasses want to go   (This would be a long *one em* dash such
boom — boom.   as precedes the signatures in all
                                                     New Yorker pieces)

or

The gathered brasses want to go   (with the booms capitalized)
Boom, Boom.

or

boom, boom.   (with the boom in lower case)

What you had on your manuscript was a hyphen, not a dash. Actually the line satisfies us as it now is printed, but we want you to be satisfied also. Let me know what you think on this and forgive me for bothering you.[1]

Where is that story I've been looking forward to reading. Do send it along.

      Yours,

          Katharine

                          The morning after the Hurricane
                                    [November 22, 1950]

Dear Katharine:

These are not my stories—but I'm finally getting someone at Skidmore to re-type it for me—these are by a young German refugee girl here, married to an English painter.[2] I think she's only been speaking English six or seven years—but already has a novel taken by I think it's Knopf. You may not like these stories at all, it may all be in my imagination—but I'm quite impressed with them. A lot of work would have to be done, commas put in, etc.—but I hesitate to make any suggestions personally. If you're at all interested I'd be glad to work on them with her—I don't think she'd mind that.

The name "Kathrine Talbot" is obviously a pseudonym and I don't like it much—her own first name is Ilse, which I think she should use for the for-eignness of it might help explain some of the oddities of the style. (If you do return them I guess it would be better to do it via me.)

(I seem to be so unnerved by the storm that I can't type—after all, one of my *walls* fell off—right by the head of my bed.)

I think the Sylvia Townsend Warner story is marvellously funny—but I don't like the end, somehow.[3]

I shall enclose one of my own works ["Song (Second Soprano)"]—which you will definitely *not* like—in fact I don't know what to do with it—

The boom - boom looked quite all right to me in the proof . . .[4]

Thank you for the idea of writing a piece about "The Owl's Journey"—

1 Bishop submitted the phrase as *boom - boom*. (*The New Yorker* Records).

2 Ilse Barker, Kit Barker's wife, submitted "Death in the Pyrenees," "Bella," and "The Sword of Darkness" under the name Kathrine Talbot. Her book, *Fire in the Sun*, came out from Putnam in 1952.

3 Warner's most recent story was "Farewell, My Love" (October 28, 1950).

4 The line ran as *"boom-boom."* When published in *A Cold Spring*, a dash was used with space on both sides.

it just hadn't occurred to me and I think I shall really attempt it, sort of à la Coleridge in Biographia Literaria or whatever it's called.

I'm ashamed to send you such a wretched looking letter. Yaddo is a complete mess and we're quite cut off with huge trees fallen across the roads—one of the biggest of all fell right across the roof of the little house where Ilse & her husband live—dented it badly, but very fortunately they were out at the time.

Sincerely yours,
Elizabeth

I hope your place in Maine wasn't damaged.

December 1, 1950

Dear Elizabeth:

I thought that you might perhaps want a prompt reply on "Song (Second Soprano)" in order to place it elsewhere if we could not use it, so I am sending it back, regretfully, before I have an answer on the Talbot stories. I haven't had time to read them yet but someone else is reading them first anyway. The poem does not seem right for us and it's a disappointment to us all to have to say so.

We'll hope for the Skidmore-typed story soon.

Yours,
Katharine

January 11, 1951

Dear Mrs. White:

I hope you are recovered from your illness now and are starting off the New Year in good health. I don't really want to keep bothering you with my little contributions and I wish you'd tell me if you'd rather have me send them in to some one else. I *still* plan to send you a story—eventually four, I guess—but I seem to keep getting held up in order to work on my real interest right now—a long poem. You might possibly be able to use this poem ["Insomnia"], though.

This clipping is from yesterday's out-of-town earliest edition of the N.Y. TIMES—I thought you might not have seen it.

With all best wishes,
Sincerely yours,
Elizabeth

Dear Mrs. White:

I'm afraid this ["The Prodigal"] will be too grim for you. I wonder, if you can't use it, if you would be kind enough to send it on to Karl [Shapiro] for me?—I promised him something months ago and I have never had anything to send him and he has just written me again. One more poem—a long one—to finish, and then I shall send you a story to look at, although I'm afraid it, too, is on the grim side.

I do hope you are well—not having heard from you I am afraid maybe you are not—or possibly you have gone to some nice warm place to recuperate.

Sincerely yours,
Elizabeth

January 19, 1951

Dear Elizabeth:

We like "Insomnia" *very* much and think it a subtle and interesting poem, although on first reading, we found it a little difficult to follow. Going over it carefully, it seemed to us that the only reasons it at first seemed obscure were its punctuation and also a slight confusion made by the parenthetical lines at the end of the second stanza. I now beg your permission to drop these lines. I'll tell you why. First of all, from the point of view of sentence structure, if the two sentences in the parenthesis are retained, the reader does not readily understand that lines #5 and #6 of Stanza #2 carry over to the first line of the last stanza or that the whole final stanza is, in fact, a part of the same sentence as the fifth and sixth lines of Stanza #2.[1] Secondly, "the sidewise well on the bureau" seems to call up a different picture to different readers.

---

1 On the last extant draft, the lines to which White refers run:

> By the Universe deserted,
> *she'd* tell it to go to hell,
> & she'd find a body of water,
> or a mirror, on which to dwell.
> So wrap up care in a cobweb
> and drop it down the well
> (the well on top of the bureau
> for it shall be its keeper)
>
> into that world inverted

The rest of the third stanza is written as it was finally published (Vassar College Library).

On studying it, I suppose you mean that this well is the mirror, but because some bureaus have a sort of well instead of drawers on each side, that image instead of the mirror at first injected itself. Also if these two lines are dropped, all three stanzas are the same length, which is possibly an advantage.

I enclose a copy of the poem that shows our suggestions for punctuation and also shows how it reads with the two lines dropped. Of course we may have misinterpreted your meaning and may have made changes in it by our new punctuation which very likely is not yet exactly right. But there would be a chance to take the punctuation up again in the author's proof. If the poem in this cut version in general meets with your approval, will you just return it to me and it will be paid for at once. If, however, you want to make changes, don't hesitate to say so, and if you feel strongly about retaining the two lines, perhaps you will see a way to punctuate and reword them for clarity. I suspect that the words "sidewise well" are the ones most difficult to grasp. We also, you'll see, suggest dropping the capital letter on "universe" and I myself would prefer it in roman, and not in italics. But possibly you will want to retain either the capital letter or the italics. To use both, seems just too much.

If you want the poem to go just as you first wrote it, please tell us, but I honestly think it didn't work out quite right. I am going to Florida and will be back in the office on February 5. Therefore, if you say yes on this yellow paper version, Howard Moss will put it through at once for payment. But if you have objections to it, your letter will be forwarded to me by airmail and we all of us here can reconsider. I shall be doing some work while away, so please don't think you should not write to me.

Sincerely,

Katharine

P.S. I am keeping the original manuscript here. K.S.W.

January 20, 1951

Dear Howard:

I have just had a letter from Mrs. White, and I think I'm supposed to answer it to you. Yes, I am quite willing to have you use this version of *Insomnia*; in fact I realize it is a great improvement. However, I don't like the parentheses in the first stanza and I should think that without them a semicolon after "smiles" would do. But punctuation is my Waterloo and I'm always willing to be advised. I must buy a book on the subject. Also I should like to retain the Capital letter in "Universe". Mrs. White says in her letter that punctuation could be taken care of in the author's proof, so maybe I don't need to worry about that now—just say "yes" to the shortened version. [The bottom half of this page and the top half of the next page are cut off.—Ed.]

Yesterday I sent Mrs. White a copy of the enclosed poem, "The Prodigal" and just after the mail went I realized I'd sent her the wrong copy—an earlier version—at least I'm pretty sure I did. This is the one I meant to send, at any rate. I'm not sure whether she'll get either copy before she comes back, or whether you'll be handling it, or what. As I said to her, I feel fairly sure it is too grim for you, and wondered if you'd be kind enough to send it on to Karl Shapiro at *Poetry* for me, since I owe him some poems, long overdue?

I can't remember whether you've ever been here or not, but I'm sure you have heard a great deal about it. It is much nicer in the winter than in the "season", I think, and much prettier. How are you and when are you going to have another book of poems out?

With all best wishes,
Elizabeth

January 25, 1951

Dear Elizabeth:

Here is the check for INSOMNIA. (The poem, not the disease.)

I was in Washington last week and kept wishing you were still there. I hope I get up to Yaddo, but if you come down to New York it would be very pleasant to see you. Please call me if you do.

Best,
Howard

February 2, 1951

Dear Elizabeth:

Here is the author's proof of INSOMNIA, and your Cost-of-Living-Adjustment check.

I left the parentheses in the first stanza, because they make it clear that the moon looks out a million miles far and away beyond sleep. A semicolon after "smiles" wouldn't work because there is no subject and predicate in the last two lines. Would a dash after "miles" and after "smiles" be any better?

I left your capitalized "Universe", but it has been questioned again by a proof reader. Anything you decide about this will be fine. We prefer it in Roman, though, since capitals *and* italics would be piling Pelléas on Mélisande.

I hope the rest of it is okay and that there'll be other poems along soon.

Best,

Howard

February 4, 1951

Dear Howard:

Thank you for the proof and the check. I'll try to make myself plain about this silly little poem. "Far & away," etc., is just supposed to be modifying—the moon is above such things, is what I meant, rather than that she was looking "far away." That's why the parenthesis still seems wrong to me. However, since the meanings do overlap considerably I'll be willing to have it stand the way it is. The reason why I wanted "universe" in caps or italics was just a matter of emphasis—the meaning being that although the speaker is being upset by being deserted by a mere human being, the moon wouldn't give a damn if the whole universe deserted *her*. Saying it makes it perfectly simple, but my punctuation can't seem to cope with it. At least, I'd like to keep the cap, if possible. At any rate it really isn't worth any more trouble, and I'll let it go as it is, because, as I said, the meanings do overlap enough to make it all right.

I have to go away for a few days next week but I hope to get you off some more things before then, or on my return. Oh—I'm sorry to bother you, but what did you do about the sonnets?

With all best wishes,

Elizabeth

February 14, 1951

Dear Elizabeth:

We all think "The Prodigal" is an extraordinarily fine poem and want to publish it. I am writing you this without waiting for the check because your answer has been so delayed. This wait was because we wanted Mr. Ross to read it and he has been way behind on his reading. Quite aside from the meaning of the poem—or the many meanings—it gives me great comfort, as almost all your poems do, just on the score of your accurate and beautiful observation of homely country things like pigs and winter barns and the natural atmosphere of weather and sky.[1] I was reading over lately your poem about catching the big fish and letting him go—things like that are what I mean. So many poets, even good ones, don't really seem to know the natural world at all, and have never encountered pigs, fish, or even fir forests.

You ask how I am. I'm fine and hope *you* are, and that you'll soon pay a visit to New York. Both Howard and I want a chance to see you. He is doing a real good job here.

Sincerely,

Katharine

April 9, 1951

Dear Elizabeth:

I forgot to ask you that day when we had lunch whether you knew the publication date of your book. We need to know it in relation to scheduling, if the poems we have of yours still unpublished are to be in the new volume. These are "Insomnia" and "View of the Capitol." Will you be kind enough,

---

1 After "The Prodigal" was accepted, Ross reviewed its slug: "Not Summer: Winter, Fall, March or April." He attached this note: "I think the slugging of this is over-scientific, and intrinsically, the poem is conflicting. The red puddles sound like hot weather, the shutting up of the cows sounds like cold weather, and the presence of the bats (which hibernate) sounds like summer. The original story of the prodigal wasn't pegged as to time (I'm advised), and I should think this poem ANYTIME" (Ross, February 20, 1951, *The New Yorker* Records).

White sent Bishop the proof on February 21. She made a few changes to the punctuation. Bishop submitted stanza one, lines five to eight, as:

> Light-lashed, self-righteous above moving snouts
> the pigs' eyes followed him, a cheerful stare,
> —even to the sow that always ate her young—
> till, sickening, he leaned to scratch her head.

White changed the lines to:

> Light-lashed, self-righteous, above moving snouts,
> the pigs' eyes followed him, a cheerful stare—
> even to the sow that always ate her young—
> till, sickening, he leaned to scratch her head.

Bishop had also given her stanzas roman numerals, which White removed. An additional change before publication was making "The lantern, like the sun, going away," "The lantern—like the sun, going away—" in stanza two, line eight (*The New Yorker* Records).

therefore, to tell me whether they are to be included and also at least the approximate date?

Where is the story? Do send it along.

Yours ever,

Katharine

Hotel Grosvenor
Fifth Avenue at 10th Street
New York
April 15, 1951

Dear Katharine:

Thank you for the lovely letter from the "adolent" fan.

No publication date has been set for my book—in fact it is all very vague, but Paul [Brooks] did say for "fall publication." So I imagine—since both of the poems you mention will probably be in the book—that any time before October would be all right for you to use them.

I seem to have been so busy doing chores, apartment-hunting, etc., since I came back to New York that I haven't done any work, or almost none. However—the story should be along next week sometime, and another poem or two before the end of the month. I'm sorry to be so slow.

Cordially,

Elizabeth

May 15, 1951

Dear Elizabeth:

I saw in the Sunday paper that you had won one of the National Institute of Arts and Letters awards of one thousand dollars and I am perfectly delighted and send you my congratulations. I suspect that it is thanks to you that I got a very nice invitation to the Ceremonial on May 25, but, unfortunately, I am going to have to send my regrets since I start off to Maine this next Sunday. Of course I'll be working from there, and will see your contributions just as usual. I'm just out of the hospital after a minor, but as it turned out not so minor, operation and I think the place I can get well the fastest is North Brooklin.

Please do send that story and any poems you have around.

Affectionately,

Katharine

P.S. By the way, two other New Yorker writers are getting the same award and I hope you will all get to know each other. The other two are Vladimir Nabokov and Brendan Gill. K.S.W.

c/o Brooks
233 East 69th Street
New York
June 2, 1951

Dear Katharine:

No, it wasn't I who sent the invitation to the "Ceremonial"—I didn't send any, having a dread of the whole thing. It *was* a nightmare, but only for a minute or so—the rest was rather like a college commencement, and the tea-party afterwards was fun. And I suppose it is ungracious to resent the nightmare, considering how useful the $1000 will be. Thank you for writing.

I'm sorry you've been sick—I wasn't feeling too well myself & went off to visit in Maryland for three weeks until I could move into this sub-let for a few months, until I can find—I hope—something else. My visit was rather lazy—but I did do some work, including a couple of poems I hope to polish off for you this week-end and some more on a story. (I seem to be always saying this kind of thing to you, but this time I really mean it.) I also have an idea for an article I'd like to approach you about as soon as I've done a little more research on it.

I did meet Nabokov and Brendan Gill but just to say how do you do to.

I'm typing where Jean Stafford just finished her novel & hoping the atmosphere still contains some of her fluency—

Affectionately yours,
Elizabeth

June 21, 1951

Dear Katharine:

I think when I last wrote to you I mentioned that I had an article in my mind and that I hoped I'd be able to interest you in it. Since then I've done some work on the subject and turned up quite a lot of fascinating—I think—material, so I think I'll write you about it right now. Has The New Yorker ever printed a piece about Sable Island, that Island off the coast of Nova Scotia? I can't remember ever having seen one. Of course if it has, my idea would be out—but here it is, anyway. I don't know how much of this you may know already . . .

Sable Island is between N.S. and Newfoundland & is known as "The Graveyard of the Grand Banks" because of the innumerable wrecks that occur there. My own great-grandfather who had a schooner in the West Indies trade was shipwrecked and lost there with all hands, so I have a particular interest in it. He himself was a rather interesting character & my idea is to combine personal reminiscences with the best parts of its history, plus a first-hand account of it now. I've just found out from the N.S. Information Bureau that one *can* get there, and I'm planning to make a trip out in August.

You've probably heard of the famous Sable Island wild ponies—my little cousins had one, a famous trick one—in fact they may still have although when last heard of she was thirty-seven years old. Then there's the Sable Island sparrow, the ornithologists' delight—they've never been able to decide whether it's a species or not, and won't know until the Island washes completely away, which it's not expected to do, and the sparrow has to go to the mainland, there to mate or not to mate with other song-sparrows. There are some wonderful ghost stories—one ghost is one of the murderers of Charles I who wanders around every May 29th singing psalms at the top of his lungs. Best of all is one Miss Dix, not a ghost—a "Boston philanthropist", who got the cities of Boston, New York, and Philadelphia—in 1850 something—each to send a tin life-boat to the Island . . . I'm trying to track down her exposé of the sad state of affairs there—lunatics were sent out to "assist" the lighthouse-keepers, etc.

The animal cycles are quite fantastic, almost allegorical. The ponies have been there since the 16th century; pigs & sheep were sent by more philanthropists for the benefit of shipwrecked mariners. The rats from the wrecks killed the rabbits; cats were imported; ate the rats and overran the place so dogs were imported; then back to rabbits again who were then killed by a species of snowy owl. I'm not sure what the equilibrium is now but hope to find out in person. In 1789 a Boston clergyman wrote a little treatise on artificial respiration for the benefit of the families sent out there to help the shipwrecked mariners again—Sable Island was then mostly owned, apparently, by John Hancock. I guess that's enough to give you the idea—and if you have already had an article about it possibly I can still do one anyway, for something else.—Of course I heard so much about it when I was little that it has haunted my imagination most of my life. I haven't been able to find any recent things about it, but I may have missed something. I thought it would be very pleasant to combine a vacation with a little work. The Archives, in Halifax, is a very nice place and I'm sure there'd be a lot more material there—I have some friends there and in the Bureau of Fisheries (just the thing!) who I think would help me.

I do hope you'll think this is a practical idea—I can't seem to think of any other magazine that would be interested although of course there probably is one—

I hope you're well. I've got about 2/3rds of my book at Houghton Mifflins and hope to have the rest of it there in a few weeks. So far it doesn't jell very well but I trust it will when I've finished the rest.

Affectionately yours,
Elizabeth

I am all out of proper paper—this is some Jean Stafford left behind.

North Brooklin, Maine
June 29, 1951

Dear Elizabeth:

Bill Shawn phoned me this morning to say that he liked the idea of a piece about Sable Island and would telephone you to fix a time to talk about it with you. So probably you have heard from him by now. He is the head of the Factual Dept. and this sort of article would come under his jurisdiction which is why I asked him to handle it from now on. Besides, I am about to have my vacation—for the month of July. I thought the Sable Island material sounded fascinating and I do hope that you'll get there this summer and can write a piece.

I'll say goodbye until August but I shall be right here in North Brooklin, so if anything comes up you want to write me about you must feel free to.

In haste to catch the mail,
Katharine

July 18, 1951

Dear Miss Bishop:

In Howard Moss's absence I am writing you about "A Cold Spring," which we all love and want very much for The New Yorker, if you will let us run it in season. I realize that this means taking it out of your book, and am very sorry that it has to be that way.

    Cordially,
      William Maxwell

P.S. I'll hold onto manuscript until I hear from you.

August 8, 1951

Dear Elizabeth:

    Now that I'm back at work after my holiday I wanted to write you a line to say how beautiful I thought your poem was that we bought when I was on my vacation—one of a kind that no one but you can do so perfectly. And I'm also delighted that Shawn was as enthusiastic as I was about the idea of the Sable Island piece. I like to think that you are there right now, gathering your material and writing your piece.

    I look forward to the book and I'm sure it will be a distinguished one.

    If you drive back from Nova Scotia by any chance, why not stop here for a night? We are right on your route west. It's possible that I may be here alone in September and if I were, I'd urge you to stay longer and would offer you Andy's desk and room. He has not quite decided yet whether he will be away then on a trip west or not. But presumably I'll be right here in North Brooklin with a going household and lots of space and quiet. I of course don't know whether this would be a good place for your asthma; I only think of it because our neighbor has just had a miserable month of asthma, but I doubt that climate has much to do with it. *He* is supposed to have an allergy to birchwood and since he gave up lobstering, he cuts more wood and has more asthma. Cortisone, when he can get it, seems to do miraculous things for him but it is terribly expensive.

    Affectionately,
      Katharine

In the R.R. Station at St. John
New Brunswick, Canada
August 18, 1951

Dear Katharine:

    I got back from Sable Island yesterday & I was very pleased to find your letter at the hotel. Thank you for your remarks about the poem & also your invitation—they were both welcome touches of civilization after my stay with Sable Islanders. It was very much the way I expected it to be—very beautiful, in its way, but certainly one of nature's mistakes—I wanted to stay a little longer but thought I had better get off while the weather held & there was a ship there—otherwise I gathered I might be there until next spring. I am on my way to stay in Stonington for about a week. If ever you come over that way I shd. be delighted to see you—I'll be staying at Mrs. George Gross's—I think—but she will know where I am. Tell your asthmatic friend to try: NOROSODRINE SULFATE,—it is wonderful—

Affectionately yours,

Elizabeth

August 22, 1951

Dear Elizabeth:

I enclose your proof of "A Cold Spring." We'd like to put parentheses around "For a Friend in Maryland" just for typographical reasons and we'd like to use all of Hopkins' name as a matter of style, if it's all right with you. The punctuation suggestions where I've x'd out the questions marks seem to me right, but those two commas where I've left the question marks are certainly optional and I suspect they may be over-punctuating, in a poem. We would put them in, in prose, but do they interrupt the movement of your lines in poetry?[1]

At (1), I think this word is usually *cow-flop*, not *cow-flap*. Mencken gives it as *cow-flop* in "The American Language."

Nothing but rain in Maine. The vegetables are rotting or going entirely to leaves. The grass is wonderfully green but the flowers are either repellantly over-size or else they pass too soon. It's very strange and rather discouraging. I hope it is different further north.

Affectionately yours,

Katharine

1 "A Cold Spring" was not edited by White or Moss before it was set in proof but by "X," who had no changes besides spelling to make. A number of changes were made between the proof and publication, including changing the semicolon after "flag" in stanza one, line twelve, to a comma, changing the semicolon after "butt" in stanza two, line four, to a comma, changing the colon after "again" in stanza three, line thirteen, to a dash, and removing the dash from the start of line sixteen. For *A Cold Spring*, Bishop kept the change to stanza one and returned her punctuation to her original form in stanzas two and three. She also removed the parentheses around line seventeen and inserted a dash at its start. When the poem was reprinted in *The Complete Poems*, stanzas two and three were run together. Stanza three begins with the line: "Now, in the evening,".

Dear Katharine:

I returned sooner than I had intended to, Sunday night—Cape Cod was a good come-down after Maine, & New York the worst come-down of all, although it always takes a few days to *see* it again & get used to the telephone, the dirt, etc. My brief visit with you was really the flower of the trip—

It is nice to have something really absorbing to start working on right away—I wish the map of Sable Island weren't blue, however—I'm afraid that color is slowly permeating my memory of it. Oh—I re-read "Anne of Avon-lee-a" on the Cape—you know, she really had some quite advanced ideas on education; I was surprised.[1] Last night I amused myself by telling Marianne Moore all about your place that I could remember,—she was fascinated by every detail & I wished I were right there. Thank you so very much & please give my kindest regards to your family—

Affectionately yours,
Elizabeth

September 6, 1951

Dear Elizabeth:

Here is a clean proof of the Maryland poem, but it is one that does not carry any of the slight changes you agreed upon in your author's proof. I send this one now just so you may write in the new line you say you want to add.[2] Then that line and the author's proof changes will be incorporated all at once in a revised proof. I hate to bother you in the midst of the Sable Island piece but wanted to be sure I got hold of that new line while I still remembered that one was to come. Are you sure you need another? The poem seems to me perfect as it stands.

Your letter came today and it gives me the chance to say that Andy and I felt guilty about your tiny visit here and feared it must have been very dull for you. I also shudder when I think how I got up and went to bed that night, leaving you and Mr. Wanning there—he must have thought I was awfully rude and inhospitable.[3] I only did it because I somehow felt that you wanted to go

1 Lucy Maud Montgomery, *Anne of Avonlea* (1909).
2 On the last extant draft, Bishop added this line four lines from the bottom: "(Later on they rise much higher.)" (Vassar College Library).
3 Tom Wanning was Bishop's friend.

over a lot of back history together that you would not have if Andy and I had stuck around but, thinking it over, it must have seemed very strange behavior on my part. You can trust me to be socially inept on almost any occasion!

My Eskimo basket is still a delight; it is one of those objects whose charm endures.

Only a day or two after you left Randall Jarrell's book manuscript arrived in the mail, sent me by Peter Taylor.[1] I read it in a gulp with considerable admiration but I am not yet sure whether any section of it is separable for New Yorker use. I've sent it back to the office with a couple of suggestions and now wait to hear what others think about this problem. Is the college Bennington?

We have had only two or three days of sunshine since you left—we had to watch the horse pulling at Blue Hill Fair in a drizzle.

Affectionately,
    Katharine

September 18, 1951

Dear Katharine:

Travel seemed to agree with me very well, but not with the typewriter, which is being repaired—I hope you'll be able to read this. I've just done something that may have been wrong—I'm not sure, but I thought I'd better let you know. I decided instead of trying to get an apartment here I'd just keep on going for a while—probably all winter—& I'm starting off towards the end of October via freighter to South America.—When I went in to get my passport re-newal yesterday I found that because it says I'm a "writer" on it that to get it renewed means I have to have a letter to the passport dept. from some publication saying I *am* a writer. Of course I couldn't think of any except the New Yorker. I thought of writing you but was afraid it might take too long—there are an awful lot of visas, etc., to get in the next ten days or so & I can't do anything much until I get the passport back. So I just called Mr. Shawn—he was out, but a girl read me the form & said she'd speak to Mr. Shawn & let me know etc. I do feel I'm being rather forward about this—but I guess it's just for the passport people, anyway, & really doesn't signify. However, I do hope to send you things, of course, poems & other things maybe.—I have a plan, not too impossible, I gather, of going all the way around the coast.

1 *Pictures from an Institution* (1954).

I've written about a third of Sable Island & shall send the whole thing to Mr. S before I leave. I'll be here till October 1st—maybe a little longer—& shall probably visit in Maryland—a nice quiet place to work—until just before sailing—at present Oct. 26th.

Please remember me to your family. I look back on my visit there as the real high-light of my trip & I've described the stencils, the geese, etc., to all my friends—I hope you're well—

Affectionately yours,
Elizabeth

September 21, 1951

Dear Elizabeth:

A hurried note before the mail goes. I talked to Bill Shawn this morning and he says he will write the note you need about your passport. I thought he would be able to get it to you sooner than I could. The State Dept. is fussy these days on sending writers but I should not think that South America ought to make any problems. To some countries, we can ask for passports for only one writer. But Bill Shawn will let you know if he has any problems. I hope you can get off and that Oct. 26 will allow enough time for you to get the Sable Island piece in and gone over in detail if we buy it. I know fact proofs take a lot of time.

I shall be back at the office Oct. 16 and do hope you'll have time to have lunch with me some day before you leave. But if you are off to Maryland, I suppose you may not. Do please be sure to send us your Maryland address.

We have had the best weather of the summer ever since you left—wonderful. This place is now a wreck with carpenters rebuilding the wood-shed and porches. That's the trouble with old houses—they disintegrate. Our shed was about to cave in, but to salvage it at all we've had to jettison my bittersweet vine that was pulling it down.

Aff'y,
Katharine

September 27, 1951

Dear Katharine:

Thank you for your letter. I am sorry about that "writer" thing—if only it hadn't said that on my old passport everything would have been much simpler, but apparently I couldn't change it.

I am in the midst of moving but hope to get to the country on Oct. 1st or 2nd, where I'll have two weeks of peace & quiet and time to work. My address there is c/o Jane Dewey, R.D. #2, Havre de Grace, Maryland. From the 19th until I leave the 26th I'll be at the Vassar Club, Hotel New Weston. I'd be delighted to have lunch with you—or have you have lunch with me—during that week.

I'll get the Sable Island thing off to Mr. Shawn from Jane's—I'm enjoying writing it but it may not be your cup of tea at all—I can't tell.

Affectionately yours,
Elizabeth

c/o Dewey
Shadowstone Farm
Havre de Grace, Maryland
October 5, 1951

Dear Howard, (if you are the one to address)

Mrs. White questioned the "And" at the beginning of the last sentence [of "A Cold Spring"], feeling that it might be unnecessary after the parentheses. However I think I still prefer it in since it takes the thought back to before the parentheses better that way—or so it seems to me.

—If you do receive this note, Howard—I'm going to write to you shortly—

Yours,
Elizabeth

The New Yorker
November 7, 1951

Dear Elizabeth:

The New Yorker is sending its 25th Anniversary Album of cartoons to a few of its writers as a memento of the twenty-five years. We have a copy for you here in the office but I thought I oughtn't to mail it until you sent me a permanent address, lest it follow you all over South America or get stuck in some post office there. Perhaps you would rather have the copy held here until your return? Anyway, please let me know your wishes about this.

I hope the voyage was pleasant and the asthma absent, and that all goes well. Do send "Sable Island" soon, and that short story soon too. We are in the midst of a scary shortage of good fiction.

Affectionately,

Katharine

November 15, 1951

P.S. Later: I held this letter up having temporarily lost your address, and now along comes your first reading agreement and the check that goes with it. Of course we hope you'll want to sign it and return one copy to us. I've told the business office that there will be a wait because you are in South America, but I do hope that this reaches you fairly promptly. K.S.W.

Alcobaça, Petrópolis
Brazil
January 19, 1952

Dear Katharine:

I think I must have left your note in Rio, but I believe I answered the business part of it, and this is just to let you know that I am still working, etc., and to wish you best wishes for 1952, good health, etc.

I was so sorry to read about Mr. Ross—I guess I saw it first in the air-edition of Time—& I saw that particular issue of the New Yorker just a few days ago.[1]

My hostess here gets the New Yorker—and she is also a fan of your husband's and has all his books and showed me the piece on how to distinguish major poets from minor poets the other night—I'd never seen it before and enjoyed it very much.[2] So she was delighted when I could tell her about the geese (she has some, too), etc. I also told her about the stenciled walls and she took me to a small tenant house here—"Alcobaça" is the name of a fazenda, or farm—and all the walls were stenciled in exactly the same way—it's very popular, only not at all comparable because the colors and patterns are so crude. I think in the letter I left in Rio you mentioned something about the New Yorker's anniversary album—that it was being held until I returned—and I wonder if possibly it could be sent to her here as a present

---

1 "End of a New Yorker," *Time* (January 17, 1951). E. B. White wrote Ross's obituary for the December 15, 1951, issue.

2 "How to Tell a Major Poet from a Minor Poet" was originally published in the November 8, 1930, *New Yorker*.

from me?—she wants one, I know. Miss Lota de Macedo Soares, Rua Antonio Viera 5, Leme, Rio de Janeiro, Apt. 1101.

The reason I have sent absolutely nothing along is that I have had a terrific—almost tropical—attack of a mysterious allergy, starting just before Christmas and stopping today. The Dr. thinks it may have been from 2 (unpleasant) bites I took of cashew-fruit, since that's the only thing I had to eat that I'd never eaten before. Anyway, I swelled and swelled—my head did—beyond belief, until I looked like something for Carnival and was absolutely blind; then my hands got it so I couldn't write or even type until a day or so ago. Now I still have asthma and eczema but I've started to work again and since I am staying here until the end of February—Rio address— I hope to be able to send you several things, including Sable Island, shortly. In spite of my appalling looks and sensations I've been having an awfully good time—the people are all so nice and absolutely crazy about sickness, remedies, etc., and all the friends and relations come to tell you about theirs and hug and kiss you tenderly even if you are looking like a pumpkin. Perhaps it's a good way to get to know a country.

I do hope you're well and not freezing—I understand it's a cold winter. I don't know what season it is here & nobody else seems to know, either—but it's a very vague country.

Affectionately yours,
Elizabeth

North Brooklin
January 30, 1952

Dear Elizabeth:

I'm writing this in bed in North Brooklin. Andy and Joe and I have been here four days and I've been in bed all the time with flu, which is infuriating since we are to have only ten days at the most here—between Joe's two terms. I'm not awfully sick either, but I do have a temperature. But when I'm angry at my fate, I consider yours and feel ashamed of myself. What a perfectly dreadful time you have had! I'm terribly sorry about it and do earnestly hope that you really are free for good of the result of those two bites of cashew-fruit. (Andy says he is more convinced than ever that no one who has asthma should ever try a new food.) I wish you'd write a piece about the way South Americans love sickness and remedies and their loving solicitude and all. It sounds very funny and, as you say, pleasant.

I've sent word to Shawn as to why the Sable Island piece has been held up. He'll be glad to hear that you hope to send it soon and will be sorry you've been so sick. You probably know by now that he is our new editor and he is a good man, as I'm sure you also know. The period of indecision since Ross's death has been hard for everyone and of course we've all had lots of extra work since then too. The loss of Ross is something Andy and I will never get over, I guess. I miss him everyday of my life, which is natural, I suppose, after working so closely with him for twenty-six years. It's a tough assignment to follow him as editor, but Shawn has been on the staff since 1933 and a managing editor since before the war.

I was interested to hear of the stencils at Alcobaça. Ours, by the way, got smeared under two windows in a recent forty-mile gale when the rain seeped through the window frames. Maine has had lots of snow, which is now almost gone, but New York has had none—it's been the mildest winter there I can remember.

Your friend Howard is to have his tonsils out when I return. This is, in fact, one reason I just must get well and get back, as he postponed the operation to let me go down to Maine. He and I and everyone will be happy when you can send us some new poems. We have only the one beautiful Maryland poem left of yours and that we're holding for spring.

I have to get well, too, and fast, in order to see what is to be done about our Brooklin Public Library's new wing, for which I got the magnificent promise of a $3000 gift from a local man who went to Massachusetts and made a fortune in baked beans. He said he would give the money once the building started. Well, it was to start in the spring and now our benefactor has died, leaving $10000 to the town to be paid up on the death of his wife who, so far as I know, is young and hale and hearty. I have the feeling that the Library trustees will hold me personally responsible for this missing $3000 since they'll think I should somehow have extracted it earlier! One other piece of local news is that Charlie Henderson, whom you met, has had worse asthma than ever since he moved into a new house in Blue Hill. He thought the old house next to us was responsible.

No more now but my love,
    Katharine

The New Yorker
March 11, 1952

Dear Elizabeth:

I am anxious to hear how your health is and to be sure that that horrible allergy has not returned. I also want to say that we long for some poems of yours and of course for the Sable Island story too.

About poetry, William Shawn, our new editor, is much interested in poetry—far more so than Mr. Ross was—and he thinks we can use serious poetry of a more varied sort than we used to. In other words, perhaps some poetry that Ross thought too "difficult", we now might be able to publish. I go into this because Bill Shawn and I do wish we could get some Marianne Moore poems. Perhaps not all of hers would be possible for us but so many of them are and so many we would have been proud to publish. I asked her a couple of times if she wouldn't contribute—this was along about 1945 and 1946—and she replied that she would eventually submit something. Our records don't seem to show that she has, although I do seem to remember in the dim past that we did reject something of hers.[1] Do you think you could persuade her to send us some new work? I thought that you could do it better than I, but if you don't want to, please let me know, and I'll write her again.

When are you coming back to New York? I wish you had been here a week ago Saturday when we gave a party for the Shawns.

Affectionately,
Katharine

> Antonio Vieira 5, Leme
> Rio de Janeiro, Brazil
> March 14, 1952

Dear Katharine:

After a really dreadful bout of allergies I have been working again for about a month. I like it so much here and feel I have lost so much time that I'll probably stay right on with my friends until returning sometime in the late spring. Anyway this address will reach me, wherever I am, and I wanted to send you some sign of life at least ["Arrival at Santos"]. If you cannot use it I wonder if Howard would be kind enough to send it on to Poetry, Chicago for me? I have promised Karl something for so long, and the mails to and from Brazil are so uncertain. I have a long piece about Brazil and a couple of short poems I'll send in a few days, I hope, and I've at last got back to Sable Island, which I like pretty well—2/3rds of it.

I want to thank you or whoever was responsible for sending the New

---

1 Pearce rejected "The Rigorists," "Four Quartz Crystal Clocks," and "What Are Years?" in 1940.

Yorker Album which has been giving a great deal of pleasure to my friends and all the callers, English-speaking or not—in fact we have to hide it from them. And thank you for the check—it was really outdone by the sum of 4¢, in stamps from Houghton Mifflin, from some anthology or other . . .

I wish I could enclose some of the butterflies for you—the brilliant kind they put into tea-trays, but on the mountainside they don't look bad. And someone gave me a toucan for my birthday—with bright blue eyes and feet, very tame—I am trying to write a poem about him. I do hope you've been and are well.

    Affectionately,
      Elizabeth

P.S.—I am *pasting* on the stamps right now—

                               [n.d.]
     [postcard: Imperial Museum and Don Pedro II's
                  Summer Palace, Petrópolis]
Dear Katharine:

Thank you for your letter which I guess crossed mine in the air—I am writing Marianne & shall say something—actually, I think she'd *like* to appear there, but I do remember her telling me about a rejection, a long time ago. She takes little cracks at me once in a while about it though! But she very carefully saved Ogden Nash's poem about the Panda, & uses it in her lectures.[1]

I shall send some more things in a week or so. I expect to be in New York during May.

This is a museum full of awful things—the public wears felt slippers over their shoes & goes sliding around, to protect the parquet floors—

    Elizabeth Bishop

                             March 31, 1952
Dear Elizabeth:

It was good to hear from you and know that you are better of that horrible allergy and well enough to be writing again. The poem is wonderful, we all think, and I enclose our check for it now. We have only a few minor

---

1 "The Panda" was part of Nash's "Animal Axis" (January 3, 1942).

queries on punctuation, and I'll take them up when I send the proof. I think it is one of your very good poems and I marvel how you do so much so simply.

I am writing this from Maine but shall not date or mail it till I get back to New York, for this is a very short trip—a week and two Sundays—and the check won't be ready till Monday when I'm back.

Maine is still wintry and very gray and raw. A huge drift of snow still covers our front hedge and is head high at our entrance gate. But spring has begun in the barn where we now have Bessie, the cow, and her new son, who is to be raised for beef, alas. Irwin, the pet gosling, whom you may remember, has just laid two eggs and so has had to be renamed Vinnie, but we still call him *he*. He is very comical still and laid these two eggs on top of another goose's nest of five eggs, after building the nest up with piles and piles of hay into a sort of skyscraper.

Joe, who is having his spring vacation, spent the day caulking his lobster boat. We now have two sheep one of which is to lamb any day and the new chicks are to arrive at the end of the week. So you see spring is *really* here.

We paid a visit to the Hendersons this afternoon in their new house. Charlie has been frightfully ill and in the hospital a lot this winter, but has suddenly shed his asthma and gained weight and is full of pep. He says he now uses no medication except the inhaler you told him about.

The promised two short poems and the long piece about Brazil have us waiting eagerly for the next mail from you. I told Bill Shawn that the Sable Island piece was two-thirds done and he was glad.

Much love to you,
Katharine

April 6, 1952
[postcard]

Dear Katharine:

I'm so glad you liked "Arrival at Santos" & now I must write Miss Breen & tell her what I've done & how I know she isn't *really* 70 (I had a glimpse of her passport by mistake & she's 69, &, I think, only 5'11"). I'm leaving Brazil the 20th for 1 week in Key West, then to NY—so possibly proof better be sent to N.Y.?

April 20th–28th, c/o Stevens, Box 668, Key West, Fla.

April 28th—Hotel Grosvenor, 35 5th Ave.

I'm glad the AEROHALER is working for Mr. Henderson—I go around with mine stuck in my face the way babies do their "comforters" here.—I am doing a lot of work & shall send some things in a few days—as soon as I "put the egg" as they so elegantly phrase it in Brazil—

Affectionately,

Elizabeth

Dear Elizabeth:

Only at (1) is there a real question on this proof. If you put the exclamation after "tourist," as you had it, it has to be "O, tourist!" and the next line must then start with a new sentence and a capital letter. But don't you perhaps mean this not in the exclamatory sense? In this case it would read:

"Oh, tourist,
is this how this country etc."

This is the way Howard and I think you meant it to be read, but we may be wrong.[1]

We made a few minor punctuation changes which I hope are all right with you.[2] Do send this proof back soon.

Affectionately,

Katharine

April 18, 1952

Dear Elizabeth:

I have your post card giving the addresses and dates and I just want to say that I have mailed, on April 7th, the author's proof of "Arrival at Santos". If you didn't receive it before you left Brazil, will you let me know at once so that I can send you another proof.

I'm glad you are going to be back before I leave for Maine and I count on seeing you then. I hope to leave about May 7th—earlier than usual because I

---

1 Bishop submitted the phrase as: "Oh tourist! / is this how". The lines ran the way White wrote them (*The New Yorker* Records).

2 White's other changes include re-punctuating the phrase "and, who knows? self-pitying", making it "and—who knows?—self-pitying", in stanza one, line three. She also removed three dashes: between "There!—Miss Breen" in stanza seven, line one; at the start of stanza nine, line four; and at the start of stanza ten, line two. She also changed the comma after "stamps" to a dash in stanza nine, line three (*The New Yorker* Records).

shall have to be coming back again in June—so if we could lunch one day between the 28th and the 7th, I'd love that.

Affectionately,
Katharine

Dear Elizabeth:

Mrs. White is on vacation at the moment so I'm sending on your cost-of-living check.

I'm sorry we didn't get to see each other again before you left. By the time I'd gotten extricated from dentists, doctors, passports, etc. and called, you'd gone. And now I suppose I won't see you unless I appear in Rio, which is hardly likely.

If you do get back for any reason, please let me know, and I hope all goes swimmingly on that mountain top.

Love,
Howard

Sitio da Alcobaçinha
Samambaia
August 17, 1952

Dear Katharine:

I believe I just missed seeing you in New York when I was there in May, and I am awfully sorry. I have been ashamed of not having been able to finish any work for so long—I am afraid you will think I am a sort of Proustian hypochondriac, but ever since I came back I have had one continuous bout of asthma and have been too full of adrenaline to think straight most of the time. I am now trying cortisone and seem to be improving some at last—at least I've been able to start writing again.

I probably shouldn't bother you with this slight poem ["The Mountain"], but I think Howard must be in Europe by now. I'm sending it rather than wait until I have a group because I have a request to make of you—Karl has written to me several times asking for something for Poetry's anniversary number & I'd like very much to send him something because I never have and he has been awfully nice about asking me. If you should want this why of course it is yours—but I think it may possibly be a little too elliptical for you—and if it is I wonder if you would do me the great favor of sending it on to Karl? If it comes back here and goes again heaven knows how long it will take—it will probably be too late for him anyway,—if you don't want it, that is—but I'd like to make the gesture at least.

I should re-type it, too, [handwritten: "I did"] but the one chance of the week to send mail to Rio has just presented itself or himself and he can't wait. The mails except for airmail right from Rio are hopeless and the first thing I learned was never to put a letter in a mailbox—they're all over the place but the letters in them haven't been touched for years. Aside from the asthma I am liking living here tremendously; I have started writing several things about it and as soon as I can I'm going on a trip to some of the old mining towns.

Pearl Kazin wrote me that she is going to work for the New Yorker in September I think. She has been a very good friend to me and I think very highly of her.

I read about the "Red Badge of Courage" with horror, fascinated.[1]

I hope you're in Maine and having a pleasant summer—we are about to get some geese here, already having three dogs, a toucan, a donkey—and plans for bees and one cow. It is "winter" and perfectly beautiful—all the flowers bloom then, and it's more like a northern Maine or Nova Scotian summer than a winter.

Affectionately yours,

Elizabeth

Sable Island is still struggling along—

North Brooklin
August 28, 1952

Dear Elizabeth:

Please forgive a longhand letter. I've been sick and I find it easier to write than to type. I was very glad to hear from you but awfully sorry to learn what a miserable time you have had. Do you really think you should be in Brazil with that terrible asthma and do they know how to take care of you there? Cortisone helped our other asthmatic friend, Charlie Henderson, I know, so it sounds as if they did know. I worry about you all the same, and do hope you're very much better by now.

1 Lillian Ross's articles on the filming of *The Red Badge of Courage* ran from May 24 to June 21, 1952.

We were so happy to see a poem of yours that I'm sorry to have to report that the decision was against "The Mountain" for the New Yorker, as you suspected it might be. I don't feel quite as badly in this instance because I thought from your letter that in a way you would really prefer it if the poem went on to Poetry, because of Karl. I have sent the two versions to him. They came attached together so I could not really be sure which one arrived second but I've asked someone at the office who should know to tell Karl this. (Or to add it to my letter to him.) In any case, I want you to know that it is always sad to have to say that anything of yours is not right for the New Yorker, and I very much hope that you'll have another poem for us soon and that you'll be well enough to finish up Sable Island. I'll tell Shawn about how sick you've been, and that you haven't forgotten the piece. We would be very much interested to read the "several things" you've started writing about Samambaia, whether prose or poetry.

Your vision . . .[1]

Much love,

Katharine

September 12, 1952

Dear Katharine:

I received the weekly batch of mail yesterday and I was awfully glad to hear from you but so sorry about your news. "Hepatitis"! Good Heavens— it sounds almost Brazilian, because here, as in other tropical countries, I suppose, the liver is the preferred organ. If you ask a Brazilian how-do-you-do he is apt to answer, "well, this morning my *figado* . . ." and go on and on. We have just seen the wild cook through a bout with *her* figado, too—but since it is located anywhere from her thigh to her sternum we really weren't quite sure what she did have, or whether it was just an excess of artistic temperament and the fact that she is about to marry the gardener, too. But jaundice is so horrible, and Nausea is no fun, no matter what Sartre says. I do hope you are feeling better.

I didn't think you'd want the "Mountain"—in fact I'm not sure that I want it myself. I am enclosing a story ["Gwendolyn"] that I'm afraid may be a little on the morbid side for you. It is the first I've finished of three or four Nova Scotian ones—the second will be along in a few days. It's better but even more morbid, I'm afraid. I don't know why this rush of stories when I

1 This letter is a typed copy of the original. The personal information that came after "Your vision . . ." was deleted.

should be finishing Sable Island and some poems, but I've had them in mind for a long time. I rather enjoyed Mary's story, "C'est le premier pas qui coûte."[1] The friend I am staying with is a product of various Sacre Coeurs, as of course most of the women one meets are, and she thought it was very true—she had her convent all wrought up when she lost her faith, too.

My New York doctor wrote me a long, detailed letter from Europe in reply to my demand that she *do* something about the asthma.[2] It came after I'd started in again with the doctor here and I was rather pleased to find—because I haven't yet learned to trust any doctor but her—that he was doing exactly what she suggested, the cortisone, etc. He spent several years at Memorial Hospital N.Y. and studied with Dr. Pack, etc., and is very nice.[3] However, the cortisone has absolutely no effect, as far as I can see—except that in between attacks—about 4 times a day, that is—I feel wonderful. It is supposed to make you feel "euphoric" so I don't know whether I really am happy or just think I am, but it is very nice and I think possibly this sudden increase in output may be due to it, too. So try it for something sometime— the literature suggests it is for just about anything, in a tentative way, saying that "improvement is sometimes felt for a few weeks or months." I read a piece about Mr. Merck, who makes it, in "Time" (all-prevalent) and it said he didn't believe in manufacturing drugs for profit—then it went on to describe his $100,000 greenhouse for orchids.[4] So I give myself a shot of Cortisone & then go out to admire the free orchids on the trees . . .

In a few weeks, before the dry (supposedly) season is over I hope to go on a trip, by jeep, to Ouro Prêto and some other Baroque old mining towns—I hope very much there will be some kind of story in it. I am also putting the cook in a story—but it again, is very sad—and should really be illustrated with her own paintings—she has proved to be a really marvellous primitive.

Ganders often seem to turn out to be geese, don't they—a neighbor just had the same problem, with both of the geese laying eggs at a great rate. He also has trouble with opossums infesting his palm-trees, which seems very strange to me. We live up higher, above the palm-line, but the donkey, Mimoso, has to be protected from blood-sucking bats with a lantern at night. I am told they don't attack human beings, but I notice my hostess sleeps with her windows closed, so I do too, now—anyway—large wet clouds come in if you don't.

1 July 12, 1952.
2 Anny Baumann.
3 George T. Pack was an oncologist at Memorial Hospital, New York City.
4 George W. Merck was the cover story of the August 18, 1952, issue, "What the Doctor Ordered" (not bylined).

I do hope you are feeling better and I shall send more things very soon.
With love,
    Elizabeth

P.S. The friend with whom I am living here, Lota de Macedo Soares, is very eager to buy a Mary Petty original painting. (She has quite a good collection of modern painters here, and also a few of the cartoonists, etc.)—I told her I'd ask you if you could give me any information as to how she should go about it—write directly to Miss Petty, or has she a dealer, or what? I remember that nice reproduction in the bedroom I slept in at your house—that's an awfully nice one; I wonder where the original of it is?

October 10, 1952

Dear Katharine:

Here is another story ["In the Village"]—and still none of the things I had planned to do first. However, that seems to be the way things often go, and I now have one more story and Sable Island going at the same time. I say here is another story because I sent one about a month ago now, I think, and I am not sure whether you received it or not—things do get lost occasionally. That was "Gwendolyn." I found I had made quite a few mistakes in typing it and left out a line, so I am sending a better copy. "In the Village" is the next one. I'm afraid all these stories will be either too gloomy or too impressionistic for you. Also I am a little embarrassed about having to go to Brazil to experience total recall about Nova Scotia; geography must be more mysterious than we think.

I keep wondering how you are and hope you are much better by now. I wish you could make use of cortisone, for something or other—I am sure all my work is due to it, and now it even seems to be starting to cure the asthma as well.

I forgot to say some time ago that Marianne Moore wrote me, when I asked her about it, that she was selecting some of her La Fontaine translations for you.

It is starting to get warm again and is perfectly beautiful. I believe that the seasons as well as being opposite, run the other way around, but I haven't been able to think it though yet. Working on these stories I get slightly homesick for the other side of the Equator, but not too much.

Affectionately yours,
    Elizabeth

Dear Elizabeth:

I'm perfectly delighted to hear that the cortisone has helped your asthma so much and excited, too, that it has made you full of energy for writing. (If only the drug will do as much for you as it has for Charlie Henderson, I shall be happy. He is a new man suddenly.) We hope that the other Nova Scotia stories you spoke of will be coming soon and we like the idea of a series of them. Do you think there would be a chance of that?

Now about the first of them, "Gwendolyn," which we admire and want to buy. There is only one major problem on it and I thought I ought to consult you about this before we put the story into type and paid for it. The problem is the episode about the soiled drawers, which we don't think we can use as it stands. It is unpleasant, I'm afraid, in spite of being true, and there is a very strong feeling here against our running such a passage. I understand why you put it in and in my opinion on the story I said why I thought you might feel it important to the story, but even so, and even though I am not as a rule squeamish on such references, I must reluctantly agree with Shawn, Lobrano, and Maxwell that the passage should come out for New Yorker publication, since it does apparently offend the sensibilities of a lot of people, and is definitely repulsive to some. Ross, as perhaps you know, was always strongly against what he called "functional" references if we could possibly avoid them and, on the whole, I think it has been a wise policy for a magazine like the New Yorker. In a book such a passage has a totally different effect. Shawn's final word on the episode was that unless you can give an absolutely answerable argument for retaining it—and he strongly doubts that from *our* point of view there could be such an argument—he feels it should be eliminated. So do let me hear soon how you feel about this, by air mail or wire. And if you feel you absolutely must keep it, then please give me your arguments for it. But I hope you won't feel that way.[1]

---

1 Bishop submitted the passage as:

> I couldn't seem to get into my side of the bed so I went around and picked up Gwendolyn's clothes where she had thrown them on the floor. I put them over the back of a chair, the blue and white striped dress, the waist, the long brown stockings. Her drawers had lace around the legs, but they were very dirty, with some brownish stains. They upset me so much that I recovered my voice.
> "Don't you use toilet-paper?" I asked, deeply shocked.
> "No," said Gwendolyn, without even opening her eyes.
> It was better after my grandmother had turned out the lamp and we had talked a while (*The New Yorker* Records and Vassar College Library).

I have read the story through again just now and it seems to me it might work all right if you simply ended that description of Gwendolyn's clothes with the sentences "Her drawers had lace around the legs, but they were very dirty." Wouldn't that statement in itself be a surprising enough flaw in the otherwise exquisite Gwendolyn, without getting into details? I should think this would remove the distastefulness but still make your point. Of course I can't answer for how this would strike the others, who may prefer the dirty underwear to come out entirely, but I think it would be worth trying out. In any case I feel sure you can see a way to fix this part, if you are willing to, and I *pray* you will be, for I just can't bear not to have us publish this story. It is beautifully written and with a most wonderful selection of detail to make your general effect. The tone is never falsified for a moment, except, apparently, for the majority of readers in this office, in this one passage. If you will therefore consent to the cut, I can have the piece set up in Varitype working proof and paid for, and then send it to you to work on this part. I would add notes about any other smaller points of editing that come up. The piece will, I think, need very little editing except for one or two small points I'd want to ask your help on—clarification etc. For instance, we feel that the Nova Scotia locale should be established earlier than it is—one can now read right ahead quite a distance without knowing that the place is Nova Scotia. Also at the very end, we have a question on the passage where you and Billy are placing flowers around the doll. You say that you can't be sure whether it was you or Billy who first suggested that this was Gwendolyn's funeral and that the doll's name was Gwendolyn. This seems to imply that Billy's preoccupation with the real Gwendolyn had been much the same as your own, which seems unlikely and rather surprising since there has been no previous mention of his having known Gwendolyn or of his being interested in her. It seems almost certain, doesn't it, that the notion occurred to *you* and not to Billy? In any case, this would be a small matter to fix and I can write you about it more clearly when I annotate the proof.

Now to answer your query about the Mary Petty covers and drawings: No covers are for sale and they have not been for a long time. She prefers to keep them herself. Years back, I tried to buy the dachshund cover you spoke of liking in the print reproduction, but though she promised me a first chance at it should she ever decide to sell it, she would not part with it. Four covers can be bought, as prints, in a portfolio of four available at $20 or in single prints at $6 each. These four are the dachshund, the maid shining silver, the artist painting the family on the lawn, and the old lady warming her legs in front of a fireplace.[1] Mary Petty's black-and-white drawings *are* for sale though, through the Walker Gallery, and Mary has agreed never to undersell this dealer. He has fixed a minimum price of $250 per drawing and often charges more. I do not know the address of this gallery but your friend could find out about the whole thing by writing Miss Daise Terry, at the New Yorker. She handles the sale of New Yorker originals for all our artists but in Petty's case, the minimum price, even if sold through the office, has to be $250 because of this Walker Gallery deal.

I do hope that you'll also soon be sending the story you mentioned about the Brazilian cook, also anything and everything you do write about your travels, whether poetry or prose. And Sable Island?

Hoping to hear right away about "Gwendolyn," I am,

Affectionately,

Katharine*

* Still in Maine and hence no proper signature but we leave for New York this week.

October 25, 1952

Dear Katharine:

Thank you for your letter, but thank you first of all for the pains you have taken with reading and re-reading what is after all a very slight story . . . Of course I was fairly sure there might be objections to poor Gwendolyn's undergarments; but I'm afraid I am not "creative" enough, and when I start telling how something actually happened I just have to go on and give every last detail. In some ways I think you're probably right—in a longer story I imagine it wouldn't seem so shocking—but it did seem natural enough to write it at the time. However, I have changed it, more or less as you suggested, so that I think the same thing is *implied*. I'm enclosing the changed paragraphs—I'm afraid this MS is getting to be an awful mess—and I do hope they will meet with everyone's approval. I had tried to lead up to the

1 The Petty cover with a dachshund is the August 4, 1945, issue; a woman sits on the beach and holds a seashell to the dog's ear. The maid cover is from the November 10, 1945, issue; the artist is from July 31, 1948; and the old lady March 14, 1942.

shocking remarks by the little privy scene, but I guess there just wasn't time enough in such a short story.[1]

In the meantime I think you will probably have received the slightly better copy of the story, with a few changes,—a few words, and a line I'd left out on the first page, about the skates, etc. I don't know what Varitype proof is—but there are one or two other words I'd like to change, and if the story is acceptable to you now perhaps I could do it on that. I am not at all sure of grammar and spelling when I am as completely on my own as I have been until recently, but Fowler and a dictionary have just arrived, and I think somewhere in the same box there is a hymnbook, so I can make quite sure of the hymns I quote. Also I recently picked up the information somewhere that insulin was not commonly used as the regular treatment for diabetes until 1922. It was given, (insulin) by doctors, but not in the systematic way it has been since. The story takes place around 1918–19—but since I say in it that I don't know what medicine she was getting I think the reference to insulin could probably be left as it is. (We had a remarkably good and advanced country doctor and it seems to me that I heard later that she *was*—but of course that's neither here nor there.)

I feel much more obstinate about the other two things you mention: not bringing in the locale right away, and the fact that at the end I say I don't remember who it was who said first that the doll's name was "Gwendolyn." I do mention Nova Scotia after three short paragraphs—and I do feel a reader should be able to wait that long. I hope you won't mind my saying so, but I think the convention of situating everything clearly and immediately can get to be boring, make the reader lazy, or else think, oh heavens, here we go again on another of those childhood reminiscences, instead of troubling to absorb the real atmosphere first. The "scene" and type of place is made plain enough, I think, and there is no mystification being prac-

---

1 Bishop rewrote the last few sentences of the passage:

> Her drawers had lace around the legs, but they were very dirty. This fact shocked me so deeply that I recovered my voice and started asking her more questions.
> "I'm asleep," said Gwendolyn, without opening her eyes.
> But after my grandmother had turned out the lamp Gwendolyn began to talk to me again (*The New Yorker* Records and Vassar College Library).

Bishop complained of *The New Yorker*'s objections to Pearl Kazin: "I have just finished a long letter to Mrs. White explaining why I said so & so in a certain story—I was too coarse as usual—she said to write, and I was frightfully tempted to cable them 'Remove Gwendolyn's dirty drawers' (that's what the trouble was about) but I thought better of it" (October 26, 1952, Vassar College Library).

ticed. The same thing, I think, holds true for the ending. In a small village (which I've said it was) among relatives, and between small children living close together and playing together all afternoon, & naturally talking about what impressed them most in the world around them—it would have been natural for both of them to have talked about the other child. I wanted to keep it deliberately vague—or, rather, have it grow vaguer towards the end—because the real drama was over and was already turning into a sort of story. That's why I said I didn't even remember "what happened to me" at the very end.

If you still think it is really unlikely-sounding I think I could put in a sentence or two a little ahead—a hint as to what Billy and I talked about, which might make it plainer, but I would still like to keep the actual remark—who made it—ambiguous.

I do hope this will solve the problems because I'd like you to be able to use the story.

The other one I sent: "In the Village," I feel sure is too poetic, and out of your line, so I won't be at all disconcerted when you return it and please don't feel you have to work over it.

I have two more about the same place and some of the same people—one a possibility for you—and one in the form of a poem as well as a story—but I'm afraid they won't make up a "series" at all, because they are all in different periods of time, some written in the first person, some not, etc. But as soon as they're done I'll send them all along. I'm awfully pleased to say that everything is still progressing, including cortisone—and the Sable Island piece.

Thank you for being so nice about the story; I imagine you feel sympathetic towards it because Nova Scotia resembles Maine in so many ways, or rather it resembled Maine at that time probably about the way Maine had been forty years earlier.

Once Sable Island and the Nova Scotian pieces are done I think I'll take a rest and go back to poetry before I undertake the Brazilian cook. The trouble with her is she keeps right on happening, so that I'll probably have to go back to Nova Scotia to do her justice.

Thank you for the information about the Mary Petty pictures which I've handed on to my friend here.

I'll send this off by a friend going to Rio tomorrow, although of course I am dying to send ambiguous cables. And I hope it meets the requirements all right. You don't mention your health and I hope you are all recovered by now—at least I feel you are working hard again, so I trust that means so.

    Affectionately yours,
      Elizabeth

The New Yorker
November 10, 1952

Dear Elizabeth:

    I was happy to have your letter about "Gwendolyn," for it cleared up our only real problem about the story, and your new passage about the little girls going to bed seemed perfect to us. We are very grateful to you for it. We all feel exactly as you do about these stories of yours about Nova Scotia; that they are and should be short stories—not reminiscences, and that this is one of their chief merits. If there is anything we do *not* want nowadays it is the conventional childhood memory piece and we agree with you absolutely about hating the beginnings of such pieces that make the reader think "Oh, here we go again!" I myself think that Nova Scotia comes in soon enough except, perhaps, for the fact you mention Boston in your first sentence, since this apparently made readers who did not know your background, as I did, place the story, by association, somewhere in New England—at least for a few paragraphs. It is unimportant and can go as is, but I have a suggestion on the notes attached to the proof that might clear up this slight red herring; that is, it might if you happened to like it. Otherwise let it go as is.

    We agree with you too about the ending to some extent and do not want it to be too explicit. The only reason the question ever came up was that Billy had not come into the story up to that point and the reader could not be sure that, though he lived in the same village, he even knew Gwendolyn as you did. I think if you introduced Billy into the story earlier as a part of Gwendolyn's and your group of playmates,—for instance, at the picnic—that this would clarify things for those who wondered about the ending. And if, as you suggest, you can put in a sentence or two a little ahead of the final episode—a hint as to what you and Billy talked about—the general feeling is that it will make the story even better. We'd be grateful for that insertion.

    This is why I am sending you the story now in "Working Proof," with a few preliminary notes and queries. On this proof, you can write your inserts and so on. Then we'll get the piece set in type and send you a regular author's proof, with the usual proofroom questions. (I do not see how there can be many of those, but one never knows.) I hate to bother you with two proofs, for I know they are an annoyance. But I also would not want to write in anything *for* you. If only you were here to talk over the proof, these minor questions, which seem so mountainous at long distance, could be cleared up in fifteen minutes![1]

I enclose our check for "Gwendolyn" now. It is a beautiful piece of writing.

I shall have to postpone until tomorrow a letter on "The Village." This story we like *even better* than "Gwendolyn"; but it does arouse some confusion. It must be kept poetic and I hope I can persuade you that it can be just that but can also be a little less puzzling in a few respects. We'll see.

When I spoke of "a series," I did not mean a series like [Clarence Day's] "Life with Father"—one episode after another. I meant a group or sequence based on Nova Scotia. We are *every one us of us* excited about these manuscripts. Do go on with others!

More to come.

Affectionately,

Katharine

"Gwendolyn" by E. Bishop—Working Proof Notes from KSW

1. As I said in my letter, the words "in Boston" are sort of a red herring here. Could you not say some such thing as "away in the States" instead? This would eliminate the thought that you were writing about a New En-

---

1 White made some corrections to "Gwendolyn" before it was set in proof. She changed "'baby' doll" to "'baby doll'" and "pencil, their names" to "pencil—their names," (*The Collected Prose*, edited by Robert Giroux [New York: Farrar, Straus and Giroux, 1984], 214). She removed the comma after "me" in "sing and sing to me, hymns" (215). She changed "I, that is about eight, and" to "I—that is, about eight—and" and "and how if they weren't more sensible" to "and of how, if they weren't more sensible," (216). One change she made on this page that did not remain was removing the comma after "bit her". She added commas around "if we were careful", made a new section with the paragraph that begins "I remember clearly", and exchanged the comma after "heroine" for a dash (217). She changed "Once we went to a church picnic" to "Once my grandparents and I went to a church picnic", replaced the comma after "Presbyterian picnic" with a dash, and in the next sentence she removed "my grandparents and I" and substituted "the three of us" (218). She removed the comma after "pass the time" and replaced it with a dash (219). On the same page she changed "I was forced to stop" to "I was told to stop". It ran as "I was made to stop". She removed the commas around the phrase "and I was there in the kitchen when he told her" and inserted dashes and added commas around the phrase "and my heart began to pound again" (221). She removed the comma after "quite large" and inserted a dash (222). She changed "dry bright-gold" to "dry, bright-gold" (223). She added a comma after "If I care to" and changed the comma after "new marbles" to a dash (224). She also changed "Everyone tried to comfort me, for what they had no idea" to "Everyone tried to comfort me—for what, they had no idea" and changed Bishop's comma-dash combination to a simple dash after "A month or so after the funeral" (225) (*The New Yorker* Records).

gland village. You could bring in the place name, Boston, too, if it seemed better to do so. It comes in later, of course.[1]

2. "a small steamer trunk" is a little misleading because it could be a *real* steamer trunk. Some real trunks used to be made of tin, I believe. The words written in are not right of course.[2]

3. Since you only give one example of hymns, don't you need "such as" or "like"?[3]

4. The varityper misread the word I had changed here. You had "we" here, and just below you again say "we," but because you have referred to Gwendolyn in the preceding paragraph, the "we" becomes ambiguous, so it seemed better to use "my grandparents and I" here rather than just below, at (4a).[4]

5. This long sentence seems to need the "and" for sentence structure, and a slight change in punctuation for clarity. Do you agree? It's a minor matter.[5]

6. Shouldn't you say here that Gwendolyn was missing, especially since she is the only friend of yours mentioned so far in the story? It occurred to me, too, that you might find it helpful to say here that your Cousin Billy was at the picnic. If you did, it would eliminate the doubt of his knowing Gwendolyn well, at the end of the story, and thus help solve the matter I wrote you about earlier. You probably would not want to put *only* Billy in, so I thought you might consider putting in some other names too—some typical Nova Scotia surnames might even add to the Nova Scotia atmosphere. Some such thing as:

"went wading in the river with mine: my cousin Billy, Jess McEach-ern, and the others; only Gwendolyn was missing, etc."

1 Bishop submitted the first sentence as "My aunt Mary was eighteen years old and away in Boston training to be a nurse." It ran as: "My Aunt Mary was eighteen years old, and away in 'the States,' in Boston, training to be a nurse." (213).

2 Bishop changed "small" to "toy," so the first sentence of the second paragraph ran as: "She had a large wardrobe, which my Aunt Mary had made, packed in a toy steamer trunk of green tin embossed with all the proper boards, locks, and nailheads." (213).

3 Bishop chose "such as" to introduce the hymns: "Then there were more specifically children's hymns, such as:" (215).

4 Bishop submitted the paragraph as: "Once we went to a church picnic." It ran as "Once, my grandparents and I went to a church picnic." (218).

5 In the same paragraph, the submitted sentence runs: "Pans of beans and biscuits and scalloped potatoes were set out on long tables; all our varieties of pickles and relishes, chow-chows and piccalillis, conserves and preserves, cakes and pies, parkins and hermits, all glistening and gleaming in the late sunshine; and water for tea was being brought to the boil over two fires." It ran as: "Pans of beans and biscuits and scalloped potatoes were set out on long tables, and all our varieties of pickles and relishes (chowchows and piccalillis), conserves and preserves, cakes and pies, parkins and hermits—all glistening and gleaming in the late sunshine—and water for tea was being brought to the boil over two fires." (218).

This isn't the way you would word it, of course, and you can do it in your own words very much better, if you think it's a good idea.[1]

7. Since you only give two instances of the remarks they made, it sounds a little as if these were the only remarks they ever made. Would some such insertion as "things like," to generalize it, be wise?[2]

8. This "never knew" must have been something you had heard an adult say. Put just this way, does it make you, the child, sound too sophisticated? Could you not perhaps give the impression that you felt that way because you had heard some grown-up say this?[3]

9. Didn't you also pick the teaberries?[4]

10. Something seems missing here—partly, perhaps, because the antecedent of "the exact sensation" gets a trifle obscured by the break preceding this sentence. It seems to need something like "the exact sensation of that disappointment", "of that grief", of that whatever it was.[5]

11. See note (1)

12. Do you think this should be amplified a little, to say you picked the chives and floated them on the water? Maybe it is clear, but I'm not sure.[6]

13. Here, or along here, you were to make the insertion of your talk with Billy. Your hint of it.[7]

November 12, 1952

Dear Elizabeth:

Here is the letter I promised about "In The Village." We all of us like its poetic quality and we all of us are *for* the story, if we can persuade you to

1 White wanted Bishop to insert the new passage after the sentence: "My grandmother settled herself on a log to talk to her friends, and I went wading in the river with mine." (218). See Bishop to White, November 23, 1952.

2 Bishop submitted the sentence as: "This was a custom of the Baptists who lived within sight of the church, and later, when they met at their own afternoon service, they would say to each other, 'They had a good turn-out this morning,' or, 'Is Mrs. Peppard still laid up? I missed her this morning.'" It ran as: "This was the unacknowledged practice of the Baptists who lived within sight of the church, and later, when they met at their own afternoon service, they would innocently say to each other things like 'They had a good turnout this morning' and 'Is Mrs. Peppard still laid up? I missed her this morning.'" (221–22). An additional query White wrote in the margin of this paragraph was whether the "window on the other side" was on the other side of the ell. It ran as: "on the other side of the ell" (221).

3 Bishop added "as people said" (223).

4 On the copy of the submitted manuscript, Bishop added "and I had" to the same sentence as White's note eight. The sentence ran as: "Blueberries grew there, too, but I didn't eat them, because I felt I 'never knew,' as people said, but once when I went there, my grandmother had given me a teacup without a handle and requested me to bring her back some teaberries, which 'grew good' on the graves, and I had." (223).

5 See Bishop to White, November 23, 1952.

6 Bishop did not make this change.

7 See Bishop to White, November 23, 1952.

clarify and strengthen the thread of narrative that it is strung on. In one or two places this thread is so thin that it seems to break entirely. We do not mean by this that you need to turn your lovely prose poem into a conventional short story, but we hope that you will at least be willing to allow the reader a little more understanding of your basic situation and give her some clues as to what the relationship is between your characters. As it now reads, without knowing you, the author, the reader can't even be sure of what the relationship is between the little girl—the "I"—and the woman who screams. I would like to quote an editorial opinion about the story because it almost exactly represents my own point of view about it. It says: "Author simply doesn't tell enough. For example, I gathered (though I could be wrong) that the woman who is having the nervous breakdown and the fittings simultaneously is the little girl's mother, and that her aunts have come home to Nova Scotia from Boston (it turns out, at the end of the story), to help the grandmother take care of her. Then the trunk comes from Boston, with the mother's clothes in it (?). And yet there is no statement to the effect that the little girl has ever known anything but the village, or that the mother *has* come home. Also, it appears that the mother's breakdown is probably the result of giving way to grief for the death of the father, whose family is referred to—but live where?—and is wealthy. I think it is reasonable and right that the little girl's mind be centered on what happens, what she sees, but the author is not limited to her point of view, and therefore can be sufficiently explicit for the reader to relax and enjoy the writing, which is wonderful. The usual sense of the richness, not to say splendor, that is found in commonplace objects, in a place strictly devoid of either richness or splendor—splendor having moved down the scale, to the miniature world—is the effect she creates."

I think a basic difficulty is that the little girl seems to be a native Nova Scotian brought up by her grandmother, even though her mother is alive and presumably has been living elsewhere. This is an odd situation and puzzling to anyone who can only guess at it. It does seem to need clarification and slight amplification. Another point we all agree on is that the dialogue is sometimes unintentionally difficult, because of your habit of using a series of paragraphs when the same person is speaking and of not using enough attribution. Often one just can't figure out who is speaking. This might be easy to fix in editing, but we would rather have you do it—that is, if you are willing to consider revising this manuscript.

About the paragraphing of some of the descriptions. Your pages 2 and 3 for example, are written like a poem rather than like a piece of prose. We presume that this is your wish and your intention. We will not raise an objection to that if you really insist because we like the piece of writing far too much to be niggling about small points. But for us it would still be poetic prose, and really better prose, if these separate single sentences were sometimes run together and written in the form of short paragraphs.

The fact that the introductory section is written in the third person and that you then make a switch to the first person at the bottom of page 3 is momentarily confusing but perhaps it is effective. I think we would prefer to have the story told either in the third person throughout or in the first person throughout but we'll accept the switch from third to first person. In fact we are willing to make all the concessions we possibly can about the piece and its form, provided you can give the reader that sense of relaxation that comes from really understanding it. One does not have to understand *everything* of course, but one ought not to be so constantly puzzled that one keeps thinking about the puzzle rather than about your words and your beautiful poetic and emotional effects.

On page 13 there is a section that bothers us again, because of the functional references. I myself feel that the cow flops should remain and that it should be said that they fascinated you. But the elaborate description of them seems to turn many people's stomachs and I am sure we could never publish the pun, "Lucy Bowels," which seems out of key with the rest of the story and far more unpleasant than amusing or charming. But as I say, I would hold out for your being allowed to mention the steaming cow flops as part of the journey behind the cow because I know from my childhood of driving behind a horse that this phenomenon is fascinating to a child. In functional reference, it all depends on how it is written: the loving description of the manure seems to go too far.

However, if you still feel strongly about keeping this in or object to any of the suggestions we make, I do hope that you will say so and give us a chance to reconsider. As I said in yesterday's letter, in many ways we like this story even better than "Gwendolyn", and we just could not bear to lose it if there is any way of our getting together on it. I urge you to change it only because I think it will certainly be a better piece of writing if you do change it, and I'm sure that the poetic quality will not be lost by so doing. The whole piece is evocative and moving and interesting provided one can figure out what is happening. But as the story now reads, the whole thing is too elusive to be understood and truly appreciated. Do let me know soon how you feel on all this.

I have left a few scribbles in the margin but have not attempted to mark all the places we feel would benefit by revision.

Affectionately,

Katharine

Dear Katharine:

Thank you for your two letters and the check and the MS, which all arrived yesterday. First, about Gwendolyn: I have followed almost all of your suggestions to the letter and I think you were perfectly right about them. (It is funny the way one can overlook such details in one's own work, I suppose because it seems so clear during the writing. I think I'd spot them myself in someone else's—or maybe I flatter myself.) I've written in my corrections and a few notes in brown pencil. I've followed your correction as to note 6, and also brought in a reference to Billy, on galley 12, that I think will make obvious that he'd be aware of the child's funeral, etc. Then on galley 16 I've put in a couple of sentences of further explanation just to clinch it—but they could be left out, if your prefer, without, I think, sacrificing any clarity now.[1]

On galley 13—the graveyard—what I had meant (I scribbled this in but you may not be able to read it so I'd better type it) was that on one occasion I had picked teaberries for my grandmother; but that my playing there, while my grandfather cut grass and talked, was something that happened over and over. I think "And so . . ." gives that idea a little better—and it could even start a new paragraph; and perhaps it would be better to leave out the three "hads" in that sentence, although I like them. But please do what you think best about it.[2]

---

1 For note six, Bishop took out the sentence "We met at tea" and inserted the following sentences: "My cousin Billy was there, and Seth Hill, and the little McNeil twins, but Gwendolyn was missing. Later, I joined my family for supper, or as all Nova Scotians call their suppers, 'tea.'" (218). For galley sixteen, Bishop made changes in the third paragraph from the end. In the submitted manuscript, she wrote: "We sipped water from jelly glasses through chives, until we reeked of them, and fought for the possession of insects in match-boxes. As it got later we grew a little bored and reckless and finally I did something really bad: I went in the house and upstairs to my aunt Mary's bedroom and brought down the tissue-paper-wrapped, retired doll." It ran as: "We sucked water from jelly glasses through chive straws until we reeked of them, and fought for the possession of insects in matchboxes. To tease me, Billy deliberately stepped on one of the boxes and crushed its inhabitant flat. When we made up after this violence, we sat and talked for a while, desultorily, about death in general, and going to heaven, but we were growing a little bored and reckless, and finally I did something really bad." (225–26).

2 Bishop submitted the sentences as: "So I had played while my grandfather, wearing a straw hat, had scythed away, and had talked to me from time to time about the people lying there." Starting a new paragraph, it was printed as: "And so I used to play while my grandfather, wearing a straw hat, scythed away, and talked to me haphazardly about the people lying there." (223).

On galley 14, note 10, I feel a real difficulty. I have inserted "of that moment" to relate it better to the paragraph before the space, but I honestly don't think it should be made any more explicit than that.[1] You know, I know, everybody knows, what I am speaking about, and to put it into words I think spoils the climax of a slight little tale completely. It would also make completely unnecessary the little illustrative example, the comparison that comes next, where the "sensation" is not given explicitly either, (so that x=x , so to speak). I tried out various phrases and I think you'll see what I mean if I give one: "If I care to, I can bring back that sensation of abrupt, inevitable abandonment today . . ." etc. Don't you think it makes the story, such as it is, entirely too obvious—and also spoils in advance the little illustration of the marbles? I hope you'll agree.

I'm so glad you liked "In The Village" because I think it's a much better story, too. I was very pleased with your quotation from an editor, and I agree with the criticism in general. I was worried about it's being too mysterious myself, so I tried it out on an acquaintance here who knew absolutely nothing of the background, Nova Scotia, etc. But since both she and your editor *did* get the story exactly as it was I can't really believe it can be *too* bewildering. But I have no interest in bewildering on purpose, and I think there are several places where the situation could be made plainer very easily without changing the story very much. [handwritten: "Where people come from, & when—etc.—the chronology *is* very confusing the way the story is now, I realize."] I'm going to get to work on it tomorrow and see, and I'll send it back in a few days. However, I'm not sure that I'll feel able to change as much as you may want changed—the paragraphing, for example, and the quotations. I worked over them for a long time to try to get a certain tempo that I *think* I've got. Better punctuation may help some, but I wanted to give the effect of nervous voices, exchanging often ambiguous remarks, floating in the air over the child's head. But I'll write again when I send the MS back.

Please don't begin to think I have a scatological obsession! I really haven't—or I don't believe I had any more than most children,—maybe

---

1 Bishop had started the section with: "If I care to I can bring back the exact sensation today; but then it is also one of those that from time to time are terrifying thrust upon us." It ran as: "If I care to, I can bring back the exact sensation of that moment today, but then, it is also one of those that from time to time are terrifying thrust upon us." (224). Apparently, Bishop also made changes to two earlier paragraphs, changing "But suddenly something happened at the church across the way." to "But now, suddenly, as I watched through the window, something happened at the church across the way." and "For a minute I stared straight through my lace curtain at Gwendolyn there, completely alone on the grass by the church door." to "For a minute, I stared straight through my lace curtain at Gwendolyn's coffin, with Gwendolyn shut invisibly inside it forever, there, completely alone on the grass by the church door." (223, 224).

less—in the country such things are taken so for granted. But I'll see what I can do about poor Nelly.[1] I'll send it back in a few days, as I said—there is one more Nova Scotia one almost done, too, I think, laid around 1900.

Thank you again for all your help, and such careful editing is an enormous help, you know—

Affectionately yours,
Elizabeth

Rio de Janeiro
December 18, 1952

Dear Katharine:

Thank you again for the contract, which I am mailing back to you in a separate envelope. It was a very nice surprise to have an extra $100 at this time of year. This is the 2nd Christmas I've spent in Brasil now and my chief impression of it is that it is HOT—but that is in Rio, where I am at the moment. But it is funny to go shopping at Sears, Roebuck—and it is even funnier that Sears, Roebuck has a fairly fashionable restaurant and *night club*.

Here is "In the Village" back again. I have made a good many corrections and re-written the first few pages where I think most of the difficulties were. I think you'll find the situation quite a bit clearer. As I think I said before, though, your editor, whom you quoted, really had the story exactly as I'd intended it, and the people here I tried it on, who knew nothing of its background—and two of them not even English very well—also "got" it quite accurately, so I really can't believe it is too mysterious.

I found it hard to put in "explanation" without spoiling the rhythm, and the same was true of the conversations, short paragraphs, etc. However, I have inserted attributions where I thought the reader should know and really couldn't tell who was speaking. But I don't think it *matters* where the other grandparents live, for example, where the mother has been, etc.—once I start giving all that it would turn into a completely different kind of piece, I think.

I still switch from the birds' eye view to the 3rd person to the 1st person—but I think by changing tenses I've made it less confusing. I've taken out the vulgar joke about the cow, but I've left in the rest—I just can't believe it could really "turn many people's stomachs"! (And I hate to think

---

1 Bishop continued to jokingly complain to Kazin: "I am having trouble with 'functional references' to the pt. I'm really getting embarrassed about it; *have* I a scatalogical obsession?" (December 10, 1952, Vassar College Library).

of their reaction to my story about the Brazilian cook—well, these things can't be helped; I don't try to startle but I feel things have to be real.)

Anyway, I hope you will try it again. I'll be sending some more things shortly after Christmas. I hope you have pleasant holidays—in case this reaches you before then—and best wishes for the New Year—I wish I could send along a pot of orchids I have blooming now, called *Lelia Tenebrisa*.

Affectionately yours,
Elizabeth

January 20, 1953

Dear Elizabeth:

I have been awfully slow in replying about your revision of "In The Village." The reason for the delay is that all of us like so much about the manuscript and differed so much in our own opinions that we have more or less agonized over it, trying to see how on earth you and The New Yorker could get together on this story that we admire so much of. We were, frankly, disappointed that you were unwilling to make the situation about the child and the mother a trifle clearer for readers who did not know any of the background facts and sorry that you did not want to make it possible for such a reader to follow and enjoy your narrative without strain and without groping. I know that you don't at all agree that it's a puzzle, but I am now convinced that it really is—at least to readers who come to this story fresh, knowing nothing about the Nova Scotia background of your childhood and without having read "Gwendolyn" as we have. We felt, and we still feel, that the poetic and literary quality of the writing could be made clear enough so that the reader would not have to work so hard merely to guess what the little girl's and the mother's circumstances were at the start of the story. I so earnestly hoped that a compromise between your way and our desire for a little more illumination could be reached that I even tried a version with the absolute minimum of editing I thought needed to make this story clear enough to *me*. I knew that perhaps you would not even like this amount of editing, but if it worked, I had planned to send it to you, just as a suggestion. Well, my version is not successful, apparently, and I was probably too close to the story, for when Mr. Shawn read the piece for the first time in this edited version, wanting and hoping to like it, he reported that he really was *too* puzzled. He is not at all literal-minded and he *is* sympathetic to unconventional writing, but he explained to me that he felt the reader just could not enjoy the story unless the circumstances at the start and at the end were made clearer and unless a few pieces of dialogue that I had not fixed in my edited version were cleared up as to who was talking.

I have decided to send you this edited version (on yellow paper) in the dim hope that you may change your mind and want to try a less elusive version. Mr. Shawn feels that if you could make clear at the start, even if in non-explicit and highly poetic words, the rather peculiar situation: i.e. that you, the child, are to all intents a real Nova Scotian, whereas your mother at that time was not; if you could it would help a lot. The reader seems to know too little about the mother, particularly. You do give some hints, of course, but they come late and are awfully vague. Then at the end Shawn feels that it is not clear why you turn away from Nate and your beloved blacksmith shop once you begin taking packages to the post office and that it is also not clear where the mother goes to at the end. Could there be a suggestion that it was to a hospital (if that is the case) so that no one would think she had returned to Worcester to live, as some readers here did?

On the matter of attributing the speeches, Mr. Shawn says he does not think they need to be attributed in circumstances where the child just hears a lot of adult voices and does not separate off who is speaking, provided you used some sort of covering device to show that the voices come as a jumble to the child. You will see that I have tried some such covering device in a few places. But wherever the mother does speak, it seems vitally important for the reader to know this. On page 20, the fire, it was really utterly confusing as to what was happening. In editing that page I just made a guess as to the circumstances. Earlier, at A1) and A2) and B) Shawn is not sure that my covering device is sufficient to make the reader able to follow the talk. Except on pages 1 and 2 where I rearranged the order for the sake of clarity, the yellow paper version is just like yours except for the pencil marks on it. Those first two pages have been recopied and I think the new order is clearer. Possibly you will, too.

Perhaps one difficulty that underlies all this is that because this story is written like a poem, you feel it will be read like a poem. But poems are not usually 26 pages long and though a reader is quite willing to read and reread a poem that is elusive and finally get to understand it, he is not so willing to reread a very long story. Instead he just gives up after one reading, feeling vaguely dissatisfied.

I am really in a state of unhappy indecision over this manuscript because I want us to have it so much, and I somehow feel it's my fault that I can't persuade you of the obscurities, in a letter. I do wish you were here, because I think you and I could make it work to your and our satisfaction if you were.

But I certainly do not want you to rework it again for nothing, or unless you are now convinced there is some merit in our criticisms. And I feel sure you won't be.

Anyway, do please let me know your final thoughts about the piece, even if you are utterly at variance with us, and annoyed too. I really only send you the yellow paper version because it has notes on it and so you will see that I did try.

I was very happy to read of your Shelley Award. That is a well-deserved honor and we are all pleased that you got it, and send our congratulations.

Affectionately,
Katharine

We very much hope for some poems and another story soon.

February 4, 1953

Dear Katharine:

I am really appalled at the amount of work you have put into my story, "In the Village." While I still don't think it's as puzzling as I guess you do, I agree that some of the conversation should be cleared up, and that probably some of it could be cut to advantage—also the situation of the mother should be made a little plainer. However, I do think that putting in "he saids" and "she saids" is going to spoil it, and I still think it's quite a good story, or may get to be, and that it has a rhythm that I don't want to lose. (I have an awful feeling that if only I didn't write poetry as well, readers wouldn't find it nearly so difficult! And may I say, although it may not be very gracious of me, that I have found those Eudora Welty stories—although I used to admire her work extremely—completely and absolutely mysterious. Who are those people and what on earth are they doing and where is that couple going and why—and that last one to reach me—the girls going calling on their relatives—the first 3000 words is nothing but padding . . . I swear my story is clearer than that . . .)[1] Well, having unburdened myself that way—I am going to do a lot more work on "In the Village" because I have hopes for it, but I'm afraid it will probably never be much closer to what you'd like. I really appreciate editing, you know, and I'll probably use a good many of

1 Welty's most recent stories, "No Place for You, My Love," and "Kin," ran on September 20 and November 15, 1952. Welty revised both stories, making significant changes to "Kin," before including them in *The Bride of the Innisfallen* (1955).

your suggestions which on the whole I think are perfectly well-founded—but I'm still afraid it won't come out the way you want it.[1]

However—I have another one, the same people and locale, laid around 1900, (no me, of course!) and I think it is much more straightforward. I shall try to send it to you just as soon as I can—in about a week. Also Sable Island, which I do so hope you will find usable, and is just straight presentation. Also one about Brazil, but I'm afraid we're going to run into difficulties with it . . .

I should answer your letter now in much more detail. I appreciate all the work you have gone to and wanted to let you know since I have the chance to send a letter today. As I said I'm going to work hard over that story—but I'm afraid it will never do no matter what.

Anyway—I'll send more things very soon—thank you for the kind congratulations about the Award—I was awfully pleased, of course.

Affectionately yours,
Elizabeth

March 3, 1953

Dear Elizabeth:

Thank you ever so much for your letter of February 4th. It is wonderful news that you will consider reworking "In the Village" and I do not feel, as you do, that "it will never do." We are all hopeful, and are eager to see it again. And I'm glad you "unburdened" yourself! We were interested in what you wrote about the Welty stories.[2]

I look forward to the new Nova Scotia story, and "Sable Island." (It may be that the letter went direct to Shawn. I forgot to ask him about it but will do so tomorrow.)

---

1 Of White's letter, Bishop wrote: "They really do want it but I refuse to put in enough 'he saids' and 'she saids' and 'it was four P.M., a very hot summer, August 16, 1917, Great Village, Nova Scotia, and my father's name was Wm Thomas Bishop. . . . The idea underneath it all seems to be that the N Yorker reader must never have to pause to think for a single second—be informed and re-informed comfortingly all the time, like newspaper writing a little—but then if one does attempt to publish there I guess one has no earthly right to complain" (Bishop to Kazin, February 10, 1953, Vassar College Library).

2 Bishop continued to struggle with White's queries. Saying Delmore Schwartz's comments were "as good as any," she typed out part of his review of 55 Stories from The New Yorker (1949) for Kazin: "The work in question is obviously not the product of a deliberate conspiracy, but the result of a profound and intuitive collaboration between the taste of numerous readers and hard-pressed editors who do the best they can, according to their lights" ("Smile and Grin, Relax and Collapse," Partisan Review, issue 7, 1950). She added, "What I'd like to know is—& maybe you are now in a position to find out—do they have complaints when they publish stories with 'functional references'? Does the circulation fall off if they print anything 'serious'?" (March 7, 1953, Vassar College Library). Her concerns came up again in a letter to Kit and Ilse Barker: "In some ways The New Yorker is not a bad writing school—in other ways of course deadly—" (Good Friday, April 3, 1953, Princeton University Library).

We are of course also hoping for more poems soon. It seems far too long since we've had any from you.

> Affectionately,
> Katharine

Dear Elizabeth:

Very likely this clipping will have reached you from some other source but I send it along just in case.

Pearl Kazin tells me that she heard from you recently and that you were finishing up Sable Island.[1] Wonderful! I trust that you got the author's proof of "Gwendolyn" and that we'll soon have it back. And of course I very much hope for more poems and stories. It's just been ages since we've had any poems of yours and we miss them badly. Did you give up the idea of fussing with "In the Village"? I still cling to the hope of publishing that story.

> Affectionately,
> Katharine

Samambaia
April 20, 1953

Dear Katharine:

I got back yesterday from a week's trip to see some old colonial towns—a wonderful trip, but rather exhausting. You can imagine what the roads are like, most of the time, when I tell you it took us 5½ hours to drive 60 kilometers. I wanted to see Congonhas and Ouro Prêto, two places famous for being the work of "Aleijadinho", the "Little Cripple"—solid baroque—18th century. He was the illegitimate child of a slave, and suffered from leprosy; and the stories are very beautiful—I'm hoping I'm going to be able to write a piece about him, although the material about him is poor and it would take an art historian to do him justice, I'm afraid. But I'm going to try.

Your letter with the proof was here and I am hastening to return it. I have written in my corrections with colored pencil. As you will see, I've agreed with most of them fairly completely, and thank you for the research on hymns—my hymn-books are here now, so maybe I won't make mistakes like that again! I've also written in my objections to, or explanations of, *your* (or

---

1 Bishop mentioned the Sable Island piece in her letter of February 10, 1953, to Kazin (Vassar College Library).

others') objections, on the yellow paper—I don't see how it could be much clearer now.

About two months ago I moved—moved my working hours, that is— into my new "studio" and I think I have been so overcome by the unfamiliar convenience and quiet and beauty of it all that I've just sat and admired and read poetry instead of working. However, I'm getting more used to it now and very soon you will receive: *Sable Island*; another story about the "Village" earlier in time & much more usable, I think; *"In the Village"* over again, with a great many changes, but not, I'm afraid, the ones you most want; two long poems I'm afraid you won't want; and a story I wrote unexpectedly last week that I think you will like called "The U.S. School of Writing" and that I'm going to start copying right now. There is also a Brazilian story that is getting longer & longer & too complicated I'm afraid,—and now I am wanting to start in on the prophets of Congonhas. (There are twelve standing in front of the church—I think I'll enclose a couple of poor postcards for you to see.)

Some time ago now I forgot to tell you how interested I was to read of Minnie's sleeping arrangements—I had a dog like her when I was small and it was very hard to keep her comfortable through winters in Nova Scotia— she would cry & my grandfather would get up over and over to tuck her in. We have one here now, too—and although Brasil is tropical, supposedly, it does get very cold and of course there are stone floors and no heat. She used to get up in bookcases until we had a high bed built for her. Then on my trip to N.Y. I bought her a sweater at Hammacher Schlemmer, which helps some in the winter—July & August—but right now she has pneumonia and we are awfully worried about her—

I also don't believe I told you that Marianne Moore wrote me how much she admired "Charlotte's Web."

I am now going to bore you, I'm afraid, by writing you two stories about children that I heard lately & that I find I can't help re-telling & perhaps you might like—

A neighboring family, *extremely* rich, nouveau riche—have a little girl— granddaughter of the fortune-founder—three years old. Of course she hears them speaking of money a great deal of the time. She asked how old she was and her mother told her she was three, and then she asked how old her mother was. Her mother said "Twenty-five," and the little girl looked pained and said, "Oh! That's too *expensive*."

Another little girl, about four or five this time, was sent into the living room to "entertain" a very old, imposing dowager caller, while her mother finished dressing. They looked at each other for some time in silence and finally the little girl said, "Do you like to fly kites?"

I am going to have some poems in a newspaper here—a literary supplement—(the poems in Portuguese-English)—I'm not quite sure which ones are going to be used yet but I think "The Prodigal" is one of them. You printed that a year or so ago—and maybe some more. Is it all right if I give "acknowledgements" to *The New Yorker*? I have done so in the note I've written for them, but I should like to make quite sure.

I hope you're all over your illness by now—and by now you must be, I'm sure,—the duplication of seasons here seeming to make time go even faster than usual.—I have settled for the very minimum of asthma, I think—cortisone really seems to have helped enormously—if I can just refrain from patting animals. I am saving my money for a trip but I think it will be to Europe first—perhaps New York on the way back if I save enough. You must be almost ready to go back to Maine now and I envy you that spring. Oh—some of the interior church walls, and niches, etc., were obviously done by stencil—I'm not sure when—but in Ouro Prêto I was reminded several times of your hall. They've spoiled the ones they've restored.

Have you heard anything of the Lucy Donnelly Fellowship this year? They wrote me about a recommendation and I am curious.

I do hope you are well—affectionately yours,
  Elizabeth

May 7, 1953

Dear Elizabeth:

Thank you for your proof of "Gwendolyn." The green pencil proved a little hard to read in some places but I think I have figured it out. I even got Pearl Kazin up to consult with me on one or two passages, and we think we have figured out what you intended. In a few places you misread our proof symbols and marks and in one place you thought we were saying that one "but" was a non-sequitur when we didn't mean that "but" at all. In any case, I'm sure it's all right now and I am grateful for your trouble.

I loved the pictures and the view from your bedroom looks to me as if I would always be looking at the view and not wanting to write. It must be heavenly. The two long poems you promise and the Brazilian story and the changes on "In the Village" and the Sable Island piece I look forward to more than I can say.

To answer your question about the Lucy Donnelly Fellowship: the news is that May Sarton got it. Was this the person you recommended?

In order to have your poems printed in a literary supplement there, you must get permission from the New Yorker business office, listing the title of the poems, unless they are poems that have appeared in book form. The reason for this is for the protection of your copyright. A mere acknowledgment to the New Yorker will not protect you or us, and the poems might thereafter be pirated. Therefore do write immediately to Mr. R. Hawley Truax, listing the poems you wish to use and he will tell you what the words are you must make them print. With every poem used must go the word "Copyrighted by the New Yorker Magazine" *plus* the copyright date. This is why we have to know the titles.

I was interested in the chilly dachshund. It would take a dachshund to be chilly in Brazil, I imagine, but they can be as cold as Greenland anywhere. Min's specially heated sleeping box works well in Maine. The one we had in New York she suddenly decided she didn't like in the middle of this winter (it was in a closet off a closet and she felt too lonely) so we now have a new arrangement. We have dedicated the chaise longue in our bedroom to Minnie. She likes the feathery pillow and she sleeps there day and night. At night we cover her with a sweater—not a dog's sweater, but a man's sweater, for her legs are too short for her to be able to wear a dog's sweater. She always gets her toenails caught in a dog's sweater and before morning is screaming in agony. After the sweater goes over her, a double blanket goes across the arms of the chaise longue with just a crack left to give her a little air. With this arrangement she is comfortable all night, and Andy and I can get some sleep. I do hope your dachshund got over her pneumonia.

Andy will be awfully pleased that Marianne Moore admires "Charlotte's Web."[1]

We are off for Maine next week but we shall be back in New York for the month of July—then back to Maine again at least until mid-October. Our Joe was married in March and all three of my children are going to be in Maine in three separate houses—none of them in our house.[2] This is much better for them and I approve of it, but we are beginning to rattle around in our big place. We are also beginning to feel closed in a little, much as we love children and grandchildren, so we think that the month in New York will be

1 *Charlotte's Web* (1952).
2 Joel White married Allene Messer.

good for all concerned. The real reason for it, though, is that Andy wishes to avoid the haying season and also wants to work on a book that he can only do in New York.

I cannot think of any amusing stories or interesting news to give you; in fact, I am depleted and haven't a thought in my brain, so please forgive a poor letter.

Affectionately,
Katharine

North Brooklin
May 16, 1953

Dear Elizabeth:

Here is a small additional check due you on "Gwendolyn." They always measure up the pieces when they get set in final form and sometimes the proof changes add length.

I am now in Maine and my last days at the office were so crowded and busy that I can't now remember whether I thanked you then for the proof of "Gwendolyn." Your changes were helpful. Sometimes the green crayon was hard to read and on a couple of spots I got Pearl Kazin to help me and see if she confirmed my reading of your handwriting. (She did.)

Maine has been cold and wet this week until today but the spring has the same purity as ever and it is more exciting than New York's headlong lushness. Andy has a whole new set of goslings to follow him about.

My very last day I was in the office I received a poem from Marianne Moore and we are buying it.[1] I am terribly pleased about it and the poem is wonderful. I was so pleased too that Bryn Mawr had the good sense to give her the M. Carey Thomas Prize and felt badly I could not attend the awarding. They asked me, but Andy is sick and I couldn't stay over for that occasion because he so much needed to get away.

Affectionately,
Katharine

1 "Tom Fool at Jamaica" (June 13, 1953).

Rio de Janeiro
May 24, 1953

Dear Katharine:

Thank you for your note and the check—I am beginning to think Gwendolyn is a most successful child-laborer! I received another note from you just when I arrived in Rio a couple of weeks ago, and I had meant to answer it, too, today. You haven't seen any of my promised work recently because, of all things, I succumbed *again* to cashew-fruit poisoning. That was what I got when I first came here, and that time I was sick with it for over a month—I'd taken two rather sour bites. Of course I never dreamed of eating it again, but someone else did, seated at the same table, and apparently I'm so susceptible to it that just the smell, or the oil from the skin in the air, is enough—anyway, the next day my head was swelled up just like a balloon, and my poor ears—they suffer worst—were just like ancient large red terra cotta casts of ears . . . So I rushed to Rio and the doctor and this time because I hadn't eaten any, I suppose, and with cortisone, the worst stage only lasted a week. It is really fantastic, but at least the dr. said now we know it *is* cashew fruit. The nuts don't bother me at all. It is strange to think there may be a root or a leaf lying in wait for any of us in Siberia or India that could kill us at "contact."—anyway, I rushed off and left almost everything I was working on up in the country, and I've only been able to work the last three days. I'm going back tomorrow, though, and I shall really be sending you several things in succession in the next few weeks. I am awfully annoyed with this interruption just when everything seemed [to be] going so well—I've written a little Brazilian sketch I must send although I don't think you'll be able to use it, but I am glad to have started writing about Brazil, anyway—

I'm so glad to hear about Marianne's poem—and the award at Bryn Mawr; I hadn't heard about that. I must write to her today.

I'm sorry about that green crayon of mine—next time I'll get some colored ink and try to be really legible—of course I always think I am, but I realize by now that it is an illusion.

No, it was [poet] Ruth Herschberger that Bryn Mawr wrote me about recommending, not May Sarton.

I envy you being in Maine now. It is still hot in Rio, although this is "autumn" and very heavy, although beautiful, and the scenery and planes and ships and bathers & umbrellas look extremely like a child's painting—an 8 year old boy's. Last night I saw from the apartment balcony—11 floors up—something that looked like burning embers right at the edge of the breakers—a spot that glowed and throbbed away, with the waves coming right up to it. Finally I decided it might be some strange phosphorescent jelly-fish and I couldn't stand it and went down in the elevator and crossed to the beach to find out. Someone had a dug a little hole, about 18 inches deep, and put a lighted candle at the bottom. I don't know whether it was just a trick, to see how high the tide was, or what—or maybe a "macumba", or voodoo—we see them around in the outskirts of Rio frequently, but usually there's a bottle of wine as well as the candle, and a dead chicken, and scraps of cloth, etc.

The Brazilian poet Manuel Bandeira is translating a poem of mine you printed, "A Cold Spring" to publish here. I shall write to Mr. Truax today about it. There are no copyright laws, of any sort, *here*, as far as I can find out . . . Bandeira is having quite a time with "dogwood" etc.—but was delighted with "cow-flop"—such words being very varied and current in Portuguese. His own poetry—he is *the* poet here, about 65, I think—is very charming, light, frequently very beautiful. I am hoping to return the compliment soon and try to do some of his which if successful would be perfect New Yorker material—and I know you have occasionally printed translations of poems.

I am sorry to say the sick dachshund died—but we have two other dogs and six mongrel puppies at the moment—and I have a young cat who caught a foot-long lizard and hid it, as a surprise for me, half-chewed, in the pocket of a jacket hanging on a chair . . .

It is wonderful to get back to work again and I hope you'll be able to use some of the material I am sending—I hope your husband is better and that Maine is as beautiful as ever—

Affectionately yours,
Elizabeth

June 3, 1953

Dear Elizabeth:

This can be only a hurried note, but I wanted to tell you how awfully sorry I am that you've been sick again from the virulent cashew. I do hope that the painful swelling has long since disappeared. Did I tell you that I had developed an allergy to fish—of all things, for a Maine coast resident! It makes me break out and itch. I am trying to develop an immunity to it by eating small amounts and taking anti-histamines. With Joe coming this week (with his bride) to spend another summer of lobstering, I just must be able to eat lobster. He and Allene will be in a little house two driveways away. He has had a new fishing boat built in Nova Scotia.

I was interested to hear about Bandeira, the Brazilian poet, and we look forward to your translations. Often translations don't work out well for us, but if they make good English poems, as yours are sure to, we sometimes do buy them. Mostly our problem with translated poems has been that the translation is not good poetry. Of course some we've had to pass up because of being too unsuited to the New Yorker. But if Bandeira-plus-Bishop proved to be right for us, that would be very exciting. We count on seeing the poems.

I can't close without telling you that we have a raccoon living in a hole high up in a cottonwood tree on our lawn. We spend our early evenings watching her emerge, wash, and descend the tree for her night's hunting. At 5 am, she is back again, resting exhausted on a limb, before she retires for the day. I say "she"—we don't know but are hoping for babies.

Only two goslings this year. Twelve of the eggs did not hatch. We think she got scared off the nest and let them cool. Andy said he thought of Marianne Moore and the poem she might have written—but that he could not—as he stood on our shore at low tide one cold, windy, wet April twilight, heaving the twelve eggs one by one—and all his hopes—out to sea, to be carried off by the tide.

I am sorry about the dachshund.

Affectionately,

Katharine

I can't wait for the new Brazilian sketch. *Please* don't fail to mail it off.

Oh, please don't use colored ink or any ink on proofs! A good, clear, soft pencil is best.

Samambaia
June 18, 1953

Dear Katharine:

I am up to my neck in typing and hope to send you some things by a trustworthy friend here for the week-end who will take them to the Post Office in Rio. It is such a job to mail things here—the stamps have no glue, or not enough, and you have to stand in line at a glue-machine, and get all covered with it—if you trust stamps to begin with; they say they are stolen in the PO often, and the mail just thrown away. (A newspaper editor friend of mine here found a cache of thousands of pieces of mail for the paper that that had happened to—imagine.) So if you don't trust stamps you have to go to the central office where there is a stamping machine—and in any case you have to go to one of the few post offices, since the mail boxes are never collected—haven't been for years. No one ever dreams of writing a letter within the country—they just vanish. Fortunately air-mail in and out is considerably better . . . If you *do* receive this, it is an earnest of more. I never used that expression before & I don't think I like it—I also rather doubt you'll be able to use this short poem ["The Shampoo"], but there are some more coming.

Heavens, I envy you a raccoon! Well—here I have a new troupe of about fifty parrots who have come to live near the studio—great big ones, just like the tame variety, bright green and yellow. They make an awful noise, but their communal life, what I can see of it, is fascinating—and they seem to be shrieking at each other in perfect Portuguese. We also have small monkeys that I hear but never see, although the gardener insists he chases them out of the garden all the time. But one neighbor has a really odd problem—opossums injuring his palm trees . . .

Poor Mr. Bandeira, the man who is doing the translations!—the last I heard he was exploring the Botanical gardens in Rio to see if he could find some Brasilian equivalent for Flowering Judas, or dogwood! Now I guess he's going to try some other poems—and I am having the same difficulties with him. In the poems that seem the simplest, and go into English so well—suddenly there is one word that can't possibly be conveyed in English . . . It is very good practice for my Portuguese, however.

I hope you are well and enjoying Maine and that you can eat lobsters. Let's see—pyrabenzamine, benadryl . . .

Affectionately yours,
Elizabeth

The New Yorker
July 2, 1953

Dear Elizabeth:

It is perfectly horrid to have to return a poem of yours, especially when we are so eager to have one to publish. But though the votes were mixed on "The Shampoo," the noes had it in the end. One reason against it for us is that this is a personal poem in which you do not quite seem to have described the occasion involved. At least it does not seem to us that you have conveyed it all; for instance, what was the dear friend too demanding and too voluble about?[1] But I guess the deciding factor was that this sort of small personal

---

1 The lines that correspond to White's comments in Bishop's papers run: "You are, dear friend, / demanding and too voluble;".

poem perhaps doesn't quite fit into the New Yorker. Thank you, anyway, for letting us read it and we look forward to the others you say are coming.

Andy and I are in New York for July. The raccoon took her three babies off about ten days ago. We miss them. Charlie Henderson tells me she may come back to the same hole another year.

I sympathize with you and Mr. Bandeira on the Portuguese-English translations.

Now that "Gwendolyn" has been published, a great many people on the staff have mentioned how much they like it. We do long for more stories as well as poems.

Affectionately,

Katharine

July 18, 1953

Dear Katharine:

Here is "In the Village" again. I let it rest for six months then re-did it, and I really think that now it as clear as such a piece of what I'm afraid is "poetic-prose" could ever be . . . I think most of your objections were justified and that I've improved it a lot—but whether it will satisfy the New Yorker now remains to be seen . . .

There is only one illogical change of tense now, on page 3—"The child vanishes"—but I don't think it's too confusing.

The conversation is paragraphed and attributed more conventionally. I *have* kept the frequent paragraphing where it was done for rhythmic effect, though. And the same is true of the punctuation—it is quite conventional I think, except for a few commas left out for effect—and I am not absolutely bound to them. Of course there are probably little inaccuracies. For example, I have no way of finding out whether it's *Moir's* or *Moirs'* chocolates. (If I were in Rio I suppose I could call the Canadian Embassy!) And the little mistakes I can't seem to help making,—but they are *not* for effect. I hope you can use it since I had much rather see it in the New Yorker than a "little" magazine.[1]

Several New Yorkers came in a bunch last week, and I was delighted to see Miss Moore's "Tom Fool." It's a wonderful piece of work—she'd sent

1 With a dash of comic indignation, but indignation nonetheless, Bishop moaned to the Barkers: "I'm so sick of re-typing my best story—I gave up after long correspondence with the N Yer last January. Now I've re-done it a little, but will not concede another comma for clarity's sake [. . .] But one tires of typing even a masterpiece I find—" July 15, 1953, Princeton University Library).

me a copy some time ago—and I hope people like it. I talked about it to some Brazilian subscriber-friends of mine, and backed it up with clippings from the N.Y. Times about the races, and they grew enthusiastic very rapidly. "Gwendolyn" also came, and along with it a letter from Robert Lowell saying he liked my "dirty girl," and that I should publish a book of stories. I have ten, I think—when I have a dozen I guess I'll try.

I got "The Shampoo" back. I somehow thought you'd like that one![1]

It is hard to think of you in hot New York, while here I sit wearing my Abercrombie & Fitch woolen underwear and feeding the fireplace. I hope you are well. I don't see how you can bear to stay away from Maine.

Affectionately yours,
Elizabeth

July 29, 1953

Dear Elizabeth:

I am writing this letter just as I depart for Maine and for four weeks of vacation, and I am so happy to be able to tell you before I leave that the answer is yes on "In the Village." I won't even be here to send you the check but it will follow shortly. The editing of the story and any questions that may come up on it in the opinion sheets will probably have to wait until September when I return to work (though not yet to the city). In any case, I can tell you now that all of us who have read the new version are delighted by the way you have clarified it, and think it is a truly wonderful piece of writing. I am sure that any queries we have will be fairly minor ones. This purchase of this particular story has made me happier than anything that's happened to me as an editor for months and I'm ever so grateful to you for your patience in doing the two, long, hard revisions on this manuscript.

A book of your short stories should *certainly* be brought out. That will be something to look forward to.

Love, haste,
Katharine

1 *The New Republic* published the poem in its July 11, 1955, issue.

Rio de Janeiro
August 12, 1953

Dear Katharine:

I'm really awfully glad The New Yorker has decided to take "In the Village", and thank you so much for your nice note about it—it's very encouraging. I have been very slow in getting started, but now I should really like to go on & try to write some *good* stories.

Then today when I arrived in Rio for a couple of days' fittings, I was very pleased to receive the check. I also found a letter here from the Aunt Mary of "Gwendolyn," saying she had liked the story and how she "hadn't thought of that poor child in years," etc. and "mother used to say," etc., verifying all my recollections—so right now I am feeling that sometimes being a writer has its satisfactions.

I'll be mailing some things next week. This is just to thank you for your interest & help—

Affectionately,
Elizabeth

North Brooklin
September 24, 1953

Dear Elizabeth:

I enclose a preliminary—not your author's proof, which will come later—of "In the Village." In it I want to ask your permission for the unusually small amount of editing the piece seemed to us to need and to ask your help on a very few wordings that aren't quite clear or spots that bother us for some reason. Near the end, there is the all important matter of the pronoun "she," for we feel that since "She" is the main figure (except for the child), it's vital that when "she" refers to the mother, the reader should know it at once.

We have kept your paragraphing almost entirely, but there are a very few places where a change has been made, for clarity or sense. I haven't tried to explain the reasons for these changes in most cases, hoping you will see them without explanation, and speak up if you disapprove.

On the whole, the story is so beautifully written that almost no editing was needed. But we thought you would want us to point out where genuine ambiguities or solecisms occurred.

If you could hurry this proof back to me, by air mail, it would be a great accommodation, for this is an extra step before the proof is read in the regular routine. This proof is just a substitute for talking it over with you. How I wish we could do that! I might even be able to convince you to give way on the lacy, watery, green cow flops!

I feel that your ennui on my queries and your annoyance with my small naggings on this story must by now be almost intolerable to you but because this is so outstanding a piece of writing, I must persist, even if you do hate me for it. We don't want a single tiny thing to mar its perfection. And of course, all our small changes of wording are tentative ones for you to make in your own way if you don't like ours.

Maine is at its most wonderful. We are deep in sheep at the moment, selling our pure-bred Suffolk lambs, showing them at fairs, and awaiting the arrival of a new ram for the flock—a fellow named Dynamite. Joe is storing his last traps today, and in two days he and his wife Allene must reluctantly head for Boston and MIT. It will be the last year there for Joe, so it may be his last lobstering for many years, since when he graduates, he will presumably be taken by the Navy—if not, by the Army. He is hopefully storing his new Nova Scotia power boat, though, in case he may have a few months next summer that he has to wait around to be taken into the service.[1] Allene has come to love it here as much as he does and seems to fit into the two worlds here perfectly.

Hoping to get this proof right back again, I am,

Affectionately,

Katharine

Samambaia
September 30, 1953

Dear Katharine:

The proof came last night (in a bundle along with books from Brentano's on top of a little negro boy's head, all the way up the mountain) and I think I am going to be able to send it back to Rio tomorrow, or the day after, which is pretty good for my messenger service here.

I was pleased to see I'd already made some of the same changes myself—besides a few more that you'll notice. The tough spot is the fire-scene but I think if you re-read it, without stopping, now, you will find it is clear at last;

---

1 Joel White received a naval architecture degree from the Massachusetts Institute of Technology. He was working at Newport News Shipbuilding & Drydock when he was drafted into the army.

the comings and goings, the 2 aunts, and the "shes." I hope so, anyway. I'll go over it a few times more and if I think of any way of improving it more I'll send it along.[1]

I think you are quite right about the "smoking" & "steaming" manure—that was decidedly unoriginal. Maybe without the adjective your editors won't object so much to Nelly's behaviour. I've had four or five "literary" friends here read it, asked them to tell me frankly, etc., etc.,—and nobody objected—and Brazilians are rather old-fashioned about their stories, you know. (On the other hand, the Portuguese language is noted for its frankness, so maybe that wasn't a good test after all!) When I see it in author's proof maybe I'll be able to part with it—but it does seem to me an essential part of any child's taking any cow to any pasture, and certainly not "repulsive"! City folks![2] Actually, my ideal in this *genre* is something like Dylan Thomas's story *"Peaches"*—you probably know it.[3] I'm afraid the New Yorker wouldn't have published it, either—In the other stories of this set

1 There are a couple of differences between Bishop's July submission and the version that ran in the magazine. Bishop sent in these lines from the fire scene as:

> "She's calling for you, mother." My other aunt.
>   "I'll go, mother."
>   "Light that other lamp, girl."
>   "No, *I'll* go." (*The New Yorker* Records).

It ran as:

> "*She's* calling for you, Mother." My older Aunt. "I'll go."
>   "No, *I'll* go." My younger aunt.
>   "Light that other lamp, girl."

When printed in *The Collected Prose*, the period after "older aunt" was changed to a colon (269).

Another change to the fire scene occurs a few paragraphs later. "She comes in and gets in bed with me" ran as: "Then my younger aunt comes into my room and gets in bed with me" (269).

2 Bishop submitted the passage as:

> Nelly, oblivious to herself, makes cow-flops.
>   Smack. Smack. Smack. Smack.
>   It is fascinating. I cannot take my eyes off her. I step around them: fine dark green, steaming, lacy and watery at the edges.

It ran as:

> Nelly, oblivious, makes cow flops. Smack. Smack. Smack. Smack.
>   It is fascinating. I cannot take my eyes off her. Then I step around them: fine dark-green and lacy and watery at the edges. (263)

3 *Portrait of the Artist as a Young Dog* (1940).

I'm working on I'd like to get even more authentic atmosphere—Nova Scotia's clearness and bareness being rather different to Wales, naturally. But "Peaches" is a magnificent little story that makes mine look pale and polite, I'm afraid.

Sometime in the next month or so you will receive a small present from me, via an architect friend of mine, Henrique Mindlin, who is doing the new Brazilian building in N.Y. It isn't much of a present—but easy to send—an old *bombilha*, the tube that maté is sucked though. I suppose you could use it for sipping iced-tea—but I find them useful for stirring small batches of Martinis, too. Maté, I think, is awfully good—and supposedly packed with vitamins, salts, etc.—but impractical to send.

It makes me homesick for the cold hard North to hear about Maine. And *Dynamite!* Well—here we have a little boy helping the gardener, who, my friend Lota remarked, has a "good old Portuguese name." It proves to be *Magellan*, and that really gave me a start. Such things console me for the things I miss.

I suppose it is never possible to skip the author's proof, is it—of course I'd be delighted to see the story soon, and it seems in pretty good shape now, as far as I can see. But it is probably illegal.

I must take this down now to see if I can persuade a neighbor to mail it for me—everyone avoids trips to the Rio P.O. whenever possible, of course.

I hope my changes meet with your approval—

Affectionately yours,

Elizabeth

October 30, 1953

Dear Elizabeth:

These cost of living adjustment checks for contributors always manage to surprise me when they come along, even though I of course know they will be turning up regular as clockwork, so I hope this check will be a pleasant surprise to you, too.

In a few days, I hope, I'll be sending you an author's proof of "In the Village." It ought to have been ready to send you before now but something seems to have held it up. We felt you *should* get a second proof on this story, since the wording is, from your point of view, as precise as a poem. From ours, too, of course but some slight change might seem an improvement to us and not to you.

I do hope a new story will be coming along soon, so that I'll have another check to send you at the end of the quarter! We'll be back in New York in four days.

Love,

Katharine

Dear Elizabeth:

Mr. Mindlin sent your present over to the New Yorker, and I am delighted with it. It is a charming little thing, and Andy and I will love using it for stirring our Martinis. I don't know that I'll ever suck anything through it, not having any maté easily at hand, but I shall always take pleasure in thinking that you sent it from Brazil and in admiring its interesting shape and its old silver engraving. Thank you ever so much for thinking of me and for going to all this bother.

I wanted to send you some small thing for Christmas, but Pearl Kazin tells me what awful times there are with things going through the Brazil customs. She thought only a book would get through without your having to pay a large duty, or else that you would never receive the package at all. I'm trying a small book anyway and hope that you may be interested to read Dylan Thomas' "The Doctor and the Devils" [as] odd a document as it appears to be.[1] (I have not had time to read it—only glance at it.) His death was a shock to everyone and a terrible loss to poetry. It is really appalling. The tales of the gathering at the hospital and all that went on there have probably by now been told you by an eyewitness. Was he a dear friend of yours? If he was, I send you my sympathy.

I had wanted also to send you for Christmas a silly gift of a box of the lovely New Yorker soft pencils most writers like so much and a box of our yellow copy paper but Pearl Kazin says they would not go through to you by mail. I therefore wrote and asked Mr. Mindlin (stupidly, I now see) if he would have space to carry them to you. But rereading your letter, I see he is to build a building here, so of course he won't be going back for a long time. I fear he thought I was very impertinent even to ask this.

Merry Christmas to you and much love,

Katharine

---

1 *The Doctor and the Devils* (1953).

Dear Elizabeth:

We have decided to use "In the Village" without sending you an author's proof and to accept the working proof version you corrected and okayed in place of your regular author's proof. This means that I have simply canceled out all the millions of conventional punctuation and style-rule and clarity queries. The piece will run just as you saw it in that varitype proof with, of course, the corrections you made there. I hope this is satisfactory to you. We would never have done it, of course, if you had not had a chance to make your changes and see our editing on that working proof. Our argument about not getting it further corrected in the normal way was that the story was really like a poem and therefore had every right to be unconventional in small matters of punctuation, usage, repetitions etc. And of course you had already taken care of all our larger problems. I am really pleased about this because it shows that the New Yorker can, for once, be flexible, but it does not mean, I'm afraid, that we would do the same thing on all your manuscripts. I think the net result is that "In the Village" should seem like a breath of fresh air in the magazine. It will be published in the issue of December 19. There were two or three minute changes we all felt needed to be made—I think entirely in punctuation, not in wording—but these were ones I was sure you would approve of, and they were no more than we would normally make at the last moment without consulting the author if they had come up on the page proof just before going to press. Anyway, for better or for worse, the story will have come out by the time you get this letter, and I do hope it satisfies you.

The very long time it takes for mail to get back and forth was what finally decided us, and we wanted and needed to use the story now.

The letter I wrote to Mr. Mindlin has come back, thank Heaven, without being delivered. So he never did receive my foolish request. Apparently he is not at the hotel Pearl Kazin told me he was living in.

Affectionately,
    Katharine

November 25, 1953

Dear Elizabeth:

You'll be tired of letters from me. This one is just a cry of hope (or despair): Haven't you a poem—or poems to send us? It is *so* long since we've had one and we need a poem of yours badly. I forgot to speak of it in my last letter.

Love,

Katharine[1]

Rio de Janeiro
November 28, 1953

Dear Katharine:

I had a letter all ready to mail to you when two from you arrived, so I am hastening to re-write it somewhat. In it I thanked you for the last check—that kind is particularly nice to get, perhaps because you feel you didn't earn it.—

I'd be extremely pleased to have "The Doctor & the Devils." Books come like ordinary mail by boat, and usually arrive in three to four weeks from N.Y. You don't have to put a customs declaration on them, just LIVROS. Because of new regulations about importing, things that have to go through the customs are more difficult. The soft pencils I'd adore. I don't write *literature* in pencil but they are so useful for everything else and I've never found any soft ones here. The reason you couldn't reach Henrique Mindlin is because he's back here now—but thank you very much for trying. He'll be going and coming while the building is going on. But sometime in the next month or so if you could give some pencils to Pearl Kazin I'd be very grateful—she'll be sending me some things via the Dept. of Foreign Affairs then.

I wish the bombilha were older & more beautiful. I may run across some someday—and send one to stir Manhattans—

Yes, I received the tragic news about Dylan Thomas—first, unfortunately, through "Time" magazine, then letters.[2] I knew him briefly when I was in Washington and I liked him very much. I still find it hard to believe.

I'm glad you think you can use "In the Village" without further proofs. When I'm in Rio I get mail often in 3 or 4 days from New York, and can get it back again that quickly, but when I am up in the country I usually

1 "Mrs. W wrote me almost a cri du coeur for some poems, particularly—I'll be sending some but only one is even barely possible—" (Bishop to Kazin, December 7, 1953, Vassar College Library).

2 Thomas's death on November 9 in New York City was announced in the November 16 issue of *Time*. Bishop probably learned more about his death from Kazin, who was his former mistress and had visited him in St. Vincent's Hospital the night before he died.

only get my mail and can send it once a week and that slows things up. I'm a little nervous about that story now and hope you will continue to like it in print.

And could I ask you—or maybe you could tell me whom I should write about things like this because I hate to keep bothering you with my business requests—I'd like to have a few extra copies of the Dec. 19th issue to give away here; it seems to be the thing to do. I see stacks of *New Yorker*s on the newsstands in Rio, but again, I might not happen to be there when it was for sale and might miss it. So I'm sending a check for $1.50 for six copies, plus postage.

I have been almost useless for about a month with another asthma-bronchitis cycle, although I have been improving a lot—but now I am back at work again. I'll be sending you both a couple of stories and some poems very shortly. I want particularly to get them off soon because in March some-time, if all goes as planned, I'm going to Europe for nine months or a year's stay. Not that I expect to stop writing while I'm away!

I hope you'll be able to use the enclosed reply to the Hamilton Basso piece.[1] I had to write it. I have no idea what the circulation of *The New Yorker* is here, although as I said, I've seen stacks in Rio—but several of my immediate friends take it, and everyone is rather put out by that piece—although not of course, as violently as I am! They just tend to say—"Well—now you see what we told you is true—Americans in foreign countries see nothing but the things that compare unfavorably with the U.S.A." I suppose about 85% of his facts are correct and naturally everyone feels the same way about them. (His little facts that aren't correct probably stand out only in Brazil, but they seem to be evidence that he didn't pay much attention to his surroundings, or check much on his details.) But the tone is so supercilious, Katharine! The mistakes do bother me because so many people have said to me that they wished they could afford a magazine as accurate and beautifully edited here, etc. But also *The New Yorker* usually comes out for tolerance, international understanding, an educated, sensitive way of looking at things—cosmopolitanism in its best sense. Mr. Basso sounds as if he were merely echoing the remarks and provincialisms of some of my compatriots here I've run into—some of the business people and the U.S. Army commission—I happened to know one or two in the United States before they came here, too,—the kind that are responsible for our present low credit in foreign countries.

1 "Letter from Rio de Janeiro" (October 17, 1953).

But the point really is that Brazilians who see the New Yorker are naturally the educated and more intelligent ones, and they are the very people who are the *only* pro-American faction in the country today. I feel that if the New Yorker had realized that fact it might not have published that piece—at least not in the style in which it is written at present.

Until fifteen or even ten years ago the culture of Brazil was open only towards Europe, France particularly. No one dreamed of travelling to the U.S. except once in a while to study engineering,—with a few exceptions. During and since the war things have changed quite a lot, but even those rich Brazilians who go to New York several times, and buy up all the "gadgets" they can, etc., feel they have to say something about "materialism." One of my neighbors and really good friends here is a young newspaper editor, Carlos Lacerda. He just came back from receiving the Maria Moors Cabot Award at Columbia. He is one of the anti-Vargas editors, and one of the few who has dared to be sensibly and courageously pro-American in his policies all along. He may even get to be the president-after-next if he isn't shot first (he's always being shot at, called a "Yankee lover," etc.). I am seeing him tonight and I am just hoping he won't want to talk about that piece with me, but he probably will—and in spite of his pro-American policies, I suspect that underneath he has probably always thought that he really liked me because I was an American-who-had-lived-in-Paris . . . & this will just confirm it.

I'm afraid you may think I'm making too much of this—and of course I know it has *nothing* to do with *you!*—but living in a foreign country is not always easy for an American these days (although they are a very polite people, as Mr. B suggests) and just by luck,—not by any natural leanings towards politics and diplomacy!—I honestly happen to be in a fairly good position to know what I'm talking about.

Did Mr. B talk to *any* intelligent Brazilians—or listen to what they are saying? He obviously has no eye for a building at all—and there is not the slightest trace of Frank Lloyd Wright here, to be carping. Wasn't he inside *one* old home in Rio?—And he never mentions the University, which, fantastic as it is for a country as poor as Brazil, is really architecturally and in many other ways, the most amazing thing going on in any country right now, that I know of. (Nothing like the one in Mexico, either!) If it were a part of a series, the mechanical breakdowns should all certainly be discussed—but it doesn't seem to be—and oh dear, it is that *tone*—Please don't mind my telling you what I think—I feel so sorry about it.

I hope you're quite well. I'd hoped to be getting to New York next year but now I'll have to postpone it another year I guess—

Affectionately (if irritably) yours,

Elizabeth

Samambaia

December 5, 1953

Dear Katharine:

I got your note—needless to say very flattering, last night, and I am hastening to answer it to say again what I said in my last letter—that I'm really getting a bunch of things ready to send before I go away. The letter I wrote you was the last I've done till now, though, since the asthma got worse and worse and I took to my bed for a week. I've now started cortisone again—with mingled pleasure and apprehension because it does make you feel too good to be true for a while but you're never quite sure what will happen next—and this afternoon I managed to get up to my studio again for the first time.

In the letter I wrote you about "Rio"—after I'd mailed it I looked at the carbon I had strangely thought to make, and I realize that in the last paragraph there is a bad spot. It should say: "But Mr. B's *'Letter'* speaks unfortunately in accents identical to those of some other resident Americans I have talked with. They are those Americans whose work keeps them here . . . etc."

I still have no idea whether what I wrote will be usable or worthwhile writing, but I hope so—one can't attack a "tone" certainly, at least not in a weekly magazine—but I thought I could point out enough errors of fact to make it all seem slightly dubious and certainly—well—"snotty" is the only word I can think of. Thank goodness he didn't hear the worst about the milk-situation, too—although how he missed it I can't imagine. I find it more shocking than any of the other things he talks about. *But*—if you stay here any length of time at all you soon begin to realize that it is not easy to change one thing by legislation—one or two or three—so many other things have to be changed first. And the country is suffering now from 14—then plus 3 more—years of Vargas. Perhaps sometime in the future when I get back here I'll be able to write a piece myself—for once in my life I think I know a good deal more about it than a journalist always seems to—

But I shall get some poems to you soon and one at least I think you will like and find amusing. A batch of magazines came last night, too, and I read

Dwight Macdonald's piece about the new Bible with pleasure—he's really awfully good—[1]

With all best wishes for the holidays—

Love,

Elizabeth

Have you struggled with children's books this year?

And here is the check for the 6 copies that I forgot to enclose last time—

December 10, 1953

Dear Elizabeth:

I passed your letter in reply to the Basso piece right to Bill Shawn. He has asked me to write you that to his regret we cannot publish it. For one thing, we could not publish it until the issue of January 9 and this is really too great a gap—October 17 to January 9—since we cannot expect our readers to remember the Basso Letter after so many weeks. The reason we cannot drop it right into an issue is that we are tied up completely these next weeks with pre-Christmas and Christmas material, and then follow the two smallest issues of the year with no space left that is not already pre-empted by "must go" material.

Bill is very sorry indeed about Basso's misstatements of fact—the number of old churches still standing in Rio and the business of the *macumba* etc.— but he does think that the Letter was never intended to be read as a serious piece on Rio but was instead a light-hearted passing visitor's account of his impressions of the city and a light recording of things he was told about it during his visit.[2] Bill feels that our checking department was remiss in not

<hr>

1 "The Bible in Modern Undress" (November 14, 1953).

2 Bishop sent a copy of the letter to Pearl Kazin, and in it she quotes a passage from Basso. "Rio has leveled just about every last evidence of its past as a Portuguese colony. If it weren't for a couple of old churches and a few other isolated remnants . . . it would be hard to realize that Rio has any past much older than Le Corbusier and Frank Lloyd Wright." To which Bishop said, " *The New World Guides to the Latin American Republics,* 'Duell Sloan & Pearce, N.Y., Vol. III, says that there are over 200 churches in Rio. Very few of them have been built since the 18th cent. The same book lists 15 as being of 'particular interest,' dating from the 16th to 18th cents. If space permitted, I could give a long list of colonial buildings still unleveled and in use." Concerning macumba, she wrote, "Mr. B gives a brief account of *macumba,* an African-derived form of worship akin to the Haitian *vodun,* and implies that it is very much in evidence & that offerings to its gods are a common sight in Rio. He saw one on the beach on his 1st morning here. In my 2 yrs stay, in the course of which I have become moderately familiar with Rio by day and after dark, I have seen 2 of these offerings, & I may have been mistaken about one of them. Brazilians who have lived here all their lives have sometimes seen only a few, and their opinion is that in the city of Rio—I am not speaking about other parts of Brazil—*macumba* is declining. And to anyone who has seen them both, regardless of their

catching the errors but he feels strongly that we have to be able to publish the personal impressions of correspondents from foreign places, even if they may represent not the best possible judgement about a country or a city. Your reply did not fit exactly under our two heads for such letters since it was neither quite a "Department of Amplification," or wholly a "Department of Correction." But that is really neither here nor there; the point is there is no space.

We are all of us of course disturbed that the Letter upset you. I can well understand why it did, and if the tone sounded supercilious that is *really* bad. I'm sure it was not meant to be.

Yours in haste, and with love,

Katharine

January 7, 1954

Dear Elizabeth:

I enclose a fan letter, which I for one particularly like because it came from the president of a ball-bearing roller pin company. *All* the readers I've encountered who have anything like a literary background speak of the beauty of your story but it's nice to hear from manufacturers too! Brendan Gill sent up an excerpt from a letter he had from Bill Cole, a bright young man at Knopf: "I'd like to tell somebody at The New Yorker that I think Elizabeth Bishop's story a few weeks ago is the best story I've ever read in the magazine." Andy thinks the story is extraordinary—"like a poem." Mary Lou Aswell spoke to me about it.[1] I know you must have heard from dozens of people direct. Pearl Kazin tells me all her friends have spoken of it and of course she must have written you about this. I hope it will make you feel that all the bother of all those letters and proofs back and forth was worthwhile. I know that, for me, to help get that story into the magazine was the thing that gave me the most satisfaction in the year 1953.[2]

It would start '54 wonderfully for me if a new one from you should arrive

---

respective aesthetic merits, the statement that 'next to the carnival' the *macumba* celebration of the Rainha de Aguas 'is the chief spectacle of the city,' is simply untrue" (1953, Vassar College Library).

1 Aswell was a fiction editor at *Harper's Bazaar*.

2 Bishop had been upset over the changes that were made to the story. In the middle of writing to May Swenson, she got up from her typewriter and walked away: "I may notice some other little changes but just now I don't think I can bear to go over it again and I dislike it, rather. Later—now I see some more of their little changes, I think, so tonight I'll go over it carefully and write the changes on a separate sheet. They decided to print it without final proofs—I was willing—but sometimes what they think is 'clarity' is just plain redundancy from my pt. of view . . ." (December 26, 1953, Washington University Library). Changes she mentioned included making "That pure note;

soon. I'm writing this in bed where I've been stewing all week with a singularly virulent bout of intestinal flu, so I need cheering up! I also look forward to the poems. When is the book to be published?

Affectionately,
Katharine

São Paulo
January 27, 1954

Dear Katharine:

I have written to you twice, & once my letter got forgotten & both times they were immediately out-dated. So I'm sending you just this card from São Paulo to tell you that I know I owe you a good many replies, business & social, & thanks for the Dylan Thomas book & several checks, by now, as well.

I'm here for a week to see the *Bienal*—over *3000* works of art, so rather exhausting, but wonderful at the same time. Going home tomorrow & straight back to the typewriter, I trust.

I've had very nice fan mail for "In the V"—some forwarded by you—of course I think I like the Ball-Bearing Rolling Pin Man the best of all! & several Nova Scotians from various parts of the globe, *all* of whom used to take the cow to pasture, apparently. I did mail the contract some time ago & the extra $200 was most welcome. Also the extra Cola check. But I shall write again from home—

Love,
Elizabeth

Samambaia
February 5, 1954

Dear Katharine:

I sent you a note from São Paulo a week ago, but I am a little dubious about the branch post-office I found there, the glue-pot, the change in stamps, etc.—and I received a note from you last night, too, so I shall write you another one just to be on the safe side. I went down to São Paulo for

---

pure & angelic." into "The pure note: pure and angelic." (26) and making the five-cent piece Miss Gurney gives her into a ten-cent piece (28). Bishop continued to stew about their changes for several weeks, but as news came in of the story's success, her mood began to lift.

about a week to see the Bienal there—over 4000 works of art or some equally crazy number, and the city was sizzling, so although it was worth it, it was rather exhausting.

I think I did thank you for the Dylan Thomas book—an awfully good job to have been done to order, I guess; and I was very glad to see it. In the two letters I wrote but that did not get mailed I also think I mentioned my Basso letter—I was sorry, of course, that you couldn't use it, but also somewhat relieved—I think I may have made a few mistakes, too. My chief complaint, and I think, a justified one, was that he was supercilious—and living in a foreign country one loathes seeing Americans make themselves *more* disliked—we are being such fools here already, with our diplomacy, etc. Well, Socrates, or HL Mencken or somebody says that no intelligent man is proud of his government, and it works both ways here, certainly.

Thank you for forwarding the "fan" letters—I have had some awfully nice ones. One curious thing—Robert Lowell wrote me the story was like a "great ruminating Dutch landscape"—he's been living in Holland recently—and a Dutch woman here, "literary," but whom I have never met, wrote me a highly emotional letter about how it reminded her of home and sent me a large Dutch gingerbread! One letter is really so good that I think I shall enclose it for you to see—the man is really appreciative, and it is nice, because he *knows*, apparently—much more than I do!

I thought the Eudora Welty story was wonderful—perhaps not quite as wonderful as "Why I Live at the P.O."—but heavens, she has a magnificent gift of gab![1] Now that is a *real* story-teller . . .

However, even if I don't consider myself as such, I'll be sending you one by next week's mail, and probably another a week after and some poems. I have lots of work under weigh. After I wrote you that I was leaving for Italy in March, I think, the cruzeiro here took a dreadful plunge—a real inflation, and awful to witness. The friend I am going with naturally doesn't know quite what to do and so we have postponed things for about a month, at least, to see what's going to happen. It will give me a chance to finish some more work, I hope. I'm hoping to get off in about two months now, though. Thank you again Katharine for the gift, the forwarding—and, I forgot—the copies of *The New Yorker*, airmail—that was very kind, and the impressive plaster of stamps was handed right over to a little boy who was calling on me at the time.—I hope you are well. I saw a very nice picture of Mr. White on the

1 Welty's most recent story was "The Ponder Heart" (December 5, 1953).

cover of the Times Book Review that also came last night but I haven't had a chance to read what it says yet.[1]

Affectionately yours,
Elizabeth

"In the V" is being read to a women's club in Toronto!

February 5, 1954

Dear Howard:

My mail arrived from Rio last night and in it was "The Toy Fair" (a lovely title) and I want to write to thank you immediately.[2] First of all—nothing whatever to do with the book—because it is the first new book of poetry I've seen in ages; and second because you'd inscribed it—the first "personalized" anything I've seen in a year or so—in English, at least. It gave me a very pleasant sensation of actually being a live American poet, myself, with some friends who haven't forgotten me. So I went to bed and read it through a couple of times, and have just read it through again this morning.

It would be rather condescending of me, I guess, to hand you out some ordinary flat compliments—but I do want to tell you one or two of the thoughts I had about the poems while I was reading them, and I hope you won't mind—I wish you were here for a small conversation and so I could just let them drop, without sounding so self-appointedly ex cathedra—I haven't got your first book here—it got lost, along with about 200 other books, mostly newer acquisitions, when I moved here—I think the NY warehouse lost them. But as I remember it, it seems to me this is really much better, isn't it?—in originality, range, everything. I agree with what Richard Wilbur says on the jacket . . .[3] I like you best of all, however, when you are being your gloomiest and most Tennysonian. Like in "Adolescent's Song" and "Burning Love Letters." When my book came out, Louise Bogan and a couple of other reviewers said oh, she should let herself be more *emotional* and write more *lyrics*, etc., and it made me rather mad—I thought they just

1 "The Wonder and Wackiness of Man," review of *The Second Tree from the Corner* by Irwin Edman (January 17, 1954).
2 *The Toy Fair* (1954).
3 "Howard Moss is both poet and musician, as his readers will discover in the fine poem 'Venice,' and even more startlingly elsewhere. In a time when lyric and song have become estranged, it is exciting to find a poet doing subtle things with syncopation and duration."

had in mind some conventional idea of the lady-poet. And anyway, one can't write pure lyrics all the time, etc. And *anyway*, the one or two I have written aren't as good as yours. But now I think I know what they did mean, possibly, and it doesn't necessarily have anything to do with being a lady-poet, either. I do think that the "Timothy, Timothy" poem ["Adolescent's Song"] is lovely and really, to me, the most moving in the book, and I wish you could sound that sad, hopeless note again—But it *is* maddening to be expected to repeat.

"Winter's End" is awfully good, and finished, etc.—but I really like you best when you give these hopeless, musical sighs . . .

Phrases:—on page 21 I like very much "cloud's applause"—clapping in the distance sounds exactly like that. "The Wind is Round" is a wonderful title—heavens, I wish I had a gift for titles. You know, I have that Klee reproduction, too, packed up here, now—and I suspect—this is mean of me—the green stuff is dill, which goes with fish—but maybe there is some parsley, too—I hope so, for the sake of your alliteration, and I haven't looked at it for some time. Page 43—"the true north of the eye"—and I like that poem ["The Lie"], very much, too. Page 52 "We cried for color as the boat went over" 55—"warrior from neighbor" 63—"moonlight that *erases*"—that gives me the proper frisson—"Venice" makes me want to go there immediately, and the last two lines are superb . . . I guess that's enough of my remarks and I'm not a critic, anyway—(I've just got the last Kenyon, PR, Hudson, etc., and decided that all US colleges must be teaching "Uncreative Criticism" now.)[1]

I wish you good luck with the book—I think you must have enjoyed your travels, too. I'm hoping to get to Europe this spring, but I'm not sure. I like it here very much, actually—once in a while I feel a little lost for some conversation, and gossip, in English. I hope you're well, Howard, and working hard—and thank you again for the book; I am awfully pleased to have it—

Love,
Elizabeth

February 26, 1954

Dear Elizabeth:

The attached bit from a letter to me from Morris Bishop was a suggestion

1 On page twenty-one, Bishop is referring to "Storm." The Paul Klee poems are "Around the Fish 1 & 2." The poem on page fifty-two is "Mariner's Song," on fifty-five is "Antennae," and on sixty-three is "Animal Hospital."

for a Talk story. I wrote Morris that the subject was reserved for you for a Reporter-At-Large, and I thought I'd send this note of his along as a reference for you for your piece, in case it happens to be of any interest to you. I own Bishop's life of Champlain but the volume is in Maine so I can't look up his Appendix C to see if it has anything particularly good in it on Sable Island, but if you should want to see it, I could get the book out of the Public Library here and have the appendix copied for you.[1] Let me know.

At this point in this letter, which I am writing in bed at home to be later typed out—I have the *mumps!*—it occurred to me to call Shawn to ask if was still reserving Sable Island for you after all this time. He said that this question of mine was a curious coincidence, for a piece on Sable had come in out of the blue a short while ago. It was no good but if it had been, he said, he would probably have figured you had abandoned your idea of the Reporter-At-Large since he had not heard from you in so long. So he wanted me to ask you about it. He is still eager to have you do it if you are still interested and said your description of the piece you had planned had sounded really good, etc., etc. So what about it, Elizabeth? Why not really finish it up? I know you once had the manuscript almost done, and your descriptions after your return from Sable are something I've never forgotten. So I hate to see you waste that material. What shall I tell Shawn? Have you lost interest in that piece? I do hope not. Such a piece is, of course, not really timely, but there is always the chance that *Holiday* would send someone there and take the cream off the subject, or there's a chance that someone else might do it for us, unsolicited. A word from you that you really will finish up your manuscript would reserve the theme for you again for a while longer. If you don't think you have enough to make a Reporter-At-Large, you could always make it into a shorter Footloose Correspondents piece. Anyway, we'd appreciate a word from you about your plans on this Sable Island story.

Naturally I don't want to urge you to do it at the expense of fiction, or poetry, for that is even more important to us and we're eagerly waiting for the next story and the poems. I just thought you might have Sable Island all written and could send it along after a day or two of work on it.

I hope the asthma is behaving. These cursed mumps won't seem to leave me. I think I'll soon have the longest case on record!

Affectionately,
    Katharine

---

1 Morris Bishop, *Champlain: The Life of Fortitude* (1948).

March 13, 1954

Dear Katharine:

PLEASE don't use Sable Island for a Talk of the Town Story! PLEASE! It is one of the things I *have* been working on lately and I didn't dare say so—however, your letter has made me go at it like a house afire. I had written about ten or fifteen pages and then stopped, getting rather sick of historical facts—however, now I think I have found a way to get around them, and I have written a lot of the end. I have shown it to some friends here who like it, and I am beginning to get enthusiastic all over again. [handwritten: "As a matter of fact, they think it is *beautiful*—I feel now is the time I must blow my own horn—"] Also—I'm not going away to Europe after all—probably not for a year. The cruzeiro has a lot to do with it, also a legal entanglement about land here—not mine, naturally, but that of the friend I was going with—so we've decided to postpone it for a while and it is really much more sensible for me to do so—I have enough work to do for two years. I honestly think, reading over what I have written on SI, that you are going to like it and it does seem a shame to condense it into a short "Talk" piece. I *will* keep it going now—may send you a few pages just to show you! I think it is really all right. Now what I want to do is go to Tristão da Cunha . . . & St. Helena—

I've also got two or three stories about ready—I dropped everything to work on two poems for HM recently—and seem to be rather stuck.

I'm appalled at the Mumps and the Shingles. I do hope you are both better. They thought I had mumps at Yaddo, once, but I was never quite sure—however, I remember how painful it was to swallow orange juice. And shingles I know are *ghastly*, having several friends who suffer from them at times—

I am also very sorry to hear about the death of your sister. And those sad, sudden trips are very hard to get over.

I can't write any more now because a caller is waiting to take this to Rio to mail. Last night—when I received your letter—I think it was so slow because of Carnival—I thought I'd cable, so strongly do I feel about Sable Island, but I thought better of it. I know myself better now than to make promises—but I can tell you honestly that I *was* very much back into it and had re-written quite a lot of it when your letter came, and I am going right on with it tonight.

First I must go to the annual flower-show, though—this is my 3rd, and I wish you could see it—it changed my ideas about orchids completely— I wish I could send you a few for the mumps.

Affectionately yours,
Elizabeth

Dear Elizabeth:

Your letter came while I was in Florida moving my old aunt out of my sister's house. The word about your work on the Sable Island piece went at once to Bill Shawn, and of course the subject will be reserved for you. We are delighted that you are working on it and we also look forward to the stories and the poems. Perhaps I didn't make it plain that we had no intention of using Sable Island as a Talk story in spite of the suggestion we received about that, but I did want to tell you that it had been so long since we heard from you that we did not know whether you had abandoned the project or not.

I'm too rushed now to write more, but I send you my love and I'm delighted that things seem to be going well for you and for your work.

Love,

Katharine

May 3, 1954

Dear Elizabeth:

I don't think I've congratulated you on your election to the National Institute of Arts and Letters. It is a great honor and a well-deserved one, and I am very happy about it. They called up from the Institute to ask for the manuscripts of one of your stories and the manuscripts of three of your poems. We sent them, on loan, the manuscripts of "In the Village," "A Cold Spring," "The Bight," and "Large Bad Picture."

Andy and I leave for Maine day after tomorrow, and I had been hoping against hope that Sable Island or some of the short stories or some of the poems would come in before I left. We are very eager to get all the things you promised, and I hope it won't be too long before something of yours is forwarded to me to read in Maine. Please don't send the manuscripts direct to me in Maine as there is more chance of their being lost that way. Send them just as usual to the office, and then they are listed and sent on after getting a first reading here.

We're going to have a terribly complex life in Maine this summer because my ninety-two-year-old aunt and her trained nurse have to come and live with us in June. Andy and I love my aunt dearly—she is like my mother—but you can see what that does in a house like ours, especially as she will have to be carried up and down stairs because of her heart. I look upon the summer with some trepidation but I am thankful that I can have her instead of her having to go to a "home."

I do hope that all goes well with you and that you have not been having any asthma.

Affectionately,
Katharine

Dear Katharine:

You are probably thinking I have gone the way of Capt. Fawcett in the Amazon or something—but this is just a note to say that I am just coming out of a stretch in the "Strangers Hospital" (dreadful name, but a good hospital) where I finally went to recuperate from a long spell of asthma, 2 months, I couldn't seem to shake off.[1] This is such a bore for one and all and sometimes I envy Proust his passivity about it all and wish *I* would refuse to see a Dr. for 4 years, the way he did, etc.—I think I'll try it next. Anyway, at the moment everything is fine; I'm just back in the country and have to work again, under mountains of correspondence, etc. I have so many things on the point of sending to you—I think I'll get at least the poems off this next week, and I have two stories to copy, and Sable Island in the last stages. I managed another story in the hospital but it will have to be re-done a lot. But I realize I should have let you hear from me long before this and I apologize.

Will you also be kind enough to send this on to the subscription dept. for me?—a friend I stayed with before the hospital, whose ambition proved to be to subscribe to the New Yorker,—I'd like her to have it for 2 years:

SRA. COSTA RIBEIRO
LARGO DO BOTICARIO, 32
COSME VELHO
Rio de Janeiro, Brazil

Every letter of the alphabet counts, and I'd feel safer sending it via you, although it's a nuisance for you, I'm afraid. It seems long ago now, but I gave "The 2nd Tree from the Corner" to the friend I live with here—Mr. White's fan—she even has clippings of his pictures—and I still think that the Classics Book Club poem of his is a masterpiece; I can recite it by heart.[2] Of course I

---

1 Colonel Percy Harrison Fawcett was a British archaeologist who disappeared along a tributary of the Amazon River in 1925 while searching for the lost city of "Z."

2 *The Second Tree from the Corner* (1954).

admire the Hemingway, too, and the death of the pig—I hadn't seen it before.[1] I saw a review in the *London Times*, in which an *English* reviewer said it made him "shed a tear," so that's really plumbing the depths of men's souls all right. I do hope you are both well and that you are having a good summer, and you will be hearing from me *very soon* now.

    Affectionately yours,
      Elizabeth

27 West 19th Street
New York
July 15, 1954

Dear Elizabeth,

I did get your fine letter, and it meant a great deal to me, as you know, that you liked some of the poems. My not answering is due only to my long-ingrained and deep sloth, and also my habit of writing letters in my head while I lie on my couch, smoking. Once the daydream has ended, the letter is as good as dispatched. Freud has some noble things to say on this matter.

The reviews have been favorable, generally, but stupid. It is unbelievable what people say about poetry—there must be a stable of morons somewhere kept exclusively for this purpose. When I find it, my home-made demolition bomb will do its usual efficient work.

I leave Monday for a month's vacation—beach, beach, beach—and am, at the moment, semi-hysterical. I'm only going to Long Island but any trip, and even the idea of travel, throws me for a loop. (Or is it loup?) I've always admired your ability—John Brinnin's, too—to take planes, ships, and water taxis to remote stations. If I go away for a week-end I have to spend the whole week getting ready, and then, shaking with compulsion and fear, I stand on railway platforms—usually the LIRR—anticipating my doom. It has something to do with a lack of love in childhood, and is, I'm afraid, persistent. Not being sure of the nest I'm in, I hesitate to get in another. Bird psychology 1.

News is dim. Everyone's away or going: Mary Lou to Folly Cove, John to Europe, Pearl to Folly Cove, etc. I've seen Lloyd [Frankenberg] and Loren [MacIver] around at parties, but haven't much of an idea of what they're up to. I offered Loren a sum of money to paint me a picture worth that much, but I think she found the whole idea depressing, if not pretentious. I would

---

1 Bishop is referring to "A Classic Waits for Me," "Across the Street and into the Grill," and "Death of a Pig."

love to own both Paris and Venice, but can't compete with museums. Eudora was in town on her way to Cambridge where she's supposed to lecture to *teachers* about teaching writing. She told me her first lecture, which I thought was sort of hilarious, since the secret gist of it is simply: why don't they just write? camouflaged under things like genre, scene, place, etc. The point peeps out everywhere. I suggested speed as a possible subject. I love writers who write things about speed—in the novel, poem, etc. The snail of effort is the title of my handbook on writing.

I'm sorry this letter is so fuzzy but I can't get over the idea that I allowed myself to go somewhere again. I've invented a psychiatric nurse called Miss Cook who takes me everywhere and believes that brandy is an antibiotic. Also a thing called Instant Leech—just add hot blood and serve.

When will you ever come back? I would love to see you again and hate to think that I might have to *travel* to Brazil to do it. Please do come back for awhile, a long shopping tour or something, the way you did last time. And where is A Cold Spring? Since I know North and South almost by heart by now, I should think, out of consideration for a fan, you'd let them bring it out. And did I tell you how much I liked THE SCREAM ["In the Village"]? I hope you'll do a whole book of Nova Scotia pieces. Do drop me a line when you can; so far everything has arrived, so the Brazilian mail may not be as far gone as you thought. Though as corrupt, I hope.

Love,
Howard

Please give my best to Lota.

North Brooklin
July 21, 1954

Dear Elizabeth:

I was so glad to get your letter of July 12, even though it brought the bad news of your stay in the hospital, for I had been worrying about you. It seems I had reason to worry, and I'm desperately sorry that this miserable asthma has laid you low again. Anyway it's good that everything is fine now and I hope to heaven it stays that way. No wonder you have been unable to write. We of course have been longing for everything and anything from you and I shall keep my fingers crossed until the poems and the stories and the Sable Island piece arrive.

Your subscription for Signora Costa Ribeiro has been attended to, my secretary writes me. If it fails to come, please write Miss Daise Terry at the office about it and she will prod the Circulation Dept.[1]

October 25, 1954

Dear Katharine:

I am truly ashamed not to have answered your nice Maine letter in all this time—I didn't answer it because of a guilty conscience, I suppose, but it didn't help much just to go on adding to it. Perhaps Pearl Kazin will have told you that I didn't get better—the asthma—even after two trips to the hospital, but instead began to get worse & worse—Then I gave in and started Cortisone, again, too, and why I refused earlier I really don't know, when it is such a wonder-drug and makes one feel the way one should all the time & so rarely does—This time I hope to be able to stop without any ill effects—I did last time, but just didn't go on with it long enough—and I even think that perhaps with care I may be able to use it four times a year—in which case I might be able to amount to something in this world, I think, and at least get enough work done during the Fool's Paradise stretches to be able to loaf happily in between them . . . It is wonderful, you know, and I recommend it all over again—one needs almost no sleep; does all kinds of unpleasant things without putting them off; and feels abnormally cheerful *all* the time . . .

I was interested in your brick porch, being very busy right now treating the brick floor of my *estudio* with muriatic acid and the Brazilian equivalent of water-glass and I don't know what all to see if I can make it beautiful— outside, too, where I also have plants, and the inevitable hammock. (I notice that most Brazilian writers seem to have their photographs taken lying in hammocks, which may be partly what's the matter with Brazilian writing.) Your porch or terrace sounds very nice, and I hope you did manage to get some servant help during the summer. That is one thing we have here—but it takes about four to do the work of one good one and one gets a little tired of so many personalities under foot all the time.

I shall never never promise anything to anyone again and I am sorry I said I was going on with "Sable Island"—even though I *am*. I'd say it was almost done if I just hadn't said that I would never, never etc. . . . When I was so miserably sick I didn't do a thing for two or three months, and then I worked almost entirely on my Brazilian translation because it was the easiest thing to do in bed, my friend Lota was around to help me, etc., and I

---

1 The carbon copy stops at this point with the note: "(Balance of this letter personal) K. S. White."

couldn't seem to work on anything original. I don't know whether I've told you about it or not, but I shall tell you a little and hope I haven't already. I don't believe it is anything the *New Yorker* could possibly be interested in, but I think that you yourself would enjoy it, and Mr. White, and also I think it would make a fine children's book—young girls', rather.

It is the diary, authentic, of a girl between the ages of 13 and 15, written in the '90s, in the colonial mining town of Diamantina, where her father was an English-adventurer-type of diamond prospector. There is a huge family, ex-slaves, animals, priests, etc.—completely poverty stricken and provincial but extremely lively and clear-sighted people. The girl, who must have been a marvellous child, writes down what has happened every day, to show her father or teacher, and she really wrote remarkably well. (—When George Bernanos was in exile here during the war he bought & gave away dozens of copies and wrote her a letter comparing her to Rimbaud, just to give you an idea—it's also given away as a prize-book at the Sacré Coeur here—)[1] The grandmother with her farms, slaves, priests, etc., is really the central character. I started in doing it rather casually and as a good way of learning Portuguese but as I've gone on I've become quite excited about it and have hopes of its success in English—in the U.S.A. or England, or both. Then I had the good luck to find a lot of really beautiful photographs of Diamantina, most of them taken just about the time the journals were being written. It is one of the best preserved of the colonial towns—heavy Portuguese Baroque, with decided oriental influences from Macao—I'm doing an introduction for the book about it. It is a *funny* book—I've seen lawyers and doctors here laughing aloud over it—and most of the literary people I've met here seem to feel it's just about the only Brazilian contribution to prose since the famous Machado de Assis, who seems to be being translated at a great rate in the U.S.A. at present—

I'm telling you about it because I thought possibly you might like to see the MS—as I said I'm pretty sure it isn't at all *New Yorker* material, being too old, etc.—but with your interest in children's books you might find it entertaining. I've sent a sample batch off to Houghton Mifflin, but I've asked them, if they aren't interested, to send it on to Pearl Kazin for me, who, I hope, is willing to act as my agent for the thing—the whole volume should be done by the first of the year, I think. I'm also making a better selection, with photographs, that I thought possibly *Harper's Baṭaar* or one of the other

1 The French novelist Georges Bernanos lived in Brazil from 1938 to 1945.

shiny-paper magazines, or even *Harper's* or *The Atlantic* might be interested in. If you'd like to, have time to, etc. I'm sure Pearl would hand it over for a few days. It's called "Minha Vida de Menina" ("My Life as a Girl"—awful) by "Helena Morley." Helena Morley is now Mrs. Brant, a wonderful old lady of 75, still talking & writing—(letters)—a blue streak. Her husband was president of the Bank of Brazil, and has recently gone back to help clean it up after the late upheavals here,—at almost 80—They are affluent now, needless to say, after the poverty of Diamantina, and social leaders in Rio—but Mrs. Brant is so excited by the thought of appearing in English before she dies, and what her grandmother and her "Aunt Madge" would have thought, that I am very eager to be able to show her something in a magazine, at least, before very long—

It is so much better than any memoirs of the sort I've ever read—that wretched [Osbert] Lancaster book, for example—or Mrs. Robert Henry—as good although worlds and wars apart, as Anne Frank, I think.[1]—I don't get excited about books of this sort, or "primitive" writing, very easily, but the longer I work on this, the more I think that it is a real find.

Since taking Cortisone—about three weeks ago now—I've got back to working very hard—my next letter will be a MS, but as I said I'm never going to say anything again about my plans. I divide my time equally between finishing the translation and my own work.

I finally received *The New Yorker* with Louise Bogan's review of Marianne's enormous book—I thought she did very well in such a short space. The best serious review was in "Poetry" I thought—Hugh Kenner, whom I usually dislike—but I thought Miss Bogan managed to imply a lot of the same conclusions in about a tenth the space. I also liked Mary McCarthy's story about the beavers better than any of hers I've seen in some time—perhaps it was a little too allegorical, but it really was awfully good.[2] I wonder if sometime you could let me have her address? I think I'd like to write her a note—or just c/o *The New Yorker* I suppose? [handwritten: "(so don't bother, please.)"]

My Brazilian friends are receiving the magazine and enjoying it very much—they almost wept when the postman handed them one empty manila slip on one occasion, and I had quickly to send down the missing copy from

1 *All Done from Memory* (1953); *The Little Madeleine: The Autobiography of a Young Girl in Montmartre* (1953); *Diary of a Young Girl* (1952).
2 Bogan's review of *The Fables of La Fontaine* ran September 4, 1954; Hugh Kenner's review also ran in September. Bishop is referring to McCarthy's story "The Appalachian Revolution" (September 11, 1954).

the country. There just aren't any magazines here at all any more—there used to be—just endless miserable newspaper supplements, and reading people really miss that particular kind of entertaining reading.

I hope you and Mr. White are both well now—and I am really sorry I haven't written you a line for so long. Please forgive me—I also hope to appear in print in your esteemed pages very very shortly . . .

Affectionately yours,

Elizabeth

The New Yorker
November 2, 1954

Dear Elizabeth:

Not having heard from you since July, when you were sick, I had begun to be alarmed about your health, especially as the stories and poems and the Sable Island piece have not arrived. I, myself, have been sick and I am only just out of the hospital and out of bed and working at home but today I called Pearl Kazin, who told me you are all right, she thinks. I do hope so. She gave me the bad news—bad news for us—that you were translating a Brazilian diary. Not that I don't think you should translate a Brazilian diary, if you think it will make a book or if it interests you to, but I am worried about that Sable Island piece because Shawn long since thought you had abandoned it because of the long delay. I swore to him it is coming, but it has not come. Dear Elizabeth, do send it! Of course I am especially anxious for more stories and more poems. Heavens, how we need you in the magazine! Are there any poems we have not seen that you have in readiness for your new book? If there are, we have much hope you will send them to us. And most of all, I long to see you bring out a book of short stories and I imagine you need a few more to make a book. It would be a most distinguished volume, and I do wish you would write us a few more. People still talk about "Gwendolyn" and "In the Village." I hate to act like a whipping boy, but honestly, it is wicked to see anybody so talented as you not producing and I can't help having the uneasy feeling that you have a lot of stuff up your sleeve that you have not sent us just because you feel that it is not perfect yet.[1]

---

1 The carbon copy stops at this point with the note: "(The balance of this letter is personal) K. S. White."

Dear Elizabeth:

I sent off a miserable letter to you yesterday and then today arrives your good letter—good except that it tells me what a dreadful time you had with asthma again. Pearl Kazin had not told me that and apparently she thought you were all right. I am dictating this letter over the phone, being back in bed again with a slight relapse of this miserable condition, so it may not make much sense, but at least I want you to know at once that we are eager to see the diary when it reaches Pearl Kazin. It sounds fascinating to me, though of course I cannot be sure that it is anything for The New Yorker. A diary of this sort that Andy and I love is one called "Maud" by a woman who lived in Cairo, Missouri (?) and this was the naïve diary of her teens. I have forgotten her name and the book is in Maine.[1] It is not a literary masterpiece but it has much naïve charm. *Your* book sounds much more of a find.

To return to your health; can't you take cortisone right along? Charlie Henderson did for a number of years without any ill effects and now he only takes it once in a great while if the asthma flares up. It remade his life. Unfortunately he has had another thing happen to him—a coronary thrombosis—but he lived through it and now is trying to learn to live a fairly sedentary life. I have had a letter saying he looks just awful and I am apprehensive about his health. I know that you liked him, so this is why I put this news in, but I especially wanted to tell you how well the cortisone worked. The heart attack had nothing to do with that; he simply did a lot of heavy lifting of blueberry boxes that he should not have done and didn't have to do on a job where he was superintendent of pickers last summer.

Please don't be discouraged by the Sable Island piece. I know that Bill Shawn will understand why you had to delay it, since you have been sick. I will tell him. I feel guilty to have been so nagging in yesterday's letter when all this time you have been so ill. Please forgive me.

Much love,

Katharine

P.S. November 11th—Mary McCarthy's address is Paradise Farm, Newport, Rhode Island, until January 1st, but if you want to write her later than that just address the letter to her in my care and I will send it to wherever she goes after the New Year. She moves around a lot. I know she will be delighted that you liked the story. I thought it was excellent.

I am back at the office for part of each day now.

1 Probably Isabella Rittenhouse, *Maud*, edited by Richard Lee Strout (1939).

Samambaia
November 17, 1954

Dear Katharine:

I hasten to send you a note to assure you that I AM working on Sable Island!—indeed, nothing BUT Sable Island at the moment, and five pages of the translation per day—that's all I can do of it without getting bored with it. Today, Sunday, I am even staying home from a long drive to buy 150 fruit trees—an expedition I'd adore—and here I am surrounded with maps, and a letter from a great-uncle, and Prowse's History of Newfoundland, etc. . . .

I think when you wrote me—the 2nd of November (I just got a big batch of mail last night)—you hadn't received my letter, maybe—I'm afraid it will only make you think I am doing nothing at all but translation, too, but I am so enthusiastic about that book that I wanted to tell you about it, too. No, I doubt, as I said then, that *The New Yorker* could use any of it, but I think, as a connoisseur of books for the "young," you will enjoy it very much if it ever appears, and perhaps you might like to see one of the sections of it sometime . . .

No—I don't mind your egging me on to finish *Sable Island* at all—and it is quite true that I have a great deal of work of different sorts that I should and could finish. You have an ally here in the friend I am staying with, who asks me about S.I. every day. And through an unplanned and quite unmerited series of fortuitous accidents I'm now in a position the first time in my life really to get a lot of work done, I think—if it isn't ten or fifteen years too late. But as I said to you last time—if I can take Cortisone every few months, and keep pretty free of asthma, and stay here in the country, I have great hopes.

I think I'll be able to send you SI before Christmas although I hate to promise. Since it's the first thing I've ever done of that sort it may need considerable re-writing, of course. I read it to two literary friends—the half or so I have done—the other night and they really seemed to like it all right. I also have about six stories going-going-going,—although of course my first and most serious interest is, as always, a few poems. But no—I'm really grateful when you write and remind me and I think you'll be seeing it soon and only hope it will be good enough.

I am terribly sorry to hear you were sick and had to be flown to New York etc.—how awful—I do hope you are recovered now, and can't you take cortisone for something?

Affectionately & gratefully—
Elizabeth

Dear Elizabeth:

I enclose a new first reading agreement for you. I am mortified to find that we are late in sending it out since your old one expired November 25th—mortified, though it is a delay of the business office, not one of my own making. We would of course have acted as if the agreement were still in effect if a manuscript had come in between the 25th and the date you receive this new agreement letter. We hope that you will want to renew the agreement, and of course are assuming so, since we include the usual $100 check. The agreement letter is just like last year's except that the minimum rates named are slightly higher. The minimum verse rate raise reflects a raise in line rates that has been in effect since last July. The prose rate raise is because we are raising your rate for fiction by 10% on January first. I hope the $100 check will reach you in time to be of some use for Christmas.

And since my Christmas is going to be an awfully complex one this year I think I should send you my Christmas greetings and love and a Happy New Year now. I am having to give up even sending Christmas cards this year because of having been ill and because the doctors have urged me to do just as little as possible. I am heeding their words for once since I want to keep well because Andy and I have to go to Boston for Christmas to bring Allene and the new baby home from the hospital in Joe's absence. I guess it will fall to me to cook a Christmas dinner. This young family is really in a tough spot this year with Joe in camp and not likely to get off at Christmas as he will have had leave earlier when the baby is born, and Allene alone in Boston awaiting the Caesarean, and her mother not able to come since she must stay in New Hampshire and take care of one-year-old Steven.

Your lovely card—the photograph of the old church in Diamatira (? spelling—I can't quite read your handwriting) has just come and I think it is going to be the most wonderful card I shall get. Did you take the photograph? It is beautiful.

I hope that cortisone is continuing to work its miracle and my New Year's wishes are for nothing but good health for you in 1955.

Affectionately,

Katharine

P.S. Please don't forget to sign and return one of the letters. And please remember that we're looking eagerly to reading the Brazilian diary.

January 12, 1955

Dear Elizabeth:

Here is a belated fan letter for you on "In the Village." Pearl tells me that you are well and working hard on your translation and that is fine news. I would like to think that in 1955 we were going to publish a lot of your prose and poetry.

Affectionately,

Katharine

March 9, 1955

Dear Elizabeth:

How is the translation of the diary coming? I am beginning to long to have a look at some of it, to see whether there is any chance of a New Yorker series there. Would you want to send us a sample, or would you prefer to wait until it is all finished?

We are of course even *more* eager to receive some poems and stories of your own. And "Sable Island"? What about that, which was so nearly finished? As usual, this letter is a plea to let us see some of the Elizabeth Bishop manuscripts that I feel certain are on your desk, all finished if only you could bring yourself to part with them. And *what* happened to the book of your poetry?

I hope you are continuing to feel better all the time. Andy has had an operation—hernia, and so not too serious, but it seems even so to have taken a lot out of us both. I am pulling now for a short trip to Europe at the end of May if he is well enough. We'd only be gone six weeks. Mary McCarthy was asking for you last week just before she sailed, to be away until August.

Much love from,

Katharine

Rio de Janeiro
April 25, 1955

Dear Katharine:

I'm sorry I've been silent for so long—I've not been quite unproductive, however, and I'll be sending you several things in a week or two. I have finally acquired a typist here—not a very good one, but I think she will help speed me up a little, at least.

I've been rather busy the past month or so getting proof, etc., back to Houghton Mifflin. After many delays and troubles I think the book of poems will appear now in *July*, I'm sorry to say. It's mostly old stuff to you I'm afraid, but I'm having them send you an advanced copy.

Tomorrow I'll be mailing the first third, the year 1893, of "Minha Vida de Menina" to Pearl Kazin, who's going to act as my agent in N.Y. for it. I sent HM some samples some months ago and they wanted to see *more*, of course; and then Pearl spoke of Mary Lou's wanting to see it, too. I really don't know who would be best to think of for the thing as a book. I've written Pearl today, too, and told her that you'd like to see what I'm sending her. I'd be *delighted*, naturally, if The New Yorker should be interested in it—I'm really afraid it couldn't be, though. However—let me make this much explanation, and please do bear it in mind if you look at the first third. The girl who wrote it was only 12–13 at the time, the book *does* get better and better as it goes along, much fuller and funnier, and also it grows by repetition and accumulation, as the same priest, the same chicken-thief, the same aunts & uncles, etc., do the same things over & over. In a couple of weeks now I am going to Diamantina, the town where it all took place, to write an Introduction. If there was any possibility of The New Yorker's being interested I could suggest the best excerpts, all the way through, and write a briefer version of the Introduction—perhaps working the present "Glossary" into it, and making it shorter, too. But you'll see what I mean. But I assure you that it really does get much better as it goes on—perhaps I shouldn't send it by thirds as I'm doing, but it's easier and I'd like to get it out of the way. I hope you like it anyway, even if it's not for The New Yorker—even after working over it a lot I still enjoy it and I think the impact of the whole book is amazing—it's real as real can be, and a marvelous detailed picture of a society in complete decadence, and such spontaneity and observation for a girl of 13–15 living the narrowest life imaginable—

I have a couple of stories I hope you'll like—I won't say any more now for fear of saying too much! I do hope you are well and that spring is there and you are enjoying it.

With love,
Elizabeth

P.S.—I forgot to say that of course I read the Peter Taylor story about the trip to New York with morbid fascination . . . It seemed very good to me—the part about the fight on the train, etc., marvellous—but I wonder how it would strike readers who didn't know the people involved? I really couldn't judge it as a story at all.[1]

May 20, 1955

Dear Elizabeth:

I am late in answering your letter of April 25th. Andy and I went to Maine for my aunt's ninety-third birthday—the aunt who is like a mother to me and who has lived in our house there since my sister died a year ago—and two days after Aunt Caroline's birthday, she had a stroke. She died eleven days later, for which we are thankful since she could never have been anything but a helpless invalid. But it did delay us in Maine and it has been quite upsetting emotionally.

About the "Minha Vida de Menina", the first third of it has arrived and Pearl Kazin read it. We want to read it but Pearl and I and everyone think that it would be fairer to the book and to our decision on whether we could use parts of it if we read the whole book straight through rather than just this first section. This is especially true since you say the book gets fuller and funnier as it goes along. Therefore to give every break to your manuscript and to the book we want to wait until the whole thing is in our office. I am sure you will understand that this is the best plan. We are very anxious to have you send, either now or when you turn in the balance of the book, your suggestions of the best passages for The New Yorker. You offered to do this and it would be a very great help to us if you did. I suggest that you do not write a brief version of the introduction now, since it would involve labor for you, but do it later if we should find that we could use any of the excerpts you suggest or any others that we might find on our own. We shall of course read every word of the book but your thoughts on the passages that are best would be of enormous value to us.

It is wonderful news that you have a couple of stories to send soon. I am going to leave your letter and this answer of mine with Bill Maxwell or Gus Lobrano because Andy and I are sailing for England in six days to be gone six weeks. When I get back I am going not to my regular New Yorker work until September 1st. The reason for this is that I have become, through so many buffets, both personal and professional, which last were just the strain of a weekly magazine, very tired nervously and that takes time to get over.

1 "A Sentimental Journey" (March 12, 1955).

Actually the extra six weeks off I am taking mostly for Andy's sake. He has been sick this winter, has had an operation, and now has some back trouble and sciatica. I have stipulated that during the six weeks in Maine they are to send me any manuscripts they know I am particularly interested in or want my advice on and yours would be among those, I am sure.

It is good news too that the poetry book is to be out in July. I can hardly wait to see it.

Affectionately,
Katharine

Samambaia
May 29, 1955

Dear Katharine:

Thank you for the letter about "Minha Vida de Menina" and I think you're quite right to wait to see it—I just wanted to start getting it out of the way. I'll follow your suggestions about indicating the best sections, too—I think possibly a fairly amusing and good piece might be made in that way—and it is true that most of the really well-done little anecdotes come later, when the girl is writing better and seeing things from a slightly grown-up point of view.

I am so glad you are going away on a trip—you must be there now, unless you went by ship—and I imagine England will be its very best now, the countryside, at least. It has probably been a long time since you've been really away like that and I hope you have a nice time—you do seem to have had a great many difficult stretches lately.

I was laid up with a fearful cold and bronchitis for 2 wks (the first I've had in Brazil) and couldn't get down to Rio to the typist with my stories, but I am going this week. I really have quite a lot of work on hand now and having someone to type for me may produce more results—I'm hoping. I have a group of four poems—2 of them I feel quite sure you'll like. I wonder if you'd rather have me send them to Howard while you're away? I am enclosing one extra one ["Squatter's Children"] that I am quite certain will be too grim for you, but I thought maybe you could send it back to me without too much trouble—or does it have to go through "channels"?

Anyway—I don't want to bother you on your holiday and I do hope you are having a nice time—maybe you're going to be there for the elections, even. Please remember me to Mr. White.

Affectionately yrs,
Elizabeth

Dear Elizabeth:

We all think SQUATTER'S CHILDREN is fine, and the author's proof and your check should be coming along shortly, unless what you told me about the Brazilian postal system is still horribly true. I always have visions of you tossing priceless manuscripts into mail boxes, only to have the stamps filched by some urchin, and the manuscripts themselves trundled, on burros, over distant mountains into oblivion. I hope it isn't so.

And speaking of things not turning up—I think that's what I'm talking about—where is A COLD SPRING? I wait and wait, and have even made a few tentative inquiries, but no one seems to know. Please let it come out, and soon.

It would be so nice if you would turn up in New York again. I look forward to that, as well as the four poems you mention in your letter.

Ever,
Howard

June 29, 1955

Dear Elizabeth Bishop:

When Howard goes on vacation, I turn up, like the nine of spades. How agreeable it is to be sending you a check. And for such a beautiful poem. Both Emmy and I are looking forward to having the new collection to refer to. We have a simply wonderful baby, born last December, and named Kate.

Bill Maxwell

July 6, 1955

Dear Howard:

Thank you for your note of June 24th—I don't know whether Katharine White is back from England yet or not so I'll address this to you. You should be getting a copy of A COLD SPRING any day now, I think—I'm afraid it is a rather thin collection and that there's nothing in it that will be new to you. *Your* title is well-thought of, though.

I have a chance to send some mail to Rio today so I think I'll send along the enclosed ["Manners"]. I have several poems about ready to send you— and they are not all so simple-minded, I trust—but at the moment I'm stuck with one and I wonder if possibly you could help me out? If I were in Rio I might be able to do this bit of research myself, or if my Encyclopedia Britannica, expected any day now, were here. Do you know who is the author of a famous quotation to the effect that all of man's troubles come from the fact that he isn't willing to sit quietly alone in his room?—those words, more or less. I thought at first it was Pascal but it doesn't seem to be, then Le Maître, but I can't check on that here, and it isn't in Bartlett . . . I'm hoping you have such resources at your finger-tips there that someone will produce the correct name for you in two minutes—or you may perfectly well *know*, of course! If I could get the name and the quotation exactly I could send another poem. Please don't think I'm getting stuck back in Nova Scotia!—but I suppose such a drastic move as to Brazil does turn one backwards for some time.

I was really touched to see your poem about Einstein—it was a nice idea, and nice to be able to say something so quickly—[1]

I'd like to make a visit to New York, too, but it's so far and costs so much—maybe I'll make it next spring. But any time you'd like to visit me, I'd be delighted to have you, really . . . The Rio apartment is rented, unfortunately, but if you'd like a stretch of quiet mountainous-country-life in the midst of a South American tour, or anything like that, come along.

Affectionately,
Elizabeth

July 11, 1955

Dear Elizabeth:

In your letter to me enclosing "Squatter's Children" you mention sending four poems and say that this one is a fifth. We *never received* the other four poems and I'm earnestly hoping that they were not lost in the mails. Please send copies, if so. Your letter came after I'd left for England. I was delighted to find on my return that we had bought "Squatter's Children", for I admire it greatly—a beautiful poem. Howard is now away until August 1st, and Andy and I go to Maine this week, but I've alerted the staff that your translated book should come to me even if I am still on vacation when it arrives. I look forward to it a lot and hope you won't forget to recommend the passages you think most promising for us.

Paul Brooks sent me a copy of your poetry book and I am excited about it. I shall read it over and over once I get to Maine. So far I've only had a chance to glance into it and thumb it through a little and to read the wonder-

---

1 Moss's elegy, "The Gift to Be Simple," ran on May 14, 1955.

ful poem to Marianne Moore. I hope the book gets all the poetry awards of the year; it deserves to.

I'm awfully sorry to hear about your bronchitis but I hope it is now completely forgotten. I also hope that the Rio typist will help you get off the stories soon. We look forward to *everything*—poems, stories, and "Minha Vida de Menina."

Our stay in England was brief and strike-ridden, but lots of fun even so. Best of all we liked our eight days in Chagford, Devon, on the edge of Dartmoor, even though the lush fields gave Andy bad hay fever.

Affectionately,

Katharine

July 19, 1955

Dear Katharine:

No, I didn't send the four poems all together; I'm sorry if I confused you. Howard wrote me about "Squatter's Children" (I'm very pleased that *you* like it, too.) and I wrote back sending him a poem for a child called "Manners", and saying that I was stuck with the others because I needed some information. Then I received a notice saying that he was away and poems weren't to be sent until August. In the meanwhile I found I did have the necessary bit of information here (a quotation) and can finish up some more. I'm not sure how many they will turn out to be, now. Here is another single one ["Exchanging Hats"] to go on with that I hope may strike you as amusing, making three so far, and more shortly . . .

The translation of the Brazilian book will be some time yet, I'm afraid— I'm only just over half-way through. But I still think it's wonderful stuff. However, I'm very much afraid it will prove too dated for your purposes. I am doing a great deal of work these days I'm glad to say and you should see some results soon.

This is just to say that I'm sorry I was so misleading and that I'm glad you're home again and hope you are both well. While you are in Maine would it be better to send poems to Howard? Stories? I wish *I* were in Maine, for a little while, at least. The book of poems is almost all old to you, I'm afraid. I'm sorry this is rather gobbledy-gooky—someone is waiting to start to Rio but I did want to send you a line—

Affectionately yours,

Elizabeth

Dear Elizabeth:

We were delighted with MANNERS, and here is the check for it, and also a cost of living adjustment check. I have been at the checking department, and they have been at their reference books, but without turning up the quotation you wrote Howard about. It seems maddening to think that it alone stands in the way of our having another poem. Are you absolutely sure it wouldn't work without the quotation?

Howard's in Millbrook. I'm sending your letter along to him.[1]

My best to you,

Bill

July 30, 1955

Dear Bill:

I don't really mean to be coy in sending poems along in this way . . . Here is another ["Filling Station"] and then there'll be another of this particular batch. You'll think I'm obsessed with filling stations, maybe, but I suppose it's because having a first car I now notice them more. I'm awfully glad to hear your nice one is in good hands.

All your checks, proofs, etc. came together last night—I get mail up here once a week now, from Rio. I'm glad you liked *Manners* and the corrections are all right with me. I think I must have been using English-style hyphenation. I think I see that someone wanted to change "Willy" to "Willie" and that would be all right, too, if it seems more natural. I just don't care for more commas than are strictly necessary, because they interfere with the rhythm, I think.[2]

The enclosed ["Questions of Travel"] may be too special and Brazilian—but I must get here sometime!

Well, if you have pages and pages, as you say, perhaps you will suddenly discover that they are a book, after all—it works that way with poetry quite often, I find. With all best wishes for it, anyway—and for your family—We have the most beautiful baby here now, Negro, or mulatto, six months old, the cook's—and named for me, more or less, "Maria Elizabeth." She can

---

1 Moss was a frequent guest at Millie and Dick Wood's upstate home. Millie Wood was a reader in the fiction department.

2 "Manners" was not edited by Moss or White but by "X," who had no changes to make. Besides the hyphenated words, one change was made between Bishop's submission and the poem's publication: removing the comma after "me" in stanza one, line one (*The New Yorker* Records).

almost sit up, tries hard, and rattles two rattles simultaneously, in African rhythms. I was going to be the godmother & then found to my disappointment I couldn't, never having been baptized myself—but I have provided the earrings for the ear-piercing ceremony.

Yours,

Elizabeth

I decided I'd better change the envelope you thoughtfully provided to the Brazilian national colors, just to be on the safe side.

Howard mentioned sending proof for "*The Squatter's Children*," but I haven't received it yet—I hope it's not lost.

North Brooklin
August 3, 1955

Dear Elizabeth:

I read "Manners" on my way through New York and am delighted that we are buying it. Thanks for your letter of July 19. In answer to your questions, it doesn't matter to whom you address poems and stories in my absence, for each editor in turn goes on vacation and anything I told you now would be out of date. Either address them to the Fiction Department or to me and they will be handled with loving care. Howard is away now; when he returns, Maxwell goes. I shall be back at work on September 1st.

Maine has been wonderful this year with a mixture of quiet hot days and an ocean warm enough to swim in, and the usual brisk cool breezy weather. Too dry, though. You really should come back for a visit.

Love,

Katharine

August 10, 1955

Dear Elizabeth:

I'm back from vacation and delighted to find all the new poems. We love STATION #2 and the author's proof and your check should be along soon. QUESTIONS OF TRAVEL is still being read, and I'll let you know about it as soon as I hear. We're returning EXCHANGING HATS, alas, which we didn't feel worked for us, though I, personally, think it's funny and touching in a peculiar way.[1]

1 *New World Writing* published the poem in its ninth issue, April 1956.

While I was in the country, one of the unexpected delights was receiving a forwarded copy of A COLD SPRING. Although I had read everything in it, I read it again, and many times since, and all I can say is that I love it. FAUSTINA seems to me especially wonderful, and LETTER TO NEW YORK says more about it than a lot of people who gas on and on about pushcarts and Rolls-Royces. And no one else but you could have thought of that moral owl—exactly right. I'm so glad all the new poems are finally under one cover and thank you for sending me a copy. I think Loren's jacket is one of the best I've ever seen, by the way, and I hope you're as happy with the book as I am.

Thanks, too, for the invitation to visit Brazil. It isn't likely, since I can't even stand flying to Boston, but if I ever can, and do, I shall certainly head for your mountain. Do please keep poems coming, and thanks for all the recent ones. And did the proof of SQUATTER'S CHILDREN ever arrive? If it hasn't I'll have a new one made up.

Fondly,

Howard

August 23, 1955

Dear Elizabeth:

QUESTIONS OF TRAVEL is fine, and we want it, of course. There are some tiny points we'd like to straighten out before we publish it.

It strikes us that the last five lines of stanza 1 seem to go more logically with stanza 2. Would you mind a stanza break after "slime-hung and barnacled" and the next five lines added onto stanza 2?

At the bottom of the first page, you have a small 2 under inconclusively and a small 1 under blurr'dly. Does this mean you want the adjectives reversed—blurr'dly and inconclusively?

The checkers can't find the Pascal quote, which is difficult since no actual words are used—from the quote, I mean. If you could tell us where it is, that would be a great help.

I won't have QUESTIONS OF TRAVEL put through until I hear from you. I hope you'll have more poems to show us soon—we're delighted with all the recent ones.

Ever,

Howard

September 2, 1955

Dear Elizabeth:

Here is the author's proof of SQUATTER'S CHILDREN. A comma has been added after "ark" in stanza 3. On the original manuscript, "rain's", in the next line, was spelled "rain s", without an apostrophe. I assume you meant "rain's" but could you possibly have meant "rains' "?[1]

I do hope other poems are on the way or coming.

Ever,

Howard

September 5, 1955

Dear Howard:

I think the changes in QUESTIONS OF TRAVEL are an improvement, probably—the change, that is. Yes, the order of adjectives should be "blurr'dly and inconclusively".

I can't find that Pascal quotation, either—but I *know* it is Pascal. While looking for it, I ran across another reference to it, too, in an essay—but not Eliot's—and now I've lost that, too. I've gone through the *Pensées* thoroughly and now I think I'll go through the *Provincial Letters* again . . . I know you have to feel quite sure, and if and when I find it again I'll let you know.

Proof for THE SQUATTER'S CHILDREN never came and I think must have got lost. Could you send it again? I'm going down to Rio today and expect to find proof of the other two in the mail. You did receive MANNERS back again, didn't you? My mail system is really breaking down—it goes through so many hands now and depends on so many conjunctions of the stars that it's really amazing I ever receive it. I am trying to develop a new system.

I'm sorry I can't be definite about that quotation but I must be getting hot, surely.

I'm glad you got the book and only wish there were more and better new poems—however, I seem to be quite productive these days and am even thinking of another book. I think when I come up I must bring you some tropical fish—do you still have them? A friend of mine here brought back

---

1 Moss also added a comma after "beguiled" in stanza four, line three (Vassar College Library). An additional change was made between Bishop's submission and the poem's publication: replacing the comma after "up" with a semicolon in stanza one, line eight.

some in a bucket by plane from the Amazon and then when he later made a trip to New York and went to Macy's found the same fish selling there for $99.98 . . .

    Affectionately,
        Elizabeth

September 9, 1955

Dear Howard:

The quotation is: "I have discovered that all the unhappiness of men arises from one single fact, that they cannot stay quietly in their own chamber."[1] It's *Pensée* 139, section II. This is the Modern Library edition, translated by W. F. Trotter.

I don't know how many times I must have read right through it without seeing it . . .

Yes, it was "rain's" in "*The Squatter's Children*." I sent the proof off yesterday. The poor Squatter's children go by the house every day wearing the blue bags that sugar comes in here on their heads, and mortally afraid of our dogs—who wouldn't touch them, really. I feel as if I should split my check with them but shall probably cheat and just give them a bag of candy.

    Faithfully yours,
        Elizabeth

September 20, 1955

Dear Elizabeth:

Here is your check for QUESTIONS OF TRAVEL. I've held it up, waiting for the author's proof, but since that still hasn't arrived, I thought I'd send it on.

How did you ever remember about the tropical fish? I don't keep them anymore, but I must say your letter made me think of starting all over again. If you do bring some up, I certainly will, but carting them around sounds like a hell of a lot of trouble, and it will be so nice to see you again that that seems like ample reward, fish or no fish.

    Ever,
        Howard

---

1 *Tout le malheur des hommes vient d'une seule chose, qui est de ne savoir pas demeurer en repos dans une chambre.*

Dear Elizabeth:

Here is the author's proof of QUESTIONS OF TRAVEL. Aside from the hyphenated words, the main problem is the word "pantomists", which doesn't seem to exist. Either one of the two alternatives in the margin is correct, through they're both rhythmically off, alas.

And then, the punctuation goes rather contrary to New Yorker style in several places. We never use dashes at the beginnings of sentences, though I've left them all in, unqueried, because I know you use them in other poems and because they seem to make sense in context. The long stanza before the last italicized ones, was re-punctuated by our grammar demons so that it made one sentence, more or less, without the dashes. An example would be:

> the whittled fantasies of wooden cages,
> never to have studied history in
> the weak calligraphy of song-birds' cages,
> and never to have had to listen to the rain etc.

Please keep it your way if you like it better, or change it if you think it's a good idea.[1] I think your way keeps the sense of someone amassing detail, so that each new thought is seen as part of a process of thinking, of someone remembering one thing after the other.

I hope you'll have some new poems to send soon.

Ever,

Howard

Caixa Postal 279
Petrópolis
October 17, 1955

Dear Howard:

I doubt that you will be interested in this ["Sestina"] . . .

I hope you received the proof of *Questions of Travel*. I thought I should get it back to you, although I was in Rio and in a hurry, and I probably made mistakes. On getting back to my dictionary I find that "humming bird" is

---

1 Bishop rejected the idea.

two words—and there were probably others. However, I approved of what you had done with the dashes, and that was the main thing.[1]

Are there any new poets or poems I should be reading?

Faithfully yours,

Elizabeth

Dear Howard:

When I went to the post office to mail you my sestina I found a letter from you in the box I share with a Portuguese carpenter. My next stop was the market; it was dark and when I got under an electric light bulb there I opened your letter just enough to see your note and the last few lines of the poem—just enough so I knew what I was looking at. Those last two lines sent a cold shudder down my spine and I stood there transfixed and incredulous while the man butchered an enormous pumpkin for me . . . I still think they're probably lines Donne wrote to Elizabeth, Countess of something or other . . .[2]

I couldn't be more flattered or pleased & of course you have my permission to do anything you want to with it. Some of your guesses aren't far off, although we don't have any *big* cats around here—the jaguars are up north. Lota says she wants to be the "benevolent patriarch", though. I tried to find a rhyme for my own name the other day for a sort of poem-letter and strange to say I didn't think of any of those—only "shibboleth"; I wonder why.

And I'd just mailed you a request for a new poem to read—it couldn't have come quicker.

The trouble is it is hard to *do* anything with such an entirely different environment, and so one falls back on grandmothers & cups of tea . . . Thank you so much, Howard—heavens, what a nice thing to have happen to one!

Faithfully yours,

Elizabeth

1 It is not entirely clear what Bishop means here, since in comparing the last extant draft to the *New Yorker* version, only one dash is missing, from the beginning of stanza one, line ten: "But if the streams and clouds keep travelling, travelling," (Vassar College Library).

2 Moss sent Bishop his poem "Letter to an Imaginary Brazil." The last two lines read: "Thin-scaled as life upon the width of death, / Who cannot read your poems, Elizabeth." See Bishop to Moss, October 18, 1956.

Dear Elizabeth:

Here is a little nightmare of a proof. First, the title is odd to grasp for an American, most people think, and Mrs. White suggests that it might possibly help if the title read something like "Station No. 2—Rio de Janeiro to . . ." (you fill in the name) OR "Station No. 2—Route 101, Brazil", using whatever route this is actually on, if it is on a route.

The rest, I *think*, is more or less self-explanatory. The question of the dash *before* a line comes up again, and the question of hyphens in the multiple words.[1]

In stanza 3, it isn't clear to us why there should be a comma after "a set" and it has been suggested that we take it out.

The complications in stanza 4 are explained, I think, by the note in the box on the side.

In stanza 5, shouldn't there be a question mark after "crochet"?

And in the last stanza, the box about 7 pt. caps means simply that the type is too big and that we plan to use a smaller type. (Though larger than the type used throughout, of course.) The business about the Esso line means this: Do you want it to read: "ESSO- SO" or "ESSO -SO" or would longer dashes do the trick?

I'm sorry to throw this on your lap, but I've refined it down to the essentials, and it's still quite a scrawly, black-marked proof.[2]

Thanks for your letter which arrived at home yesterday. I plan to answer it from there.

Ever,
Howard

Dear Howard:

Here's the proof—I've put in my corrections—mostly agreeing with those already made—in blue, just to try to keep it clearer. About the title—I hadn't thought of it as being an especially Brazilian poem—couldn't it be

---

1 Bishop submitted the poem with dashes starting stanza one, line two, and stanza five, line four (*The New Yorker* Records). Only the dash in stanza one remained for publication.

2 Moss made a couple of corrections to the poem before it was set in proof. He added a comma to the end of stanza two, line one. He changed "(It's a family filling-station.)" to "(it's a family filling-station)" in stanza two, line six. He also inserted a comma between "big" and "dim" in stanza four, line four, but the comma was deleted before publication.

equally true of an out-of-the-way filling station anywhere? The only difference is that here, of course, it's on one of the 2 or 3 driveable roads in the country . . . If you agree with me, I should think it could be called just "*Filling Station*", if not, perhaps "*Station #2, Rio to Bahia.*" (No one would ever dream of driving to Bahia, but that's what the signs say.) They do have a system of numbering the stations, as I see you have surmised, and I was just being literal about the one nearest me here. But I think it could be in many parts of the world, after all—don't you?

I think the longer dashes, set in the middle of the space, take care of the ESSO business—ESSO — SO — SO etc.—best.[1]

In stanza 5, "embroidery", etc., is a sort of parenthetical description, not a question. If it started with the dash and a small "e", couldn't that sentence end with a stop?—I don't like a question mark after "crochet," if it's avoidable.[2]

I think the rest is clear—and I'm awfully sorry that my typewriter has decided to crack up this very morning, which isn't making this letter any clearer, I'm afraid—it's more or less hand-printed.[3]

Since I've heard from you twice now since sending you the first copy of the enclosed poem, I think it must have got lost. This is the same as the first one with two small but important changes—in case you did get the first one. In any case, I'm sure it is not the *NYer*'s cup of dark brown tears—

Faithfully yrs,
Elizabeth

November 15, 1955

Dear Elizabeth:

I'm happy to say that we like SESTINA very much, and I should be sending you your check and the author's proof soon.

I'm also enclosing this pink proof of FILLING STATION so that you can see what it will look like. The author's proof got to be such a mess that you couldn't see the poem for the proof marks.

We've followed your directions throughout, except that we felt the best

---

1 Bishop submitted the line with hyphens with single spaces on either side. When the poem ran, no spacing was used between the dashes or the "so's."

2 Bishop submitted the lines as: "—Embroidered in daisy-stitch / with marguerites, I think, / and heavy with gray crochet."

3 Other changes between Bishop's submission and the poem's publication include: changing "This" to "this" in stanza one, line two; removing the comma after "set" in stanza three, line four; and removing the comma after "color" and inserting a dash in stanza four, line two.

solution to the problem of the last three lines of stanza 5 was using parentheses. I hope you think it's all right; if you don't, please drop me a line so we can tinker with it some more, perhaps. The trouble is that the question mark after doily does end the sentence definitely. So using a small e on embroidered wouldn't work. This way the whole parenthesis is like an afterthought, or qualification, and obviously refers to doily.[1]

We'll be happy if new poems as good as this one and SESTINA keep coming along at the same rate.

Ever,
Howard

November 20, 1955

Dear Howard:

I think the parenthesis after doily? works very well—stupid of me not to have thought of it. You don't need the pink proof back, do you—it all looks right to me now.

I'm glad you can use SESTINA—I never thought you would. I'd like to change what the almanac says to the present tense: "*I know what I know*", says the almanac. Also, it occurs to me that it begins with the "Line storm" of September, and says September, which means that *The New Yorker*, a rigid house, will use it in September. Unfortunately, the opposite line storm comes in June, does it not?—June 25th (I'm writing this in bed with a slight cold, and can't get up to the study to check up), which doesn't fit very well—so I'm afraid I'll have to wait until September after all. I'd gladly change it for "rains of March"—or something like that, which would go even better with the "planting" idea later on, literally speaking, but I'm afraid would not go with the mention of the equinox . . .

When am I going to receive that personal letter? Be sure you personalize it hard.

Faithfully yrs,
Elizabeth

P.S. I thought Dick Wilbur's Baroque Fountain had some lovely stanzas in it—if you're writing him I wish you'd tell him so for me.[2]

---

1 The lines ran as: "(Embroidered in daisy stitch / with margeurites, I think, / and heavy with gray crochet.)"
2 "A Baroque Wall-Fountain in the Villa Sciarra" (October 8, 1955).

November 24, 1955

Dear Howard:

This ["Manuelzínho"] is an impossible size and shape for any magazine, I'm afraid.

If *The New Yorker* can't use it, I wonder if I could ask you to send it on to the *Partisan Review* for me? They probably couldn't, either, but if you'd be good enough it would save two or three weeks and the risks of the mails both ways.

Perhaps, in any case, you could show it to Katharine White?—I think possibly she might enjoy it.

This may be an insult—but to be on the safe side—"Manuelzínho" is "little Manuel," and "h" is pronounced like "y" in English.

Faithfully yours,

Elizabeth

November 25, 1955

Dear Elizabeth:

I've changed "I knew what I knew" to "I know what I know" in SESTINA. As for the other change, we'd prefer to keep the original September line, unless there's some reason to print it before next September, like an English book you want to include it in, or something like that.[1]

I am writing you a personal letter—God, how words get to seem awful!—though I keep hoping you'll arrive in person soon so we can talk. I find it hard to divide myself into the executive me and me, and sometimes it gets all mixed up so that I feel I should enclose a check in every letter I send. Not a bad idea, really.

I don't understand what's happening in Brazil, but I hope and trust you're all right. Do come up soon. I promise at least one big party, and a magnum of small ones.

Ever,

Howard

1 Moss sent Bishop the proof on December 2nd. He inserted a number of commas: after "light" in stanza one, line two; after "small" in stanza three, line two; after "dark" in stanza four, line four; and after "But" in stanza six, line one. The only comma that remained for publication was the one added to the first stanza (*The New Yorker* Records).

November 28, 1955

Dear Howard:

This is a bad habit and I promise I will nip it in the bud . . .

If you received *Manuelzinho* and still have him on hand will you make the following corrections for me? Beginning of the third paragraph, "You steal my telephone wires, or someone does. You starve" etc.—It just happened again, and I think the present tense adds to the tone of exasperation. The same is true for the last line, which I think should read "Again I promise to try." (That was what I had to start with, of course.)

If you have returned it to me or sent it on to PR, it's all right. I'm sorry to be such a nuisance.

Faithfully yours,
Elizabeth

P.S. Brasil, in Brazil, is spelt with an *s*. But in English I think it is correct with a *z*, isn't it? I like it better, if it's right.

The New Yorker
December 7, 1955

Dear Elizabeth:

Your Sestina enchanted me, and I am so glad we have it to publish. I have rarely seen as skillful and effortless a handling of the form, and the poem itself is very moving. (Perhaps I've already written you this.) "Manuelzinho" is still in process of being read but in this case I dare give my personal opinion ahead of time (which of course is not to be taken as acceptance since the poem is so long). To me, it is one of your best poems. It absolutely delighted me. You will hear from Howard about the final decision very shortly. This last leads me to explain that when I came back from my vacation on September 1st, I did not take over from him the correspondence with you on your poems and the handling of your verse proofs (though of course I have read all the poems for opinions and made my usual comments on the proofs), just because I rather foresaw the change in my working habits here at the magazine that I am about to explain to you: After January first I shall no longer be reading poetry and fiction for opinion, or editing either verse or prose; I am leaving this department of the magazine and shall instead be working only on general policy and on other matters that concern the magazine as a whole. This was a terribly disrupting and difficult decision for me to make and I am full of grief about it, chiefly because it means that I shall no longer be working with writers like you. It is, even so, a necessary step for me to take and it is going to be much better for Andy's writing, and for my own health and happiness, that I be freer, able to move about when he wants to and with me less weighed down with the detail of the Fiction Department work than I am now. Yet when I think of the happiness and rewards I have had from working with you on a story like "In The Village," or from being able to cast a vote on your poems, or from your letters, the whole idea of stopping such work still seems to me almost unthinkable. Yet I must. (I hope that I shall still hear from you sometimes, though.)

For you, everything will go on at the New Yorker just as always. Every other editor here is just as eager as I am to have you contribute, and everyone admires your poetry and your fiction just as much as I do, I know. Howard will continue to be your verse editor. You should send your stories to G. S. Lobrano, who will decide who is to edit them.

I have one more pleasure to look forward to, though, and that is reading the manuscript of your translation of the Brazilian diary. Pearl tells me it will soon be along, which is good news. Since it isn't fiction, and *is* translation, I shall read it whenever it arrives, even if it is after January 1st. I do hope that parts of it may be possible for us. Please remember, too, that I shall be right at the office (or in close touch with it) and be sure to call on me if there is anything I can do for you in a general way. We still hope for the Sable Island piece of course, and for more short stories. It would be wonderful luck for me if a new short story arrived in the mail this month so that I could have the pleasure of writing one more opinion on one of your stories. And of course, Elizabeth, I shall be reading everything we buy from you with the same intense interest as always. It has been a joy to have you sending us so many poems again after such a long lapse—and such beautiful poems!

Faithfully always,

Katharine

December 20, 1955

Dear Katharine:

I think your letter must have been delayed in the Christmas rush at that end; I just received it yesterday and certainly there's no comparable rush here, and I've been getting letters from New York in four or even three days. This is by way of saying that I am answering it right away. I am awfully sorry to hear that you are giving up the editorial part of your work on the magazine. (At least I think that's what it amounts to, doesn't it?) I don't know much about the workings of The New Yorker, nothing at all, really, but I do know it was wonderful to feel that there was someone there I knew and liked and who couldn't have taken a kinder, or more personal, or more meticulous interest in everything I sent in. And it makes me very annoyed with myself for having planned things so badly—just when I've made up my mind to have 1956 be my Prose Year, and was just going blithely along, I discover, counting on having you there!

But I've never been able to understand how you and E. B. White do so much, anyway, and surely it is a wise decision for both of you. And for heaven's sake don't feel you are "giving up" any friends! That must be just an additional fantasy of the present moment, as you must know quite well and nip in the bud immediately!

If I had worked just a bit harder and not felt I had to take on a rush translating job this past month—but I did have to—I feel I might have been able to get a couple of stories in your tender hands, too, before you left:—An architect friend who had helped me out of visa difficulties, etc., is doing the first large complete account of contemporary Brazilian architecture.[1] It should be an important book and should appear before another one, or two, do, and he wanted his Portuguese text in good enough English to serve as a basis for the other translations, including Japanese, I think. His wife is having their first baby; the mass of material is fearful; and the deadline January 8th—I think we'll make it all right, but it has certainly been occupying my mind and time. I dropped everything for it, including Minha Vida de Menina, but that is almost done—I'm going to mail Pearl the 2nd section tomorrow or the next day, and the rest, I imagine, by the end of January, now.

I had one idea about it, or rather a Brazilian friend had,—heavens, maybe now I shouldn't go on about such ideas, but write them to Mr. Lobrano. Well, this once—If the New Yorker doesn't think it can use any of the diary directly,—fairly possible, I think,—I still believe that I could use some of the more interesting sections from it to make two stories, or at least accounts. The first, the finding of the diary; meeting the extraordinary old lady the author of it is now, and her extraordinary family and the whole funny business. The second, my trip to Diamantina, the dead and beautiful old town it happened in in the '90's, and looking up the places mentioned, etc. Well, I might try one, anyway. (Please skip this if you should . . .)

I am very happy that you like "Manuelzinho." Yours is the first outside opinion I have had and I was in the completely blank frame of mind in which

1 Henrique Mindlin, *Modern Architecture in Brazil* (1956).

the whole thing might have been Hickory Dickory Dock, as far as I could tell. But I do realize what a strange-looking page or is it three pages! it would make, for your purposes, so I won't be at all surprised if they feel they can't use it. That diminutive is awkward, too—but "zinho" this and that is so much a part of things here I found it impossible to think of anything else. (The friend supposed to be saying it was talking to me in English the other day and taking over an exclamation from me, said "heavenzinhos!" without even realizing it.) American readers are fairly familiar with the Spanish double *l*—*ll* sounding like *y*; but the *h* sounding like *y* is strange. This same friend, by the way, is the one who is so devoted to E. B. White's writings and is gradually spreading them around the intelligentzia of Brazil . . .

In the middle of this letter I made a trip to the Post Office and found the November 27th New Yorker, the Thanksgiving number. I am delighted with Pearl's story—all I knew was that she'd written one—and I think it is very good: very funny, very sad, and altogether nice—and telling a great deal more about life in Brownsville than many more solemn tales I've read. I'd always thought she could write something "funny" well—that isn't exactly the word, nor is "comic"—and I'm glad to see she has begun.[1]

Another friend of mine—I may have said this before, I'm not sure—who's done some nice stories lately, is Calvin Kentfield. He has a very nice, I think, touch of surprise and a surprising "naturalness" sometimes—Nabokov surprises, of course, but in a stranger way—and I like the change of strata in society Calvin has introduced.[2]

Thank you for your kind remarks about my book of poems—they seemed to come along at just the right moment, too, when I was in a sort of slump about the whole thing. Chatto & Windus is bringing out a small selection in England and they've also taken an option—sight unseen, as far as I know—on MVDM, which is nice. The old lady is ¼ English and that plays quite a part in her diaries and even now she keeps saying, "Oh, if only my Aunt Madge could have lived to see me have a book in *English*!"—As for poetry, I hope to have another book much sooner than that last one and I think I shall—Brazil, or my perpendicular stretch of it, seems to be the best, or maybe first, place I've found to work in steadily.

But I really feel so sad, Katharine, that you are changing your role at the New Yorker—and I'm sure many other writers are feeling the same way and wish you'd given two or three years warning, at least! There have been some

1 "We Gather Together" (November 26, 1955).
2 Kentfield's most recent story was "The Bell of Charity" (July 16, 1955).

exceptionally good things in the magazine lately, but at this moment the only one I can think of right off—and it will seem long ago to you—is Edmund Wilson's "Dead Sea Scrolls."[1] It must have been a success everywhere—I found a Brazilian friend, laid up from a heart attack, reading about the Bible in the Encyclopedia Britannica just because of that article, and planning to go on to the Bible itself next—& in Catholic countries you know, that is really amazing, for the ordinary reader.

Please don't feel this requires any reply, but also please don't feel it's any kind of farewell address! Thank you so much for your letter.

Affectionately yours,
    Elizabeth

December 28, 1955

Dear Elizabeth:

We are buying MANUELZINHO, thank God. It is *the* best poem I've read in ages, and I think the tone is handled marvelously—one of those absolutely right poems where the sense of someone's life is all there, and, as you know, it's very funny in that special way you have, without ever going against the grain of what it's doing.

I'll send you your check and the author's proof—which will probably look like the inside of Proust's pillowcase—as soon as they are ready.

I love MANUELZINHO, and my personal "personalized personal" letter is awaiting a revision of that poem I sent you too hastily. I'm afraid to send it again until I let the new version weather in a drawer.

Happy New Year, and love,
    Howard

December 31, 1955

Dear Howard:

Happy New Year.

This is a little bastard sonnet ["The Wit"], perhaps too much so for your more correct taste. "Bidden" would be the correct form, too, but under these circumstances (according to Fowler) I think "bid" will do.

I haven't heard about "*Manuelzinho*", but I know it would make an impossible-looking page for your purposes. I'm only mentioning it because I

1 "The Scrolls from the Dead Sea" (May 14, 1955).

hope it didn't get lost if you returned it to me—but there may be a bottle-neck in Rio at present; quite a lot of mail we expected at Christmas time hasn't appeared yet. Oh—I think I asked you to send it on to PR, didn't I?—if you have, that is all right, but if you haven't, please just return it to me. I don't know what to do with it, if anything, as far as a magazine goes.

No—the political situation, after our anti-revolution revolution, is quiet, but unpleasant—and the N.Y. papers seem to have all the issues completely reversed, so don't go by them. If you should happen to meet, at a party or anywhere, one of my best Brazilian friends, Carlos Lacerda, who's in exile in New York now for six months or so—do talk to him; he's awfully nice. (I've mentioned you to him, too.)

Your idea of a party appeals to me strongly—after so many party-less years. Maybe I'll make it in 1956. So also does your idea of a check in every letter—rather like Cyril Connolly's for having admiring readers send small monetary contributions to writers.

With all best wishes, yours,
Elizabeth

January 9 or 10, 1956
[The stationery reads in glitter:
"UNIDOS SEREMOS FELIZES"]

Dear Howard:

I just received your letter and I am so pleased that you can use "Manuel-zinho" after all. I was afraid you wouldn't be able to because of its length and width. I am afraid it may have cost you a good deal of work on my part, too, and this is a private note to say so & thank you . . .

I'm also very pleased that *you* seem to like it. I'll probably snow you under with poems now.

I liked what you said about your poem "weathering" in the bureau drawer. Think of the storms that rage in bureau drawers! But do take it out pretty soon.

My motto says "United we shall be happy"—so *true*, don't you think?
Yours,
Elizabeth

January 13, 1956

Dear Elizabeth:

I can't remember whether I wrote you that I am still at my old desk in the Fiction Department, because Gus Lobrano has been sick for over a month. He is now recovering from a gall bladder operation, in a hospital in Boston.

His illness is the reason that your first reading agreement has been delayed. You have been being paid for your contributions as if the agreement had been renewed on November 25, when the old one expired. Here is the new agreement now, with many apologies for the delay. I also enclose the hundred dollar check that goes with these agreement letters. We hope you will sign one of the letters and return it promptly.

I am hoping that one of the products of your "prose year" will soon be along, while I am still able to read it. Of course each new poem is a delight. You will hear from Howard on them. When I read the two-thirds of the diary, which is still being read by Pearl, I'll discuss with Shawn the prose pieces about it that you suggested in your last letter to me, and write you about them. I'm eager to read the diary.

Affectionately,
    Katharine

January 20, 1956

Dear Elizabeth:

Thanks for both of your letters.

THE WIT, which we all liked, caused some consternation here, since there were as many interpretations as there were readers. We felt, finally, that we shouldn't leave it up to *our* readers to decide what you intended, when we couldn't reach an agreement ourselves. Here are some of the alternatives: this is a comment on the birth of a quotable remark; it is a comment on a remark whose antecedents slowly come into consciousness; it is a poem on the birth of a wit—the punster, having been applauded, begins to shine.

I'm sorry we finally decided against it, especially since it may be our denseness, rather than a real ambiguity in the poem, that led to a negative vote. In the future, when we reject a poem, if you want me to send it on to PR, let me know. I hate to think of the poems stuck in that scheming bottleneck that I gather the Brazilian P.O. has come to be.

I am still getting joy and comfort from MANUELZINHO, and please do send us more poems soon.

Ever,
    Howard

January 24, 1956

Dear Elizabeth:

Here is the author's proof of MANUELZINHO. On the second page, New Yorker style would omit the quotation marks around Klorophyll Kid, but if you want to keep them, just cross out the pencil marking in the margin.[1]

I hope more poems are coming.

Ever,

Howard

January 27, 1956

Dear Katharine:

Here is the contract and I am most grateful for the check. I am also grateful for the copy of the Cartoon Album that came about a week ago—it would be fun to have anywhere, of course, but I am sure you have no idea how much they are appreciated here and how many captions I've been trying to turn into Portuguese for the benefit of ailing neighbors, etc.—it is an extremely useful book here.[2] Brazilians are very witty people, but it is strange—their own cartoons are horrible.

I was so glad to hear that you are staying on a while at your old job. I am finishing up *Minha Vida de Menina* just as fast as I can go now and hope to be able to get some other things off to you while you are still there. I am going to Diamantina—where MVDM took place—sometime in February, or just as soon as the rains are over, for a few days, to see it with my own eyes and write an introduction. It is odd to think that about 100 years ago the name of

---

1 Moss's punctuation changes to this poem are extensive. In stanza one, he removed the comma from the end of the first line and inserted a dash. He made the same change to the end of line six, and he deleted the dash at the start of line seven. In stanza two, he inserted commas at the ends of lines two and nine. In stanza three, he removed the commas after "loud" in line eight and after "potatoes" at the end of line nine. He also deleted the comma after "potatoes" inside the closed quotes in line sixteen and the comma after "vanished" in line seventeen. A change that did not stand was inserting a comma after "time" in line fifteen. In stanza four, he inserted commas after "hat" in line seven and after "you" in line nine. A change that did not remain was the removal of the comma after "happen" in line one. In stanza five, he placed commas around "briskly" in line twelve and changed the comma after "earth" to a dash at the end of line twenty-five. In stanza seven, he inserted a comma after "standing" in line six and removed the dash at the start of line eight. Two changes that did not stay were inserting commas after "horse" in line ten and after "Formoso" in line eleven. In stanza eight, Moss deleted the commas after "paint" in what became line eight. In the same line he deleted the comma after "why" and inserted a dash, which he had removed from the start of line nine. He also inserted a comma after "small" in line twelve and a comma after "while" in line sixteen (Bishop had submitted the line as "For a while one was gold,". In stanza nine, Moss deleted the period from the end of the penultimate line and inserted a semicolon. The period was restored prior to publication (*The New Yorker* Records).

2 *The New Yorker 1950–1955 Album* (1955).

that place was well known all over Europe, in England, etc.—and now, I gather, it is a sort of ghost town—it is certainly hard to get to, at any rate.

I hope you are well and that we'll be communicating again soon—
Affectionately yours,
    Elizabeth

January 31, 1956

Dear Howard:

I'm sorry to make so many corrections on this. I did send you a slightly improved version shortly after sending the first one—in which I changed the last line back to "Again I promise to try," and, I think, made most of these other small changes, too—but it must have got lost.

Yes, I prefer Klorophyll Kid without quotation marks. In the 3rd paragraph I'd like to change "bring" to "fetch", if you approve. It's the word the "speaker" would use and it goes better with the general "f"-ness. But perhaps it will strike you as an anglicism, or affected, and if so please leave "bring."[1]

I don't feel that commas are necessary in

> "in dim moonlight, the horse
> or Formoso, stumbling after."

But perhaps the New Yorker does?[2] I put it, "The strangest things happen, to you" because that's the way one should say it, implying that they happen to him especially. But perhaps the comma does not do that?[3]

Otherwise I think the punctuation is all right now and I think the poem looks very nice and thank you for all your work on it. None of this is worth writing me again about—I'll be guided by New Yorker usage. [Handwritten: "'bright-blue' should have a hyphen—I was wrong. I've also inserted one line, in parentheses, after, 'She has gone over & over / (Forearmed is forewarned.) / your pair of bright-blue', etc.—"][4]

---

1 Bishop submitted the line as: "and bring me those potatoes,". Bishop wrote *"fetch?"* in the right margin of the last extant draft (Vassar College Library). The poem ran with "fetch".

2 The lines ran as Bishop submitted them.

3 The line ran as Bishop submitted it.

4 Additional changes between Bishop's submission and the poem's publication include: removing the comma after "week" in stanza one, line fourteen; changing the commas to dashes at the end of stanza two, lines three and four; changing "I see you all up there, / twined in the wisps of fog," to "Twined in wisps of fog, / I see you all up there" in stanza seven, lines one and two; and adding "along" to the start of stanza seven, line three, changing "today /

I'm afraid that sonnet *is* confusing. I meant that making a pun is unlike logical thought; instead of building up, it fractures, in a contrary way—as we might imagine the birth of a star, or creation itself, as taking place against or outside the order of human thought . . . But without the sonnet to refer to, you'll find this explanation equally confusing. Thank you for being so obliging when I've asked you to send things on for me, but you were right to return this. It's probably not etiquette or something, anyway, to ask you.[1]

Please forgive me for sounding carping, won't you—but perhaps you'd better tell whoever types envelopes for you to type my address the way it is above. It's Petrópolis, in the State of Rio de Janeiro (like the State of Washington, etc.). I think one or two of your letters have gone to the city of Rio de Janeiro for a few days because the address was typed Petrópolis, Estado do / Rio de Janeiro (R. de J. on a separate line, so at first glance they thought it was the city, not the state). It's confusing, I know—but the Post Office is already confused enough!

Faithfully yours,
Elizabeth

February 17, 1956

Dear Elizabeth:

I'm going off day after tomorrow for a five weeks vacation with Andy, who has been sick. Yes, I'm still at my desk after all, and it is only because we have been so short-handed here that I haven't written you before now about "Minha Vida De Menina." I have read the sections that are here almost all the way through, but not quite all the way. I found the book delightful, and the translation is so pure and simple and so completely without any sense of its being translation that I know you have a small work of art here, both in the original and in your version. I do think, though, and I believe Pearl agrees with me and the other editors in this decision, that excerpts of the diary will not work out well as a series of pieces for The New Yorker. I had so hoped they would, but the difficulty is that the effect of the book is cumulative. The reader becomes enthralled in the little diarist and her family after a time, but it does take time and space—more than is available in a weekly magazine— to do it, and so far as I've read there seem to be no separatable incidents that

your limbs" to "and these days / your limbs" in stanza eight, lines six and seven, in addition to flip-flopping "For a while, one was gold," to "One was gold for a while," in stanza eight, line sixteen.

1 *The New Republic* published the poem in its February 13, 1956, issue.

are not too gentle and mild to stand alone. (Not that Helena was gentle! She *really* had fire.) Also, the greatest pleasure in the book, of course, is to watch Helena Morley grow up, and develop as a personality, and this would not be possible to achieve in our space, we're afraid.

However, it may well be that in the sections I have not read there are little short stories that do stand alone. If so we hope you will point them out. Also, in the two pieces you are going to write that you described to me in your letter—your story of finding the diary and of the diarist today, and your visit to Diamantina, which, as I understand it you are to use as an introduction—it just might be that there would be New Yorker material, especially if you illustrated your own essays with telling excepts from the diary. I felt it fair to tell you this, yet at the same time I don't think it would be conscientious of us to suggest that you put in days and days of work on the selection of excerpts, just because we all feel that the material is rather far afield for The New Yorker. I have discussed it with Shawn. He feels, and I agree, that we would be wrong to encourage you to put a lot of time on a venture that would be so speculative. On the other hand, he hopes very much that you will let us read your preface material; it might change his mind, and since you are writing it anyway, we hope you will do this. But for making a special version including excerpts of the translation, we do feel quite strongly that, both for you and for us, the time would be better spent on your own fiction and on your projected fact pieces, like the one on Sable Island. This is to be your fiction year, you say, and this is wonderful news for us.

My own plans are still unsettled but it does not now look as if I would be entirely out of the picture after all, though when I wrote you, it was, I thought, a fact. In any case, do continue to send me your fiction and your poetry. We long for more of both, as we look forward to the diary preface material, too. When I am on vacation, please address manuscripts to me just the same, and Howard or William Maxwell will read them.

Poor Howard has had a painful but not dangerous operation this week but should be working at home next week and back here the week after.

Much love,
Katharine

February 24, 1956

Dear Katharine:

I found your letter at the Post Office this morning on a marketing expedition—it is the "summer season", carnival is just over, and school holidays are on, and the little town of Petrópolis is so crowded that we've cut down our marketing to once a week, which means mail once a week, too—and I was delighted to hear your reactions to "Minha Vida de Menina." You are my first outside "straight" audience and it seems to me you feel about it just the way I hoped you would. It has encouraged me a great deal and I am sitting up late tonight putting some final polish on the last section, but interrupting myself to type you this note of thanks.

What you say about it in connection with The New Yorker is exactly what I've felt myself all along and believe I've said to you, more or less, too. It takes too much of it to produce an effect, for your purposes, I'm sure. This last year, 1895, however, she does write better and more at length, and there are a few longer episodes—five or six pages each—but I still don't think they'd be too good. When I mail it to Pearl I'll indicate them, though.—She writes better, but adolescence is rapidly overtaking her and a note of sentimentality does creep in from time to time, although she is still the same tough-minded child underneath. I had also had exactly the same idea you had about my showing you the introduction first. Any kind of excerpt-ing and hitching together like that is very hard and time-consuming, and I think it would be much better for you to look at the Introduction first to see if you think it would be worth it at all—or for one piece, if not two. I was going to Diamantina day before yesterday, then it started raining again so I've postponed it until next week—it would be pretty deadly there if it rained.

I'd hoped to get it all off two or three weeks ago but the friend doing the copying has been sick and I myself have been held up somewhat by the fact that we now have three small children here—1, 2, & 3 years old—two of them adoptive grandchildren, or however one might put it, of the friend I live with (she has an adopted son)—their mother has been very sick, and is now about to arrive too, with a new one, aged 4 weeks . . . And although we have plenty of room and even "*babás*" as nursemaids are called, it does mean a great deal of rushing about and reading Dr. Spock and Dr. Gesell! I find my spoken Portuguese is just about right, conversationally, for a child aged 17 months . . . rather disillusioning. They are very good children and we like having them very much, thank goodness.

I am sorry to hear Howard's been having a difficult time. I hope he received the proof of "Manuelzinho" safely—it looked like something the cat brought in, but I think it was all legible. I also hope your husband is better by now—this is a dreadful time to be in New York, I think.

I'll be mailing the rest of MVDM very shortly, I hope, and then I hope I'll be mailing you a good many things—work seems to be going very well these days. I have some Brazilian sketches outlined, three, or four, possibly, the first one roughly written, and although they are rather wild I am hoping you'll find them entertaining—and I must confess that much as I enjoy Helena's remarks and philosophy (I'm like Proust's grandmother & Madame de Sevigné about her by now), I am dying to get back to some of my own.

Always affectionately,

Elizabeth

—I forgot, last night, to wish you a pleasant rest & holiday—

March 22, 1956

Dear Katharine:

Just the day before your letter came I read in TIME of Mr. Lobrano's death and I was terribly surprised and realized it must mean a very great loss to you.[1] I am awfully sorry, for you, and for the magazine's sake. (Even though I don't contribute to it in any great quantity I do have a deep and somehow personal feeling for it.) I do hope you can find the kind of editor you want and it must be an extremely hard task, I know. I'm overwhelmed by being asked if I know of anyone, and flattered—but most of the "literary" people I know are the poets or critics, who all seem to teach, these days, and have no practical editorial experience—and of course, I'm very out of touch now, anyway.

I've meant to tell you I've thought Dwight MacDonald's pieces and reviews awfully good the past year. Sometimes I like Anthony West & sometimes I don't, but I did think he did a fine job on that book about the Boston politician—not even the "left" magazines I see here seemed to see it as it really must be. "*The Last Hurrah.*"[2]

I hope that you're having a nice vacation and both feeling well. Here is a little story I just heard: a man I know here has a mother-in-law who recently celebrated her 100th birthday. Apparently she's a lively old lady, very interested in politics (& if she can keep up with them *here* for 100 years she must be strong), listens to the radio, watches television all the time and argues with everyone. The son-in-law wanted a little celebration for her and sent an announcement to the newspapers, etc., and when she found out what he'd

1 "Milestones" (March 12, 1956).
2 Edwin O'Connor, *The Last Hurrah* (1952), reviewed by West (February 11, 1956).

done she took him aside and said couldn't he please change it just a little bit? Couldn't he please make it her eightieth birthday? 100 sounded so *old*.

With that inspiring thought I'll say goodbye. I hope to be sending you some things shortly now.

Affectionately yours,

Elizabeth

March 23rd

Since I don't believe my letter will get mailed for a day or two I'm going to add a note to it.

I know that Miss Bogan is very happy with her reviewing job for you—at least a few years ago she once told me she was, what excellent employees she'd found you always, etc. But just on the chance that some day, some year, she might want to stop—I wonder if I could put my name on your *list of applicants* as a possible poetry-reviewer? I never wanted to do any reviewing before, and I haven't done very much—some for the Library of Congress publication, and a few besides (in *Poetry* and *The New Republic*, I think) but lately I've been thinking I'd like to, after all. I think it has something to do with distance making one feel one doesn't give a damn, perhaps—or helping one to get the contemporary poets in better perspective,—at any rate, I've felt I'd like to do it, and could do it fairly easily. But *The New Yorker* seems to be the only publication I'd like to write a review for. For one thing, Miss Bogan's reviews only mention those books that really seem to be of some importance; for another, they are brief reviews and don't attempt to write like Kenneth Burke every time, the way reviews in the "little" magazines do,—Burke, or Empson, or imitation Jarrell—which I've always felt was unnecessary. Also, it seems to me to be something I could do perfectly well at long distance, if I keep on living in Brazil,—which I probably shall, part of the time, at least.

This is just an idea and I hope it is all right to mention it—Miss Bogan may be eager and able to keep on for twenty years more, and I think she is very good at it, in general; she's kept up a very high level. But I thought there would be no harm in mentioning it to you and if the possibility ever did come up you might think of me and give me the opportunity to write a "sample" or two, perhaps.—Also there's the fact that books do come here safely, in about three weeks—the only thing that does, apparently.—It's just an idea—Please don't feel you have to reply to it at any length—

April 4, 1956

Dear Elizabeth:

Thank you very much for your good letter of March 22nd and for what you said about Gus. I passed your anecdote about the 100th birthday on to The Talk of the Town and will let you know about that later. The P.S. about the poetry reviewing went to Shawn, of course. So far as I know Louise does not want to give up doing the reviews now but we are very much interested to have your name as a person to do them if Louise wanted to stop for one reason or another. Thank you for making this suggestion.

I am of course now hoping earnestly that your year of prose has started and that we shall soon have a short story or two. Just now I am swamped in trying to get squared away on the new job, so this can't be a real letter.

Affectionately,
    Katharine

April 26, 1956

Dear Elizabeth:

The Talk of the Town department returned your anecdote with regret— the one I had copied and attach. I'm sorry.

Spring isn't here even yet, this year. It's probably waiting for one of your prose pieces to get here first.

Love,
    Katharine

May 18, 1956

Dear Elizabeth:

It is a sample of what my life is like now that I have had to wait all this time to write you how much I rejoice about your having won the Pulitzer Prize. The morning I read it in the paper my spirits rose, for it has seemed to me that you have deserved all the prizes for poetry this year. And I found myself saying, "At last!"

This can be only this small note, to congratulate you and say how happy I am. We are using "Manuelzinho" in the issue that goes to press this week. I hope that you like its appearance on the page; we fussed about with the layout and I think it now looks well.

Affectionately,
    Katharine

Dear Howard:

Thank you so much for writing me a note about that prize . . . Naturally I feel it probably should have gone to someone else, that never, never, has it been awarded for so little work, etc., etc., and your note was one of the things that helped me derive a small amount of normal satisfaction from it all . . . We've had lots of fun here, though, being televised and news-reeled and radioed and the waxed floors are just beginning to recover. What I liked best was being asked to pose with *Miss Concurso Hippico* (Miss Race Track)—a Horse Race—a runner-up for Miss Universe. You'd love her— very tall, a tiny, tiny head, blue eyes and very *fuzzy*—I think it's either the latest style or we were all fuzzy once & it wore off. I hope to send you some poems very soon now.

Much love,
Elizabeth

P.S.—I saw a lovely, long, musical poem by you recently—an extra-nice one.[1]

June 1, 1956

Dear Howard:

I *did* thank you for your kind and cheering note, didn't I? I am fairly sure I did but if you didn't receive it please let me thank you again—it meant a great deal to me.

I am writing to tell you about something just plain *dumb* I have just done. Some time ago, over a year I think, a Mr. Alfredo Rizzardi (who has probably been in touch with you, too—he seems to know all American poets) asked me to contribute something to a Pound 70th birthday number of a magazine he gets out, in Bologna. I considered a piece of prose, couldn't get it going, and finally refused, firmly. The deadline was last October or November. Well, a short while ago I found my name announced as a contributor, in POETRY, and then he wrote again, saying that he *had* announced me, was "blackmailing" me, that he'd held up the magazine because of me, etc. (I don't really know why he thought I had anything to contribute about Pound, but anyway . . .) So being weak-minded as well as absent-minded, apparently, I sat

---

1 Moss's most recent poem in *The New Yorker* was "Local Places" (April 21, 1956).

down and wrote him a poem ["Visits to St. Elizabeth's"], or a kind of a poem—wrote it and sent it off in 24 hours. In about ten days I received it back, all translated into Italian. (I hadn't realized that the magazine was printed in Italian.) So I sent it back to him a few days ago and still don't know whether he is definitely using it or not—but I suppose so—and it wasn't until I had done all this that I realized with horror that I'd done something unethical and completely forgotten my *New Yorker* contract. I don't know how I could have been so thoughtless. I'd hate to have you see a poem by me somewhere that you hadn't seen first, or even see anything announced . . . What consoles me somewhat is that I don't think you could possibly be interested in it. I'm enclosing a copy of the poem—if you can call it that; I'm not very proud of it—and you can see what unlikely material it is. If there is the faintest chance of your wanting it—I can't believe there is, but just in case—perhaps I could cable Mr. Rizzardi, or you could, at my expense, and tell him not to use it. Or, if it's just appearing in Italian, maybe it wouldn't matter. But anyway I hope to goodness it will be all right and I am awfully sorry to have been so careless—he really rather hounded me, and I suppose Bologna and New York just didn't connect in my mind at all when I blithely mailed this to him—

May Swenson mailed me the page with *Manuelzinho* on it and I am very pleased with the way it looks. I liked her poem you used recently, about the reflections in the water in Central Park—one of her best, I thought.[1]

Please do let me know if this is all right. I really can't imagine this bitter jingle in your pages so I'll hope for the best.

Faithfully yours,
Elizabeth

His address is VIA MENGOLI, 5, BOLOGNA

June 3, 1956

Dear Katharine:

Thank you so much for your note about the Pulitzer. I was really and truly surprised—I had the idea it had been given out long before and I'd missed the announcements! And it's been a lot of fun here, where they take "literature" and The Poet much more seriously than we do in the U.S.A.—

---

1 "Water Picture" (April 14, 1956).

We—everybody, that is, including the cook's black baby and my black cat—got in on the act, and were even in the newsreels. But now the excitement is dying down and I am getting back to work. I'm sending Pearl the introduction to my translation this week. It's rather short and simple, but the middle section—I'll ask her to show it to you—is the part that just possibly might be developed into a piece for you. I could add quite a bit to it—things not relevant to the introduction.

May Swenson (I've liked some of her recent poems in The New Yorker, particularly that one about reflections) sent me the page with "Manuelzinho" on it and I am very pleased with the way it looks. It must have been hard to fit in properly, I'm sure. I have just finished writing a note to Howard, explaining something rather *stupid* I did—if necessary he can explain it to you, but I trust and hope it will be all right. But I can imagine how fearfully busy you must be at present. I enjoyed Mr. White's article about Florida very much—and I love the ones about Lillian Leitzel that we've just received now. I saw her many times when I was little and thought she was the ideal of glamour and skill.[1]

Thank you again for being so nice and writing me a note—I hope I'll be sending you or Howard some things very soon now. I hope you are well and tough after your vacation.

Affectionately yours,
Elizabeth

P.S.—I believe that every single remark of Harvey Breit's so far has been wrong—in case you ever read him![2]

June 12, 1956

Dear Elizabeth:

Though we admire the notion and the ingenuity of the Pound poem, you were right in thinking it wasn't for us, so there's no harm done. I do hope, though, you'll have some others you'll want to send us soon.[3]

---

1 "Letter from the South" (April 7, 1956) and Robert Lewis Taylor, "Star-I" and "Star-II" (April 21 and 28, 1956).

2 Bishop is referring to Breit's May 20 and 27 "In and Out of Books" columns in *The New York Times Book Review* in which he discussed Bishop and her Pulitzer Prize. In his May 20 column, he addressed a letter to Bishop answering her poem, "Letter to N.Y." In his May 26 column, he reports on an "agent" (Mario Silviano) he sent to Samambaia to meet her. Bishop later wrote a friendly note to thank him for mentioning her in his column and to correct him on a few details from Mr. Silviano's visit.

3 *Nuova Corriente: Rivistas di Letteratura* published "Visits to St. Elizabeths" in 1956.

I was intrigued, by the way, by your notion, that we were once, perhaps, all covered with fuzz but that it wore off. I have investigated the matter carefully, and you may be right.

Love,
Howard

August 15, 1956

Dear Howard:

Here is a Nature Note ["The Armadillo"]. Since I realize you really don't want to run a Brazilian column, I won't be surprised if you feel you can't use it. Send it back and I'll save it for a Brazilian group I'm working on.

Perhaps you are away now on your vacation. If so I hope you're having a nice time and writing. I liked the sad little elegy by you I saw some time ago now.[1]

I think May Swenson is doing better all the time. A young Negro girl named Gloria Oden recently sent me some poems in which I see great possibilities.[2] I suggested that she try sending a few short ones to you, so perhaps you might keep an eye out for them.

Affectionately,
Elizabeth

August 24, 1956

Dear Elizabeth:

We love THE ARMADILLO, which is charming and much more.

We would like, if you don't mind, to put "Brazil" in parentheses under the title to place the poem, and a word from you about what "time of year" these fire-balloons are used would help us run it at the right time to go with the suggested sub-title.

Many thanks for THE ARMADILLO, and we are anxious, as always, to see others. I received some poems from Gloria Oden, which weren't right for us, but which I liked, and I have asked her to send us more. I hope she does.

Ever,
Howard

1 "Small Elegy" (June 16, 1956).
2 Oden's first book was *The Naked Frame: A Love Poem and Sonnets* (1952).

September 3, 1956

Dear Howard:

I'm glad you liked *The Armadillo*. I wish I wrote prophetic poems some-times instead of the recollected kind—the fire-balloons start appearing in June. They are used mostly to celebrate St. John's day—that's either June 14th or 15th—the biggest holiday here. I think they are also used for another saint sometime in August—anyway, one sees them frequently in the month of June, and occasionally in July and August.

I think that perhaps the last stanza would look better italicized; what do you think? If it is, perhaps I could leave off the final exclamation point. I also think that "escaping" in the fifth stanza would be better exchanged for "for-saking". I trust that's my final tinkering.[1]

Gloria Oden wrote me that you wrote her a "lovely letter" that was very kind of you and I hope she sends you some more short poems sometime. I've only seen three, I think, but I thought they were pretty good. And I hope that I'll be sending you a batch fairly soon now.

With all best wishes,
    Elizabeth

September 18, 1956

Dear Katharine:

A few days ago I mailed the introduction to my translation to Miss [Ber-nice] Baumgarten, the agent [at Brandt & Brandt]. I asked her to send a copy of it to you and I imagine you'll be receiving it in about a week. I'd like you to see if you think it couldn't be expanded into a short travel piece about Diamantina (the town where the book I translated took place) for you. There is a longish second section—twelve pages—about Diamantina, and some material from the last sections could be used too, I think. I'd leave out all ref-erences to the book, or "Helena" (the girl it was written by, as you may remember—or well may not, by now!), and just make it a travel piece. Besides what I tell in the introduction there's quite a bit more I could include—I did make a trip to a big U.S. owned mine and stayed with the driller and his wife (apparently famous characters in the U.S. mining world), and saw and did quite a lot that of course wasn't relevant to the introduction. While I have all the facts in mind, and the books here (& Sir Richard Burton

---

1 In the last extant draft, the line runs: "and steadily escaping us,". Bishop wrote by hand "forsaking" next to the line (Vassar College Library).

has some wonderful stuff, too) I think I could easily expand it about ten pages for you—if you think it would be of enough interest. Anyway, I'd like you to see it.

I feel we've been out of touch for far too long. Now that I've at last got that translation out of the way (and never again!) I've started on some stories—you'll be getting the first very shortly. The first is not the best—I'm working up to that—but I fear *it*'s much too long and wild.

I hope everything has been going well for you this past summer and that you had a vacation and that Maine was as nice as ever. I wonder if Howard ever received my letter about the "Armadillo" poem—I answered his immediately but I haven't heard and maybe mine got lost. But I should write to him, of course.

With love and best wishes,
Elizabeth

September 21, 1956

Dear Elizabeth:

Here's the proof of THE ARMADILLO, and your check.

We've had a change of mind about the title. We think it looks better if Brazil is put into the title after a dash—rather than the sub-title I first suggested. We also think putting the last stanza into italics is a good idea, and if you still think so, we'll have it set up that way before it comes out.

I think all the other suggestions are clear, except I'm not sure about the commas in the last line of stanza 3. It depends, I think, on whether you mean Mars to be going down, as well as Venus, or whether you're simply qualifying Venus, then refer to Mars with no qualification, and then go on to the pale green one. I hope that makes sense, but please do what you want with the punctuation. I think the line is clearer with the commas if you're referring to three separate things, each with or without its own qualifiers.[1]

We hope, as always, that there will be more poems coming soon, and thanks again for this one.

Ever,
Howard

1 In the last extant draft, the lines run: "Venus going down or Mars // or the pale green one." It ran as "Venus going down, or Mars, // or the pale green one." (Vassar College Library).

September 22, 1956

Dear Katharine:

I don't know whether you'll be able to use this true, but awfully simple, autobiographical sketch or not . . . Perhaps it should be called *"Rachel & The U.S.A. School of Writing"* since it is divided evenly between the two—
Elizabeth

October 5, 1956

Dear Howard:

If you can't use this ["Sunday, 4 A.M."]—& I don't imagine you can— would you be kind enough to send it on to PR for me? And thank you very much.

Thank you for the recent check. I hope to send you some possibilities very soon now.
Faithfully yours,
Elizabeth

October 12, 1956

Dear Elizabeth

I enclose a copy of a letter I have just had to send to Bernice Baumgarten. I'm so very sorry about the preface, and so were the editors in the Fact Department, but the piece is really a bit out of our way and for our purposes it would have had to be rewritten, and it all seemed impractical, especially in view of the awkward coincidence of our having just finished running that very long series of pieces by Emily Hahn on mining towns in South Africa.[1]

Meanwhile your manuscript "The U.S.A. School of Writing" has come in and is now in Shawn's hands, to read this weekend. I shall be writing you soon on that, I hope.
With love, and in haste,
Katharine

1 "Diamond" ran from April 7 to September 29, 1956.

Dear Katharine:

I am sorry about the Diamantina piece (I'd planned to have such fun quoting Burton!) but I see what you mean, of course. I'm afraid I was so busy with my own little diamond-digging researches that I completely forgot about Miss Hahn's enormous ones. However, now I've started in on South America I'm going on—I believe I told you I have a small book planned out and begun—and after a while I'd like to send you a section or two to see.

Last week I received a book to review from *The New Republic*, air mail,—for their fall book supplement, and of course they wanted it done immediately. Since I don't believe that book reviews or criticism are included in my contract with you—and since I'm quite sure you wouldn't be interested in it (Wm. Jay Smith's translation of Laforgue), I did do it, and mailed it back yesterday. I felt quite sure you wouldn't object. However, I'd like to tell you that I've been asked to do a monthly review of U.S. books or periodicals—a sort of literary letter—for a new review starting here soon. I don't believe *The New Yorker* would have any objection to that, would it?—or be interested in my efforts—pieces about 2000–3000 words, probably, and of course to be put into Portuguese. But I thought I'd better let you know.

I have two stories almost ready to send to see what you think—one, I *think*, as good as *In the Village*, but both better than the U.S. Writing School sketch, certainly. I hope you are well and not working too hard.

Love & best wishes,
    Elizabeth

Dear Howard:

I hasten to thank you for your beautiful poem ["Letter to an Imaginary Brazil"]. I picked it up at the Post Office last night and read it through at the local café, with a lump in my throat. I was so pleased and touched that I couldn't make much sense out of it then, although I saw that you'd made some changes. Today I've been comparing it with the first version. "Improvement" is so rare, in anything, I suppose—but you have improved the poem, enormously, I think—of course I'm hopelessly prejudiced.

The second stanza is much better, don't you think—says much more to me, at any rate. "ironed out among the dark crevasses" I like, and the "naturalism / That cannot weigh the difference between / A feather and a leaf." / But I like particularly the last six lines—they are lovely, and so like a "samambaia" (giant fern)—for which the land where I live is named.[1] (Too bad I can't send you one to fill one end of your apartment and hang a hammock from.) You are quite uncanny; the house is "modern" and has lots of glass, of course, and one of the unplanned-for but nice things about it is that at night the windows do reflect back and forth: the sunset, the mountains, each other; and the living-room *is* "hung up" between the mountains just as you say. I'll try to send you a snapshot. We are just ending the season of "sulphurous yellow" trees, too. I think you should pay me a visit and write a companion poem: *Letter from a Real Brazil*. Seriously—we'd love to have you, or you and a travelling companion (it's too far to come alone), for as long as you cared for a really extremely quiet country life . . .

And speaking of explorers—when I next see you I must tell you about the lost scout-master here and the night we spent waiting for him to be rescued from a "dark crevasse"—a funny story, fortunately.

I'm afraid I sent you a poem "too fast" last week—I don't know why it seemed good at the time. And the minute I saw *Sestina* again [in *The New Yorker*] I thought of a change that makes it much better, I think.[2]

We really hope to get to New York for some months, by next September . . . I hope everything is going well with you.

Thank you again; love,
Elizabeth

Here's a feather, an owl's—or is it a leaf?

October 19, 1956

Dear Elizabeth:

I had better warn you at once that this letter is full of bad news, except for the small "COLA" (cost of living adjustment) check I now enclose for your earnings on verse in the last quarter.

---

1 The last six lines are:

> You'll see, as fine as fern, a single tree
> Which, sprouting all its foliage at once,
> Will seem to move beneath a microscope
> Until each cell is separate to the eye,
> Thin-scaled as life upon the width of death,
> Who cannot read your poems, Elizabeth.

2 Bishop changed two words after "Sestina" appeared. "Heartless almanac" became "clever almanac" at the end of the third stanza, and "Like a bird," became "Birdlike," at the start of the fourth.

First, I'm terribly sorry to have to report that the decision went against "The U.S.A. School of Writing." The vote was mixed, and the piece seemed to arouse two quite opposite sets of opinions among the four editors who read it. The deciding one was Shawn's, of course, and he felt that both this kind of correspondence writing school and the character of Rachel were familiar as subject matter. Another point made against the piece was that, in a way, it broke in two between the school and Rachel, about half the piece being devoted to each. One trouble I myself found, although I was entertained throughout, was that from the way you wrote the piece, one could not be quite sure how much was fact and how much fiction, but this I felt you could clarify. Perhaps you intend it as a short story, but if it is all true, as you said in your letter, I think you could make this plain to your reader, and that the piece would gain by it. Indeed, what I had hoped was that, if treated as fact, the story might make an "Onward and Upward with the Arts" piece for us, but Bill Shawn didn't agree. He felt it needed more humor for that and less familiar material. Anyway, none of us thinks it works as fiction, so the answer has to be a regretful no. I'm terribly sorry.[1]

Now what I need to know is whether to return the manuscript to you, or whether to send it to Bernice Baumgarten, to sell elsewhere, or whether you would like me to send it direct to some other magazine you will name. Distrusting the mails, I'll hold the manuscript here for you until you write. I think Bernice would like to handle it if you wanted her to.

I have reason for distrusting the mails because a dreadful thing has happened. Your preface, which was mailed to Bernice the day I wrote you last—October 12th—has apparently been lost in the post. We at once put a tracer on it, and I feel sure that it was missent and will turn up eventually. This happened to a manuscript envelope we sent out about a year ago. It was correctly addressed but took one month to arrive at its destination. But that it should happen to this preface is *miserable*, since apparently you sent Bernice only one copy. If she agrees, I'll send a cable asking you to send a copy to her by air mail. She and I have already discussed it but decided to wait a day or two longer on the chance the manuscript would turn up at her office.

Writing you this big bundle of bad news makes a miserable day for me. The gloom will linger because I am so terribly anxious to have you writing prose for us again. I hope you can forgive me—and the magazine.

1 *The New Yorker* published the story after Bishop's death as "The U.S.A. School of Writing" (July 18, 1983).

The poems have been beautiful—a great source of pride and pleasure to us all. "Sunday: 4 A.M." is with Shawn so I have no answer on that yet.

    Affectionately,

      Katharine

Later: Bernice is sending you the cable. The book ms. is with H&M and she doubts that the delay will matter much. I do hope not. KSW

October 23, 1956

Dear Elizabeth:

    We love SUNDAY, 4 A.M. and I hope to have a proof and a check for you very soon. The last line, to single something out, is a dream.

    Thank you for sending it, and we hope others will be along soon.

    Ever,

      Howard

October 24, 1956

Dear Katharine:

    The Brazilian friend I live with here happened to be the one to go the Post Office yesterday and get the cable from Miss Baumgarten. Thinking it might be something she should telephone back to the house about, send a reply to, etc., she opened it, of course. After several years of my, and other Americans' (including Mr. Basso's), unkind remarks about the Brazilian mail system, I think it was really rather cheering to her . . . It's even rather cheering to me, in an unpatriotic way. So please don't worry about the lost Introduction—except that I'm afraid you already have.

    At the same P.O. she had just mailed another copy of the Introduction, as it happened, to Miss B for me, enclosing a letter saying that as it's so hard to get good copying, in English, done here, and since my typing is so slow and bad, I wondered if Miss B could get the necessary copies for me in N.Y. (Never having had an agent before, I'm not sure how these things should be arranged.) So now I just hope *that* copy doesn't get lost between Petrópolis and N.Y.

    Also please don't feel badly about the U.S. School of Writing!—I had a feeling it wouldn't do, but it was something I wanted to get down. Maybe sometime I'll do it over again, at greater length, I think, and "make something of it." Your objections are perfectly right. Will you send it back here, please?

I am so sorry to hear about Howard and I think I'll write him a note. He had a very nice poem, uncannily accurate about Brazil, & dedicated it to me, in the last *Hudson Review*, and I was very pleased and touched.

Now that it's been straightened out, through Mr. Melanson's kind offices, I can tell you that we haven't been getting *The New Yorker* for some time—I missed the last of the diamond mining pieces and all of Mary on Venice—but they're sending back copies, so now I can catch up.[1]

Now I'll write Miss Baumgarten and then get back to the other stories. I do hope you're keeping well, but have a feeling you are probably working too hard. Thank you for the check.

Affectionately yours,

Elizabeth

[nd]
[postcard: trolley above Largo dos Prasinha]

Dear Howard:

Katharine writes me that you've been sick & may have to have a gall-bladder operation. I'm so sorry to hear this & hope the operation proves unnecessary. However—I believe that lots of people get along much better without gall-bladders than with them (including a neighbor of mine here, age 76, who is blooming like a rose after having hers out last year). This is just to send you my best wishes.—& to show you a thrilling trolley ride you could take, in Rio— Elizabeth

October 26, 1956

Dear Elizabeth:

Doubtless Bernice has already told you that the preface is not lost—that it turned up in the mail, delayed beyond explanation. Thank God it isn't lost. I am so sorry you had to be disturbed about it.

Your October 18th letter raised the matter of your reviewing books. By your agreement you are perfectly free to do this without ever raising the question with us. Also your literary letter for the new Brazilian review would not come under the heading of "poetry, prose fiction, humor, reminiscence,

---

1 McCarthy's essay on Venice, "The Revel of the Earth," ran July 7 and 14, 1956.

or travel essays," which are the only sorts of writing you agree to let us read first.

I am so happy to hear you have two short stories nearly ready to send us. I can hardly wait for them to get here.

And I must not fail to tell you how really wonderful I thought the dream poem was, "Sunday, 4 A.M." It seems to me that your poetry is getting constantly more beautiful, yet I would not have thought that possible; it was so good to start with. It is a great source of pride to all of us to publish these poems.

Affectionately,
Katharine

October 31, 1956

Dear Elizabeth:

I was glad to get your letter and, following your instructions, I now return "The U.S.A. School of Writing," with our thanks and with many regrets.

I thought Howard's poem delightful. He submitted it in an earlier version to us, but we had to say no because of its being too intramural. We felt that if The New Yorker published a poem by its Poetry Editor, written for one of its major poets, then perhaps all of them would expect us to publish poems written especially for them. All in all, it seemed a poem that we should yield to another publication.

Dreary, rainy day here and the news so frightening.

Much love,
Katharine

November 8, 1956

Dear Howard:

Thank you for the check.

Perhaps you can catch the poem before it is set up, in which case I'd like to change the first stanza to:

> An endless, flooded
> dreamland, lying low;
> crucifix- and wheel-studded
> like a tick-tack-toe.

—leaving it without a verb, but I think greatly improved, because it makes it plainer that that's the landscape and background. I'll try to stop this second-thought habit! If the poem's been set up I can correct it in proof, if it's all right with you.[1]

I do hope you are well and didn't have to have that operation after all. I've had some very impressed letters about your poem.

Being the ordinary variety of egg-head, not the new one (N.Y. Times) I'm very disappointed in the election . . .

Faithfully yours,

Elizabeth

December 4, 1956

Dear Elizabeth:

Thank you for your charming letter, and for your tempting invitation to visit Brazil. It seems unlikely, but it is certainly something to nurse as a possibility when the world seems sour, which is about three times a week, on schedule.

I'm enclosing SUNDAY, 4 A.M. with your changes incorporated into the first stanza. There were some other punctuation suggestions I took off: a comma after "wheel-studded", a comma between the two "dreams" in stanza 7, which would change the meaning completely, as I understand it. The ones I've left seem to me at least worth considering.[2]

I do hope there will be some new poems from you soon.

Ever,

Howard

1 Bishop submitted the stanza as:

> Endless and flooded,
> the dream is lying low,
> crucifix- and wheel-studded
> like a tick-tack-toe.

She changed the stanza again for *Questions of Travel*. The first line became "An endless and flooded" and the "crucifix-" became a "cross-".

2 Two other punctuation changes were made between the time Bishop submitted the poem and its publication. Moss had changed "Dream dream confronting,—" to "Dream dream confronting," on the submitted manuscript. During author's proof the last line of the fifth stanza, "On the bed a smutch:" became "On the bed a smutch". When included in *Questions of Travel*, a dash was inserted at the end of the line. Bishop also rejected Moss's idea of changing the first line of the sixth stanza, which would have made the "black and gold gesso" "black and golden" (Vassar College Library). The phrase was "black-and-gold gesso" when printed.

December 7, 1956

Dear Elizabeth:

Enclosed is your new first-reading agreement for the coming year. I sincerely hope that you'll want to continue this arrangement. And, as always, we hope to see more poems.

All best wishes,
Howard

December 14, 1956

Dear Howard:

Here's the proof and I hope I've made it clear. You are quite right, of course, about no comma between the "dreams." And one after "wheel-studded" isn't necessary, to my way of thinking.

I'm also sending back the contract & check that came two days ago. I'm sure you'll understand my reasons for doing this. *Partisan Review* gave me that fellowship for poetry, although I haven't appeared in their pages for a good many years now. Naturally I feel that since they were so generous I am really obliged to send them some poems when I can. If I were more prolific, had a big "back-log", etc., it would be different. Also, & I believe it's partly due to your fine work as poetry editor, the range of poems published by *The New Yorker* has widened so that one can no longer say (in spite of Mr. Gregory's comments), "The *NY-er* will take this, but won't take that . . ."[1] So I can't count on having enough poems, of different sorts, in the next few months, for both places, and yet I certainly feel I should be represented in *PR*, if I can, by a poem or group of poems while I'm still enjoying the benefits of their fellowship. I'm sure you'll see my position.

Of course this doesn't mean I'm going to stop sending you poems, when I have any. It's just that for the next few months (until the fellowship will be over) I feel I shd. send them to PR first, if they seem possible for it. If *The New Yorker* wants me to go on with a contract then I'd be willing to, or if, by any chance, they'd care to make it for *prose*, now (I'm working on several stories I hope to send Katharine in a month or so), that would be all right— You & Katharine have both been most kind & helpful, always, and I don't want to appear to be ungracious to either of you . . .

How are you? I hope you're all right now.

Faithfully yours,
Elizabeth

---

1 Bishop is referring to Horace Gregory's review-essay, "The Poetry of Suburbia," *Partisan Review* (Fall 1956).

December 20, 1956

Dear Elizabeth:

Mr. Shawn and I have seen your letter to Howard, returning the agreement and check. All three of us understand your position exactly, and see why you feel you must send *Partisan Review* a poem or poems. At the same time we very much want to continue the first reading agreement if you are willing to, and so we are sending you a new agreement with an exception clause, which will permit you to submit, without our first reading, "a poem or group of poems" to the *Partisan Review.* The quote is from your letter and I hope it expresses your wish in this matter. You have for so long been so valued a poet of ours and we all of us so greatly admire your work that we can't bear at this point not to have *you* have the financial benefits of a first reading agreement and *us* not to have the first chance at any poems you may write after your obligation to the *Partisan Review* is fulfilled. If we had realized your dilemma earlier, we could, perhaps, have solved it sooner. I hope this will do it for you. We of course are also eager to have the agreement apply to your prose, but it would be a bitter disappointment to us if it could only apply to the stories, because we have been so proud of every poem of yours that we've published. We space them out in our scheduling, knowing that you are not a poet who produces prolifically, and I'm thankful that we still have three that we have harbored. While you fulfill your obligation to *Partisan Review*, we shall be using "Squatter's Children," "The Armadillo," and "Sunday, 4 A.M."

Let me know whether the new agreement seems fair to you. I earnestly hope that it will. And meanwhile Merry Christmas and Happy New Year.

Affectionately,
Katharine

December 21, 1956

Dear Elizabeth:

Your dilemma in regard to the Partisan fellowship is very understandable, and, now that I think of it, it surprises me that none of us ever thought of it before. We feel the situation can be handled to everyone's satisfaction all round by changing the first-reading agreement as we have done.

For me, personally, not having your poems to look forward to is a rather dismal prospect, since publishing you is one of the really unalloyed joys of my job. Our enthusiasm for your work is no secret, and we would do almost anything within reason to be in a position to publish your poems. I do hope that this compromise will seem satisfactory to you.

I am enclosing a new agreement, which covers both your prose and poetry, and includes the PR exception. I'll look forward to hearing from you about it. In the meantime, all my fond wishes for a Merry Christmas and a Happy New Year.

Ever,

Howard

December 29, 1956

Dear Howard:

Thank you for grasping my position with *Partisan Review* so well—you & Katharine both. The phrase "a poem or group of poems" that I used without thinking may be a little vague, i.e.—one batch, but I think I understand the circumstances it will serve, don't you? I intend to send them a fairly large "group" as soon as I can—whether they'll take them all, or use them *as* a group of course I can't tell—anyway, I'll let you know now that that's the way I'll be doing it, so you'll understand. They also took the one on Pound that you couldn't use, but of course that doesn't count. I am free of my translation now at last and only wish I could produce enough for five magazines . . .

I'm looking forward to seeing your book—I saw a lovely lyric in *Poetry* recently—I liked the song and *A Marriage* particularly—I should think the composers would welcome you—[1]

Christmas has gone by—just a pleasant ripple here, thank goodness— New Year's is more of a whirlpool, though. With all best wishes for it for you—

Faithfully yours,

Elizabeth

January 25, 1957

Dear Howard:

This is a personal note, so I'll send it to your home address. My friend Lota de Macedo Soares & I are planning to come to New York around the

---

1 Moss had three poems in *Poetry*'s October issue: "Swimmer in the Air," "A Song to Be Set to Music," and "A Marriage."

first week or two of April—I don't know the exact date yet. We're going to be staying six months (have to stay six months to bring back a car with us, for one reason) and we want to sublet a furnished apartment, if possible. I know it's an awkward stretch of time, etc., but I thought I'd write to you because I know you have a vast circle of friends and might possibly know of someone going abroad then . . . We'd like two bedrooms or three rooms, anyway— or two big ones with a kitchen—and could pay from $200–250 a month,— the less the better, naturally. We'd rather not be *in* the Village (around where you live is all right, though), nor *away* up town—(Riverside Drive, etc.)— but I know we can't be too fussy.

I'm an excellent housekeeper. We have to buy quite a lot of linen, dishes, etc., anyway, so we'd be using mostly our own shortly after we got there.

Probably you know of absolutely no one, now—and don't bother to answer this. But I'm just trying to think of all the likely possibilities. I like to be up high—& I'd probably also be buying an air-conditioning unit to bring back here, too—

I've had four fan letters about *your* poem—I hope to get a couple of my own off to you soon. I hope you're all over the gall bladder trouble—my 83-yr old aunt writes of hers as her "Gaul bladder."

With love,
Elizabeth

If we couldn't move in right away—or had to move out a little early—it would still be all right. And I see I haven't said that it's going to be awfully nice to see you again.

February 21, 1957

Dear Howard:

You are an angel. I would have answered your letter immediately but I was in Rio for a few days—passports, etc.—when it arrived. Lota and I have been talking it over, passing judgements on the tastes of the other friends I'd written to about apartments, etc., and we've come to the conclusion that you are the friend whose taste in views, bathrooms, table-lamps, etc. is *by far* the most likely to coincide with our own . . . This is a great compliment, but a rather unlucky one for you, I'm afraid, because we really would very much like you to get a place definitely, before we get there, if you can, and if it doesn't mean too much work or worry for you. I think I'll enclose a check for $200 for you to pay a deposit out of. But if you feel too dubious, or it means running around a lot, please *Don't.* I'm just hoping that your agent (that sounds as if you really knew a lot about these things, too—no one else mentioned their agent), or someone at *The New Yorker*, will have something that sounds all right, right off, and that it will only mean a very little work for you. If it begins to get complicated at all, *don't*—we'll go to a hotel for a few days and apartment-hunt ourselves. We were extremely touched by your offer to move out for us, too, but I think that is really carrying it too far. However, I've described your terrace, etc., to Lota and she is looking forward to that party . . .

As I think I said before, but I'll say again in tedious detail: we'd like three rooms if possible, or two big ones (so that I'll have a place to work in). Anywhere in your district, or uptown as far as 86th St., East Side,—or Central Park South! I don't like the idea of the Village proper, it has too many depressing associations for me, I think; or way up town, or around Columbia, etc., although I know it's hard to be choosy. I also like being *up*— although a friend once had a lovely sub-let, with garden, on Washington Square. I really do trust your judgement, though. (Lota would like to be "near the theatres"!—although I tell her that's impossible. I think the Plaza and Times Square are the two big landmarks for Brazilians.)

I think I said between $200 and $300 a month, didn't I? Of course the closer to $200 the better—but I'll mention the bigger amount just in case you hear of something that sounds worth it—a pent-house, say, or air-conditioning, or a part-time maid thrown in . . .

I think that sublets usually come with a certain amount of linen & silver, of sorts, don't they? If it happened to be the place of an acquaintance at *The New Yorker* you could even say that we'd need very little of either—just enough to start off with, and then we'd put it away. We have to buy so many things to bring back here with us, sheets, towels, dishes, etc., that in a week or so we'd probably have enough of our own and not have to use the apartment-owners' any longer. That might make a difference to some people . . .

Now I hope I'm not just indulging in a day-dream of New York, and that it is much more difficult a place to live in than it was when I last saw it, even, and I'm really asking a nerve-wracking and impossible favor of you. Please don't hesitate to say *no*, right away, if I am—

I'm leaving Rio between the 10th & 15th of March—this address will reach me until the 10th, anyway. I'm going north by stages, and for the last week in March my address will be c/o Mrs. M. C. Stevens, Box 668, Key West, Florida. Then probably on April 3rd, I'll fly to New York, and Lota will arrive straight from Rio on the next day. The dates aren't exact, but that address will reach me all right from about March 22nd. (And I really wish I had lived long before the air-age . . .)

It is nice of you to offer to get theatre tickets, too—I'll probably have to go to Boston for a few days shortly after I get to N.Y., depending on that Gaul bladder, so I think I'd better not accept, much as I'd like to.

We both thank you from the bottom of our hearts and we are debating whether you'd like a bag of coffee beans or a butterfly tray as a suitable reward. I'll take this letter down to the house & see if there is anything I should add—

Love, & see you soon—
Elizabeth

March 10, 1957

Dear Howard:

The Americana visiting here says that sub-lets *never* come with sheets, silver, etc. . . . But that doesn't matter, since we do intend [on] buying more of our own immediately. I just hope I haven't brought on that annual breakdown you spoke of by my demands. This is just to say that I am not going travelling here first—I'll be at this address until about the 28th or 29th—Lota and I are going *straight* to NY about April 1st.

Please don't worry about finding us something—if you haven't, or have too many doubts, or are working hard, etc.—please rest assured that we won't mind a bit. I am quite sure your taste in apartments is better than my own, though, and that we'll be happy in anything you might offer . . . honestly—

If you have written—the carpenter who shares box 279 with me says it is crammed with mail, and I'll be picking it up when I mail this tomorrow—We are awfully eager to get there.

With much love,
Elizabeth

115 East 67th Street
New York
[n.d.]

Dear Howard:

We haven't acquired any writing-paper yet, as you see—but I have just—

two hours ago—acquired a new typewriter. First things first. May Swenson sent up a man with it from some discount place in the Village—I can't understand how it's possible—about ½ an hour after I'd phoned her vaguely saying I must get one—and it's $35 cheaper than list price and has so many innovations—an exclamation mark of its own!!!! and a number IIII of its own, too—oh I now see this = +++ Wonders will never cease.

I haven't even thanked you politely enough for your new book, I feel.[1] I think I'll just write down here all the things I've liked a lot so far, higgledy-piggledy, but more or less from page one on—(May was very enthusiastic about the book, loved "Rounds", and said she'd written you about it, to your apartment.)

> "intrinsic as the crickets are to night,
> The summer night is music made by them."

> "sandy heads"

I like the sea purses like "old-fashioned sleds", too—it's over a little before one can appreciate it, though . . .

The first two lines of THE FALLS OF LOVE are lovely, particularly—but that whole poem is successful, I think.

I've already admired the Einstein one, haven't I? Particularly the first stanza and the fine line "We save so plain a story for great men."

A MARRIAGE is Spender-like, I suppose, only better.

"The sheets of time have a common wrinkle" 1 !!! I do like that!

A BOX AT THE OPERA is awfully good.

UNDERWOOD—the Underwood and the Hindu dancers I like particularly—it's funny, I have an unfinished desk-litter poem, too, and it also brings in Bali—or some rice growing region. What is this? But *I* have a uni-cycle rider with bushy hair (see if you can figure that one out) in mine.

1 *A Swimmer in the Air* (1957).

I think Lennie one of the best things in the book—I want you to read the first stanza sometime because I have trouble scanning line 3 but I do think that for its kind of poem it's almost perfect—

Of course page 49 thrills me to the marrow—

"And kept one scale"—THE SWIMMER IN THE AIR is successful, too—

I seem to have lost momentarily something I liked very much about the breakers or rollers like "blue barrels"—this isn't a nice way of doing it but I have to get down to Grand Central to meet my aunt shortly and thought I'd put this in the mail for you there—[1]

I saw a very young man in Bloomingdale's yesterday studying an hour-glass for eggs—turning it up and down over and over for a long time—and I had the feeling he'd just read your poem and was wondering if he bought one would he, too, write a poem—

Lots of love and I'll probably get there about the time this does—

Kisses to Miss Karo—didn't you like it when she said it was the nurse speaking? Perhaps the friend on the other end thought you'd had your voice out—

    Elizabeth

North Brooklin
June 10, 1957

Dear Elizabeth:

I am writing this from North Brooklin, where I'll be during June, doing my regular New Yorker job at long distance. Then I'll be back in the city again for July and I do hope I can get you and Lota to come and sit on our Turtle Bay porch with us and drink some gin-and-tonics or vermouth cassises on a hot summer evening. I had hoped to do this in May, but the month turned out to be a wildly busy one for me, thanks to a new upheaval in my plans. What has happened is that because of Andy's health and happiness, we've decided to move to Maine on a year-round basis as of October 1st. I

---

1 Bishop is referring to: "A Summer Gone," "The Falls of Love," "The Gift to Be Simple," "A Marriage," "Chalk from Eden," "A Box at the Opera," "Underwood," "Small Elegy," "Letter to an Imginary Brazil," "A Swimmer in the Air," and "Aside by the Seashore."

shan't stop working for the New Yorker but it means, of course, that I must give up my present job of running the Fiction Department, and also I shall no longer be able to edit manuscript and handle proofs. I shall, though, be reading and casting my vote on what you contribute, in both poetry and prose, before the manuscripts go to Shawn, just as I do now.

I shall miss the close contact with people like you most awfully. For you, it won't make much of a change, for Moss will handle your verse, as now, and we'll find a good editor for your prose—probably Maxwell. That will be up to Bill Shawn as he is not now appointing anyone to take my place as Fiction Editor. What I'm earnestly hoping is that you'll have both short stories and poems to submit between now and October, so that I can have the pleasure of editing at least one more of your stories before I stop. Also, we need you most awfully, Elizabeth—we need both your poems and your prose. The two poems we've been hoarding are now both of them scheduled for use this summer—"The Armadillo" in June, and "Sunday, 4 A.M." in August. So very soon we'll have none of your poems on the bank, and of course no prose. Dare we hope for some of both before long?

When I saw you, your summer plans were still vague. Will you let me know what they are now? I'll be in Maine during August, so if you and Lota should be going to Nova Scotia by car then, I hope you'll stop in here to pay us a call en route. And most of all, I hope you'll still be in New York in July.

Affectionately,

Katharine

June 28, 1957

Dear Elizabeth:

A line from a letter from Frances Lindley, who is an editor at Harper's: "It seems to me that the Elizabeth Bishop *Fire-Balloons* poem is one of her very, very best."

And then Jean Stafford spoke of you highly, indeed, last night over the phone.

Have you finished that poem you were working on? And can we get together soon? Maybe after the 4th when I go to Milbrook? I shall call you when I return.

Love,

Howard

November 8, 1957

Dear Elizabeth:

Here is a new first-reading agreement that seems to include every form of human writing except doodling. We hope, of course, that you will want to sign it.

I forgot how many days you were to be at sea—nineteen, I think—and have lost track, though, on numerous occasions, I have imagined you and Lota surrounded by books in a square cabin, walking up a slanting deck, and looking at the sea interminably. I hope it was fun. Someday, I would like to hear about the other "ten."

The play [*The Folding Green*] is going to be done at the Poet's Theatre in Cambridge either in January or April. Then, less definite, but very likely, off-Broadway in the spring. I have my fingers crossed. It will probably sound like hell on stage, and I'm sure I can't think of anything more for all those people to say, if I'm asked to rewrite. In fact, since I finished it, I can't think of anything to say at all.

Do write me a letter when you get settled and tell me how things seem and if you made a dinner using *all* the casseroles. And nothing would make everyone here happier than to see new poems and stories.

Affectionately,
Howard

Petrópolis
November 27, 1957

Dear Howard:

Thank you for the contract, etc.—I'm slow about answering because we were kept in Rio for some days off and on to see about the horrible Customs.

I'm so pleased about the play. Now I want to do one, too!—but I know I have no trace of talent in that direction. Our trip went on forever—Lota called it "The Long Voyage Home." I think I'll have to write you a letter about it sometime. This is just to say I did get that letter and I do hope to be sending you some things very soon now, and the blue sauce-dish has already made a triumphant appearance on our black marble table . . .

Oh—I just read "Justine"—mostly sitting on a crate in the customs' shed. I am very eager to see what you say of it. Since you've probably already said it I can say right out I thought it was lousy—except for lots of unrelated sentences, poetic ones, I think he must have taken from his note-books and just stuck in . . .[1]

Affectionately yours,
    Elizabeth

Oh—I wonder how you're liking "Helena"?[2]

                                                                March 10, 1958

Dear Howard:

Thank you so much for sending me your review—it arrived on the day it was to appear in the U.S.[3] I sympathize with you completely about that stupid practice of cutting reviews—it's happened to me, too, and it's one of the reasons why I hate to write reviews. But at least yours didn't turn out to be quite nonsensical or contradictory, the way the Sunday reviews often are. And I think you certainly said more than any of the other reviews, really—they've been very "favorable" but rather disappointing, I feel—you did attempt to give reasons why you enjoyed the book, and also gave by far the best quotations . . . Thank you very much and I do hope it wasn't too onerous and maddening. No one else tried to explain its "charm" at all. Someone sent me another copy yesterday, and I must send it off to the old lady today . . .

I have several poems crowded on my one-burner stove and I hope I'll be able to send you a couple soon. Lota joins me in love and good wishes—
    Elizabeth

                                                                 May 8, 1958

Dear Elizabeth:

The bookkeeping department keeps reminding me that you haven't yet returned your first reading agreement. I tell them that you are a poet, but you know bookkeeping departments, so if you could, without too much trouble, lay your hands on it, and slip it into the mail, we'd be grateful, though I'd be a lot more grateful if you included a story in the envelope.

As ever,
    Bill

---

1 Bishop may be referring to Lawrence Durrell, *Justine* (1957).
2 Bishop probably gave Moss an advance copy of *The Diary of Helena Morley*, which was released in December.
3 "Childhood in Diamantina," *The Reporter* (March 6, 1958).

August 21, 1958

Dear Bill:

Yesterday I got back from a four-day trip to see the brand new capital of Brasil, Brasilia. I went on a party with Aldous Huxley and his wife [Laura Archera] (who happens to be an old friend of mine) and an oddly assorted group of people, which made it quite a bit more interesting than it would otherwise have been. We also doubled the distance of the trip with a long flight to the west to the Xingu River (over where Col. Fawcett disappeared) to an Indian post, and spent a day with the Indians, the most primitive people left on earth—before flying back to what is supposed to be "the most modern city in the world." I am writing up my journal of the trip and I really think it has the makings of a fairly good and entertaining travel piece. I imagine that you are not the right person to address about this—but could you possibly find out for me if *The New Yorker* would be interested in seeing it?

I shall write up the trip anyway, but I should like to find out if by any chance *The New Yorker* has already assigned a piece on Brasilia to anyone; if they haven't if they would please wait for me—I could send it in within two weeks—and if they are interested in the subject at all. A proper piece on the city, architecture, etc. couldn't really be done for six months or a year, because so little is yet constructed. But I find I have quite a lot to say on the subject, and combined with the irony of the next stop being the Indians, Huxley being the guest of honor, etc. (and he has told me I can say whatever I want about him) I think it might do for a "Footloose reporter" or some other department—or even as a story. But I don't want to work on it too long *as* a *New Yorker* piece unless there is some possibility of their taking it, as you can understand.

I hope you and your wife and your family are all well—I also hope to send you some stories presently—

Sincerely yours,
   Elizabeth

August 28, 1958
[Western Union cablegram]

NO ONE DOING A PIECE ON BRASILIA STOP SHAWN SAYS IT SOUNDS HOPEFUL AND INTERESTING AND THAT YOU SHOULD BE ENCOURAGED TO GO AHEAD WITH IT, WITH THE WARNING THAT WE CAN'T BE SURE IT WILL WORK STOP EVERYTHING SEEMS IN ITS FAVOR, THOUGH

BILL MAXWELL

September 2, 1958

Dear Bill:

Thank you very much for the wire. The piece is done but I want to hold it until the end of the week when I can see a newspaper editor friend who will check on the facts for me—so I think I'll be mailing it about the 8th or 9th. I hope they like it—although I could understand if they'd prefer a full-scale Lewis-Mumford-treatment of Brasilia—if it's still going—in two or three years.[1]

With all best wishes—
    Elizabeth

October 1, 1958

Dear Bill:

I am sorry to be so slow about sending you that piece about Brasília, etc. There proved to be so much more fact-checking necessary than I'd realized and it is so hard to get hold of people here that it takes a long time. However, I think everything is *correct* at last and as soon as I get it copied again I'll mail it—and *hope* you'll find it interesting enough to use.

Faithfully yours,
    Elizabeth Bishop

October 8, 1958

Dear Elizabeth:

I was beginning to worry. I'm glad it was only checking that was holding it up. Though I will not be adding my opinion to the others, since it is a factual piece, I long to have the pleasure of reading it. The prose of poets is the only kind that gives me intense pleasure.

Yours,
    Bill

October 14, 1958

Dear Elizabeth:

It has been such a long time since I've heard from you that I've had to resort to spies. I've learned little: Aldous Huxley went to Brasilia with you.

---

1 Lewis Mumford was the architectural critic for *The New Yorker* and a specialist in the development and design of American cities.

And today I read the de la Mare review in Poetry, which I liked.[1] I wish Knopf would send it to me. They send me a lot of things I don't want.

Things are dullish in poetry, and one of the reasons I'm writing is to beg for some poems. I do wish you'd send me something. I feel the larder is empty when at least one poem of yours isn't on the "bank," and when we used up the dream poem, it depressed me. What happened to the poem about the typewriter eraser that I liked so much? The one about the unicycle? And if there are others, please, please let us see them. We need poems, and it would cheer me up enormously to have some from you.

The play is now supposed to go in December, and I am revising. It *has* to go sometime before May 1st, but December seems likely if the casting goes smoothly, etc. This is for Cambridge. As for New York, that's still in the dream days stage, two people waiting (with an option, they say) for the revision of the third act. Not all of the theatre's illusion is on stage.

Kunitz's book is good, and I hope you've seen it. He's being given the full bandwagon treatment. I also liked Philip Larkin's book, which I had briefly read in its English edition, but really read in the American. He's quiet, formal, etc. but the best of that whole lot for me. Cummings' new book is not up to snuff, as far as I'm concerned, and you know, of course, how much I liked May's.[2]

I still dream of arriving in Brazil someday on one of those new Moore-McCormack floating palaces. Would you kill all the snakes if I came? And would you show me things? I went to California this summer, and discovered I really wasn't a bad traveller after all. Straight across in a Volkswagon, and not a bone broken. I wasn't mad about California, though. It seemed pretty in a mild way, sometimes beautiful, and often garishly ugly. It has a fascination, though; something like changing your whole life and being utterly different and no one knowing or caring. It struck me as awfully anonymous, if that makes any sense.

Katharine told me the other day that Andy was reading "Helena Morley" and adoring it.

Do write me a letter, here or home, and poems would be lovely to get. Love to Lota and to you.

Howard

1 "I Was But Just Awake," review of *Come Hither: A Collection of Rhymes and Poems for the Young of All Ages* by Walter de la Mare (1957), *Poetry* (October 1958).

2 Moss is probably referring to Stanley Kunitz's *Selected Poems, 1928–1958* (1958); Philip Larkin's *The Less Deceived* (1955); E. E. Cummings's *95 Poems* (1958); and May Swenson's *A Cage of Spines* (1958).

Dear Bill:

I am mailing you the piece about Brasília, etc. today. At the same time I am mailing two pen and ink drawings of the presidential palace there, made by a friend who went on the trip—I don't know whether *The New Yorker* would be interested in using them or not—one of them, that is—something of the sort seems like a good idea because of the difficulty of conveying the appearance of the palace in words—and it's [Oscar] Niemeyer's best, and the only thing worth seeing there, so far. The girl who did the sketches, Maya Osser, would be willing to do them again, any way the magazine might suggest, I know—

It is kind of you to say you like poets' prose—but I have many doubts about this sample of it. For one thing, the items are so diverse, and for another Huxley never *said* anything!—or no general reactions, that is—he does speak at length once in a while on mescaline, say—in real life, that is, not in my article.

If the magazine can't use it, would you be good enough to send it over to the Brandt & Brandt agency for me? That would save so much time and waiting to see if it arrives safely, etc.

The titles are just suggestions. I see I have spelt Brasil like that all the way through—that's the way Brasil prefers it, but maybe you prefer Brazil. It has been checked by several people including an architect and the newspaper editor—who's very careful—and I think it is accurate. I have also been assured that it will not make me *persona non grata* here. Of course it is very mild compared to what some newspapers here print every day, but I am somewhat critical—

My September 6th copy of *The New Yorker* has just come and I see there is a long long piece about African natives in it—oh dear![1]

Now I shall try "creative writing" for a while—

Cordially yours,

Elizabeth

The sketches are to be returned, naturally—

---

1 Alan Moorehead, "A Drop into the Stone Age."

Dear Howard:

I owe you two letters and I am very ashamed—we enjoyed your first longer one so much and then I meant to write immediately when I got the second one a week or so ago—but I had, have, a poem just on the brink and I thought I'd be sending it along, too. My brinkmanship doesn't seem to be so good and I think I had better write you a note anyway. The poem, or poems, will follow shortly I trust—maybe even today, with luck.

I have just got back from two weeks in Rio—Lota and I have taken back her apartment there and have decided never to rent it again, no matter to what heights rents soar. In spite of the last tenant's best efforts, it is still a wonderful apartment, and Lota wants me to tell you that if ever you want to take a trip this far we'd love to have you stay in it for a month or more if you wanted to. (Perhaps you and your friend George would like to come sometime.) It is the top floor, 11th, with a terrace on two sides, and a view overlooking all that famous beach and bay. You go down in the service elevator in your bathing suit, out through a little tunnel alongside the café in the ground floor, and you're on the beach—(that is if you're not run over crossing the street). The bathroom has an outside entrance to use when you return from the beach so you won't drip through the apartment. There are five rooms—lots of stores in the neighborhood deliver—you can buy pasteurized milk now for the first time; food is very cheap compared to N.Y.—there's a telephone, so you could call us up for instant translation of any word you needed . . . And then you could come up here for week-ends. The new Moore-McCormack takes about a week, I think—and the new planes take *nine hours* (I think I prefer the nice old planes). It is fearfully hot from December to March—in Rio, that is—cool up here—and actually the Rio apartment is very cool, always has breezes—But almost any time of year is all right; it's apt to rain more in the rainy season, naturally—Dec.–March—Do please consider it sometime, won't you. Perhaps you'd like Carnival time best—I should think you'd love the Negro Samba Schools—George would be interested in the music, too. Everyone does the samba day and night for 72 hours—women with their babies in their arms—and the Samba Schools are worth seeing. Imagine several hundred Negroes got up in Louis XVI costumes, with silver wigs, all blue and white and silver and small electric light bulbs concealed in their coiffures and buttons . . . dancing all night long.

Yes, I like Philip Larkin, too—Robert Lowell gave me the paper English edition last year. I haven't seen Kunitz's book but I have liked occasional poems of his very much. I have Cummings' new one—well—I find him hard to judge, you know, he is such an institution—but I do like some of them as much as ever—you have to pretend you've never seen a Cummings poem before, and that is difficult.

I have never been West at all—do you think one *should?* I like San Francisco in detective stories and in the movies—and I'd like to see the desert, certainly. May Swenson wrote me a descriptive letter from Sausalito—and Calvin Kentfield lives there and likes it, too. (I don't know whether you know him or not.)

Marianne Moore wrote she had a poem in the New Yorker—so, [I] think, did I, but neither of those copies has arrived yet (they take over six weeks). I agree with you that things are "dullish" in that line. But Robert Lowell has a whole new book, mostly autobiographical. I had a surprise visit from Kimon Friar here—I'd never met him before—who was lugging along a 333,333-line translation he had just finished—a continuation of Homer, by Kavakis (?).[1] Simon and Schuster are publishing it—I can't quite imagine how the American public will feel about it. Kimon Friar arrived just as we moved into the apartment—and it was really a wreck, then—so if by any chance he tells you I live in a slum in Rio don't believe him!—The tenant had stolen furniture, seven windows were broken, and all the walls painted horrible rich *shiny* colors. We were trying to get it cleaned and scraped when he appeared—

Here is a memento for you—I'm afraid this was almost the least attractive of the Indians. I went on a trip a while ago, when Aldous Huxley was here, to see the new capital and then further west to see some Indians. I liked them very much—everyone does—I want to go back and stay a week sometime. The men are much better-looking, I'm afraid. They are short and almost plump, a nice color—very clean—they go swimming all the time—quite naked—a little red paint in the hair, and a necklace. One friend of mine was watching an Indian, a man, paint himself for a party—black and red lines all over his body—He admired the work and the Indian, in his enthusiasm, grabbed him and hugged him, so that he had red and black paint all over his clothes—

---

1 Moore's poem "The Arctic Ox" ran September 13, 1958. "Sunday, 4 A.M." ran September 20, 1958. *Life Studies* (1959); Nikos Kazantzakis's *The Odyssey: A Modern Sequel* (1938) was 33,333 lines long. Friar's translation was published in 1958.

Lota sends her love. We'd both love to see you. I must get to work, as you well know!

Elizabeth

How's the harpsichord?

There's a record of Sylvia Marlowe playing a de Falla harpsichord concerto—do you know it?[1]

November 19, 1958

Dear Elizabeth:

Bad news. Three of the factual department editors read the piece and all of them feel that it starts off well and that from the point where you get involved in the architectural descriptions everything "tails off badly". Also that Huxley doesn't come through. I was in such a hurry to get it read by them that I didn't stop to read it myself, and have been sending memos and reminders once or twice a week ever since, to—as it turned out, to my horror—the wrong editor. When it finally came back to me, I dropped everything and read it. I found so much to enjoy in it, and to wonder at, and I thought the Indians were beautiful to read about, especially the young man who politely took off his clothes to have his picture taken. I think, as apparently you do also, that it suffers as a piece from Huxley's taciturnity and non-attachment to everything and everybody. To make it work out for The New Yorker he should have been as attached and attaching and as talkative as our two year old daughter, and I am so sorry he wasn't.[2]

I read the manuscript before I looked at the drawings and was delighted (with you as a writer, I mean) when the kite-shaped pillars turned out to be just as I imagined them from your description. So much hard work has gone into the writing that I hate to think about it—except that I also feel quite sure that the piece will be published. But it would have been such a pleasure to have you in The New Yorker again.

I have just talked to the Brandt & Brandt office and am sending the manuscript and the drawings over to Mrs. Brandt this afternoon. I hope I don't

1 Sylvia Marlowe was a celebrated harpsichordist.

2 Of the essay, Maxwell wrote White: "And all the time I was badgering Shawn about Elizabeth Bishop, I was barking up the wrong tree. He didn't have it. I read the piece carefully when it came back, to see if there was a casual there, and there didn't seem to be. Almost, but not quite. Huxley simply never opened his mouth apparently, except once, on the bedroom of King George V, and that alas she didn't record; perhaps couldn't remember. In any case, it was a long way from being a successful reporter piece, though the writing was often good, and here and there was a nice detail" (n.d., Bryn Mawr).

have to tell you how much we would like to have a poem or a story from you. Or twenty poems and twenty stories.

As ever,
Bill

November 19, 1958

Dear Elizabeth:

Here is the renewal of your first-reading agreement, which we hope very much that you will want to sign. I keep thinking of those people who had not yet conceived of the idea of punishment. It probably goes back to the beginnings of human slavery, don't you suppose? I can't wait to tell my brother-in-law, who has arrived at something like the same position himself, but the hard way.

Yours,
Bill

January 13, 1959

Dear Elizabeth:

I'll be writing from home soon to answer that lovely last letter, with its tempting invitation. It would be wonderful if it could be arranged.

In the meantime, it would be so nice to see some poems, even *a* poem. What happened to the one I liked about the typewriter? I hate leafing through the poetry file and not finding one of yours, ready to go. My best to Lota.

Ever,
Howard

June 11, 1959

Dear Howard:

Are you there? If you can't use this anthropological number ["The Riverman"] perhaps you'll be kind enough to send it on to *Partisan Review* for me?

I'm really going to write to you very soon. I hope you're well—and what are your summer plans or travel plans?

With love,
Elizabeth

BUYING RIVER MAN. WONDERFUL.

THE NEW YORKER

North Brooklin
July 6, 1959

Dear Elizabeth:

Howard took off just before he could put through for payment of your *beautiful* poem, "The River Man." At least he had the excitement and pleasure of reading and voting on it. It is your first poem since 1956, I believe, and I can't tell you how happy we are—all of us—to have it. Worth waiting for! For me, it's a magical poem that casts a spell—one of your very best.

I enclose our check for it now and soon I'll be sending you your author's proof. During this year when Howard will be away, I shall be writing to you in his place, for I've agreed to do it again for a short list of poets whose work I used to edit. This will mean, I'm afraid, a delay of about four days for you, but if a poem is very timely, someone in the office will handle it.

I shall have to put off writing you a real letter until the next time. I wanted to get this right into the mail, and I hope you will forgive the longhand scribble and the very inadequate expression of my wonder at the beauty of the poem and my happiness that we again have a poem of yours to publish. I hope there will be another soon.

Affectionately,

Katharine

There will be more than the usual delay on your getting this check—not because of my working from Maine but because the office is having a three-day holiday over the Fourth. Please address your poems to me at the New Yorker, not at North Brooklin. I go back and forth quite often.

And I'm asking the office to cable you about this poem. It is too exciting not to let you know about it at once.

July 18, 1959

Dear Katharine:

I am very glad you liked the River-Man, and thank you so much for the check and the nice letter I finally got last night. I had been spending some time in Rio and all my mail got held up and confused in the Petrópolis P.O.—someone did bring the cable to me in Rio, however, just before I came back, three days ago, and I felt very cheered to get it. It has been a long arid stretch, certainly, and I hope now things will go better—if not exactly an Amazon of verse, at least a small steady trickle—

Since you like that particular poem I would very much like to dedicate it to you, with your permission. I don't think *The New Yorker* uses dedications, does it?—and probably certainly not to its editors—but if you could use initials, or however you cared to indicate it—you that is—I should be very pleased. Then when the poem appears eventually in a book I'll do it properly—that is, of course, always if it is agreeable to you—

After I'd mailed the poem I got the announcement about the poetry department's slowing down for the month of July—then learned that dear Howard was going to be away—I'm glad I managed to get something to him before he left. I am also very glad that you are going to edit during that stretch—and I hope I'll be sending you several more things to consider soon now—A delay of four days, or many more, I'm afraid, doesn't mean very much to me here, where the mails are very irregular and I can get my mail very irregularly, too—and send it off the same way. I'm about to write to Marianne Moore about her Russian poem, so you see how slowly I catch up with things—I think from something she wrote me you may have even published another one of hers by now (unless we were both speaking about the same poem in entirely different words!). I've seen a beautiful one by Roethke, two nice ones by Howard, a good Nash—and the marvellous one he signed Nashe—the best in years, I thought.[1]

I hope both you and your husband are well—I wish we could get back to Maine sometime. Lota wishes to be remembered to you. You'll be hearing from me again, I trust—

    Yours faithfully,
      Elizabeth

---

1 Moore's poem was "Combat Cultural" (June 6, 1959). Her next poem, "Leonardo da Vinci's," appeared on July 18, 1959. Roethke's most recent poem was "The Early Flower" (April 25, 1959). Moss's two most recent poems were "Torches" (May 2, 1959) and "Light and Dark" (June 27, 1959). Nash's most recent poem was "Sticks and Stones May Break My Bones, but Names Will Break My Heart" (June 13, 1959). He signed "Capercaillie, Ave Atque Vaillie" "Nashe" in the April 25, 1959, issue.

Dear Elizabeth:

I feel both touched and honored that you should want to dedicate "River Man" to me. Nothing could please me more. I am afraid you'll have to wait to do it, though, until the poem comes out in a book, for you are right that the *New Yorker* tries to avoid personal dedications and it would be particularly bad, of course, if the dedication were to an editor. My initials won't hide my identity from contributors and staff, and to use them in a dedication in the magazine would seem to us too intramural. But to have a dedication in your next book, and especially above that most beautiful poem, would mean more to me than I can say.[1]

It was cheering to have you name so many recent poems in the magazine that you liked. Yes, there was a second poem by Marianne Moore, in the issue of July 18, a beauty, about Leonardo da Vinci's drawing of St. Jerome and the lion. I especially loved the poem on the Moiseyev dancers, because of its description of that extraordinarily funny fight, between two little boys, all done by one dancer. Did you see it? Watch for another good Nash poem in the issue of July 25.[2]

I'm in bed with a grippe cold—of all things to have midsummer—so this scribbled letter will have to go to New York to be copied and then back here again to be signed. Andy is sick, too, so we are in the doldrums at the moment. By the time you get this letter, everything ought to be different. Your letter, with its good news of more poems to come before long, and its generous gesture that you dedicate the poem to me has lifted my virus-depressed spirits. Thank you, dear Elizabeth. Please remember me to "Lota," if I may use her first name so familiarly.

    Affectionately,
      Katharine

The New Yorker
August 3, 1959

Dear Elizabeth:

Here is your proof of "The Riverman". We have followed Webster, as always, in the matter of your hyphenated words, making them a compound word or two separate words or leaving them with your hyphen as this dic-

---

1 The dedication did not appear in *Questions of Travel*.
2 Moore's poem was "Leonardo da Vinci's" and Nash's was "Paradise for Sale."

tionary says. I speak of it only because you have so many hyphenated words in the poem that I thought it just possible you might be trying for an effect. But I do think it makes the poem look and read better to follow the normal spelling, don't you? It is always "Riverman," as one word, for example, and always "river mist" and "river dolphin" as two words. To hyphenate these words looks somehow too eccentric. O.K.?

We have followed Wagley in the matter of accents and spellings of the foreign words and names. (You yourself were not consistent in the accents.) Apropos Wagley, Shawn has made what seems to me a good suggestion for a slight change in wording in the attribution to "Amazon Town" in your sub-title. He suggests, at 1), that the final sentence be put in parentheses and read as follows: "(The *sacacas* named were famous fifty years ago. These and many other details on which this poem is based are from 'Amazon Town,' by Charles Wagley.)"[1] His comments on this is that you have used three *kinds* of information in your note—the story that the poem tells, some facts about details in the poem, and finally the source. He thinks that the above change in wording might solve the problem. Do you agree?

At 2) and 3) he notes that we have not been told who "they" or "we" are, but he guesses this is allowable in a poem—even a narrative poem. I had assumed so, thinking it clear that the "they" were the river spirits—the dwellers under the river. But you might consider whether it would be better to say "The river spirits" here in place of "they." Do it just as you like, of course.

On punctuation, whether already incorporated in the type or suggested in pencil, I have kept only such changes of your original that seem to me to make the poem easier to read and follow. Excuse all this fuss. The poem is such an important one that we want to get it entirely right.

I am in New York at the moment, because Andy is in Harkness, having tests to see what is back of weeks of indigestion. It is very likely no more than nerves, but when it goes on too long, one has to be sure.

Affectionately,
Katharine

---

1 Macmillan, 1953.

August 24, 1959

Dear Katharine:

I am sorry to be so very slow about getting the proof back this time. I was spending some time in Rio and couldn't get my mail until I got back to Petrópolis.

In the poem itself I have agreed with every correction except one. I didn't like the comma after the first line and took it out. The lines are so short, anyway, and the end of the line seems to serve as a sort of weak comma, usually, and I didn't like the looks of it right at the beginning. But otherwise I agreed.

I know my accent marks seemed inconsistent and I should have explained what I was trying to do, I'm afraid. (Wagley himself is slightly inconsistent, I think—but I am in Rio again and haven't the book with me.) My idea was to give accent marks, in that subtitle, for each of the foreign words used in the poem, in order to help the reader scan it right as he read along. Now I see I just made things more difficult rather than easier. I think they can all be omitted with the exception of *pirarucu*—the Indian names for things almost always end on a heavily stressed syllable and *are* printed with the accent. The others haven't any—you are quite right—and I put them in merely as aids—but if you think they aren't necessary I'll be happier without them. The *h* after a consonant being pronounced like *y*—"Lu-an-*deen*-ya"—I don't know how many U.S. readers would know about that. We are growing more used to Spanish double *l*'s and *ñ*'s, etc.—but since A. Huxley said that Portuguese "looked like a bad joke" (!) I've thought maybe the reader did need help.

I don't think it is necessary to say "river spirits" right out—paragraph 2; the sense seems clear enough after that introductory paragraph, surely, and the omission was deliberate, since it seems that such creatures are *not* spoken of by name but always in veiled terms.

I hope that covers everything. I think the changes in the introductory paragraph improve it.

I am so glad you like it and when it appears in a book—whenever that may be—I'll remember our agreement. I was so sorry to hear you'd been sick and I hope you are better now. I've seen Marianne's second poem now and like it *very* much—one of her best in a long time, I think, a really beautiful poem. Both Lota and I liked the Owl & the Pussycat in French very much, too—a brilliant piece of poetry-translation, wasn't it—scarcely a syllable missed![1] She sends you her best regards, you and your husband both.

1 Edward Lear, "Le Hibou et le Poussiqette," translated into French by Francis Steegmuller (June 20, 1959).

Thank you for all your pains with the poem—I hope to send some more soon and perhaps a better letter—

    Affectionately,
      Elizabeth

September 8, 1959

Dear Howard:

Thank you for your nice letter and first of all let me say that you may use my name for the Guggenheim application if you want to—I'll try to say the right things, if they apply to me. I should think you could get one easily, but one never knows, do one, as Fats Waller said.

I like getting the news. I haven't seen those books of poems although I've seen many poems from them all; and I have been reading in *The Human Condition* off and on for some time.[1] It was kind of you to think of sending it, but I can get books here—I order them from time to time from N.Y. or England—that's cheaper than buying them directly here, although just about everything one wants does show up here sooner or later. Your one item of news that baffled me was "Jean & *Joe's*" leaving for Europe—and that was cleared up when I asked D. Labadie, who came to lunch here yesterday— I've never laid eyes on Mr. Liebling but it does seem an odd marriage—or doesn't it?[2] But now Jean will surely never suffer from malnutrition again, as I remember she once did. I'm also surprised at your meeting with Huxley, somehow—he was always extremely pleasant when he was here, gentle, polite, etc. but not very communicative. Perhaps once or twice on that Brasilia expedition I went on he did insist a bit too much on the superior Inca culture of the west coast and how altitude and *cold* air probably had a lot to do with it (very English, I thought), for a Brazilian audience, but in general he was very nice. (Probably the theory he was developing for you.)

The weather has been perfectly awful lately, unseasonally hot and with a thick pink haze over our best feature, the view. Don might as well have been in Yonkers on a hot day. He took a lot of photographs of the disc of a sun showing through the haze and I'm sure they're going to look like advertisements for a North Cape cruise—Right beneath the sun were seven amazing mountain peaks, completely hidden for days now. He seemed a bit uncertain as to whether he should like Brasil or not, I thought!—but he has had awful

---

1 Hannah Arendt (1958).
2 Perhaps Bishop means art critic Donald W. LaBadie.

weather and nothing is looking its best. The day before we had had the Calders here and that visit was more successful, I'm afraid—they've spent some time in Brasil before, and they love to *samba*.[1] Calder went samba-ing all over the terrace, wearing a bright orange shirt, just like a calendula swaying in the breeze—All our guests these days seem just to have seen *Orfeo of the Carnival*, that French-Brazilian movie that got the prize at Cannes this year.[2] Have you seen it, too? It is not very good, being more French than Brazilian—at least that's one reason it isn't good—but there are some lovely shots of Rio (in clear weather) and I think you should see it & be tempted again to visit us. And the music is pretty good.

I am answering you promptly for business reasons—real estate reasons, again. You say you know some available sub-lets. Do you think you know of any that might be free from the middle of December until the end of March? It looks now as though Lota and I might get back to N.Y. for that stretch—more or less the time people go to Florida in. If you will be kind enough to pass on any information you have to our friend Mary Morse (I think you met her) who's in the U.S. now, she could go to look at them and perhaps engage one for us before she comes back to Brasil, the first part of October. She is on the Cape until the end of this month but you could send her a list (that is, if you plan to leave town October 1st or something like that) to M. S. Morse, c/o PAGE, Route 2, Buzzards Bay, Massachusetts. She'll come back to town probably about when you do and it might be easier just to talk to her. That address is also c/o Mrs. Kate S. Page; 116 East 66th St. The telephone is in the book. This time we'd like something a bit bigger if possible—there may be three of us, and if so I think we could pay up to $300 a month—although much less would be much better, of course. But a lot would depends on the charms of the sub-let—and if Mary could see it first and even engage one, that would relieve you of any responsibility—If you don't know of anything perhaps you could tell her your agents' names—strange, but I've forgotten—and thank you very much—

Lota and I liked a poem of yours about *eyes* that we saw lately—I'd like to be more detailed but our recent N Yorkers are in Rio—and I have seen several more good ones by you. I liked Miss Moore's St. Jerome one very much.[3] Thank you for your kind remarks about my Amazon poem—it's not a type I really approve of but maybe it will do—and I have a few more going

---

1 Alexander and Louisa James Calder.
2 *Black Orpheus*, directed by Marcel Camus, received the Palme d'Or 1959 Cannes Film Festival. It went on to receive an Academy Award for Best Foreign Language Film in 1960.
3 "Light and Dark" and "Leonardo da Vinci's."

I like better, I think. I do hope the plays are going well—maybe now we'll even be seeing them. Please don't go to Europe before we get there—maybe with some luck we all might go, in the spring—If I don't go travelling soon, *my* travel nerves will be beyond me I'm afraid. What bothers me is not transportation but things like porters and anti-Americanism . . . Perhaps travelling with a Brazilian will take the blight off me?

Your summer sounds awfully nice and I hope you're doing some more sea-pieces. Thank you again for the letter, and I'll be very grateful if you'll let Mary know of any apartments you can think of. As we drove Don La B up our mountain road yesterday he began musing out loud about how maybe it was just as well you hadn't come to Brasil (it is a startling road the first time; after that no one minds it)—but when you do we shall take very good care of you—

With love,
Elizabeth

27 West 10th Street
October 1, 1959

Dear Elizabeth,

Mary Morse and I tore a few ambiguities over the phone; she is uncertain about leaving for Brazil, now that you are coming up, and the apartments I had in mind are no longer available. She will let me know by next week whether or not she is going to Brazil. If not, she and I will look at what's available. Actually, I called my agent, who has registered you and Lota as potential sub-leasees, but he says it is too early to get anything good for the period you want. The best time, according to him, is the middle of November, when the Florida gangs have decided to depart. In any case, he will be looking for a suitable apartment for you from now on, and will let me know of all his finds.

I asked, by the way, for two bedrooms. Is that right? And I assume that you would prefer to be on Lower Fifth Avenue, or up on the East Side. And do you still want to be high up, if that's possible? I remember something about your being disappointed in the kitchen last time, so I will try to get a functioning one, as stainless steel as possible, or marvelous in an old-fashioned way. I will stop short of a wooden stove, of course.

Thanks so much for the Guggenheim. I am struggling at the moment, with my "plan." The point is all I want to do is write. I hate the idea of making up some pretentious bit about a long poem etc. etc. I'll do my best, though I wish they could distinguish more clearly between scholars and what they choose to call "creative artists." I noticed that, last year, someone won a Guggenheim for "creative painting." As distinguished from the real thing, of course.

It is raining, the tail end of Hurricane Gracie. And it is thick gray out no matter where one looks. I hope by the time you arrive something will have stirred.

Are you serious about Europe in the spring? I am, and it would be fun to go over on the same boat. (The idea of having two nurses is heady.) And I would like to drive around, especially England and Italy, in a rented car. Or a boughten one, if you and Lota can ever get past the custom authorities. Why don't you *make* a car, and fool them all? You might even get a Guggenheim in "creative engineering."

No word from Jean, who is either starving in Greece or stuffed in Turkey. I imagine she is being passed from one expensive hotel to another in a litter, though, if she is really true to form, it will be one expensive hospital to another. How I understand that girl!

Don is back, and though he loved seeing you and Lota and the house, he seems somewhat shaken by the whole South American experience. He managed to catch several diseases, spent days in waiting rooms and at airports, and doesn't seem to be able to explain anything clearly. I assume the fog will lift. He did say one thing: he claims that the phrase "more or less" is the clue to South American culture, society, weather, etc. I wonder. Anyway, I would love to come down some day, and go all funny on my own.

I will keep in touch about any apartment developments (I don't mean the physical structures.) Until then, love to you and Lota.

     Howard

October 15, 1959

Dear Katharine:

Here are a couple of things from a new batch; I thought I'd send one of them now because just possibly you might be interested in the "January" one ["January 1, 1502" and "Electrical Storm"]. If you are it would have to say "Brazil" I suppose—the other one the place doesn't matter. If you are not interested would you please send them back to me?

Lota and I think we are coming to New York the first of the year—for three months. If you happen to know of anyone who would like to sublet us an apartment for that stretch (I think it coincides with the Florida season) I'd be very grateful if you'd let me know. I'm a pretty good housekeeper and would be willing to take over one cat, or any number of birds . . .

I've been enjoying Mary's Florence pieces very much—Florence seems to have been more sympathetic to her than Venice, perhaps—anyway, they're awfully good.[1]

We hope you are well and flourishing—and it must be beautiful in Maine these days.

Affectionately yours,
Elizabeth

North Brooklin
October 26, 1959

Dear Elizabeth:

I enclose your quarterly "COLA" check and I only pray that there will be another to send you at the end of the next quarter, for this would mean that you had sent us a poem or poems and that we had bought it (or them). I certainly got involved in *that* sentence! I shan't rewrite it, though, because there is so much to do today—a golden, crisp cold autumn day, which makes one hurry to put the last spring bulbs into the ground. We seem to be due for an early winter. Often I wish you were here, and almost as often I wish I were in Brazil to see you both in your beautiful surroundings.

"The Riverman" was scheduled to run in a September issue but at the last minute had to give way to something more timely. From Maine I can't do much about the jigsaw of the schedule, but I know that everyone who can is anxious to publish the poem and are watching for that full page opening.

Affectionately,
Katharine

November 3, 1959

Dear Elizabeth:

Here is a contract, which we hope very much that you will want to sign. I saw an apartment-wanted memo being prepared for the bulletin board, and was delighted to learn that you are coming north. After Christmas, Pearl said over the phone, when I called her. We agreed that it was lovely to be able to choose not to see Saks' and Lord & Taylor's celebration of the Nativity. I am

1 Mary McCarthy, "A City of Stone" (August 8 to 22, 1959).

always surprised that at Easter they don't do the Crucifixion in papier-mâché. We are now living in town, and would be so happy to see you, if you are in a mood for seeing people.

Affectionately,
Bill

Dear Elizabeth:

We are very happy about the two new poems and are buying them both. "Brazil, January First, 1502" is an absolute beauty and if we can get the proof to you in time and get it back here in time we would like to use it, in principle, in the New Year's issue, which this year will come out on January 2nd. Of course we can't swear to that.

We agree with your suggestion that Brazil should be in the title, and I have put it in first, but you may prefer to have it come last, in this way "January First, 1502—Brazil." Let me know which you prefer. We also ask you if you will please, for your subtitle quote, give us the title and date of the Kenneth Clarke book from which the quoted words are taken. We think they should appear after the quote. A reason for this is that not all readers will at once know that Sir Kenneth Clarke is contemporary. Also it seems to us that a modern date in the subtitle helps point up the "theirs" of line 2—shows that they were in the far past. By the way, are these eyes that were theirs the eyes of the Christians of stanza 4, or merely of the natives of Brazil in 1502? If you mean the Christians, it might be clearer if they could come into stanza 1 by name, rather than by a pronoun, but this involves a knotty poetic problem and the question should be disregarded if you much prefer to have "theirs" stand as is. I only point out that there *is* a slight ambiguity to those who do not know Brazilian history or know when the Christians did enter Brazil.

I should be giving you these queries on proof, not in a letter that precedes the proof, but because there may be a slight rush to get the proof ready and back and forth in time for this year's use, I thought I'd ask ahead of time so you can be thinking about these queries. I don't think there is any problem on "Electrical Storm" and the check for that should be along any day. The one for the long poem may be a week later as Mr. Shawn got to read it a week later than the short poem. I love that cat, by the way.

I am in New York now for two weeks and wish that you and Donna Lota were here already. It is wonderful news that you are coming for a real stay and I'll surely be here again to see you before you leave. I have been working in a dim way to find you an apartment, but living as I do in Maine I shall probably not be the one who will find you one in the end. I have posted notices on the three New Yorker bulletin boards asking for one for you, with two bedrooms; occasionally such notices do bring results. I also called Bowden Broadwater to see whether by any chance his and Mary's would be available. She is abroad now and he follows, but he comes right back soon after Christmas and Mary before your three months are over, so that won't do. Pearl and Howard are on the lookout, I know, and I feel that something will turn up. I mentioned the cat and the birds in my notices. Jean (Stafford) and Joe Liebling are in Greece now, but I'm pretty sure they'll be back before April. I shall ask, though. For all I know their apartment may be sublet right now.

Much love, and our grateful thanks for the poems.

Katharine

November 13, 1959

Dear Elizabeth:

I enclose two proofs and also the checks for the two poems. As I said in my earlier letter this week, we are anxious to have you mail the proof of the "Brazil, January 1st, 1502" poem right back, for it is now scheduled for the issue of January 2, so do hurry it into the mail if you can. About the attribution in the subtitle, pay no attention to the blanks left there but make it read, if possible, to show what Sir Kenneth was talking about, for this, I now perceive, would explain the "theirs" of line 2. Couldn't it go somewhat this way, if I guess the facts correctly—it's the merest guess from the Britannica account:

"Sir Kenneth Clark, describing, in 'title of his book' the land seen by Portuguese explorers when they first entered the bay of Guanabara."

I suggest bringing in this about the bay because the Britannica says that *Brazil* was discovered in 1500, but that it is probable that the explorers entered the bay of Guanabara on January 1st, 1502. Worded this way, no date of his book would be needed, but however you do word the subtitle, the checkers want to know where to find your quoted words. Naturally I don't mean that my wording is the best one—just something along that line.

The punctuation changes suggested seem to me right and I hope they will to you.

There is no hurry about the proof of "Electrical Storm" as we won't use it in winter but we'd like the proof back at your convenience. The punctuation mark at the end of line 2 here was obscure in your manuscript so I made it a comma, but it now occurs to me that perhaps you mean the "Cra-aack" was dry and light, not the house. If so, the comma is wrong. If dry and light apply to the sound of the lightning crack I suppose the punctuation should be "Cra-aack—dry and light." Will you tell me which way you intended? I don't think it works to have those three words make a sentence: "Dry and light," that so the reader can't know what the adjectives apply to. I hope that the reason for the few other punctuation changes is clear. If you don't approve, please be sure to say so.[1]

I'll hurry this off now so no more but my love.

Katharine

November 17, 1959

Dear Katharine:

I am very glad you can use the poems . . . I've waited a few days to answer you because I thought probably the proof of the JANUARY FIRST one would be coming along, but it hasn't appeared. Do you suppose that— for the first time—a proof has got lost? [handwritten: "NO—"] So I shall answer the questions in your letter, anyway, and let you know that so far it hasn't arrived—then if I find it at the P.O. today I'll enclose it, re-corrected—

I like the title as you suggest: BRAZIL, JANUARY 1st, 1502. Underneath the quotation, to make it shipshape, the title can be LANDSCAPE INTO ART, by Sir Kenneth Clark (no e, as I think I had it), 1949. (The book title does much more explaining—probably why I left it out—but it does no harm, either, I see.)

If you think it makes it clearer, the first line could read "Januaries, Nature greets our eyes . . ." etc.[2] It seems to me that makes it all pretty plain. Saying that it still looks very much the same to us, in January, as it did to the discoverers, the Christians who arrived on New Year's Day, 1502, (and gave Rio

---

1 In the last extant draft, the line runs: "*Cra-aack!* Dry and light." (Vassar College Library). It ran as White's second option.

2 In the last extant draft, the line reads: "Januaries, Nature greets the eyes" (Vassar College Library).

the name of "River of January of Saint Sebastian"—although there is no river; a slight mistake). I didn't want to drag in the story of the founding of Rio de Janeiro because I had to keep it *in the country*, for purposes of comparison—Rio naturally looking very different, these days! It might help to put a double space before the paragraph that starts off with "Just so the Christians"—showing that everything has been leading up to that, and the rest before is just description. I realize that it is a little vague—however, it seems to me it is obviously a comparison between *some* important Brazilian date and the present time—what it means is not too important—and I think most readers do associate "Janeiro" with "January", even if they don't know the facts. I wanted to keep it as general as possible in order to emphasize the general historical truth (as Toynbee might say),—the moments when one realizes what it must have been like in 1502—[1]

I think there should be a comma after "found it all"—4th stanza, line 3. But probably when I do receive the proof there will be more punctuation changes—I hope the delay doesn't mean that someone is having such a hard time making any sense out of it that it has taken days of work—

Everything after the semicolon at the end of stanza 1, line 2, up to "Just so the Christians"—is just description and hangs on that semicolon, really—if you can think of a better way of indicating it (than my idea of the double space) I'd be delighted—[2]

I see on page two of your letter you say that there might be a delay with this poem—so maybe it isn't lost—but here is what I can do before seeing the proof, at least.

I hate to say it—but the trip to New York has had to be postponed. After I had alerted everyone I know, too, and everyone had been so helpful about apartment-finding. The dollar has just gone zooming, lately, making it very hard for Brazilians to leave the country, and also Lota has a large land deal going on now and it seems better to stay and see it get off to a good start. We speak hopefully of the spring, but I think it is probably better not to speak at all. Since she adores New York, and loves *all* Americans (including callers who sometimes strain my patriotism a bit) Lota really minds not going much more than I do—but I did want to see my friends, again, including you—

---

1 Arnold J. Toynbee was a historian and the author of *A Study of History* (New York: Oxford University Press, 1934–1961).

2 Since the submitted manuscript does not survive, it is not clear what Bishop is referring to, since she used a colon, not a semicolon, at the end of the line in all her drafts. The line was printed with a colon in *The New Yorker* and there was no additional line spacing.

We got a whole batch of New Yorkers this week—sometimes they seem to come in batches—and have been catching up on them. Lota wants me to tell you she thinks your gardening reviews (this last, and one much earlier one) are *excellent*—I haven't read this one yet. But I did enjoy Andy's piece about Khrushchev very much, the Kreuger articles, and one odd one about the Russian army sculptors that I found quite enlightening.[1] Gardening is more L's department than mine and she is very busy changing over from the "winter" garden to the "summer" one right now. There isn't too much difference, actually—only things that will be spoiled by heavy rains can't be planted in the "summer"—Lettuce, spinach, celery, etc. we can have all year—and last night we had strawberry shortcake—

November 19th—

The proof & the check did come yesterday, and I am hastening to mail it back to you today—or whenever I can get to the Post Office, because we are having a rainstorm—

I have approved of all the small changes, I think. "blue-green" should be like that, shouldn't it?—since it is an adjective applying to the leaves? The comma after "wealth"—next-to-last stanza, last line, is unnecessary, I suppose—I had it just to make the pause. Take it out if you prefer.[2]

Now I'm in a slight quandary as to what to do about Sir KC and his book—I think the title of it does suggest the (very simple) idea behind the poem: 15th and 16th century artists (& people) tended to see nature as a background, a thickly filled-in tapestry or embroidery, and nature here, in the summer season, at any rate, still looks exactly (and obviously) like a tapestry or embroidery . . . So that to the people who actually set foot in these regions in January, 1502, it probably didn't look too surprising, but just like what they had enviously seen on the castle wall back home . . . The trouble is there is no particular sentence in the Clarke chapter that says *that*—He's not talking about Brazil, just art—but I think the two odd phrases, plus the title of the book itself, ought to give the reader enough to go on. Also, I have kept bringing in the idea that it looks "worked", "rich", etc.—right up to the next-to-last stanza—or I think I have! I do think giving the title helps a lot,

1 White's garden pieces were "Floricordially Yours" (March 14, 1959) and "Before the Frost" (September 26, 1959). Bishop also refers to E. B. White, "Khrushchev and I" (September 26, 1959); Robert Shaplen, "Annals of Crime: Kreuger" (September 26 to October 10, 1959); and Simon Peter Karli, "My Most Durable Translation" (October 10, 1959).
2 The comma was left in.

Edit and handle M)   AB-3047

~~Elizabeth Bishop~~
~~60 Brattle Street~~
~~Cambridge, Massachusetts, 02138~~

Set Slug   DEC. 28 1973   7=M   HANDLE M   Dc   SAND

FIVE FLIGHTS UP   #6

FEB 25 1974

Set in 11-pt verse style line for line on 27 picas. No indents.

Still dark.
The unknown bird sits on his usual branch.
The little dog next door barks in his sleep
inquiringly, just once.
Perhaps in his sleep, too, the bird inquires
once or twice, quavering.
Questions—if that is what they are—
answered directly, simply,
by day itself.

Enormous morning, ponderous, meticulous;
gray light streaking each bare branch,
each single twig, along one side,
making another twig, of glassy veins...
The bird still sits there. Now he seems to yawn.

No italics next Roman HM

The little black dog runs in his yard.
His owner's voice arises, stern,
"You ought to be ashamed!"
What has he done?
He bounces cheerfully up and down;
he rushes in circles in the fallen leaves.

Obviously, he has no sense of shame.
He and the bird know everything is answered,
all taken care of,
no need to ask again.
—Yesterday brought to today so lightly!
(A yesterday I find almost impossible to lift.)

whi li

Elizabeth Bishop

[Draft 12]

11-pt C+S.C.
flush right
w. longest
line above

Elizabeth Bishop's submitted manuscript of "Five Flights Up," with her return address in the upper right-hand corner. The top of the manuscript reads "Edit and handle M," showing that Howard Moss was in charge of the manuscript. According to the slug, *The New Yorker* decided to buy the poem on December 28, 1973; the poem was to be published in the front of the magazine ("7=M"); and the poem was serious ("sand") as opposed to light ("lake"). Moss put the poem into the house style by taking the title and quote out of italics and changing the punctuation in stanzas two and three. Someone else wrote instructions for setting type for the galley proofs. Galley proofs were circulated in various departments and returned to Moss, who collated any questions and comments and had an author's proof made for Bishop's review, after which the poem would be readied for print. The manuscript is stamped "FEB 25 1974," the issue in which the poem appeared. (New York Public Library)

Katharine White in her *New Yorker* office, 1950s. (Photograph by William Mangold)

BELOW: Elizabeth Bishop, 1951. (Photograph © Rollie McKenna)

Harold Ross, editor and founder of *The New Yorker*, 1948. (Bachrach Photography, Hulton Archive, Getty Images)

Howard Moss, 1983. (Photograph © Thomas Victor, courtesy of Harriet Spurlin)

William Shawn at his desk, late 1970s. A photograph of Harold Ross sits behind Shawn's office lamp. (Photograph by James Stevenson)

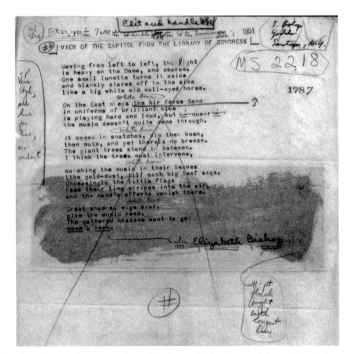

Slips like this one were attached to manuscripts as they went through the editing process. Underneath the slip, upside down, is the date and time the manuscript was sent to the typesetter—October 27 at 5:50 p.m.—and the date and time the galley proofs were to be returned to the office—on October 28 with the first delivery. (New York Public Library)

Elizabeth Bishop's submitted manuscript of "View of The Capitol from The Library of Congress," with her return address in the upper right-hand corner. The top of the manuscript reads "Edit and handle," showing that Howard Moss ("M") handled the manuscript before Katharine White ("KSW") did. The slug shows that *The New Yorker* decided to buy the poem on October 27, 1950, that the poem was to be published in the front of the magazine ("7=M"), and that it should be published during the summer. Moss put the poem into the house style and made changes in punctuation, and someone else wrote instructions for setting type for the galley proofs. The manuscript is stamped "JUL 7, 1951," the issue in which the poem appeared. (New York Public Library)

Mr. Wigglesworth

November 7, 1950

Mr. Ross's Notes on Bishop's "View of the Capital From the
Library of Congress"

1. Fact matter: Is the uniform of the Air Force band
brilliant? Mr. Weekes, old Air Force man, says they
were dull blue in his day, as he recalls—sort of a
postman's blue.

H. W. Ross

The 'brilliant' must be allowed the poet I think—It is how they looked to her in the sun—KSW

Harold Ross's memo to Katharine White concerning the color of the Air Force band's uniforms, with White's reply: "The 'brilliant' must be allowed the poet I think—It is how they looked to her in the sun—KSW". Hobart "Hobey" Weekes was a longtime editor at the magazine. (New York Public Library)

Nov. 8. 1950

Air Force has no official designation of type of blue. They say it
is a light powder blue, and that it might seem brilliant in the bright
sunlight with bandsmen wearing special bright insignia and such.
Ones I see around I would call bright light blue, but not brilliant.
They are considerably bluer and less gray than postmen's uniforms.

Packard

The matter of the uniforms' color was still not settled. Frederick "Freddie" Packard, head of the fact-checking department, weighed in on their brilliance. (New York Public Library)

Bishop in New York, 1943. (Photograph © Josef Breitenbach)

Elizabeth Bishop's studio in Samambaia, Brazil, 1962. (Harry Ransom Humanities Research Center, University of Texas, Austin)

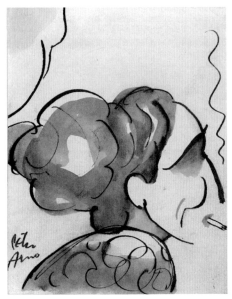

E. B. and Katharine White at work on *The Subtreasury of American Humor*, early 1940s.

Drawing of Katharine White by Peter Arno.
(Used by permission of the Estate of Peter Arno)

Katharine White's notes to Elizabeth Bishop about her story "Gwendolyn." Bishop's notations are on the bottom half of page two. The crossed-out lines refer to White's note ten. They read: "If I care to, I can bring back the exact sensation: of irremediable solitude abject, inevitable abandonment: today, just by thinking of about it; but then". The other lines refer to White's note thirteen: "To tease me, B. stepped on one of them and crushed its inhabitant. When we had finally made up after this violence we [sat & talked] talked, [for a while] desultorily, about death and going to heaven, but as it got later we grew we were growing [a little] bored & reckless,". (New York Public Library)

Howard Moss reading manuscripts in his office, late 1970s or early 1980s. (New York Public Library)

Author's proof of "Santarem" without Bishop's replies. On galley 1, "WEB" stands for *Webster's* dictionary and means there is a question about Bishop's spelling. The number sign—#—means the magazine would like to take the hyphen out and use a space instead. On galley 2, the checking department wrote, "Cannot verify: "Philips Electric" not official name. In Netherlands: N.V. Philips In Brazil: Philips S.A. do Brasil." Next to the last stanza, there are questions about the name Mr. Swan. The checking department wrote, "unidentifiable. Dutch spelling would be Zwaan. Ckg." The legal department added, "A REAL PERSON? If so, is he still living?" (New York Public Library) and hope you will, too. They found the landscape looking like their contemporary ideas of "art" and "riches" (what they were after), but without some of the usual romantic trappings and conveniences, of course—

I am sending back the other poem, too, since there's so little to do to it; also the contract—all my eggs in one basket. I think I'll try registering it to see if you receive it any quicker—Thank you for all your help and if there's any more I can do to this poem let me know—

Affectionately—
Elizabeth

North Brooklin
December 2, 1959

Dear Elizabeth:

The two proofs came and I hope and believe all is clear and in order. I think the subtitle is all right as you fixed it. If any further questions are raised, I'll let you know. *I* thank you for your care and *we* thank you for the signed agreement.

I am *dreadfully* disappointed that you are not coming, but understand the reasons. Let's hope that you can be here in the spring. I was very much encouraged to hear that Donna Lota approved of my gardening pieces. I've done just three in all—last summer's, last spring's, and one in the spring of 1958, and I'm due to write a new one in January if I can manage it, on the 1960 spring catalogues. This silly business takes endless time for small results as I must garden and garden in summer and grow plants all winter if I'm to know from experience what I'm writing about. Each time I fear that it will be the last and that I'll run out of fresh material. The clutter all these catalogues and books make in my study is appalling, not to speak of correspondence, for my readers are my best source for new nurseries and seed companies. And of course it is all a side issue to editing. Just now I have a new extra task—lining up New Yorker stories of the past decade for a possible third book. If we decide to publish one, your story, "In The Village," will be in it as we are all of us in agreement on that. I do the rounding up but we try to make the choice as near as possible to what will suit everyone in Fiction, and, of course, Bill Shawn, so this means everybody has to yield on some choices and also there is length and duplication to contend with.

I am home in No. Brooklin but only temporarily. My sister is in the hospital—better than she was but grave problems remain for me to settle with her about her way of life when she comes out.

I pray for some new poems from you soon. You will have another book soon I'd hope.

Affectionately,
    Katharine

P.S. Had a wonderful lunch in New York with Marianne Moore and [fiction editor] Rachel MacKenzie—Miss M. and I talked fondly of you. What courage she has! I did not even know until that day that she had had a slight stroke.

December 4, 1959

Dear Howard:

I went to Rio for two days, supposedly, and stayed for ten, and while I was there I did write you a note to say we are NOT coming, but now I think it did not get mailed . . . For some reason it is much harder to get to a Post Office in Rio than it is here, where we have to drive five miles—and then, too, I think I was very embarrassed to have to tell you we aren't coming after all that ballyhoo and all the trouble you went to about apartments. Lota has a big Land Deal started now, and the dollar took a rocket-like leap (things would cost over twice as much as they did for her in N.Y. our last visit—and *then* they were twice as much as they'd been in 1952, so you see how it goes) and it seems the better part of valor to stay put, although she is very unhappy about it—

When I finally collected my mail yesterday there was your letter of November 24th and also the forms from Mr. Moe—and I am answering both this morning.[1] I'll register the Guggenheim letter, too, to make it a little safer. I am glad to see you stuck to the point so well in your "Statement"—and it seems to me you should get one, but one never knows and I have frequently been surprised and displeased—You must just about have a new book out, haven't you? Or is it out and I am away behind as usual?

I didn't want to get N.Y. for Christmas, if we had gone, so I took particular delight in showing Lota your letter about it—but she just said well, we Americans are used to it, but when Brazilians go and see those electric reindeer, etc., for the first time, or at five year intervals, it's very different. Also,

---

1 Henry Allen Moe was the principal administrator for the John Simon Guggenheim Memorial Foundation.

she adores SNOW. I had wanted to get through Christmas at Lima, but probably would have yielded and found myself doing Christmas shopping in a state of nervous exhaustion on December 23rd in N.Y.—But thank goodness—we are going to Cabo Frio ("Cold Cape") for two weeks and do nothing but swim and fish and read.—Speaking of snow—a young lady I know here, very young, went last year to Europe for the first time, in February. Before leaving she said, "I know this probably is very silly, but can you tell me—when it snows, does it snow in the cities, *too*?"

That Academy! I am now on their mailing list for something called the *Poetry Pilot* which has little guessing games every month, like, 2 B or not 2 B—etc.—but the $5000 does command respect!

You must go to see "Orfeo do Carnaval"—maybe I said this before? It is not very good and carnaval isn't much like that—it's much, much better, actually—but the views of Rio are marvellous and the hero and heroine adorable—particularly the hero. The music is fair, too—although the words, being written by a real poet, aren't right. Sometime I'm going to try to get a Samba record to you—when someone's flying up—do you think you would like that?

The *NYer* has a poem of mine with a secret reference to you in it—I found upon reading proof. It is supposed to appear January 2nd—I'll give a small prize, of a Samba record, when you spot it—As Christmas approaches I find my U.S. correspondents getting rather gloomy—then they cheer up towards spring. Here we maintain even keels more or less—and Lota has just acquired a Siamese kitten who is taking our minds off our troubles very well. He is called Suzuki—Japanese, but never mind—sometimes "Zenzinho"— Tobias, my cat, is fearfully jealous, and I have to be cruel to poor little S whenever he's around to make him feel better. Mary is staying with us while she builds a new house and *she* has a cat, and we each sit and talk to our respective cats—(Better not tell anyone.)

With much love,
Elizabeth

I love your flattery and wish I could believe 25% of it—

December 14, 1959

Dear Howard:

I forgot to tell you when I wrote that I did get the little Keats you edited—the reason I forgot was because I already did write you about it in

Rio—then mislaid that note—or did you get it—or did I tell you about it before?[1] I can't even blame this lamentable state on Christmas, since I haven't given it a thought yet . . . But I did take the Keats to Rio to keep in the apartment there—I have four or five of that series now and thought it would be a good idea to have a set of The Poets in Rio as well as here—"to settle arguments" maybe . . . Thank you very much for sending it—I thought your introduction very good, lucid, to the point, etc.—and it must have been hard to do, there is so much material on Keats. The section about the nightingale particularly good—But since I adore Keats anyway—even *all* the poetry— you could scarcely go wrong with me . . . (not that you did, I'm sure). He makes almost every other poet seem stupid, don't you think his letters do, that is.

I had a lovely time "recommending" you—finally quoted the first two and last two stanzas of "Lennie"—which I've always admired—as does Cal Lowell, or did I tell you that before?—I said I thought your elegies would be a good plan—you sometimes reminded me of a 20th century Thomas Gray—I hope you like that? And hope it means something to the committee—

I went to see "The Bridge on the River Kwai" one off-afternoon in Rio— it's a maddening kind of nationalistic affair—but to my surprise Ceylon looks *exactly* like Brazil. I haven't seen a river quite that good so far although I'm sure there are some—but the scenery, plants, everything, is exactly the same—so if you go to see it and superimpose the best sections of Black Orpheus on top of it—you'll soon find a visit to us irresistible—It is beautiful "summer" now—the woods full of blue, blue lilies three or four feet high—frogs as big as your hat singing love songs to each other—and my chin all over blisters from eating too many mangos—

Let us skip Christmas, shall we? I'll just send love and best wishes,

Elizabeth

May 10? 1960

Dear Howard:

Your book finally arrived two days ago—I gather from my correspondence with Scribner's that there had been some trouble about presentation copies—WHY is there, always?[2] It is part of that general conspiracy. The

1 *Keats* (1959).
2 *A Winter Come, A Summer Gone: Poems, 1946–1960.*

book looks very impressive and I want to thank you for it right away and tell you how pleased I am to have it—even if others have had it for months now. I've already stated my simple thoughts and praise about many of the poems, but I do like some of the new ones very much—some I've seen, or am about to see, in *The New Yorker*, I think—I meant to write you when "Tourists" appeared how much I liked it—particularly the two [lines] about Copenhagen and Hostels—they are wonderful—your best manner. I am still awfully fond of poor Lennie. Both Lota and I were very much taken with "A Song Struck from the Records", particularly the first stanza. Maybe you hate to be told you should be funny oftener—I think I'd be—but you do do that kind of thing so well and somehow "too old at the Hostel" hits me much harder these days than even the evanescence of perfect love, oh dear.

I'd like to say something brilliant, of course—but the truest and really most complimentary thing I can say is that your book makes me fearfully homesick for New York, all of it—all the excitement and confusion and fatigue and messiness and stylishness and horror and noise and romance and everything—and all the people—"The Feast" gives me the creeps. I hope I'm not the Hermit—"O miseries and appetites of the world"—but there are plenty, too many, of both, right here—

You look sweetly solemn on the jacket—don't you know that rubber tree is trying to get your attention?

Perhaps you have gone abroad already?—or are about to go? I do wish you'd write me a letter when you have time; in fact I'd like a long private conversation. Since I last wrote I have made a trip on the Amazon and now am living to go back there again—it was much more beautiful than I'd imagined and I liked the people very much. I want to take a long and very tough trip *up*-river next time, into Ecuador and Peru—it can be done. I suppose I should be studying the stones of Florence, but geographic curiosity leads me on and on and I can't stop. Last night I dreamed there was a narrow road that began at Tierra del Fuego and went straight north, and I had started to walk it, quite cheerfully.—A large primitive stone coffin was being carried on mule-back alongside of me, ready for me when I gave out—the mule driver had a toothache. (I can't understand that part.)

Thank you again for the book—much love, and please write us soon—
Elizabeth

June 9, 1960

Dear Katharine:

Here is a poem ["Song for the Rainy Season"], but I am afraid it has missed *your* rainy season, probably.

In April I finally made a trip to Amazonas—down the Amazon from Manaus to Belém. I was afraid I'd find I'd made mistakes in "The River-man", but I hadn't. I saw a great many "dolphins" (river porpoises, really), pink and black—the pink ones bring good luck. Now I'm working on a post-Amazon Amazonian poem. I have not forgotten my intentions for that poem when it comes out in a book—

I hope you and Andy are both very well and enjoying the beauties of spring up in, or down in, Maine—

Affectionately,

Elizabeth

P.S.—I just received Miss Moore on "The Tailor of Gloucester"—wonderful—[1]

June 29, 1960

Dear Katharine:

I don't know whether you'll be able to use this ["From Trollope's Journal"] or not—but if you can, it obviously should appear in January or December—or late November—of this year. (That is, if you conform to your usual system of topicality!) If you'd like it, but couldn't use it for *another* year, I think I'd rather send it some other place—because it seems a shame to waste Trollope's fantastic patness . . . don't you think?

I hope you and Andy are well. It is very, very cold for here—in the 30's, I suppose. I am typing with a cat in my lap to keep us both warm.

Affectionately,

Elizabeth

Fourth of July, 1960

Dear Katharine:

When I went to mail you a couple of sonnets taken from Trollope, I found your letter of June 22nd at the Post Office. I also received a note from

1 "Tell Me, Tell Me" (April 30, 1960).

Bill Maxwell about the story. I am glad it is to be used again, of course. There is one correction—but if it is impossible to make it (as well may be) it won't matter too much. It was the *five*-cent piece, rather than the ten, that was called a "fish-scale." (It was much smaller than the ten, which was the size of the U.S. ten. Now they have an ugly five, the size of our nickel.) Not even my Aunt noticed this, but one always likes to be accurate (and I know The New Yorker does!).[1]

I read a probably highly in-accurate account of an article by Andy, in TIME—and now I am eagerly waiting to see what he really said. I am so sorry your expedition with Marianne fell though, and I hope you are all better, and I hope she is all right. She will not take care of herself, except in very mysterious ways . . . And please accept my congratulations on being "cited"; does that mean a degree, too? I liked that last poem of Marianne's and I must write her about it right away. [2]

Your note said you had received the "Rainy Season" poem. I thought you would probably like the first part, at least—but that rather syncopated meter may give trouble. Perhaps I shall hear from you today—I'm about to leave for Rio for some dismal dentistry and shall stop at the P.O. on the way—It has warmed up a bit here and is really the most beautiful time of year,— clear, brilliant, dry—but I think I prefer the hot and rainy season, when everything blooms. Please forgive this hasty letter; I just wanted to let you know I had heard from you. Maine sounds wonderful and I wish I were celebrating the Fourth there—

    Affectionately yours,
      Elizabeth

                                            July 5, 1960

Dear Elizabeth:

I hasten to tell you, without waiting for your check to come through, that we are delightedly buying "Song For The Rainy Season." And to hurry up the news, which has been delayed by a four-day office holiday over the Fourth, I shall ask that this letter be signed for me at the office, since it has to

1 The correction was not made.
2 The *Time* article, "Disarmament: Strange Climate" (July 4, 1960), quoted E. B. White's "Letter from the West," *The New Yorker* (June 18, 1960). Katharine White was to be with Moore at the Bryn Mawr graduation ceremonies. She was to be honored with Moore and other alumnae as part of the college's seventy-fifth-anniversary festivities. Bishop refers again to Moore's poem "Tell Me, Tell Me."

be copied for me there. Please forgive this and remember that I shall not have read over the letter after it's typed.

Except for a couple of minor points that will turn up in proof we have only two general queries on the poem. It is perfection, really. We do, though, hope you will be willing to *place* this rainy season in the title, or in a subtitle, which we believe should carry the word "Brazil" or a recognizable Brazilian place name. The natural scene here is so exotic that the reader really craves to know the locale, and it is not given in the poem itself. I have just added the word "Brazil" to the title as a dummy wording for you to fix up, to suit your-self when you get your author's proof. (No need to write about it until then.) What are the dates of your rainy season, by the way? I don't think we have to restrict publication to this period and I'd hate to have to hold the poem too long. It would read all right in the magazine almost any time of year except midwinter, but I'd like to know the dates even so just for reference in case the point is raised by the checkers.

The other query is that in the next to last stanza there's a difference of opinion here about your intention in the words "later era." [fifth stanza, lines five and six]. If by them you mean just the next dry season, the mind makes a larger jump in time than you perhaps want it to, and "season" might perhaps be a more exact word than "era." But *I* feel that you mean both the next season and a much later era, when geophysical changes, or even merely aging, will have turned a lush wet land into a dry one. (Bill Shawn inclines to agree with me.) So if you do have a double of philosophical meaning here, your words must by all means stand. And they must of course stand if you prefer them whatever your meaning or intention. I rather hope my interpre-tation is right, but I'd like it either way. This poem leaves me full of wonder-ing admiration.

Affectionately,
Katharine

July 17, 1960

Dear Katharine:

First of all, please give my congratulations and Lota de Macedo Soares's to Andy because of the Academy honor—That was very nice.[1]

"Song For The Rainy Season"—of course you are quite right about the word "era," and I'd like to keep it the way it is, please. Theoretically the rains

1 E. B. White received the gold medal for essays and criticism from the American Academy of Arts and Letters.

begin around October,—here that is—it's a very varied country!—so I should think if you wanted to use the poem any time from September through November you would not be being wrong in Brazil, *or* in New York City . . . However, the poem is not specific. In fact, I think it could apply to any rainy season, any place that there was a big rock and a brook and a waterfall or two. (It works equally well for a month I once stayed in the Great Smokies in a mountain house, when it rained a lot.) I would very much like to avoid labeling more poems "Brazil" and in this case I don't think it's necessary really,—I think the poem is clear enough without it. (The New Year's poem, for example, wasn't, of course, being about a real historical event and the real landscape it took place in.) I don't want to become a local-color poet any more than I can help. If you wanted to change the title to "Song for *a* Rainy Season" perhaps that would help disassociate it from Brazil in the minds of any readers who do associate me with Brazil? But I think it is better to let the reader make his own references whenever possible and by adding "Brazil" I'm afraid of cluttering his mind with extraneous palm-trees, deadly snakes, etc. If you pretend my poem came with a New Hampshire—or West Coast address on it, I am sure you will see what I mean . . .

The Trollope poem I sent you about two weeks ago should have a comma at the end of the next to last line and an exclamation point after the word "sick" in the very last line—I think I sent you by mistake a copy that omitted both.

I do hope that Andy is better and that you are having a good summer. Don't you think sometime you should make a possibly botanically-minded trip here? We have orchid-growers and anthurium (?) growers all around us. I hope you'll agree with me about the "Song" and I am glad you like it. I've just enjoyed the piece about [Pier Luigi] Nervi—[1]

With love,
Elizabeth

July 18, 1960

Dear Elizabeth:

This is an unusual and unhappy situation: I must return a poem of yours, for the decision has gone against "Trollope in Washington." I detect from your letter that you thought this might happen, and because you say you

1 Winthrop Sargeant, "Maestro di Costruzione" (June 11, 1960).

want it published elsewhere in late 1960 or in January, 1961, and refer to Trollope's "fantastic patness," I know you will want as quick an answer as possible. This is why this letter will be signed for me in New York as I haven't time to type out a neat letter with carbon before the next mail leaves. You did not tell me to turn the poem over to anyone else in this country or where to send it except to you, so here it is, with many regrets. Our general feeling is that the intention of the poem is obscure and we fear it could be badly misinterpreted. There were various interpretations here, as a matter of fact.

I am told that Maxwell is taking care, if he can, of your change about the "fish-scale." He'll write you about it, I feel sure. I hope it wasn't too late for him to make the change.

Time did manage to distort Andy's "Letter From The West" by quoting those few sentences from the disarmament section out of context. They wholly omitted his main argument. As one reader put it, "they beat his plough into a sword for their own militaristic purposes." But you may well not agree with him even when you read the whole piece.

We've been having a week of thunderstorms. In one of them lightning hit the power pole near us and travelled in on the telephone wire, utterly destroying the innards of our telephone instrument. We were lucky it didn't set the house on fire. The television set survived and I almost wish it hadn't, because the Democratic convention has kept us up till all hours. I am not too happy about the Kennedy-Johnson ticket, for I doubt it can win.

Affectionately,
Katharine

I hope you received my letter saying how much we liked the rainy season poem. If the check for the poem has come through, I shall ask my secretary to enclose it.

August 5, 1960

Dear Katharine:

Thank you for the check. I am sorry the Trollope poem didn't work out for you, but I had the feeling it might not. Perhaps it would have been clearer if *all* in quotation marks, and probably it needs some additional lines . . .

Here is the proof of "Song for a Rainy Season." I agree to the changes in punctuation, etc.—and Oh! those O's. I do know about them, of course, but grow careless and forget.

I don't believe I have ever mentioned that I like the jazz reviews very much. They're not only a great help when I can manage to get some records, but I save them all to hand on to Lota's nephew, a young fan.

On re-reading the proof, I think the only thing I'd question is your Pt. 3. I meant "kills much, or intimidates much" [in the fifth stanza] but in order to imply that everything would not be killed outright I put in the comma, thinking I was making it clearer thereby. If you don't think so please leave it as you have it—but now it seems to me it is saying "kills all and intimidates a great deal"—

I think Lota wants to enclose a note in this. It is a rainy season day today with a vengeance and the frogs began last night, two or three couples in a pool by the dining-room, which they use as a sort of honeymoon hotel—

With best wishes—affectionately,
    Elizabeth

P.S. John Brooks and his wife were here last week and we had a very nice time—at least I did, and I think they did, too—

[Handwritten:] Dear Mrs White, Please be very kind to tell E. B. White how much I admired his piece in The New Yorker! How very satisfactory the blend of intelligence, common sense and sensibility . . .
    Affectionately yours,
    Lota de Macedo Soares

                                                                August 7, 1960
Dearest Howard:

I haven't heard from you, not even a postcard, for ages it seems—is it a year? I gather from something Katharine wrote that you are about to go back to the magazine and I hope you've had a good time wherever you've been and that the drama flourishes. Did you ever get the enthusiastic letter I wrote you about your book? I do hope you didn't misunderstand anything I said then? I got a card from the publisher, you know, saying that some hadn't been sent (the same thing that happened to me and to Merrill's book and I don't know how many others)—and I filled out the card and then shortly after that got *two* copies . . .

Last week John Brooks and his wife were here, with some other PEN people—I'd never met them before. They didn't seem to know your whereabouts, either. Before he came I bought a paper edition of "The Man Who

Broke Things"[1] and thought well at last maybe I'll learn something about high finance and proxies, etc.—maybe in novel form I'll be able to understand it—but I wasn't—It was a cold and rather dismal day when they were here—but at least they will be able to tell you we have fires, and that there's plenty of room for you if ever you decide to pay us a visit. I think March and February are the prettiest months, even if it does rain—all the flowering trees appear then, and carnival usually takes place in one of those months.

This is just to send you Lota's love and mine, and to say I hope I hear from you soon—maybe my letters were lost, or maybe your reply was, who knows—

Elizabeth

August 17, 1960

Dear Elizabeth:

I have placed the commas around "or intimidates". It might be even better with no commas there at all, it seems to me, now that I'm sure of your meaning. If you happen to agree, please write me right away and I'll remove both commas. Also would you want me to add the usual comma after "small" in "our small, shadowy / life!"? This is your choice, of course, but our usual style is a comma between two adjectives.[2]

Whitney Balliett will be pleased that you like his jazz column. I, too, think it's awfully good.

Andy was grateful for Lota's postscript to me and I glowed at her wording. Please thank her warmly and give her my affectionate regards.

I'm struggling to write a September garden piece and I think I am failing this time.[3] Too many interruptions, too many anxieties, too many beloved children and grandchildren around.

Affectionately,
Katharine

1 John Brooks (1958).
2 The lines ran as:

> (O difference that kills,
> or intimidates, much
> of all our small shadowy
> life!)

3 "War in the Borders, Peace in the Shrubbery" (September 24, 1960).

The New Yorker
October 11, 1960

Dear Elizabeth,

Here is a COLA check, for the past quarter. It comes to you, from me, with more than the usual guilt and remorse. I know I owe you a long letter, especially after the lovely one you wrote after the book came out. And then the one that hoped you hadn't . . . I can't go on with this. The truth is that I have, somehow, forgotten how to write letters. All I can think of saying is what I had for lunch, or what kind of day it is. I am hoping whatever small gifts I had in that direction (I say that with a Chinese smile) will come back. In the meantime, all my love, which you need never worry about, and all my hope that you will make an appearance on these shores soon.

I loved SONG FOR THE RAINY SEASON.

Love,
    Howard

January 26, 1961

Dear Elizabeth:

Here is a surprise check, an adjustment on your 1960 cost of living bonus.

Is it true that you and Lota are going abroad in March? And does that mean you will be in New York around that time? If so, I'll try to make up for all the letters I've meant to write—not by bending your ear but by taking you out. If you'll have me.

New poems from you would be a delight. It is still five degrees here, the coldest I remember. Still, we'd rather have the iceberg than the ship.

Love,
    Howard

April 23, 1961

Dear Howard:

I now owe you two notes, I think and to my surprise the latest—I think—is dated January 27th. That was to tell me about Mr. [Donald] Hull's arrival—although he didn't actually come till Carnival time—and it rained constantly and I was in Rio so really just found him by chance and I'm afraid I wasn't much use to him—but perhaps he has told you how I rushed him off to call on a friend to see her nice old house and instead we fell into the clutches of a mad Russian lady who has a not-nice old-new house next door, and she talked his ear off about botany for a long time . . . He was very polite about it all and I liked him and I am sorry I couldn't see him again or do more for him.[1] I'll tell you again, just in case—if you ever want to send any-one else to us, do you think you could give them our telephone numbers, the Rio one and the one up here? Otherwise they are apt to write me a note from Rio and it is apt to take a week to get up here—or more—by which time they are in Lima or back in New York. I like to be hospitable, really, and hate to lose guests like that. The numbers are: Petrópolis 3663, Rio 57-3412. Ask for Dona Elizabetchy; if that doesn't work, Dona Lota. Please put this in your address book! Lota is working in Rio now and so we are spending almost every week from Tuesday to Friday there—also quite often no one is around to attend the phone up here—Or—if I know *what hotel* travellers will be at of course *I* can call up—the Rio apt is near all the probable ones, anyway— And when are you coming yourself—or did Donald give you too dreary a picture? I have one wonderful place I want to take you to with a good place to stay at, too—

The new governor of the new state of Guanabara (the old Federal State, before they moved the capital) is a friend, and he has asked Lota to take charge of—her title is Chief Co-ordinatress, really—a huge new long park development on the Rio bay—play-grounds, restaurants, everything.[2]—She is handling all the difficult engineers and brigadier-generals, and architects, etc., very well, so far. I think she'll either end up *in* politics for life and be a senator, like her pa & uncles, or else she soon won't be able to stand politics a minute longer and we'll find ourselves in Athens after all, where we were about to go when this job came along. I am writing, somehow or other, after a long halt,—you'll be getting some things soon now. We had planned to go abroad for at least six months, but this job seems more important for the time being.—I have no idea what you did with your sabbatical—except I know you wrote poems—I have seen some good ones and I did admire the one about the boy who got drowned.—If I were up in my study I'd be much more specific, since I cut out the ones I like and keep them—but there are no lights there since the last storm and I am using the card-table-reading-lamp method this evening—I do hope you are well & cheerful—write me a real letter soon.[3]

With love,
Elizabeth

1 Hull was *New Yorker* art editor James Geraghty's asistant.
2 Carlos Lacerda asked Lota to head the development of Parque do Flamengo.
3 Moss's elegy, "Water Island," ran August 6, 1960.

Dear Bill:

When I first received your recent note about the "agreement" I thought that it had been lost and that I'd never received that check, etc. (I was in Rio, as I am now; I have been spending most of the time here and that has added to the slowness of my correspondence.) When I got back to Petrópolis I went through papers and I am very much ashamed to say I found it, still unanswered.

This year—only I'm afraid it's already *last* year—I have decided not to renew the agreement because I want to try some experimental poems and some other kinds of prose, as well, neither at all in the line of *The New Yorker*, so that it seems simpler just not to sign the agreement. This is far from meaning I don't intend to send things to the magazine—I have just sent Howard a poem and I mean to send others fairly soon. It is just that, partly because of distance and mailing difficulties as well as my plans, it really seems easier, for me and for you, not to renew it for this time, at least.

I have seen splendid reviews of your new book[1] and I am going to receive it soon now, I think—and am looking forward to it very much, even if it sounds a bit too appropriate for someone living in foreign parts—Please remember me to your wife—

Faithfully yours,
Elizabeth Bishop

Rio de Janeiro
June 28, 1961

Dear Howard:

I have just this minute scrubbed my hands after changing the ribbon for what I hoped was a BLACK one, and it's much paler than the old one. WHAT is the matter with ribbons these days?—or is it just that my eyesight is getting dim and gray and this type is really black, black?—It's a ribbon from the U.S.A., too, and says "black" on the tin . . .—

Your letter of May 4th arrived just at the right moment and cheered me up so much that I should have thanked you for it immediately. Now maybe you are about to take off for London, and I hope this reaches you before you go. I wish I'd been able to get some poems into your hands before you left—I have two or three about ready to mail but not quite—I'm sure you know how it is.

---

1 *The Château* (1961).

I am not renewing my New Yorker contract this year—or last year, I believe, since I just realized I'd forgotten all about it for months, and then they wrote me again. But that doesn't mean I'm going to stop contributing when I can, by any means.—I felt I should branch out a bit more—as I undoubtedly should have done before, I suppose—and also I want to be free to do some prose-work, not New Yorker things at all—and it just seems simpler this time to leave myself free. I have some poems to send you, and I also have a couple of stories going that I'll certainly send there first, if ever I get them finished. I am sure you will understand this situation—and I hope actually I'll appear in print in the N Yer more this year than last, if anything. I'm sorry to hear about Katharine's being sick and I must write to her right away.

Loren sent me a catalogue—but it's hard to tell much, of course, since one her best qualities is her coloring—but some do look lovely. I've at last acquired one of those projector-lights—you probably know them—for my favorite of hers, "The Waters"—and at last it's decently lit and at night particularly it is marvelous—a sort of pale, abstract, mystical aquarium at one end of the living-room—And now they're in Paris, I think, and we were going to have met them in Athens or Rome until Lota decided to do her civic duty. (She likes your idea for cement statues of parents very much.)[1] She is working awfully hard; we spend all the week-days, almost, here in Rio (in Portuguese they are "useful" days), and I scarcely see her at all—or else I just watch her talking on the telephone (and using the left hand for gestures). She is getting more and more involved in the 6 kilometers of park, and other projects as well—and people call up requesting steam-rollers, or a private helicopter, or a word in the governor's ear, etc., all the time. *I* am getting involved in a money-making project that we think will bring us to New York in October for a short visit—I'd better not say anything more than that until it's all settled.[2] It will be wonderful to see you then—please don't stay in London too long. Maybe it's because I read the English reviews a lot—but it does sound like the place to visit these days—I just refused to go to hear "The Importance of Being Oscar", being given here tonight—the same En-

---

1 Moss wrote James Merrill about Lota Soares's park: "A lovely letter from Elizabeth Bishop yesterday, saying she will not be coming up this spring after all. Lota has been given some sort of governmental chore—to build a series of parks and playgrounds along the coastline in, or just outside of, Rio. She is already deep in bribes, graft, and other political maneuvers, or so it seemed to me, reading above and between the lines. Elizabeth, whose passion for travel is no secret, is slightly miffed, I think, but will end up supplying a list of birds and plants to be included, as well as designing the 'furniture' for the children's playground. My idea for the proper equipment for a playground is a series of mothers and fathers made out of cement" (April 29, 1961, Washington University Library).
2 Bishop is referring to her Time-Life book *Brazil* (1962).

glish actor—but I didn't feel I could sit through the Ballad of Reading Gaol in its entirety—[1]

I am pleased to hear about the Proust book and wonder what the 60 pages are to be about—with pictures?—what *aspect*, etc.—Have you ever read Mme. de Sévigné at all? This may be insulting you, like those *young* people who annoy me by telling me to read "War & Peace" or "Anthony & Cleopatra"—but if you haven't, I think you'd like it a lot. I have recently acquired three props for old age: 1) a rocking chair, a beautiful old Brazilian one 2) a warm, *purple* sweater 3) all three Pléiade volumes of Mme. de Sévigné.[2] I haven't settled down to all three simultaneously yet but probably soon shall—

I've been going over poems and trying to put together a new book for 1962. This old little poem ["A Norther—Key West"] has never been printed and it occurred to me that perhaps you might like it—for the "winter-travel season"—anyway I'll send it along to you instead of to the office, and you can see what you think.

Please when you write tell me what brand of typewriter ribbon you use! It is so nice and black.—And thank you again for the kind things you said. You really have no idea how they stiffened my moral fibres.

I was glad to see that David Jackson had a story taken at last—but I do hope Europe is not going to be quite like that when I finally get back there again. And are there that many poets around?

I'll confess I haven't touched my clavichord for a year or more, too—

Lota and I hope you have a wonderful trip—the *Statendam* sounds safe and peaceful, to me. We saw a friend off by jet Sunday night and I am really terrified by them—the awful solemnity combined with violent speed of that take-off—and the tiny, piggy, little eyes the things have. Did you know that a Brazilian *really* flew before the Wright brothers?—in Paris— Santos-Dumont?—It was the only thing the Brazilians lay claim to like the Russians—He was a tiny, neurotic little millionaire, who made the first dirigible, and then the first power-plane, called "Demoiselle"—and then in 1932, seeing the way things were going, he hung himself with his necktie . . . (I don't know what this is all about now—but be glad you're going by ship, and do have a nice time!)

Much love—send us a postcard or two—

Elizabeth

---

1 *The Importance of Being Oscar* was a one-man show based on the writings of Oscar Wilde starring Micheál MacLíammóir. The show toured around the world.

2 *Madame de Sévigné: Lettres*, edited by Émile Gerard-Gailly (1953–1957).

Dear Elizabeth:

I understand perfectly about the agreement. Don't give it a thought. And if you ever find that there is a reason why you would like to have it again, all you have to do is tell me.

Though I am glad you are where you want to be, it is a matter of sadness to me that Emmy and I can never see you. On consulting Howard, I find this is shared. There is no point in quarreling with people's destiny and yours seems to be to live in Brazil. Meanwhile, at odd moments, I recite to myself *Nothing that I can see belongs to me* . . . and think of you.

Affectionately,
Bill

Three

1961–1967

Then the Economies—
Lower, Middle, Upper;
Five Islands, Five Houses,
where a woman shakes a tablecloth
out after supper.

A pale flickering. Gone.
The Tantramar marshes
and the smell of salt hay.
An iron bridge trembles
and a loose plank rattles
but doesn't give way.

On the left, a red light
swims through the dark:
a ship's port lantern.
Two rubber boots show,
illuminated, solemn.
A dog gives one bark.

A woman climbs in
with two market bags,
brisk, freckled, elderly.
"It's a'grand night. Yes, sir,
all the way to Boston."
regarding us amicably.

Moonlight as we enter
the New Brunswick woods,
hairy, scratchy, splintery;
moonlight and mist
caught in them like lamb's wool
on bushes in a pasture.

The passengers lie back.
Snores. Some long sighs.
A dreamy divagation

July 26, 1961

Dear Elizabeth Bishop,

Here is a check for A "NORTHER." KEY WEST, and here is the author's proof. Mr. Weekes suggests that the quotation marks around "Norther" be dropped and that the period be replaced with a dash, so the title would read, A NORTHER—KEY WEST. Then the quotation marks would come out in the third stanza. That's all, except once again our thanks for the poem.

Sincerely yours,
Rachel MacKenzie

September 19, 1961

Dear Elizabeth,

A hurried note. The author's proof of "A NORTHER." KEY WEST doesn't seem to have been returned to us. At least, it never arrived. Did you *get* a proof? Did you send it back? If it *is* lost, let us know, and we can send on another.

I hope, how I hope, you are coming up in October. Please do. I thought of you often when the news from Brazil was so moment to moment. But then, the whole world seems to be in the same boat. A cave in Vermont may be the final answer. Some poems from you would, of course, not only make my day, but a whole series of them. My best to Lota.

Love,
Howard

Petrópolis
September 22, 1961

Dear Howard:

(If you are back—and I think you must be.) I have two poems here ["First Death in Nova Scotia" and "Sandpiper"], one of fifty lines and one of twenty, that I'd like to send you and that I think you'd probably like. However, first I'd like to bring up a rather difficult subject with you . . . (Probably you have to bring it up with someone else.) I've had poems in The New Yorker as long ago as 1940, I think, and I had a contract with them for, I think, about fifteen years. I'm not sure of the dates because I am writing in Rio and can't look things up. But I am fairly sure that for at least ten or twelve years my rates haven't changed at all. I know that the COLA is supposed to make up for this, but, at least for poetry, I don't think it quite does. I also think I can claim to be one of the better poets The New Yorker publishes. Everything else has gone up, including rates from other magazines where I'd also like to appear from time to time—even if they aren't as good as the New Yorker's. Don't you think it is about time my rates were raised?

The mails have been extra-bad lately. I haven't received a check yet for that little poem THE NORTHER you took some time ago. The New Yorker is always so prompt that I am telling you, not to complain, but because I think it must have got lost.

This isn't the time to write you a letter. However—I do want to say that Lota and I are coming to New York around the first of November and will be staying at Loren's place on Perry Street for about a month. It will be wonderful to see you—and I hope you are well and had a nice trip—

Love,
    Elizabeth

Rio de Janeiro
October 4, 1961

Dear Howard:

In my greed for gold I forgot to say that I hadn't received the proof, either, of course . . .

I'm so glad you're there and we'll be almost neighbors for a while—Lota is coming, too, I'm relieved to say—we're leaving in about a month.

Love,
    Elizabeth

October 6, 1961

Dear Elizabeth:

First, we stopped payment on the check for A NORTHER. Since two months have passed, it seems almost certain that it is lost. I'm having a new check made up and will send it along as soon as it's ready.

Second, about line rates. I showed Mr. Shawn your letter and he suggested the following. Your present line minimum is $2.30. You have never been paid this minimum, but always a higher rate, usually $2.50 a line. From now on, your minimum will be $2.50 a line. As in the past, it is almost a certainty that you will always be paid a higher rate, in this case $2.90 a line. To put it simply, your minimum will go up from $2.30 to $2.50. In actuality, your line rate, in cold cash, will be changed from $2.50 to at least $2.90 or higher. Do let me know how this strikes you, and if it should make you reconsider signing a new agreement in November, we'd all be happy.

I am delighted you and Lota are coming in November and will be so close. I promise at least one good party, and one good—at least the attempt will be—dinner.

And do please send those two poems. I'm dying to read them.

Love,
Howard

October 15, 1961

Dear Howard:

Thank you for your letter of October 6th—a batch of mail just came, via [a] friend from Petrópolis . . . At the moment I am quite incapable of figuring out lines and rates, etc.—in fact I always am, being either very feminine or very dumb about such things but it does look all right to me. I sent you another note last week saying that I hadn't received the proof for the NORTHER poem either (naturally)—so perhaps you'll be good enough to send another one? The mails are getting worse all the time, along with everything in poor dear Brazil.

Here are two poems ["Sandpiper" and "First Death in Nova Scotia"]— if the DEATH one is too grim for you, perhaps you could send it on to PR for me?

I'm afraid Lota and I won't get there until about November 15th. It will be wonderful to see you and we can discuss both pleasure, mostly, and a little business thrown in—

Faithfully yours,
Elizabeth

October 31, 1961

Dear Howard—

How very cosmopolitan—to receive a cocktail party invitation for New York in Rio de Janeiro.—I'm afraid we won't get there in time, however—I think we're leaving the *7th* now—arriving that same night—

I mailed you the proof of THE NORTHER some time ago—hope you got it.[1] I imagine there is a letter from you in Petrópolis now—I'll be getting it this week and will attend to anything attendable before leaving—

Lota and I look forward to seeing you—I hope maybe Loren's telephone will be turned on when we get there—Do you know of anyone who has an extra cot bed? (I asked May Swenson, so maybe she has found one by now—but just in case.)

How pleasant to exchange the national worries of Brazil for the international ones of N.Y. for a while—

Much love,
Elizabeth

October 31, 1961

Dear Elizabeth:

How wonderful to get those two poems! We are taking them, of course. I'll hold on to the checks and the proofs until I see you, since I'd hate to have them cross.[2]

Thanks for sending them. And we're dying for more. See you soon.

Love,
Howard

61 Perry Street
December 12, 1961

Dear Katharine:

I have been in New York for about three weeks—no, four—and I have to go back to Brazil day after tomorrow. This is just to say that I am awfully sorry to have missed seeing you in town and how terribly sorry I was to have heard from Howard Moss that you had been sick and in the hospital. He

---

1 Bishop agreed to the changes regarding the punctuation of the title.

2 On the submitted manuscript of "First Death in Nova Scotia," Moss inserted a comma between "cold cold" in line one. He removed a comma from the end of line eight, after "loon" (Vassar College Library).

seemed to think that you were feeling much better now and much relieved, and I do hope he was right—

I don't know whether there is airmail to you—probably to Bangor, of course—but this seems to be the only paper here—and I am using a marvellous typewriter of about 1920, I think, that I can scarcely see over. Lota de Macedo Soares is with me and sends you and Andy her kindest regards. I have seen a few people in the general rush—Mary McCarthy and her new husband [James West], Marianne, the Lowells, etc.—Marianne looks frail to me and I am worried about her. I am saving her baseball poem to read on the way home—I'm afraid it's beyond me, though.[1]

From what I have seen this trip I think you are very wise to live in Maine—although the city looks very handsome it certainly can be uncomfortable—and the general richness of everything and everybody is particularly upsetting after poor Brazil—

With love to you—and I do hope you are feeling well—
    Elizabeth

Howard has a couple of poems I think you'll like—one more coming that is right up your alley I think—

February 8, 1962

Dear Elizabeth:

This is a fine time to be answering your note of early December. I was desolated not to see you when you were here, but at that time I was still convalescing from that October operation. I still am, as a matter of fact, for the after effects of having an artery slit open in the throat are fairly brutal. Even now I'm not any good for any continuous work; and fatigue, whether physical, mental, or emotional, sends my heart and circulation and head into a dither. But very slowly I'm getting better all the time and I hope eventually to be able to write my garden pieces again. I tried to start a piece in January but soon saw I couldn't write one I myself would like in time for spring. Perhaps I never can again but this isn't what the doctors say.

I simply love the two last poems we bought of you—the sandpipers and the Nova Scotia one. I don't know which I admire more. Where is that "one more coming" that you spoke of? I trust it will be along soon. And short stories?

1 "Baseball and Writing" (December 9, 1961).

This is just to send my love and to hope you and "Lota" will have a good year. 1961 was a wicked one for us and we were glad to see it go—a lost year for me what with five hospital sessions and two major operations. And for nine months the doctors assured me I had a brain tumor. They were wrong; an occluded artery gave the same indications. So I suppose, even though I'm not well yet, that I'm lucky. We are on our way to Florida now and two months there should make us both better. The worst of the past year for me has been that my illness has seemed to prevent Andy's writing anything. It's awful to be a burden.

Much love to you,
Katharine

P.S. I long to hear how you like Mary McCarthy's husband. I missed seeing Mary, too, of course.

Petrópolis
October 30, 1962

Dear Katharine:

I think I asked you about this once before, but I can't seem to remember your answer. Does *The New Yorker* ever accept translated stories? I don't remember any off hand. I have discovered a novelist & short-story writer here whose stories, I am sure, if written in English, would delight you— extremely original, light, Tchekovian-yet-Brazilian, funny, slightly sinister, etc. . . . really good. I am translating a group of them; Spender wants some for ENCOUNTER. I thought that if there is any possibility of your using them I'd like to give you an opportunity to see them, too. But if you have a rule about translations I won't bother you with them. The author is Clarice Lispector—I think she's having a book come out in the U.S. next year— one or two have appeared in France.[1] She has a wonderful turn of phrase that goes into English very well—quite unlike most other Latin-American writers.

We have had a very preoccupied summer/winter here, with many guests, etc.—but everything is back to normal more or less now and I am preparing quite a bit of work to send out. I hope you will be seeing some of it soon. I hope you have been keeping well and had a nice summer. Everyone here,

1 Bishop is probably referring to *The Apple in the Dark*, translated with an introduction by Gregory Rabassa (1967).

almost everyone, is pleased with the late turn of events and people congratulate *me* on our President's actions . . .'[1]

Lota wishes to be remembered to you and your husband—

Always affectionately,

Elizabeth

November 14, 1962

Dear Elizabeth:

It was good to hear from you. I am referring your letter on the Lispector short stories to William Maxwell, for I'm not up to date on Shawn's current policy on translations, but Bill Maxwell will answer you at once, I know. To me the stories sound most interesting and promising, especially in your exquisite translation, which we all admired so much in The Diary of Helena Morley, but whether the magazine now favors using anything that has previously been published in any language I don't know.

I have been in very poor health and it has been a battle to keep going at all on the things I like to do—i.e. desk work and garden work. Whether my garden article of last June will have to be the last of the series I don't yet know. The operation of a year ago to remove the block in an artery leading to my brain was a perfect success and I am just back in Maine after a checkup. The tests proved that the old brain is O.K. but I have new blocks—one in my left leg and perhaps one in my left arm. These, of course, are much less serious than the first one and may correct themselves but we've been ordered to a warm climate for the winter and this is a pest. I had hoped to stay here and get started on a book. Instead, I find myself a partial invalid, a drag on and anxiety to poor Andy, and a pain in the neck to myself.

Andy has a new book out—old Letters from the East and *other* points and I'll try to send you a copy as thanks for the pleasure your books have given us.[2] It's wonderful news that you are sending out "quite a bit of work." I earnestly hope that most of it is headed toward *The New Yorker*.

You are lucky to live where you are congratulated on our President's actions in the Cuba situation. In Maine, that G.O.P. stronghold, everything he does is suspect. However, the elections at least brought us a recount of the

---

1 Bishop is referring to President Kennedy's handling of the Cuban missile crisis.
2 *The Points of My Compass: Letters from the East, the West, the North, the South* (1962).

Maine governorship, and while I fear the weak Republican incumbent will win out, at least the recount will give the Republicans a month of discomfort. There's *a* Blue Hill newspaper now, with Goldwaterish editorials that often arouse my ire, but the reporting of the area it covers, including your old favorite Deer Isle, is quite good.

    Affectionately,

      Katharine

P.S. As I told you earlier, I'm really out of editing except as a consultant once in a while.

November 14, 1962

Dear Elizabeth:

    Katharine White sent your letter down to me, and I showed it to Mr. Shawn, who said to tell you that if you were going to translate the Lispector stories anyway, we would like very much indeed to see them, and that the fact that they are translations would not keep us from publishing them.[1] We would however, as with any other material, want to publish them before they have appeared either in a book or in *Encounter*. The usual arrangement is that English magazines wait until six weeks after the story has come out in The New Yorker.

    We are happy to learn that there is a possibility of not only these stories but other things as well coming before long. As perhaps you forget to tell yourself when you wake up in the morning, you are the phoenix. Of if you aren't, I don't know who is.

    Yours affectionatcly,

      Bill

[n.d.]

Dear Elizabeth:

    I will be keeping a weather eye out for the stories. Whether they are or are not at all our line, it will be an absolutely dizzying pleasure to read anything you have had a hand in.

---

1 Maxwell wrote White: "Elizabeth has been written to, and I am pleased that the way is now clear to our publishing translations when we feel like it" (n.d., Bryn Mawr College Library).

I conveyed your compliment to Emmy, who smiled and didn't say a word. The kites *and* the beach is what I'd like to have.

Yours, ever,

Bill

Rio de Janeiro

December 15, 1962

Dear Howard:

We have to stay in the city this week-end; Lota is off with the Governor somewhere, probably looking at a tunnel or a new sewer—and I have had a very pleasant, rainy, lonely Saturday afternoon reading straight through your Proust book.[1] It came from Petrópolis a few days ago and I thought I'd save it to take to the seashore with me for over Christmas, then I thought today well, I'll just read the first chapter—and now it's six o'clock and I've read the whole thing. So you see you certainly held my interest. I think you have managed to say an enormous amount in very little space—and without cramming or ungainly technical-critical language—it is just *elegantly concentrated* and I hope the critics will realize it and not think that because it is a small book it is a slight book—It is also very "poetic" in the right way—and I think the "Gardens", "Windows" and (particularly) "Steeples" arrangement is very effective. ("Windows" and "Gardens" made me consider some very profound thoughts (so I think) about Alice in Wonderland . . .) I am only sorry the photograph on the jacket isn't used as a frontspiece, too. I'm sorry, for personal reasons, that the subject of asthma isn't brought up—however, that is more the other Mardel, I suppose—although I've always liked very much that scene on the train with his grandmother when he gets into a state of "euphoria"—following his doctor's advice.

Now I want to read some Proust right away and have none here in Rio. Is the 2nd volume of Painter out yet? I must get it—The book I interrupted to read yours is one about the same period in Paris and I think you might even enjoy it: SANTOS-DUMONT, a Study in Obsession, by Peter Wykeham.[2] They moved in the same circles and probably knew each other—although they would not have had much in common. Santos Dumont's aeroplanes were called "Dragonflies"—and his dream was the utmost simplicity, light-

1 *The Magic Lantern of Marcel Proust* (1962).
2 London: Putnam, 1962.

ness, perfection of construction, etc.—one wishes things had developed more according to his dreams than the Wright brothers! He himself was about 5'4" and weighed 50 kilos—I have seen his tiny boots and panama hat in a museum here—

And he was so appalled by the development of the plane and its use in war that he hanged himself with his necktie, in 1933. Forgive me if you know all this—I had never heard of Santos-Dumont until I came here.

Two weeks ago I sent you, boat mail, a couple of odd wood-cuts as a sort of Christmas card. Since the envelope wouldn't go in any slot, I handed it over to a fat cranky lady knitting at a table (instead of selling stamps or whatever she should have been doing), and I feel very doubtful of its ever reaching you . . . I have also read this afternoon the 50th Anniversary POETRY and I admire your SILENCES—I like some of the rhymes especially—Just in general, too, I admire your productivity!—I do hope the Proust is well-received & thank you very much for sending it. With much love—Lota would send hers, too, if she were on hand—Write me if ever you have time—

    Elizabeth

Do you know if Rollie [McKenna] has been sick?[1] We haven't heard from her in ages—

January 15, 1963

Dear Katharine:

Howard had written me some time ago about your operation and illness—but I hadn't dreamed how awful it had all been. I am so sorry to hear of it and I do hope you are recovering—such a damnably unpleasant kind of thing. I think you must be back in Florida again—and if so of course I have a very clear picture of what that is like, from the LETTERS . . .

We went away to Cabo Frio to stay in a friend's empty beach house over Christmas (with servants, dog, and garden), and while we were there a friend arrived bringing Christmas mail from Petrópolis, including Andy's book. It was just the right thing to have to read there—I read it straight through under a beach umbrella on a lonely little beach without another soul on it—a beach that is almost like a segment of the Maine coast, except that the water is

---

1 Rollie McKenna was a photographer famous for her portraits of Dylan Thomas and other poets of the 1950s and sixties.

warm, and the cacti, were all in bloom—rocks, islands, a turtle swimming around and raising his head every once in a while, even a small waterfall,— Thoreau—or Andy—would have felt quite at home and pleased that there *is* a great deal of the world still pretty much untouched, even if it is not in the U.S.A. . . . Of course I was especially interested in the postscripts. I had missed the piece about Alaska, too—that number must have got lost—and I liked it very much—a wonderful bit of recollection! Then Lota read the book straight through, too—and since then it has been read by a good many Brazilian friends and always makes a deep impression—they always seem surprised by any kind of American "dissent," even such a graceful one. One of the few things I am of two minds about—however—after living here so long and seeing how deadly it is to have a spoken language *and* a written language, widely divided—is the problem of "correct" English. I'm all for it— nevertheless I have decided that one thing that keeps English poetry—and prose—alive and real is the fact that there has never been an "Academy" and that writers in English are free to chose their words wherever they want to. I found I was backed up in this by [Otto] Jesperson's "Growth & Structure of the English Language"—but you probably knew that wonderful little book long before I did.)[1] Thank you so much for the book—I am delighted to have it, and mostly can only groan & agree . . . One day when I was sick an American friend brought me a huge batch of American magazines—the ladies' magazines, etc., the kind I never see—and after wading through them I suddenly felt extremely happy to be living in an "underdeveloped" country.

I have liked a lot of things in *The New Yorker* lately—the follow-up on jet planes, Dwight's pieces,—and although it's long ago now, for you, "Silent Spring"—I am sure she knows what she is talking about![2]

Bill Maxwell wrote me a very nice note about the Lispector transla- tions—I have a batch of five ready, but unfortunately Clarice got sick and is in the hospital for a minor operation now. I think I'll be able to get them off in a week or so, though—they may not be usable at all, but she does have a great deal of originality & humor—rare here—

Brazil goes from bad to worse—to worse—to worse—until one doesn't see what keeps things going at all. The government now seems to be trying to please the U.S.A. as well as the communists, however. One witty old jour- nalist, retired now, was interviewed & asked what he thought about the

1 *Growth and Structure of the English Language* (1926).
2 Bishop may be referring to John Bainbridge's profile of pilot Harold Blackburn, "Like a Homesick Angel" (November 10, 1962). Macdonald's most recent piece was "The First Editions of T. J. Wise" (November 10, 1962). Rachel Carson's "Silent Spring" ran June 16 to 30, 1962.

Alliance for Progress. He said he thought it was a very nice idea—for all the Latin American countries to get together and help the United States to progress—A friend of ours in the Foreign Office (Brazilian) was with a Minister when he flipped over the pages of a fat Christmas-time New Yorker and remarked "And all this is at *our* expense . . ." But you shouldn't think the ruling class here is all that stupid, by any means—there are some wise, hard-working, honest men—but the demagogues have won out for so long that it looks pretty hopeless—Meanwhile, how most of the population manages to eat—to keep alive at all—is a mystery.

My friend Lota was one of the 10 "Women of the Year" in the newspapers, for her work for Rio's huge new waterfront park—3 more years to go on it, if the governor manages to stay in. She works without pay. I copy out huge sections of Mumford for the governor, and terrifying books like "The Squeeze", etc.—he'd never have time to read the whole book—it is strange to be in such a role. He—Carlos Lacerda—has his faults, but he's much the most intelligent man in the country—according to Raymond Aron, too, not just my impression![1]

I didn't mean to bore you with the Brazilian situation. I do hope you are both feeling better and having a pleasant winter somewhere. Aren't *you* going to write something now? With all best wishes from Lota and from me for 1963, and thank you again—

Love,
Elizabeth

March 19, 1963

Dear Elizabeth:

Mr. Shawn has the feeling that anything in translation ought to be noticeably superior to the ordinary material of the magazine to explain our publishing it, and that, though there are wonderful and really quite unforgettable flashes in these stories, they don't quite measure up to that I dare say peculiar standard.[2] "A Hen" came the closest to it.

Could we see more of them?

Affectionately,
Bill

1 Edward Higbee, *The Squeeze: Cities Without Space* (1960). Raymond Aron was a French political commentator.
2 Bishop submitted her translations of Clarice Lispector's stories, "A Hen" and "The Smallest Woman in the World." *Kenyon Review* published the stories, along with her translation of "Marmosets," in its Summer 1964 issue.

Dear Howard:

It was nice to hear from you again—and I hope you did receive the letter I wrote you about your Proust book, long ago now. I won't say how long because I find I am always saying something happened a "few months ago" and then discovering that it was two years ago. I don't know whether this is the effect of Brazil or of age. I did like the book very much, and it started me reading Proust again. Of course Rio society would make him sick with envy and frustration—but he did do quite well with the small complexities he knew . . . I've seen many nice references to your book.

Yes, I want to renew this gift subscription and I'm enclosing a check for it.

Well, you asked me what I read and whom I see. I read plenty of everything; I am what is known as a bookworm. I also have plenty of real bookworms in the books I read, and I have at last, after twenty or so years in the sub-tropics (counting Florida) got the recipe for an excellent poison for killing them—from the British Council. The British have probably been keeping worms out of their books for centuries in India, and other parts of the Empire, but of course they are so discreet about telling one these things. It smells awful, and one ingredient is oil of cloves, so when you enter Lota's or my library you wonder (like Proust) why you suddenly feel as if you had a tooth-ache. I see—Lota, lots of movies, and many people like Greek City Planners, architects, engineers, sewer experts, Governors, and an occasional wandering poet or sight-seer. That's here. Up in the country I see mostly Lota. She's a wonderful mixture these days of Mumford, Galbraith, and perhaps Mayor La Guardia.

How odd—she came in just this minute and gave me a handful of *fresh* cloves, just off the bush, from her "park." I've never seen them before—have you? I'd enclose some but I'm afraid they'd make little bumps that might arouse someone's curiosity too much. Just imagine a dried black clove covered with a thin layer of rose-red flesh and smelling divinely—a mixture of clove and jasmine. The mails are dreadful—last week I got two New Yorkers from last September, and a big pink letter addressed simply to: "The Bishop of the Methodist Church of Brazil, Petrópolis, Brazil."—My own mail I don't seem to get at all, or never all of it.

You said you'd like a poem, so no sooner said—or not much—than done. It ["The Burglar of Babylon"] is last week's news in the form of poetry—like TIME magazine. I won't be the slightest bit surprised or hurt if you can't use it, but I thought I'd send it to you first, at least. If you can't use it, because of the mail situation referred to above, would you mind very much sending it on for me?—that will cut the possibility of loss by about 50%, won't it? Sonia Orwell wanted me to send something to ART & LITERATURE. I thought the 1st number was to appear in March, but now she has written again and it is already out and apparently my copies are among the lost items of mail. She wanted something on Brazil. Since I haven't seen the magazine I have no idea whether this would serve, or even fit the pages—but anyway—I'd be awfully grateful if you'd send it to her if you don't want it: 38 rue des Sts. Peres, Paris, 7e.

We did have a nice peaceful Christmas & New Years, up in the country, the longest we've been able to stay there for ages,—and I did get your card. One Christmas story I think you'd like (or maybe the Talk of the Town would next Christmas): In Rio the garbage collectors usually write a poem for Christmas—each section of the city—and have the poem printed on a little card, "I am your faithful garbage man," etc. Then you're supposed to give them a tip. This year the poem appeared, full of fine sentiments, and I meekly obliged. But those who didn't got another card a week later that said just "Merry Christmas. Second Notice."

1964 seems to have started with a lot of work,—writing, I mean—for me, and I hope it has for you, too, and that you're well.

With love from Lota and me,
 Elizabeth

P.S.—If you saw "Black Orpheus" (not good at all)—a lot of it was taken on the hill of Babilônia.

February 11, 1964

Dear Elizabeth:

What a pleasure to see a poem of yours again! And what a splendid one! We're taking it, of course. I have two tiny suggestions:

In the second and third stanza on page 2, and in the last stanza on page 4 and the first on page 5, I think I'd use quotation marks so the reader knows the speech is continuing. It's a conventional matter, but I'll have it set up that way, and if you don't like it, you can remove the quotes on the A.P.

On page 2 [stanza fifteen], the phrase "Some climbed the wall" led to a bit of confusion. It was read, at first, as referring to people, other people running away like Micuçú. You mean it, I'm almost sure, to refer to the freighters passing by. Would "They" be all right? That would make it absolutely clear.

I hope, in the next book, you put all the Brazilian poems together: Manuelzinho, the one about the gasoline pump—is that the one with the word "comfy" in it—the squatter one, the sort of tapestry one, and Micuçú. And, of course, the river god. The next book should be a wow,—but then what one hasn't been?

Did you ever finish the poem about the typewriter eraser I liked so much? I have been, on and off, writing another poem to you called SAUDADES, each section is supposed, ha ha, to correspond to one of the Milhaud pieces.[1] Since I haven't the faintest idea of what any of the places look like, I make them up. It will be, in the end, the most inaccurate poem ever written.

I'm finishing a book of critical pieces called Writing Against Time— reviews and essays.[2] And working on poems. And then The Folding Green is to have some "workshop" off Broadway performances in April. They are about to unveil my albatross again.

Aside from that, I lead a sedentary life. I went to Europe last summer, but stayed in London for the most part, with the exception of a four day drive through Ireland, which was wonderful. I fell in love with a place called Cobh. It's high on a bluff overlooking the Atlantic, with a big church, a little park right on the water, a statue of three men drowning, tenders going off into the blue, followed by gulls, and a funny hotel that faces the sea. The rest are little lace shops and candy stalls, etc. Some of the houses are pastel. You'd like it.

I still dream of arriving in Rio in a white linen suit off one of the Moore-McCormacks, twenty years younger and ten pounds lighter. The facts are against me.

Do send more poems soon and thank you for this one, which we are overjoyed to have. My love to Lota and to you.

All best wishes,
Howard

Petrópolis
February 16, 1964

Dear Howard:

I'm glad The New Yorker likes my simple ballad . . . Yes, the quotation marks at the beginning of stanzas are all right with me. Page 2, stanza 7—I

---

1 Moss may be referring to the piano piece, "Saudades do Brasil," by French composer Darius Milhaud.
2 *Writing Against Time: Critical Essays and Reviews* (1969).

was trying to make a distinction between freighters "passing by", horizontally that is, north or south, and those going out to sea, vertically (the way it does appear from a height). Now I have it:

> "Flat as wall, and on it
> Were freighters passing by,
>
> Or climbing the wall, and climbing
> Till each looked like a fly
> And then fell over and vanished" . . . etc.

Clearer now?

In that footnote—it should say "the folk-name of a large deadly snake in the north." I'm not very up on Tupi language, but I know that *mico* means big. I put in both possibilities just for interest.—The newspapers said "Dirty Marmoset", but petty gangsters usually go in for fearsome names and probably if anyone had called him that he would have answered with a bullet.—I hope they use ç ç's—cedillas. (Your letter says Micucu . . .) However—all this can easily be corrected on the proof.

I'm glad to hear you've travelled some more. I'm thinking of making a trip to England myself in a month or two to see a lot of touristy, literary things I've never seen. Have you any suggestions? Any suggestions about a place to stay in London? I haven't been there for so long—probably before you were born—when I saw Cobh, too, and loved it, too. But now you really must come here—while the political situation allows it. It would be very cheap for you here. No pure white suits any more, alas—It seems they have gone out of style for the upper classes because of the high cost, relatively, of servants.—Only low-class men, whose wives or mistresses will iron a suit for them every day, wear them now, and the *gran finos* wear only a white *jacket* with flannel trousers . . . (Just consult me as to fashions before you come!) Occasionally one sees an old man of the old school, and they do look nice. I saw a very fat old man the other day, all immaculate white, with a big panama with a black band, black necktie, and fanning himself with a small black lacquer fan . . .

Please send me "Saudades". I'd love to see it. "Writing Against Time" is a good title, too. I've been hunting around here to find a New Yorker that had a shortish poem of yours I liked very much—very *musical*—but probably it is in Rio, and perhaps it isn't as recent as I thought,—the mails are hopeless, as I've said before.

Would you like a good samba record to get you in the mood for South American travel? Or can you get them all in New York? Or do you dislike them, anyway? I am serious—I have an American Embassy friend who will kindly send things for me, so that they really arrive.

Affectionately,

Elizabeth

Lota sends her regards—

Rio de Janeiro
March 23, 1964

Dear Howard:

I've just been told by telephone that there's a note & a check from you at Samambaia (I'm spending the week-end in the city) thank you, & I hope the proof hasn't gone astray . . .

I was catching up on magazines yesterday and I saw your piece on Nathalie Sarraute's book, in Kenyon Review.[1] I haven't read the book, but I've read some of *her* and an article or two I think must be in the book—and I couldn't agree with you more.

Thank you for sending *Inventario*. I suppose I must write to Miss Petinella. The word "shell" in my poem ["The Map"] is a misprint—should be "shelf", so she is right. But she *still* hasn't put the poem back in its stanza form . . . It is true she couldn't get in touch with me—rather, I finally gave up writing to her, in despair—and I never gave her my permission to publish the translations, that I know of. She started sending me things about three years ago. I thought she did the hard part of translating very well, words and shades of meaning, etc.—but she wouldn't pay *any* attention to *my* punctuation, stanza form, italics, repetitions, etc. . . . the purely mechanical parts. Translators are very strange—they work so hard, and then overlook the obvious.—I am warning you, because I am sure she will translate you well if *you* pay attention to the details . . . The prize example was a man here who translated a sestina of mine, infinite labor, *without repeating a word*. (They're taught not to, in school—not for two pages, or hours, or something.) And yet [I have] come to find out he knew all about sestinas and could recite some old Portuguese ones—

We saw Alastair Reid several times when he was here two weeks ago—

1 *The Age of Suspicion: Essays on the Novel* (1963).

and I have a feeling you're going to get a poem by him about *futebol* on Copacabana Beach. He's a fan, and it's too bad there weren't any real games going on while he was here. He wired me at Petrópolis—the wire turned up in my mail box, days later—and we met here in Rio, just by chance. So if you ever do have any friends coming here you'd like to have call, my Rio address is Rua Antonio Vieira 5, Leme; 57-3412. Petrópolis phone: 3663. I have a feeling I have annoyed you with all this before—but it is maddening to miss seeing old friends (which I've done) when they're staying right next door in Rio, trying to get me by writing or wiring Petrópolis . . . Life's lonely enough here without that! In fact I am finding Rio so tedious I am going to England about the end of April, just for a month or two. I don't know whether I can bear to leave Lota, in the political mess here—but if it gets too bad she can fly to join me. Any suggestions?—I haven't been to London for 25 years.

A young Brazilian I know if going to the U.S. for 3 months, invitation of the State Dept., and is going around seeing "magazines", etc.—I'm not sure what-all, really. He is very bright, speaks excellent English, writes good criticism, and knows a lot about English and American poetry. I've taken the liberty of giving him your address. I rather doubt you'll ever hear from him—the State Dept. sends these people off on wild itineraries—but if you do I think you might not mind talking with him for an hour or so. His name (poor man) is Alexandre Eulália Pimenta—He comes from Diamantina & his relatives figure in that "Diary," the Pimentas, or "Peppers."

As you see—I'm so lonely I'm garrulous!

Love,

Elizabeth

Postscript, March 25th—

Mr. Eulália Pimenta is in the Brazilian State Dept. publications—and they do very nice books, bi-lingual Pound & Cummings, etc.—He'd probably want to put you in the next anthology.—He's translating Nathanael West now, I think—

Our plans have changed & we're probably both going to Italy, just for a couple of weeks, alas, May 20th; then I'll go on to England alone for a visit.—But Lota can get away for a little, we hope (I'm giving you all this because I hope to see you somewhere!) E.

April 21, 1964

Dear Elizabeth,

Here is the proof of THE BURGLAR OF BABYLON. I don't think there are any special problems though there seems to be some confusion about the pronunciation of the name of your hero.[1]

I was delighted to get your wonderful letter and would have answered at length except that I have been ill in the hospital and am still in traction at home. I go in and out of strings and weights but as soon as I am out for good I'll write.

Jimmy[2] called last night on his way to Greece and I'm sure you've seen the marvelous long poem which we hope to print soon. I hear his new novel is splendid.[3]

Will you be coming to New York on your way to England? I hope so, and if you are I'd love to give a party for you and Lota, in or out of traction.

Stay away from Brazilian politics, and I do hope somehow I'll be seeing you soon.

All my love,
Howard

May 3, 1964
[postcard: carnival parade samba school]

Dear Howard:

I haven't rec'd the proof of the ballad yet & I wonder if it got lost? I'm leaving May 13th. American Express, Milan, will reach me from then till June 12th—after that Am. Exp., London, until Aug. 1st.

I at last found the poem of yours I was so taken with I cut out of the New Yorker—and mislaid. "On the Library Steps." I think it's one of your very best . . . Seems to me it would make a lovely song.[4]

This was taken at dawn, this year—

Affectionately,
Elizabeth

---

1 Moss made a number of changes to Bishop's punctuation. He removed the comma after "hysterics" in stanza twenty-two, line three. He changed the colon after "said" in stanza twenty-three, line one, to a comma and removed the comma after "God" in line three of the same stanza. In stanza twenty-four, line two, he removed the period after "heaven". In stanza thirty, line one, he removed the comma after "beaches". In stanza forty, line one, he removed the comma after "respected" and inserted a period. And in stanza forty-three, line four, he removed the comma followed by a dash after "times" and inserted a dash. He also added quotes at the start of new stanzas when a character's speech continues (*The New Yorker* Records).

2 James Merrill.

3 "The Thousand and Second Night" (June 13, 1964) and *The (Diblos) Notebook* (1965).

4 November 23, 1963.

Florence
May 20, 1964
[postcard: to Howard Moss]

I'm mailing you the proof of Micuçú today. I got it just as I was leaving. I agreed with everything, I think except questions of "style"—which was, of course, repetitious & a bit clumsy on purpose . . .[1] We are so sorry to hear you've been sick and it sounds awful—I hope you weren't in an accident. "Traction" is what we've been needing, though, since that plane trip— planes are rather like slave-ships these days. How full-grown men survive I can't imagine.

We've been having a wonderful time and haven't thought of politics or Brazil, except to give it a sigh, for a week. I'll be in England about June 15th. With love from L & me—E.B.

Milan
June 13, 1964

Dear Howard:

I received your duplicate proof and letter here but I hope by now you have the one I sent you early in my trip—about three weeks ago, I think. As I think I said—it came to Rio just before I left and I didn't have time to do anything about it then. If you did not receive it—let me know at Hotel Pastoria, St. Martin's St., London, WC2—and I'll re-do the proof, using this extra copy.

Duplicate letters have an odd effect—this second time I am sure you have been *dreadfully* sick, and that Jimmy's poem is the poem of the age . . . And I wish I were going to New York but can't make it this time. Day after tomorrow Lota, *coitada*, goes back to Brazil and her job, and I go to England until August first. Then back to Rio by slow boat—I'm rather looking forward to

---

1 In stanza five, line two, Bishop agreed to changing "The Skeleton" to "the Skeleton". In stanza nineteen, line three, she agreed to removing the comma after "skyline". In stanza twenty-four, line two, she agreed to "Heaven" instead of "heaven". In stanza twenty-five, line two, she agreed to changing the semicolon after "no" to a comma. In stanza twenty-nine, line two, she agreed to ending the line with a dash instead of a comma. In stanza forty, line three, she agreed to removing the comma after "baby". There were additional issues with stanzas fourteen and fifteen, which Bishop had previously addressed in her February 16 letter. An "a" had been inserted into stanza fourteen, line two, so it read "Flat as a wall, and on it". The proofreader suggested removing the comma after "wall" in stanza fifteen, line one, but Bishop rejected this idea. With questions of style, Bishop is probably referring to the query about the repetition of the word "another" in stanzas forty-two and forty-three (Vassar College Library). There were three additional changes between the proof and publication: changing "The Chicken" to "the Chicken" in stanza four, line three; changing the comma after "shelter" to a period in stanza thirty-six, line three; and changing "Taurus gun" to "Taurus revolver" in stanza thirty-eight, line one.

collecting my wits and my "impressions" of our trip. We had a lovely time, confined ourselves to northern Italy—and Lota drove a weird white rented car nobly and safely through cities and over mountains—

We send our love and do hope you are better, Howard. Oh—I saw the Giottos in Padua that Proust writes about so beautifully—the allegorical figures—remember?

Love,
    Elizabeth

London
June 28, 1964
[postcard]

Dear Howard—G. Baro gave me this [East Hampton] address for you.[1] *Did* you receive that 1st proof I sent you from Florence? If not, I'll send the 2nd from here. My address is Hotel Pastoria, St. Martin's St., WC2. I do hope you are better now? This will reach me till Aug. 1—Much love, Elizabeth Bishop

Rio de Janeiro
September 30, 1964

Dear Howard:

I hate to keep bothering you about that one ballad, but here I go again about it. The Brazilian affiliate of ENCOUNTER, called *Cadernos Brasileiros*, wants to use it, in a Portuguese translation done by a friend of mine (Lota's nephew, who writes very nice poetry). I wonder if you have any idea when *The New Yorker* will be using it, so that the *Cadernos* could plan ahead? It's a monthly. At least, I suppose there'd be no objection if the proper credits are given? This is to ask the permission as well as the date, if you yourself know that.

How are you? I do hope you are quite recovered and had a nice summer on Long Island. I saw quite a few poets in London—and Gene Baro was very hospitable. He spoke about you a lot. Dick Wilbur happened to be there, too, and I was delighted to see him again,—looking younger and handsomer than ever, I swear.

---

1 Gene Baro wrote fiction and reviews for such publications as *Botteghe Oscure*, *The New Yorker*, and *Book Review of the New York Herald-Tribune*.

The mails seem to be a little better since our "revolution" and I think you could safely answer me at the above address. It does save a bit of time—unless foreign mail happens to coincide with a week-end in Petrópolis. I'd love to have a real letter from you and promise to answer one right away.

With love,

Elizabeth

October 9, 1964

Dear Elizabeth,

First, I was delighted that you'd won the Academy [of American Poets] fellowship. In fact, a picture of you and the story that goes with it is pinned up on my bulletin board this very minute. You look clean-cut, slightly austere, and ready to say something strongly worded about something.

Second, the ballad. We've scheduled it for our November 21 issue, and I hope it will stay there. The rest of the issue is still uncertain, so it's always chancey. But we can promise to run it before the end of the year in any case, and as soon after Nov. 21 as possible, if that issue should have to be changed at the last minute. I say that in case they want to use the poem in December or January. I'd love to see it in Portuguese when it comes out, if it isn't too much trouble.[1]

This is not the "real" letter you ask for but I will try to write one from home. In the meantime, please do send us some poems when you have them. I miss reading them, and try to find them whenever one comes out. Will there be a new book soon? How I would love to see MANUELZINHO and the squatter poem, the Brazil poem, and so many others safely bound together in one precious volume! All my best wishes to Lota.

Love,

Howard

December 6, 1964

Dear Howard:

I wonder if you'd be good enough to speak to the right person there, and have me sent two (2) copies of the November 21st *New Yorker*? Ordinary mail will do. I did get the airmail copy, and thank you. I'd also like a copy sent to my aunt:

1 Flavio Macedo Soares translated the poem for *Cadernos Brasileiros* (November–December 1964).

Mrs. William W. Bowers
c/o Snow
2231 Scott Street, Hollywood, Florida

I don't know how much postage will be but I think this check for $2.00 should cover it. If not, please let me know. If too much—put change in a Salvation Army tambourine . . .

You'd be amused by the reception of the "Burglar" poem here—it has been mentioned in the newspapers and by the "columnists." Some think I'm helping Brazil, some harming Brazil—one thinks I'm morbid.

I envy your prolifacy—prolificacy these days. (Can that be right? I almost write it profligacy.) "September Elegy" reminds me a bit of [Louis] MacNeice, although you are more graceful, or gracious, about it all. But oh dear I don't like your aging hand—[1]

Your aging affectionate friend,
    Elizabeth

P.S. How do writers get those "off-set" copies of things they are always showing me? I have no idea—is it easier or cheaper than whole copies? Perhaps you can enlighten me so I'll be more professional.

December 14, 1964

Dear Elizabeth,

It was sweet of you to send this check, but, honest injun, we don't need it, and it might do something dreadful, like complicate the "tax structure." How would the lawyers ever explain those two extra dollars to the feds? No, no, it's best destroyed quietly in some secret nook of South America. I've sent two copies of the issue on to you, and one on to your aunt in Florida.

I've heard nothing but good things about the Ballad, and I'm sure the news has been trickling down to you. So many people have asked for you in the past two weeks. Among them: Harold Leeds, William Goyen, Marguerite Young.[2] I keep telling everyone you're fine, which I hope is true.

Will you ever come back again? I hope so, and soon. In the meantime, a merry Christmas and a happy New Year to you and Lota—if they have happy

---

1 October 17, 1964.
2 Harold Leeds was the head of the interior design program at the Pratt Institute. His partner was Wheaton Galentine. William Goyen was a novelist, lyricist, and playwright. Marguerite Young was a novelist.

new years in Brazil. On my one New Year outside the USA, in Bermuda, no one seemed to care. They were celebrating something else, like Boxing Day or Guy Fawkes' Retreat, or Mothers Over Greenland Day, or something.

A new poem from you would make me forget a lot of horrors.

Love,

Howard

December 30, 1964

Dear Elizabeth,

A tiny question has come up in regard to a subscription for Miss Rosalina Azevedo Leão. She expires, as we say, on February 13, 1965. Should she be renewed? And if she is not, will the gods be angry?

A word from you could set the enormous clock-work of our subscription department in motion. And, anyway, she has a month of grace, which she needs, living in Brazil.

How was Christmas? I was out at East Hampton, which was more exhausting than I'd hoped, though nice, too. No snow. Spring weather with lots of rain.

I saw the back of Cal's and Elizabeth's heads at "Tiny Alice" last night, two rows in front of me.[1] We never met, oddly, in the intermission crush. They looked pretty good from the back.

I wish you'd send me a poem as a New Year's present. I thought Jimmy's last poem about not buying a carpet in the last NY Review of Books splendid.[2]

Happy New Year to you and Lota, and think of me sometimes, stuck up here among the canyons and the pushcarts and the bars.

Love,

Howard

Petrópolis
1965

Dear Howard:

Yes, please go ahead with the subscription for Miss Rosalina Azevedo Leão: I forgot about it, of course, and I'm glad you reminded me. I'll try to

1 Edward Albee's play *Tiny Alice* premiered December 29 at the Billy Rose Theatre starring John Gielgud and Irene Worth.
2 "A Carpet Not Bought" (December 3, 1964).

figure out the right amount—or perhaps they'd bill me, do you think? I always get it wrong the first time and that means more note-writing for everyone and more Post Office work here. Not that I mind writing notes to *you*, Howard—but I don't seem to have Marianne's gift for getting 20 or 30 business letters out of the way in one morning, and I wish I did right now . . .

I have always loved Jean's "Lottie Jump" story—and a couple of others in her new book, too.[1] It's funny—she's one of the few natural "writers" or "born writers", I think, around these days and I wish she'd do much more.

Well—we spent ten days up in the country—at the unusable address, actually the name of our house [Sitio da Alcobacina]—and it rained almost constantly but we liked it anyway. Peace—It rained so hard the telephone stayed out of order a lot of the time and we couldn't get to the nearest train stop to get the newspapers more than twice—So for once in a way I stopped worrying about Brazilian politics, etc., and looked at Nature, and polished brass, and brushed the cats and listened to the hi-*fee*—Oh—that reminds me—almost the only Rorem song I've listened to on that record he sent, besides my own, is yours—that is a lovely poem, I think—real classical!— My song (if you've listened to it) seems a bit too fast & hysterical—but he wanted it that way, I suppose—[2]

I won't make any promises—I've learned at last—but I do have quite a few poems on hand now—

What can "Tiny Alice" be? The reviews will tell me in 2 or 3 weeks . . . I'm sorry I didn't see Jimmy's poem—I subscribe to the NY Review and *never* get it—other subscribers here in the same fix—& it is the fault of the magazine, because I do get everything else. Well, I'm about to write & complain bitterly—I did receive a picture of his house in Athens, however.

Keep well, Howard—I hope you're over all your trouble of last year—

I just got a lovely book I recommend—ARCHITECTURE WITHOUT ARCHITECTS—Rudofsky—Museum of Modern Art—maybe you know it already?[3] He makes one feel there is much to be said for "underdeveloped countries"—no—now we called them "less developed." But there should have been some Brazilian examples in it—Brazil is less & less developed, but has its compensations—An advertisement for stoves, for example, that shows the black cook kissing the white mistress because she likes the new stove . . . She's still *only* the cook—but there *is* a lot to be said for this country when

1 Jean Stafford, *Bad Characters* (1964).
2 Ned Rorem, "Visits to St. Elizabeths: (Bedlam)," *Songs of Ned Rorem*. Bishop's poem is in the same group as Moss's "See How They Love Me," Robert Hillyer's "Early in the Morning," and Gertrude Stein's "I am Rose."
3 Bernard Rudofsky (1964).

no one thinks anything of such an ad—Lota didn't even notice it, for example—(After the kind of articles I get in all the US magazines these days, particularly.)

Well—if they will kindly bill me I'll send a check immediately—Lots of love & my best wishes for the new year—

Elizabeth

January 12, 1965

Dear Elizabeth,

A brief note to tell you that I've sent Miss Rosalina Azevedo Leão a new subscription. But I sent it under my name, not yours, since it's $8.oo for me and would have been $16.oo for you. (I can't find her renewal card. She *does* live in Brazil or Portugal, doesn't she? Anyway, when they finally check with the files downstairs—this sounds like a Maigret novel—it will all be straightened out, and it's always cheaper if I get it, anyway.)

So you owe me eight dollars. Instead of sending it to me, which would involve us both, I imagine, in deals so complicated that we might never write again, why don't you hold off, and if you ever find any more cinnamon soap with the sun carved on it, send that to me instead. And—by the byebye—if the magazine is a gift from you to Leão, you might drop her a note explaining how simple life really is. I mean I don't want her to get the idea I'm some sort of international stage-door Johnny.

Love,
Howard

P.S. *Please* send some *poems!*

Rio de Janerio
February 18, 1965

Dear Howard:

I did find your letter of January 12th at last—and also some un-opened letters the maid carefully put away while I spent two weeks or so in the "interior"—She's a nice maid, but *analphabetica* and attaches no importance at all to printed papers, and I'll just have to be more careful. I did send you the $8.oo, however, on January 29th, and I hope you received it? Thank you once again. I see Rosalina frequently and I gather she is still getting the magazine—no lull.

On the other hand—I can find no record in my checkbook for the past two years of my own subscription to *The New Yorker* and I wonder if you would be good enough to call them up about that? (I feel like DH Lawrence, always asking impossible things from his friends—I try not to but sometimes it is hard to resist, and my correspondence with *your* subscription department is always so difficult.) We have been getting it, but I have a *feeling* it has stopped. (Now I'll probably get up there this week-end and find five.) *This one I WANT TO PAY IN FULL—of course!—*

My mailing address for all magazines is the old permanent one: Caixa Postal 279, *Petrópolis*, Estado do Rio de Janeiro, Brasil

This is scarcely your line of work and I do apologize. After you have been here to visit us—as we hope you're going to do—I think you'll understand how nice it is to get magazines, and particularly New York magazines, in this now very provincial city . . . I haven't received any notification, but I'd like to know when the magazine is due to stop, and how much I should send them if it has stopped, etc. . . . *Coitado de Howard!*

That cinnamon soap—well it has deteriorated sadly and no more sunfaces, only *walnuts* now—but I'll send you some by Richard Kelly, probably,—Lota's park-lighting-expert,—when he goes back to New York.[1] What I'd like to send you, if you think you'd enjoy it, is a *samba* record? Do you still have your gramophone, or a bigger one by now? There is one fairly old record that's really good—gives the exact effect of the street parades—and it will set you samba-ing even if you never have. Or any other Brazilian music you'd like? They have recently discovered masses of baroque—rococo, really, I'd say—church music composed and performed—mostly by Negroes and slaves—in the late 18th century in Minas (where I've just been). You may not be interested in this kind of music, but I find it diverting that when we were just about up to Wesleyan hymns, the Negroes here were singing whole masses that sound very much like Hayden. That remark is not original—was made by Ashley Brown, the very nice Fulbright Prof. here this year, who went with me on my last trip to see all the churches, etc., over again. I am actually writing some prose pieces about them, and one I hope to send to your prose Dept. soon—we'll see—(Also some poems to you, I hope—but I never make promises any more. (I hope.)) If there is anything else from here you'd like, just tell me—too bad palmit (hearts of palm) is so heavy to take by air—it is good, too. I'll send a small bottle of palm oil, though, *dendé*—to give your shrimp soufflés or any fish dish, gumbos, etc.

1 Kelly was the lighting designer for Parque do Flamengo in Rio de Janeiro.

that je ne sais quoi—rather, ils ne savent quoi. Forgive this untidy letter—I've had many interruptions. Tell me, —you never did—how you like your song set by Rorem—and don't you think mine is too *fast?*+—

    With love,
        Elizabeth

+I never meant it to be hysterical—

Dear Elizabeth,

You are on the complimentary list of New Yorker subscribers, which means the magazine sends them to you for free, and that's why you have no record of paying for them. You have always been a complimentary subscriber and I think the confusion arose out of our tangled correspondence in regard to Rosalina. So there is no need to worry. If you *haven't* been receiving the magazine, though, do let me know and I'll check further. And if you are missing any issues, let me know which ones, and I'll have them sent to you. I did find out one tiny horror in my "investigation": the subscription department was leaving out the phrase "Estado do" in the Petrópolis address, so, maybe, some of the magazines went to Rio instead of to Petrópolis. The address is now absolutely accurate.

I would love a Brazilian record madly and will dance around my apartment while I play it. I need something new to dance to anyway. Are you a member of PEN? I am, though I've never gone to a meeting or cocktail party, God help me. Anyway, they're having a "congress" in Bled, Jugoslovia, "a high, Alpine resort," and I'm thinking of going. Why don't you come? It would be wonderful to meet on a terrace overlooking a lake, snow mountains all around, and *not* discuss literature. The congress lasts a week—July 1–7—but there is a boat trip after that down coast to Dubrovnik. Optional. Do think about it. Jean Stafford and Edward Albee may turn up and we could all have *fun*.

    Love,
        Howard

Dear Howard:

Richard Kelly flew up to New York last night, and by the time you get this you probably will have received a samba record and a letter from me. I think he said he'd met you . . .

Before he left, he handed over a lot of odds and ends, the way our visitors usually do—match-folders from the Yale Club, extra US cigarettes & Kleenex, paper-backs, etc.—and also the March 13th *New Yorker*. My own copy of course hasn't got here yet, and won't for several weeks. If he hadn't given me that March 13th one, and I hadn't looked at it last night, instead of this letter you'd be getting a long poem called CRUSOE AT HOME . . . It is a bit unnerving, isn't it . . . Or is it just "great minds," even so far apart? Well, they aren't really exactly alike, because mine is in the first person, more realistic and un-organized, etc. I'll send it someplace else, and I'll send you a copy when I have time to make copies.

Yours ["Robinson"] is very lovely—the cork image particularly fine, I think.

I re-read Crusoe not long ago and found it morally appalling, but as fascinating as ever. Have you ever read the travel memoirs of Woodes Rogers, the young captain who picked up Selkirk?[1] The parts about him are brief, but very moving.

Telepathically yours,
Elizabeth

March 29, 1965

Dear Miss Bishop,
Howard Moss just called in on his way out of town to ask me to ask you to please, please, please send the Robinson poem to us.

Sincerely yours,
Elizabeth Hawes

May 8, 1965

Dear Howard:
I just had a telephone call from the country and I hear there's a new book of poems of yours waiting for me there.[2] Thank you—I am looking forward to seeing it on the week-end . . . & I hope to be sending you a book of my own, probably next October.

1 *A Cruising Voyage Around the World* (1712).
2 *Finding Them Lost and Other Poems* (1965).

This is to ask a sort of favor of you—please don't worry if you haven't any suggestions. I've written a friend who lives uptown, and May, for the Village—and surely something will turn up. It is about a *room* for 3 weeks—for a friend of Lota's and mine to stay in during her stay in New York. She will arrive June 14th. She is an architect here, Polish-Brazilian, a very cultivated, polite, and intelligent lady of about 40 named Maya Osser. She is also quite a successful architect and shop-designer, etc.—but the $$$ is just impossible for anyone with Brazilian money now, and although she has plenty for her trip, hotels *are* impossible, really. (She bought her ticket at a bargain, a year ago, and now has to use it up before it expires!) She told me she had a room with a friend-of-a-friend-of-an-acquaintance, a Polish lady who takes "roomers" out somewhere near the World's Fair—and I thought that sounded grim, and as if she'd have to spend all her time on the subways, so I said I'd ask around for her and see if I could find something in Manhattan. She was in NY with her family, just before the war under very different circumstances, of course. She gets to Europe every 3 or 4 years, has relatives (her mother was the niece of Henri Bergson) in France, and lives here with a Count (with 3 years in the mines in Siberia behind *him*—but they can't marry, being Catholics and he having a wife somewhere in the dark past. She didn't even know until the war started, apparently, that her maternal grandmother was Jewish. She is a very interesting and quite amusing person, and I think would be no trouble at all—very independent—also, she has introductions to architects, etc. I hope—even if you don't know a place for her to put her head—perhaps you will see her, have lunch with her or something? I have given her your name and address. She wants to see paintings, mostly, — (you might be able to tell her more about the small galleries now than I can,)—and, of course, contemporary architecture.

If you do know of anyone with a spare bedroom, that rarity—could you let me know at the Rio address? She'd pay for it, naturally—

I shall send you my Robinson Crusoe poem as soon as I give it a good dusting, —maybe this week.

Are you really going to Jugoslavia, and if so tell me how much you think it might cost, your plans, etc. I am serious; I might go—We are supposed to be in Italy now, but had to postpone it until the fall, because of Lota's job. I might go somewhere first, and meet her in Italy—

I wonder if you got the *disco* I sent up by Richard Kelly, and if it was so AWFUL you're afraid to mention it? I did listen to one of them all the way through and it seemed all right, then I lost patience. The one I took home for myself couldn't be worse—a great blur—and I do hope yours wasn't like that. Brazilian products *vary*. I promise you I'll do much better next time—perhaps Maya will take you a better one. I hope you are well and flourishing, and I know you are writing a lot—

Much love,

Elizabeth

Maya is very well read in Proust, etc.—but not, I'm afraid, in poetry—

May 18, 1965

Dear Howard:

I have lost so much mail lately that I am beginning to worry for fear you haven't received any of my letters, that AWFUL record—except that Kelly is very reliable!—etc. . . . and so I'll just write it all over again . . . I am so sorry about that record. The one I wanted was not in stock and those *are* good old sambas and marchas—but when I played mine last week in the country it was really unbearable. Please throw it away and I'll try to get you a better one sometime.

I wrote you about ten days ago about a friend of ours who is coming to N.Y. the 14th of June, Maria Laura Osser (Maya). I'll repeat this, too—She is an architect here, very successful (especially for a female, in Brazil) and she came here when she was about 13, I think, escaping from Poland with her family—a hair-raising tale, but she never tells it. She once was in N.Y., just before the war, travelling in luxury then, poor dear. Last year she bought a bargain round-trip ticket to NY and now has to use it up before it expires. She has plenty of money for her trip, etc.—but I did ask you in my first letter if by any chance you knew of a "spare room" she could rent for three weeks. Hotels are really beyond the reach of anyone with Brazilian money these days, except the politicians. (I have asked other friends, too, so please don't think that I am demanding you think of a place!—something will probably turn up.) She is very bright, speaks many languages and reads them, too. She doesn't read much poetry, I'm afraid—but she knows Proust very well, and I think that you and she might lunch out pleasantly on that. Lota and I would be very grateful if you could see her, just once even. There is no divorce here, you know—but for all practical and—here—social purposes she is married to another Pole, a count, this one—who spent three years in the mines in Siberia.—She is coming alone, however. Oh—her mother was Bergson's niece. That is enough to go on, I think . . .

I shall send you the Crusoe poem shortly. I am off to Minas tomorrow for a week or ten days, but I usually get much more done there than in Rio—and I'll get it copied and in the slow Minas mails—

Now I have repeated everything and can start all over again—

Dear Howard:

Thank you very much for your book.—I read it through a good many times in the long rainy days I spent up in the country last week. I like the title, type, etc. very much—and as for the rest of it, I think you have every reason to feel very proud—even if you are looking quite modest in that photograph. Of course the poem I like best is ON THE LIBRARY STEPS—the one I cut out of the New Yorker, lost, found, lost, and found—and now have in permanent form, thank goodness. I really think the first eight lines of that one are perfectly beautiful—I know them by heart. I like all of it but especially the first two thirds.—THE SILENCES is quite lovely—and where is that one about the stars—oh, LOOKING UP. The "sprayed from a hose" image is wonderful. I like these very simple lines you have been using. I also feel a great pathos—so many of your poems are a city-man's summer-poems—and you are so aware of summer and vacation and the country when you have them all together. I want to write more about the translation [of Paul Valéry's "The Cemetery by the Sea"] and a lot of other favorite lines. But this is the first chance I've had to mail a letter in ten days and I just wanted you to know I had received the book, and to thank you—I'll really write about it again when I get back—

With much love,
    Elizabeth

June 8, 1965

Dear Howard:

How nice to have a real, almost super-screen size letter from you again, —but I'm awfully sorry to hear you've been sick. I know exactly how you feel about craving a mother-figure and a refuge—in fact I have made another trip to Minas, where I stayed much too long, in search of just the same atmosphere. There are no telephone calls, or none for me—the air is cold and clear; our friend there [Lilli Correia de Araújo] has a large old-fashioned Brazilian farm-yard full of assorted poultry, and even the remains of a gold-mine in her garden—and everything is nice and untidy and leisurely and 19th-century and when I do get the afternoon paper the news makes no sense to me at all—compared with the arrival of a visiting saint that evening in the town square or the acquisition of *three* old cupboards (where am I going to put them all?)

I stayed too long and so I didn't receive your letter until two days ago and now I'll send this answer (and token gift) to you by Maya herself. Thank you for your information about places to stay—but I had great luck—my old friend Frani Muser has a room vacant, since her son is off crossing the continent or something—so Maya will stay, at least to begin with, with her, on 52nd Street. Then Sylvia Marlowe has just arrived in Rio and she, too, has offered her apartment if necessary, since she'll be off in Connecticut. So I think Maya will not lack a place to put her head and she is feeling very cheered up about her trip . . . (I've been an "honorary member" of the Cosmopolitan from time to time—but you know I am so far removed from the affluent society now that it strikes me as fearfully expensive . . . much too much to pay and watch the Lindberghs drinking tomato-juice . . .)[1]

I'm giving Maya all the information—you'll hear from her some-time next week, I think. I do hope you are feeling better—hepatitis is one of *the* diseases here—and I know there are many varieties and all make you feel awful, and even the dogs get it, they say . . . It is rather rare and wonderful for American citizens to have LIVERS though—I don't think I have one—almost like a Bourbon chin or Hapsburg nose or something—Maya drove Sylvia, S's "tuner," and me, up to the country Sunday just to show her the house, etc.—and while we were there I went to the study to look for your Proust book to lend M—she'd like to read it. Unfortunately, Alberto (our boy or man or whatever his rank is) had been treating all my books for bookworms, and most of them were put back upside down or inside out, and I just didn't have time to find the M's again.—I'm awfully sorry because I am sure she'd like it. This is one of the troubles we have with analfabetas—(It is worse, even, when a telegram arrives at the wrong address and can't be read to us—)

I feel awfully flattered that you may write about me—and I'd like it to be in Kenyon, too. The new book [*Questions of Travel*] will be out in October.—If you'd like I could probably get you copies of those you mention before then, however. Just give me a few days here, until we get Sylvia's (unscheduled) concert over with, and I promise to write again—at the moment I feel almost as if I were in New York, all this telephoning, jotting down of numbers, forgetting everything, etc. I also want to say a lot more about your book—I think that very clear simple voice is lovely, but I want to

1 The Cosmopolitan Club is a private women's club on East Sixty-sixth Street.

say more than that—Do take care of yourself, Howard.—Lota & I talk about you a lot,—you'd probably be surprised if you knew how often!—If you feel like seeing Maya, do—if not, I am sure she will understand, being very polite and old-world—

    Lots of love,
        Elizabeth

                  C/O Correia de Araújo
                      Caixa Postal 118
                      Ouro Prêto
                September 28, 1965

Dear Howard:

I'm sorry I promised you *my* Robinson Crusoe poem and then changed my mind about it . . . Perhaps I'll like it better again after a while. In the meantime, here is another one ["Under the Window"] I hope you can use.

I've been up here for quite a long visit—Lota could only make it for one weekend, *coitada*—She is killing herself with work, I'm afraid, but after the elections—October 3rd—we'll know where things stand—whether she's in or out, +etc. I'm going to stay away from Rio until they're over—I'm of no use to anyone when political hysteria is in the air. [handwritten: "+of her job. She's not running for office"]

You should be getting a copy of my book sometime in October—I wrote to Bob Giroux that you were planning to write a piece about me and should be sent an "advance" copy, if they have such things.

If you do want to use this poem, I'd be awfully grateful if you'd just let me know—here until October 8th, after that in Rio—but mail takes longer to get here than to Rio, of course—and send the check directly to my Massachusetts bank. Could you do that, do you think? To be deposited to my account? I'm not sure.—But it would save a great deal of time for me, mailing back and forth—and the mails have taken a turn for the worse lately.

I suppose you've read the 2nd volume of the Proust biography—?[1] I hope my copy of it will be in Rio by the time I get back. I'm doing a lot of work here, I'm glad to say—perhaps you'll be seeing some more of it. I hope you're well—had a nice vacation somewhere?

    With love,
        Elizabeth

---

1 George D. Painter, *Marcel Proust: A Biography, Volume 2* (1965).

I apologize for the local typewriter ribbon—& the lack of a dictionary, too—

October 5, 1965
[postcard]

Dear Howard: I see by my carbon copy I made a mistake in that poem I sent you the other day. It should be—in the next to last stanza—"the seven ages of man"—of course.

I wish you'd come here some time—it lacks the social attractions of Europe, but it [is] such a beautiful town—and also has the best hotel in South America in it—or as one of my well-travelled friends said: "One of the few great hotels left in the world . . ." Lota and I would love to have you up in Samambaia, too—that being our chief "residence", I suppose—

Can you tell me to whom I should send a story now at the NY?? It has been so long since I did any prose I really don't know any more. I've been getting quite a bit of work done here, I think, and hope to get some things sent off this month—

How are you—I hope you're quite recovered from your last trouble— Here we have just had a disastrous election—and rumors of more "revolution" from Rio—I take these in my stride now, however, but for L's sake I hope not—Much love, Elizabeth

October 12, 1965

Dear Elizabeth,

UNDER THE WINDOW is, simply, wonderful, and we are overjoyed to have it. It makes me wild to get my hands on ROBINSON CRUSOE. I've made the change in the next to last stanza, and the check will be sent to your bank in Massachusetts.

One tiny thing: We are against dedications, as you know, and they have been cropping up more and more frequently on poems. The simple theory is that the dedicatee means nothing to the reader and is only relevant in magazine publications when it is relevant to the poem. (I mean a poem like CLAIR DE LUNE dedicated to Achille-Claude Debussy.) Would you mind terribly if we removed the dedication? I'm speaking here for the policy of the magazine. Do let me know.

As for the story, do send it on to me and I will get it to the right places as quick as a flash.

The book hasn't arrived yet, but I keep looking forward to it. And please do send a poem along with the story if you can. It gave me such real pleasure to read UNDER THE WINDOW.

Love,
    Howard

October 26, 1965

Dear Elizabeth,

Here is a check for UNDER THE WINDOW, OURO PRÊTO, and thanks again for a poem I love.

Still no sign of the new book, but I've put a call through to Bob Giroux and I hope to get an early one, since Kenyon wants the review or essay-review by January. Of all the books of poems I see and know are coming out, it's the one I look forward to most.

(While I was writing this, Bob Giroux called. I should have "Questions of Travel" some time next week.)

Please do send the new story—if it's anything like IN THE VILLAGE, I'll buy myself a split of champagne—and I still await Robinson Crusoe. He deserves to be rescued. And whatever did happen to that little poem that fascinated me about the typewriter eraser that kept travelling up and down the machine, and looked like an English guardsman's hat, if I remember correctly?

My best to Lota, and I hope the elections weren't too wrong. From here, Brazilian politics is about as clear as the Hudson River.

Love,
    Howard

Rio de Janeiro
November 8, 1965

Dear Howard:

I'm sorry to have been slow about this [author's proof]. I stayed on in Minas for a long time—an extra week because no planes could get out, for one thing—and I've just got back to Rio and my correspondence. I'm so glad you like the Ouro Prêto poem. I think it should be "seven ages of man"—or however it is in Shakespeare, as someone says in the margin . . . If S says "life" it can be life—but I think he says "man"—I don't have S at hand in the apartment here.[1]

---

1 It ran as "man". Bishop maintained Moss's insertion of a comma after "Meanwhile" in stanza thirteen, line two. It appears she rejected his other changes. He inserted a comma between "whip-lash" and "blinded" in stanza ten, line three. The phrase ran as "whiplash-blinded". In stanza fourteen, line two, Bishop had a colon after

One thing—if it is at all possible I do want to keep that dedication. In this case I know the name means nothing to the reader—however it is obviously a *Brazilian* name (although a Dane bears it) and so I think gives just a bit more color, mystery perhaps, etc. For another—your policy is fairly new, I think— maybe because poets are going in too much for dedications these days? But I have only done it one other time and you did use the name, "Jane Dewey," that time, I remember. Also—in the batch of *New Yorkers* I find here, I see a poem dedicated—to initials, at any rate—also another, obviously Stevenson's initials—etc. etc.[1] Thirdly—it is almost the only re-turn my friend Lilli will let me make for endless hospitality and kindness and she is so proud and pleased that I can't bear to disappoint her . . . It is out my window at her house, and when I showed her the poem she took a long time to read it and then said it was the first poem she had ever understood in her life—and I was so touched I immediately said I'd dedicate it to her. I don't know whether these arguments—objective ones and personal ones together—can convince you, but I hope in this case they can. The name is Lilli Correia de Araújo— and your Brazilian readers at least (not many, but some surely subscribe) will recognize the family name at once—it's a famous old one, etc. [handwritten: "Oh—*The NYer* with May's letter poem just arrived. I like it—but shall try to improve my letter writing style in the future . . ."[2]]

I imagine you've received your copy of my book by now—since I got one airmail yesterday and another today. I am so curious to see what you'll say I can scarcely stand it until January.—I think the book is pretty thin, myself—wish it were twice the size—but can't really judge the contents otherwise. I DON'T like that picture on the back—but it was either that or a lot of blurbs, or a large photograph—and I thought this at least a bit impersonal.

Lota finally came and *got* me in Ouro Prêto—it is a terribly long drive, too, so I was properly impressed. I'm hoping we can both go back next month for a stay, or in January—she needs a rest badly and is very upset by elections and everything else here at the moment, and never stops working and has lost her voice, etc. etc. But she's done a wonderful job—even all the enemies agree to that—But oh lord—Brazilian politics . . . I wish we could

"passersby:". Moss substituted a comma. It ran without punctuation. Bishop ended the penultimate line with a colon. Moss had a dash set. It ran as a colon (*The New Yorker* Records and Vassar College Library). There were two additional changes between Bishop's submission and the poem's publication: the comma after "laughed" in stanza four, line two, was removed, as was the comma after " 'godmother' " in stanza nine, line one.
1 Recent poems with dedications include: "On the Marginal Way" by Richard Wilbur (September 25, 1965), dedicated to "J.C.P.," and "Envoy" by L. E. Sissman (September 4, 1965) dedicated to "A.E.S."
2 "Dear Elizabeth" (October 9, 1965). Swenson used Bishop's letters to write the poem.

get to Italy as we planned to, but I'm afraid not—but some place out of the country is the only way for her to stop fretting about them and really rest.

Thank you for the check. As soon as I get *both* typewriters overhauled you shall have one story at least and maybe two—I do hope you're well Howard—much love,

Elizabeth

Dear Howard:

Another note to you—although I'm not sure my proof and first letter have got off yet. I got a batch of mail from Petrópolis last night and in it is your note of October 29th and the photostats of your other two letters. Oh dear—I think Mark Strand has put you to a lot of unnecessary trouble—what possessed him? He came over to Ouro Prêto for one day while I was there, and talking about The New Yorker, you, etc., I must have happened to say I hadn't heard from you about a poem I was expecting to hear about. I haven't any recollection of this and certainly didn't mean to complain—if I *will* bury myself in these antique spots I have to expect to slow down my life even more than usual—

I think all my friends have to visit me, sooner or later, and preferably by boat—so they can really understand how very far away Brazil is! The mails, that improved enormously for a while after the "revolution", have been getting very bad lately, too—and then Ouro Prêto is remote—it wouldn't be at all in the USA, but here it is—and the Post Office very dreamy and absent-minded. If I tried to mail more than three letters at a time the postmaster would sigh heavily, and ask if I *really* wanted to send them airmail, or register them, because it would cost a great deal. But this is one of the things I like here—the dreadful salesmanship, or none at all—so I have to accept the results cheerfully.

Along with yours I had a letter from May—very nice about my book but obviously a bit hurt and worried because I hadn't said anything about her letter-poem for me.* Well—I got that New Yorker at the same time, too, so you see!—I live in a backward country with a very backward clock.

I've just been reading in the morning papers all about the black-out in New York. Heavens—please tell me what it was like and what *you* did during it. Lota, for some reason, refuses to believe it and says it's just newspaper exaggeration—but I still believe a bit in United Press.

Mark admires you and your poetry very much; we like some of the same poems. I don't mean to complain about him and he undoubtedly didn't mean to confuse things, just trying to help—

Love and best wishes,
Elizabeth

* I like it very much—she sent me a copy when she was working on it. But again—what about "dedications"?

Rio de Janeiro
December 1965
[postcard]

Dear Howard—thank you for your card. I am about to leave—tomorrow, the 27th—to be a poet-in-residence at The University of Washington, Seattle, Washington, 98105. PLEASE write me! Why do they call it that—sounds like Longfellow's house in Cambridge, at least. I'll mail this to you from Miami or one of those many horrid stops . . . I hope Lota will join me, in May. Then I hope we can come east by *Vista-Dome*—but I suppose I couldn't lure her aboard anything like that. She frightened the public horribly even on a short bus-trip (taken in an emergency). I wonder if you got my letter with the proof, long ago now, and my insistence of having a dedication if possible, etc.—Or is it your reply that is lost this time? I think Jim Merrill's new book is very good.[1]—I wonder how you are and hope you are well—Don't YOU ever go on those reading circuits like the other poets?—and if you do, why not come to Seattle? (I just read in the National Geographic that he was an Indian chief.) Forgive this hasty note and please let me hear from you. Love and best wishes for the New Year—Elizabeth

January 28, 1966

Dear Elizabeth,

Here is an adjustment on your 1965 cost of living adjustment—whatever that means. I think it's an annual overall second look on the quarterly payments of the year before. Beyond that, one needs an MIT education to figure it all out. *I* say, though, never look a gift horse in the mouth.

I felt I was rather a pale telephone pal the other evening when you called. I was delighted, but having just been working on the piece about you, I was

1 Bishop is probably referring to *The (Diblos) Notebook*.

shocked suddenly to hear your voice. I felt that maybe I had conjured you up, and since my magical powers are already dangerously neurotic, I was afraid that if I thought or said the wrong things a whole series of natural disasters might occur.[1] I hope Seattle looks better by now—where is all the water? Puget Sound, and all that? I thought it was a sort of northern Eden, but I suppose there are factories and such. Tell me if it's awful, so that I won't have to go. That's *my* question of travel.

Marianne Moore has moved to 9th Street and there have been interviews and pictures in almost every paper and magazine. Two of them have her on the same page with a picture of one of the Beatles getting married. Mrs. Beatle is wearing the shortest wedding dress I've ever seen.

May has written a play I like.[2] No word from Jimmy since his reading. I read at NYU on Sunday, and have already begun the countdown on tranquilizers and injections. I've now read 6 times in the past 2 years. That should be enough to prove I'm not a coward, but I think I'll go back to my policy of total withdrawal.

That rain storm in Brazil sounded absolutely horrible. I hope they'll do something at last about the favelas (?). Mark wrote me a letter describing some of the worst of it. The only tiny ray of sunshine, as far as I was concerned, was that you weren't there.

How are your students? And especially that Japanese one.[3] I have the proof of my Kenyon review (joke) but you said you wanted to be surprised. And whatever happened (business) to the Robinson Crusoe poem? I'll die if it suddenly comes out somewhere else.

I'll be in Minnesota in April. If you were the brave girl you say you are, you'd meet me in Minneapolis. Further west, I cannot go. At least in my present condition. I hear it's all mud and filth in April, but we could wear rubber skis and trip across the mudflat.

Do write me when you can.

Love,

Howard

1 After relating a "disconcerting" incident Bishop had had with a student, Moss told Merrill: "*I* was disconcerted, since I was just finishing a review of Questions of Travel, and had just written a sentence like 'Elizabeth Bishop is . . .' Then the phone rang, there she was, I said, '*Eli*ʒabeth!'" (February 28, 1966, Washington University Library). See note 3 below.

2 May Swenson's one-act play, *The Floor*, was produced on May 11 at the American Place Theater.

3 Moss wrote to Mark Strand of his conversation with Bishop earlier that month: "Elizabeth called me last night from Seattle and seems to be settling in, though I think she is rather alarmed by the ugliness of the city. She hasn't seen any water yet. She has a Japanese student who told her it made him very nervous to be working with a 'fairly well-known poet.' She didn't say it made her nervous to be working with a fairly unknown student, which is what I would have said" (January 4, 1966, *The New Yorker* Records).

Dear Howard:

Happy George Washington's birthday—& I presume this state was named for him . . .

This is just to ask you a question. I've been asked here to recommend poets for this job, and I wondered if by any chance you would consider it sometime. I have already given your name to Robert Heilman, the head of the English Dept. (& very nice, too), so he may even have written you by now for all I know, because he seemed to take to the idea. I had heard a rumour (I think from May Swenson) that you were leaving *The New Yorker*—or perhaps if not you could have a leave of absence.—You may not like the idea at all, but when they asked me about "poets" I thought of you. *The Poet* can come for one, two (like me), or three "quarters" and the pay is $7,000 a quarter—which seems very good by my humble standards. That is $7,000 each ten weeks, more or less. There are only 2 small classes—15 to 20—and they meet for 50 minutes, supposedly 4 times a week but I have cut the writing class to 3 times a week. This part of the world, and the breezy western manner, and teaching, rather staggered me at first— but now I am beginning to enjoy most of it except the classes—but then you did teach before, didn't you? [handwritten: "They are *very* nice to one, too—"]

Well—I am not urging this on you! I just thought I'd explain how it came about, in case you do hear from Mr. Heilman or a Mr. James Hall . . . Also— one is a full professor for the term, because Roethke was. One does feel a bit like his ghost, of course. This year Henry Reed is here—he had this job, too, 2 years ago—and he brightens things for me a great deal.[1] I wish you would get him to send you something for The New Yorker—I am sure he has some poems somewhere, and I think he is a beautiful poet, don't you? c/o the Eng. Dept. here would reach him.

If you can think of anyone else who might like it—Anthony Hecht?— you might let me know—The biggest drawback is that one has no time for one's own work, or I don't—perhaps someone more experienced at "teaching" would. (I feel a complete fraud as far as teaching goes.) May has a job for next year or I might suggest her. Who else?

---

1 The British poet Henry Reed was famous for his poem "Lessons of the War."

I hope you are well and cheerful—and I hope to see you in New York sometime before I retreat to the other side of the Equator again—

With love,

Elizabeth

Dear Elizabeth,

And here's one more [clipping] to add to the collection, which must be getting almost unwieldy by now. It's reassuring to see good things appreciated.

I was delighted you called and so pleased you liked the piece.[1] I'll try to write a proper letter soon. At the moment, I'm having the same difficulty you are—letters seem too long to do, or long to send. Elizabeth Bowen once told me that she wrote lots of them in the bathtub—marvelous ones—and then completely forgot them the minute she got out of the tub.

Love,

Howard

1966

[postcard]

Dearest Howard: No doubt this plea will come too late—but I do wish "Under the Window, OP," could appear while I [am] still here!—before June 7th that is—although I'll be around probably until almost the end of June. I feel the DEPT. is sadly disappointed in me for not winning any prizes etc. and a bit of publication might help—although why I care I can't imagine! I'll be trying to grind out scholarly articles at this rate—and I am already so absent-minded I feel sorry for myself—found the dish of butter on the back of the toilet the other day, to give you an example. Well, when it gets too bad I go to bed and re-read your review and never fail to arise the next morning feeling a wiser and more cheerful woman. I have heard several people say how beautifully written it is, by the way—of course it is hard for me to see it objectively.

With love,

E.B.

1 "All Praise," *Kenyon Review* (March 1966).

Dear Howard:

I had a letter from Mark Strand several weeks ago now in which he said you had just got back from someplace—I'm sorry I can't remember where and left the letter up in the country . . . Anyway, I gather you had been away for quite a long time or on quite a long trip? . . . I got back in July but stayed up in the country at first, then went up to Minas to see my OLD house there that a friend is re-modelling for me. It is a totally unnecessary indulgence but I just had to have it—and it would have fallen down if someone hadn't "restored" it quickly, and it may well be the very oldest house in town—around 1720 they think—Well, someday I hope you'll see it and sit on the blue balcony with me overlooking six or seven baroque churches, etc.—a perfect tiny 18th century town, and it *can't be changed*, by law—that's the great thing—Heavens, I got sick of those freeways and that "cheap" electricity—cheap enough so that it never got dark in Seattle at night as it should, at all.

I wonder if you got my rather querulous note or postcard about publishing my poem? I felt that when I didn't receive the National Book Award (I didn't mind, except that it would have meant a trip to New York) the University—and my "students"—were disappointed in me, and I did hope something by me would appear while I was still there, so at least they'd see I hadn't given up entirely.[1] Now it is too late for that, but I am wondering when my poor poem will appear—it's almost a year now and I feel I need a little encouragement badly, at the moment.[2] I'm working at a prose book—odds and ends—on Brazil, with pictures, a sort of grab bag, but haven't done anything for so long it is hard to get going.

Lota has been really very ill and is just gradually getting better now, day by day. It is the "labyrinth" that is troubling her, mostly, but I blame about 90% of it on Brazilian politics and have decided we must get away, the sooner the better, for a real change for her. We were to fly to Amsterdam tomorrow but have had to put it off for a week—till the 16th—[but] she still isn't strong enough to go. We are going just to Amsterdam and London—about a month or six weeks—The hysterical atmosphere here is enough to kill anyone—

Besides the poem, will you do something else for me? I forgot to renew my friend Rosalina Leão's subscription to *The New Yorker* when the time

---

1 James Dickey received the award for *Buckdancer's Choice* (1965).
2 "Under the Window" ran December 24, 1966.

came around and now I'd like to do it again and have you *bill me,* because I can't remember how much it is. She can catch up the back copies with mine here. The name and address is: well, again,

Rosalina Leão
Largo do Boticário 34
Cosme Velho
Laranjeiras
Rio de Janeiro GB, Brasil

and thank you very much.

I have seen a good many poems by you since I came back and have been getting caught up—I didn't read anything except for classes while I was away, nor write any letters. When we get settled again I'll try hard to write you a decent letter and tell you all the many things I've liked. There is a possibility that someone here may translate your piece on me—or part of it—for the best local review—I'll let you know about it—an old friend, a very good critic, admired it very much—[next part illegible in margin, then:] how Louise Bogan is? I heard she was well again. I hope so—

With much love,
Elizabeth

March 1, 1967

Dear Howard:

I received my two copies of the *NYer* with my poem in it & thank you. I know I shouldn't ask you to perform such chores, but when I write the subscription department I never seem to get any replies . . . I also realize it has been such a long time since I heard from you that I am beginning to be afraid you are sick . . . I hope you did receive at least one of my thank-yous for the lovely Kenyon article—I wrote *twice,* from Seattle, and surely that much *U.S.* mail doesn't get lost, too . . .

I'd like very much to have a copy of the poem sent to the dedicatee of the poem:

Dona Lilli Correia de Araújo
Caixa Postal 118
Ouro Prêto, Minas Gerais, Brasil

She is very thrilled with her one and only appearance in print . . . She is remodelling my OLD house there for me—where Lota and I hope some day you will visit us—as well as our MODERN house . . .

I have written you, AND the subscription dept., both, and can't seem to get any results. I wanted to renew my friend Rosalina Azevedo Leão's subscription for her—she's missed almost a year now! The address is Largo do Boticário 32, Cosme Velho, Laranjeiras, Rio de Janeiro GB, Brasil. (I realize these addresses are hell—)

Hope to send you a long poem very soon now, —I've seen a couple of lovely ones by you, and think there are more waiting for me up in the country this week-end. I do hope you have not been sick and that all goes well with you.

Love,
Elizabeth

March 30, 1967

Dear Howard:

This is not the poem I spoke of a while back—it is a more serious effort and I'll be sending it in a week or so—but I thought you might like this sad little true-story ["House Guest"] . . . IF you are hearing from me these days—I have been out of touch with you so long and I don't feel you have been getting my letters at all. I do hope you are not sick. We both were— Lota very seriously—but are back in the country and recovering now. At last I am back at work after much wasted time.

Do write me sometime—I've heard nothing except one item from Mark Strand, ages ago now, and I am really worried about you.

Love,
Elizabeth

April 11, 1967

Dear Elizabeth,

What a pleasure to get a new poem from you! We all breathed a sigh of relief, a sigh of pure joy, really, at reading it. Of course we're taking it. It's so good. I'll be sending along an author's proof and a check shortly.

I'm sorry if I've caused you worry. I have had a rotten year, not as bad as yours sounds by far, but a rather dispiriting one, and I have not been able to write letters beyond the ones I do here. It will all pass, is passing, but it's been an odd time, what with small illnesses like plagues, and other complications not so easily describable. But I've been working and hope to have a new book ready next fall.

I plan to go to Europe for the summer and will be taking off July 6th if things jell the way they seem to be dong. Please do send the new poem soon, and stay well. My love to Lota and to you.

    Howard

April 24, 1967

Dear Howard:

It was awfully nice to hear from you again and I hope you are well and that everything is going well with you . . . I wonder where you are planning to go this summer in Europe.

This ["Going to the Bakery"], again, is not the poem I have in mind to send you, but something that sort of turned up. The real one I think you'll like—almost done. My Crusoe poem didn't please me when I finished it but maybe I'll re-write [it] sometime.

I rather liked the poems by someone named, I think, Amable (?) Aimble?—we get the *New Yorker*s so late, and often out of order—but one came yesterday with Ted Hughes in it. I've admired some of his poems very much but these (don't tell him) strike me as dull . . .[1] The thing both Lota and I have liked best in all the last numbers was the *sloppy* air-stewardess cartoon—I've done so much flying lately and am so tired of them![2] Even crossing the Channel—about 45 minutes—the English ones managed to put on pinafores like Alice in Wonderland and serve TEA, to 200 or so people . . .

We are in Rio actually but return to Petrópolis the 27th—staying on here to see [Margot] Fonteyn and [Rudolf] Nureyev once more. She is part Brazilian; her name is really Fontes—as perhaps you know—and of course she is extremely popular here.

I'm sorry my typing does not improve. I wish you'd write me a letter from 10th street—and I'll reply from the country, where I can really write letters.

    With love,
    Elizabeth

1 George Amabile, "Snowfall: Four Variations" (March 4, 1967). Bishop may be referring to Hughes's recent group: "Small Events," "You Drive in a Circle," "Thaw," and "Fern" (March 18, 1967).
2 Probably Donald Reilly, "You should see the pilot!" (March 11, 1967).

June 19, 1967

Dear Howard:

I hope this reaches you before you take off for Europe, and I wonder where you are going this time. Lota and I want very much to get back to Venice, next time for a really long stay, & would like to go in Sept. or Oct., but I don't know—she is taking on a new job this week for the city-government—unless it turns out to be entirely too boring.

I went off on a long—endless, in fact—trip on the Rio São Francisco, on a stern-wheeler, tiny, made in the USA 70 years ago . . . I am now writing all the details for a "chapter" (so far the book is so formless I'm using the quotes) for my book in prose about Brasil. I *think* the NY-er might like it—possibly other sections as well—although I've never tried this kind of thing before and may not have the knack at all. Should I send it to William Shawn? If you get this before you leave, maybe you'll let me know—otherwise I suppose I shall, anyway. It's a travel-piece, whatever department they come under.

THE poem I want to send you so much still isn't quite done, but I may yet get it off to you before you go.—I feel sure you'll like it—more than those other minor efforts. Maybe today or tomorrow (how tedious I am getting) . . .

I also want to ask another question. After several very lean years I seem to be doing a lot again, and I think, because of living here, mail complications, etc., that—if they want me—I'd be willing to renew a New Yorker contract. Do you think they would offer me one again?

I do hope you're feeling very strong and up to sight-seeing—or maybe you don't do that. I might get to New York a little later on, so I wonder how long you'll be away. Meanwhile—*Boa Viagem*, dear Howard, and have a lovely time.

Love,
Elizabeth

June 27, 1967

Dear Elizabeth,

A hasty reply. We'd be delighted to renew the agreement, of course—in fact nothing would make me happier. Our lawyer returns from vacation next week, so it will have to wait until then, but I wanted to let you know—in case I was gone before it could be arranged. I'm not going to Europe, by the way, but to a house I've rented at Amagansett for the summer. My address will be P.O. Box 758, Amagansett, N.Y. 11930.

And Mr. Shawn would very much want to see any part or all of the book on Brazil. I guess the best thing would be to send it to him direct, since I won't be back until September.

Do have a lovely summer, and if you're anywhere near New York, please, please call me in Amagansett—Long Island—and come out. Information will have my phone number. I don't even know it yet.

Love,
Howard

Four

1967–1979

(Edit and handle M)   AB-3047

Elizabeth Bishop
60 Brattle Street
Cambridge, Massachusetts, 02138

Set Slug   DEC. 28, 1973 ½ 7 = M ½ HANDLE M ½ DC & SAND

FIVE FLIGHTS UP   #6

FEB 25 1974

Still dark.
The unknown bird sits on his usual branch.
The little dog next door barks in his sleep
inquiringly, just once.
Perhaps in his sleep, too, the bird inquires
once or twice, quavering.
Questions — if that is what they are —
answered directly, simply,
by day itself.

while it

Enormous morning, ponderous, meticulous;
gray light streaking each bare branch,
each single twig, along one side,
making another twig, of glassy veins...
The bird still sits there. Now he seems to yawn.

The little black dog runs in his yard.
His owner's voice arises, stern,
"You ought to be ashamed!"
What has he done?
He bounces cheerfully up and down;
he rushes in circles in the fallen leaves.

Obviously, he has no sense of shame.
He and the bird know everything is answered,
all taken care of,
no need to ask again.
—Yesterday brought to today so lightly!
(A yesterday I find almost impossible to lift.)

— Elizabeth Bishop →

Set in 11-pt verse style line for line on 27 picas. No indents.

No italics none. Roman HM

11-pt C+S.C.
flush right
w. longest
line above

[Draft 12]

Dear Miss MacKenzie:

Mr. Moss told me that you were taking care of the poetry department while he is on holiday. You have a poem of mine called GOING TO THE BAKERY. I can't remember now whether I have seen proof of this one or not—I think not—but anyway, would you please hold it for a while? I have decided I don't like it. I have made some small changes, but am not sure whether they improve it or not. I'll let you know in about a week, and I may want to give you the money back and withdraw it.

The above will be my address until further notice.

Here is a very, very light poem ["Trouvée"] you might just possibly like for the summer season . . .

Sincerely yours,
Elizabeth Bishop

July 24, 1967

Dear Miss Bishop,

We're all delighted with "Trouvée" and we love having it. Thank you for it.

I've asked that "Going to the Bakery" be held for your revision. It can wait as long as you like. The author's proof will not be made up until after we have heard from you.

I wrote Howard a note the other day and told him about "Trouvée." He will be so pleased.

Sincerely yours,
Rachel MacKenzie

Havre de Grace
August 7, 1967
[postcard]

Dear Howard: This is just to apologize & say how sorry I am I didn't feel I could make it that week-end and I hope Jean will understand and have me again some time. I have been feeling *very* lousy, with my concussion and other ailments. I finally came down with an old friend and collapsed for a few days. I am NOT in Florida—just stole this card from her desk . . . I'll be back in New York by the 11th or 12th probably, and I shall get in touch with you then. I still hope to get to Long Island (or Short Island, as Lota puts it) sometime—but feel it needs a clear head, don't you? (my 1st experience with an electric typewriter isn't clearing it much . . .) With love, Elizabeth

August 11, 1967

Dear Miss MacKenzie:

I have made a good many small changes in this poem and I think I have improved it. I believe you said it had not been set up yet—I am away on a visit & do not have your letter with me—anyway, I hope this will be all right. (Again, when I do see it in proof I may still feel I should buy it back . . .)

If you think the enclosed, from WOMAN'S DAY, is funny enough, you might hand it on to the right department.

I am sending the carbon because the ribbon is very pale—also, I have never used an electric typewriter before—that is why my typing is worse than usual, if possible.

Sincerely yours,
Elizabeth Bishop

On September 19, Lota de Macedos Soares arrived in New York for a visit with Bishop, who was staying at Loren MacIver and Lloyd Frankenberg's home on Perry Street. That night Lota took an overdose of valium. When Bishop found her, she and MacIver's neighbors Wheaton Galentine and Harold Leeds rushed Lota to St. Vincent's Hospital, where she died in a coma on the evening of September 25.

September 26, 1967

Dear Elizabeth,

Two proofs ["House Guest" and "Going to the Bakery"] to cast your eye over—mostly the usual problems of what's hyphenated and what's not.

I'm still gurgling and side-clutching. I'll see you before these come back.

Love,

Howard

61 Perry Street
September 30, 1967

I am enclosing the proof for HOUSE GUEST. I am revising a bit more the poem called GOING TO THE BAKERY and shall send it along in a few days—I think I have improved it quite a lot.[1]

Elizabeth Bishop

October 13, 1967

Dear Elizabeth,

I called you—you had probably just left—to thank you for the custard: no lumps, no air foam, absolutely delicious. I devoured all three samples in three days, and I'm saving those very attractive little brown pots for your return. I hope Maryland turned out to be stoic and soothing.

Here's TROUVÉE, practically clean as a whistle. Should the title be in italics, considering it's a word from a foreign language? Thus the thinking goes here. I think it would look funny, and I'd just leave it.[2]

1 Bishop made a number of changes before sending back the author's proof of "Going to the Bakery." Some of her changes brought the poem back to her April 24 version, like returning "strange to her" to "new to her", in stanza two, line one. Her other changes were to lines she already revised in her August 11 version. The first two lines of stanza three, "whose tin hides wear their iridescence / of dying, puckering toy balloons.", became "whose tin hides have the iridescencē / of flaccid, dying, toy balloons." before running as "(The tin hides have the iridescence / of dying, flaccid toy balloons.)". The poem's last two lines, "from force of habit. The moon, perhaps, / could frame a phrase more apt or bright.", became "—sheer force of habit. Senhora Moon / could coin a phrase more apt or bright." before running as "from force of habit. Oh, poor habit! / Not one word more apt or bright?". She changed the first line of stanza four an additional time. On April 24 it was "wry influence, are taking off". On August 11, it was "blind authority, take off". In the March 23, 1968, *New Yorker* it was "compulsiveness, are taking off,", and in *The Complete Poems* it was "magnetic instances, take off" (*The New Yorker* Records and Vassar College Library). In addition, four of Moss's changes to the April 24 version stayed: inserting a comma after "nights" in stanza one, line two; inserting a comma after "electricity" in stanza four, line four; changing the colon after "faint" to a dash in stanza five, line one; and changing the semicolon after "money" in the second line of the last stanza.

It does not appear that Bishop typed this letter herself. The arrangement of the letter does not correspond to her usual format and her signature appears above her full name.

2 Rachel MacKenzie edited the poem and had no changes to make, except the usual changes to Bishop's hyphenated spelling. The title was left roman.

I'm better, though still not the laughing boy I once was. Please call me when you get back.

Love,

Howard

1559 Pacific Street
San Francisco, California
January 17, 1968

Dear Howard:

I sent you a postcard, I think, when I was still staying at an hotel here. Now I've moved to the above address—taken a "flat" for six months. I think I'm going to like it here—for a while, at least, although I haven't done much or seen very many people yet—just trying, once more, to get unpacked and settled. I've done nothing, of course, but pack & unpack and pack again for three months. Maybe it is all to the good—I am really dying to get down to serious work now . . .

This morning I had a long communication from the Rockefeller Foundation asking me for a recommendation for a grant for next year, for "Imaginative Writing and Literary Scholarship." They want only one name. I'm writing you right away to see if by any chance you'd like to be nominated. This probably is not the way to go about it—so perhaps you had better not speak of it!—but I thought there might be a possibility of your wanting to take a year off from your job and devote yourself to a book of poems or a play or something, and if so I'd send in your name and also attempt some other nominations for you. So will you just let me know as soon as possible? You may have no intention of ever stopping your present work—just let me know, and if not I'll think of someone else. Or—I wish you'd make a suggestion for me—I do feel very much out of things in US writing, you know, after all the years in Brazil, and may not know of some very obvious choices . . .

I think I asked you on that card but I'm not sure—COULD you be good enough to let the subscription department or whatever one I come under know my change of address? I think I did write them from Brazil—I was still getting New Yorkers there, of course—but I was in such a state of fatigue and sadness I'm not sure that I did—and if I did, they may not have received it.

Have you ever been here? I like the city a lot, so far—and the light is lovely, and it's all rather small scale and slower and much much cleaner than New York. I've just bought an occasional NYer since I've been here—

getting no periodicals yet (damn Brentano's, as usual) and there is also a newspaper strike on—so I feel even more cut off at the moment, or much more cut off, than I ever did in Rio.

I hope you're well & lots of love,
    Elizabeth

January 19, 1968

Dear Elizabeth,

I did get your postcard and was glad to know you were settled somewhere, even if temporarily. Yes, I've been to S.F. and liked it, though I never felt it was a place I could settle down in. Why that should be hideous New York, I don't know. Yes, I do: I was born here. It's the only place I really know, he said, great sobs wracking his tiny chest, but goddamn, it's true. Santa Fe struck me as a place I could live, oddly. It was like the sea by being its opposite, and small and large enough to somehow manage in. That is, depending on certain other domestic arrangements. The idea of living in Santa Fe alone, and not driving, would drive me mad.

I thought of you often, very, when you were in Brazil, not even contemplating what horrors might have awaited in each packing box and every closet. Not to mention rooms, mirrors, views—and people. I think you've been really brave in the face of a situation that many people would simply collapse under, and since you always had my undying admiration, you now have that part of it that is immortal, too.

I did notify the subscription dept. about the change of address. It takes a little time, though, for the computers to do their stuff. I hope you'll be getting the magazine soon.

I've been going through a rough time emotionally but staying above water most of the time. My stories are all old. The only trouble is that I'm getting old, too, which should, you'd think, make me more sensible. Well.

I turned in a new book of poems [*Second Nature*] to Atheneum this week who claim it's on their fall list even though they haven't seen it. They may have second thoughts now. It is an odd book, the oddest one for me. We'll see.

Yes, by all means, recommend me for a Rockefeller. I'd love a year off. I've been at this job for 20 yrs. and no one has given me the untold marvels I deserve. Though rumor has it that the Institute has awarded me its poetry prize this year.[1] It is not official, but I've heard the buzzing twice.

---

1 Moss received an Academy Award in Literature from the American Academy and Institute of Arts and Letters.

The light is lovely in S.F., especially in the afternoon, seen from Berkeley, when the fog lifts. I mean it. I know a charming woman in S.F. you might like called Marjorie Brush. I don't have her phone number or address here at the office but if you look her up in the phone book, call her and tell her you're a friend of mine that should do it.

And I'll be waiting for new poems as I always do. S.F. should be full of things the color of turned down gas, or, if you listen closely (and were Baudelaire) marimba music.

Love,

Howard

January 23, 1968
[postcard]

Thank you for your letter & it should be done immediately . . . I'm sorry, but my OLD address book is en route from N.Y. & I can't remember your street no.—I'll call your friend this week. Brazil was even worse than you can imagine, I think, & alas, will drag on for months or years—I am liking it here, thank heavens & all goes well.[1] I'll write again—

Love,

EB

February 20, 1968

Dear Elizabeth,

Have you seen either of these? In case you haven't, I send them on.

There's a lot of untidy activity going on here, and I don't mean the recent garbage strike.

Have you met Marjorie?

Jean and I talked of you last night at dinner. Compliments all.

Whatever happened to that poem you showed me that I liked so much? You, as a child, sitting in a doctor's office, as I remember, and something to do with the National Geographic? I'd love to see it. And you.

Love,

Howard

---

1 Many people, including Mary Morse, held Bishop responsible for Soares's death and rejected her upon her return to Brazil. Bishop lost many friends, and Soares's family contested Lota's will, which divided her property between Bishop and Morse.

February 25, 1968
[postcard]

CAN'T SEEM TO FIND MY OLDER BOOK WITH YR HOME
ADDRESS IN IT SO PLEASE EXCUSE THIS & IN OTHER WAYS
TOO: I WOULD HAVE WRITTEN BEFORE BUT 3 WKS AGO I FELL
& BROKE MY RIGHT WRIST IN SEVERAL PLACES: PERFECTLY
SOBER & IN MY RIGHT MIND I THINK BUT A STEEP WET SIDE-
WALK & HIGH HEELS: ON MY WAY TO CITY LIGHTS SHOP
WHICH I NOW HAVEN'T SEEN YET: I DON'T SEEM TO MIND
TOO MUCH BUT CANT WORK ALAS: HAVE A LOT OF ALMOST
DONE WORK ON HAND TOO I WROTE TO THE R'S FOR YOU A
MONTH AGO I THINK & THEY REPLIED SO NOW I HOPE
YOU'LL HEAR FROM THEM: THANK YOU FOR THE CLIPPINGS:
C & W DOES SEND OR RATHER C CARVER DOES: THEY'VE
BEEN HAVING AN ABSURD CORRESPONDENCE IN THE TLS
OVER ME MOSTLY: ENGLAND MUST BE REALLY IN A DECLINE! I
LIKE SOMEONE YOU MUST MEET IS DR CZERNY & MANY
OTHER LINES TOO & HOPE IT WAS YOU PRACTISING: I
HAVEN'T CALLED YOUR FRIEND YET BUT SHALL SOON &
NOW THINK THIS IS ABOUT ALL FOR TODAY WITH MY LEFT
HAND: MUCH LOVE
    Elizabeth B.

September 7, 1968

Dearest Howard:

    I was awfully sorry not to have seen more of you while I was in New
York. At first I was feeling just too miserable to see anyone at all—and by the
time I was more or less back to normal you of course had left . . . It was a
rather bad summer—I do hope yours was a lot better than mine. I finally got
back here and am at last getting back to work—real work, I think—after
doing next to nothing for over two years, I think.

    I wonder if you received that Rockefeller Grant?—I was allowed one
nomination and you were it . . . and I wrote the strongest recommendation I
could, but I have never heard what the outcome was . . . Perhaps they have
not been announced yet—I can't seem to get their schedule of nominations
and awards straightened out. Anyway, of course I certainly hope you did
get one . . .

    Everyone I know, including myself, terribly depressed by the [Republican and Democratic presidential] conventions, etc. The first time I've been able to vote in years & years—and no one to vote for. I am going to the circus this afternoon to see what that will do for the spirits.

With love, as always—

Elizabeth

September 19, 1968

Dear Howard:

I'm enclosing a copy of HOUSE GUEST in which I've made two changes . . . Will you please change it for the magazine before it appears?—if you can, that is if it hasn't been printed yet. I'm getting out a Collected Poems with Farrar, Straus & Giroux in March, so I hope it will appear sometime before then . . . I hope to send on one or two more shortly, too—we'll see.

I heard from the Rockefeller Foundation the other day, and yes they had received my nomination safely back in February—I was worried about it.

I hope you are not sick or anything, and that your summer was nice. You know I have never even been to Fire Island . . . I haven't seen Marjorie since I got back, but I hope to next week.

Love,

Elizabeth

P.S. How did you like the Ginsberg pieces?[1]

P.P.S. The changes are in the third stanza, line 5; and the fifth stanza, last line.[2]

January 31, 1969

Dear Elizabeth,

I've been meaning to write for weeks—months—but correspondence (I hope not in all its meanings) has eluded me, and I have simply been unable to write letters. Maybe because I write so many of them here. But I did have to tell you how beautiful that translation of Andrade is.[3] I love it. And if you have any others, please do send them my way.

---

1 Bishop is probably referring to Jane Kramer's profile of Allen Ginsberg (August 17 and 24, 1968).
2 Bishop changed "quite well, and we are stuffing" to "quite well, and we're stuffing" and "a comic-book, a yacht!" to "a comic book, a car!". An additional change between Bishop's submission and the poem's publication is changing the ellipses after "foods" to a period in stanza three, line six.
3 "The Table," *The New York Review of Books* (January 16, 1969).

Do forgive me for not writing, and I hope Farrar, Straus is smart enough to bring out a book of the translations.

Love,

Howard

February 3, 1969

Dear Howard:

This is a brand new typewriter and it is behaving so badly I think I must take it back . . .

Thank you for writing me about the Carlos Drummond de Andrade translation. It has one mistake but that will be corrected when Farrar, Straus & Giroux publishes a "collected" book of me this spring. ARE YOU interested in translations? In the past, a few of mine, both prose and poetry, were rejected and The New Yorker wrote me then that they never published translations. However, since then I did see that very nice poem by Borges, so perhaps the magazine's policy has changed?[1]

We had a very amusing evening with Marjorie not long ago—she showed us some of "old San Francisco." Her stories of her family and early life in California are very funny. Before Christmas she thought you might be coming out this way and I am sorry you didn't. I am really rather liking this city—and poets are as plentiful as blackberries here.[2]

With love,

Elizabeth

February 7, 1969

Dear Elizabeth,

Yes, we would be interested in translations—especially yours.

There is a man here, Sandy Campbell, who is a great fan of yours and every time there is a rumor that you will be coming to NYC to give a reading, he brings me a copy of *Questions of Travel* in the hope that I'll give it to you so that you'll sign it.[3] Well, last spring, I kept it for a few months, when

---

1 Bishop is probably referring to Jorge Luis Borges's poems "Hengest Cyning," "Afterglow," "Plainness," and "The Dagger," translated by Norman Thomas di Giovanni (November 16, 1968).

2 Bishop's papers at Vassar contain two drafts of this letter, the first of which contains a note about her contract and an article she was preparing based on an interview she had conducted with Kathleen Cleaver. *The New York Review of Books* expressed interest in Bishop's essay and Bishop wanted to know whether *The New Yorker* would release it.

3 Campbell was a fact-checker.

the reading was postponed, and then when it turned out you would not be coming in the next few months, returned it to him. Then he came up and said he'd heard you were coming again. And I said, ok, let's try again. And so I hope you will sign his copy for him. My, what a long-winded story.

I spent a lazy, pleasant week-end in Rye at my sister's, playing ping-pong and drinking. They go very well together.

The piece I did on you in the *Kenyon* is coming out in a critical book this spring.

Why doesn't FSG reprint *The Diary of Helena Morley?*

I am trying to translate a poem by a Mexican poet named [José] Gorostiza. He's very good—but so hard! I have a literal version and a Spanish dictionary and the rest is piece work and guesswork.

I'll be out to SF sooner or later, now that I fly. I'm going up to Cambridge by plane next week all by myself with no drugs or friends. (On the plane.) A big step forward in the late forties. (I mean mine.)

Love,

Howard

February 23, 1969

Dear Howard:

I'll be glad to sign Mr. Campbell's book when I get to New York— around May 6th I think now . . . I'll only be there for a week or ten days, probably, but of course I hope and expect to see you somehow during that stay.

I have a few more, mostly rather short, translations from Brazilian poetry here—I am polishing them up now—but I don't think they are the kind of thing you'd like at all . . . However, when they're done I'll probably send them on to you just in case. (I'm pretty sure they won't do, though.) I was interested in learning that you have been doing some translating, too, because it hadn't occurred to me that you did it. Now I am wondering if perhaps you'd undertake some for me when we (my co-editor & I) [Emanuel Brasil] get around to the younger poets for the anthology we are working on . . . The 1st volume, older poets, is about done now (that's what I did the Drummond de Andrade for) and I tried to get poets who knew Spanish, at least, and the two or three rare ones who know some Portuguese.[1] Now I find you are tackling something with those "literals" (awful word to me now) I

1 *An Anthology of Twentieth-Century Brazilian Poetry* (1972).

am happy to think maybe you'll undertake a young poet for me—but we'll speak of this in New York, and I'll know much more who and what by then.

The DIARY is out of print and F, S & G doesn't seem to want it anymore—it didn't sell at all you know . . . Obtuse public.

Well, *do* fly out here—have you ever been here? I think Marjorie's reminiscences of you are all of Baja California? It's a pretty city, poets thick as blackberries, universities all on strike, & the city of the *voyeur par excellence* . . . (French)

Lots of love,
Elizabeth

Caixa Postal 79
Ouro Prêto
August 5, 1969

Dear Howard:

I don't know whether you will be back from your vacation by now or not—I have lost all track of time. I wanted to write to you long ago to say I was sorry our last meeting was a bit confused, and that I hadn't had more time to talk to you. I'm afraid it couldn't be helped. And now this note is looking a bit confused, too, and because this machine seems to have been hit by the tropics, that can't be helped, either . . .

Here is a little advertisement from a restaurant in Manaus that I thought someone at THE NEW YORKER might like. If not, I think you will like it, anyway. Will you hand it on to the proper authorities?

My house here is so beautiful I can't believe it, and I hope that next year or the year after you will visit me in it. I am still not in it myself, but expect to move and sort of camp out in it this week. Please come sometime—NOT during July, however—we have just come through a month's "Art Festival" and the praças (plazas to you) looked just like the Berkeley campus. It was cold and everyone wore blankets—the idea was ponchos, I suppose, but very few had ponchos so they just used pink and blue blankets. I thought of wearing my electric one, transistorized.

I hope you had a nice holiday and did a lot of your own work. I am also hoping to get down to mine soon now, and shall try to send you something.

With love como sempre,
Elizabeth

August 8th: P.S.

I have just decided to call my house "Casa Mariana" in honor of MM—also, it is on the road to Mariana, a very pretty tiny town about 8 miles away, so it all works out very nicely. Only don't put it on my address because then any letter might GO to Mariana to the archbishop there—it is an ecclesiastical center—

September 12, 1969

Dear Elizabeth,

I don't know whether the Saturday Review gets to Ouro Prêto but, in case it doesn't, here's a review of the "Collected" I thought you might want to see.[1]

Marjorie called me long distance from S.F. to say she just finished reading the "Collected" and was over-whelmed. She wanted your address so she could write you a letter. I didn't have it at home but have finally air-mailed it to her from the office.

And when are *you* air-mailing yourself back. Let me know so that I don't send things south that should go west.

I laughed, by the way, over that menu—*very* funny. I hope they like it downstairs, as Kafka said to his mother.

Do send me a poem. I'm holding off sending *you* the new book with that essay-review of you in it. As soon as you say it's safe, I'll send it on.

What happened to two poems I keep asking about, as if I'd read them in a dream. (I wish it had been *my* dream.) The one about the doctor's office and the National Geographic, and the one about the typewriter eraser? I'd love to see them, along with anything else.

The house sounds—it must be—lovely. Someday, I will get to Brazil, that is, if they stop kidnapping ambassadors, hijacking planes, and planting bombs in everybody's candy.

Love,
Howard

---

1 Dan Jaffe, "Voice of the Poet: Oracular, Eerie, Daring," *Saturday Review of Literature* (September 6, 1969).

November 6, 1969

[postcard: "Olímpia, traditional person from Ouro Prêto"]

Dear Howard: Thank you for your note of Sept. 12th which for some reason took an extra-long time to reach me, but which I have had on hand for 2 weeks, I think . . . Thank you for the clipping; I hadn't seen it, in fact have seen almost nothing except John Ashbery's fine review . . .[1]

May S [Swenson] wrote me you had a lovely poem in the Oct 11th, I think, New Yorker—and of course I haven't seen it—they are all piled up in San Francisco. "Menage à Trois" . . . She also reports on poems of her own. I have been so completely taken up with problems of house-building, law-suits in Rio, troubles with neighbors & workmen (Mineiros—that is the people of this state are notorious for being difficult, & I am learning it all the hard way.) that I haven't written a line so far and don't even see when I'll be able to, alas.

Here is a picture of one, a very decayed and slightly mad although not so mad as she puts on—who has been a town character for years. There are many such at loose here which I think is rather nice on the whole . . . I am going to meet the kidnapped ambassador [C. Burke Elbrick]—Much love, Elizabeth

Please do send your book—registered, AIR MAIL—PLEASE!

November 28, 1969

Dear Elizabeth,

The "newsbreak people"—I always think of them as a tiny group hud-dled under an umbrella—have decided to use that wonderful menu from the "Chapeau de Dalha," though I would simply have reprinted it myself. And so here is a tiny check to go with the tiny people and maybe in Ouro Prêto you can buy something with it. Something tiny.[2]

Did you get the copy of my book I sent you?

Did you get a copy of the NYer anthology I sent you?[3]

There is an announcement of your book in this week's NYer—in that Christmas list of work by our contributors.

1 "The Complete Poems: Throughout Is This Quality of Thingness," *The New York Times Book Review* (June 1, 1969).

2 It is unclear whether the newsbreak ran.

3 *The New Yorker Book of Poems* (1969).

I'd wish you'd send me a new poem. For Christmas, or for the winter blues. And do let me know when you're coming back.

Love,

Howard

December 7 or so, 1969

Dear Howard:

On my last trip to the PO, three days ago, I found your letter, your book, and the *other* book . . . These all brightened my week-end very much and especially *your* book—really. (Well, I suppose $5.00 isn't going to brighten anyone's life very much, and it isn't even mine—an English friend receives that—and the collection of poetry is so BIG, and there are too many poets in the world one never heard of—However, I do rather like the arrangement of it, and I was delighted to see EBW[hite]'s poem about the Book Club again ["A Classic Waits for Me"], one of my favorite poems . . . & I read it and a few other funny ones aloud to Suzanne [pseudonym] and shall get down to the serious ones over the years . . . I imagine you were one of the "editors", if not the leading one . . .)

But your book is a personal pleasure. I had read all *The New Yorker* essays and a few of the others, and of course I like mine best of all. Perhaps one should not confess such things, but what you say about little cousin Arthur strikes *me* as very true, and just goes to show how much poetry comes from the—is it—*para* conscious? Because I'm sure you're exactly right about it and yet I swear I didn't think those things when I wrote it—I just have naturally always remembered that little scene much too clearly. (Little Arthur's mother died recently, aged 86, so now I can go ahead and finish, and perhaps publish, a story about her . . .)

We agree so well in general about our favorite writers that re-reading the Chekhov, Keats, Lear, etc. were almost as good as having a pleasant conversation with you. The "Notes on Fiction" I hadn't seen, and like very much, too. I read the "The Pilgrim Hawk" [by Glenway Wescott] when it first came out and didn't like it; now someday I'll try it again. I was very touched to see my own name hit me in the eye, too, in your contribution to the "Symposium." I've never read Daniel Fuchs, either, but shall some day.[1]

Well, all together, I think you are a fine critic who has not been properly recognized as such and last night I turned back and read [Edmund] Wilson's

1 Perhaps Bishop is referring to fiction and screen writer Daniel Fuchs, whose stories appeared in *The New Yorker*.

"Shock of Recognition" for a couple of hours and it struck me that the pieces in that that are still alive and endearing and enlightening, are much more the kind of thing you write than the dreadful quarterly analytical stuff . . . I really mean this. I think you have helped start me off again on my half-done notes on Marianne Moore, too—if I ever have time to write anything here at all. So I thank you very much and shall cherish both copies, hard and soft cover, and only lend the soft cover . . .

The seven months, is it, so far here have been too awful to talk about at all. I have the most beautiful house in the world and my one idea now is to sell it as soon as possible and get away. It is still, Ouro Prêto, one of the most beautiful small-towns, or city-towns, too—but I have had so many misfortunes here and in Rio so far, that I can't even *see* it any more. I never intended to make it a permanent home, anyway; it was to be a sort of hobby for Lota and me, since we always wanted an old house, too (this dates from, they now think, about 1690, at least all the outside walls do); then I thought I might keep it as a half-time place, to work in, but see only too well it is not going to work out. It is much admired, praised, written about, and so on—and the town is becoming more and more of a tourist attraction, even has two art festivals yearly, etc. . . .

So—will you do something for me? I have no back files of *New Yorker*s here, but I know a rather fancy outfit advertises in them, something like "Pre-View Homes"—that specializes in selling the exotic to the rich and slightly eccentric. Do you think you could find me one of their ads so I could write them? They advertise villas on the Greek Islands, Max Beerbohm's house, I think, that sort of thing.—I am preparing a group of photographs. I'd also sell quite a lot, or most of the antique furniture—mostly 18th or early 19th century.—4 or 5 bedrooms, fireplace, study with stove, 3 baths . . . (In case you have a millionaire friend who might be interested . . .) And if you can send me that address I'll be grateful—of course I have an agent in Rio, probably São Paulo and Belo Horizonte as well—but I want to try everything. I may eventually make it back to New York, with my 3,000 or so books . . .

Forgive my personal paragraphs and thank you again so much for "Writing Against Time."

With love,
Elizabeth

Dear Elizabeth,

After that lovely, long letter from you, you'd think that I would have written back, pronto. But I was almost instantly seized by a 10th Street version of the flu that put me to bed for two weeks, left me dangling, fever-crazed and semi-idiotic, in the apartment for another week, and from which I am just recovering. The first day I went back to the office I held on to the sides of walls and to any umbrella that happened to pass by, and, of course, when I first arrived, thirty thousand manuscripts, proofs, complaints, and letters threatening my person needed almost instant attention. Since my attention wandered and my strength, the variety observable in a bird thrown out of a nest, was reserved for begging people to get me a cup of water, I haven't been very organized. I'm just beginning to be, and so I pass on the tiny bit of information you requested: PREVIEWS, INC. / 49 East 53rd Street / NYC, N.Y. 10022.

For some reason not quite clear to me, I hate to see you give up the house in Ouro Prêto. It sounds so incredibly beautiful, and I think I had some secret idea of throwing myself on your mercy, at the age of about fifty-five, and arriving, on mule back, with my nurse, to settle into Minas Gerais for good. It is only one of many dreams that have been shattered. But if you find it hard to write there, you need no other reason, God knows, to get out. Your absolute fan, Sandy Campbell, by the way, has left copies of The Complete Poems and The Diary of Helena Morley on my desk for you to sign. I told him you were in Brazil but that didn't seem to make any difference. He's nice and bright and rich, and my other secret plan is to get him to give you a million dollars since he thinks you are the, or one of the best writer(s) in the world. And so do I.

I had a drink yesterday with, of all people, Djuna Barnes, who is ill and confined to her apartment at the moment and wanted my advice about something. I'd never met her before and found her fascinating. Did you ever know her? We talked about "Nightwood," she showed me a painting, and talked about Joyce, Eliot, Gide, and so on. I was afraid, for a moment, that she might say something like, "When Marcel and I . . ." at which point I would have fainted, or, as John Hall Wheelock once said, describing his meeting with Swinburne, swooned.

I was pleased as punch—no, more pleased—that you liked "Writing Against Time."

Do write me again, and I'll answer more promptly, unless I get the Hawaiian version of some dread disease.

It snowed last night but today it's sunny, cold, and one of those odd, absolutely clear days that make other days in New York seem so tacky.

Love,

Howard

Washington's Birthday, 1970

Dear Howard:

Your nice letter came the first of last week and I am answering you very soon, partly to tell you how much it cheered me up in this endless, awful stretch I have been living through here—with no signs of a let-up so far. I'd like just to complain, complain, complain, I'm afraid . . . but I'll try not to. It is partly that life has grown very hard here—or maybe it always was, *here*— I never stayed longer than a month, as a visitor, before, so didn't realize the full horrors of the *mineiros* character . . . Please don't think I am being paranoid—it is well-known; there are books on the subject . . . I believe it comes from the fact that for two hundred years or more everyone here was busily engaged in steeling gold and diamonds from the Portuguese crown, so the habit of stealing, lying, concealing, etc. is ingrained. Everything disappears . . . We just wonder what will go next. You can't leave a hammer or a knife alone for two minutes. Then, when I put on a horrible scene, sometimes things re-appear equally mysteriously. Well, after some woeful trials (I do sound just like Mrs. Carlyle, I know—and feel like her) we at last have two maids, sisters, who are honest, so far, and quiet, and clean, and almost pretty . . . Of course they don't know how to do anything, but at least the other qualities almost make up for that . . .

I was so sorry to hear about your awful time with the "flu"—we have been spared that, at least. I just ache from the dampness (Mrs. Carlyle again) and Suzanne and her child, being blond, are eaten up by all the tropical insects: fleas, ticks, mosquitoes, and so on—that I seem to be completely immune to. Insects I never even heard of before have turned up in the yard and we are constantly trying out different unguents, repellants, & sprays. I thought at first it was because the poor dirty old man who lived here before me for 50 years or so had kept hens, cats, dogs, burros, and so on right in the house with him—but I've been in residence now for some months and if anything the insect population is growing. I feel almost coarse and thick-skinned, when nothing bothers me at all.

There is a local legend that there is gold in this house—whether a pot of it, or just gold ore, I've never learned. But we have to watch the workmen every minute—they keep vanishing into the cellar, and then we find more big holes dug in all the foundations . . . Come help dig . . . I suspect that there *is* gold, in very small quantities, since they used to pan it in my brook, I think—but probably not worth extracting. Oh, but a pot of golden guineas!—one was found in a garden in the next little town not long ago. They think that a slave had stolen it and hidden it. Well, as I've been told, I have the "largest slave quarters in OP"—poor things, the cellars, apparently—but so far nothing but old iron pots, stirrups, and two branding-irons have turned up.

I am not getting any magazines—they are all piling up in San Francisco, because I thought I'd be getting back much sooner—so I am afraid I have been missing poems by you, something else I would find very cheering, I'm sure. I am writing this again partly to ask you about the poetry-critic situation—I read about Louise's death in TIME.[1] I never knew her at all well but I am very sorry; I had a long talk with her in Washington last spring and she did seem very sick then. I wonder if any one else has been appointed to the job, or if perhaps you have, or what . . . If there is any possibility of it, at the risk of sounding just too pushy, perhaps, I'd like very much to "try out" for it. But perhaps it has already been decided. I've always thought it was one critical job I could do—since apparently Louise didn't have to discuss a lot of books she *didn't* like, or make the kind of attack-in-general that I dislike so much. Anyway, I'd be willing to try a sample one, if there is any possibility of it . . .

The "cultural attaché", US, from Belo H[orizonte], the capital, dropped in yesterday with two more of them with him, one from Berlin, one from Iran—it is really a strange world, isn't it—and there we were, playing Janis Joplin to some young Brazilians. (She is in Rio now—was forbidden to sing in a plaza, as she had planned—but not because of her, because of her popularity and the government's fear of such a large assembly of the young that she'd draw.) The attaché drops in fairly often; I think he displays me as an example of American culture.

The house is gradually getting put together and in running order. It IS beautiful, and I do wish you could see it. I'd like to have all my old friends see it once. However, my one desire is to get away—something has gone sadly wrong with life, and my life, here, and I feel I can't endure it much longer. Please do write again when you have time, just a note, even—it helps

---

1 *Time* (February 16, 1969).

a lot. I am half considering New York again—although I know all the draw-backs, too. Can you think of any good place to live? Live and work. I am at last getting a little work done and trying to organize my "book"—have a great deal, too much, material. Well, eventually I shall be sending a few chapters to The New Yorker, I think. But poetry—well, at least Mrs. Carlyle didn't have that problem. (I am assuming you've read her letters; I re-read them bit by bit, to let her do my complaining for me.)[1]

I must go down to the PO—fight with the *mineiro* there, who once just flatly refused to register more than 4 letters in a day—said I had too many . . . I do hope you are quite recovered now, no relapses, and please take care of yourself.

Much love always,
Elizabeth

P.S. I realize that registered letters are an awful nuisance, at your end, but I have lost so many mailed from here—forgive it.

1970
[postcard: native Kaiapato holding a giant frog]
NEXT DAY: I have just found yr. letter & see I forgot to thank you for the PREVIEWS address. I'd already picked it up somehow & have been in com-munication with them—they are too rich for me, I think, but I'll see. Among the pound of gorgeous colored brochures they sent is the home outside Paris of the Duke & Duchess of Windsor. If you threw out a lot of bric-a-brac it would be quite comfortable—maybe they'd consider an exchange. Also an ancient abbey in Portugal I wouldn't mind at all. But perhaps one would have all the same problems one has here. It would have been so nice to have you and your nurse come to stay, too—well, maybe it will still happen—but I'm afraid I want honest help, and people who will be polite to me, and if possible love me dearly, in my old age . . .

Who is Sandy Campbell?

No, I have never met Djuna Barnes—I sold two or three of her early books many years ago when hard up and I've regretted it since. When she returned to the USA Marianne told me she'd met her on the steps of the Pub-

---

1 It is unclear to which edition of Jane Welsh Carlyle's letters Bishop is referring. Carlyle's letters went through many printings, some of which also included Thomas Carlyle's letters.

lic Library, and I asked what she was like. Marianne hesitated a bit and then said, "Well . . . her shoes were beautifully polished . . ." That was all I ever learned. But Cummings was very fond of her.

Shall I bring you an Amazonic Frog? You could train it to go on a leash—

With love,

Elizabeth

The New Yorker
February 27, 1970

Dear Elizabeth,

Mr. Shawn thinks your being the poetry reviewer of The New Yorker is a splendid idea, and so do I, and so it seems like a sure thing. He'll be writing to you separately about arrangements. My only worry at the moment is about getting books to Brazil, but maybe the best thing to do is to start reviewing when you get back. What do you think? I'll be on the lookout for an apartment for you here, though everything is tighter than a drum and hideously expensive.

This is merely a note to say how delighted I am that you'll be reviewing poetry and I'll write again from 10th Street.

Love,

Howard

March 24, 1970

Dear Howard:

Forgive this paper—it seems to have been aging in an old trunk for many years. It is impossible to get any paper in Ouro Prêto except school notebooks and air-mail "blocks"—and I've run out of those, now—and even Belo Horizonte can't provide much better. (And I have to write to our Ambassador—C. Burke Elbrick—isn't that a wonderful name?—and I think I'll have to make some rag paper and engrave it myself . . . He sent a correctly flowery telegram, or his secretary, more likely, did, on the occasion of the NBA.)[1]

I received your letter of February 27th and was delighted that The New Yorker would consider me as a poetry-reviewer—The reason I haven't answered sooner is that I thought probably I'd be hearing from Mr. Shawn

---

1 Bishop won the National Book Award for *The Complete Poems*.

fairly soon. Since I haven't, I don't know of course if he changed his mind, or if his letter got lost, or what . . . but I think it is time I wrote you, at least.

At present, although my house-plans are still rather up in the air, I expect to stay on here for quite a while longer, in hopes of being able to work at last, since things are a bit more settled. I don't really think there'd be any trouble about my receiving books by mail—they're the one thing that does come safely, even to Ouro Prêto. (maybe because no one wants to steal them) In about 18 years of ordering books, and being sent books, to Petrópolis, Rio, and occasionally to here, I have only lost two—and they were sent by friends, non-professionally, so to speak—and they probably didn't label them BOOK, or something else . . . When sent in those book-mailers and labelled *LIVRO* all over, in big letters—and preferably sent air-mail, if that isn't too expensive (but fortunately most poetry books are fairly light)—I have never lost a one. Boat mail takes from two weeks to a month or more—and those always came safely, too, to Rio or Petrópolis—but here—well, the mail troubles are mostly between here and Rio, or here and Belo Horizonte (50 miles away) so air-mail *is* safer . . . There; I have covered that only too well, I'm afraid.

When I looked at last week's TIME I was appalled to see how near you had been to that explosion on West 11th Street . . . It had been mentioned in the Rio papers, but no details given. I do hope you weren't at home when it happened. I hope Marianne wasn't close enough to be aware of it, too. Oh, the horrors . . . Also, this same number of TIME is all about American "inefficiency"—this has cheered me up a bit about Brazilian inefficiency, almost to the point of thinking, what with that and explosions, and so on, I am just as well off here. They do hold up banks here at the rate of two or three a day—and I am on my way to the bank now—but haven't got involved in a hold-up yet.[1]

Well, I am really delighted about the poetry-reviewing and do hope no one has had second thoughts about my abilities, etc. I even find myself making up phrases for imaginary reviews, the idea appeals to me so much.

I am so glad I didn't try to get to NY for the NBA affair—although if I had felt I could have made it at 24 hours notice, I suppose some of the excitement I read about in the N.Y. Times wouldn't have taken place . . .[2] These

---

1 "The House on 11th Street" (March 23, 1970). The cover banner reads: "Inefficiency in America: Why Nothing Seems to Work Anymore."

2 When accepting the award on Bishop's behalf, Robert Lowell read "Visits to St. Elizabeths" to protest Ezra Pound's never receiving the award. Kenneth Rexroth, who was one of the judges, then called Lowell an "anti-Semitic fascist" (Henry Raymont, "Criticism Mounts Over Book Awards Procedures," March 5, 1970).

things are nice *here*, because they make a big impression—unfortunately, you & I know too much about them . . . I do hope you weren't anywhere near that dynamite and take care of yourself, and I'll be hoping to hear from you or someone soon—

    With love, as always,

        Elizabeth

                                                May 6, 1970

Dear Howard:

I sent my maid out to get me some air-mail paper, without lines, and envelopes with a note to the paper-store and everything—and this is the result . . .

I have been having a very tough time here—Suzanne, my secretary, is quite sick and will be going home in a day or two—it is time for her to go, anyway, to take her little boy back to his father. She is in the hospital in Belo Horizonte and I have "had my hands full" as mothers & grandmothers say.[1] My papers and affairs are in great disorder. I am writing you this personal note, hoping you will answer it soon and put my mind at rest a bit . . . Please don't tell Mr. Shawn . . .

I had a very nice note from him, dated April 15th, and a day or two afterwards I received a copy of Stanley Burnshaw's *The Seamless Web*.[2] I have been reading away at it—kind of fascinating, the sort of tedious work about poetry that most poets are too lazy to do for themselves—but don't really know what I think yet—in fact, because of Suzanne's illness and having to stay in Belo Horizonte (the world's ugliest city) with her, I haven't been able to concentrate today. Shawn's letter is nice, but vague. I suppose that is the way The New Yorker proceeds? I don't know—and I'm not *complaining*, either—I'd just like to know a little bit more. Do you know if one gets paid at the usual prose rates, or what? He doesn't mention anything like money, or dates, etc.

Should I write and ask him? Will you tell me? Or am I just being too coarse?

Also—would you please, Howard—I think I am always asking favors of you—get my New Yorker transferred to the above address [Ouro Prêto]? I never dreamed I would be staying here this long, so all magazines have been

---

1 Bishop believed Suzanne Bowen was having a nervous breakdown and had her forcibly hospitalized. Their relationship ended soon after. For a more detailed look at Bishop's relationship with Bowen, see Brett Millier's biography of Bishop, *Life and the Memory of It* (1992).

2 *The Seamless Web* (1970).

piling up in San Francisco. But now heaven knows when I'll be able to get away, so I might as well settle down and get to work.

Since I not haven't seen your family magazine for a year—I wonder if you'll remember if Louise reviewed that book about Hart Crane, published by Farrar, Straus & Giroux, quite some time ago now?—I don't remember the author's name.[1] They are sending it to me, and I thought—if I find it interesting enough, and if Louise did not discuss it—it might be worth writing about. Perhaps in connection with the Burnshaw book. ANY articles by her of the past year I'd appreciate very much . . . I promise that from now on I shall be quite independent and not ask you to do anything more for me for a long, long time.

I shall be all alone here for some time—rattling around in a rather big old house—with my rather incompetent but clean maid . . . Why don't you come to visit? NOT July—there's an awful arts festival here then—but any other time. I think you'd like looking at the town, at least—it is beautiful, and so is my house—though I can't say much for the characters of the native population, and it *is* a bit lonely—or you could bring a friend. Plenty of room.

Much love, and I hope you're well and cheerful—

Elizabeth

Did you receive the registered letter I sent you in March?—10th, I think, but I can't read the date. Maybe you did, & have answered it, too. If not, I want to make inquiries—I've been losing too many letters lately—

May 18, 1970

Dear Howard:

I am awfully tired of sitting on this egg and thing maybe it has hatched, after all ["Crusoe in England"] . . . It is quite unlike your Crusoe, as I remember him. I won't mind if you can't use it, however.

Abraços,

Elizabeth

P.S. on page 3—should it be "Which is the bliss" or "That is the bliss"? I have Wordsworth here somewhere, but can't find him, and I am always uncertain about which and that—please don't tell any one. [handwritten: "I hope I haven't stolen your title? If I have, I'll change it. E."]

---

1 Bishop is probably referring to John Unterecker, *Voyager: A Life of Hart Crane* (1969).

May 19, 1970

Dear Howard:

I was awfully tired yesterday when I mailed you the Crusoe poem. This morning, I think I've improved it quite a bit, so if you happen to want it, will you please use this version?

I'm afraid, without Suzanne here to type for me, my work looks very untidy. And—believe it or not—the carbon paper they sell in Ouro Prêto is carbon on both sides. I went back to the paper store, and the man was surprised I didn't like it—he said it was "more practical" that way . . . Now don't you want to come visit me in a town that thinks like that? But this explains why I'm sending you the carbon, since the first copy is printed on both sides.

With love and all,

Elizabeth

May 19, 1970

Dear Elizabeth,

Here's a new first-reading agreement we hope you'll want to sign. *I* hope you'll want to sign it, too.

I've sent Mr. Shawn a memo asking for further information. I'm almost sure the book reviews would be separate from the fiction rates, but I'm not absolutely certain. The information should come from him, of course, since you'll be dealing with him. I mentioned the question of money, deadlines, and so forth, and I do hope he'll write to you soon.

Life here has had a hospital edge all round: my sister's been ill, my mother is being flown back from Genoa, having suffered a stroke, and things are as bleak here as Belo Horizonte sounds there. It is a name one distrusts on instinct instantly.

I saw Jimmy the other night and he said something about going to Peru and then on to you, possibly, though he is afraid of the Amazon, as I am. You, of course, weren't and aren't. But I think if I set out on it, a la Mr. Dickey's Deliverance, I would be delivered, belo horizontally to a lot of angry natives.[1] Not the nice Indians, but an undiscovered tribe just waiting up the bend a bit, for ME.

Love,

Howard

1 James Dickey, *Deliverance* (1969).

June 2, 1970

Dear Elizabeth,

We're delighted with CRUSOE IN ENGLAND and, of course, we're taking it. I hope to be able to send you a check and an author's proof before I take off for the summer, which will be on June 20.

I was particularly fascinated by the poem because of mine. No, my title (I think) was simply ROBINSON. I'm hesitant about that because I know I changed it several times. It definitely was not CRUSOE IN ENGLAND. (I don't have any of my books here.)

Last night I bought your poems in the 8th Street Bookshop, the paperback edition, to take with me to the island. I do love those Andrade translations so—perhaps because they are the least familiar to me. They'll be very familiar by the end of August. We'd love more poems from you.

Love,
    Howard

June 15, 1970

Dear Howard:

I'm glad you can use CRUSOE. I want to change one word, but shall do it on the proof. I seem to be working again at last, after three years, and hope to send you a whole batch of things. Meanwhile here is another I think I once spoke of ["In the Waiting Room"].

It cheats a bit, and so you may not want it for your super-honest weekly. When I was in New York I went and looked up The National Geographic for this date and strange to say I had actually remembered it for 52 years . . . It is all about "The Valley of Ten Thousand Smokes"—well, I tried that, but went back to a preferred version based on another or almost any number of the magazine . . . If you do want it, however—I doubt very much that anyone else would look it up except a junior English major or something like that—again, would it have to wait until *February*? *5th*? I wonder. Well, maybe you won't even like it.

I keep thinking of your arrival Belo Horizontally and wish you were here to say things like that to me. Maybe I could say a good thing or two to you, too—I am absolutely alone and occasionally startle my 18 year old maid by laughing to myself at my own witticisms. I have told her not to pay any attention when I talk to myself—that I am "working." That's good, don't you think.

More soon I hope and a smallish bit of prose—do I send it to Mr. Shawn?

    With much love,

      Elizabeth

P.S.: I hope you get this before you go on your holidays. Should I just keep any other offerings until you come back, & when will that be? My paperback—I didn't even know about it & was surprised to receive some copies recently. I think Drummond's TABLE is a good poem, don't you? He has some extremely funny early ones, but very untranslatable—

June 30, 1970

Dear Elizabeth Bishop,

    Your poem arrived before Howard left for the summer, but he left before it had gone through, and so it falls to me to tell you how much we all liked it, and that we want it for the magazine. We can't see that the fictitious "National Geographic" magazine matters at all. And we don't feel bound to publish in a February issue.

    Howard will be back in September, and perhaps you should hold your new poems until then. You may send the prose to William Maxwell, or to Mr. Shawn, or to me.

    Thank you for an extraordinarily fine poem.

    Sincerely,

      Robert Hemenway

February 13, 1971
[postcard]

Dear Howard: I'm terribly sorry I got in such a rush those last 2 days in N.Y.—I really had meant to have a whole week there but had to go back to Cambridge to finish packing.[1] This is the trouble with living in so many places. But it was lovely to see you at the party, anyway, & I only wish I'd had more time to talk to you—without interruptions. I do hope you are all right, & well—

    You'll receive poems by 2 young men—I'd like to see what you think of

---

1 Bishop started teaching writing and modern poetry at Harvard University in the fall of 1970.

them, but I doubt that you can use either. J. [John] Peech was a student—very brilliant—Give the poems back to Emanuel Brasil, will you please?—But do tell me what you *think*.

When I get my typewriter back I'll write to you soon again. *Please* let me hear from you—

Much love,
Elizabeth

February 17, 1971

Dear Elizabeth,

Have you seen this? I send it on, just in case.

And I was sorry not to see you. I tried some point or other at the Cos Club when I thought you'd be there. They had you paged and then told me you weren't staying there. They were kind, if peculiar.

I leave tomorrow for a few days in Florida, the state with the prettiest name. It *would* be nice to see you.

Love,
Howard

P.S. I'm also enclosing a second set of the *Partisan Review* tear sheets.[1]

March 16, 1971

Dear Elizabeth,

Have you seen this one from the TLS?[2]

I'm reading some of your Brazilian translations, which I love. The decision [to publish them] hasn't been made here yet but as soon as it is, I'll let Betty Kray know.[3]

I'd like to do one, if there's still time. Maybe a tiny one. I got stuck in Mark's Mexican anthology with a poet I couldn't understand, didn't like, and finally shelved the whole project.[4] A poem about the soul and a glass of

---

1 Moss may be sending Bishop David Kalstone's review of *The Complete Poems* (1969), which had recently appeared in *Partisan Review*.

2 Probably Irvin Ehrenpreis, "Loitering between Dream and Experience," *Times Literary Supplement* (January 22, 1971).

3 Kray was executive director of the Academy of American Poets, which sponsored Bishop's translation project.

4 *New Poetry of Mexico* (1970).

water, starting somewhere in the millionth canto, and about as sympathetic to me as pineapple upside-down cake seen as a universal analogy.

    Love,
       Howard

P.S. Peech sent me poems on his own and I'd been dealing with James Martin, not realizing he was the other student. So I'm dealing with both of them directly, after asking Emanuel Brasil if I might on the poems of theirs *he* sent me.

March 18, 1971

Dear Elizabeth,

    I'm happy to say we're taking two of the Brazilian translations that Betty sent us: SONNET OF INTIMACY (Vinicius De Moraes) and CEMETARY OF CHILDHOOD (Joaquim Cardozo)—both absolutely splendid, but the first is a miracle of translation. My God! I read it over and over—really you are the most incredible translator! The Brazilian government should give you a billion pesos (or whatever) and a free cruise to the Greek Islands and back. I'll send the check to you—right?—and the proofs, too. We'll publish the poems under the title TWO BRAZILIAN POEMS and under the second and last we'll say "(Translated, from the Portuguese, by Elizabeth Bishop)."

    You might be pleased to know we've bought a long poem by your John Peech—LETTER TO ZBIGNEW CYBULSKI, which is the one I liked best of all.[1]

    How is Ouro Prêto? And You? I wish you'd drop me a note and send me a poem. (I read THE FISH aloud the other night to a poet from L.A. who had never heard of you! He has, now.)

    Love,
       Howard

P.S. The lawyer here has asked me to ask you for a letter saying two things: that you're authorized to submit the translated versions of these poems, and that you have the authority to accept full payment for their publication. I think he's trying to avoid a trial that would take place completely in Portuguese.

---

1 Peech's poem appeared in the November 12, 1973, issue.

Dear Elizabeth,

It seems to me your letter box must be crowded with letters from me, and here's another, the author's proof of IN THE WAITING ROOM. The queries are all routine but I should explain that our style is to put the titles of novels, poems, plays, operas, and so on, in Roman and caps, but we italicize the names of newspapers and magazines. So it should be the "Long Pig" but the *National Geographic*.

This is a beauty—I remember first reading it on Perry Street a long, long time ago—and I hope you'll send us other poems soon.

Love,
　　Howard

March 26, 1971

Dear Howard:

I am delighted you've taken a poem by my dear John Peech. I'm going to write to him right away. He is quite an amazing boy; I don't remember whether I told you about him or not at that dinner party? [handwritten: "(Physicist & concert-pianist)"]

Of course I'm also pleased about the translations. I'll get permission from Vinicius and Cardozo. *This may take some time!* In the meantime I think you might as well go ahead with the printing because I'm sure neither will object. It's just a matter of locating anyone in this country.

I wrote to Mr. Shawn a few days ago and I hope the idea I presented to him will be acceptable. At any rate, I'm working on a Marianne Moore memoir now.

I'm pleased to have you spreading my name in Los Angeles but I wish you'd chosen another poem! I'm declaring a moratorium on that one.

Do you think you can send The New Yorker here? Also, may I meekly inquire about what has happened to my two poems? I felt you were hounded enough that night in New York and hate to do the same thing, but *something* in print would do me good right now.

Ouro Prêto—well, you'll just have to come to visit.

With much love,
　　Elizabeth

P.S. I loved your story of your Mexican translation. If mine are good, it is LUCK—or I just pick those that *will* translate easily. And thanks for the clippings—that TLS one is the best I've ever had, I think. *How is your health?*

Dear Howard:

I think our letters crossed . . . I wrote you a note last week—rather, *dictated* one—my correspondence situation got so desperate I got an American to help me—he does "Speedwriting" and needs the work, etc.—But dictating accounts for any strangeness you may have felt about my note . . .

I managed to get a telephone call through to Rio to Vinicius Moraes about the permission, etc.—I never did get him, but left messages with a friend here who has a telephone—and he did call back that night. I hope she got it straight. I also hope he does something about it. He's pretty hopeless about things like that, and was also supposed to go to Europe the next day— maybe not; also hopeless about sticking to plans. In his case I think it would be perfectly all right just to go ahead—we are very good friends.

Joaquim Cardozo—well—this is a drama. He's 76, I think—and the head of a house of "calculations"—whatever that is, or whatever we call it. (*I* only now learned all this.) A pavilion his firm had done the calculations for, in Belo Horizonte, fell down last month—killing 56 workmen . . . The papers every day have more attestations from various writers saying what a fine man Mr. C is, how honest, and what a good poet, and how it wasn't his fault . . . He, meantime, is in a rest-home-sanitarium place. There was a hearing and he went accompanied by four doctors . . . A friend of mine from here went to Rio yesterday morning and took a letter to him for me—about the permission—but I don't know if the poor man is in any shape to think of such things or not. We'll see . . .

I'm glad you liked the translations. I think the sonnet turned out pretty well, too—and I wonder if I am not the 1st person to use that last word ["piss"] in your family magazine? However—I'm *not* a brilliant translator— I just stick the very rare poem that IS translatable—once in a while one does seem to go into English, but not often.

No—I won't be in SF—probably never again. (Have furniture in storage there, however.) I'll be here—with just *possibly* a trip to Europe, very brief, in May-June—until the end of August. Then I go back—by way of Peru, I think—to teach another fall term at Harvard. If you see Marjorie— give her my love. I was there for 5 awful days last October (?)—just packing up the apt.—and had so much to do I saw no one. Here it is very lonely and I am again thinking of selling the house, much as I love it. Meanwhile, I go on working away at it, getting ready for some American visitors for Holy Week . . . It is the best time to visit here & I wish you could be here, too.

I agree with all the corrections in the proof. I found one mistake—it should be *knew* (page 2) and I have put in one word, a "the" (page 2)—Was her name really Osa Martin? Must have been.[1] (I did some research on this poem, as I may have told you—very strange story . . .) I'm glad you like it, because I'm not sure that I do . . . I am actually working on some more poems—first in eight months or so—

I hope you're well, Howard—I felt concerned about you at that party and wish I could have seen you again. I'm so glad about Mr. Peech—and I'm sure it will make him happy, too.

Lots of love,
Elizabeth

P.S. Maybe I mis-spelled it? & I think you did—Isn't it CEMETERY?

April 6, 1971

Dear Elizabeth,

Here's the proof of CRUSOE IN ENGLAND, and there are a few sticky spots, the stickiest of all being the Wordsworth quote on page 2, which has so many queries attached to it, I can hardly make out the trees for the wood.[2] Here they are, as I dope them out:

First, the whole quote is an anachronism. Is that ok?

Second, the first "They" should be capped. There should be a comma after eye. "Which", on the other hand, should be in lower case. The mark "tr" followed by a question mark means should the quotation marks precede the three dots or follow them? And should the following "the" be capped? In other words, should it look like this:

("They flash upon that inward eye,
which is the bliss" . . .The bliss of what?

OR

1 Robert Hemenway edited this poem. The only changes he made before having it set in galley proof were removing the indentations to the first lines of the second, third, fourth, and fifth stanzas. Between Bishop's submission and the poem's publication, the following changes were made in stanza three: removing the colon after "similarities" and inserting a dash at the end of line twenty-four; changing "boots, hands, a family voice" to "boots, hands, the family voice" in line twenty-five; making the comma after "breasts" a dash in line twenty-eight; and removing the comma after "worse" in the last line. In the second line of the last stanza, a comma was added after "Outside" (*The New Yorker* Records and Vassar College Library).

2 Bishop submitted the sixth stanza lines as "they flash upon that inward eye / Which is the bliss:—the bliss of what?" (*The New Yorker* Records and Vassar College Library).

("They flash upon that inward eye,
which is the bliss . . ." The bliss of what?

If you have a Wordsworth edition that uses different caps and lower case let-
ters from the ones we suggest, I'd stick to whatever the printed edition says.
I do think, though, that the quote should come *after* the three dots and that
the following "The" should be capped.

I think all the other queries are clear.[1]

Yes, your poem introduces a new word to *The New Yorker*. It's a first.

The story about Cardozo is a horror, so ghastly it's almost funny, as is
almost anything that occurs in Belo Horizonte. I simply don't believe it really
exists. Poor man. What is there to say?

Yes, it *is* "cemetery."

I hope someday to get down to Brazil, but I wish you'd come back and
live on Spring Street, with that little terrace, the harpsichord, and Varick
Street hard by.

Love,
Howard

April 9, 1971

Dear Miss Bishop,

Yes, we'd like very much to have a look at your memoir.

I'm sorry we missed each other.

Best regards,
William Shawn

May 25, 1971

Dear Elizabeth,

Here are the proofs of TWO BRAZILIAN POEMS and I think, aside
from messiness, everything is pretty clear. One thing: Somebody's queried
"Joaquim" or "Joaquin," and to confuse matters further, wonders if there

---

1 Moss made additional changes. In stanza two, line one, he removed the colon after "fifty-two". In line two, he
added a comma after "miserable". In line three, he removed the comma after "strides" and inserted a dash. In
line six, he removed the comma after "others" and inserted a comma after "up". In stanza five, line ten, he put com-
mas on either side of "at a distance". In line twenty, he inserted a comma between "and" and "dizzy". In stanza
eight, line eight, he removed the commas from either side of "or". In line nine, he removed the period after
"names". In the last stanza, five lines from the end, he removed the comma after "work" and inserted a comma after
"but" (*The New Yorker* Records and Vassar College Library).

should be an accent over the last syllable? I assume "Joaquim," which is the way it was on the ms. But I am not up on the latest Portuguese dope, or even the earliest.

And I'm enclosing a new first-reading agreement I hope you'll want to sign.

My terrace is in bloom—that is, I put the blooms in recently—and this morning, appropriately, the morning glories started through the ground with that peculiar look they have, as if they were hanging their heads in shame. (Or chagrin, maybe—a city terrace when they should be out in the country. Or out *of* the country, more likely.) For the usual Cheap Irony Dept., it turns out I have a raving allergy to dust. I plant; I sneeze; I die.

Tomorrow, the Institute do and I wish you were going to be there. Cocktails and speeches.

I'll probably end up in London in July. I'm about to start a book on Virginia Woolf. An old love.

Love,
Howard

Kirkland House, Harvard University
Cambridge, Massachusetts
June 15, 1971

Dear Howard:

Your letter with contract & proof went to Brazil, Athens, and then reached me here . . . where I received it two or three days ago. I was supposed to go to Rotterdam the 1st week of June, then to visit Jimmy Merrill in Athens until the end of the month. However, I had been sick in Brazil for some time, and getting sicker, and I finally decided to go to Europe by the "triangular" route, stopping off to see drs. in N.Y. It was just as well I did; I had—still have—amoebic dysentery and three other kinds as well—so it's no wonder I had been feeling poorly and unable to work for two months or more. I came over here just to see my flat for next September, signed the lease, and then collapsed at the apartment of my friend Alice [Methfessel] for ten days or so. I'm much better now but had to give up the trip. I'll be here until the end of the month, when I have to return to Ouro Prêto. I'll be there all July, then travelling for 2 or 3 weeks, then back to OP, then here again around the first week of September. I have a friend staying in the OP house and he naturally sent a large batch of mail to Greece—and Jimmy sent it back to Cambridge . . . I think that covers my late wanderings . . .

I wonder if the proof of Vinicius' sonnet means that you did receive the permission from him? I wrote to the Brazilian Embassy in Paris, where he was last reported to be, and to a friend of his in Paris who would know where he is if anyone does. However—I'm positive it would be all right to publish the poem. We are very good old friends. However—*The New Yorker* may be too correct for that.

I don't have the Portuguese poems with me. I tried to stick to the Portuguese punctuation when it wasn't too different from the English, and I think the ;;;'s in the Cardozo poem are all right as they now are. The name is just JOAQUIM in Portuguese; JOAQUÍN (with accent) is the Spanish form of it. I don't think that "from the Portuguese" should be set off by commas (line at the bottom)—perhaps that's what another reader meant when he or she wrote STYLE after it? Otherwise, all is correct.

I am in some distress about the contract. I'd like to sign it and would certainly like the money and the 25% bonus, etc. On the other hand, I am quite sure that if I had sent the two poems I sent you last June or July (?) to any other of the magazines that keep asking me for poems, they would have appeared some months ago. When I sent the WAITING ROOM I asked especially, since it mentions February, if it would have to wait until a February to be published, and whoever answered for you then (you were on vacation) said no indeed, it could be published in any month, and also spoke admiringly of the poem—as you did later, when you sent me the proof. And February came and went. If I were a prolific writer, I suppose I wouldn't mind this waiting, but since I'm not, naturally I'd like to see the few poems I do send out published—well, while I'm still alive . . . People now say to me, "You've stopped writing entirely, haven't you?" and it sounds a bit feeble to say, "Well, not quite . . ." So I'm going to return the contract & check this year, at least, and see if I can get some poems published soon.

If the contract could say that any poems—or prose—accepted would be published within three months, and if not I'd have the right to send them some place else, I'd be glad to sign it. I'd also like to because I have two pieces or more of prose coming along well now—one a Marianne Moore Memoir I hope to get done while here.

I'd also like to receive *The New Yorker*. I wrote about this twice, but maybe to the wrong people. I can see it while I'm here, of course, and friends have watched out for my poems all this time—but I'd like it when I get back to Caixa Postal 79, Ouro Prêto, Minas Gerais . . .

I don't believe I have corrected proof for the Robinson Crusoe poem, have I? (I can't remember.) There are two or three small changes I'd like to make before it is published.

I missed even the account of the Institute ceremonies. I got to NY a day or two after them, I think—but I was there only four days and I was feeling so sick I saw almost no one.

What will happen to your nice terrace if you go to London? (I was going there for a few days, too.) I remember some very nice gatherings there, especially one with Jean in which we all talked at length about TEETH. Have a nice time in London, and I'll be seeing you sometime in New York, come fall.

With love,
Elizabeth

P.S. If by chance THE WAITING ROOM is now waiting for *next* February—maybe I should take it back and refund the payment? I am much better now, but after feeling that my end was approaching, just last week, I'd really like to see something published, to cheer me on my way a bit—

June 18, 1971

Dear Elizabeth,

Your letter opened three or four Pandora's boxes, and I hasten to screw the lids on a few of them, at least. Before that, though, let me say how sorry I am about the amoebic dysentery—I know from other friends of mine what a plague it can be. I hope you're on the mend and on a bland diet and are being well taken care of.

Lid 1—I understand about the time lag—I know it from firsthand experience—it's partly the result of our buying more poems than we can use in a reasonable time, and partly our scrupulous respect for book deadlines, a respect not so scrupulous in other places. However, I've talked to everyone concerned and I can promise that, from now on, any poem of yours will be printed within six months of our buying it. (IN THE WAITING ROOM is scheduled in July or August.) Is this a satisfactory arrangement—an understanding between us about not holding the poems for more than 6 months? I can't make it official, put it in the agreement, that is, but I can definitely promise it. I hope you'll reconsider the agreement on this basis, and I'm enclosing it with this letter.

Lid 2—The author's proof of CRUSOE IN ENGLAND was sent to you in Brazil on April 6th. It has never been returned, and I'd hate to have it all redone. Do you think it's lurking around somewhere in Brazil? Harvard? Wherever? If we have to, we'll have another one made up, but it means going through the whole process of several people reading it again. If you find it, please make the changes you mention in your letter. If not, could you let me know? And also what changes you want? I'm enclosing an *uncorrected* proof of the poem for you to look at. It is NOT an author's proof.

Lid 3—We no longer publish seasonally, by the way, and haven't for ages. Your remark about our not printing WAITING ROOM one February and suggesting that means we'd have to hold it until the next February isn't so. All poems are published without regard to season, though once in a while, we'll print a poem relevant to an occasion. A poem called NEW YEAR'S EVE is more likely to be published, if possible, around New Year's Eve. But not necessarily.

Lid 4—I've received no permission from Vinicius or from Cardozo about the translations. This is important, especially since there is going to be, I gather, book publication. Unless we get permission, we're in the position of having the publisher ask us where we got permission to publish those two poems. Do you have the authority to give it to us? If so, fine. But we'd prefer for you to get it, which is the usual case. Wouldn't you want it copyrighted—isn't the Portuguese copyrighted?—to protect everyone involved? Please let me know about this. Or if you hear from either of them.

Lid 5—I've gone to the subscription people and asked to have the magazine sent to Brazil. I think it went from Brazil to San Francisco to Cambridge—confusing the computer, not to mention others.

I leave for London within a week and a half from now. I do hope, Elizabeth, you feel better. And do please reconsider the agreement. Everyone here is a fan of yours. The cheering section is led by me.

Love,
Howard

June 24, 1971

Dear Howard:

Thank you for your letter of the 18th and I am writing in time, I hope, for you to receive this before you go to England. (I'm leaving for Ouro Prêto a week from today, no, yesterday. I'll be there through July, then travelling, and for another week, the last week in August; then to Cambridge . . .)

Taking it paragraph by paragraph: I didn't receive the proof of CRUSOE

IN ENGLAND, just that of IN THE WAITING ROOM. I've usually had good luck with mail from The New Yorker, but this time it must have got lost. (Or the censors decided to open it and then they lost it or didn't bother to re-mail. This happens now sometimes.) I'm sending my corrections on a separate sheet. I'm sorry this will put you to the extra work, but it can't be helped—I'm positive I didn't get it; the WAITING ROOM came by itself, and I've had a man doing secretarial work for me almost every afternoon, and he kept track of things very well.

Well, I'm glad to hear about the change in policy about seasons and months, etc. . . . I hadn't realized it had been changed.

Cardozo wrote me promptly, as I said, and his letter (slightly shaky English), I thought, implied he had written *you* right away, too. Today I'll write to the "secretary," staying in my house just now, and ask him to send on the letter Cardozo wrote me, to The New Yorker. It gives the permission, etc. I've done all I can for the moment about Vinicius (who is also holding up the anthology I'm doing); however, the friend of his in Paris will be staying with me the month of July in Ouro Prêto, and as soon as he gets there I'll know if he has an address for this hopeless (but nice) man, and I, or we, shall try once more . . . (He hasn't even cashed the checks Betty Kray sent him months or years ago, and she is desperate—nor one of mine sent *four years* ago . . .)

Thank you so much for seeing about the subscription. I need all the agreeable reading I can get in OP & like to keep up with the NY-er—but I never received it in Cambridge. I'll see about transferring it, *very carefully*, when I return . . .

Oh—re-reading point #4: Yes, Cardozo's letter does give me permission. And I know Vinicius would—he'd love to be printed in the NYer—I'm sure it would be all right. Even if he never writes—the friend is returning to Paris in August and he can *tell* him.

Now back to #1: Well, all right . . . Thank you, too. I am signing the contract, mostly because I do expect to be sending along at least two prose pieces very soon—poetry is more uncertain always, of course. And I don't seem to mind much waiting for prose, and I can stand 6 months, anyway—unless I catch another tropical disease, when I think I'd have everything printable printed immediately on handbills just to see how it looked while I waited for the end. But really, Howard—don't you think that over a year is a bit too much? Are all those David Wagoners and James Dickeys and so on publishing books every year? Yes, I suppose they are . . .

I hope I've improved this a bit. I didn't realize how sad it is until I saw the proof—ye gods! Bits of it are about the Galápagos—taken from *The Voyage of the Beagle*, and did I tell you I'm going there, in August? I'll send you a color picture of a blue-footed booby. While you're being civilized in England, I'll be sitting on a lava beach with a sea-lion—they say they're so tame they come and sit right down beside you on the beach when you go swimming—join the party and grunt sociably—

Have a nice holiday and do keep well.

Love,

Elizabeth

Elizabeth Bishop
CORRECTIONS FOR *CRUSOE IN ENGLAND*
(or approval of those made in copy sent me June 18th, 1971)

Galley 1: bottom of page. The word *cloud*—singular.
  " " "   As set.[1]

Galley 2: 1st questioned line OK (. . . hours apart.)
Same paragraph, last line: "a ~~faltering~~ stammering philosophy."
3rd paragraph, last line: omit "badly".
Last paragraph, 2nd line, shd. be a stop.
  " " "   1.8: "or" is *not* italicized.
  " " "   1.9: please change to "(I'd time enough to play with names),"
  " " "   4th line from bottom—no indentation.[2]

Galley 3: next to last line—no punctuation at the end of the line:
" . . . measles seventeen years ago come March."[3]

E.B.

---

1 In the third stanza, six lines from the end, the proofreader questioned whether "their heads in cloud" should be plural and the spacing of the ellipses between "glass" and "I" three lines from the end (*The New Yorker* Records).
2 Bishop is referring to the proofreader's questioning either the period at the end of "I tried it, one by one, and hours apart." or the period in "(I think it had the weirdest scale on earth.)" in the fifth stanza, lines thirteen and nineteen. Bishop changed "my indistinct philosophy" to "a stammering philosophy" at the stanza's end. In the last line of stanza seven, Bishop removed "badly" from "got badly on my nerves." In stanza eight, the proofreader questioned the period at the end of the second line: "like a big tree in a strong wind, its leaves." In line eight, someone questioned whether "or" should be italicized between *"Mont d'Espoir"* and *"Mount Despair"*. Bishop changed line nine from "(I had enough time for full names)," to "(I'd time enough to play with names),". She also wanted "His pupils, perpendicular, narrowed up" flush left.
3 Bishop had submitted the poem's second to last line with a comma after "measles".

July 6, 1971

Dear Elizabeth Bishop,

I enclose the author's proof for CRUSOE IN ENGLAND—the proof that was lost last April—along with a copy of Howard's letter that accompanied it. I have made all of the corrections on the proof that you asked for in your letter from Cambridge of June 24th, so that you need deal only with Howard's questions and the few queries on punctuation and the like.

I've seen the page proof of IN THE WAITING ROOM, which will be in the July 17 issue.

Sincerely,

Robert Hemenway

Ouro Prêto
July 21, 1971

Dear Mr. Hemenway,

I am sorry to be so slow about answering you & returning this proof. It is not my laziness however; my mail has been being held up for about a month now because of things I had rather not go into in a letter—you can guess, perhaps—and it has just started coming again, in out-of-sequence bunches.

Thank you for the proof—I didn't receive the first copy, last April—and I was amazed to see all the other corrections, too.* I didn't know there had been a problem about "anachronisms"—& Wordsworth. Apparently those objections were dropped along the line, and some of the punctuation troubles, etc., as well—I don't remember them at all on the copy Howard sent me in Cambridge, in June. If you can look at that copy—I did correct EVERYTHING on it. I don't know your usage as to some hyphenated words, but I am sure that "cloud-dump" should be hyphenated, since it's a made-up word; also "left-over" is hyphenated, in the SOED (but maybe you don't use that). So is "home-made". I don't care one way or the other about the hyphens—but of course they should be consistent.

One important correction, please, is on galley 2, last line of the 2nd paragraph, or 1st complete paragraph: please have it read: "a miserable philosophy." (I seem to have had trouble with that adjective.)

And just after that, I did correct, on the copy I returned to Howard (not a proof, he wrote), line 3 in the next paragraph, and I see it is the only thing *not* appearing corrected on this proof you sent me. It should read: "Greek drama or astronomy?"—[1]

1 Bishop had originally submitted the phrase in the sixth stanza as: "Greek, or astronomy, preferably."

*There are several "anachronisms," and several islands combined, on purpose—the date is obviously later than Alexander Selkirk's experience, and the island not his.

The W quotation shd. read as I've corrected it—or agreed with your reader.[1]

I wonder if you'd be kind enough to see that I get a few *New Yorkers*? I've asked, various people & departments, for two years now—since they wrote they were sending it, and did for many years, but I haven't seen any except when I get to the USA, or a rare copy here through friends. Of course, I'd like the July 17th issue—2 copies, if possible—air mail? These may have possibly been sent me already, boat mail. I am going away the 1st 3 weeks in August; back here briefly, then to Cambridge in early September. I'll get them when I get back if so—Now that I think of it—there is no point in sending any copies here *except* that July 17th one. I need it—the poem is being translated into Portuguese & I have no final copy here.

Thank you very much.

Sincerely yours,

Elizabeth Bishop

July 26, 1971

Dear Miss Bishop,

Thanks so much for the proof. I think nearly all of those hyphens should be there, and I've pretty much left your punctuation and the like, rejecting the proof-reader's suggestions. Subject to Howard's review when he returns, of course.[2]

I understand about the delay.

Tearsheets of IN THE WAITING ROOM went off to you today under separate cover, and a couple of copies of the July 17 issue as well.

Enclosed is a copy of my letter of June 29, which you may not have received. It has to do with that vexing matter of the permission for the translations.

If you are to be in Cambridge in September, we will arrange to have the magazine sent to you there.

---

1 It ran as: 'They flash upon that inward eye, / which is the bliss . . .' The bliss of what?

2 One of the suggested changes that Bishop did not include in her letter was made. Hemenway initialed changing the fifth line of the first stanza from "and then a black fleck, basalt, probably," to "and then a black fleck—basalt, probably—". One suggested change he initialed did not appear; he okayed a dash instead of a comma at the end of the seventh line of the fifth stanza: "over the one variety of tree".

We hope that you are in good health now.
Sincerely,
    Robert Hemenway

Dear Elizabeth,

This is my first day back and I've just read through the proofs of and the correspondence on CRUSOE IN ENGLAND. My God! Espionage and codes seem simple by comparison. Anyway, I think I've got it all doped out now, and what I'm sending you is the overmatter—or the version we now think is absolutely correct. Incorporating your changes, your responses to our queries, and so on and so forth. NOTHING NEED BE DONE ABOUT THIS PROOF. I send it on to reassure you, and myself, that we now have the poem as you would like to see it printed.

A word, though, saying it's o.k. would be nice. And I'd love to know how you are, where you are (I assume in Cambridge) and whether you still want a subscription to go to Brazil. Wouldn't that be silly if you're going to be in Cambridge for a semester? The reason the subscription is fouled up is because you move around so much. Let me know where it arrives now, and *if* it arrives.

I had dinner with Mark and Antonia [Strand] last night and he said he thought the waiting room poem was the best poem you'd ever written, which seems an impossible topping of the top.

Do write, when you can, to tell me you're all better. I'm back now for good.

    Love,
        Howard

P.S. We received written permission from Mr. Cardozo about the translation and have decided to go ahead about the Moraes poem. So we'll print them both in time to meet the book deadline.

P.S.S. I'm sending a copy of this letter (but not the overmatter version of CRUSOE) to Brazil, just in case.

Dear Howard:

Thank you for sending me the "overmatter"(?!) copy of the Crusoe poem. I'm sorry; I hadn't realized I'd made it so difficult. It looks quite all right now and thank you.

I'm now here—have been for about ten days—and have an apartment at the above address. I'm going to teach two seminars again, the fall term, as I did last year. The apartment is still rather chaotic, but I think it will be quite nice when I get a table, say, or a desk . . .

Please don't worry about my subscription now—I did get one or two copies in Brazil, but not very many I'm afraid.—I can always see the magazine here easily, and I'll let you know when I have to go back to Brazil again, etc.—

It's nice of Mark S. to like my poem that much—but I do think he's exaggerating a bit!

And—thank goodness poor old Cardozo did write directly to you, finally. You'll never know the idiotic complication I've been involved in about Vinicius's address, present tel. no, present lady-friend—and so on.—I finally gave up—although I heard he "wanted to see" me.—Anyway—I'm sure it's all right to go ahead—and I'll write once more to 2 friends of his who see him often—and so I'm again sure it *will* be. Oh dear—if the man came to NY and you met him I think you'd like him . . . !

I hope you had a nice trip to England? I had a marvellous one—to the Galápagos—& Machu Picchu—I'll be coming to NY fairly often, I hope, and I hope I'll be seeing you—

Love,

Elizabeth

December 7, 1971

Dear Elizabeth,

Here is a letter I thought you'd want to see—but it is only one of the many comments I heard about "Crusoe" after it came out. Everyone I know, practically, thought it remarkable, including James Schuyler, David Kalstone, Jimmy M [Merrill], Ed White—and a host of others. In fact, so many people mentioned it, that I assumed the same thing was happening in Cambridge.

Did you get that invitation to the screening of a movie based on "Helena Morley"? I told the man, after talking to Bob Giroux, to wire you in Cambridge. I never thought of it as a movie, but now that I do, I can see the possibilities. If I *had* thought of it, I would have asked for a grant for a trip to Diamantina. And from *that* height (and here comes my favorite and standard joke) there is always Belo Horizonte.

Is there any chance of seeing you over Christmas? Or seeing you at all? I was really terribly disappointed not to see you when I was in Cambridge and Duxbury. It seems like ages since we've talked.

Love,
Howard

February 18, 1972

Dear Elizabeth:

I have been waiting to get your address from Howard Moss in order to send you my sympathy and share my own sorrow in Marianne Moore's death.[1] I loved her dearly, though I suppose she never knew it, and to have been her editor for eight years when she was contributing to *The New Yorker* was one of the most rewarding experiences I had in my nearly forty years of editing. It turns out that we published twenty-three of her poems if Howard's records are accurate. To you her loss must be hard to bear for I know very well how much she meant to you and you to her. I have been so sick and so out of touch with New York and *The New Yorker* for the past three years that I really don't know just how long she has been only half in this world after her series of strokes or how long she has been a complete invalid. If she was suffering and had lost her wonderful wit and mind I suppose we must take comfort in her death and think of it as a mercy, but the thought of no more Marianne Moore and no more of her poems ever leaves the world a poorer place. It's a miserable enough world without this loss. One of our giants is gone. And with Auden moving back to England (with very good reasons, it seems to me) it means that you are one of our few major poets left, Elizabeth. Marianne admired your poetry and loved you. She often spoke to me about your poems. I think I read that you were teaching but I hope you are writing too.

I knew M.M. long before I became her editor. In fact when I was in Bryn Mawr and the co-editor-in-chief of the two college literary magazines—a

---

1 After several years of illness, Moore died in her sleep on February 5.

fort-nightly that we revived that year and *The Lantern*, a literary annual to which we asked alumnae to contribute—I wrote to the even then famous Miss Moore and asked for a poem for *The Lantern*. Promptly one came back and we published it. Somewhere in our attic that copy of *The Lantern* is buried but I can't climb the attic stairs to search it out and, shamefully, I can't remember the poem *at all*. I would like to see whether she ever put it into one of her early books.[1] Later, in New York, she was a friend of my sister Elizabeth and I saw her off and on until she became my friend too—because I was her editor.

I shall always be grateful to her for liking my garden pieces. She kept urging me to collect them into a book—a project I'm still working at but doubt that I'll ever finish. Writing is hard for me now and too many extraneous things have interfered, but mostly my rotten health and age. Also I can't write decently any more. But I shall never forget her generosity and encouragement. Or her zest for life and her humor. She will live on, both as a poet and as a wonderful and unforgettable person.

If you come to Maine this summer, I do hope you will stop by to see me, but call up first. My days are queer as I now am surrounded by nurses and get about only on a "walker"—osteoporosis—and have just about every affliction. Nevertheless I am up and about and working (mostly now to help Andy on his correspondence so he will have time to write) but because I have lost the knack of sleeping at night I have to waste two hours of the afternoon napping to make up on sleep. We'd therefore love to see you, Andy and I, for luncheon or cocktails.

I suppose you will have heard from your Maine or Deer Isle friends of the big blow that almost wrecked the Deer Isle Bridge. Heavy trucks can't go over it now. It is being temporarily patched up and will need real rebuilding when it warms up, but the photos of bent and cracked girders and frazzled cables give one the creeps, especially now that the high school children of Brooklin, Sedgwick, and Brooksville are bussed over the Bridge every school day.

Ever affectionately,
Katharine

[Handwritten: Since dictating the above messy & ungrammatical letter, it has come to me that the most wonderful tribute The New Yorker could give

1 It is not entirely clear to which poem White is referring. White was co-editor of *The Lantern* for the 1914 issue; however, no poem of Moore's was included in that issue. The following year, three poems of Moore's ran: "Isaiah, Jeremiah, Ezekiel, Daniel," "To Disraeli on Conservatism," and "The North Wind to a Dutiful Beast."

Marianne Moore would be a memorial poem by *you*. The magazine no longer writes obits of its contributors as they once did occasionally. I suppose the reason for this is that by now every issue would have to carry an obit for all its early stars have lived to be old enough to die. I have no authority to ask you to do this as I am not an editor but I shall suggest it to Bill Shawn. He has had a heart attack from which he made a good recovery, but he's working at home & will be back in the office March 1st. Anyway, if you feel impelled to write such a poem, which you may not, I hope you'll let The New Yorker see it. KSW]

March 21, 1972

Dear Howard:

Thank you so much for your kind letter. I thought I might see you at Marianne's funeral—maybe you were there, and I missed you. I had a very nice letter from Katharine White, too, the first news I had had of them in ages.

Here is an old-fashioned umpty-umpty nostalgic poem that perhaps you'll be able to use ["Poem"]. Now that I am through teaching for the year—last year—I'm at last getting some work of my own done and I hope this is just the first of several.

I saw your Chekhov poem—and I wish I would write one about him, too—we do pick the same subjects sometimes; I've noticed this.[1] I am crazy about him, too—have you read his book about Sakhalin island? Perhaps I'd better say *don't*—until I've finished my poem talking about that . . .

I'll probably be seeing you on the 13th of April, won't I?

Lots of love,
    Elizabeth

March 28, 1972

Dear Elizabeth,

What a beauty POEM is! I love it, and so does everyone else here who's read it. I wish I could read a poem like that every day for the rest of my life.[2]

I saw Jimmy Sunday night, which was a pleasure—I hadn't seen him with

---

1 "Chekhov" (February 26, 1972).

2 Moss made three punctuation changes to the poem: adding a comma to the end of the first line; adding a comma after "gray-greens" in line three; and removing the comma from the end of the thirteenth line of stanza two (*The New Yorker* Records and Vassar College Library).

his new beard. He looks like Debussy. Without the hydrocephalic forehead, of course.

I'll have a check and an author's proof to be sending you shortly, and *please* do send me some new poems, soon. I'd be fascinated, naturally, to read the Chekhov one. I haven't read the Sakhalin Island book. I'm in the middle of reading *all* the stories—an unbelievable number, even in English—but I'm not complaining.

I'll see you on the 13th.

Love,

Howard

P.S. I'm editing a book of stories by poets and wonder where I can find THE FARMER'S CHILDREN.[1] Do you have an extra copy? I remember reading it years ago in Harper's Bazaar—and liking it enormously. The idea of the book is to save stories that have never been collected.

May 10, 1972

Dear Howard:

While trying hard to finish a longer poem, I occasionally turn out a short one on the side—and perhaps you will be able to use this ["Night City"] . . .

Jimmy Merrill was here to give a reading yesterday. The weather was awful, a blustery storm, but the reading went well and then we had a nice party afterward—a party that went on & on and on. He came to eat some black beans and rice with me today, in memory of Brazil.

I hope you're well. I'm afraid I won't be able to get to the Academy function—I wanted to, just to see friends. I hope you'll meet Octavio Paz. He & his wife [Mary Jo] have been here this term and I like them both a great deal.

With love,

Elizabeth

P.S. When you write, will you please give me the Whites' address in Maine? I *know* I have it somewhere, but can't find it and want to write to them. Thank you.

1 *The Poet's Story* (1973).

Dear Howard:

Enclosed is another by-product poem—on my way, I hope, to sending you a really long one in another week or two. I remember telling you a bit of this fancy, long ago—it started out as a very short "poem"—not very good; now it's turned into this ["12 O'Clock News"]. You may not like it at all. However, if you *can* use it, the words in the margin should be printed in that tiny type *The New Yorker* sometimes uses for foot-notes, I think. And the body of it should have perfect margins both right and left, like a newspaper column . . .

I'm sorry I can't be seeing you today at the "ceremony." It's a lovely chance to see a lot of friends—unfortunately, I am too broke. I hope you meet Octavio Paz and his wife . . . They are both adorable. I did a few small translations for him here—they'll be put into a very small booklet, I think—and although his poetry does not have the fashionable appeal of Borges', say, or Neruda—I may try sending you the one or two I think you might like.

I hope you're keeping well. I'm fine, except for rheumatism?—might as well call it that, I think . . . The lilacs, after stalling a week, are really coming out, right under my bedroom window. This is the first northern spring, real one, I've seen in 21 years . . .

Love,
Elizabeth

May 19, 1972

Dear Elizabeth,

I've read a trillion poems about planes flying over cities and what it all looks like and *is* like, and so on. But yours is the one. We're taking it, of course; in fact, by a miracle of dispatch, the author's proof just came up and so here it is. As you can see, I've taken out the hyphen in the title and changed "the" to "a" in the sub-title. If you disagree, please change them back. A payment for the poem should be coming along soon.

I'm enclosing a new first-reading agreement, which we hope you'll want to sign, too. I won't go into the details, which you know so well.

I'm anxious to see the long poem. Please try and send it on before I take off. I'll be out in Watermill for six weeks because Albee's directing a play of mine [*The Palace at 4 A.M.*] in East Hampton. It opens on August 9 for two weeks. Will you be anywhere close by?[1]

Love,
Howard

May 23, 1972

Dear Howard:

Thank you for the proof, check, etc. and the contract—I am sending all back to you directly. I wonder where the proof for POEM is? I haven't received it yet. By now you will have received a third poem, fairly short, and in a few days a longer one, I trust. I just wish I could keep on like this forever . . .

Congratulations about your—or for?—your play being put on—I'd love to see it, but I'm afraid I'll be travelling then. I'll be in Brazil from June 18th or so until the end of July—then I hope to make a trip, I'm not quite sure where yet.

I approve of your change in the title—everything else looks all right, "bitumen" with an E must be English—I looked it up in the OED—so have it your way—[2]

With love and best wishes—hurriedly (rudely—but I'm on my way to the dentist's)
Elizabeth

May 26, 1972

Dear Elizabeth,

12 O'CLOCK NEWS is marvelous and we're delighted to have it. It's simply grand, and I was particularly happy to see that "unicyclist" back. I've been waiting for him for years. Where did you first show me that poem— Spring Street, up in the seventies somewhere, on Perry Street? He's finally found a place to get off his bike.

I'll be sending on a check and an author's proof soon, and I look forward with pleasure to the long poem.[3] Every poem of yours brightens the day for

1 The play was performed at the John Drew Theater. The cast included Beatrice Straight and Christopher Walken.
2 Moss changed the subtitle from "(From the Plane)" to "(From a Plane)".
3 In stanza one, Moss changed Bishop's colons to semicolons after "light" and "poor". In stanza three, Moss inserted a comma after "calcareous". The semicolon after "poor" was changed to a period before the poem was published (*The New Yorker* Records and Vassar College Library). One additional change was made between Bishop's submission and the poem's publication. In stanza seven, "He appears to be, rather, to have been, a unicyclist-courier" became "He appears to be—rather, to have been—a unicyclist-courier".

me. Like Beethoven's father, I'd simply put you in a room and make you work all the time if I could. Of course, I wouldn't be that strict. A little gin, a few sandwiches . . .

Love,
    Howard

June 9, 1972

Dear Elizabeth,

Here's a check for 12 O'CLOCK NEWS, and thanks again for sending it. I hope for others, and soon.

I've been trying to reach you by phone for several days. No luck, though I did talk to a nice lady—Brazilian?—who understood nothing of what I said, and I little of what she said. She apologized sweetly for not understanding English. I should have apologized for making her flunk the test.

Anyway, what I'm hoping is that you'll be able to get to a dinner Atheneum is throwing for me on the 20th—6:30, the Wine Room of the Pierre Restaurant on 53rd between Park and Madison. It's a small dinner, the room is charming, and you'll see people you know, and if you'd like to bring someone, please do. Could you let me know? I'd love you to be there to celebrate my winning the NBA, or half of it [for *Selected Poems*].[1] You get a *whole* dinner, though—or at least so I've been led to believe.

Love,
    Howard

June 15, 1972

Dear Howard:

The Harvard Alumni Bulletin would want to use this ["The Moose"] in September . . . I think. Anyway—it doesn't matter about the HAB, as far as I'm concerned, although of course it would be nice to have them use it if they want to.

The editor is John Bethell—Wadsworth House, Cambridge, 02138. (H Wadsworth Longellow?)

I don't know how soon you could print this—* (I think my agreement was 6 months)—maybe he could use it in the September issue of the Bulletin, or whatever one comes after that?—

1 Moss shared the award with *The Collected Poems of Frank O'Hara*, edited by Donald Allen (1971).

And maybe you'll find it entirely too 19th centuryish, anyway—

You may get this before I get to NY—maybe not. I'll try to talk to you, anyway, before I leave—and I hope you have a lovely party—it does sound rather grand & I wish I could be there—

Love,

Elizabeth

*publication within six months, that is—

June 26, 1972

Dear Elizabeth,

Since we plan to run this, now, in the July 15th issue, I thought I'd *ignore* your warning about the Brazilian mails and send this [proof of "The Moose"] down to you no matter, since there *are* a few tiny decisions to make that you would ordinarily like, I know, to be in on. But *heeding* your warning, on the other hand, I've had Xeroxes made of practically everything, including the top of my desk, so that another copy has gone to Bob Giroux in case yours is stolen by angry Indians, incensed by the title, and I'm holding on to still *another* Xerox, in case we all have heart attacks at the same time.[1]

If you could get *your* copy back to me pronto, that would be a great help and blessing. I may be gone by the time it arrives but if it's addressed to me, it will get into the right hands.

I hope all goes well at the house, though I imagine there are a thousand things that need doing after all this time. I hope the tools and the silver aren't disappearing and re-appearing in that mysterious way you once described to me. Have you made any trips to Belo Horizonte?

I'll be reachable through the office all through the summer, since mail will be forwarded, and it would be wonderful to see you in August.

Love,

Howard

---

1 In stanza five, line four, Moss inserted a comma after "neat". In stanza ten, line two, Moss substituted the colon after "Economies" with a dash and inserted a comma after "Houses" in line four. In stanza twenty-five (four from the end), line three, Moss substituted the colon after "softly" with a comma. In stanza twenty-seven, line three, Moss changed "r's" to "R's" (*The New Yorker* Records and Vassar College Library).

June 30, 1972

Dear Elizabeth,

Here's the author's proof of POEM, and I've taken the same precautions, with the exception of sending a copy to Giroux. I have a Xerox of it in a basket I'm handing over to the editor who'll be taking care of unfinished business.

We're printing THE MOOSE, by the way, in the July 15th issue, and if we don't hear from you by then, we'll simply print it exactly as it was in the manuscript. The few queries aren't terribly important, in any case— hyphens, wood in one place, woods in another—that sort of thing.

On this proof, do forgive those scrawls made by the typesetters in Chicago. We can't do anything about them, since they come over a machine in indelible ink. Just ignore everything that isn't in pencil.

This is my last day here and things have piled up somewhat. If I seem semi-hysterical, it's because I am.

By the way, I've asked Mr. Henderson to hold your check (or checks) for you until you get back from Brazil. O.K? If you want them or need them, just write to Mr. Robert Henderson, c/o The New Yorker. You might send this proof back to him, too, though anything addressed to me will eventually get into the right hands—those last five words being the title of my new Jesus-freak rock musical.

Love,
Howard

Ouro Prêto
July 7, 1972

Dear Howard:

The proof of THE MOOSE came yesterday, and I corrected it as best I could (don't have my dictionary with those *marks* in it here . . . I always have to look them up, except for "delete.") I'd already made some small changes that I think improve it a *lot*, so I added those, and put it right back in the mail—it should have gone out last night. I didn't have time to write you a letter to go along with it, but I think I can remember the proof-reader's chief objections and explain myself.—Letters seem to be arriving pretty well these days—5 or 6 days—so I do hope you get it. And I'd love a copy air-mail, if possible! (Conceit)—I'm getting the *New Yorker* again, but still haven't caught up with those I saw before I left Cambridge—they take at least 6 weeks & I'm only here this month. I have quite a file here, but they won't be wasted—several people are clamoring for them. Oh dear—you say July 15th—well, it may get to New York by the 10th or 11th, with luck.

I'll give my changes, in case it gets lost. (If the corrected proof doesn't arrive—well, I guess the 1st version isn't too bad.)

Stanza 7: The light / grows richer. Then the fog, / shifting, etc.

Stanza 9: / to their wet white string / on the whitewashed fences; / the bumblebees creep / inside the foxgloves. / Evening commences.

Stanza 11: / Then the Tantramar marshes /

Stanza 13: / "A grand night. Yes, sir / all the way to Boston." / She regards us amicably. /

Stanza 15—It should be divagation, I think—at least according to the OED. I had it "divigation" and so did *The New Yorker*.

Stanza 22: / stops with a jolt and / turns off his lights. /

Stanza 26: / (we all feel) this sweet / etc. (I think I forgot to change this—to omit the "it"—on the proof, but I like it better without.)[1]

The proof-readers' objections: —"journeys *west*" was questioned. Well, driving from Nova Scotia to Boston, one would have to go west for quite a while—to get onto the mainland (NS is almost an island) before turning south—where New Brunswick begins. For the ΦBK occasion, I gave the poem the subtitle of *Back to Boston*, but I don't like that very much. It seems to me it makes things *too* clear—and simplicity is the biggest fault of this poem, anyway, I'm afraid. What do you think? You can put it in if you want to.

I liked Red Sea with a capital, two capitals—otherwise it loses its good old Baptist significance entirely and is just descriptive—and it isn't the "sea", anyway—it's the Bay of Fundy *looking like* the Red Sea (which it does, that

---

1 Bishop submitted the lines in stanza seven as: "The light / is deepening; the fog, / shifting,". She submitted the lines in stanza nine as: "to wet white string / on the whitewashed fences; / bumblebees creep / inside the foxgloves, / and evening commences." She submitted the line in stanza eleven as: "The Tantramar marshes". She submitted the lines in stanza thirteen as: " 'It's a grand night. Yes, sir, / all the way to Boston,' / regarding us amicably." She submitted the lines in stanza twenty-two as: "stops with a jolt, / turns off his lights." And she submitted the line in stanza twenty-six as: "(we all feel it) this sweet". The "it" is crossed out by hand (*The New Yorker* Records and Vassar College Library).

is, if the Red Sea is RED). "Led them with unmoistened foot / through the Red Sea waters . . ." (I'm afraid you aren't apt to be familiar with one of my favorite hymns!)

"Tantramar Marshes"—well, the NY-er couldn't find it on the map, and neither could I (I used one). Nor could the Harvard Library map room. However—I know I'm right, and they used to be called that, at any rate. I had it firmly in mind, but couldn't prove it, when I finished the poem, and the next day I went to Bermuda for the week-end. This is uncanny. In the one bookshop I saw in Hamilton, the first book that caught my eye was a very crude Canadian re-print of a Methodist minister's travels in Nova Scotia and Bermuda, in the early 19th century . . . It had page-headings, one of which was "The Tantramar." (This was just a day or two after I'd been going crazy in Cambridge trying to find some reference to them . . . and didn't know whether I could use the word or not—and I like it a lot.) Well, the missionary crossed the marshes and his horse sank in them and he sank, and they had to be pulled out, etc.—and apparently at that time there was even a place called "Tantramar"—it probably comes from the time of the Acadians, a French corruption . . . (Frank Bidart, who was along, went back and bought the book for me—it was much too expensive—like an angel.) So—I do think that's all right.

Someone objected to using "woods" in stanza 14, and just "wood" in stanza 23—but I think that's rather silly. There are, or were, miles and miles of what we'd surely call "woods"—but the moose emerged from one spot in them, of course, and I think it is more natural to call that "wood"—If there has to be a change, they shd. both be "woods"—but the second one sounds ugly, followed by "and stands . . ."

They had also corrected "rolling his r's." next to last stanza, to "rolling his Rs"—which looks awful. I think a small italicized *r* would be best.

I think that's all. I do hope they can catch that "it" in stanza 26. Frank liked it—I'll blame him—but now I think it doesn't go, metrically.

I am a fuss-budget—but you already knew that.

Oh—they also questioned stanza 20: "half-groan, half-acceptance." / STYLE! Well, I had already tried various other words in place of "acceptance" to make the construction *parallel*, which I suppose is what they mean—but none of them seemed to have the right meaning; "acceptance" does, and I hope it can be kept.

* * * * * * *

Now I'll confess to one deliberate inaccuracy, but don't tell anyone. (Whoever used the map must have had a small one and so didn't spot this—it would only be on a large-scale one.) The "Economies"—real places, near where I used to live, down the bay, would really come in the other order, driving to Boston—"Upper, Middle, Lower" and I changed them around for the sake of a rhyme.—Imagine living in "Middle Economy . . ."

Everything was in remarkable good shape here, except for a lot of chipped dishes—but not of much value—I just can't have more than 3 people to dinner, if I should want to. But the house was fearfully dank and half the light bulbs burned out—I don't think it had been aired in ten months, or a bulb replaced. I arrived alone (from Belo H—but just from the airport—I didn't have to see that ghastly city but suppose I shall, once at least) and there was no one here. Freezing cold. I wanted to start two fires and there were no matches, and all the wood was damp. I had five left in a folder, and found a big bottle of cachaça under the sink, so I threw it on the wood and it worked beautifully, bright blue flames—Turned on the electric blanket and went to bed . . . But finally my maid, Vitoria, who is really awfully good for here, did show up.—She had left roast chicken, etc. but had expected me a day earlier.

We have been having a sort of New England spring-cleaning ever since and everything is shining. You must really come to visit sometime—it is now better than when Jim [Merrill] was here, I think. However—I am trying to sell the house, alas—but it may take years. The trip is too long; in general it is too lonely, and although I don't seem to feel ancient the way Auden seems to—it would be nice to know there was a doctor one could trust not too far away—an hour's flight, say . . . But—I don't want to end my days in Cambridge. Or New York. Oh dear—where to go next?

I hope you're having a nice stay on Long Island—but it seems not to have stopped raining since I left the USA. Here it is "winter," but not a cold one so far, and the sun is marvellous. You're probably all wrapped up in being a playwright and I do wish you a great success with your play and a lovely summer. I'm coming back the last day of July, probably—but shall leave Cambridge almost at once for a trip—back there again in September. But anything else, not too urgent could wait for my return August 1st—(I think I have 2 more proofs coming sometime.)

With love,
Elizabeth

July 13, 1972

Dear Mr. Henderson:
I'm mailing this proof back to you a day after I received it—I don't

know why it took so much longer, apparently, than the first batch I received here . . . (one never does know).

I always have trouble with hyphens. The Shorter Oxford Eng. Dictionary is the only one I have here and I believe *The New Yorker* goes by Webster— so however you corrected the hyphenated, or non-hyphenated words is quite all right.

The only change I'd like to make is to italicize the small words at the left-hand side of 12 O'CLOCK NEWS. The same size type—but in italics. I think they'd look more unobtrusive and possibly more mysterious.

Howard Moss told me to address this to you. I'll be leaving here the 29th, probably—at any rate, I expect to be back at 60 Brattle Street, Cambridge, on September first, so any further communications—(or checks)—can be sent to me there. Thank you.

Sincerely yours,

Elizabeth Bishop

Forgive this erratic typing; my good machine broke down.

July 18, 1972

Dear Miss Bishop:

Thank you for the proofs of POEM and 12 O'CLOCK NEWS, which arrived today. I'm very sorry to say that we didn't get the proof of THE MOOSE until too late to make the changes. The poem was already in the magazine. Howard is still in the vicinity, has seen your proof, and will write you at greater length.

Sincerely,

Robert Henderson[1]

---

1 Henderson wrote this note at Moss's request. Moss knew Bishop would be upset and wrote in a memo: "I *will* answer her long letter from here, and explain that the proof came too late. But *please* file it with her check. It may be valuable when she puts her next book together. It might even be sent to Robert Giroux after telephoning him, at Farrar, Straus & Giroux. But all that's really necessary is a) to hold on to it in her file b) for Bob [Henderson] to write her a short note saying it came too late, and c) my explaining further and more personally that it was too bad, etc. and that her check *and* proof are being held at the office" (Moss to Nancy [Novogrod], July 16, 1972, *The New Yorker* Records).

Dear Howard:

John Brinnin tells me that you are going to the MacDowell Colony—perhaps you are already there?—but I'll send this to your New York address & trust it will reach you. I hope you had a good summer and that you are getting lots of work done at MacDowell, or wherever you may be. I wonder if you ever got that letter of corrections for THE MOOSE that I sent you from Brazil? It arrived too late to be used—if you ever did get it—but most of the changes weren't very important and whoever edited the thing finally did NOT use all the changes that had disturbed me on the proof. So all's well that ends well as I suppose Marxists say—[1]

I don't know to whom I should address this letter, really, except that I don't think it's you. I want to make a complaint. Perhaps you can hand it along?

You must have seen the September 16th number of *The New Yorker*. My poem NIGHT CITY appears on page 122, that is, just as far back as it could be put. I'm vain enough to think it's better than the other two poems in that issue. I'm not sure whether it was wounded pride or simple bafflement when I found it relegated to the back pages—the first time that this has happened to me, I think, in the more than thirty years I've been appearing in *The New Yorker*.[2]

I hope they do better by the other two poems they now have on hand—if not, I'll just start sending work to other magazines. I don't want to scold *you*—you may have absolutely nothing to do with make-up—but I think I should really register disapproval somehow.[3]

I've just seen a charming little poem by May Swenson at the back of this week's issue—so I'm not the only one![4]

---

1 Although "The Moose" ran without any of the suggested changes on the author's proof, it did not run as Bishop had submitted it. It ran as Moss had edited it before it was set in the author's proof. Bishop kept all of his changes except in the penultimate stanza. She changed "rolling his R's" back to "rolling his r's" when she put it in *Geography III*. Bishop made additional changes before printing the poem in *Geography III*. She changed the lines in stanza seven to: "The light / grows richer; the fog, / shifting,". She changed the lines in stanza nine to: "to their wet white string / on the whitewashed fences; / bumblebees creep / inside foxgloves, / and evening commences." She returned the lines in stanza eleven and twenty-two to how she originally submitted them. She kept the lines in stanza thirteen as she sent them in July. She also put "Red Sea" in lowercase.

2 The other poems were Anne Sexton's "The One-Legged Man" and John Updike's "Insomnia the Gem of the Ocean." "Chemin de Fer" and "Trouvée" were also printed in the back of the book.

3 Enclosing copies of paragraphs two, three, and four of Bishop's letter, Moss told Henderson, "Make-up should be told not to publish her B of B again—it would be silly to risk losing her" (Moss to Henderson, October 7, 1972, *The New Yorker* Records).

4 "September Things" (September 30, 1972).

Do you know how Jean Stafford is? I heard she was in the hospital and I'd like to know if it's true & which one, etc. if you know.

I envy you your year off—I really don't have to work too hard, I suppose, but the beginning is always trying—and today I have to finish reading and judging about 40 sets of poems, oh dear . . .

With love,
Elizabeth

The MacDowell Colony
Peterborough, Massachusetts
October 8, 1972

Dear Elizabeth,

Your letter finally reached me here yesterday, and, of course, I did see the poem and was puzzled and displeased and apprehensive. But I haven't been near the magazine since the end of June and so I'm out of things. I have sent the relevant paragraphs of your letter off to Bob Henderson at the office and it will never happen again. I know (I think) what *did* happen: Poems that are one-column wide are sometimes slipped by Make-Up into the back of the book at the last minute, and since I tried to obliterate the distinction between front and back (in the good cause of being able to publish more poems), they have taken me literally, without weighing each instance or being able to know, it seems, that poems of yours, even if they're only a nailfile wide, don't go in the back of the book. I *am* sorry, and if I were there it wouldn't have happened. But I *do* have to take some time off and I had no idea they'd do something so silly.

I keep thinking of coming into Cambridge and/or Boston—certainly I'll have to get away from here sooner or later, sooner, I think, and I hope to see you. As a matter of fact, [poet] Robert Mazzocco and I have vague plans to meet in Cambridge *and* see you—we just haven't told you. Would that be something you'd like? Or would it be just more poetry added to poetry?

Here, everything's autumnal and nice but regimented. When I hear the bell strike for breakfast at 7:30, I ask myself: What are you *doing* here? But I work all day in my studio, the people are nice (as an old song says), though hardly electrifying, and I write facing a big window framing two absolutely beautiful birch trees that go way up into the sky. Around them, it's all gold and red with green at the edges. The trouble is that sometimes I just keep staring . . . My lunch just arrived in a basket. Ugh!

Love,
Howard

P.S. I'm reading Christopher Ricks's book on Tennyson.[1] I had no idea his life was so awful! Do you know a poet who had a, more or less, *happy* life? Wallace Stevens—rushing from one insurance agency meeting to another? Laforgue? Larbaud, with all that money?

October 1972
[postcard]

Dear Howard: Thank you so much for yr. letter & card. I think you will have received my permission for that story—but—do you really think it's any good? I'd like to write you a letter but I am "working"—I mean working, not for pleasure but for $$$$$ . . . But I hope I'll be seeing you in Duxbury on the 5th of November. Love, Elizabeth

[Handwritten: "I'm determined to conquer this new machine, but haven't yet . . ."]

[n.d.]

[card: "Harvard Yard in Snow (detail)" by Chiang Yee]

Dear Howard: I thought I gave up Christmas cards long ago, but this does seem like a good time to send you love & best wishes for another year.—It looks much worse here than *this*—I am homesick for my back-yard in Brazil—just to sit in the *sun* & watch the mustard-greens grow & accept the blessings of the passing beggars (one is supposed to say "Amen", not "Thank-you", but I find it hard to).

Another complaint, too—it is *over* 6 months since *12 O'Clock News* was accepted . . . But I haven't yet seen the last N.Y. . . .

I hope to see you in January sometime—

With love,
Elizabeth

October 17, 1973

Dear Howard:

I went to Dartmouth College last Thursday to give a reading (not exactly a wow, I'm afraid) and in the afternoon they had something called a "conver-

---

1 *Tennyson* (1972).

sation" in the library, or a library.—But maybe you've been there and done all this, too? People asked questions; Dick E. [Eberhart] rather annoyed me by saying from time to time "Now, when you and I began to teach, Elizabeth, almost forty years ago . . ." and so on; one militant young lady asked me if I feel like a—guess what—*woman*—(*of all things!*), when I write poetry, etc. etc. . . . And there was once nice older professor there, a Mr. Laing, who had a magazine with him and asked me if I'd seen it and when I said I hadn't he proceeded to read some sentences from it. They were from an interview with you, by a girl, I think, I don't know who, and you said some extremely kind things about me.[1] Although I blushed modestly, I hope, I was delighted—a compliment couldn't have come at a better moment, honestly—my heart was sinking. And after the far-from-wow reading the same Mr. Laing was at Dick E.'s and spoke of it again . . . It has cheered me up immensely and I am very touched—in fact I think I got a bit weepy at the "conversation" but I was against the light so probably no one noticed. I've tried to find the magazine here—I'd know it if I saw it—in fact, in the past I *have* seen it—the *"NY"* something-or-other, isn't it?—but I've been looking for it since I've been back and can't find it. Please do let me know soon what it is and what issue so I can get a copy, and maybe frame that page to hang at the foot of my bed . . . That was awfully nice of you, Howard, and thank you very much.

I'm not teaching this term, thank heavens, although I suppose I should be—I begin in February. I'm trying to get ready to move—that means get floors laid and bookcases built in my "condominium" down on Lewis Wharf, in Boston—I can't remember whether I knew about this when I last saw you or not—it's been dragging on for a long, long time. Anyway, if ever I do get there, it will be wonderful, I think—a marvelous old warehouse building and a view of the harbor & up the Mystic River.

Cal [Robert Lowell] is here, living in Brookline with his wife [Caroline Blackwood], infant son, and the wife's youngest daughter, and teaching away . . . From what he tells me of his classes I discover that my best pupils are now handing in their poems—the ones I know by heart, almost—all over again, to him . . . I think they think if they can only manage to take the course enough times, *some* poet is going to like the poems. However—John Peech and Anne Hussey—two of my pets—have both made good impressions and have written pretty good new poems—you may be seeing some of them. Or

1 Moss was asked which poets he reads for pleasure. "The two contemporary poets I read with the greatest pleasure are Elizabeth Bishop and James Merrill [. . .] I've read Elizabeth's poems a million times." "Craft Interview with Howard Moss," *New York Quarterly* (Summer 1973).

did you get the fearful backlog used up?[1] You wrote me such a good letter from Yaddo—now I'm afraid I won't have another such nice long letter for years to come . . . I'd like to know how you are, however, and what all you did during your leave of absence.

Jean Stafford was here last week-end—but I saw her only briefly at Peter Taylor's—also here for a term. We go round & round in a little social circle with occasional forays.—The *Paz*-es are here, too, and I am very fond of both of *them*. He & I are so tired of getting bad books and being asked to translate, etc., that we are going to start a Poets' Lib Movement—want to join?

Thank you again, dear Howard—I am really overcome by the quotes I only *heard* from your interview and I *must* see all of it with my own eyes.

Lots of love,
Elizabeth

December 14, 1973

Dear Howard:

I have had so many interruptions in trying to get the Marianne Moore piece copied out and revised a bit for you . . . I am still hoping to get it to you before I leave for Brazil, on Christmas day, but I don't know if I'll be able to or not.[2]

In the meantime, here is a short, sad poem that *maybe* you'll like ["Five Flights Up"]. Since I usually write poems in threes, I hope it means, at least, there'll be some more soon.

I didn't like Mr. M's piece on you too well—I thought he ignored some very important things about your poetry—one being your absolutely lovely ear, and the fact that you are one of our few melodious-*if*-modern poets . . . John lent me the Poets' Stories and I have read most of them now. Heavens, but they are grim, aren't they—I do like the Schuyler one, *very* much—[3]

1 With 130 poems on the bank, Moss called a moratorium on new poems while he was on his year's leave of absence.

2 Moss received "Efforts of Affection: A Memoir of Marianne Moore" after Bishop's death and rejected it. "I was disappointed in it," Moss said. "I thought it wasn't really Elizabeth's top prose. There was a struggle going on there. The struggle was still there after she was dead. It wasn't what I read Elizabeth for." In Gary Fountain and Peter Brazeau, *Remembering Elizabeth Bishop: An Oral Biography* (1994). The essay was published in the June 1983 issue of *Vanity Fair*.

3 Bishop is probably referring to Robert Mazzocco's review of Moss's *Selected Poems*, "Very Different Cats," in *The New York Review of Books* (December 13, 1973) and to James Schuyler's story "Life, Death, and Other Dreams."

I'll be at the Cos Club for 3 nights before the 25th—perhaps we can at least talk on the telephone, if you will be in town then.

With lots of love,

Elizabeth

P.S. Could you send me a copy of POET'S STORY? F, S & G has written me that because I said I didn't want any more anthologies some time ago (no more room) it is impossible for them to get a copy for me . . . No hurry, & perhaps it had better go to Kirkland House—packages here sometimes get stolen.

PAGE TWO

Another postscript—& forgive the tattered envelope—that was my last stamp, that's why . . .

I have just learned that ESQUIRE wants me to see a French photographer who has made a set of "spectacular" photographs of Brazil. That is, they want me to see his photographs—he's in the vicinity, I gather—and then to write some "impressions" of them, sort of captions, not more than 1,000 words all together. Since I have masses of Brazilian material and probably several 100 pages of my long-procrastinated book on Brazil on hand, this should be fairly easy, I think, and, I hope, profitable—but I wonder if THE NEW YORKER would object? I don't think that a set of captions would interfere with any work I might want to send THE NEW YORKER when the book, or some chapters of it, are publishable—but I certainly am duty bound to ask first. Since I need all the money I can make these days, for laying floors, building bookcases, and moving from South America—I hope the magazine will agree?

Of course, if I don't like the photographs, I won't do it anyway . . . Thank you for your help—

E.

The New Yorker
December 18, 1973

Dear Elizabeth,

A quick note to say that there would be no conflict in regard to the Brazilian text for the photographs and a *New Yorker* piece. I called Mr. Shawn and he just called back. Will write again later this week and hope to see you when you're in town for Christmas.

Love,

Howard

January 4, 1974

Dear Elizabeth,

You're probably in Brazil at the moment, but you do have to have *some* mail to come back to, and this is a note to say we're delighted with FIVE FLIGHTS UP, and you should have a proof and a check shortly. I assume you've already received that tiny previous note saying Mr. Shawn thought there was no conflict with the *Esquire* French photographer project.

I'd love to read the Brazil piece.

I wish I'd called you when you were here at the Cos Club, but your letter was attached to the ms. of FIVE FLIGHTS UP, and I forgot to write a note to myself. In all the Christmas brouhaha, I forgot a lot of things. Anyway, a belated merry Christmas, and most certainly a happy new year.

I'll try to get a copy of POET'S STORY to you. But a copy *was* sent to F, S & G for you. What did they do with it? They don't have to *get* a copy; they've *got* one.

Yes, the stories were rather grim. I'd like to do another anthology of cheery poems by short story writers. It would probably be the saddest little package imaginable.

I hope you're not giving up the ping-pong table in the new apartment. One of my dreams of glory is to return to Cambridge, and beat everyone.

Love,
Howard

P.S. Here is your check.

January 25, 1974

Dear Elizabeth,

Here's the author's proof of FIVE FLIGHTS UP and it is miraculously free of the usual six hundred "suggestions." We'd like it back, as soon as it's convenient.[1]

And I hope you've recovered and are out of Stillman [Infirmary] (though, from what I hear, it sounds like one of the best places to be). The day after I spoke to you, I came down with the second act of my cold, which is a sort of permanent wash and dry machine, with very little emphasis on the dry, and it goes on and on and on. I make another foray this afternoon to the doctor's.

---

1 Moss removed the colon at the end of stanza two, line one and inserted a semicolon. At the end of stanza two, line three, he changed the semicolon to a comma. In stanza three, line two, he changed the colon after "stern" to a comma and took line three out of italics (*The New Yorker* Records and Vassar College Library).

I'd love to see the new poem you mentioned, or any, and I'm delighted to have this one. Thanks again, stay well, and I hope we'll see each other soon, inside or outside of an infirmary.

Love,
Howard

March 26, 1974

Dear Howard:

I spoke to you some time ago about sending some translations of Octavio Paz & you said, I think, that you'd like to see them . . . He picked a group of four or five short ones I've been working on—they haven't been translated before—In the meantime, however, he was asked to write a poem for a book on Joseph Cornell (the Paz-es were very fond of him and have some of his work, etc.) to be published by Viking—I'm not sure when, but this year sometime.[1] My brains are disintegrating so fast here at dear old Harvard that I don't remember whether I told you all this before or not . . . Anyway, here is my translation of his poem—he has approved it and has already written Dore Ashton or Viking making the change in stanza order, etc. I thought you'd better see it—as soon as I heard from him (yesterday)—I don't know whether you'll want to use it or not, but if by chance you *do* you could call Viking to learn the publication date of the Cornell book.

Since I broke my shoulder & couldn't go to Brazil for Christmas vacation as I'd planned—I'm going Friday for one week—the "spring break." But I'll be back by the 10th of April. I'm hoping to see you on *some* of the various trips I have to make to NY this spring—Forgive a quite sparkle-less note!— It's 7:30 in the morning & I have *Income Tax* next . . .

With love,
Elizabeth

Jenny Colon—*I* didn't know, but maybe you do?—was Nerval's love. I'll be sending the other translations when I get back, & a couple of my own poems I hope.

---

1 Dore Ashton, *A Joseph Cornell Album* (1974).

Dear Elizabeth,

The Paz translation ["Objects and Apparitions"] is beautiful and we're taking it. It took me two weeks to straighten the whole thing out with Viking who weren't quite sure when the Cornell book was due to appear. It's now coming out in November.

I'm having half of the check made out to Paz and half to you. Is that ok? That's what we've been doing with other translations. The government, unfortunately, will take a slice out of Paz's check even before he gets it—it has to do with international tax agreements or the lack of them—but then, of course, it takes a slice out of all of us eventually. I don't pass that on as a profundity.

I'd love to see other Paz translations, and, of course, poems of yours. I hope there will be new ones soon. And I look forward to seeing you this spring. In fact, maybe the night of the reading at the New School. I'm not sure of the date but will call Danny Halpern today.[1]

Love,
Howard

April 30, 1974

Dear Elizabeth,

Here's a check for the Paz poem minus the payment we're making to him. Unfortunately, that only adds up to $92.92 because the U.S. government makes us take out 30% withholding. Mexico doesn't have a tax agreement with us. I hope this half and half arrangement is ok with you. If not, please let me know. I'm sending his check to his Mexican address.

It was lovely seeing you and Alice on Sunday and being assistant cook in various ways. Though as far as the gravy goes, I think Alice and I were equals. (Equally culpable, I mean.)

Love,
Howard

May 7, 1974

Dear Elizabeth,

Here's the author's proof of OBJECTS & APPARITIONS with our

---

1 Halpern is a poet and the editorial director of Ecco Press at HarperCollins.

usual fussy details, some puzzling, some routine. We can't find "hexadron" in either Webster 2nd or 3rd, for instance, and Jenny Colon turns out to be Jenny Colonne, which is an improvement, I would think, at least from her point of view.

If the source of the Degas comes to mind that would be a help to the checkers—or even a guess as to where you saw it. The Hotel is called "Grand Hotel de la Couronne" without the "The" but one could always leave the article out of the title—we prefer roman and quotes here to italics, but as you say.[1]

I'm sorry you won't be at the *New Yorker* poetry festival in the park, but I understand very well that it would put more pressure on a tight schedule. Again, it was lovely to have that day with you and Alice. I hope for another soon.

Love,
    Howard

June 7, 1974

Dear Howard:

I'm going to make use of this sturdy New Yorker envelope (already stamped) to write you a note. I have wondered, over the years (& especially in Brasil) if that RUSH! has any effect on the Post Office Department? It has struck me as increasingly pathetic—

I forgot to say when I last saw you—no, I think it was the time before the last time I saw you—how much I had liked "At the Masseur's".[2] Not only as *poetry*—Sometime I hope you'll tell me if it is all true, and if you think it would benefit—massage—my many broken and aching bones? I had one massage, once, that I could endure—any other attempts, in hospitals, etc.— have driven me crazy—

I also wanted to tell you how impressed I was with you at the Institute meeting and how sorry I was to be late. You handled it all so well—and it was nice the way us poets agreed so promptly, I think, about our contemporaries. (I heard for the first time the hideous expression "peer pressure." Have you heard that before?)

Well—later today Alice and I are driving, gratefully, to Duxbury. If I don't have to get back to Lewis Wharf to supervise the staining, etc., of my

---

1 "Hexadrons" ran as "hexagons". It was later changed to "Hexahedrons" for *Geography III*. The name of the hotel ran without "The."

2 April 22, 1974.

new-old floorboards, I hope to stay there until Thursday, to try to get some work done. Alice comes back Sunday—graduation is the 13th, & she may take her parents down for two days after that. But otherwise I'll be there, I hope—and please do call, *and* come by—I can't remember when you planned your Provincetown trip. A & I also thought we might take the Provincetown boat from Boston some day—call on the Strands, etc.—but when will *you* be there?

    Love,
      Elizabeth

Sabine Farm
North Haven, Maine
July 18, 1974
(until July 30th—)

Dear Howard:

    I'm not sure whether your magazine has declared another moratorium on poetry or not—I rather think it has. But I'll send this along, anyway ["The End of March"]. It's my version of The Lake Isle of Innisfree. (And Dickey would say it is too contrived for words, probably . . .) I was hoping to see you in Duxbury one of the days I was working on it, or earlier, or later—but you didn't appear.

    The SABINE FARM is absolutely beautiful—I've never had such luck with a summer rental before—it is almost too good—magnificent views, all high-brow books in 1st editions, fire-wood, lobsters, even our own row-boat and, this afternoon, a sailing dinghy . . . John [Brinnin] and Bill [Read] are expected Sunday—if John's mother is all right. North Haven is a haven for the *very* rich, mostly, but somehow we have infiltrated. We brought bags and bags of groceries from a supermarket with us—probably we shall be socially ostracized if we don't buy *some* supplies, soon, from the one general store where everything costs at least 33% more than on the mainland . . .

    I hope you're enjoying your holidays on Long Island—I should know your address there but I don't seem to have it with me. I'm sending you the poem in carbon copy because I also forgot to bring along a new typewriter ribbon—

    With love,
      Elizabeth

August 5, 1974

Dear Miss Bishop:

THE END OF MARCH seems to us a fine poem, and we are taking it, very gratefully. (Howard is away, as perhaps you know, and forwarded it to me.) I am, I'm afraid, duty bound to mention a matter of policy, leaving the decision up to you. Our present custom is to avoid dedications except in the case of major figures—statesmen, for instance, or people of some especially large accomplishment—when the poem would substantially lose meaning without the name. It was a pleasure to me to see John Brinnin's and Bill Read's names, there, but they don't, as individuals, affect the meaning of the poem to most readers.[1] John's being a frequent contributor makes the reference somewhat intramural, and the unidentified "we" is a common device. But—having said all this—we will leave the dedication or lack of it entirely to you. I merely thought, and Mr. Shawn thought, that we might at least mention it. If you do decide to drop the names, I think the inclusion of Duxbury, in title or subtitle, would be useful. In any event, thank you once more for the poem.

Sincerely,

Robert Henderson

437 Lewis Wharf
Boston, Massachusetts
August 15, 1974

Dear Mr. Henderson:

I am very glad you like THE END OF MARCH. I know about the policy on dedications—and I've withdrawn one or two, and once, only, insisted on including one because it seemed like part of the poem . . . This time, if there isn't too much objection to it, I'd like to insist again and include the names . . . (even if they aren't statesmen). The poem is really a thank-you letter for their great hospitality to me (the "we" is actually someone else . . .) and they seemed very pleased with it and pleased that you'd liked it. (They were here for dinner two nights ago and we discussed this.) So—unless there is a great deal of objection—I'd really like to put in the names. If I had a book coming out soon I could save them until then—but the prospects of a book are rather remote right now and so I'd rather not wait.

---

1 Bill Read was John Brinnin's partner.

I'm in the process of moving, which explains the mixed paper—I can't uncover anything else today—and you'll see my new address at the top.

Sincerely yours,

Elizabeth Bishop

Dear Miss Bishop:

Thank you for your letter. No, the objections aren't that substantial, and we'll keep the dedication.

Best wishes,

Robert Henderson

September 24, 1974

Dear Elizabeth,

Here's the author's proof of THE END OF MARCH, and I think all the problems are fairly routine, with the exception of the sub-title, where Mr. Shawn objects to the period followed by "Duxbury"—possibly misread as a mistaken dedication, or part of Bill's name, especially to people who haven't the faintest idea where or what Duxbury is. I think a better idea than putting "Duxbury" first is to transfer it to the title, which would read "The End of March, Duxbury"—at least that makes more sense to me.[1]

In stanza 3, the proof readers say the dashes aren't coordinate, and suggest putting a comma after "green," taking out the dash before "a sort of," and leaving the dash before "are they railroad ties?" As you wish, of course.[2]

I'm delighted to have this poem for all the reasons you can imagine. I hope the new apartment is finished. I bought a house in East Hampton and so I have a faint idea of the terrible struggle. Do we have your new phone number? I'm not sure.

---

1 The poem was edited by Robert Henderson, who made no changes before it was set in proof.

2 Bishop submitted these lines as:

> set up on pilings, shingled green
> —a sort of artichoke of a house, but greener
> (boiled with bicarbonate of soda?),
> protected from the spring tides by palisades
> of—are they railroad ties?

(*The New Yorker* Records and Vassar College Library)

And forgive the businesslike tone of all this. I can hardly lift my head from my desk, or put it down, really, so high is the pile of manuscripts.

Love,

Howard

September 30, 1974

Dear Howard:

(If you see this) Yes, I think that putting DUXBURY in the title is much better—I forgot it isn't known the world over . . . I suppose Webster has it about the words "seabirds" and "offshore" & I really should get another dictionary besides the Oxford, which leads me into such variations, usually. The dash before "a sort of artichoke" etc. shd. also come out.* I like the comma after "icy", however, and have put one in after "far" in the next to last line of the third stanza.¹ It should have been "a palisade"—my mistake, I think. Everything else seems all right. I spent Saturday night & most of yesterday with the dedicatées (?) and I think they like it.

As you may know, Bill has been really very poorly, with an awful cough for some weeks. John finally got him to go to some sort of specialist and the x-rays showed that he has a hernia—I've forgotten the correct name for it— in the diaphragm. He's to see the specialist himself—who'd of course gone away for the week-end—today or tomorrow, so then we should know more exactly what kind it is and how serious . . . He's being very brave but I'm sure he feels miserable.

I've heard about your East Hampton house and I'd love to see it sometime. BUT—it is furnished, I gather, and luxurious, too.—Well, mine has touches of luxury mixed in with the usual shoddy contemporary construction—but it will be months before it is at all finished. I put in my own floors, shutters, and so on—and, worst of all, my "goods" have taken over five months to get here from Brazil—and even now are only on the high-seas, or so I hope . . . (omit hyphen no doubt)

This is a borrowed typewriter, both of mine having collapsed on the same day—this accounts for *some* of the bad typing. Take your flu shots and please keep well—Another poem soon, I hope.

With love,

Elizabeth

*with a comma after "green"—

1 Bishop is referring to "The rackety, icy, offshore wind" in stanza one, line six, and "even to get that far," in stanza three, second to last line.

Dear Howard:

John Peech has just been here to show me his last version of a poem now called *The Hardness of the Wind* (originally, I think, *Aspects of the Cannon* [*sic*]—)—I don't think I've ever drawn your attention to a particular poem before—but I really think this is an awfully good poem—and it gets better as it goes on—I know you get thousands of poems—I don't know how you can possibly read them all personally, or what the system is—but please don't miss this one! (It will probably take him 2 or 3 days to get it in the mail.) He has 2 or 3 more good ones, too—but this is the best I've seen for a long time by him—and I hope you'll agree with my opinion of it—

Classes have begun—how I hate to work—I have one extraordinary girl, however—1st in years, it seems to me—

Everyone I know feeling very saddened by Anne Sexton's death—oh dear, oh dear—I wish people would *stop* doing this . . .[1] And here at Lewis Wharf (where you must come sometime soon) it is a gorgeous fall day, high tide, and a huge freighter from London, named, improbably, the "Act III" has just gone by—

Love & best wishes—

　　Elizabeth

October 22, 1974

Dear Howard:

I'm afraid I'm being a nuisance—but I don't think I have done this kind of thing very often, have I? The last stanza of THE END OF MARCH never had pleased me, so this morning I've made some changes that I think improve it a lot. I hope you'll agree.

I don't think I ever told you that I was glad to see you got *something* out of Yaddo, apparently (with "Saratoga"?)—the beginning is certainly a different aspect to me of that place—but I haven't been there since 1950—and I think they have taken down the very last old hotel now, haven't they? Dear me—change & decay—and your poem about "Lower Fifth Avenue" certainly made me feel old . . .[2] Do you remember when dining at the Brevoort was a great treat?—and I used to stay at the—hm—just up the street, huge,

---

1 Sexton committed suicide on October 4.
2 "Saratoga" (August 19, 1974) and "Memories of Lower Fifth" (October 14, 1974).

nice rooms—now a hostel or a dormitory for delinquent women or some-
thing—oh, the Grosvenor!

    Well—more poems soon, I hope—if ONLY I didn't have to teach . . .

    With love,

        Elizabeth

P.S. John Brinnin mentioned the other day that *The New Yorker* has some
kind of investment fund for its contributors—I am vague about how it
works—never heard of it, in fact, but he said small amounts of money pile up
for him over the years. Do I get this, too?—or—what *is* it?

To replace the last stanza of THE END OF MARCH:

> On the way back our faces froze on the other side.
> The sun came out for just a minute.
> For just a minute, set in their bezels of sand,
> the dim, occasional stones
> were all of different colors,
> with all those high enough throwing out long shadows
> and, after a minute, pulling them in again.
> They could have been teasing the lion sun,
> except that now he was behind them
> —a sun who'd walked the beach the last low tide,
> making those big, majestic paw-prints,
> who perhaps had batted a kite out of the sky to play with.[1]

    Elizabeth Bishop—

---

1 Bishop had originally submitted the last stanza as:

> On the way back our faces froze on the other side.
> The sun came out for just a minute
> and for a minute the embedded stones
> showed what colors they were
> and all those high enough threw out long shadows,
> individual shadows, then pulled them in again.
> They could have been teasing the lion sun,
> except that now he was behind them
> —the sun who'd walked the beach the last low tide,
> who'd made those big, majestic paw-prints,
> who'd batted a kite out of the sky to play with.

October 24, 1974

Dear Elizabeth,

I think the changes in THE END OF MARCH are all splendid, and they are being put into proof. The ending is really much more beautiful this way and yet nothing essential is changed.

As for The New Yorker Participation Plan: at the age of sixty, one is no longer eligible to join it, and the people who *were* eligible drop out—it's the cutting off date. At the time *you* would have been eligible, which would have been in 1971, you were over sixty. You gave up your first-reading agreement in 1961, and then went back on it in 1968. If you'd stayed on, you would have been eligible in 1965 or 1966. But there's a consolation: the Plan is based on whatever is earned during a given period and what you are losing is benefits based on only the five or six years between 1966 and 1971. It's all as clear as mud to me, but I hope you at least, understand it. The one thing that *is* clear, after consulting the people here who do seem to understand it, is that you are not, alas, eligible for the Plan.

I hate to pass on this blunt news but it is not a loss, I assure you, of millions. Or thousands. Or even hundreds.

I hope new poems are simmering away. And thank you for your nice words on SARATOGA and FIFTH AVENUE.

Love,
Howard

March 8, 1975

Dear Howard:

This is a rather difficult kind of letter to write to a dear old friend . . . However, I am assuming that you'd really like to have my clavichord—and I can't think of anyone I'd rather have *have* it & there's also the chance that I may be able to see it again, occasionally, and even hear you play it . . . Well, I've been doing some research on the subject, because I really had no idea what the poor little thing is worth these days.

I ordered it from [Arnold] Dolmetsch—THE Dolmetsch—in 1934. It took him months & months to make it and entailed endless correspondence with Mrs. Dolmetsch, who did the painting in those days. I wanted it just like [Ralph] Kirkpatrick's (& it is) but she wanted to paint a motto, in gold, on the inside of the lid. I didn't want one, and she tried & tried to convince me, and sent many mottos, in Latin, Old French, etc. . . . (The white and rose one at Vassar said PLUS FAIT DOUCEUR QUE VIOLENCE, I remember . . .)

I was so poor I paid for it in installments, $25.00 a month—and it took me 14 months, I think—at least, it cost $350 then, with maybe more for the case; I've forgotten. Anyway, it finally arrived—in Paris. The case has now become a work of art, too, I think. (Octavio Paz said he liked the case better than the clavichord.) It's rather like a Harnett[1]—pasted all over with torn and faded labels from its worldwide travels.

I asked various musical friends—then I had the idea of talking to William Dowd—he's very famous here, makes harpsichords & occasionally clavichords, here and in Paris. He said what my two friends had said—that things have gone up 300% since 1934 and that a real Dolmetsch, by Arnold himself, should be worth $1,000. That's what he has been getting for *his* for some years, I gathered, and that their re-selling price doesn't change when he takes one back and re-sells it. He also suggested that you might like to speak to the New York harpsichord maker, Henry (??) *Hough* (you may even have got your harpsichord from him?). His telephone number is 741-0250. You could ask him what *he* thinks is a fair price. There's another Boston man, too—Hubbard—but I haven't been able to reach him.

My clavichord has been put into good condition at least three times over the years—maybe four. The last time was in 1969 or '70, in San Francisco—a harpsichord maker there whose name I can't remember—anyway—I paid him $100, I remember, and he did a beautiful job, all new strings, re-gluing, and so on. (It's undoubtedly very out of tune now, of course—especially the lower notes—but they're easy to tune.) There *is* a small crack in the sounding board—has been for years—but according to Bill Dowd, this makes no difference at all, unless it *buzzes*—& it doesn't do that.

Now if you *really* want it, I'll see about getting it sent over to you . . . I have a nice, rather hippy, young man who does carpentry, etc. for me and he told me yesterday that he and his wife would be driving to New York in a few weeks and would take it to you in their station wagon or truck or whatever it is . . . But maybe you know of someone going from here, too—even to Long Island instead of New York? (You can take the case & legs in a taxi, you know.)

I'll send along quite a lot of early keyboard music I have here, if you'd like—since I probably won't have any more use for it. One little book, if it turns up, had parts for alto recorder, etc.—Frani & I used to play together occasionally and that was fun—if you have friends who play another instrument that goes with a clavichord . . . There's a tuning fork, etc.—the only

1 The painter William Harnett was famous for his trompe l'oeil still lifes.

thing missing seems to be a green stick that propped the lid part-way open, to throw sound into the room or something—however, any wooden spoon would serve . . .

However, I'd feel better about the whole thing if you would consult Mr. Hough, too . . . It may seem like too much money. (Of course I'd gladly take three or four *installments* . . .) Anyway, let me know what you think—I simply have to sell it as soon as possible, because of lack of space, but I'd like you to have the first chance at it—

You *must* be about to get out a new book of poems . . . Heavens—I envy you. Now *I* work two days a week, too—why can't I write as many poems as you can—or even a quarter as many? I hope "The End of March" will appear the end of March—it came in like a lion here—and apparently will be going out the same way . . . I hope you haven't had this AWFUL flu—I've had it, endlessly, it seems—all my senses went, one after the other—today they seem to be creeping back—

With much love,
    Elizabeth

Sunday afternoon

Dear Howard:

Thank you very much for the check . . . I do hope you find the clavichord in good shape—I am sure it will be somewhat out of tune, especially the lower notes—but those you can probably tune yourself . . . Most piano tuners won't touch a clavichord—but undoubtedly Sylvia [Marlowe] would know of, or have, a tuner who will . . . (She brought her own along to Brazil.) And once tuned, it does stay in tune for a remarkably long time . . .

One of the long bolts on the case—I *think*—is missing—or maybe it was bolted & unbolted so many times one wore out—I've forgotten. Probably any "handy man"—like that Greg—could replace those long screws or bolts so that they would work better.—I hope Greg took along the music I had turned up—I really haven't checked—but if I find any more I'll certainly send it along, also one rather magnificent, if old, German book of keyboard music when *it* appears as I unpack my 40 cases of books here . . . You might as well have all the useful music I can find here.

No—the case isn't "The Monument"—It had begun to look more like a Harnett (?) to me . . . And who is your composer nephew? John Peech is giving a concert next week—an extremely difficult [Elliot] Carter—some Vila-Lobos—I've forgotten what all, although I certainly shouldn't have! Please do let me know if you *think* you're going to be in Boston—

    With love,
        Elizabeth

March 24, 1975
[postcard]

Dear Katharine & Andy: I hope you will forgive me for having been remiss about writing you for so many years . . . I certainly have not forgotten you, and I loved that piece about Maine in The New Yorker not so long ago.[1] I've been teaching—something I put off until old age—at Harvard since 1970 or '71—and it seems to take up all my time and energy—this is my only excuse.

    I shall be on North Haven Island this summer for the month of July—a *beautiful* place (c/o Pettit—I've rented one of their houses there.) I know that you are not in very good health, but I do hope that sometime while I'm there, or at the end of July, you will let me come to call on you, even if very briefly.

    With my affectionate greetings for Easter,
        Elizabeth Bishop

P.S. I make ALL my students MEMORIZE "Strunk & White" . . .

April 14, 1975

Dear Katharine:

    I was very pleased & touched to receive such a nice letter from you, after my shameful neglect. I started teaching in the fall of 1970, two seminars, for one term, and kept that up until this year when I am teaching *two* terms—and shall do so until 1977, I think it is . . . I don't like it very much, I'm afraid—although I do like some of the students a lot—but perhaps because I'm not a real teacher, I find it takes up almost all my time and I rarely get any writing done—even letters—except occasionally during vacations. However, I suppose compared to most jobs, it is really very agreeable . . .

---

1 White's most recent essay was "Letter from the East" (February 24, 1975).

Thank you for liking the Duxbury poem—I did have a much better last stanza that I forgot to send Howard until it was too late.[1] The "Duxbury Clipper"—the little weekly newspaper—wants to re-print the poem. I think that's rather nice.

I'd love to come to call on you and Andy and thank you for inviting me. Since I don't drive, I'll have to be toted by a friend—and probably it would be either just before July 1st, or just after July 31st, when I'm leaving—because once I get out to North Haven I'll probably stay put, to make the most of my month there. As soon as I know my plans more exactly, I'll let you know.

I hadn't read the Brendan Gill book but after your letter, and after similar stories from friends, I bought it on my way to New York last week, and read it going and coming back.[2] Some of it, that is—I don't think I'll ever read all of it and I regret the $12.75 or whatever it was! It's amazing it's on the Best Seller list—but I suppose that reflects more on the good reputation of *The New Yorker* than on the merits of the book—or maybe it is just due to the insatiable greed for gossip. Anyway—I concluded after observing a good many mistakes, repetitions (he tells some of the same stories twice), *awful* clichés, etc., etc.—that what the book really needed was a careful *New Yorker* editing. I never thought he could write that badly—& of course there are mistakes, I'm sure, that I don't know about. I'm going to sell it back tomorrow, I hope . . .

I haven't seen Andy Wanning for many years, but I do see Tom Wanning in New York from time to time & hear about the family.

I'm so sorry to hear about your back troubles. Well, I have other friends using "walkers", too, and I sometimes think they should also wear those padded ring-things on their heads that one sees in Breughel paintings, on the small children—so they won't get bumped and bruised. The brain is what matters most, after all, and I'm glad yours is "still with you" as you said, and as I'm sure it is. I have arthritis (like everyone else) but just the hands; so far my legs are holding out quite well! And it's not very bad—

---

1 Bishop revised lines five to eight:

> the drab, damp, scattered stones
> were multi-colored,
> and all those high enough threw out long shadows,
> individual shadows, then pulled them in again.

(Vassar College Library)

2 *Here at The New Yorker* (1975).

I love living here on the Wharf and right now I am looking out on high tide, a very sunny day at last, and two tankers with attendant tugs going by. (Of course they're almost always tankers.)

Please remember me to Andy and I'll let you know about my possible visit as soon as I can. I'd love to see the geese again—there are Canada Geese, hundreds of them, in Duxbury; they even come up and waddle across the lawn.

With love,
Elizabeth

May 20, 1975

Dear Elizabeth,

Here's a new first reading agreement I hope you'll want to sign, and since you know all the terms, I won't go into my uncertain song and dance.

I hope to see you tomorrow at the annual bash at the Institute, and, if not then, soon. More on the clavichord later—I mean money, too.

Love,
Howard

North Haven
July 22, 1975

Dear Howard:

I feel guilty about interrupting your summer—vacation or not, I don't know—with "business", but it has just occurred to me that there is something I should write you about . . . John & Bill are here—came yesterday, for a week—and they know your LI address—I didn't have it.

Well—Octavio Paz recently sent me a poem, my translation of which I'm enclosing ["January First"]. (This may not be its final form—I've sent it to him to see if he approves of it.) He intended it to be given to PLOUGH-SHARES magazine—a magazine I've only seen once, but apparently it varies greatly from number to number, depending on who is doing the editing that quarter. It's in Cambridge—or Boston. He is doing this just as a favor to the magazine and of course I was pleased to translate it for him. Then I thought of course I should show it to you first—I can't remember if the contract specifies translations or not . . . If it doesn't (I haven't it with me, naturally)—all well & good. If it does—perhaps you will release this translation—but if by some chance you *want* it—I can probably do another Paz translation that you *wouldn't* want (!) before September 1st, the deadline. So will you please let me know as soon as possible?

It is my idea of heaven here, and today, after days of Maine fog, is clear, warm, and the whole of Penobscot Bay is like a sheet of pale-blue milk—almost white—with a scattering of sloops & schooners, motionless, all dreaming of a breeze, one presumes . . . I hope you like where you are as much as I like where *I* am—

Love,
Elizabeth

—Here until the 31st of July—then Lewis Wharf—

30 Springwood Lane
East Hampton, New York
July 28, 1975

Dear Elizabeth,

I read JANUARY FIRST and talked to Shawn about it on the phone, and I think we'll let it go and hope for the opposite arrangement from the one suggested in your letter. That is, the next Paz (all the next ones) be sent to us and to let this one go. It is so specifically dated that we'd have to wait to run it until New Year's and since it's promised, and since I don't like it quite as much as that other wonderful one we published, I send it back, with thanks and in hope that you'll send along any new ones. I'll be back in harness right after Labor Day.

But I'm also teaching a poetry class at Barnard in the fall and at Columbia in the spring, and I'm beginning to get cold feet about both. What do you say? What do you do? I did two short story writing classes at Vassar but can hardly remember them, and took over workshops at Iowa, but all I can think of saying right now is "You sit down at your typewriter, take out your gun, and aim for the forehead." Not exactly the sort of thing Barnard's looking for. Any advice would be welcomed.

The house is lovely but also a mixed blessing—it takes an enormous amount of time to organize it all, gardens, furniture, gardeners, planks rotting on the deck, a pine tree with a white disease, rhododendrons longing for water. And so on. But I think I've got it in control now, and would love to have you come visit. I'm hoping J. & B. will arrive sometime in August—they've never seen it.

And Sabine Farm sounds heavenly—from your description and from

John's. What I miss here is being right on the water, and the very sloops, schooners, and bluish milk glass you mention. I'm in the trees and may trade it all for sand and sea.

John mentioned something about a story. I'd love to see *that*. And, of course, poems and poems. Love to all, and especially you,

Howard

The New Yorker
November 4, 1975

Dear Elizabeth,

ONE ART is fine—upsetting and sad, too. But everything in it is handled with such skill, feeling, and just the right amount of distance that it comes off marvellously. I'll be sending along a check and an author's proof shortly.

Please, *please* send more poems soon. My class *adored* "Little Exercise"— that's the right word—and were stunned by "At the Fishhouses." My brightest student is doing her term paper on you. You have 12 new fans.

Love,
Howard

December 1, 1975

Dear Elizabeth,

Here is the author's proof of ONE ART, a poem we're delighted to have.[1]

And I enjoyed David Kalstone's remarks about you in PLOUGH-SHARES.[2] I'm waiting for a "term" paper from one of my students on you, too. If it's halfway decent, I'll send it on.

And I'll send the rest of the clavichord money, too. Soon it will be all mine and if you come to New York, I'll play you something. Something easy.

Love,
Howard

---

1 Moss made three changes before the poem was set in proof. In line one, he replaced the colon after "master" with a semicolon. In line eleven, he added a comma after "next-to-last". In line seventeen, he removed the comma after the close-parentheses (*The New Yorker* Records and Vassar College Library).

2 "Questions of Memory—New Poems by Elizabeth Bishop" (Volume 2, Number 4, 1975).

Boston

December 7, 1975

Dear Howard:

I am so glad my poem has been cleared for libel . . .

I hope I've made my corrections—(changes rather, since the proof is actually correct—the way I sent the poem)—clear. I do think there should be at least as much space between the title and the first line as there is between the stanzas—if not a bit more. It looks squeezed the way it is now, don't you think? And, in print, I've decided the two words in italics in the last line are a bit too much, so I've indicated that *it* should be in regular type & only the word *Write* italicized.

(Jimmy M. can switch to italics, I understand, on his IBM, but my other choice is something else. Perhaps I shd. purchase an italic-ball, or whatever one calls them. (Delicate ground here.))

If there is time—I never can understand the clues at the top—before you intend printing this, I wonder if you'd be kind enough to send me a second proof so I can see if it really looks better the way I've decided it might?

Below freezing here this morning—oh dear oh dear—I'm so glad I'm going to Florida for a while on the 21st of the month. Keep well—

Love,
Elizabeth

January 5, 1976

Dear Elizabeth:

I just don't know what to say about the fact that the enclosed letter, which I dictated and read over, was never signed and mailed. My secretary, in a New Year cleanup, came across a large handsome folding writing board that I seldom use, and this August letter was folded up in that. All this time I had thought I had sent this letter and I have worried because I have not heard from you. I was already worrying when I wrote the letter, but the worst thing was that I seemed to think I had not written you something about your stopping here on your way back from the Island. My secretary tells me that I wrote this at a time when Andy's new young editor at Harper [& Row] (with the wonderful name of Corona Machemer) was visiting, and we were all three of us working on proofs of Andy's Letters book, and everything was scattered about. Since I can no longer type anything because of my spine, I have turned what used to be my office over to Isabel Russell, who is a very good secretary who gives us help three or more mornings a week. She says I am not to blame about the letter because we were in terrible confusion and anguish over the book at that time.

Corona wanted an enormous "apparatus" as part of the book and at that time Andy felt the best thing to do was to go along with her. Apparently she is Cass Canfield's new assistant. All was smooth at Harper with the book when Beulah Hagen, who is Glenway Wescott's sister, was Cass's assistant. She is now retired, as of last February, because of over-work, low pay, and age. Cass is so old he doesn't even go into the office any more, and since he is Andy's editor at Harper, his assistant is actually Andy's editor. After Beulah's retirement there was a total silence and nothing happened—no proofs or anything else for about four months.

Meanwhile, this fall I stopped everything on November 4th by waking up in the morning and being unable to breathe and then passing out. It was a matter of fluid collected around my heart and lungs, and it's a miracle my life was saved. The real name for the trouble is congestive heart failure. I think you will like to hear that it was the Volunteer Fire Dept. of Brooklin that really saved my life by getting here in five minutes and giving me oxygen until the ambulance arrived from Blue Hill. I remember nothing at all about the first thirty-six hours there, when I was in Intensive Care, but I soon bounced back from this and my heart seems to be O.K. The real miracle was that there was no damage to either my heart or brain, or so the doctors say. I think that the fact that I forgot to sign and mail your letter proves my brain *was* damaged!

We've had a bad fall season because after the heart business I had to have two teeth extracted, and they crumbled during the process and I had to have minor surgery on the jaw and this meant being on antibiotics for two weeks. The gap in the gums doesn't show but it has made eating difficult, and I am waiting for it to heal so I can get a partial plate and have better chewing power. This deterioration of teeth is due to the cortisone I have had to take for my weird dermatitis.

I do have considerable anxiety about you because I fear you got sick and never got to Maine, so I hope you'll just drop me a postcard to tell me how you are.

Ever so much love and my continued admiration.

Happy New Year. May 1976 prove better than it looks right now.

Affectionately,

Katharine

August 19, 1975
(dictated August *15*)

Dear Elizabeth:

I know I answered your letter of April 14, and here it now the 15th of August and I suddenly realized that you never did come to see us early in July. I thought of it at that time and expected to hear from you, but this has been a killing summer for us and I failed to write you saying how disappointed Andy and I were not to see you. He was all prepared to pick you up wherever you wanted to be met, either on your way to the island or when you came off.

I am writing now just to ask whether you are all right. Perhaps you never came to Maine and perhaps you are sick. This is what is on my mind and I would appreciate just a postcard to tell me that you aren't sick but just failed to make it to Blue Hill and Brooklin.

It's been the worst summer for weather I have ever known in Maine, and both of us have suffered in health because of it, and perhaps also because of other things. My son Roger Angell and his family were here all of July in a rented cottage and that was very nice. This month has been bad for Andy; he is not well and he is at this very moment struggling on footnotes, etc. on his book of Letters. At this point he would like to abandon the book entirely but unfortunately he can't because he has an editor and co-worker on the book—Dorothy Lobrano Guth. She was marvelous at collecting the letters but there are about twice too many, and the book is still having to be pared down to reasonable size. When it gets that way I am not sure at all what will develop because of the apparatus. Andy refuses to write the introductory notes because he finds it difficult to speak of himself in the third person, but he will help give the facts, and we fear that the apparatus may overwhelm this collection of very personal and almost totally unliterary letters.

Anyway, I missed you and I'm sorry, but I hope you are back at the Wharf and are going to teach at Harvard again.

Affectionately,

Katharine (signed Jan 5, 1976)

P.S. My difficulty about not knowing why you didn't turn up is because I don't keep carbon copies of my personal letters—and I should, especially when they involve arrangements with someone. I have the awful feeling that there was something I was supposed to do in the way of communicating with you that I didn't come through with, and that this is why I didn't hear from you. If this is so, do please forgive me and tell me what I did say, that I failed to follow through on. I am hoping that you just didn't have time to get here or didn't feel like it when the time came. K.S.W.

Ft. Meyers Beach, Florida
January 16, 1976

Dear Katharine:

Your two letters, of August 19th and January 5th, were forwarded and reached me here yesterday . . . I am so sorry to learn you have been having such a tough time and I think *I* am the one who should explain—and apologize—about not writing, not you at all . . . I'll begin with that:

I did get to North Haven, for the month of July this time, and all the time I was there I thought of ways of getting over to see you and Andy, but somehow I could never work it out . . . I don't drive, have no car, and so was entirely dependent on my guests—who came for week-ends, mostly—and always had to get right back to Boston or other points south. One friend stayed two weeks with me, but she, too, doesn't drive—we merely took bicycle rides every day to the town dump and back . . . I had hoped somehow to combine a trip to North Brooklin with a trip to Nova Scotia, to see my one remaining aunt (age 86) but hard as I studied bus schedules, ferry schedules, etc., I could never work it out. And of course I should have written you all this, long ago—while I was on North Haven, to be exact. It is stupid of me never to have learned to drive—I was afraid to in Brazil and probably now I'll never learn . . . I adore North Haven—the nicest place I have found in the USA, I think—but it was a very hot July for there—I even went swimming a few times, unheard of before. No—I was very well up there and worked very hard—but none of this is any excuse for my not having written to you. And again—when I left—the "ride" I got back was with a friend who had to get right back to Boston . . .

I feel miserable about your illness and thank heavens for the Brooklin Fire Department . . . I *feel* for you about the teeth, too—I went through almost the same thing a few years back. And while here, *four* caps fell out, making me look like a retired lady-boxer for a while. Fortunately, the friends I'm visiting have a nice young dentist who stuck them back in again better than before, I think and was also much more encouraging about my dental future than my famous Boston dentist has been lately!

I am still teaching two seminars at Harvard—this next one and one more year to go, and I think I'll be through—at least, that will make ten terms in all and then I'll be eligible for their "medical benefits"—which of course are extremely important. This last term I was lucky—had almost all very good students, one class really exceptionally bright—I'm correcting their term papers now and can't believe my eyes . . . I also can't believe I'll ever be so lucky again.

I am delighted to hear about Andy's letters—and of course can scarcely wait to read the book. (I use him often as an *example* in my spring prose-writing course—and as I said before, I think—I *force* the students all to buy STRUNK & WHITE—even give it to them if they say they can't afford to buy it.) How I wish I had a secretary named Corona!—but one by any name would help a lot, and this coming year—or fall—I'm going to try to hire a student-one, at least. As it is, I never seem to write anything but postcards any more.

I took off from Boston in a blizzard—the airport was officially closed for three days and I didn't dream I'd get away, but they called me with 45 minutes to spare and said *my* plane might get off—and it did. But this explains this typing paper—all the local drugstore provides—I packed in such a hurry many things got left out—including writing-paper—

I am having a poem in your magazine fairly soon, I think—the one and only villanelle of my life. It is very SAD—it makes everyone weep, so I think it must be rather good, in its awful way, and I hope you will like it. Adrienne Foulke telephoned a New York friend of mine about it—I have only met Adrienne once, I think, and I have no idea what she does on *The New Yorker*, but she seems awfully nice . . .[1]

I do hope you are both getting along as well as you possibly can. In late October or so it will be time for me to visit my Canadian aunt again—and again I'll try to work out some way of getting there by way of North Brooklin, Maine. Oh—in the guest house where I am staying there is a copy of Jean Stafford's *Collected Stories* and last night I read it all, right straight through until 4 AM—I knew some of them, but some I hadn't seen before—and what a good writer she is—especially, I think, the "middle period"—I wish she'd do more stories.[2] I was very pleased to see that the book is dedicated to you. I have recently got to know, in Boston, Penelope Mortimer, who is teaching at Boston University this year. I have liked some of her stories very much, too—better than the last novel, I think.[3]

---

1 Foulke was a copy editor at the magazine.
2 *The Collected Stories of Jean Stafford* (1969).
3 Mortimer's most recent novel was *Long Distance* (1974). Her stories regularly appeared in *The New Yorker*.

I MUST get to work on the remaining term papers. Thank you so much for your letter(s) and please don't think for a minute that this requires an answer. I just send you both my love and my very best wishes—

Elizabeth

Boston

March 5, 1976

Dear Howard:

First, this is to invite you to dinner on the 18th . . . about seven o'clock? Penelope, of course (who just failed to get off to England by *daylight*, because of the fog here), and I don't know who else yet . . .

Second, to thank "The New Yorker"—(I don't know whom I should really be thanking, but perhaps you can convey my thanks to whomever responsible) for the beautiful flowers I found at my door when I came back from New York last Saturday.[1] It really was one of the prettiest assortments of "spring flowers" I've ever seen, and there were all those I like especially— anemones, white tulips, freesias, etc. The freesias and little poppies are still holding up very well—after almost a week.

Last night I read at the "St. Botolph" Club here—a 99 yr. old Boston Establishment place—I didn't expect to have a good time but I *did*, after all, everyone very talkative and almost too poetry-loving. John was there and brought me home later. My last hour in New York I fell down and tore a ligament in my foot—I have no idea how; I was walking with a man on either side of me, & it was all over in a second, they caught me up so quickly—but by the time I got to Boston I knew something was wrong. So I went to the reading with a wheel-chair and crutches. I just realized this morning that I didn't *explain* to the audience—just a few people I knew or met—& probably the audience in general thinks I'm a cripple and wonder how I did some of the things I say I did in those poems . . . oh dear!

I'll be all over it before the 18th—and it would be nice to see you at greater length than I could in New York—

With love,

Elizabeth

---

1 Bishop had received the *Books Abroad*/Neustadt International Prize for Literature.

Dear Howard:

Before I go to the corner to get the Sunday papers I want to write you a short note. I woke up thinking about you, for one thing! & you have been on my mind, maybe my conscience, since a week ago . . . But first—thank you for A SWIM OFF THE ROCKS.[1] You really do have the gift for "light verse", of which there should be much more in the world, I think. Some of my favorites are in this book—"Lennie"—one of my *very* favorite of your poems—rather, "Small Elegy" I think it's called; "Geography"—the 1st two of the "Double Dactyls" . . . (Not that I think ED is sacred—I think the 1st two come off best).[2] I read quite a few of the poems to my "Advanced Verse Writing Class"—a very smart class, this time, and they appreciated them very much . . . It was the day after the election, so then we all wrote a "light verse" poem about *that* for half an hour. Those who did do it "lightly" turned out very well.—I have two really witty boys, & if I had their efforts here (one obscene) I'd quote them for you . . .

I'm sorry I won't be able to get to the party for you on the 3rd. There was a point at which Penelope and I thought we'd go together, although I knew I shouldn't—and then she decided quite suddenly to go to England, Thursday, to see "Kate", the new grandchild—but you probably know this. I'd love to be there, but I have been sick a lot lately—1st teeth, then asthma—and I have a great deal of work to catch up with—and also shouldn't spend the money. But—and this brings me to the theme of my letter—

John told me, last Sunday, I think it was, about your treatment at the hands or pen of that incredible Miss (or Mrs.?) Estess . . . SYBYL SIBYL—(I can't think how to spell it.) Whoever she is, she must be quite mad. "Editing"! I think you did the only possible thing—withdraw your paper.[3] I know nothing about her—or knew nothing about her—until she 1st wrote to me, early last spring, and sent me a paper she'd written on me—maybe it was a thesis or part of one, I don't know. She said she had sold it to the Southern Review. It was so AWFUL I couldn't believe it—full of mistakes, factual and grammatical, & quotes from people I'd never heard of who were equally mistaken about me & everything else. I wrote her a very severe letter, correcting all the mistakes, and I also wrote to the editor of the SR [Donald

1 *A Swim Off the Rocks* (1976).

2 Moss's "Three Double Dactyls" were on Sergei Rachmaninoff, Sergei Diaghilev, and Emily Dickinson.

3 Moss was to give a talk on being Bishop's editor at the Modern Language Association annual convention in New York.

Stanford] (a friend from college days)—Later by chance I met him in London & warned him all over again. Well—I frightened her off, I think, because except for one more letter about the MLA project, I never heard a peep from her again until just a week or so ago when I had a very brief, polite note, *hoping* I could attend the affair in New York . . .

BUT—she somehow got the names of many friends—and telephone numbers!—and has hounded almost everyone one could think of with *long* letters, telephone calls, etc. Frank Bidart & I studied one of her 3-page letters to him and decided that her prose was so odd she must be from eastern Europe—possibly Hungarian, from the sentence structure.—But it later turned out she is from Kentucky, and, I suspect, very young—Well—brash?—pushy?—words fail me. I'm just sorry you had to become involved with her.

It certainly will be FUN to meet her on December 28th! Whatever & whoever she is—she *has* raised the money to get the Speculum Musicae group to perform the Carter music again—& I'd like to hear that again.[1] I'll read for ten minutes, *leave*, and come back for the music, and afterwards there's to be some sort of "reception"—this, I think, thanks to Farrar, S & G.—The music is "open to the public" and I do hope you'll come, and to the reception part of the thing . . . I hope I can bring myself to be *civil* to *Sybil*—that will be my motto for the evening. But I'm afraid one doesn't like to "serve a purpose" in this obvious way. The music hasn't too much to do with the poems but it is fascinating & I want to hear it again. Please come if you can bear to—under another name, if you want.

With love,
Elizabeth

December 31, 1976

Dear Elizabeth:

How wonderful it was that "The Complete Poems" were not complete after all. Every poem in this new book [*Geography III*] is a joy to read and reread. Thank you for asking your publisher to send me a copy. If all the poems appeared in *The New Yorker*, I must have missed reading the copy containing "The Moose" for it was new to me. It particularly fascinated me

---

1 Elliot Carter's *A Mirror on Which to Dwell* included "Anaphora," "Argument," "Sandpiper," "Insomnia," "View of the Capitol from the Library of Congress," and "O Breath." It premiered at the Hunter College Playhouse on February 24, 1976.

because two sisters who live near us had a similar experience during deer hunting season with a huge-antlered buck deer. They were driving on a back road and had to stop because the big fellow came trotting toward their car, attracted I suppose by the car lights. The deer sniffed the car all over but instead of jumping off into the woods, when they got going again he followed them for half a mile. This is far away from your poems. Andy and I both love the sad villanelle—but there's no point in singling out poems as every one is a perfect poem.

Are you still teaching at Harvard, I wonder, and still living in Boston? Perhaps it's better if I send this letter care of *The New Yorker* and the office will know your most recent address. Reading the book made me wish that the magazine still had a regular reviewer of poetry. I miss Louise Bogan. If you were not still engaged at Harvard, would you by any chance be interested in doing occasional poetry reviews for *The New Yorker*? I have no right to ask this question because I have nothing to do with the magazine now, of course, and have been retired for years, but I did recently write Bill Shawn saying I wished he could get someone to review poetry in the way Louise did, sometimes just short blurbs and sometimes full pieces, and if it at all interests you, I would like to suggest your name. It seems to me that Howard Moss cannot do such reviews because he buys the poems from the authors he would be reviewing, and that wouldn't work.

For all I know, you may be miles away in one of those northern or southern lands that you so beautifully recover in your poems. Perhaps the old address on a Boston wharf is still correct, but just in case it isn't I'll send this to my secretary at *The New Yorker* and have it forwarded. We are inundated with letters—or rather Andy is and I have to help him answer them so have little time to write long letters of my own. Winter here has become a matter of survival for me, but I'm doing all right, and the more I stay indoors, the better I am. However this year I have the added pleasure of a very small greenhouse Andy gave me as a wedding anniversary present last year, and each day now he brings in a camellia blossom. We are still green at running a greenhouse, but so far the only disaster was one night when the power went off for four hours and I lost a huge angel wing begonia. I have a cutting of it, though. Now we have a special kerosene heater to use out there when the electricity goes off.

Forgive a very mixed up and rambling letter that doesn't half tell you how much I admired your new book.

Affectionately,

Katharine

January 4, 1977
[postcard]
Dear Howard: I think I said the same thing the other night, but I do think it was really NOBLE of you to be there at that rather absurd occasion . . .

Did you hear the music—or maybe it was for the 2nd time? That's really all I wanted to go for—no, I suppose I wanted to lay eyes on SYBIL . . . Actually, she isn't as bad as one might have thought—is she? Just—well—I don't know, and I hate the word but maybe it's the right one—*naïve?*

I suppose you must have met the excitable Ivar Ivask?—& I am very eager to read *your* piece in his magazine, whatever it is called now.[1] (You had by far the best title, to begin with.) I saw a piece by Harold Bloom (whom we must talk about sometime) yesterday—and he ended by saying that "A Swim" . . . is a "superb book of light verse"—but of course you are so *au courant* you've seen this.[2] *I* think you're good as Praed . . . So—lots of love— & if you come to Boston, let me know—Elizabeth

February 15, 1977
Dear Elizabeth,
I'm almost sure you've seen this but I send it on, just in case.[3]

I was sorry you and Alice weren't at Duxbury last weekend—mostly cooking, movies, reading, and so on. The bay was frozen over but ridged so that an ice-skater would have had to jump hurdles as well. Penelope arrived Sunday morning and drove me back to Boston.

Could the poet you mentioned to me on the phone be named Avner Strauss? I have two poems from him, and he's in Cambridge. I thought the name was Avram Shapiro.

And a poem from *you* would really make me feel that maybe this winter *will* end.

Love,
Howard

1 "The Canada-Brazil Connection," *World Literature Today* (Winter 1977).
2 *A Swim off the Rocks* is "a superb book of light verse which culminates in a marvelous poem, not so very light, called 'Horror Movie,' with its sublime closing couplet: 'Make the blood flow, make the motive muddy: / There's a little death in everybody.'" In "The Year's Books: (Part I)," *The New Republic* (November 20, 1976).
3 William McPherson, "The Famous Eye," *Washington Post Book World* (February 6, 1977) or "The Literary Scene," *New York Post* (February 10, 1977).

Dear Howard:

You got a letter written to *me* before I managed to get the one I've been planning for several days written to *you* . . . I am sorry; I never seem to get caught up with correspondence and if it is possible I'll spend part of eternity writing letters to be sent back to earth. I'm sorry to have missed you last week-end—Alice & I and a couple went to New Hampshire—where we had a marvellous snow-storm Sunday, while you had rain, I think, in Duxbury—

Yes, I had seen that review—do you know who William McPherson is? It was used in another newspaper, too, I think. The reviews so far, those I've seen, have all been so favorable it makes me nervous—there's bound to be an abrupt change in the near future, I'm sure. I'm pessimistic—but I agree with Forster that it's better to be pessimistic—one is always so surprised when anything—or anybody—turns out well.

Did you get a copy of *Geography III*? You were on my list but I have had several complaints already. This always seems to happen, as I'm sure you know. Two days ago I received a copy of "World Literature Today" (formerly "Books Abroad") and so I've been able to read your piece at last. I like it very, very much—in fact you and Helen Vendler—and Octavio, in a different way—take all the honors, I think—and you are by far the most entertaining—or maybe the *only* entertaining contribution. But I'm scarcely the person to judge, I suppose, only I know I like what you say and don't find it embarrassing the way I do most things about me, and also you don't make mistakes—I'm amazed at how critics & reviewers can't get simple facts, or quotations right . . . Thank you very much. Alice loved you calling me a "cool customer"—& so did I—

The young man's name is *Amram Schapiro*. The poem I thought especially good was called something like "Our Visit to Times Square." I suggested that he cut it a bit & perhaps it still needs more cutting—but parts of it, certainly, are good, and I suggested that he send two or three more along with it—shorter poems. I may be prejudiced because I like him so much—but I do think he has a gift and he has never had anything published as far as I know, although Richard Howard kept the Times Sq. thing for several months, until that magazine [*American Review: The Magazine of New Writing*] expired.

I was to have John & Bill to dinner last week but some horrible dentistry has kept me from any dining-entertaining for two weeks now. I'll see them after Washington's birthday I hope. I *am* working on a poem—a childish one—and maybe I'll get it done by Washington's Birthday—I've become a Sunday poet.

With love and many thanks—

Elizabeth

Amram S. lives in East Boston. Oh—Sybil wanted to interview me for the Paris Review . . . 1st I said yes and then retracted it the next day . . . wiser, don't you think?

May 16, 1977

Dear Elizabeth,

Here's a new first-reading agreement we hope you'll sign. Whenever it's convenient.

And I'm delighted—honored and flattered would be closer—at the idea of our joint reading at the Y in October. How lovely!

Love,

Howard

North Haven
July 27, 1977

Dear Andy:

I was awfully saddened to learn of Katharine's death (indirectly) just yesterday . . . I don't get newspapers here, but a neighbor found her July 22nd *New York Times* for me last night.[1]

I hadn't seen Katharine for many years, but she had written, or dictated, a long letter to me almost annually, and always when I had published a book or a poem she liked—I remember how shy & frightened I was the first time I met her—but she was unfailingly kind and generous to me, and unfailingly perceptive about my work. It breaks my heart to think of how much she suffered physically—

I had been meaning to write to you about how much I have liked the "Letters"—but that can wait until later.[2]

With affection and sympathy,

Elizabeth

1 White died July 20 at Memorial Hospital in Blue Hill, Maine.
2 *Letters of E. B. White* (1976).

Dear Elizabeth,

I am enclosing the New Yorker's piece about Katharine, since your let-
ter mentioned that you were not receiving papers. It was written by Bill
Shawn and is an awfully good obituary, I think.[1] Katharine loved you, and
had an extra warm feeling for you as she did for all writers whose work
she respected. The mail keeps pouring in from all over. I try to keep abreast
of it, but there isn't a chance. Thank you, Elizabeth, for your kind words
about K.

 Yrs,

  Andy

                Boston

           October 1, 1977

Dear Howard:

Here is a poem—or maybe just an endless "description" ["Santarem"]—
I don't know, and I haven't been able to get much done the past few months.
I *wish* I could write a poem for, or about, *you* before the 10th!—but this New
York University thing is very trying and I can't seem to concentrate on any-
thing but how to tell 22 young people that something does exist beside "free
verse", etc. . . . .[2]

I'm so glad you could get to see Bill & John off on their trip—I'm sorry
it was impossible for me to make it. So far, two cards from each, sounding
rather cheerful, on the whole . . .

This "poem" may be over-punctuated—& have other faults, too, of
course. I do hope to send you more things soon. I meant to write you about
"Gravel" but of course never did—but I'll be glad to hear you read it—[3]

 À bientôt—

  Elizabeth

           October 12, 1977

            [postcard]

SANTAREM: line 3: That golden evening I really wanted to go no farther;
 line 20 (end of 2nd stanza): in that watery, dazzling, etc.

1 August 1, 1977.
2 Bishop taught at New York University from September 1977 to January 1978.
3 August 15, 1977.

3rd stanza, 3 lines from end—omit "all"—just "dampered by golden sand",

Beginning of 4th stanza—shd. read "riversfull" I think—if it doesn't already.

Page 2, end of 5th stanza: *Graças á deus*—he'd been etc.[1]

    E. Bishop

(I could have done this perfectly well on the proof!—Love, & see you soon.)

November 3, 1977

Dear Elizabeth,

Here's a check for SANTAREM. And it lovely to know there's another poem of yours waiting to be published.

And what a terrific story UNCLE NEDDY is! I read it in *The Southern Review* and thought it marvelous. Was it submitted here? I hope not. I mean I can't imagine anyone turning it down.[2]

I began to write a letter to you about how I felt reading with you that night at the Y, but it became rather soppy. It meant a great deal to me for a thousand reasons but two are obvious: you are my favorite poet, and because (I figured out) we have known each other now for something like thirty-five years!

Candace MacMahon (?) kindly sent me a photograph of the painting of yours Dr. Baumann has in her office.[3] It looked splendid, extraordinary, as a matter of fact. Are there any others? Mark Strand claims there are. But where?

---

1 Bishop originally submitted line three as: "I really wanted to go no farther that golden evening,". The last line of stanza two was "in the watery, dazzling dialectic." In the third stanza, the line was "all dampered by golden sand,". In the fourth stanza, it was "riverfulls". And in the fifth stanza, it was "*Graças a dios*, he'd been" (*The New Yorker* Records and Vassar College Library).

2 Of the story Moss said, "When it came out in *Southern Review*, I saw it first, then the editor of fiction saw it. It killed us. He said, 'Did we get it?' And it turned out we had. There were seven people reading prose at *The New Yorker* at that time. I still don't know what had happened" (Fountain). All the correspondence for the story is missing from Bishop's *New Yorker* file.

When Bishop submitted the story to her old friend and *Southern Review* editor Donald Stanford, she said, "Here is the story I think I promised you some time ago . . . I feel I shd. tell you it was rejected by The New Yorker (I have a '1st reading' contract with them); although they were extremely flattering, they said they had too big a back-log of 'family stories.' (They do seem to have published at least one a week for some time now!) And critical friends have said that 'nothing happens.' So please don't think I'll be crushed if you can't use it, or if you make suggestions as to how to improve it" (April 19, 1976, Stanford University Library).

3 MacMahon is the author of *Elizabeth Bishop: A Bibliography, 1927–1979* (1980). The painting may be "Brazilian Landscape" in *Exchanging Hats: Paintings*, edited with an introduction by William Benton (Farrar, Straus and Giroux, 1996).

I have had a virus. My "swanky" dinner is on a back burner, and is not mere "talk." Maybe in a week or so? I've tried you at the NYU number but am not sure when you're here. I've tried Boston, too, without success. Would you call me when next you're in?

Love,

Howard

February 2, 1978

Dear Elizabeth:

Here is the author's proof of SANTAREM, which we'd appreciate getting back, corrected and signed, as soon as possible, since we want to run it in the anniversary issue of February 20th. If you just cross out the question mark that precedes or follows a suggested change, it will be put into the text. If you don't want it, just lightly pencil out BOTH the question mark AND the suggested change. I say that only because there may be some rush on this and the clearer we are about whatever punctuation changes we're going to make the better.[1]

Thank you again for this wonderful poem, which I'm so delighted to have. I'll look forward to other poems and to seeing you, I hope, either here or in Duxbury or Boston.

Ever,

Howard

February 15, 1978
[postcard]

Dear Howard: I made an overnight train-trip to N.Y. & spent most of Mon. in the waiting rooms of 2 doctors—Each had the last *N. Yorker* so I managed to read yr. article fairly well—That no. hasn't reached Boston yet—no mail since the 4th now!—but when it does I'll write you a proper

---

1 Moss made several changes in punctuation to this poem before it was set in galley proof. In stanza two, line sixteen, he changed the semicolons between "death" and "right" and "wrong" and "male" to commas. In stanza three, line three, he changed the semicolon after "river" to a comma. In line five, he added a comma after "yellow". In line eight, he added a comma after "rain". In stanza four, line one, he removed the semicolon after "shipping" and inserted a dash. In line two, he removed the commas around "apparently". In line six, he removed the comma after "names". In line seventeen, he added a comma after "ferried". In line twenty, he removed the comma after "sails". In stanza five, last line, he changed the comma after "deus" to a dash. In the third line of the last stanza, he added a comma after "white" (*The New Yorker* Records and Vassar College Library).

thank-you note.[1] I *did* get the proof one day—(perhaps I had some mail the 6th, having a very nice mailman). *Graças á deus.* All ok.[2] I returned Mon. with "flu"—not bad, however—

    With love,
      Elizabeth

May 21, 1978

Dear Howard:

I'm sending this contract to you. Perhaps you aren't the right person, but I'm sure it will "fall into the right hands". Now that I have a lovely Guggenheim and don't have to teach—*maybe* I'll be getting some work done for a change, and maybe you'll hear from me once in a while. That's my plan, at any rate.

I didn't go to the Academy Ceremonial—as you no doubt know. Probably I should have. I talked to John the next day and he told me all about it—and how much his mother had enjoyed herself . . . (I've never met her!) I'm glad he could go. I'm really worried about him. The last time I was there—Duxbury—two weeks ago, I think,—he seemed terribly on edge and tired—and, of course, no wonder. I wish to goodness he'd consent to have a practical nurse or housekeeper at least, come in every day for a while—but he wouldn't hear of it when I dared bring up the subject. Have you suggested anything like that to him? It would be so much better to do it—hire someone helpful—now, than when it might become an emergency call.

Well—please tell me on a postcard where you saw the review of HELENA MORLEY, will you? I've only seen one or two newspaper clippings ECCO sent—but nothing very interesting. Yes—I do remember your review—in fact I have it in *File?*—Another thing I'm doing with my free time is arranging papers, or having them arranged, etc.—about time, too.

I hope you're well. *I'm* well at last, or so it seems, and hope to stay this way.

    With love,
      Elizabeth

---

1 Moss reviewed Richard Poirer's *Robert Frost: The Work of Knowing* and David Kalstone's *Five Temperaments* in "The Poet's Voice" (February 13, 1978). In his discussion of Kalstone, Moss talked about "In the Village" and "In the Waiting Room."

2 Besides spelling, Bishop agreed to the proofreader's suggestion of adding a comma after "proud" in stanza three, line nine (Vassar College Library).

Postscript: Probably the TV ads are the same in New York as here, and if so, probably countless others have commented on this one to *The New Yorker*—but—if you didn't see it, you'll like it, and possibly think it worth passing along.

During the week before Mothers' Day, last Sunday, I saw an in-between kind of ad for Mothers' Day. The scene was a middle-aged lady rocking in a Victorian-style rocking chair—beside a small round table with a bunch of flowers on it. Another chair, vacant, Fathers?, was on the other side of the table. The lady was knitting or crocheting. The Voice reminded us not to forget Mothers' Day and concluded its comment by quoting, "Age cannot wither her, / Nor custom stale / Her infinite variety . . ." E.

May 29, 1978

[postcard]

Dear Howard: Now of course I know what you meant by this nice review of "H.M."—at least I think you must have meant the Alastair Reid piece?—My *New Yorker* didn't come until 2 or 3 days later.[1] Of course I am awfully pleased. I'll write him a note & send it to you (?) at the magazine, to be forwarded—since I have no idea where he is. He was in Brazil—oh, over ten years ago—and we saw a little of him then. Perhaps his review will help *sales* . . . I'd been slightly disappointed that Ecco has stopped listing it with their favorites. Summer has come—a beautiful Memorial Day here. Will you be going away?—or just to Long Island? With love, Elizabeth

September 12, 1978

Dear Elizabeth,

We're taking NORTH HAVEN, of course, and I agree that the dedication "(In Memoriam: Robert Lowell)" should be spelled out and also that this should run soon.[2] We don't publish poems seasonally at all anymore, with the exception of something so obvious it would be peculiar not to. Say a poem called NEW YEAR'S EVE.

In line 4, of stanza 1, I found "sidewise" a bit odd—instead of the more usual "sideways," but I'll set it up as you have it, and if you agree, we can change it on the author's proof.[3]

---

1 "Immortal Diamond" (May 29, 1978).
2 Lowell died September 12, 1977.
3 It was left "sidewise."

I'm delighted to have this, as you can imagine, and hope for other poems soon. Thanks for sending it.

And forgive the rushed tone of all this. Two hundred poems have been submitted in the last two days on top of the usual million. What I need is a grant to run a nice hamburger stand in New Jersey. My best to Alice.

Love,
Howard

September 21, 1978

Dear Elizabeth,

Here is a check for NORTH HAVEN, which we're delighted to have. I hope there will be other poems along soon.

I'm not sure whether John has taken off yet or not, and I suppose you will be using the Duxbury house on weekends. I hope so; it would comfort me to think you're there. If I'm ever up, floating among the autumn leaves, I will ring you up for some tea and a madeleine.

Love,
Howard

P.S. And here is the author's proof, too—it just arrived.[1]

October 12, 1978

Dear Elizabeth,

Just to say—again—how delighted we are with SONNET. I'll put it through as is, in spite of that mysterious word you mentioned on the phone that you think needs changing. We can always do *that* in author's proof.[2]

---

1 In preparing the poem for galley proof, Moss took all of the proper names of the birds and flowers out of initial caps. In stanza two, he removed the comma at the end of line two and inserted a dash. He added a comma after "south" and removed the comma and inserted a dash after "sidewise" in line four. In the last stanza, line four, he made "songs" singular (*The New Yorker* Records and Vassar College Library). Three additional changes were made to the first stanza between the time of Bishop's submission and its appearance in the magazine. Bishop submitted the last two lines of stanza one as: *the pale bay wears a milky skin, the sky / no clouds, except for one long, carded, horse's-tail.*" It ran as: "*the pale bay wears a milky skin; the sky / no clouds except for one long, carded horse's tail.*" When Bishop reprinted the poem as a broadside, she kept one of Moss's changes: making "song" singular in the last stanza. She also returned the first stanza to how she originally submitted it in addition to starting stanza two, line three, with a dash and widening the space between stanzas one and two and stanzas four and five.

2 Moss sent Bishop the proof on October 26 and had no changes to make before the poem was set in galley proof (*The New Yorker* Records). Between the time of Bishop's submission and its publication, one change was made: changing line three from "a creature divided;" to "contrarily guided;".

Thank you again for this, and I hope to see you on or around the 19th.
Love,
   Howard

January 3, 1979

Dear Elizabeth,

We're taking PINK DOG, of course, and plan to run it in the February 26th issue, the closest to Carnival on the one hand and to Ash Wednesday on the other.[1]

I hope to have a check and a proof for you shortly, and thank you, as always, for sending it on. I hope you've heard all the good things I have about NORTH HAVEN.

Love,
   Howard

January 25, 1979

Dear Elizabeth,

Here's the author's proof of PINK DOG, which we'd appreciate getting back, corrected and signed, as soon as possible.[2]

We're not sure whether "Rio De Janeiro" should stay as it is, as a sort of sub-head, or be put in somewhat smaller type, with caps and lower-case letters in parentheses, as a way of clueing a reader in, and setting the poem. The latter would be the more usual procedure for us—and this would be particularly true if there were to be a series of Brazilian poems with different settings. And then there's the possibility of including the place name in the title, which is what we did with "Under the Window." It was titled "UNDER THE WINDOW: OURO PRÊTO." I don't mean to confuse you but these are the possibilities and you may want to consider the alternatives.[3]

I'm not sure whether "four-legged" should have an accent mark or not. Up to you, of course.[4]

---

1 There was some internal debate over taking "Pink Dog," but Moss and Shawn voted to take the poem.
2 In stanza six, line one, Moss removed the comma from the end of the line. In line two, he added a comma after "sewage" and removed the comma after "nights". In stanza eleven, line two, he removed the comma after "come" (*The New Yorker* Records and Vassar College Library). Between Bishop's submission and the poem's publication, a comma was added after "drunk" in stanza seven, line two.
3 "Rio de Janeiro" ran in caps in parentheses.
4 "Four-leggèd" ran with the grave accent mark.

Thanks again for this poem, and we hope for others. And I hope to see you when I'm in Cambridge week after next.

Ever,

Howard

February 22, 1979

Dear Howard:

A very nice former student has been re-doing my "library" for me—that is, she does all the hard work while I advise, decide, discard, etc.—the past three days and I've turned up a good many forgotten things. One is a large really large, & *heavy* book of early music, German, I've had for years and used to use a lot when I could play the clavichord a little. I meant to send it along with the clavichord but I overlooked it. It will take some time to get it properly wrapped & to the PO—but wd. you like it? I also have a nice but battered little book "for Anna Magdelena Bach"—green, just the right size & shape—but you probably have that already? Anyway, they're both yours & maybe some more if you'd like them. (Sheet music of Count Basie? etc.— all have re-appeared.)

My genius-former-student, John Peech, has recently telephoned me twice from Ithaca (his hometown) where he is under contract with the Un. there (which?) doing a two-year research job on disposal of nuclear wastes & other such dangerous wastes. He seems in very good shape and talks about his project at length and very interestingly. He would like to write an article about it all and of course would also like to sell it to *The New Yorker*. What he wants to know is: should he write up an outline, etc. to send first? 2. To whom should he send such an outline, or such an article?

I hate to bother you, but I have no idea. He just might do something very good, I don't know—at least it's a good subject and he certainly knows a chilling amount about it. What I've seen of his prose wasn't exactly [John] McPhee, but it was very good.

Thank heavens it's getting a bit warmer here—parts of the harbor were frozen over, (melting, now), and all the ducks, several varieties, come into my piece of it then. I can't understand why when the marina on the other side of me is frozen, dozens of people throw beer bottles or cans on the ice. If I were Flannery O'Connor, whose letters I am reading as hard as I can these days, I'd probably *know* why . . .[1]

---

1 *The Habit of Being: Letters of Flannery O'Connor*, edited by Sally Fitzgerald (1979).

My stay in NY for the National Book Critics Circle was very brief and I mostly found it much too cold to go out. I'll be back fairly soon, though, for longer, and when it's better weather, I hope, and then we'll have that meal together. I hope you're well—

With love,

Elizabeth

27 West 10th Street

March 2, 1979

[card]

Dear Elizabeth—I'd love the early music books for surely my clavichord will be tuned shortly, now that spring is glossing the windows. (Along with lots of other stuff.) I've sent the Peech suggestion down to the "fact" dept. and am waiting to hear; in the end, it will probably be decided by Mr. Shawn. The chances of outsiders doing fact pieces are not good. But this one sounds special, so maybe. I thought PINK DOG looked terrific, and all the type the right size and in the right places—a weekly triumph. I am frantically trying to finish up some work, get ready for California, handle my mother's ever-more complicated estate, do my income taxes, read at least the best of the over 1000 poems that now arrive at the NYer, and try to live what's left of my life, singing and humming. Dinner tonight with Jimmy and David at Harry Ford's—always a delight—though the three wines leave one totally aluminum the next day.[1] I must be careful. There is also a pub. party for Bernard Malamud first. The w. round goes on. Forgive the brevity and crowdedness of this. Love, Howard

The New Yorker

March 6, 1979

Dear Elizabeth,

I received an answer today on the Peech idea for a piece on "the disposal of nuclear wastes" and the answer, I'm afraid, is no. It seems a staff writer on the magazine has "reserved" nuclear wastes (this is all beginning to sound absurd) for a piece he plans to do, and there are other related ideas also "reserved" by other staff writers of the magazine, and the Peech piece would be in conflict

---

1 Moss is referring to James Merrill and Merrill's partner, David Jackson. At the time, Harry Ford was the poetry editor at Atheneum.

with what is already, however rudimentary and tentative, in the works. I'm sorry; he'd probably do a fine piece. Thanks for sending the idea along.

I've heard nothing but good things about PINK DOG and I hope you have, too. I was amused by your turning up old sheet music of Count Basie—of? by? . . . I have a little closet full of old songs, mainly Gershwin but a few "Tip Toe Through the Tulips," too. Someday, we ought to combine our collections and play them on E. Power Biggs' organ.

Love,
Howard

May 17, 1979
[postcard: "Prize Yoke of Oxen, Nova Scotia"]

Dear Howard: This inappropriate card is the only one I have left from my recent Nova Scotian trip—I didn't even see these creatures, either. I've been meaning to write you to thank you for yr. kind remarks about me in the APR (?) I've seen 2 "columns" & I think John says there'll be another.[1] Aside from *me*—I think they've been very good—and a *treat* after most of the articles in that paper. We've seen John in Duxbury—& last night at dinner—and he reported on Laguna Beach, etc. It will soon be over, I gather. Alice & I leave tonight for London and the isles of Greece—back June 10th—I think I might pack now—

With love,
Elizabeth

North Haven
July 27, 1979

Dear Howard:

A few days ago I had a letter from a Mr. [William] Goodman of Godine's asking me if I'd like to make a selection of Sarah Orne Jewett's work—to have an introduction, photographs, etc. He said this was at your suggestion. I wrote and told him I'd have to read a lot more—or all—of SOJ's work, also biographies, etc. (I think I *have* read one—somewhere, a long time ago) before I could make up my mind. Of course I read *The Country of the Pointed*

---

1 "The First Line," *American Poetry Review* (November/December 1978) and "From a Notebook" (March/April 1979). In "From a Notebook," Moss says, "The truest changes in art are not changes of technique but of sensibility. And so the real pioneers are rarely recognized as such. They are too subtle to make good copy. Examples: Henry Green and Elizabeth Bishop."

Firs many years ago.[1] Well—yesterday Alice discovered quite a few SOJ books in the North Haven Library—very old little books, quite nice—and brought back three. I've read the two books of stories already and started on a novel—*A Marsh Island*—but can't seem to get very interested in it.[2] I'll look at the other volumes in the library today or tomorrow. Now—I wonder what *you've* read? I can see why you might have thought of me as a suitable selector—there are many bits in *The Country of the Pointed Firs* that are reminiscent of the few stories I've done about life in a Nova Scotian village—but I wonder if you've discovered good things I haven't?—Because to tell the truth I think that very little of what I've read is very good . . . This may be heresy—and I may find more good stories—I'm sure there are a good many more books. I've always meant to go to see her house in North Berwick—but it is open at very odd hours and we're always catching a ferry or trying to get home or something like that . . .

Well—I'm not asking your help! I'll read all the works and see what I think then, and thank you for thinking of me. I do like The C of the PF—all of *that*, as I remember it—and some of the stories in that book, but not all. The same is true of the 2 little books I read last night. The stories are too much alike and woefully sentimental . . . But then—some of the description in some of the very worst ones is superb . . . Well—I'll see. Mr. Goodman mentioned "contemporary photographs"—I'm not sure what that means, but I hope he meant old ones—there are hundreds available, I think—some albums in the library here, even.

Most of the above, as they say, is quite unnecessary . . . I've been meaning to write you for some time—months, probably—to thank you for your really much too kind references to me in *American Poetry Review*. (If that's its right name. I don't have a copy here and there are two or three of those tabloid-like magazines that I confuse . . .) I think someone (John B?) told me you were writing only three such pieces—and I may not have seen the last one—but I thought the two I did see were extremely good. (That is—apart from your speaking of me in such a flattering way!) I also wanted to speak of one fairly recent poem of yours I liked a lot—and I haven't that magazine with me, either. I'm afraid you'll have to take my word for these kind thoughts and good intentions.[3]

Since Alice & I got back from our Swann's Trip in Greece I seem to have

---

1 *The Country of the Pointed Firs* (1896).
2 *A Marsh Island* (1885).
3 Bishop is probably referring to "The Night Express" (July 2, 1979).

been in a sort of daze and always a month behind myself. I imagine you're at East Hampton, but I don't know—at any rate I hope you're some place cooler than New York. Here it is cool—but we've been fogged in, completely, a real Maine fog, for days. It's quite beautiful but I am sick of feeling damp. The typewriter feels damp. Harold Leeds & Wheaton Galentine have been here all week (I think you know them), very superior guests—but I think they've only seen our truly magnificent view once or twice—& then through a haze.

Day before yesterday I read Jean's *The Mountain Lion* for the 1st time (also in our very superior library here). It does sound youthful and I think one foresees the ending—but nevertheless—it's awfully good. She certainly could write.—I felt she developed some unfortunate mannerisms later— they appear slightly in this book—but she could really *write*—a natural-born writer, I think. I wish she'd done more.[1]

I have a poem I've almost sent but I've turned against it. Before the end of August I hope to get a couple of things done. I hope you're well—cheerful— etc.—I gathered from John that California was rather awful.

With love,
        Elizabeth

East Hampton
August 2, 1979

Dear Elizabeth,

How lovely to hear from you! Yes, I did suggest you for the Jewett but in rather casual way when David Godine and I were bandying about possibilities for a series he plans of New England—maybe all-American—writers. (I asked for Henry James and have heard nothing. Mr. Edel is probably busy at them now in Hawaii.) And I hasten to say I am no expert on Jewett. All I know is THE COUNTRY OF THE POINTED FIRS. But it *seemed* right because of something in the descriptive passages, your being at Cambridge at the time and summering in Maine, the possible connection with the village in Nova Scotia, and so on. It was more a matter of intuition than my being familiar with work of hers no one would know outside of what is laughingly called the scholarly community. And so. As for Godine, he is a charming man and does wonderful books but my experience with him is not reassuring. He is reprinting my Proust book in the "Non-Pareil" paperback series, and an

---

1 Stafford died March 26, 1979.

excellent series it is. But the book was announced for April publication, this is August, and I have yet to see a copy. In fact, I was grimly amused to see the new fall Godine catalogue in which the paperback "backlist" is proudly announced. And, of course, the Proust is on it. But how can you be "back" when you haven't even gone "forward?" Well, the compensation is these paperbacks have no acid in the paper and are sewn rather than just glued, so they are books intended for eternity. Or something damn close.

Here, everything is hot, wet, sticky, and icky. I'm not having a very good summer. I can't seem to write—or finish anything I start—the paper sticks to the typewriter, envelopes won't unglue, my toothbrush is mushy, and there hasn't been any rain in about three weeks. I spend most of my time racing about from one wilting bed of flowers, one more rhododendron with its head down to another. My gardener hasn't appeared since May, but leaves me little tearful notes saying he knows how badly he's treating me, and the only thing that's saved my summer—or the summer garden—is a visit from a friend in California who is a groundskeeper at UCLA. It wasn't all peaches, however. He had a novel that needed editing, to put it mildly. And while he liberated my pines, and fertilized the petunias, I edited away on his novel. (A bunch of grackles—I hate them—just settled on the gravel making their hideous noises. Peacocks are nightingales by comparison.)

I've been in touch with the permissions editor at Farrar, Straus about reprinting poems for my New York City anthology—a tough lady, and FSG charges the biggest prices in the business, and they want a cut of the royalties, too, or something like it.[1] But they never say who's to figure it all out, and how. Anyway, I wanted to put all your New York City poems together: VARICK STREET, LOVE LIES SLEEPING, LETTER TO N.Y., the Marianne Moore poem, FROM THE COUNTRY TO THE CITY, and THE MAN-MOTH. (The only missing one, as far as I can make out, would have been the one about the dead bird on 4th Street ["Trouvée"].) I will probably end up with less than the whole and I hope you will give your permission, once the fee is established. Avon has given me $10,000 for fees and it all has to come out of that. So far, I'm doing fairly well but we'll see. I'm also using Lowell, Jarrell (THE SUBWAY FROM NEW BRITAIN TO THE BRONX), Walcott, Valentine, Berryman. (These are all Farrar, Straus, & Giroux.) It should be a good anthology. I'm trying to print a lot of foreign poets in it: Guillen, Lorca (of course), Mayakovsky (the Brooklyn Bridge poem), Cruz, Jiminez, etc. and a lot of new poets no one's ever heard of. Did

1 *New York: Poems* (*1980*).

you—by the way—see those 5 Poems by Nicholas Christopher in The NYer recently? I think he's wonderfully gifted.[1]

A letter from John yesterday, from Venice, where he sounds fairly contented, is working hard, and leading a social life we once talked about. It sounds almost like a parody but he really has dinner with Baroness Muffy Contini, or something, races over to Peggy's [Guggenheim] for a nightcap, brunches the next day with the Tunisian ambassador, and meets Countess Lafitte-Syringe for secret cocktails at Florians. And so it goes. I wonder if all those same people *winter* in the Virgin Islands, slightly disguised. (An idea for a play?—)

I spoke to Jimmy just before he left and he sounds in fine fettle, rather casting about, I think, for something to work on after DIVINE COMEDIES, a real problem.[2] What did Dante do after he finished you-know-what?

The New Yorker seems remote—I haven't been there since March—though they keep sending checks, thank God, and still consider me one of their own. California was alternately awful and charming. If it weren't for Charles Wright and his wife, Holly, both of whom I adore, and a very interesting poet named James McMichael and *his* wife, and some very attractive students [at the University of California, Irvine], bright, unspoiled, and madly sincere, I think I might have simply packed up and taken off.[3] Orange County is not for me, and I was a half hour away from the Campus and had to *drive* there in a *Pinto* through hideous traffic. I imported friends to help since it meant getting up at 6:30 to get on a gas line. In fact, I seem to be importing help everywhere. Maybe I should stay on 10th Street, tending my window boxes, there, where I need no help at all.

This letter is a true ramble. Maine sounds lovely, even in fog. Maybe I'll sell this house and just go places in the summer—I think I'm getting sick of East Hampton, with its chic, its little expensive boîtes, and too many writers and painters. Not to mention rich young couples tearing around in Rollses. Love to Alice, and to you,

    Howard

August 14?, 1979
[postcard]

Dear Howard: your summer sounds rather like mine—except Rolls-Royces

---

1 "Heat," "Nocturne for Miranda," "Providence," "Double Solitaire," and "Rimbaud Crossing the Alps" (July 16, 1979).
2 *Divine Comedies: Poems* (1976).
3 Yusef Komunyakaa was also a student in Moss's class.

and *boîtes* wd. not be considered the thing here . . . The raggeder, & the older one's car, the more lofty one's social position . . .

I, too, heard from John & wonder how he keeps it up. (There *was* a Countess here 2 yrs. ago but she was really Minnie somebody from Minneapolis.) I've had several letters from Godine's—and even 3 very valuable, I think, old books—& I've read the 4 or 5 books in the local library. There's a lot more to read—when I get back—Aug. 26th—but on the whole I think I *won't* do it . . . (Don't say anything to G's.) W. Cather chose the best things yrs. ago, I'm afraid—much of it is very weak.[1] I hope the anthology goes well. With love, Elizabeth

[Handwritten: "The sun has come out!"]

Elizabeth Bishop died of a cerebral aneurysm on October 6, 1979, in her Lewis Wharf apartment.

The New Yorker
November 27, 1979

Dear Alice,

Here is a Xerox of the author's proof of SONNET. The change at the left-hand top is in Elizabeth's handwriting, as is the injunction to me about leaving the hyphens, and the initials at the end of the poem. The handwriting actually incorporating the change into the text of the poem is the collator's—that is, the person who collates all the final changes on a proof before it is printed.

In a phone call, in which I told her how much I liked the poem, Elizabeth said one line needed to be changed. She also told me, which you probably know, that the mirror in the poem is the one at the door of the house in Duxbury.

In any case, the change is unquestionably hers. The earlier line was read over the phone to Lloyd Schwartz because I was using the original galley of the poem rather than the author's proof, which had already been filed away.[2]

I'm sorry I won't see you at the Academy on Friday, but I hope to when I'm next in Cambridge.

Best wishes,
Howard

1 *The Best Stories of Sarah Orne Jewett*, edited with an introduction by Willa Cather (1925).
2 Methfessel had contacted Moss about the version of "Sonnet" that ran in the October 29 *New Yorker*, since it differed from the version Moss dictated to Schwartz for Bishop's memorial service. The line to which Moss is referring is "a creature divided;" which ran as "contrarily guided;". When printed in *The Collected Poems*, Bishop's original submission was used.

Dear Alice,

These are the sort of letters I used to send on to Elizabeth with a copy of our reply. And so I send this on to you. If you don't want to receive others, just let me know.

All good wishes,
Howard

Acknowledgments

I wish to express my deepest thanks to Condé Nast and the late Alice Methfessel, literary executor of the Elizabeth Bishop estate; *The New Yorker* magazine; Allene White and Martha White, literary executors of the Katharine S. White estate; and Anne Simmons, literary executor of the Howard Moss estate, for their support of this book, and to Jonathan Galassi for his enthusiasm and careful editing—may everyone be so lucky. I also wish to thank Jesse Coleman, David Chesanow, Jonathan Lippincott, Susan Mitchell, and Christina Ward.

My thanks to everyone I spoke to and corresponded with for this project: Edward Albee, Roger Angell, John Ashbery, David A. Bell, Jane and Burton Bernstein, Frank Bidart, Katherine Bouton, Nicholas Christopher, Joni Evans, Dana Gioia, Ann Goldstein, Anne Hall, Richard Howard, Vickie Karp, Fran Kiernan, Mary D. Kierstead, Yusef Komunyakaa, Philip Levine, Charles McGrath, Sheila McGrath, Elizabeth Macklin, Candace MacMahon, W. S. Merwin, José Alberto Nemer, Nancy Novogrod, Mary Painter, Stanley Plumly, Alice Quinn, Alastair Reid, Ruth Rogin, Lloyd Schwartz, Dave Smith, Mark Strand, Allene White, Richard Wilbur, Charles Wright, and Herb Yellin. The information they provided was invaluable in understanding Bishop, White, Moss, the magazine, and the relationships between them all.

My thanks to the librarians at all of the collections I used. Special thanks to Patricia Heron at the University of Maryland, College Park, who helped me start this project, and to Nancy MacKechnie and Dean Rogers at the Vassar College Library, William Stigone, Thomas Lannon, and Thomas Lisanti and the entire staff at the Manuscripts and Archives Division at the New York Public Library, Isaac Gewirtz at the Berg Collection at the New York Public Library, and Marianne Hansen at the Bryn Mawr College Library. Their help was indispensable. For their help with researching photographs, I wish to thank Leslie Calmes and Tammy Carter at the Center for Creative Photography at the University of Arizona; Katherine Feo at the Harry Ransom Humanities

Research Center at the University of Texas, Austin; and Lizanne Reger at the National Portrait Gallery, Washington, D.C.

For permission to publish unpublished material, I wish to thank the estates of Louise Bogan, John Malcolm Brinnin, William Maxwell, Marianne Moore, Aurelia Plath, Philip Rahv, Theodore Roethke, Karl Shapiro, and William Carlos Williams. I also wish to thank Richard Wilbur, the Houghton Mifflin Harcourt Publishing Company, and *Poetry* magazine.

For permission to reproduce artwork and manuscripts, I wish to thank the Josef and Yaye Breitenbach Charitable Foundation, Condé Nast, and the estates of Peter Arno, Rollie McKenna, and Thomas Victor.

I would also like to thank the following libraries for the use of their collections: Bryn Mawr College Library; University of Chicago Library; Cornell University Library; University of Delaware Library, Newark; Henry W. and Albert A. Berg Collection of English and American Literature, New York Public Library; Manuscripts and Archives Division, New York Public Library, Astor, Lenox and Tilden Foundations; Princeton University Library; The Rosenbach Museum and Library; Stanford University Library; Vassar College Library; Washington University Library; the American Heritage Center, University of Wyoming; and The Beinecke Collection at Yale University.

For their hospitality while I visited various libraries, I would like to thank Marie and John DiGuardia, Rebecca Dunne, Christine and Rick Meyer, and Ingrid and Otto Siegwarth.

The following books were especially helpful and I wish to thank their authors: *Onward and Upward: A Biography of Katharine White* by Linda H. Davis; *Remembering Elizabeth Bishop: An Oral Biography* by Gary Fountain and Peter Brazeau; *Genius in Disguise: Harold Ross of The New Yorker* by Thomas Kunkel; *Elizabeth Bishop: A Bibliography* by Candace MacMahon; *Elizabeth Bishop: Life and the Memory of It* by Brett Millier; and *About Town: The New Yorker and the World It Made* by Ben Yagoda.

I also wish to thank Richard Cross and Stanley Plumly for their years of guidance and generosity, which has meant more to me than I am sure they know. Special thanks to Michael Collier for first suggesting this project and his many insights. My thanks to Deborah Digges, John Fyler, Elizabeth Bergman Loizeaux, Martha Nell Smith, and David Wyatt for all they taught me about poetry and manuscripts. My thanks to Elizabeth Spires and Gail Walter for their support and to Allison Kimmich, Monica Hoesch, Nadève Ménard, and Michele Osherow for their friendship while I worked on this book. To my parents, Joann and Richard Biele, to my brother David, to Katie, Andrew, and Erik, and to my husband, Kirk Siegwarth, all my love.

Index

Academy of American Poets, 321n3; fellowship, 266

accent marks, 214, 392

Adams, Léonie, 45

advertisements, viii, xxxviii–xxxix

Albee, Edward, 272, 341; *Tiny Alice*, 268 and n1, 269

Algonquin Hotel, New York, xi, xii, xviii, xxvii, 17, 22; "vicious circle," xi

Allen, Donald, *The Collected Poems of Frank O'Hara*, 343n1

Alliance for Progress, 256

"A lovely finish," lv

Amabile, George, "Snowfall: Four Variations," 290 and n1

Amazon River, 229, 230

American Academy of Arts and Letters, xlii, 232 and n1, 299

American Poetry Review, 396; "The First Line," 395 and n1; "From a Notebook," 395 and n1

American Review: The Magazine of New Writing, 384

Ames, Elizabeth, xxix, 45

Amsterdam, 287

"Anaphora," xxxi, 381n1

Andrade, Carlos Drummond de, xl, 302n3, 303, 304, 319

Angell, Roger, xi, xiii, 376

Anthology of Twentieth-Century Brazilian Poetry, An, 304 and n1

"Apartment in Leme, Copacabana," xlix

Araújo, Lilli Correia de, xl

Archera, Laura, xxxiv, 202

architecture, 164, 203n1, 269

Arendt, Hannah, *The Human Condition*, 215 and n1

"Argument," 20, 221, 381n1

"Armadillo, The," 180, 181 and n1, 182 and n1, 192, 199

Arno, Peter, x, xxxviii

Aron, Raymond, 256 and n1

"Arrival at Santos," 77, 78–79, 80 and n1

art, x, lv–lvi, 87–88, 387 and n3; *see also* cartoons; covers

Ashbery, John, xxvii; "The Complete Poems: Throughout Is This Quality of Thingness," 307 and n1

Ashton, Dore, *A Joseph Cornell Album*, 357 and n1, 358

asthma, xiii, 68, 69, 75, 81, 82, 84, 86, 106, 134, 137, 141

"As We Like It," 35 and n1

Aswell, Mary Lou, 126 and n1

Atheneum, 29, 343, 394n1

Athens, 327

Atlantic Monthly, The, x, 21n1, 139

"At the Fishhouses," xliv–xlvi, 28, 29, 373; editing and revision, xliv–xlvi, xlix, 29, 30 and n1

Auden, W. H., xxii–xxiii, xxiv, 337, 348; "September 1939," xxii; "Song," xx

Austen, Jane, xii

author's proof, xliii, xlviii, lxii, 16, 41, 61, 80, 104, 118, 120, 148, 155, 156, 169, 245, 280, 295, 342, 373, 391, 400

Bahamas, 31, 32, 33

Bainbridge, John, "Like a Homesick Angel," 255n2

Balliett, Whitney, 236

Bandeira, Manuel, 110, 111, 112, 113

Barker, Ilse, xii, xxiv, 57 and *n2*, 103*n2*; *see also* Talbot, Kathrine

Barker, Kit, xii, 57*n2*, 103*n2*

Barlow, Perry, xxxix

Barnard College, 372

Barnes, Djuna, 310, 313

Baro, Gene, 265 and *n1*

Basic Cookbook: A Completely Revised and Enlarged Edition of Good Food Made Economical (Heseltine and Keezer), 34 and *n1*

Basso, Hamilton, 122–23, 124, 125 and *n2*, 128

Baumann, Anny, xxxiv, xli, 84 and *n2*

Baumgarten, Bernice, 181, 183, 186, 187, 188

Beats, xxvii

Beerbohm, Max, 309

Bendel, Henri, xxxviii

Benét, Stephen Vincent, "Nightmare for Future Reference," xx

Bennington College, 71

Benton, William, 387*n3*

Bermuda, 268

Bernanos, George, 138 and *n1*

Berryman, John, 398; "Homage to Mistress Bradstreet," xxvii

Best American Short Stories, The (1949), 44 and *n2*

Bethell, John, 343

Bevington, Helen, xix

Bidart, Frank, liv, 381

"Bight, The," 35, 36, 37 and *n1*, 38, 42, 133

Bishop, Elizabeth, xxii; artwork by, lv–lvi, 387 and *n3*; asthma of, xiii, 68, 69, 75, 81, 82, 84, 86, 106, 134, 137, 141; awards and fellowships, ix–x, xiv–xv, xlii, 12, 64–65, 102, 133, 176, 177, 178–79, 191–93, 266, 314*n1*, 379 and *n1*, 389; in Brazil, lv, 74, 77, 82, 84, 85, 99, 104, 109–12, 118, 119, 122–24, 125 and *n2*, 127–28, 132, 136, 138, 148, 149, 162, 169, 171, 187, 200, 202, 206, 207, 211, 215–17, 226–28, 232, 237–38, 254–59, 262, 267, 271, 272, 282, 289, 300 and *n1*, 305, 306, 307, 309, 310–13, 315, 316, 319, 331, 348; breaks contract with *The New Yorker*, xxxix, xl; clavichord of, 366–68; contracts and money issues, xxv–xxxiii, xxxix–xl, xlii–xliii, 3, 15–16, 22, 32 and *n1*, 33, 38, 42, 46, 64–65, 99, 108, 118, 121, 127, 143, 185, 194, 195, 210, 219, 236, 239, 246–47, 267, 270, 271, 278, 283, 328, 330, 331, 345, 358, 366, 389; critical writing by,

xl–xli, 188–89, 201, 314, 317; critics on, xxxiii, 20, 21 and *n1*, 129, 321*n1*, 323; death of, liv, lvi, 400; dissatisfaction with *The New Yorker*, xxxii–xxxviii, xxxix–xlii, 89*n1*, 103*n2*, 113*n1*, 126*n2*, 328–29, 350 and *nn2–3*; editing and revision process, xliii–lvi, lxi, lxii; first-reading agreements, xviii–xix, xxxi–xxxv, xxix–xl, 22, 32, 45–46, 74, 143, 168, 191, 192, 200, 201, 209, 239, 318, 327, 341, 366, 371, 385, 387*n2*; Guggenheim Fellowship, 389; hands of, lv; health problems of, 45, 75, 109, 134, 296, 301, 327; Houghton Mifflin Poetry Prize Fellowship, ix–x, 12; Gustave Lobrano and, 11, 14–15, 163; love poems, xxvi–xxix, lv; Robert Lowell and, xlix–lii, liii, 128, 315*n2*, 353, 390; William Maxwell and, xxxix, 11, 12, 19, 35–37, 67–68, 148, 201–203, 208 and *n2*, 209, 219–20, 239, 242, 252–53, 256; memorial service for, liv, 400*n2*; Alice Methfessel and, liv, 327, 358, 359, 384, 396, 400 and *n2*, 401; Marianne Moore and, 5, 35, 150, 207, 231 and *n2*, 309, 323, 337–39, 354 and *n2*; National Book Award, 314*n1*, 315 and *n2*; National Book Critics Circle Award, xlii; National Institute of Arts and Letters award, 64–65, 133; Neustadt International Prize for Literature, xlii, 379 and *n1*; 1934–1936 correspondence with *The New Yorker*, 1–23; 1947–1961 correspondence with *The New Yorker*, 25–242; 1961–1967 correspondence with *The New Yorker*, 243–92; 1967–1979 correspondence with *The New Yorker*, 293–401; *Partisan Review* fellowship, 191–93; Charles Pearce and viii–ix, 3–12; pen names, ix, 11*n1*, 36*n1*; as poet-in-residence at University of Washington, 283, 284 and *nn1–3*, 285, 286, 287; as Poetry Consultant to the Library of Congress, 43–44, 50; as poetry critic for *The New Yorker*, xl–xli, 314–15, 317; posthumous poems, lv; prose style, lv, 18–19, 22–23, 44, 83–84, 85–103, 117, 140, 184, 191, 202, 239, 240, 354 and *n2*, 387; Pulitzer Prize, 176, 177, 178, 179 and *n2*; punctuation and, xliv–liv, lxii, 16, 29, 41, 55*n1*, 56–57, 60–62, 63*n1*, 69 and *n1*, 80 and *n2*, 92*n1*, 117*n1*, 120, 156, 158 and *nn1–2*, 159 and *nn1–3*, 169 and *n1*, 170 and *n4*, 190 and *n2*, 212–13, 214, 222, 223 and *n2*, 245, 248*n2*, 263*n1*, 264*n1*, 280–81*n1*,

297*n1*, 325, 326*n1*, 332*nn1–3*, 334 and *n2*, 339*n2*, 343*n3*, 344*n1*, 356*n1*, 373*n1*, 386, 388*n1*, 391*n1*, 392*n2*; recognition, xlii–xliii; rejections from *The New Yorker*, xxiv–xxvi, xxxi, lv, 5–12, 19–23, 28, 36, 47–50, 53, 56, 58, 83, 112–13, 152, 168, 171, 186, 233–34, 354*n2*; Harold Ross and, xv, xviii–xix, lii, 13, 41, 54*n2*, 63 and *n1*; "second-thought" habit, xlvii; sexuality of, vii, xxiv–xxvi, lv; William Shawn and, xxv, xxxiii, xliii, 67, 68, 71, 72, 77, 100, 101, 140, 141, 172, 186, 208*n2*, 213, 247, 291, 292, 314, 316, 320, 326, 329, 355, 392*n1*; six-month agreement, xliii, 329, 331, 352; Lota de Macedo Soares and, xxiv–xxv, 75, 85, 193–96, 200, 206, 212, 216, 223, 226, 227, 235, 236, 238, 240 and *n1*, 246, 248, 256, 257, 262, 264, 265, 274, 278, 281, 287, 291, 296, 300 and *n1*, 309; as teacher at Harvard, 320 and *n1*, 324, 343, 357, 369, 377, 382; as teacher at New York University, 386 and *n2*; time lag in *The New Yorker* publication, xli–xlii, 328, 329, 331, 352, 354 and *n1*, 387*n2*; titles of, 3, 4, 5, 17, 18, 49–50, 233, 342*n2*; translations by, xl, 48 and *n1*, 140, 144, 145, 150, 163, 171–73, 201, 251, 252, 256 and *n2*, 302–305, 321 and *n3*, 322, 324, 341, 357–59, 371–72; typewriters of, 49, 50, 51, 71, 197, 239, 282, 296, 304, 363; *see also* editing and revision; Moss-Bishop correspondence; *specific poems, essays, reviews, translations, and books*; White-Bishop correspondence

Bishop, Morris, 130–31; *Champlain: The Life of Fortitude*, 131*n1*

"Bitter Day—Key West, A," 10

Blackburn, Harold, 255*n2*

Blackburn, Paul, xxvii

Black Orpheus (film), 216 and *n2*, 258

Blackwood, Caroline, 353

Bloom, Harold, 383 ands *n2*

Blough, Frani, viii, xxxiii

bodily subject matter, xxvii–xxviii, 86 and *n1*, 87, 88, 89 and *n1*, 96, 98, 99

Bogan, Louise, xiv, xx, xxii, xl, 21, 29, 51 and *n1*, 129, 139 and *n2*, 175, 176, 288, 312, 317, 382; "Hypocrite Swift," xxi; as Poetry Consultant to the Library of Congress, 44 and *n1*; "Verse," 21 and *n1*

Bologna, 177

Book Review of the New York Herald-Tribune, 265*n1*

Books Abroad/Neustadt International Prize for Literature, xlii, 379 and *n1*

Borges, Jorge Luis, 303, 341; "Afterglow," 303 and *n1*; "The Dagger," 303 and *n1*; "Hengest Cyning," 303 and *n1*; "Plainness," 303 and *n1*

Boston, viii, xxx, 91, 92, 93 and *n1*, 346, 353, 378, 379

Boston Post Magazine, 47 and *n2*

Botteghe Oscure, xxxi, 265*n1*

Bowen, Elizabeth, 286

Bowen, Suzanne, 316 and *n1*, 318

Brandt & Brandt, 208

Brasil, Emanuel, 304, 321, 322

Brasilia essay, xxxiv, xxxvii, 202, 203, 205, 291

Brazil, vii, xv, xxx, xxxiv, 122–23, 221–24, 255–56, 355; Bishop's life in, lv, 74, 77, 82, 84, 85, 99, 104, 109–12, 118, 119, 122–24, 125 and *n2*, 127–28, 132, 136, 138, 148, 149, 162, 169, 171, 187, 200, 202, 206, 207, 211, 215–17, 226–28, 232, 237–38, 254–57, 262, 267, 272, 277, 282, 289, 300 and *n1*, 305, 306, 307, 309, 310–13, 315, 316, 319, 331, 348; *see also specific cities*

Brazil, xl, 240 and *n2*

"Brazil, January 1, 1502," xxxiii, 218, 220; editing and revision, 220, 221, 222 and *n2*, 223 and *n2*, 224 and *n2*, 225

"Brazilian Landscape," 387*n3*

"Breakfast Song," lv

Breit, Harvey, 179 and *n2*

Bridge on the River Kwai, The (film), 228

Brinnin, John Malcolm, xxix, xxx, xxxi, xlvii, 350, 360, 361 and *n1*, 363, 365

British Museum, 55

Broadwater, Bowden, 221

Brooks, Gwendolyn, xl

Brooks, John, 235; "The Man Who Broke Things," 235, 236 and *n1*

Brooks, Paul, 64, 149

Brooks Brothers, xxxviii

Brown, Ashley, 271

Brush, Marjorie, 300

Bryn Mawr, x, xv, 50, 108, 109, 231*n2*, 337–38

Bryn Mawr Fellowship, 50, 51–52, 53–54, 55

"Burglar of Babylon, The," xl, xliii, lxiii, 257, 266, 267; editing and revision, 258–59, 263 and *n1*, 264 and *n1*

Burke, Kenneth, 175

Burns, Katharine (pen name), 36*n1*

Burnshaw, Stanley, *The Seamless Web*, 316 and
n2, 317

Cabo Frio, 254
Cadernos Brasileiros, 265, 266n1
Calder, Alexander, 216 and *n1*
Calder, Louisa James, 216 and *n1*
California, 204, 207, 298
Cambridge, Massachusetts, viii, xxx, 136, 200,
320, 327, 335, 336, 347, 351, 353
Campbell, Sandy, 303 and *n3*, 304, 310, 313
Camus, Marcel, 216n2
"Cancelled Dream, A," 7
Canfield, Cass, 375
Cannes Film Festival, 216 and *n2*
Cape Breton, 31, 39–43, 45
"Cape Breton," lii, 38, 39; editing and
revision, 39 and *n2*, 40–42
Cape Cod, 70
capitalization, lii–liii, liv, 13, 14, 15, 36–37, 61,
62, 392 and *n3*
Cardozo, Joaquim, "Cemetery of Childhood,"
322, 323, 324, 325, 326, 327, 328, 330, 331,
335, 336
Carlyle, Jane Welsh, 311, 313 and *n1*
Carlyle, Thomas, 313*n1*
Carson, Rachel, "Silent Spring," 255 and *n2*
Carter, Elliot, 369, 381; *A Mirror on Which to
Dwell*, 381 and *n1*
cartoons, xxxviii–xxxix, 73–74, 290 and *n2*;
1955 Album, 169 and *n2*; 25th Anniversary
Album, 73–74, 75, 77–78; *see also specific
cartoonists*
Casa Marianna, xl, 306
Cather, Willa, *The Best Stories of Sarah Orne
Jewett*, 400 and *n1*
Chatto & Windus, 165
Cheever, John, xxxvi
Chekhov, Anton, xxxv, 308, 339, 340
"Chemin de Fer," xviii, 17, 350n2; title, 17, 18
Chicago, 345
Christopher, Nicholas, 399; "Double
Solitaire," 399 and *n1*; "Heat," 399 and *n1*;
"Nocturne for Miranda," 399 and *n1*;
"Providence," 399 and *n1*; "Rimbaud
Crossing the Alps," 399 and *n1*
Ciardi, John, xxvi, xxxi, xliv, xlvii; as *Mid-
Century American Poets* editor, 51 and *n1*
"Cirque d'Hiver," viii–ix, xviii, xxi, xxxiii, 3–
5; title, 3, 4 and *n1*, 5

Clarke, Kenneth, 220, 221, 222, 224
Classics Book Club, 134
Cleaver, Kathleen, 303n2
"Close close all night/the lovers keep," lv
Coates, Robert, "Return," xxxviii
"Cold Spring, A," lii, 67–68, 133; editing and
revision, 69 and *n1*, 70 and *n2*, 73;
translations, 110
Cold Spring, A, xvii, xxxii, xxxiii, lii, 37n1,
55n1, 57n4, 69n1, 148, 153
Cole, Bill, 126
Coleridge, Samuel, 58
Collected Poems, The, 400n2
Collected Prose, The, 117n1
colons, xlv, xlvi–xlvii, 117n1, 280–81n1,
297n1, 343n3, 356n1, 373n1
Columbia University, 123, 372
commas, xliii, xliv–xlv, xlvi, xlviii, liii, 29,
55n1, 69 and *n1*, 80n2, 92n1, 151 and *n2*,
158n2, 159n3, 161n1, 169n1, 170 and *n4*, 190,
214, 222, 223, 236, 248n2, 263n1, 264n1,
280–81n1, 297n1, 326n1, 332n3, 339n2,
344n1, 356n1, 363, 373n1, 388n1, 389n2,
391n1, 392n2
communism, 255
Complete Poems, The, liv, 69n1, 297n1, 310,
314n1, 321n1, 381
Condé Nast, xxii
Congonhas, Brazil, 104
Connolly, Cyril, 167
contracts, 38, 51, 99, 219, 239, 240, 242, 246,
283, 291, 328, 330, 331, 389; cost of living
adjustment, xl, 38, 42, 118, 185, 219, 237,
246; first-reading, xviii–xix, xxxi–xxxv,
xxxix–xl, 22, 32, 45–46, 74, 143, 168, 191,
192, 200, 201, 209, 239, 318, 327, 341, 366,
371, 385, 387n2; six-month agreement, xlii,
329, 331, 352
copyright laws, 107, 110
Cornell, Joseph, 357 and *n1*, 358
correspondence between Bishop and *The New
Yorker, see* Moss-Bishop correspondence;
specific correspondents; White-Bishop
correspondence
Cosmopolitan Club, 277 and *n1*
covers, ix, 87–88; dachshund (August 4,
1945), 87, 88 and *n1*; Petty, 87, 88 and *n1*
Crane, Hart, 317 and *n1*
critical writing, xl–xli, 188–89, 201, 314, 317
"Crusoe in England," xlvii, lxii, 273, 274, 275,
278, 279, 280, 284, 290, 317, 318, 319, 325;

editing and revision, 325 and *n2*, 326 and *n1*, 328–29, 330, 331, 332 and *nn1–3*, 333 and *n1*, 334 and *nn1–2*, 335, 336

Cuban missile crisis, 251*n1*, 252

Cummings, E. E., xxii, 207; *95 Poems*, 204 and *n2*, 207

Dante, 399

Dartmouth College, 352–53

dashes, xliv, xlv–xlvi, xlviii, lii, liii, 56, 57 and *n4*, 80*n2*, 92*n1*, 158 and *n1*, 159 and *nn1–3*, 169*n1*, 190*n2*, 245, 297*n1*, 391*n1*

Davis, Linda, xii

Day, Clarence, "Life with Father," 92

"Dear, my compass/still points north," lv

Deaths and Entrances, xxxi

dedications, 211, 212 and *n1*, 279, 281 and *n1*, 283, 361, 362

de la Mare, Walter, 204; *Come Hither*, xl, xli, 204 and *n1*

Democratic Party, 302

De Moraes, Vinicius, "Sonnet of Intimacy," 322, 323, 324, 328, 330, 331, 335

Depression, xx

De Vries, Peter, xxvii

Dewey, Jane, ix, 73, 281

Dewey, John, ix

Diaghilev, Sergei, 380*n2*

Diamantina, 138, 139, 145, 164, 169, 172, 181, 184, 262

Diary of Helena Morley, The, xvii, xxxiv, 201 and *n2*, 251, 304, 305, 310, 337, 389; film of, 337

Dickey, James, xxiii, 331, 360; *Buckdancer's Choice*, 287*n1*; *Deliverance*, 318 and *n1*

Dickinson, Emily, xl, 380 and *n2*

dictionaries, xlviii, lii, lxi

Dolmetsch, Arnold, 366, 367

Donne, John, 157

Dowd, William, 367

dreams, xlvi, 53

Duell, Sloan and Pearce, ix

Duke University, 56

Durrell, Lawrence, *Justice*, 200, 201 and *n1*

Duxbury, Massachusetts, xlvii

Ecco Press, 358*n1*, 389, 390

Ecuador, 229

Edgar Allan Poe & The Juke-Box, lv

editing and revision, xxiii–xxv, xliii–lvi, lxi, lxii; "At the Fishhouses," xliv–xlvi, xlix, 29, 30 and *n1*; "Brazil, January 1, 1502," 220, 221, 222 and *n2*, 223 and *n2*, 224 and *n2*, 225; "The Burglar of Babylon," 258–59, 263 and *n1*, 264 and *n1*; "Cape Breton," 39 and *n2*, 40–42; "A Cold Spring," 69 and *n1*, 70 and *n2*, 73; "Crusoe in England," 325 and *n2*, 326 and *n1*, 328–29, 330, 331, 332 and *nn1–3*, 333 and *n1*, 334 and *nn1–2*, 335, 336; "Electrical Storm," 222 and *n1*, 223; "The End of March," xlvii–xlviii, xlix–lii, 361, 362 and *nn1–2*, 363 and *n1*, 364, 365 and *n1*, 366, 370 and *n1*; "Filling Station," 158 and *nn1–2*, 159 and *nn1–3*, 160 and *n1*; "Five Flights Up," 356 and *n1*; "Going to the Bakery," 296, 297 and *n1*; "Gwendolyn," 86 and *n1*, 87, 88, 89 and *n1*, 90, 91, 92 and *n1*, 93 and *nn1–5*, 94 and *nn1–7*, 97 and *nn1–2*, 98 and *n1*, 104, 106, 108; "House Guest," 302 and *n2*; "The Housekeeper," 29–30; "Insomnia," 59 and *n1*, 60–62; "In the Village," 94–96, 98, 99–102, 103 and *nn1–2*, 104, 105, 113 and *n1*, 114, 115–16, 117 and *nn1–2*, 118, 120, 121, 126*n2*, 127*n2*; "In the Waiting Room," 323, 325 and *n1*; "Large Bad Picture," 16 and *n1*, 17; "Little Exercise," 13–14, 49–50; "Manuelzinho," 169 and *n1*, 170 and *nn1–4*, 171, 173, 176; "The Moose," lii, 344 and *n1*, 345, 346 and *n1*, 347, 349 and *n1*, 350 and *n1*; "A Norther—Key West," 245, 248 and *n1*; "North Haven," lii–liv, 390 and *n3*, 391 and *n1*; "The Owl's Journey," 53 and *n2*; "Poem," 342 and *n2*, 345, 349; "The Prodigal," 63 and *n1*; "Questions of Travel," 153, 154, 155, 156 and *n1*, 157 and *n1*; "The Riverman," 212–13, 214, 219; "Santarem," 386, 387 and *n1*, 388 and *n1*, 389 and *n2*; "Sestina," 160, 161 and *n1*, 185 and *n2*; "Song for the Rainy Season," 232, 234, 235, 236 and *n2*; "Sonnet," liv, 391 and *n2*, 400 and *n2*; "The Squatter's Children," 154 and *n1*, 155; "Sunday, 4 A.M.," 189, 190 and *nn1–2*, 191; "12 O'Clock News," 342 and *n3*, 349; "Under the Window: Ouro Prêto," 279, 280 and *n1*, 282; "View of the Capital from the Library of Congress," 54, 56, 57 and *n4*; *see also* capitalization; grammar; punctuation; spelling; *specific editors and works*

Edman, Irwin, "The Wonder and Wackiness of Man," 129 and *n1*

"Efforts of Affection: A Memoir of Marianne Moore," liv, 354 and *n2*

Ehrenpreis, Irvin, "Loitering between Dream and Experience," 321*n2*

Einstein, Albert, 149

Eisenhower, Dwight D., xxxvii

Elbrick, C. Burke, 307, 314

"Electrical Storm," xlii, 218, 220; editing and revision, 222 and *n1*, 223

Eliot, T. S., xii, xix, xxviii

ellipses, xlv, 332*n1*

Ellis, Sally, "U.S. Poetry Chair Holder Tells How She Courts the Muse," 47 and *n2*

Encounter, 252, 265

"End of March, The," xlvii–xlviii, 360, 361, 368; editing and revision, xlvii–xlviii, xlix–lii, 361, 362 and *nn1–2*, 363 and *n1*, 364, 365 and *n1*, 366, 370 and *n1*

England, 146, 147, 150, 165, 218, 257, 259, 264, 265

Esquire, 355, 356

Estess, Sybill, liv

Eulália Pimenta, Alexandre, 262

Evergreen Review, xxxi

"Exchanging Hats," xxvi, xxxi, xliv, xlvii, 150, 152

Exchanging Hats: Paintings, 387*n3*

fact checking, xxii, xxiv, xliii, 16, 153, 203, 208

Fact Department, xxii, 67, 183, 208

"False Scent," 52*n1*

fan letters, 64, 126, 128, 144

"Farmer's Children, The," 19, 23, 44 and *n2*, 340

Farrar, Straus and Giroux, 302, 303, 304, 305, 317, 349*n1*, 355, 356, 398

"Faustina," xxi, 27, 28 and *n1*, 153

Fawcett, Percy Harrison, 134 and *n1*

55 Stories from The New Yorker, 103*n2*

"Filling Station," xvii, 151, 158; editing and revision, 158 and *nn1–2*, 159 and *nn1–3*, 160 and *n1*

"Fine Examples," *see* "Chemin de Fer"

"First Death in Nova Scotia," xl, xlvi, 246, 247, 248 and *n2*, 249

first-reading contracts, xviii–xix, xxxi–xxxv, xxxix–xl, 22, 32, 45–46, 74, 143, 168, 191,

192, 200, 201, 209, 239, 318, 327, 341, 366, 371, 385, 387*n2*

"Five Flights Up," xlvii, 354, 356; editing and revision, 356 and *n1*

Florence, 219

Florida, viii, ix, 23, 27, 38

Foley, Martha, 44 and *n2*

Fonteyn, Margot, 290

Footloose Correspondent, 131

Ford, Harry, 394 and *n1*

"For M.M." ["Invitation to Miss Marianne Moore"], 35 and *n1*

Fortune, xi

'47, 33, 34

Foster, Sarah (pen name), ix, 11 and *n1*

Foulke, Adrienne, 378 and *n1*

foul language, xxiv

Fountain (Gary) and Brazeau (Peter), *Remembering Elizabeth Bishop: An Oral Biography*, 354*n2*

Fowler, Henry Watson, *English Usage*, xxiv, xliv

Fowlie, Wallace, 48

France, 123, 250

Frank, Anne, *Diary of a Young Girl*, 139 and *n1*

Frankenberg, Lloyd, 135

Freud, Sigmund, 135

Friar, Kimon, 207 and *n1*

"From Trollope's Journal," xxxvii, xlix, 230, 233

Frost, Frances, xxvii

Fuchs, Daniel, 308 and *n1*

"Full Moon, Key West," 11, 20, 21 and *n2*

Galápagos, 331, 336

Galentine, Wheaton, 267*n2*, 296, 397

galley proofs, xliii, xliv, liv, lxii, 391 and *nn1–2*

Gannett, Lewis, "Books and Things," 27 and *n1*

gay poetry, xxv–xxvi

Geography III, xxxix, xlii, lii, 350*n1*, 359*n1*, 381, 384

Geraghty, James, 238*n1*

Gerard-Gailly, Émile, *Madame de Sévigné: Lettres*, 241 and *n2*

Gibbs, Wolcott, x, xxiii, xxiv; "Theory and Practice of Editing *New Yorker* Articles," xxiii–xxiv

Gielgud, John, 268*n1*
Gill, Brendan, 65, 126; *Here at The New Yorker*, xivn, 370 and *n2*
Ginsberg, Allen, xxxi, 302 and *n1*
Gioia, Dana, lv
Giotto, 265
Giroux, Robert, liv, lv, 278, 280, 337, 344, 349*n1*
Glück, Louise, xxvii
Godine, David, 397, 398, 400
"Going to the Bakery," 290, 295; editing and revision, 296, 297 and *n1*
Goldwater, Barry, 252
Goodman, William, 395, 396
Gordimer, Nadine, xii
Gorostiza, José, 304
Goyen, William, 267 and *n2*
Graham, Jorie, lv
grammar, xxiv
Grand Cayman, 31, 32
Grand Central Terminal, New York, 47 and *n1*
Grant, Jane, xi
Graves, Robert, xxii
Greece, 263, 327, 396
Green, Henry, 395*n1*
Greenslet, Ferris, ix–x, xix, 12, 23
Gregory, Horace, ix, xxxiii, xxxv, xxxvii; "The Poetry of Suburbia," xxxiii, 191 and *n1*
Guanabara, 238
Guggenheim, Peggy, 399
Guggenheim (John Simon) Memorial Foundation, 215, 217, 218, 226 and *n1*, 389
Guiterman, Arthur, "Lyrics from the Pekinese," xix
Guth, Dorothy Lobrano, 376
"Gwendolyn," xxiv, xxxiv, 83–84, 85, 86–97, 100, 108, 109, 113, 115, 140; editing and revision, 86 and *n1*, 87, 88, 89 and *n1*, 90, 91 and *n1*, 93 and *nn1–5*, 94 and *nn1–7*, 97 and *nn1–2*, 98 and *n1*, 104, 106, 108

Hagen, Beulah, 375
Hahn, Emily, "Diamond," 183 and *n1*, 184
Haiti, 42
Halpern, Daniel, 358 and *n1*
Hancock, John, 66
Harcourt Brace, viii
Hardwick, Elizabeth, xii, xvii

Harnett, William, 367 and *n1*, 368
Harper & Row, 374, 375
HarperCollins, 199, 358*n1*
Harper's Bazaar, xi, 6*n1*, 23, 126*n1*, 138, 139, 340
Harvard Alumni Bulletin, 343
Harvard Library, 347
Harvard University, 320 and *n1*, 324, 343, 357, 369, 377, 382
Havre de Grace, Maryland, ix, 73
Hawes, Elizabeth, 273
Heaney, Seamus, xxvii, lv
Hecht, Anthony, 285
Heilman, Robert, 285
Hellman, Geoffrey T., viii, 52*n1*
Hemenway, Robert, 320, 325*n1*, 333, 334 and *n2*, 335
Hemingway, Ernest, 31*n1*, 134
Hemingway, Pauline Pfeiffer, 31 and *n1*, 35, 36
Henderson, Charlie, 76, 79, 82, 86, 141
Henderson, Robert, xxxix, 37, 43, 345, 348, 349 and *n1*, 351, 361, 362 and *n1*
Henry, Mrs. Robert, *The Little Madeleine: The Autobiography of a Young Girl in Montmartre*, 139 and *n1*
Herschberger, Ruth, 110
Higbee, Edward, *The Squeeze: Cities Without Space*, 256 and *n1*
Hillyer, Robert, "Early in the Morning," 269 and *n2*
Holland, 128
Houghton Mifflin, ix, xix, 12, 16, 18, 20, 23, 78, 138, 145
Houghton Mifflin Poetry Prize Fellowship, ix–x, 12
"House Guest," 289, 297; editing and revision, 302 and *n2*
"Housekeeper, The," ix, 29–30; editing and revision, 29–30
Hudson Review, 188
Hughes, Langston, "Mean Old Yesterday," xxvii
Hughes, Ted, xxiii, 290; "Fern," 290 and *n1*; "Small Events," 290 and *n1*; "Thaw," 290 and *n1*; "You Drive in a Circle," 290 and *n1*
Hull, Donald, 237, 238 and *n1*
Hussey, Anne, 353
Huxley, Aldous, xxxiv, 202, 203, 205, 207, 208 and *n1*, 214, 215
Hyman, Stanley Edgar, xx

hyphens, xlviii, lii, liii, 57 and *n1*, 151 and
n2, 158, 159 and *n1*, 212–13, 333, 334, 349,
400

Importance of Being Oscar, The (show), 240,
241 and *n1*
Ingersoll, Ralph, x
"In Prison," 23 and *n1*
"Insomnia," 58, 61–62, 63, 381*n1*; editing and
revision, 59 and *n1*, 60–62
"In the Village," xvi, xxiv, xxxiv, xxxv, 85, 90,
92, 94–96, 98, 99–105, 106, 114, 115, 126
and *n2*, 127, 129, 133, 136, 140, 144, 163,
184, 225, 280, 389*n1*; editing and revision,
94–96, 98, 99–102, 103 and *nn1–2*, 104,
105, 113 and *n1*, 114, 115–16, 117 and *nn1–2*,
118, 120, 121, 126*n2*, 127*n2*
"In the Waiting Room," xlii, xlix–l, 319, 328,
329, 330, 331, 334, 335, 389*n1*; editing and
revision, 323, 325 and *n1*
Ireland, 259, 260
Iroquois, xxvii
italics, 36, 37*n1*
"It All Depends," 51*n1*
Italy, 128, 177, 178, 218, 262, 264, 265
Ivask, Ivar, 383 and *n1*

Jackson, David, 241, 394*n1*
Jacob, Max, 48, 49; "Banks," 48 and *n1*; "Hell
Is Graduated," 48 and *n1*; "Patience of an
Angel," 48 and *n1*; "Rainbow," 48 and *n1*
Jaffe, Dan, "Voice of the Poet: Oracular,
Eerie, Daring," 306 and *n1*
James, Henry, 397
"January First," 371, 372
Jarrell, Randall, 27, 29, 398; *Pictures from an
Institution*, 71 and *n1*
Jesperson, Otto, *Growth and Structure of the
English Language*, 255 and *n1*
Jewett, Sarah Orne, 395–96, 400 and *n1*; *The
Country of Pointed Firs*, 395–96, 396*n1*, 397;
A Marsh Island, 396 and *n2*, 397
Johnson, Lyndon B., 234
Joplin, Janis, 312
Junior Bazaar, xxvi

Kalstone, David, 321*n1*, 336; *Five
Temperaments*, 389*n1*; "Questions of

Memory—New Poems by Elizabeth
Bishop," 373 and *n2*
Karli, Simon Peter, "My Most Durable
Translation," 224 and *n1*
Karp, Vickie, xxviii
Kazantzakis, Nikos, *The Odyssey: A Modern
Sequel*, 207 and *n1*
Kazin, Pearl, vii, xiv, xxv, xxvi, xxx, xxxvi,
xxxvii, xxxix, lxi, 82, 89*n1*, 99*n1*, 104 and
n1, 106, 108, 119, 121 and *n2*, 125*n2*, 126,
137, 138, 140, 141, 145, 146, 168, 179; "We
Gather Together," 165 and *n1*
Keats, John, 227–28, 308; "This Living
Hand," lv
Kelly, Richard, 271 and *n1*, 272, 274
Kennedy, John F., 234, 251 and *n1*, 252
Kenner, Hugh, 139 and *n2*
Kentfield, Calvin, 165, 207; "The Bell of
Charity," 165*n2*; "A Good Example,"
xxxii
Kenyon Review, xl, 256*n2*, 261, 284, 288, 304;
"All Praise," 286 and *n1*
Key West, viii, ix, 38
Khrushchev, Nikita, 224 and *n1*
Kinnell, Galway, "The Porcupine," xxvii–
xxviii
Kirkup, James, "Sendai Sequence," xlii
Klee, Paul, 130 and *n1*
Knopf, A. A., 57, 126, 204
Komunyakaa, Yusef, 399*n3*
Korean War, xxxvii
Kramer, Dale, xi
Kramer, Jane, 302 and *n1*
Kray, Betty, 321 and *n3*, 331
Kunitz, Stanley, *Selected Poems, 1928–1958*,
204 and *n2*, 207
Kunkel, Thomas, xi

LaBadie, Donald W., 215 and *n2*
Lacerda, Carlos, 123, 167, 256, 238 and *n2*
Lancaster, Osbert, *All Done from Memory*, 139
and *n1*
Lantern, The, x, 338 and *n1*
"Large Bad Picture," xv–xvi, xviii, liv, 12, 13,
16, 18, 133; editing and revision, 16 and *n1*,
17
Larkin, Philip, 206; *The Less Deceived*, 204
and *n2*
Laughlin, James, viii, ix, 5
Lawrence, D. H., 271

Leão, Rosalina, 287–88, 289

Lear, Edward, "Le Hibou et le Poussiqette," 214 and *n1*

Leeds, Harold, 267 and *n2*, 397

legal department, xxiv, xliii, 322

"Letter from Rio de Janeiro," 122 and *n1*, 123, 124, 125 and *n2*, 126, 128

"Letter to N.Y.," ix, 6 and *n1*, 153, 179*n2*, 398

Levertov, Denise, xli

Levine, Philip, xxvii

Library of Congress, 46, 49, 175; Poetry Consultant to, 43, 44 and *n1*, 50

Liebling, Joe, 221

Lindley, Frances, 199

Lispector, Clarice, xl, 251, 252, 255; *The Apple in the Dark*, 250 and *n1*; "A Hen," 256 and *n2*; "Marmosets," 256*n2*; "The Smallest Woman in the World," 256 and *n2*

"Little Exercise," xviii, xxxi, 13–14, 49–50, 373; editing and revision, 13–14, 49–50; title, 49–50

Lobrano, Gustave, xvi, xxiv, 14, 86, 146, 164, 168; Bishop and, 11, 14–16, 163; death of, 174

London, 259, 260, 262, 264, 265, 287, 329

London Times, 135

Longchamps Restaurant, New York, 37

Look Stranger, xxxi

Lorca, Federico García, 398

Lord John Press, liii

love poems, xxiv–xxvi, lv

Lowell, Robert, xvii, xxxi, xxxiii, xxxviii, xl, xlix, 114, 206, 207, 249, 353–54, 398; Bishop and, xlix–lii, liii, 128, 315*n2*, 353, 390; death of, 390 and *n2*; *Life Studies*, 207 and *n1*; *Lord Weary's Castle*, 27*n1*; "My Last Afternoon with Uncle Devereux Winslow," xxxii; "Sailing Home from Rapallo," xxxii

Lucy Martin Donnelly Fellowship, xiv–xv, 106, 107

"Lullaby," 12 and *n1*

"Lullaby for a Not Very Bright Child," 12 and *n1*

Macauley, Robie, xl

Macchu Picchu, 336

Macdonald, Dwight, 174; "The Bible in Modern Undress," 125 and *n1*; "The First Editions of T. J. Wise," 255 and *n2*

MacDowell Colony, 350

Machado de Assis, Jaoquim Maria, 138

Machemer, Corona, 374, 375

MacIver, Loren, xxx, 135, 240

MacKenzie, Rachel, xxxvii–xxxviii, 226, 245, 295–96, 297*n2*

MacLíammóir, Micheál, 241*n1*

MacMahon, Candace, 387*n3*; *Elizabeth Bishop: A Bibliography, 1927–1979*, lxii, 387*n3*

MacNeice, Louis, 267; "Barroom Matins," xx

Maine, x, xviii, 20, 44, 64, 76, 79, 82, 90, 107, 110, 116, 118, 133, 198, 251–52, 338, 360, 369, 372, 377

Malamud, Bernard, 394

Mallarmé, Stéphane, xxxvii

"Manners," xvii, 148, 150, 151 and *n2*, 152, 154

Mansfield, Katharine, xxxv

"Manuelzinho," xvi, xvii, xxxviii, xxxix, 161, 162, 164–65, 166, 167, 168, 177, 179, 259, 266; editing and revision, 169 and *n1*, 170 and *n1–4*, 171, 173, 176

"Map, The," xlvii, 261

Marcel Proust: A Biography, Volume 2, 278 and *n1*

Maria Moors Cabot Award, 123

Marlowe, Sylvia, 208 and *n1*, 277

Martin, James, 322

Massachusetts Institute of Technology, 116 and *n1*

Maxwell, William, xiii, xxi, xxiv, xxxv, 37*n2*, 56, 86, 146, 172, 199, 231, 234, 251, 252 and *n1*, 255, 320; Bishop and, xxxix, 11, 12, 19, 35–37, 67–68, 148, 201–203, 208 and *n2*, 209, 219–20, 239, 242, 252–53, 256; *The Château*, 239 and *n1*

Mazzocco, Robert, 351; "Very Different Cats," 354 and *n3*

M. Carey Thomas Prize, 108, 109

McCarthy, Mary, ix, xii, xiii, xxxvi, xli, 13, 141, 144, 249, 250; "The Appalachian Revolution," 139 and *n2*; "A City of Shame," 219 and *n1*; "The Revel of the Earth," 188 and *n1*

McDonald, John, 42

McKenna, Rollie, 254 and *n1*

McMichael, James, 399

McPhee, John, 393

McPherson, William, 384; "The Famous Eye," 383 and *n3*

Mencken, H. L., 69, 128

Merck, George W., 84 and *n4*

Meredith, William, xxiii

Merrill, James, xxvi, xli, 240*n1*, 263, 327, 336, 339–40, 348, 353*n1*, 394 and *n1*; "A Carpet Not Bought," 268 and *n2*; *The (Diblos) Notebook*, 263 and *n2*, 283 and *n1*; *Divine Comedies: Poems*, 399 and *n2*; *The Firescreen*, xli; "The Thousand and Second Night," 263 and *n2*

Merwin, W. S., xxiii, xxxi

Messer, Allene, 107*n2*, 110, 116, 143

Methfessel, Alice, liv, 327, 358, 359, 384, 396, 400 and *n2*, 401

Mexico, 358

Mexico City, 9

Miami, 45

Mid-Century American Poets (anthology), 51 and *n1*

Milhaud, Darius, "Saudades do Brasil," 259 and *n1*

Millay, Edna St. Vincent, xii

Miller, Margaret, 54*n3*

Millier, Brett, *Life and the Memory of It*, 316*n1*

Mindlin, Henrique, 118, 119, 120, 121; *Modern Architecture in Brazil*, 164 and *n1*

"Minha Vida de Menina," 145, 146, 150, 164, 169, 171–73

Minor, Audax, 45*n1*, 46

Modern Language Association, 380 and *n3*, 381

Moe, Henry Allen, 226 and *n1*

Montgomery, Lucy Maud, *Anne of Avonlea*, 70 and *n1*

"Monument, The," viii

Moore, Marianne, viii, ix, xxi, xxii–xxiii, xxvi, xxxv, xlvii, liv, 55, 70, 77, 78, 85, 105, 107, 111, 207, 214, 226, 249, 269, 284, 313–14, 398; "The Arctic Ox," 207 and *n1*; "Baseball and Writing," 249 and *n1*; Bishop and, 5, 21 and *n1*, 35, 150, 207, 231 and *n2*, 309, 323, 337–39, 354 and *n2*; "Carnegie Hall: Rescued," xxxvi; "Combat Cultural," 211 and *n1*; death of, 337 and *n1*, 338–39; *The Fables of La Fontaine*, 139 and *n2*; "Four Quartz Crystal Clocks," xxii, 77*n1*; "Isaiah, Jeremiah, Ezekiel, Daniel," 338*n1*; "Leonardo da Vinci's," 211 and *n1*, 212 and *n2*, 216 and *n3*; "Light and Dark," 216 and *n3*; "A Modest Expert," 21 and *n1*; "The North Wind to a Dutiful Beast," 338*n1*; "The Rigorists," 77*n1*; "Tell Me, Tell Me," xxxvi, 230 and *n1*, 231 and *n2*; "To Disraeli on Conservatism," 338*n1*; "Tom Fool at

Jamaica," 108 and *n1*, 109, 113–14; "What Are Years?" xxi, xxxvi, 77*n1*

Moorehead, Alan, "A Drop into the Stone Age," 205 and *n1*

"Moose, The," xliii, xlvii, lii, lxii, 343, 381–82; editing and revision, lii–liii, 344 and *n1*, 345, 346 and *n1*, 347, 349 and *n1*, 350 and *n1*

Morse, Mary, 216, 217, 300*n1*

Mortimer, Penelope, 378; *Long Distance*, 378*n3*

Moss, Howard, vii, xii, xvii, xxii, xxv–xxxi, lv, lxi, 151 and *n1*; "Adolescent's Song," 129, 130; American Academy of Arts and Letters award, 299 and *n1*; "Animal Hospital," 130*n1*; "Antennae," 130*n1*; "Around the Fish 1 & 2," 130*n1*; "Aside by the Shore," 198 and *n1*; "At the Masseur's," 359; "A Box at the Opera," 197, 198*n1*; "Burning Love Letters," 129; "Chalk from Eden," 197, 198*n1*; "Chekhov," 339 and *n1*; "Childhood in Diamatina," 201 and *n3*; death of, lv; "The Falls of Love," 197, 198*n1*; *Finding Them Lost and Other Poems*, xxx, 273 and *n2*; *The Folding Green*, 200; "The Gift to Be Simple," 149 and *n1*, 197, 198*n1*; *Keats*, 227, 228 and *n1*; "Lennie," 380; "Letter to an Imaginary Brazil," xxx, 157 and *n2*, 184, 185 and *n1*, 189, 198 and *n1*; "Light and Dark," 211 and *n1*; "Local Places," 177 and *n1*; *The Magic Lantern of Marcel Proust*, 253 and *n1*, 257, 397; "Mariner's Song," 130*n1*; "A Marriage," 193*n1*, 197, 198*n1*; "Memories of Lower Fifth," 364 and *n2*, 366; National Book Award, 343 and *n1*; *New York Poems*, 398 and *n1*, 399; "The Night Express," 396 and *n3*; "On the Library Steps," 263, 276; *The Palace at 4 A.M.*, 342 and *n1*; poetry by, xxix, xlii, 129 and *nn2–3*, 130 and *n1*, 157*n2*, 185, 189, 193 and *n1*, 197, 198 and *n1*, 228–29, 259, 364, 380; as poetry editor of *The New Yorker*, xxvi–xxxi, xxxiv–xxxv, xxxix, xl–lv, 60–62, 81, 129–30, 148–49, 152–62, 166–71, 177–209, 215–18, 226–29, 235–41, 245–48, 253–54, 257–92, 296–332, 335–37, 339–48, 350–74, 379–401; "Robinson," 319; "Saratoga," 364 and *n2*, 366; "Saudades," 259 and *n1*, 260; *Second Nature*, 299; "See How They Love Me," 269*n2*; *Selected Poems*, xxix, 343 and *n1*, 354 and *n3*; "September Elegy," 267; "The Silences," 254, 276; "Small Elegy," 180 and *n1*, 198 and *n1*, 380; "A Song to Be Set to Music," 193*n1*; "Storm," 130 and *n1*; "A Summer Gone," 197, 198*n1*; "Swimmer in the Air," 193*n1*, 198 and *n1*; *A Swimmer in the Air*, 197 and *n1*, 198 and *n1*; *A Swim Off the Rocks*, 380 and *n1*, 383 and *n2*; "Three Double Dactyls," 380 and *n2*; "Torches," 211 and *n1*; *The Toy Fair*, 129 and *n2*, 130 and *n1*; "Underwood," 197, 198*n1*; "Venice," 129*n3*; "Water Island," 238 and *n3*; *A Winter Come, A Summer Gone: Poems, 1946–1960*, 228 and *n2*, 229; "Winter's End," 130; *Writing Against Time: Critical Essays and Reviews*, 259 and *n2*, 260, 309; *see also* Moss-Bishop correspondence

Moss-Bishop correspondence, xxvi–xxxi, xxxix, xl–lv, 56, 172; of 1947–1961, 60–62, 81, 129–30, 148–49, 151–62, 166–71, 177–209, 215–18, 226–29, 235–41; of 1961–1967, 245–48, 253–54, 257–92; of 1967–1979, 296–332, 335–37, 339–48, 350–74, 379–401

"Mountain, The," xxxii, xxxiv, 81–82, 83

Mulligan, James, xxxix

Mumford, Lewis, 203 and *n1*, 257

Munn, Orson D., viii

Museum of Modern Art, New York, 54, 269

music, 47 and *nn1–2*, 269, 271, 272, 273, 366–69, 381, 393, 394, 395

Nabokov, Vladimir, ix, xii, xxvii, 40, 65, 165; "Portrait of My Mother," 39 and *n1*

Nash, Ogden, 78; "Animal Axis," 78*n1*; "Capercaillie, Ave Atque Vaillie," 211 and *n1*; "I Will Arise and Go Now," xix; "The Panda," 78 and *n1*; "Paradise for Sale," 212 and *n2*; "Sticks and Stones May Break My Bones, but Names Will Break My Heart," 211 and *n1*

Nation, The, xxxi, 21*n1*, 27, 28*n1*

National Book Award, xxix, 287 and *n1*, 314, 315 and *n2*, 343*n1*

National Book Critics Award, xlii

National Book Critics Circle, 394

National Geographic, 319, 320, 323

National Institute of Arts and Letters award, 64–65, 133

Nemerov, Howard, xxii

Neruda, Pablo, 341

Nervi, Pier Luigi, 233

Neto, João Cabral de Melo, xl

Neustadt International Prize for Literature, xlii, 379 and *n1*

New Directions Yearbook in Poetry and Prose (anthology), viii, ix

Newhouse, S. I., xxii

New Orleans Item, The, xi

New Poetry of Mexico (anthology), 321 and *n4*

New Republic, The, x, xx, xxvi, 114*n1*, 171*n1*, 175, 184, 382*n2*

New World Writing, xxvi, xxxi xliv, xlvii, 152*n1*

New York, viii, xi, xxiv, lv, 20, 37, 38, 64, 178, 193–96, 223, 226, 248, 274, 282, 301, 315, 342

New York: Poems (anthology), 398 and *n1*, 399

New Yorker, The, 265*n1*; advertising, viii, xxxviii–xxxix; back pages, 350 and *nn2–3*, 351; Bishop's contracts and money issues with, xxxiii–xxxv, xxxix–xl, xlii–xliii, 3, 15–16, 22, 32 and *n1*, 33, 38, 42, 46, 64–65, 99, 108, 118, 121, 127, 143, 185, 194, 195, 210, 219, 236, 239, 246–47, 267, 270, 271, 278, 283, 328, 330, 331, 345, 358, 366, 389; Bishop's dissatisfaction with, xxxii–xxxviii, xxxix–xlii, 89*n1*, 103*n2*, 113*n1*, 126*n2*, 328–29, 350 and *nn2–3*; Bishop's 1934–1946 correspondence with, 1–23; Bishop's 1947–1961 correspondence with, 25–242; Bishop's 1961–1967 correspondence with, 243–92; Bishop's 1967–1979 correspondence with, 293–401; Bishop's poetry criticism for, xl–xli, 314–15, 317; blind spots of, xii, xxvii–xviii; bodily subject matter shunned by, xxvii–xxviii, 86 and *n1*, 87, 88, 89 and *n1*, 96, 98, 99*n1*; business prospectus, xix; cartoons, xxxviii–xxxix, 73–74, 75, 77–78, 169, 290; circulation, 122, 137; Condé Nast shake-up of, xxii; copyright issues, 107; covers, ix, 87–88; criticism of, xxxii–xxxviii, 103*n2*; dedications, 211, 212 and *n1*, 279, 281 and *n1*, 283, 361, 362; editing and revision process, xxiii–xxv, xliii–lvi, lxii; fact checking, xxiv, xliii, 16, 153, 203, 208; first-reading contracts, xviii–xix, xxi–xxxv, xxxix–xl, 22, 32, 45–46, 74, 143, 168, 191, 192, 200, 201, 209, 239, 318, 327, 341, 366, 371, 385, 387*n2*; gentility of, xxvii–xxviii, xxxvii–xxxviii, 86, 87; legal department, xxiv, xliii, 322; Moss as poetry editor at,

New Yorker, The (*cont.*)
xxvi–xxxi, xxxiv–xxxv, xxxix, xl–lv, 60–
62, 81, 129–30, 148–49, 152–62, 166–71,
177–209, 215–18, 226–29, 235–41, 245–48,
253–54, 257–92, 296–332, 335–37, 339–48,
350–74, 379–401; offices, vii; original
"nucleus" of, x; parodies of poets, xix–xx;
poetry rates, xviii–xix, xxii, xxxiii–xxxiv,
xxxix, xlii–xliii, 15–16, 32 and *n1*, 33, 143,
246–47; procedure for discovering new
talent, viii–ix; prose rates, xviii–xix, xxii,
xxxiv, xxxix, xliii, 143; punctuation style,
xliv–liv, lxii, 29, 41, 56, 120, 156, 213; "The
Race Track," 45*n1*, 46; rejection policy, xx–
xxiii, xxiv–xxvi, xxvii–xxviii, lv; Harold
Ross as founding editor of, xi–xii, xviii–
xiv, xxxviii, xl, 32*n1*, 39–40, 41, 47, 86;
serious poetry, xx–xxiii; William Shawn as
editor of, xxii, xxiv–xxv, xxvii, xxviii,
xxxvi, xxxvii–xxxviii, xl, xli, xliii, xliv, 76,
77, 86, 100, 125, 131, 133, 168, 176, 186, 199,
251, 256, 372, 382, 386; six-month agree-
ment, xlii, 329, 331, 352; subscriptions, 134,
136–37, 268, 270, 271, 272, 287–89, 298,
328, 330, 331, 336; "Talk of the Town," viii,
xxii, 3 and *n1*, 47*n1*, 52, 54, 131, 132, 176,
258; time lag in publication, xli–xlii, 328,
329, 331, 352, 354 and *n1*, 387*n2*; Katharine
White leaves Fiction Department, xviii,
162–64, 165–66, 199; Katharine White as
literary editor at, x–xix, xx–xxiii, xxv,
xxxiii, xl, xliii, 12–23, 27–34, 37–60, 62–
152, 162–89, 254–56, 385; World War II
and, xx; *see also specific authors, editors,*
departments, and works
New Yorker Book of Poems, The (anthology),
307 and *n3*
New Yorker Festival (2002), lv
New Yorker 1950–1955 Album, The, 169 and *n2*
New Yorker Participation Plan, The, 366
New York Herald Tribune, xivn, 27 and *n1*
New York Post, "The Literary Scene," 383*n3*
New York Quarterly, "Craft Interview with
Howard Moss," 353 and *n1*
New York Review of Books, The, xl, 302*n3*,
303*n2*, 354*n3*
New York Times, The, 58, 190
New York Times Book Review, The: "The
Complete Poems: Throughout Is This
Quality of Thingness," 307 and *n1*; "In and
Out of Books" columns, 179*n2*

New York University, 55; Bishop as teacher at,
386 and *n2*
Niemeyer, Oscar, 205
"Night City," 340, 350
North & South, x, xxxi, xxxiii, 14, 21, 27*n1*,
51*n1*; reviews of, 20, 21 and *n1*
North Brooklin, Maine, x, 68, 76, 198, 225,
378
"Norther—Key West, A," 241, 246, 247, 248;
editing and revision, 245, 248 and *n1*
"North Haven," lii–liv, 390, 391, 392; editing
and revision, lii–liv, 390 and *n3*, 391 and *n1*
North Haven, Maine, xviii, 360, 369, 377
Notes and Comments, 34
Nova Scotia, xvii, xlix, 31, 39–43, 44, 45, 65–
66, 86, 87, 89, 90, 91, 93, 95, 98, 100, 101,
103, 105, 118, 346, 395, 396
Nuova Corriente: Rivistas di Letteratura, 179*n3*
Nureyev, Rudolf, 290

Objectivists, xxvii
"Objects and Apparitions," 358, 359, 360
and *n1*
"O Breath," 43 and *n1*, 53*n1*, 381*n1*
O'Connor, Edwin, *The Last Hurrah*, 174
nd *n2*
O'Connor, Flannery, 393 and *n1*
Oden, Gloria, 180, 181; *The Naked Frame: A*
Love Poem and Sonnets, 180 and *n2*
Olds, Sharon, xxvii
"One Art," xxvi, xlvi–xlvii, 373 and *n1*, 374
"Onward and Upward with the Arts," 186
Orwell, Sonia, 258
Osser, Maya, 205, 274, 275, 277
Ouro Prêto, Brazil, viii, xl, 84, 104, 106, 279,
280, 282, 307, 309, 310, 315, 316, 327, 331
"Over 2000 Illustrations," 35, 36
"Owl's Journey, The," 52, 53, 54–55, 56, 57;
editing and revision, 53 and *n2*
Oxford English Dictionary, xlviii, lii, lxi

Pack, George T., 84 and *n3*
Padua, 265
Painter, George D., 278*n1*
Panama City Star and Herald, The, xi
Paris, xi, 240, 241, 253, 313
Partisan Reader: Ten Years of Partisan Review,
The, 23 and *n1*
Partisan Review, xxxi, xxxiii, xxxv, 12*n1*, 21*n2*,

35, 36n2, 43 and n1, 52, 53 and n1, 161, 191, 192, 193, 209, 321n1; "The Poetry of Suburbia," xxxiii, 191 and n1

Partisan Review Fellowship, xxxiii, 191, 192, 193

Pascal, 153, 154; *Pensées*, 154, 155

Paz, Mary Jo, 340, 341

Paz, Octavio, 340, 341, 357, 367, 384; translations, 357–59, 371–72

Pearce, Charles, vii, viii–ix, xxi, xxxvi, lxi; Bishop and, viii–ix, 3–12

Pearl Harbor, bombing of, xx

Peech, John, 321, 323, 325, 353, 364, 368–69, 393, 394; "The Hardness of the Wind," 364; "Letter to Zbigniew Cybulski," 322 and n1

"pegging" rule, xxiv

periods, xlv, 332n2

Peru, 229, 318

Petrópolis, Brazil, viii, 171, 173, 253, 257, 262, 266, 272, 282, 290, 315

Petty, Mary, 85, 87–88, 90; covers, 87, 88 and n1

Phillips, William, 22n1, 43

"Pink Dog," 392 and nn1–2, 294, 295

Pinsky, Robert, xxvii, lv

plain style, xx, xxvii–xxviii

Plath, Aurelia, xxviii

Plath, Sylvia, xxvii, xxviii; *Ariel*, xxvii; "Daddy," xxvii

Ploughshares, 371, 373

Plumly, Stanley, xxvii

"Poem," xlii, 339 and n2; editing and revision, 342 and n2, 345, 349

"Poem on Dolls," 6–7

poetry: parodies, xix–xx, plain style, xx, xxvii–xxviii; rates paid by *The New Yorker*, xviii–xix, xxii, xxxiii–xxxiv, xxxix, xlii–xliii, 15–16, 32 and n1, 33, 143, 246–47; seasonal, xli–xlii, xlix, 67–68, 330, 390; serious, xx–xxiii; *see also* editing and revision; punctuation; *specific poets, poems, editors, and publications*

Poetry, xx, xxii, xxvi, xxvii, xxxi, xxxii–xxxiv, xl, 46n1, 48 and n1, 49, 61, 77, 81, 83, 139, 175, 177, 193 and n1, 204 and n1; "I Was But Just Awake," 204 and n1

Poetry Pilot, 227

Poet's Story, The, 340 and n1, 355, 356

Poet's Theatre, Cambridge, 200

Poirier, Richard, *Robert Frost: The Work of Knowing*, 389n1

Poland, 275

Pollit, Katha, lv

Pound, Ezra, xix, xxv, xxviii, 177, 178, 179, 315n2; *A Draft of XXX Cantos*, xix

"Prodigal, The," xxxii, 59, 61, 62, 63, 106; editing and revision, 63 and n1

Proust, Marcel, 134, 241, 253 and n1, 257, 275, 278 and n1, 397

Pulitzer Prize, 176, 177, 178, 179 and n2

punctuation, xliii–lvi; Bishop and, xliv–liv, lxii, 16, 29, 41, 55n1, 56–57, 60–62, 63n1, 69 and n1, 80 and n2, 92n1, 117n1, 120, 156, 158 and nn1–2, 159 and nn1–3, 169 and n1, 170 and n4, 190 and n2, 212–13, 214, 222, 223 and n3, 245, 248n2, 263n1, 264n1, 280–81n1, 297n1, 325, 326n1, 333nn1–3, 334 and n2, 339n2, 343n3, 344n1, 356n1, 386, 388n1, 391n1, 392n2; *The New Yorker* style of, xliv–liv, lxii, 29, 41, 56, 120, 156, 213; *see also* accent marks; colons; commas; dashes; ellipses; periods; question marks; quotation marks; semicolons; *specific poems*

Quarterly Review of Literature, 35 and n1

question marks, 69, 325

"Questions of Travel," xvii, xxxi, xliv, 151, 152; editing and revision, 153, 154, 155, 156 and n1, 157 and n1

Questions of Travel, 190nn1–2, 211n1, 277, 280, 303

Quinn, Alice, lv; as poetry editor of *The New Yorker*, lv

quotation marks, 245, 325

Rabassa, Gregory, 250n1

"Rachel and the U.S.A. School of Writing," xxiv, xxxiv

Rachmaninoff, Sergei, 380n2

Rago, Henry, xli

Rahv, Philip, xxxi–xxxii, xxxiii, 22n1, 36

"Rain Towards Morning," 53n1

"Rainy Season: Sub-Tropics," xl

Read, Bill, 360, 361 and n1, 363

"Reassurance," 3n1

Red Badge of Courage, The (film), 82 and n1

Reed, Henry, 285; "Lessons of the War," 285n1

Reid, Alastair, 261–62; "Immortal Diamond," 390 and n1

Reilly, Donald, "You should see the pilot!," 290 and *n2*

rejections, ix, lv, 394; of Bishop by *The New Yorker*, xxiv–xxvi, xxxi, lv, 5–12, 19–23, 28, 36, 47–50, 53, 56, 58, 83, 112–13, 152, 168, 171, 186, 233–34, 354*n2*; *The New Yorker* policy on, xx–xxiii, xxiv–xxvi, xxvii–xxviii, lv

Reporter, The, 201*n3*

Reporter-at-Large, 131

Republican Party, xxxvii, 301

revision, *see* editing and revision

Rexroth, Kenneth, 315*n2*

Ribeiro, Costa, 134, 137

Rich, Adrienne, xii, xxxiii

Ricks, Christopher, *Tennyson*, 352 and *n1*

Riley, James Whitcomb, xix

Rio de Janeiro, viii, 74, 75, 82, 99, 109, 110, 122–24, 125 and *n2*, 132, 171, 206, 211, 223, 237–38, 240, 262, 309, 315

"Rio de Janeiro," 392 and *nn3–4*

Rittenhouse, Isabella, *Maud*, 141 and *n1*

"Riverman, The," xvii, xxxiv–xxxv, xlii, 209, 210, 211, 212, 230; editing and revision, 212–13, 214, 219

"River Rat, The," 36

Rizzardi, Alfredo, 177–78

Robinson, Edwin Arlington, xix

Rockefeller Foundation, 298, 299, 301, 302

Rodman, Selden, xxxiii, 27 and *n1*

Roethke, Theodore, xxii, 285; "Dirge," xxxvii; "The Early Flower," 211 and *n1*; "The Storm," xlii

Rogers, Woodes, *A Cruising Voyage Around the World*, 273 and *n1*

Rorem, Ned, 272; "Visits to St. Elizabeths: (Bedlam)," 269 and *n2*

Ross, Harold, viii–ix, x–xii, xxvii, 3*n1*, 48, 77; Bishop and, xv, xviii–xix, lii, 13, 41, 54*n2*, 63 and *n1*; death of, xxii, 74 and *n1*, 76; editing style, xxiii–xxiv, xliv; as founding editor of *The New Yorker*, xi–xii, xiv–xviii, xxxviii–xl, 32*n1*, 39–40, 41, 77, 86; obituary by E. B. White, 74 and *n1*; poetry rates and, 32*n1*; Katharine White and, xi–xii, xvi, xx, 76

Ross, Lillian, 82*n1*

Rudofsky, Bernard, *Architecture Without Architects*, 269 and *n3*

Russell, Isabel, 374–75

Ryall, George, 45*n1*

Sable Island, xvii, 65–67, 68–69, 131

Sable Island essay, xvi, 65, 67, 68, 70, 72, 73, 74, 75, 76, 77, 79, 83, 84, 85, 103, 104 and *n1*, 105, 106, 131, 132, 133, 134, 137, 140, 141, 142, 163, 172

Sacramento Union, The, xi

Salinger, J. D., "Seymour: An Introduction," xxxvi

Salt Lake City Tribune, The, xi

"Sandpiper," xl, 246, 247, 249, 381*n1*

San Francisco, viii, 207, 298, 367

Santa Fe, 299

"Santarem," xliii, lxii, 386; editing and revision, 386, 387 and *n1*, 388 and *n1*, 389 and *n2*

Santos-Dumont, Alberto, 253–54

São Paulo, 127

Saratoga Springs, viii, 45, 46, 52

Sargeant, Winthrop, "Maestro di Costruzione," 233 and *n1*

Sarraute, Nathalie, *The Age of Suspicion: Essays on the Novel*, 261 and *n1*

Sarton, May, 107, 109

satire, xix, xx

Saturday Review of Literature, The, x, xxxi; "Voice of the Poet: Oracular, Eerie, Daring," 306 and *n1*

Schapiro, Amram, 383, 384, 385

Schapiro, Meyer, 55

Schuyler, James, 336; "Life, Death, and Other Dreams," 354 and *n3*

Schwartz, Delmore, 103*n2*

Schwartz, Lloyd, liv, lv, 400 and *n2*

Scientific American, viii

Scribner's, 228

seasonal poems, xli–xlii, xlix, 67–68, 330, 390

Seattle, viii, 283, 284

"second-thought" habit, xlvii

semicolons, xlvii, 154*n1*, 169*n1*, 223 and *n2*, 297*n1*, 343*n3*, 356*n1*, 373*n1*, 388*n1*

serious poetry, xx–xxiii

"Sestina," xvii, 156, 157, 159, 162; editing and revision, 160, 161 and *n1*, 185 and *n2*

Sévigné, Mme de, 241 and *n2*

Sexton, Anne, xxiii, xxviii; death of, 364 and *n1*; "In Celebration of My Uterus," xxviii; "The Nude Swim," xxviii; "The One-Legged Man," 350 and *n2*

sexuality, vii, xxiv–xxvi, lv

Shakespeare, William, *Love's Labours Lost*, liv

"Shampoo, The," xvi, xxiv–xxvi, lv, 112 and
    n1, 113, 114 and *n1*
Shapiro, Karl, xx, xxii, xxvi, xxxii, 31, 59, 61,
    77, 81, 82, 83; as Poetry Consultant to the
    Library of Congress, 44 and *n1*
Shaplen, Robert, "Annals of Crime: Kreuger,"
    224 and *n1*
Shawn, William, xii, xiv*n*, xvi, xx, xxii; Bishop
    and, xxv, xxxiii, xliii, 67, 68, 71, 72, 77, 100,
    101, 140, 141, 172, 186, 208*n2*, 213, 247, 291,
    292, 314, 316, 320, 326, 339, 355, 392*n1*; as
    editor of *The New Yorker*, xxii, xxiv–xxv,
    xxvii, xxviii, xxxiii, xxxvi, xxxvii–xxxviii,
    xl, xli, xliii, xliv, 76, 77, 86, 100, 125, 131, 133,
    168, 176, 186, 199, 251, 256, 372, 382, 386
Shelley Award, 102
Silviano, Mario, 179*n2*
Simon and Schuster, 207
Sissman, L. E., "Envoy," 281*n1*
six-month agreement, xlii, 329, 331, 352
"Slot Machine, The," 8 and *n1*, 9, 10
Smith, Dave, xxvii
Snedens Landing, New York, x
Soares, Flavio Macedo, 266*n1*
Soares, Lota de Macedo, xvii, xxv, xxxiv, 75,
    85, 193–96, 200, 206, 212, 216, 223, 226, 227,
    235, 236, 238 and *n2*, 240 and *n1*, 246, 248,
    255, 256, 257, 262, 264, 265, 274, 278, 281,
    287, 291, 309; death of, 296, 300 and *n1*
"Song (Second Soprano)," 57, 58
"Song for a Colored Singer," 12 and *n1*
"Song for Sina," 12 and *n1*
"Song for the Rainy Season," xxxiii, lii, 230,
    231, 236; editing and revision, 232, 234, 235,
    236 and *n2*
"Sonnet," xxvi, xlii, liv, 391; editing and
    revision, liv, 391 and *n2*, 400 and *n2*
South America, xv, xxx, 71, 72, 74, 218, 229,
    230; *see also* Brazil
Southern Review, The, viii, 380, 387*n2*
Speculum Musicae, 381
spelling, xliv, lii, 55*n1*
"Spleen," *see* "Cirque d'Hiver"
"Squatter's Children, The," xvii, 147, 148,
    149, 150, 152, 153, 192, 266; editing and
    revision, 154 and *n1*, 155
Stafford, Jean, xii, xxxvi, 45, 46, 65, 199, 218,
    221, 272, 351, 354; *Bad Characters*, 269 and
    n1; *The Collected Stories of Jean Stafford*,
    378 and *n2*; death of, 397 and *n1*; *The
    Mountain Lion*, 397

Stafford, William, xxii
Stanford, Donald, 380–81, 387*n2*
Stars and Stripes, xi
"Station #2," 152
Steegmuller, Francis, 3*n1*, 214*n1*
Stein, Gertrude, "I Am Rose," 269*n2*
Stevens, Wallace, xxii, 352
Stevenson, Anne, 4*n1*
Stonington, Maine, xvii
Straight, Beatrice, 342*n1*
Strand, Antonia, 335
Strand, Mark, xxvii, xxx, xxxi, xl, 282, 284*n3*,
    287, 289, 335, 336
"Street by the Cemetery, The," 7
Strout, Richard Lee, 141 and *n1*
Strunk and White, *The Elements of Style*, 369,
    378
subscriptions, 134, 136–37, 268, 270, 271, 272,
    287–89, 298, 328, 330, 331, 336
"Summer's Dream, A," 34
sun, xlix
"Sunday, 4 A.M.," xlvi, 183, 187, 189, 192,
    199, 207*n1*; editing and revision, 189, 190
    and *nn1–2*, 191
"Sunday Morning," 5–6, 7
Swenson, May, xxvi, xxxvii, xliii, 126*n2*, 179,
    180, 197, 207, 248, 282, 285, 307; "All That
    Time," xxiii; *A Cage of Spines*, 204 and *n2*;
    "Dear Elizabeth," 281 and *n2*; *The Floor*,
    284 and *n2*; "September Things," 350 and
    n4; "Water Picture," 178 and *n1*

Talbot, Kathrine, 57 and *n2*, 58; "Bella," 57*n2*;
    "Death in the Pyrenees," 57*n2*; *Fire in the
    Sun*, 57*n2*; "The Sword of Darkness," 57*n2*
"Talk of the Town," viii, xxii, 3 and *n1*, 47*n1*,
    52, 54, 131, 132, 176, 258
Taylor, Peter, 71, 354; "A Sentimental
    Journey," 145, 146 and *n1*
Taylor, Robert Lewis: "Star-I," 179 and *n1*;
    "Star-II," 179 and *n1*
Teheran, xxvii
Tennyson, Alfred, Lord, 129, 352 and *n1*
Terry, Daise, 88, 137
Thanatopsis Literary and Inside Straight
    Club, xi
"The Race Track" column, 45*n1*, 46
Thomas, Dylan, 127, 128, 254*n1*; death of, 119,
    121 and *n2*; *The Doctor and the Devils*, 119
    and *n1*, 121; "The Peaches," 117 and *n3*,

Thomas, Dylan (*cont.*)
118; *Portrait of the Artist as a Young Dog*,
117 and *n3*
Thurber, James, x, xii, 38–39, 40; "A Friend
of the Earth," 38, 39*n1*; "Joyeux Noël, Mr.
Durning," 38, 39*n1*; "Our Own Modern
English Usage," xxiii; *The Years with
Ross*, xi
Tilley, Eustace, x
Time-Life, xl, 240*n2*
Time magazine, xxvi, 84 and *n4*, 121 and *n2*,
174, 257, 312 and *n1*, 315; "Disarmament:
Strange Climate," 231 and *n2*, 234; "End of
a New Yorker," 74 and *n1*; "The House on
11th Street," 315 and *n1*
Times Literary Supplement, 321 and *n2*, 323
Tipyn O'Bob, x
Town Hall, New York, lv
Toynbee, Arnold J., 223 and *n1*
translations, xl, 48 and *n1*, 110, 111, 140, 144,
145, 150, 163, 171–73, 201, 250, 251, 252, 256
and *n2*, 261, 302–305, 321 and *n3*, 322, 324,
328–30, 331, 341, 357–59, 371–72; *see also
specific works*
travel essays, xvi, xviii, *see also* Brasilia essay;
Sable Island essay
Trial Balances, xlvii
"Trip to Vigia, A," lv
Trollope, Anthony, 230, 233–34
"Trollope in Washington," 233–34
"Trouvée," 295, 297 and *n2*, 350*n2*, 398
Truax, R. Hawley, 107, 110
"Twelfth Morning; or What You Will," xl
"12 O'Clock News," 341, 343, 352; editing and
revision, 342 and *n3*, 349
Two Brazilian Poems, 322, 326–27, 328
typewriters, 49, 50, 51, 71, 197, 239, 282, 296,
304, 363

"Uncle Neddy," 387
"Under the Window: Ouro Prêto," xl, 278,
286, 287 and *n2*, 288, 392; editing and
revision, 279, 280 and *n1*, 282
"U.S.A. School of Writing, The," lv, 183, 184,
186 and *n1*, 189
University of Washington, Seattle, 283, 284
and *nn1–3*, 285, 286, 287
Unterecker, John, *Voyager: A Life of Hart
Crane*, 317 and *n1*
untitled (August 21, 1954), 52*n1*

untitled (October 13, 1956), 52*n1*
Updike, John, xxiii, xxxvi; "Insomnia the
Gem of the Ocean," 350*n2*

"Vague Poem," lv
"Valentine II," xlvii
Valéry, Paul, "The Cemetery by the Sea," 276
Vanity Fair, 354*n2*
"Varick Street," xxi, 27, 28 and *n1*, 398
Vassar College, viii, xxvi, xxx, lv, 7*n1*, 303*n3*,
372
Vendler, Helen, 384
Venice, 188 and *n1*, 219, 291, 399
"Verdigris," 46, 47, 48
Viereck, Peter, xx
"View of the Capitol from the Library of
Congress," lii, 49, 50–51, 54 and *nn1–2*, 55
and *n1*, 63, 381*n1*; editing and revision, 54,
56, 57 and *n4*
Viking, 357, 358
"Visits to St. Elizabeths," 178, 179 and *n3*,
315*n2*
Vogue, xxiii

Wagley, Charles, 213, 214; *Amazon Town*, xxxv,
213
Wagoner, David, xxiii, 331
Wakoski, Diane, xxvii
Walcott, Derek, xxvii, 398
Walken, Christopher, 342*n1*
Walker Gallery, New York, 88
Waller, Fats, 215
Wanning, Tom, 70 and *n3*, 370
Warner, Sylvia Townsend, "Farewell, My
Love," 57 and *n3*
Washington, D.C., viii, 46, 47 and *n2*, 48
Washington Post Book World, 383*n3*
Webster's Dictionary, xlviii, lii, 212
Weeks, Edward, "Prize Poet," 21 and *n1*
Welty, Eudora, xxxvi, 102 and *n1*, 103, 136;
The Bride of the Innisfallen, 102*n1*; "Kin,"
102*n1*; "No Place for You, My Love,"
102*n1*; "The Ponder Heart," 128 and *n1*;
"Why I Live at the P.O.," 128
Wescott, Glenway, "The Pilgrim Hawk," 308
West, Anthony, 174 and *n2*
West, James, 249, 250
Westminster Magazine, xxv
Wharton, Donald, 3*n1*

White, E. B. "Andy," x, xi, xvii, xliii, 42, 68, 75, 107, 108, 144, 146, 147, 163, 164, 165, 198, 204, 235, 251, 254, 338, 369, 370, 374, 375, 376, 382, 385–86; "Across the Street and into the Grill," 135*n1*; American Academy of Arts and Letters medal, 232 and *n1*; "Before the Frost," 224 and *n1*; *Charlotte's Web*, xvii, 105, 107 and *n1*; "A Classic Waits for Me," 135*n1*, 308; "Death of a Pig," 135 and *n1*; death of wife Katharine White, 385–86; *Elements of Style*, 369, 378; "End of a New Yorker," 74 and *n1*; "Floricordially Yours," 224 and *n1*; "How to Tell a Major Poet from a Minor Poet," 74 and *n1*; "Khrushchev and I," 224 and *n1*; "Letter from the East," 369 and *n1*; "Letter from the South," 179 and *n1*; "Letter from the West," 231 and *n2*, 234; *Letters of E. B. White*, 385 and *n2*; *The Points of My Compass: Letters from the East, the West, the North, the South*, 251 and *n2*; *The Second Tree from the Corner*, 129 and *n1*, 134 and *n2*

White, Joel, 107 and *n2*, 110, 116 and *n1*, 143

White, Katharine, vii, ix–xix, lv, lxi; blind spots of, xii; death of, xviii, 385 and *n1*, 386; ill health of, xviii, 18, 37, 75, 83, 248–49, 250, 251, 254, 375, 385; leaves Fiction Department, xviii, 162–64, 165–66, 199; as literary editor of *The New Yorker*, x–xix, xx–xxiii, xxv, xxxiii, xl, xliii, 12–23, 27–34, 37–60, 62–152, 162–89, 254–56, 385; marriage to E. B. White, 68, 75, 107, 146, 147, 163, 198, 251, 338, 382; Marianne Moore and, 337, 338 and *n1*, 339; obituary in *The New Yorker*, 386 and *n1*; retirement of, xxiii, xxvii; role and influence at *The New Yorker*, xii–xvii, xx–xxiii; Harold Ross and, xi–xii, xvi, xx, 76; "War in the Borders, Peace in the Shrubbery," 236 and *n3*; Wolfe's articles and, xiv*n*; *see also* White-Bishop correspondence

White-Bishop correspondence, xii–xix, xxv, xxxiii, xliii, li; of 1934–1946, 12–23; of 1947–1961, 27–34, 37–60, 62–152, 162–89, 192, 198, 210–26, 230–36; of 1961–1967, 248–52, 254–56; of 1967–1979, 337–39, 369–71, 374–78, 381–82

Whittier, John Greenleaf, xix

Wilbur, Richard, xxii, xxix, xxxiii, xxxvii, 129, 265; "A Baroque Wall-Fountain in the Villa Sciarra," 160 and *n2*; "October Maples," xxxvii–xxxviii; "On the Marginal Way," 281*n1*

Wilde, Oscar, 241*n1*

Williams, William Carlos, xx, xli; "The Deceptrices," xxi

Wilson, Edmund, ix, 13; "The Scrolls from the Dead Sea," 166 and *n1*; "Shock of Recognition," 308–309

Wilson, Jane, ix

Wilson, Ted, viii

"Wit, The," xvii, 166, 168

Wolfe, Tom: "Lost in the Whichy Thicket," xiv*n*; "Tiny Mummies! The True Story of the Ruler of 43rd Street's Land of the Walking Dead," xiv*n*

Wood, Dick, 151*n1*

Wood, Millie, 151*n1*

Wordsworth, William, xxvii, 317, 325, 326, 333, 334 and *n1*

working proofs, 91–92, 120

World Literature Today, 384; "The Canada-Brazil Connection," 383 and *n1*

World War I, xi

World War II, xx

Worth, Irene, 268*n1*

Wright, Charles, xxvii, 399

Wright, Frank Lloyd, 123, 125*n2*

Wright, James, xxiii

Wykeham, Peter, *Santos-Dumont, a Study in Obsession*, 253 and *n2*

Xerox, 345

Yaddo, xii, xxix, xxxii, 45, 46, 54, 58, 132, 354, 364

Yagoda, Ben, xxviii, xxxvi

Yeats, W. B., "The Lake Isle of Innisfree," xix, 360

Young, Marguerite, 267 and *n2*

Zabel, Morton, xx

PERMISSIONS ACKNOWLEDGMENTS

Grateful acknowledgment is made for permission to reprint quotes from letters, memoranda, manuscripts, and journals by the following individuals:

Elizabeth Bishop, copyright © Estate of Elizabeth Bishop, used by permission of the Estate of Elizabeth Bishop.

Louise Bogan, copyright © Estate of Louise Bogan, used by permission of Mary Kinzie, Literary Executor, Estate of Louise Bogan.

John Malcolm Brinnin, copyright © Estate of John Malcolm Brinnin, used by permission of David Wolkowsky, Literary Executor, Estate of John Malcolm Brinnin.

Ferris Greenslet, copyright © Ferris Greenslet/Houghton Mifflin Harcourt Publishing Company, used by permission of the Houghton Mifflin Harcourt Publishing Company.

William Maxwell, copyright © William Maxwell, used by permission of the Wiley Agency, agents for the Estate of William Maxwell.

Marianne Moore, copyright © Estate of Marianne Moore, used by permission of David M. Moore, Administrator of the Literary Estate of Marianne Moore. All rights reserved.

Howard Moss, copyright © Estate of Howard Moss, used by permission of Anne Simmons, Literary Executor, Estate of Howard Moss.

The New Yorker staff, copyright © *The New Yorker* staff/Condé Nast, used by permission of Condé Nast.

Aurelia Plath, copyright © Estate of Aurelia Plath, used by permission of Susan Plath-Winston, Literary Executor, Estate of Aurelia Plath.

Philip Rahv, copyright © Estate of Philip Rahv, used by permission of Betty Rahv, Literary Executor, Estate of Philip Rahv.

Theodore Roethke, copyright © Estate of Theodore Roethke, used by permission of Carol Christiansen, Random House, Inc., on behalf of the Estate of Theodore Roethke.

Karl Shapiro, copyright © Estate of Karl Shapiro, used by permission of Robert Phillips, Literary Executor, Estate of Karl Shapiro.

Karl Shapiro, copyright © Karl Shapiro/*Poetry* magazine, used by permission of *Poetry* magazine.

Katharine S. White, copyright © estate of Katharine S. White, used by permission of The White Literary LLC.

Richard Wilbur, copyright © Richard Wilbur, used by permission of the author.

William Carlos Williams, copyright © 2011 by the Estates of Paul H. Williams and William Eric Williams. Used by permission of New Directions, agents for the Estate of William Carlos Williams.

GALENA PUBLIC LIBRARY DISTRICT
GALENA, IL